Artificial Intelligence for Cloud-Native Software Engineering

Pethuru Raj Chelliah
Reliance Jio Platforms Ltd., India

Ramamurthy Venkatesh
NETS International, UAE

N.A. Natraj
Symbiosis International University, India

Rathinaraja Jeyaraj
University of Houston-Victoria, USA

IGI Global
Scientific Publishing
Publishing Tomorrow's Research Today

Vice President of Editorial Melissa Wagner
Managing Editor of Acquisitions Mikaela Felty
Managing Editor of Book Development Jocelynn Hessler
Production Manager Mike Brehm
Cover Design Phillip Shickler

Published in the United States of America by
IGI Global Scientific Publishing
701 East Chocolate Avenue
Hershey, PA, 17033, USA
Tel: 717-533-8845
Fax: 717-533-7115
Website: https://www.igi-global.com E-mail: cust@igi-global.com

Library of Congress Cataloging-in-Publication Data

LCCN: 2024054514 (CIP Data Pending)
ISBN13: 9798369393567
Isbn13Softcover: 9798369393574
EISBN13: 9798369393581

British Cataloguing in Publication Data
A Cataloguing in Publication record for this book is available from the British Library.

Table of Contents

Preface xviii

Acknowledgment xxvii

Chapter 1
A Technical Perspective of Artificial Intelligence for the Ensuring Knowledge Era 1
B. Sundaravadivazhagan, University of Technology and Applied Sciences, Oman
P. Ashok, Symbiosis Institute of Digital and Telecom Management, India
U. Arunkumar, Karpagam Academy of Higher Education, India
N. A. Natraj, Symbiosis Institute of Digital and Telecom Management, India

Chapter 2
Artificial Intelligence: Augmented Integrated Development Environments for Boosting Programmer Productivity 29
P. Ashok, Symbiosis Institute of Digital and Telecom Management, India
Ravi Gorli, GITAM University, India
S. Parameswari, Sri Sairam Institute of Technology, India
Lakshmi Sridevi, Chennai Institute of Technology, India
N. Janaki, Vels Institute of Science Technology and Advanced Studies, India
S. Gopinath, Karpagam Institute of Technology, India
Harishchander Anandaram, Amrita Vishwa Vidyapeetam, India
K. S. Shreenidhi, Rajalakshmi Engineering College, India
Samaya Pillai Iyengar, Symbiosis Institute of Digital and Telecom Management, India

Chapter 3
AI-Powered Software Engineering for Cloud-Native Environments 57
M. Swathi Sree, Stanley College of Engineering and Technology for Women, India
C. Kishor Kumar Reddy, Stanley College of Engineering and Technology for Women, India
Kurella Vaishnavi, Stanley College of Engineering and Technology for Women, India
Vallapureddy Harika, Stanley College of Engineering and Technology for Women, India

Chapter 4
Generative AI for Source Code Creation: Revolutionizing Cloud-Native Software Engineering.. 87
C. V. Suresh Babu, Hindustan Institute of Technology and Science, India
Kathari Hima Kishore, Hindustan Institute of Technology and Science, India

Chapter 5
A Study on AI Tools That Can Generate Software Source Code 117
C. R. Rathish, New Horizon College of Engineering, India
S. Aaron Dennis, New Horizon College of Engineering, India
S. Arjun, New Horizon College of Engineering, India
Nithin Shiva Vanka, New Horizon College of Engineering, India
Akhilesh R. Mohan, New Horizon College of Engineering, India
Aryasree Madhukumar, Cambridge Institute of Technology, India

Chapter 6
AI-Powered Tools to Enhance the Stages of Software Development 133
Taye Iyinoluwa Adeyinka, University of Science and Technology, Beijing, China
Kehinde Iyioluwa Adeyinka, University of Science and Technology, Beijing, China

Chapter 7
Enhancing Lifecycle Stages and Navigating Implementation Hurdles for AI-Powered Tools and Challenges in Cloud-Native Software Development 171
C. G. Buluji, Symbiosis International University, India
Sivaram Ponnusamy, Sandip University, Nashik, India
S. Menaka, SRM Institute of Science and Technology, India
G. Rajeswari, Sathyabama Institute of Science and Technology, India
Harsh Jain, SRM Institute of Science and Technology, India

Chapter 8
AI-Driven Enhancements in Cloud-Native DevOps Boosting Automation, Deployment, and Monitoring 203
Nikhil Subodh Nagmoti, Symbiosis Institute of Digital and Telecom Management, India
Ishita Srivastava, Symbiosis Institute of Digital and Telecom Management, India
Madhavi Damle, Symbiosis Institute of Digital and Telecom Management, India

Chapter 9
Artificial Intelligence in Software Testing 237
Subash Banala, Capgemini, USA
Sudheer Panyaram, Fisker, USA
P. Selvakumar, Nehru Institute of Technology, India

Chapter 10
Top AI-Powered Tools for Software Test Automation 263
R. Adline Freeda, Department of Information Technology, KCG College of Technology, India
K. Sudha, Department of Artificial Intelligence and Data Science, Velammal Institute of Technology, India

Chapter 11
Harnessing AI for Scalable and Adaptive Cloud-Native Applications 283
C. R. Rathish, New Horizon College of Engineering, India
Yelam Ethi Sai Sreevathsav, New Horizon College of Engineering, India
Akhilesh R. Mohan, New Horizon College of Engineering, India
Nithin Shiva Vanka, New Horizon College of Engineering, India
L. Jeevan Bharadhi, New Horizon College of Engineering, India
Aryasree Madhukumar, Cambridge Institute of Technology, India

Chapter 12
Leveraging AI and Hyper-Automation for Cloud-Native Process Optimization in Healthcare for Hospital Admission and Discharge Automation 295
Madhavi Damle, Symbiosis Institute of Digital and Telecom Management, India
Achlendra Raj, Capgemini, India

Chapter 13
Leveraging AI and Hyper-Automation for Optimizing National Health ID Registrations: A Framework for Enhancing Public Sector Efficiency 331
Madhavi Damle, Symbiosis Institute of Digial and Telecom Management, India
Srimanta Pandit, Symbiosis Institute of Digital and Telecom Management, India

Chapter 14
Data Security With Replication for Cloud Computing 357
Cigdem Bakir, Dumlupinar University, Turkey
Mecit Yuzkat, Health Institutes of Türkiye, Turkey

Chapter 15
Best Practices, Ethical Challenges, and Regulatory Frameworks for AI Integration in Banking: Navigating the Future 377
R. Vettriselvan, AMET University, India
Palanivel Rathinasabapathi Velmurugan, Berlin School of Business and Innovation, Germany
Jimmy Carter Regins, Bishop Heber College, India
S. Uma Maheswari, Sathyabama Institute of Science and Technology, India
R. Joyce, Sathyabama Institute of Science and Technology, India

Chapter 16
A Hybrid Approach Employing Coded Caching-Based Federated Learning (HA – CCFL) for Multiparameter Optimization in Cloud Frameworks 411
Vaishnavi Bhardwaj, Siksha O Anusandhan University, India
Narayan Patra, Siksha O Anusandhan University, India
Sushree Bubhupprada B. Priyadarshini, Siksha O Anusandhan University, India

Chapter 17
AI-Powered Tools to Enhance the Stages of Software Development 435
S. Roobini, SNS College of Technology, India
M. Kavitha, Sri Krishna College of Engineering and Technology, India
Hema Deenadayalan, Sri Ramakrishna College of Arts and Science for Women, India
A. Muthusamy, Kongu Engineering College, India

Compilation of References 479

About the Contributors 519

Index 533

Detailed Table of Contents

Preface xviii

Acknowledgment xxvii

Chapter 1
A Technical Perspective of Artificial Intelligence for the Ensuring Knowledge Era 1
B. Sundaravadivzhagan, University of Technology and Applied Sciences, Oman
P. Ashok, Symbiosis Institute of Digital and Telecom Management, India
U. Arunkumar, Karpagam Academy of Higher Education, India
N. A. Natraj, Symbiosis Institute of Digital and Telecom Management, India

This chapter examines artificial intelligence technologies and their role in the emerging Knowledge Era, focusing on the evolution from traditional computing to AI-driven systems. It analyzes fundamental AI components, including machine learning architectures, deep learning innovations, and natural language processing, alongside essential infrastructure requirements. The discussion covers AI integration frameworks for knowledge management, exploring automated discovery, information extraction, and semantic reasoning mechanisms. The chapter examines cognitive computing platforms, predictive analytics, and decision support systems that enable sophisticated knowledge processing. Emerging technologies such as explainable AI, federated learning, and autonomous systems are explored, along with their impact on knowledge management.The chapter concludes with future directions emphasizing bio-inspired systems and edge-cloud integration, providing insights for researchers and practitioners implementing AI in knowledge management.

Chapter 2
Artificial Intelligence: Augmented Integrated Development Environments for Boosting Programmer Productivity 29
P. Ashok, Symbiosis Institute of Digital and Telecom Management, India
Ravi Gorli, GITAM University, India
S. Parameswari, Sri Sairam Institute of Technology, India
Lakshmi Sridevi, Chennai Institute of Technology, India
N. Janaki, Vels Institute of Science Technology and Advanced Studies, India
S. Gopinath, Karpagam Institute of Technology, India
Harishchander Anandaram, Amrita Vishwa Vidyapeetam, India
K. S. Shreenidhi, Rajalakshmi Engineering College, India
Samaya Pillai Iyengar, Symbiosis Institute of Digital and Telecom Management, India

AI is transforming software development with technologies that improve speed, quality, and productivity. AI-powered technologies and their use in software development are covered in this abstract. NLP algorithms help extract and categorize requirements from unstructured documents during requirements collecting and analysis. Machine learning algorithms forecast hazards and resource needs using past project data, improving planning and estimating. In addition, machine learning models trained on massive code repositories may produce code snippets and functions from natural language descriptions. AI algorithms produce test cases, prioritize test scenarios, and anticipate defect-prone code for testing and quality assurance. Automatic bug detection technologies use deep learning to spot bugs before they hit production. This research article brings in more insights about the various tools and softwares that are utilized in various stages of software development life cycle for efficient product development.

Chapter 3
AI-Powered Software Engineering for Cloud-Native Environments 57
M. Swathi Sree, Stanley College of Engineering and Technology for Women, India
C. Kishor Kumar Reddy, Stanley College of Engineering and Technology for Women, India
Kurella Vaishnavi, Stanley College of Engineering and Technology for Women, India
Vallapureddy Harika, Stanley College of Engineering and Technology for Women, India

Software engineering has been transformed by the rise of cloud-native architectures, which make it possible to create scalable, adaptable, and robust systems. Using serverless computing, microservices, and containers, cloud-native software engineering provides a dynamic and modular method of system development. Concurrently, the incorporation of Artificial Intelligence (AI) in cloud-native settings is revolutionising the process of software engineering, upkeep, and evolution. Automation, resource optimisation, and decision-making processes are all greatly improved by AI-driven tools and techniques like machine learning, automated code creation, predictive analytics, and intelligent monitoring. The merging of cloud-native architectures and AI approaches is examined in this study, which offers a systematic examination of how AI improves the design, testing, deployment, and operations phases of the software development lifecycle.

Chapter 4
Generative AI for Source Code Creation: Revolutionizing Cloud-Native Software Engineering.. 87
C. V. Suresh Babu, Hindustan Institute of Technology and Science, India
Kathari Hima Kishore, Hindustan Institute of Technology and Science, India

This study explores the integration of Generative AI in cloud-native software engineering, aiming to enhance the efficiency and effectiveness of source code creation. Targeting software developers, engineers, and organizations leveraging cloud technologies, the research employs a multi-disciplinary approach, combining qualitative interviews and case studies from successful implementations of AI tools like GitHub Copilot and OpenAI's Codex. The findings reveal that Generative AI significantly reduces manual coding efforts, automates routine tasks, and allows developers to focus on complex problem-solving and innovative design. Furthermore, the study highlights the transformative impact of cloud-native architectures in facilitating scalable and flexible software development processes. The conclusions underscore the necessity for developers to adapt to new roles that emphasize critical thinking and creativity, while also addressing potential challenges such as code quality and security.

Chapter 5
A Study on AI Tools That Can Generate Software Source Code 117
C. R. Rathish, New Horizon College of Engineering, India
S. Aaron Dennis, New Horizon College of Engineering, India
S. Arjun, New Horizon College of Engineering, India
Nithin Shiva Vanka, New Horizon College of Engineering, India
Akhilesh R. Mohan, New Horizon College of Engineering, India
Aryasree Madhukumar, Cambridge Institute of Technology, India

AI is revolutionizing software development with tools that automate tasks like code suggestions, completions, and full code generation based on minimal input. Advanced machine learning models, such as Transformers, power tools like GitHub Copilot and TabNine, enhancing productivity and reducing coding errors. These tools use vast code repositories and natural language processing to help developers focus on complex problem-solving. However, AI-generated code presents challenges, including concerns over code quality, maintainability, and security. Ethical issues, like ownership, plagiarism, and biases in training data, also arise. Despite these hurdles, AI is set to play a crucial role in software engineering, pushing research toward improving scalability, ethical guidelines, and model generalization. As AI continues to evolve, it is expected to become a key component in future software development tools, transforming how developers work and optimize code. Its growing influence will shape the next generation of programming.

Chapter 6
AI-Powered Tools to Enhance the Stages of Software Development 133
Taye Iyinoluwa Adeyinka, University of Science and Technology, Beijing, China
Kehinde Iyioluwa Adeyinka, University of Science and Technology, Beijing, China

AI operates at the heart of cloud-native software engineering and is now transforming traditional software development methodologies by introducing intelligent automation and optimization along the SDLC. The present chapter focuses on the specific opportunities and issues that the unique characteristics of containerized applications and microservices architecture introduce, with particular emphasis on AI-based tools that make developers more productive in cloud-native environments. Some critical research areas include AI-driven requirements analysis, intelligent system design, automated code generation, and advanced testing frameworks. The chapter also covers using AI to facilitate cloud-native platforms, such as Kubernetes, anomaly detection, dynamic resource management, and continuous integration and deployment

Chapter 7
Enhancing Lifecycle Stages and Navigating Implementation Hurdles for AI-Powered Tools and Challenges in Cloud-Native Software Development 171
C. G. Balaji, Symbiosis International University, India
Sivaram Ponnusamy, Sandip University, Nashik, India
S. Menaka, SRM Institute of Science and Technology, India
G. Rajeswari, Sathyabama Institute of Science and Technology, India
Harsh Jain, SRM Institute of Science and Technology, India

This chapter examines the transformative impact of artificial intelligence (AI) on software development within a cloud-native context. As the adoption of AI tools has intensified, their integration throughout the Software Development Lifecycle (SDLC) offers both opportunities and challenges. It explores the benefits of AI in areas like requirement analysis, design, implementation, testing, and maintenance, each experiencing advancements in efficiency, accuracy, and scalability. AI aids in automating processes, predicting system issues, optimizing resource use, and enhancing software quality, bringing substantial changes to conventional methods. It emphasizes the specific challenges posed by AI adoption, such as data quality, skill gaps, integration complexity, ethical considerations, and technical scalability. Key sections address the research questions and methodological approaches to understanding the integration barriers. The findings underscore AI's potential to enhance the SDLC but highlight the need for robust strategies.

Chapter 8
AI-Driven Enhancements in Cloud-Native DevOps Boosting Automation, Deployment, and Monitoring 203
Nikhil Subodh Nagmoti, Symbiosis Institute of Digital and Telecom Management, India
Ishita Srivastava, Symbiosis Institute of Digital and Telecom Management, India
Madhavi Damle, Symbiosis Institute of Digital and Telecom Management, India

This paper looks into the incorporation of Artificial Intelligence into cloud-native DevOps practices dealing in automation, workflow optimization, and proactive monitoring. The paper also outlines AI-based tools that support some of the main points in DevOps practice areas like CI/CD, infrastructure management, security, and observability. Additionally, it elaborates on new developments that shorten workflows in cloud environments. This study on AI-driven automation shows how these systems can help mitigate repetitive works, speed CI/CD Processes, and increase deployment efficiency. It further explains the possible AI contributions in the areas of real-time monitoring, anomaly detection, and rapid root-cause analysis. The paper also examines the existing challenges under which impeding aspects like scalability constraints, data issues, and overlook, as well as interpretability by human experts must be highlighted. Future research directions would also be mentioned at the end, intended to pave the way for practitioners and researchers to adopt artificial intelligence to develop.

Chapter 9
Artificial Intelligence in Software Testing 237
Subash Banala, Capgemini, USA
Sudheer Panyaram, Fisker, USA
P. Selvakumar, Nehru Institute of Technology, India

AI which is reshaping the landscape of quality assurance (QA) by enhancing efficiency, accuracy, and coverage. Traditionally, software testing has relied heavily on manual and semi-automated processes, often leading to time-consuming and error-prone tasks. AI introduces a new paradigm in software testing, offering advanced methodologies and tools that significantly improve the effectiveness and efficiency of QA practices. Additionally, AI enhances test maintenance and evolution. Traditional test suites require manual updates as software evolves, which can be labor-intensive and prone to oversight. AI-powered tools can automatically adjust test cases and scripts to accommodate changes in the software, reducing the manual effort required to maintain and update tests. By leveraging AI to detect changes in the software and adjust tests accordingly, organizations can ensure that their test suites remain relevant and effective throughout the development lifecycle.Another significant advancement brought about by AI is the optimization of test execution.

Chapter 10
Top AI-Powered Tools for Software Test Automation 263
R. Adline Freeda, Department of Information Technology, KCG College of Technology, India
K. Sudha, Department of Artificial Intelligence and Data Science, Velammal Institute of Technology, India

As software systems become more complex, there is also an acute need for efficient, accurate, and scalable testing solutions. While traditional test automation is indeed quite powerful, it very often has to struggle against the demands of more advanced development environments that rely on continuous integration and delivery pipelines. We will compare these tools with a number of real-world case studies, underlining the improvements in how these tools enhance software quality and reduce the time-to-market along with the ability to perform continuous testing.Of course, we also touch upon the related issues when adopting AI-driven testing solutions-the challenges of data privacy and the integration complexity of new tools into existing workflows. By the end of this chapter, you will understand in clear-cut terms the main benefits and limitations and the scope of AI-powered tools, thus making them better decision-makers when it comes to choosing and applying such technology to their software testing processes.

Chapter 11
Harnessing AI for Scalable and Adaptive Cloud-Native Applications 283
C. R. Rathish, New Horizon College of Engineering, India
Yelam Ethi Sai Sreevathsav, New Horizon College of Engineering, India
Akhilesh R. Mohan, New Horizon College of Engineering, India
Nithin Shiva Vanka, New Horizon College of Engineering, India
L. Jeevan Bharadhi, New Horizon College of Engineering, India
Aryasree Madhukumar, Cambridge Institute of Technology, India

Software engineering is changing as a result of artificial intelligence (AI), which makes decision-making easier, automates activities, and creates more intelligent, adaptable systems. AI can now write code, debug programs in real time, and run continuous software tests—all of which increase productivity and decrease error rates. AI-driven solutions also improve risk assessment, resource allocation, and project management, which results in improved planning and more efficient project execution. However, issues with bias, transparency, and data privacy arise when implementing AI. For AI to be used in software development in a responsible and moral manner, these problems must be resolved. In the future, artificial intelligence will propel developments like quantum computing and self-healing systems. These developments will push the limits of software engineering, increasing accessibility to development and redefining the industry's future.

Chapter 12
Leveraging AI and Hyper-Automation for Cloud-Native Process Optimization in Healthcare for Hospital Admission and Discharge Automation 295
Madhavi Damle, Symbiosis Institute of Digital and Telecom Management, India
Achlendra Raj, Capgemini, India

Hospitals face challenges with inefficient paper-based workflows, manual data entry, and fragmented communication in admission and discharge processes. This section introduces a blueprint for cloud RPA to address these issues, enhancing hospital operations with cloud-native software practices. RPA, combined with OCR, speeds up digitization and integrates hospital data, enabling data-driven decisions. The section also discusses the risks of RPA and cloud implementation but highlights their benefits, especially in reducing human contact. This transformative technology improves productivity and patient care while supporting compliance and governance.

Chapter 13
Leveraging AI and Hyper-Automation for Optimizing National Health ID Registrations: A Framework for Enhancing Public Sector Efficiency 331
Madhavi Damle, Symbiosis Institute of Digial and Telecom Management, India
Srimanta Pandit, Symbiosis Institute of Digital and Telecom Management, India

This chapter explores AI and Hyper-automation's potential to revolutionize National Health ID registration within cloud-native frameworks. It examines integrating these technologies to address public sector challenges in managing health information systems. The study discusses aligning cloud-native principles with health ID registration, challenges of implementation. It proposes using RPA and cognitive technologies to streamline registration, identity creation, and verification processes essential for the national growth

Chapter 14
Data Security With Replication for Cloud Computing 357
Cigdem Bakir, Dumlupinar University, Turkey
Mecit Yuzkat, Health Institutes of Türkiye, Turkey

Cloud computing is an advanced technology that provides access to different services via the internet. These services include applications such as servers, networking, data storage, databases, and software. Instead of storing files on local storage device, cloud-based storage makes it possible to store files in a secure database. As long as an electronic device has access to the web, it has access to data and the software programs to run it. For this reason, this technology is very popular for institutions and individuals for many reasons such as cost, production, efficiency and speed. However, with the advantages of cloud computing, some security risks also arise. At the beginning of these security risks are data breaches and data losses caused by malicious software applications. In this study, data replication is discussed in order to solve security breaches in cloud computing technologies.

Chapter 15
Best Practices, Ethical Challenges, and Regulatory Frameworks for AI Integration in Banking: Navigating the Future 377
R. Vettriselvan, AMET University, India
Palanivel Rathinasabapathi Velmurugan, Berlin School of Business and Innovation, Germany
Jimmy Carter Regins, Bishop Heber College, India
S. Uma Maheswari, Sathyabama Institute of Science and Technology, India
R. Joyce, Sathyabama Institute of Science and Technology, India

This chapter explores the transformative impact of artificial intelligence (AI) and cloud-native software on the banking sector. It examines how AI enhances customer service, fraud detection, and risk management through technologies like virtual assistants and predictive analytics. However, these advancements introduce ethical challenges, including data privacy concerns, algorithmic bias, and the need for transparency in AI decision-making. The chapter reviews relevant regulations, such as the General Data Protection Regulation (GDPR) and the California Consumer Privacy Act (CCPA), and offers strategies for compliance and ethical AI integration. Through case studies, it highlights successful implementations of AI in banking, illustrating effective management of ethical and regulatory issues. The chapter concludes with a look at future trends and proactive strategies to address emerging ethical and regulatory challenges, aiming to guide stakeholders in balancing innovation with ethical practices in the evolving landscape of banking technology.

Chapter 16
A Hybrid Approach Employing Coded Caching-Based Federated Learning (HA – CCFL) for Multiparameter Optimization in Cloud Frameworks 411
Vaishnavi Bhardwaj, Siksha O Anusandhan University, India
Narayan Patra, Siksha O Anusandhan University, India
Sushree Bubhuppradа B. Priyadarshini, Siksha O Anusandhan University, India

Federated computing refers to the method of combining multiple distributed user groups and training models together without distributing data sets to client devices. In this chapter, the authors discussed a caching-based federated learning coded in fog computing called HS-CCFL, which is used as a content distribution artificial intelligence strategy with a single server connected to other devices through common constraints. They established an estimate of the long-term average speed of shared data for many users, each with a certain amount of memory. In this chapter, the authors show the experimental results by increasing the latency of fog points, which leads to an increase in latency and hit rate. Federation learning algorithm based on coded caching is discussed, where instead of local cache optimization, the closest term is added, which is related to the distance between local caching strategies. The experimental results justify the effectiveness of the method.

Chapter 17
AI-Powered Tools to Enhance the Stages of Software Development 435
S. Roobini, SNS College of Technology, India
M. Kavitha, Sri Krishna College of Engineering and Technology, India
Hema Deenadayalan, Sri Ramakrishna College of Arts and Science for Women, India
A. Muthusamy, Kongu Engineering College, India

The rapid evolution of Artificial Intelligence (AI) has significantly impacted the software development lifecycle (SDLC), introducing tools that enhance efficiency, accuracy, and innovation. This chapter examines the integration of AI-powered tools across SDLC stages, including planning, design, coding, testing, deployment, and maintenance. AI automates tasks like code generation, bug detection, and test case creation, reducing errors and accelerating development. It also enhances decision-making, fosters team collaboration, and optimizes resources through predictive analytics and intelligent project management tools. The chapter highlights AI's role in software quality improvement, using machine learning to detect anomalies and predict failures early. Ethical and security challenges are addressed, stressing responsible AI use and human oversight. By chapter's end, readers will understand how AI-powered tools reshape software development, enabling the creation of robust, scalable, and user-friendly applications while navigating ethical and quality challenges effectively.

Compilation of References 479

About the Contributors 519

Index 533

Preface

INTRODUCTION

In recent years, the role of artificial intelligence (AI) has evolved dramatically, becoming a transformative force in numerous industries. One of the sectors experiencing the most profound change is software engineering. As the digital landscape continues to shift, AI tools and techniques are emerging as indispensable in automating and enhancing various stages of the software development lifecycle. With the advent of cloud-native architectures, the synergy between AI and software engineering is more evident than ever, driving both innovation and efficiency.

In this book, *Artificial Intelligence for Cloud-Native Software Engineering*, we aim to explore the many ways in which AI is revolutionizing the field of software development. From the early stages of requirements elicitation to the final phases of deployment and enhancement, AI is streamlining processes, reducing cognitive overload, and enabling the creation of high-quality software applications. We delve into AI-powered tools that assist software architects and engineers in developing software that meets modern standards of scalability, reliability, and security, all while reducing the time and effort typically associated with traditional software engineering practices.

The integration of AI into cloud-native principles marks a significant shift in how software products, services, and solutions are developed. The move towards microservices architecture, combined with AI-driven testing, debugging, and monitoring tools, offers unprecedented opportunities for improvement across the software engineering lifecycle. As cloud-native approaches continue to mature, AI is positioned to play an increasingly central role in the way we design, develop, and deploy software applications.

This book provides a comprehensive overview of AI applications in various aspects of software engineering. We cover AI in areas such as requirements management, code generation, testing, deployment, and software monitoring, offering valuable insights into how these technologies can reduce development time while enhancing software quality. We also examine the challenges associated with AI implementation and the emerging tools and methodologies that can help address these obstacles.

Our primary goal is to provide software engineers, architects, developers, and project managers with practical insights into the integration of AI in their work. Additionally, this book will be of great value to academic researchers, students in computer science and software engineering, and IT professionals working within the realms of cloud-native architectures, DevOps, and software testing.

By showcasing the transformative impact of AI in the field, we hope to foster a deeper understanding of how AI can drive innovation, accelerate delivery times, and improve software quality. As the field of AI continues to evolve, we believe this book will serve as an invaluable resource for professionals and researchers alike, helping them navigate the ever-changing landscape of AI-augmented software engineering.

We invite you to explore the cutting-edge technologies, best practices, and emerging trends presented throughout this book, and to join us in advancing the future of cloud-native software engineering with the power of AI.

ORGANIZATION OF THE BOOK

Chapter 1: A Technical Perspective of Artificial Intelligence for the Ensuring Knowledge Era

This chapter explores the pivotal role of artificial intelligence (AI) in the emerging Knowledge Era, where AI is reshaping the landscape of knowledge management. It traces the evolution from traditional computing systems to AI-driven technologies, delving into the key components such as machine learning, deep learning, and natural language processing. The chapter emphasizes AI's integration into knowledge management frameworks, particularly through automation, information extraction, and semantic reasoning. Additionally, it highlights the transformative potential of cognitive computing platforms, predictive analytics, and decision support systems in managing sophisticated knowledge. The discussion also examines cutting-edge technologies like explainable AI and federated learning, alongside future directions such as bio-inspired systems and edge-cloud integration, making it an essential resource for researchers and practitioners in the AI and knowledge management space.

Chapter 2: Artificial Intelligence: Augmented Integrated Development Environments for Boosting Programmer Productivity

AI's impact on software development is accelerating, with AI-powered tools significantly enhancing the speed, quality, and productivity of programming. This chapter discusses the integration of AI in various stages of the software development lifecycle, including requirement gathering, project estimation, code generation, testing, and quality assurance. It examines how natural language processing (NLP) algorithms assist in extracting and categorizing requirements from unstructured documents, while machine learning models predict potential hazards and optimize planning. By automating repetitive tasks, AI tools allow developers to focus on more complex problem-solving, thus improving overall productivity and product quality. The chapter provides insights into the practical application of AI tools, such as code completion and bug detection, that streamline the software development process.

Chapter 3: AI-Powered Software Engineering for Cloud-Native Environments

This chapter focuses on the intersection of artificial intelligence and cloud-native architectures, which have redefined software engineering practices. It explores how AI is leveraged within cloud-native environments—encompassing serverless computing, microservices, and containers—to enhance software development, maintenance, and evolution. By incorporating AI tools such as machine learning, automated code generation, and intelligent monitoring systems, software engineering processes become more efficient, adaptive, and scalable. The chapter emphasizes AI's role in automating resource management, predictive analytics, and decision-making, thereby transforming every phase of the software lifecycle from design to deployment.

Chapter 4: Generative AI for Source Code Creation: Revolutionizing Cloud-Native Software Engineering

This chapter examines the revolutionary potential of Generative AI in cloud-native software engineering, particularly in source code creation. By leveraging tools like GitHub Copilot and OpenAI's Codex, AI significantly reduces manual coding efforts and automates routine tasks, allowing developers to focus on more innovative aspects of design and problem-solving. The research draws on case studies and interviews to illustrate how Generative AI has reshaped the development process, enhancing efficiency and scalability in cloud-native environments. The chapter also discusses the emerging role of AI in cloud technologies, highlighting the need for developers to adapt to new roles that emphasize creativity and critical thinking while addressing challenges related to code quality and security.

Chapter 5: A Study on AI Tools That Can Generate Software Source Code

AI-driven tools are transforming the way developers approach software source code creation. This chapter explores the capabilities of advanced machine learning models like Transformers, which power tools such as GitHub Copilot and TabNine. These tools assist developers by suggesting code snippets, completing functions, and generating entire code segments from natural language descriptions. While AI-generated code improves productivity, it also raises concerns related to code quality, maintainability, and security. The chapter addresses the ethical implications of AI in software development, such as ownership issues and biases in training data, and examines the future potential of AI tools in shaping the next generation of programming practices.

Chapter 6: AI-Powered Tools to Enhance the Stages of Software Development

This chapter delves into the significant role of AI in transforming traditional software development methodologies by enhancing the efficiency of the Software Development Lifecycle (SDLC). It highlights AI tools that optimize various stages of development, from requirements analysis to automated code generation, system design, and advanced testing frameworks. Special attention is given to AI-powered tools that cater to the unique needs of cloud-native environments, such as Kubernetes and microservices architectures. By utilizing AI to automate workflows, detect anomalies, and optimize resource management, the chapter demonstrates how cloud-native platforms are enhanced, improving the overall efficiency of software development processes.

Chapter 7: Enhancing Lifecycle Stages and Navigating Implementation Hurdles for AI-Powered Tools and Challenges in Cloud-Native Software Development

As AI becomes more integral to software development, its adoption within the cloud-native software development lifecycle (SDLC) presents both opportunities and challenges. This chapter explores how AI can optimize the SDLC by automating tasks, predicting issues, and enhancing software quality across different phases, including design, implementation, and testing. However, integrating AI also presents significant challenges, such as addressing data quality concerns, skill gaps, and integration complexities. The chapter offers valuable insights into overcoming these obstacles and provides a roadmap for effective AI adoption, making it an essential resource for researchers and practitioners seeking to implement AI in cloud-native software development.

Chapter 8: AI-Driven Enhancements in Cloud-Native DevOps Boosting Automation, Deployment, and Monitoring

This chapter examines the integration of AI into cloud-native DevOps practices, focusing on how AI-driven tools are enhancing automation, deployment, and monitoring processes. By automating repetitive tasks and improving workflows, AI tools enable faster continuous integration and delivery (CI/CD) cycles, which is crucial in cloud-native environments. The chapter explores AI's contributions to anomaly detection, real-time monitoring, and rapid root-cause analysis, enhancing operational efficiency and software reliability. While AI offers significant benefits, challenges such as scalability constraints and data interpretation issues remain, which are also addressed in the chapter, along with future research directions in AI-driven DevOps practices.

Chapter 9: Artificial Intelligence in Software Testing

AI is significantly transforming the field of software testing by improving the efficiency and accuracy of quality assurance (QA) practices. This chapter outlines how AI enhances traditional software testing methods, such as automated test generation, test execution optimization, and predictive defect detection. AI tools can adapt test cases and scripts as software evolves, reducing manual effort and ensuring that test suites remain relevant throughout the development lifecycle. The chapter also explores how AI is reshaping test maintenance and evolution, helping organizations maintain robust QA practices that improve software quality and accelerate time-to-market.

Chapter 10: Top AI-Powered Tools for Software Test Automation

As software systems grow in complexity, AI-powered tools are becoming essential for efficient, accurate, and scalable testing. This chapter compares various AI-driven testing tools, providing real-world case studies to illustrate their effectiveness in enhancing software quality and reducing time-to-market. It addresses the challenges of integrating AI-driven solutions into existing workflows, including data privacy concerns and the complexities of tool adoption. The chapter concludes with a comprehensive understanding of AI-powered tools, offering guidance for organizations seeking to optimize their software testing processes.

Chapter 11: Harnessing AI for Scalable and Adaptive Cloud-Native Applications

AI is revolutionizing cloud-native application development by enabling intelligent decision-making, automating activities, and improving scalability. This chapter examines how AI-driven tools enhance software engineering practices, such as real-time debugging, continuous testing, and risk assessment. It also discusses challenges related to data privacy, bias, and transparency in AI implementations. Looking ahead, the chapter explores how AI will drive future developments, including quantum computing and self-healing systems, pushing the boundaries of cloud-native application development and transforming the industry's future.

Chapter 12: Leveraging AI and Hyper-Automation for Cloud-native Process Optimization in Healthcare for Hospital Admission and Discharge Automation

This chapter introduces the integration of AI and hyper-automation into hospital operations, focusing on optimizing admission and discharge processes. By leveraging cloud-native technologies and Robotic Process Automation (RPA), hospitals can streamline workflows, reduce manual data entry, and improve patient care. The chapter explores how AI-driven solutions enhance productivity and governance in healthcare, while also addressing risks associated with RPA and cloud implementation. This blueprint demonstrates how AI and automation can revolutionize healthcare operations, leading to improved efficiency, patient outcomes, and compliance.

Chapter 13: Leveraging AI and Hyper-Automation for Optimizing National Health ID Registrations: A Framework for Enhancing Public Sector Efficiency

This chapter explores the transformative potential of AI and hyper-automation in optimizing national health ID registrations within cloud-native frameworks. By integrating AI-driven technologies and automation tools, the registration process can be streamlined, making it more efficient and reducing administrative burden. The chapter examines the benefits of automation, such as enhancing data security and reducing processing time, while also addressing challenges such as privacy concerns, data accuracy, and accessibility. This framework offers insights into how AI can play a crucial role in improving the efficiency of public sector services in a digitally transformed landscape.

Chapter 14: Data Security with Replication for Cloud Computing

Cloud computing has become a cornerstone of modern digital infrastructure, offering scalable and efficient access to services like storage, networking, and software. However, the adoption of cloud-based systems brings with it significant security challenges, particularly in terms of data breaches and losses due to malicious software. This chapter addresses these challenges by exploring the critical role of data replication in enhancing security within cloud computing environments. By replicating data across multiple secure servers, institutions can mitigate risks associated with data loss and unauthorized access. The chapter delves into how data replication, as a strategic security measure, can bolster the reliability and integrity of cloud systems, ensuring that organizations and individuals can continue to benefit from cloud computing's advantages—such as cost-efficiency, speed, and accessibility—without compromising data security.

Chapter 15: Best Practices, Ethical Challenges, and Regulatory Frameworks for AI Integration in Banking: Navigating the Future

As the banking sector undergoes a transformation driven by artificial intelligence (AI) and cloud-native technologies, this chapter examines the revolutionary impact of these innovations on customer service, fraud detection, and risk management. It highlights the ethical challenges arising from AI integration, such as concerns over data privacy, algorithmic bias, and the need for transparency in decision-making processes. With a focus on regulatory frameworks, the chapter reviews key regulations such as GDPR and CCPA and offers practical strategies for ensuring compliance while implementing AI solutions. Through insightful case studies, readers gain a deeper understanding of how financial institutions can navigate the complexities of AI integration and maintain ethical standards. The chapter concludes with a forward-looking perspective on future trends, emphasizing the importance of proactive strategies to balance technological advancements with ethical responsibility.

Chapter 16: A Hybrid Approach Employing Coded Caching-Based Federated Learning (HA-CCFL) for Multiparameter Optimization in Cloud Frameworks

This chapter explores a cutting-edge approach in federated learning, where data remains decentralized and user privacy is preserved while optimizing multiple parameters in cloud computing environments. Specifically, the authors introduce a hybrid strategy called HS-CCFL, which integrates coded caching with federated learning to enhance content distribution across fog computing systems. By analyzing the long-term average speed of shared data and addressing latency challenges, the chapter presents innovative solutions to improve the efficiency and scalability of federated learning systems. Experimental results validate the effectiveness of this approach, which leverages both local caching strategies and a federated algorithm to optimize data distribution. This method is shown to significantly reduce latency while improving data accessibility, making it a valuable contribution to the advancement of cloud and edge computing technologies.

Chapter 17: AI-Powered Tools to Enhance the Stages of Software Development

Artificial Intelligence (AI) is rapidly reshaping the software development lifecycle (SDLC), introducing powerful tools that streamline each stage of development, from planning and design to coding, testing, deployment, and maintenance. This chapter explores how AI-powered tools automate tasks such as code generation, bug detection, and test case creation, reducing errors and accelerating development timelines. AI also supports smarter decision-making and fosters better collaboration among development teams through predictive analytics and intelligent project management systems. Furthermore, the chapter examines AI's role in enhancing software quality by identifying anomalies and predicting system failures early in the development process. As AI becomes increasingly embedded in the SDLC, it is crucial to address ethical and security concerns, ensuring responsible AI use and appropriate human oversight. By the end of this chapter, readers will have a comprehensive understanding of how AI tools can transform the software development process, creating high-quality, scalable applications while navigating the challenges that come with these technological advancements.

CONCLUSION

In conclusion, this reference book offers a comprehensive exploration of the evolving landscape of technology and its multifaceted impact across various sectors. Through its insightful chapters, we have seen how innovations in cloud computing, artificial intelligence, federated learning, and software development are not only reshaping industries but also presenting new challenges in data security, ethical considerations, and regulatory frameworks. The contributions presented within this volume underscore the importance of responsible adoption and integration of these technologies, with an emphasis on balancing innovation with ethical practices. As we look toward the future, the chapters highlight the ongoing need for proactive strategies to address emerging risks and capitalize on the opportunities that these advancements present. We hope this book serves as an invaluable resource for researchers, professionals, and practitioners seeking to navigate the complexities of these technological transformations, offering both practical solutions and a forward-looking perspective on the challenges and opportunities that lie ahead.

Acknowledgment

The creation of this comprehensive volume on Artificial Intelligence for Cloud-Native Software Engineering represents the collaborative efforts of many talented individuals and organizations. We, the editors, would like to express our sincere gratitude to all those who contributed to bringing this project to fruition.

We express our profound gratitude to Dr. Ramakrishnan Raman, Vice Chancellor of Symbiosis International (Deemed University), for his visionary leadership and unwavering support of academic excellence and research innovation. His guidance has been instrumental in fostering an environment conducive to scholarly pursuits.

We are deeply thankful to Professor Dr. CA. Abhijit Chirputkar, Director of Symbiosis Institute of Digital and Telecom Management, for his exceptional leadership and constant encouragement throughout this project. His insights and support have been invaluable in shaping this work.

Special appreciation goes to Professor Dr. Giri G Hallur, Deputy Director of Symbiosis Institute of Digital and Telecom Management, for his steadfast support and valuable contributions to the development of this book. His academic expertise and guidance have significantly enhanced the quality of this work.

First and foremost, we extend our deepest appreciation to all the chapter authors who shared their expertise, insights, and research findings. Their dedication to advancing the field of cloud-native software engineering and artificial intelligence has made this book a valuable resource for practitioners and researchers alike.

We are particularly grateful to our respective institutions - Reliance Jio Platforms Ltd., NETS International, Symbiosis International (Deemed University), and the University of Houston-Victoria - for providing the supportive environment and resources necessary for this academic endeavor.

Special thanks go to the technical reviewers who devoted their time and expertise to ensuring the accuracy and quality of each chapter. Their thorough feedback and constructive suggestions have significantly enhanced the final manuscript.

We would like to acknowledge the team at IGI Global for their professional guidance and support throughout the publication process. Their commitment to excellence in academic publishing has been instrumental in bringing this work to completion.

We also wish to thank our colleagues and research associates who provided valuable feedback during the development of this book. Their informal discussions and insights have contributed significantly to shaping the book's content and structure.

Finally, we express our heartfelt gratitude to our families for their unwavering support and understanding during the many hours dedicated to this project. Their encouragement and patience have been essential to the successful completion of this work.

Editors:

Pethuru Raj Chelliah

Ramamurthy Venkatesh

N. A. Natraj

Rathinaraja Jeyaraj

Chapter 1
A Technical Perspective of Artificial Intelligence for the Ensuring Knowledge Era

B. Sundaravadivzhagan
University of Technology and Applied Sciences, Oman

P. Ashok
https://orcid.org/0000-0002-5859-6041
Symbiosis Institute of Digital and Telecom Management, India

U. Arunkumar
https://orcid.org/0000-0002-4119-1996
Karpagam Academy of Higher Education, India

N. A. Natraj
https://orcid.org/0000-0002-8726-5284
Symbiosis Institute of Digital and Telecom Management, India

ABSTRACT

This chapter examines artificial intelligence technologies and their role in the emerging Knowledge Era, focusing on the evolution from traditional computing to AI-driven systems. It analyzes fundamental AI components, including machine learning architectures, deep learning innovations, and natural language processing, alongside essential infrastructure requirements. The discussion covers AI integration frameworks for knowledge management, exploring automated discovery, information extraction, and semantic reasoning mechanisms. The chapter examines cognitive computing platforms, predictive analytics, and decision support systems that enable

DOI: 10.4018/979-8-3693-9356-7.ch001

sophisticated knowledge processing. Emerging technologies such as explainable AI, federated learning, and autonomous systems are explored, along with their impact on knowledge management.The chapter concludes with future directions emphasizing bio-inspired systems and edge-cloud integration, providing insights for researchers and practitioners implementing AI in knowledge management.

1. INTRODUCTION

The dawn of the 21st century has witnessed an unprecedented acceleration in artificial intelligence (AI) capabilities, marking a transformative shift in how we process, analyze, and utilize information. As we transition into what scholars increasingly recognize as the Knowledge Era, AI technologies are becoming fundamental enablers of intelligent information processing and knowledge management systems. This chapter presents a technical perspective on AI's evolution, current capabilities, and future trajectories, with particular emphasis on its role in shaping the emerging Knowledge Era (Zhang & Lu, 2021). The field of Artificial Intelligence (AI) stands at the forefront of technological innovation, marking a pivotal transition in how we approach computation, knowledge processing, and problem-solving. As we advance into the Knowledge Era, understanding the technical foundations and implications of AI becomes increasingly crucial for both practitioners and researchers in the field (Xu et al., 2021).

1.1 Historical Evolution of AI and Its Technical Foundations

The journey of AI has been characterized by significant technological paradigm shifts since its conceptualization in the 1950s. Initially, AI systems relied heavily on symbolic reasoning and rule-based approaches, where knowledge was explicitly encoded through logical frameworks. The 1980s witnessed the emergence of expert systems, which attempted to capture human expertise in specific domains through complex rule sets and inference engines. However, these early approaches faced limitations in handling real-world complexity and uncertainty (Li, 2017). A fundamental transformation occurred in the 1990s with the rise of machine learning approaches, particularly statistical learning methods. This shift marked the beginning of systems that could learn from data rather than rely solely on predefined rules. Though initially limited by computational constraints, the development of neural networks laid the groundwork for modern deep learning architectures. The current AI renaissance, beginning in the early 2010s, has been driven by three crucial technological advances: the availability of massive datasets, significant improvements in computing power, and breakthroughs in deep learning architectures. These developments have enabled unprecedented achievements in areas such as natural language processing, computer vision, and autonomous systems.

1.2 The Transition from Traditional Computing to AI-Driven Systems

The shift from traditional computing to AI-driven systems represents a fundamental change in how we approach problem-solving through technology. Traditional computing systems operate on predetermined algorithms with explicit instructions for every possible scenario. In contrast, AI-driven systems employ learning algorithms that can adapt to new situations and improve their performance through experience. This transition has necessitated significant changes in system architecture and development approaches. AI-driven systems require different considerations for:

- Data management and processing capabilities
- Computational resource allocation and optimization
- System testing and validation methodologies
- Performance monitoring and improvement mechanisms
- Error handling and reliability assurance

The infrastructure supporting these systems has also evolved, with the development of specialized hardware accelerators, new approaches to distributed computing, and advanced data storage and retrieval systems. This evolution has enabled real-time processing capabilities and enhanced security frameworks necessary for modern AI applications.

1.3 The Emergence of the Knowledge Era and Its Technological Demands

The Knowledge Era represents a transformative evolution beyond the Information Age, marking a crucial shift in how we perceive and utilize digital resources. While the Information Age focused primarily on data accessibility and storage, the Knowledge Era emphasizes the intelligent processing and application of information to generate actionable insights. This fundamental transformation is driven by the growing recognition that mere access to information is insufficient; organizations and individuals need sophisticated mechanisms to derive meaningful value from the ever-expanding digital universe. The distinction lies in the transition from "what" (information) to "how" and "why" (knowledge), requiring advanced technical frameworks that can process, analyze, and synthesize information into valuable knowledge assets.

1.3.1 Technical Requirements for Knowledge Processing

a. Natural Language Understanding and Generation

Advanced natural language processing capabilities form the cornerstone of Knowledge Era systems. These systems must possess sophisticated abilities to comprehend human language in its various forms - from formal documents to informal communications. Modern NLP systems need to understand context, handle ambiguity, recognize sentiment, and generate human-like responses (Lu et al., 2024). This requires deep learning architectures capable of processing semantic relationships, contextual nuances, and linguistic variations across multiple domains and languages.

b. Pattern Recognition and Analysis

Sophisticated pattern recognition systems serve as crucial components in knowledge discovery. These systems must be capable of identifying complex patterns across diverse data types - structured, unstructured, and semi-structured. Through advanced machine learning algorithms, particularly deep neural networks, these systems can detect subtle correlations and relationships that might escape human observation. The ability to recognize patterns extends beyond simple data mining to include temporal patterns, spatial relationships, and complex interdependencies across multiple dimensions.

c. Knowledge Extraction and Synthesis

Automated knowledge extraction mechanisms represent a critical technical requirement for processing vast information repositories. These systems must efficiently extract relevant information from diverse sources, including text documents, databases, multimedia content, and real-time data streams. The synthesis component involves combining extracted information to create new knowledge, requiring sophisticated algorithms for information fusion, conflict resolution, and knowledge validation. This process must maintain semantic consistency while generating meaningful insights that can be practically applied.

D. Intelligent Filtering and Prioritization

The overwhelming volume of available information necessitates intelligent filtering and prioritization systems. These mechanisms must go beyond simple rule-based filtering to incorporate context-aware algorithms that understand user needs, organizational priorities, and temporal relevance. Machine learning models must continuously adapt to changing requirements and user preferences, ensuring that only the most relevant and valuable information reaches the intended recipients. This includes real-time processing capabilities to handle streaming data and dynamic priority adjustments based on evolving contexts.

e. Context-Aware Knowledge Delivery

Context-aware delivery systems represent the final crucial component in the Knowledge Era technical framework. These systems must understand not just the content but the context in which knowledge will be applied. This includes user roles, organizational hierarchy, security clearances, device capabilities, and environmental factors. The delivery mechanism must adapt content presentation based on these contextual factors while maintaining information integrity and ensuring optimal user experience across different platforms and devices.

1.3.2 Technical Challenges and Considerations

The implementation of these technical requirements presents several significant challenges that must be carefully addressed:

a. Scalability Challenges

Knowledge processing systems must scale efficiently to handle growing data volumes and user bases. This requires sophisticated architectural designs that can distribute processing loads while maintaining system responsiveness (Dwivedi et al., 2019). The challenge extends to both computational resources and storage systems, necessitating innovative approaches to resource management and optimization.

b. Quality Assurance

Ensuring knowledge quality and relevance requires robust validation mechanisms and quality control systems. These must include automated verification processes, consistency checks, and feedback loops to maintain high standards of accuracy and reliability in knowledge assets. The challenge involves balancing automation with human oversight to ensure optimal quality levels.

c. Lifecycle Management

The knowledge lifecycle presents unique challenges in versioning, updating, and retiring knowledge assets. Systems must track knowledge evolution, maintain historical records, and ensure seamless transitions between different versions while preserving relationships and dependencies (Borges et al., 2020). This requires sophisticated metadata management and version control mechanisms.

d. Interoperability Requirements

System interoperability remains a critical challenge, requiring standardized protocols and interfaces for seamless knowledge exchange across different platforms and organizations. This includes semantic interoperability to ensure consistent interpretation of knowledge across different contexts and systems. The challenge extends to maintaining compatibility with legacy systems while adopting new technologies and standards.

e. Security and Privacy Considerations

Protecting intellectual property while ensuring appropriate access requires advanced security frameworks. These must include granular access controls, encryption mechanisms, and audit trails while maintaining system usability. Privacy considerations must be embedded in system design, ensuring compliance with regulatory requirements and organizational policies while facilitating necessary knowledge sharing and collaboration.

1.4 Current State of AI Technologies and Their Impact on Knowledge Management

The contemporary landscape of Artificial Intelligence has evolved to achieve unprecedented levels of sophistication, marking a significant milestone in technological advancement. This evolution is particularly evident in several key areas that have demonstrated remarkable progress. Large Language Models (LLMs) have revolutionized natural language understanding and generation, enabling human-like text processing and creation. Computer vision systems have advanced to recognize and interpret visual information with exceptional accuracy, while speech recognition and synthesis technologies have made natural human-machine interaction a reality. Reinforcement learning has opened new frontiers in complex decision-making scenarios, and multimodal AI systems have successfully integrated various forms of information processing, creating more comprehensive and nuanced artificial intelligence capabilities (Waghambare et al., 2023).

These technological advances have catalyzed transformative changes in knowledge management practices through several innovative mechanisms. Automated content creation and curation systems now efficiently process and organize vast amounts of information, significantly reducing manual effort while maintaining high quality standards. Intelligent information retrieval mechanisms have evolved beyond simple keyword matching to understand context and intent, delivering more relevant and accurate results. Predictive analytics and decision support tools leverage advanced algorithms to forecast trends and provide data-driven recommendations, enabling more informed decision-making processes. Personalized knowledge delivery platforms adapt content and presentation based on individual user preferences and needs, while enhanced security and privacy frameworks ensure the protection of sensitive information through sophisticated AI-driven monitoring and control systems (Goul et al., 1992).

The practical implications of these AI advancements in knowledge management are both substantial and far-reaching. Organizations have witnessed dramatic improvements in information processing efficiency, with AI systems capable of handling larger volumes of data at unprecedented speeds. Knowledge extraction accuracy has significantly improved through advanced natural language processing and machine learning algorithms, reducing errors and increasing the reliability of automated systems. User engagement has been revolutionized through sophisticated personalization mechanisms that tailor content and interactions to individual preferences and learning patterns. Perhaps most notably, the cognitive load on human operators has been substantially reduced, as AI systems increasingly handle routine tasks and complex data analysis. This automation has facilitated more effective knowledge sharing and collaboration mechanisms, enabling teams to focus on higher-value activities while AI manages the underlying information infrastructure.

The synergy between AI technologies and knowledge management has created a new paradigm in organizational learning and information utilization. By combining advanced algorithms with sophisticated data processing capabilities, modern AI systems have transformed how organizations capture, process, and leverage knowledge assets. This transformation extends beyond mere automation to include intelligent analysis, predictive capabilities, and adaptive learning systems that continuously improve their performance through experience. The result is a more dynamic and responsive knowledge management ecosystem that can adapt to changing needs while maintaining high standards of accuracy and security.

These developments represent not just technological advancement but a fundamental shift in how organizations approach knowledge management. The integration of AI technologies has enabled a more nuanced and sophisticated approach to information handling, where systems can understand context, learn from experience, and provide increasingly relevant and personalized solutions. This evolution continues to drive innovation in both AI technology and knowledge management practices, creating new opportunities for organizational efficiency and effectiveness (Pedro et al., 2019).

1.5 Chapter Objectives and Organization

This chapter aims to provide a comprehensive technical perspective on AI's role in the Knowledge Era by:

- Examining the fundamental technical components enabling modern AI systems
- Analyzing frameworks necessary for AI integration in knowledge management
- Exploring emerging AI technologies and their potential applications
- Discussing technical challenges and potential solutions
- Providing insights into future developments and their implications

The subsequent sections are organized to build understanding progressively, starting with fundamental technical components in Section 2, moving through AI integration frameworks in Section 3, examining emerging technologies in Section 4, and concluding with future directions and recommendations in Section 5. Each section builds upon the previous ones, providing increasingly detailed technical insights while maintaining practical relevance. The chapter structure enables readers to focus on sections most relevant to their specific interests while understanding the interconnections between different aspects of AI in the Knowledge Era.

2. FUNDAMENTAL TECHNICAL COMPONENTS OF MODERN AI

2.1 Core AI Technologies

The foundation of modern artificial intelligence rests upon several core technologies that have evolved significantly in recent years, each contributing unique capabilities to the AI ecosystem. These fundamental technologies form the backbone of advanced AI systems and continue to drive innovation across multiple domains of application.

2.1.1 Machine Learning Architectures and Frameworks

Machine learning architectures represent the fundamental building blocks of modern AI systems, encompassing a diverse range of approaches from traditional statistical methods to advanced algorithmic frameworks. These architectures have evolved to include sophisticated ensemble methods, gradient-based optimization techniques, and probabilistic modeling frameworks. Contemporary ML frameworks such as TensorFlow, PyTorch, and scikit-learn have democratized access to these capabilities, providing robust implementations of various algorithms while offering high-level abstractions for rapid development. These frameworks support both traditional machine learning paradigms, including support vector machines, random forests, and gradient boosting, as well as more advanced architectural patterns that enable scalable and distributed learning systems (M. Waghambare et al., 2024).

2.1.2 Deep Learning and Neural Network Innovations

Deep learning has emerged as a transformative force in AI, characterized by revolutionary advances in neural network architectures and training methodologies. Modern deep learning systems incorporate sophisticated architectural innovations such as attention mechanisms, residual connections, and transformer models. These innovations have dramatically improved the capacity of neural networks to learn complex patterns and representations from data. Recent developments include efficient architecture search mechanisms, neural architecture optimization, and novel training approaches that address traditional challenges such as vanishing gradients and computational efficiency. The emergence of foundation models has further revolutionized the field, enabling unprecedented transfer learning capabilities and few-shot learning applications.

2.1.3 Natural Language Processing Advances

Natural Language Processing has witnessed remarkable progress through the integration of advanced neural architectures and sophisticated linguistic modeling approaches. Modern NLP systems leverage transformer-based architectures and pre-trained language models to achieve human-like performance in tasks such as text understanding, generation, and translation. Recent advances include improved contextual understanding, better handling of cross-lingual applications, and more efficient processing of long-form text. The development of large language models has revolutionized how systems process and generate human language, enabling more natural and context-aware interactions while supporting increasingly sophisticated applications in content generation, summarization, and semantic analysis.

2.1.4 Computer Vision Systems

Computer vision technologies have evolved to achieve exceptional accuracy in visual data processing and interpretation through the development of specialized neural network architectures and advanced image processing techniques. Modern computer vision systems incorporate convolutional neural networks (CNNs), vision transformers, and hybrid architectures that can effectively process and analyze visual information across multiple scales and contexts (Bharathi et al., 2024). These systems excel in tasks such as object detection, image segmentation, and scene understanding, while recent innovations in self-supervised learning and multi-modal integration have extended their capabilities to more complex visual reasoning tasks. The integration of attention mechanisms and efficient neural architectures has also improved the computational efficiency and accuracy of vision systems.

2.1.5. Reinforcement Learning Mechanisms

Reinforcement learning represents a distinct paradigm in AI that enables systems to learn optimal behavior through interaction with their environment. Modern RL mechanisms incorporate sophisticated approaches such as deep reinforcement learning, multi-agent systems, and hierarchical learning frameworks. Recent advances include improved exploration strategies, more efficient policy optimization methods, and better approaches to handling sparse reward scenarios. The development of advanced algorithms such as Proximal Policy Optimization (PPO) and Soft Actor-Critic (SAC) has enhanced the stability and efficiency of RL systems, while innovations in model-based RL and offline reinforcement learning have expanded the practical applicability of these techniques across various domains. Each of these core technologies continues to evolve rapidly, driven by theoretical advances, practical innovations, and the increasing availability of computational resources. Their integration and synergistic application enable the development of increasingly sophisticated AI systems capable of addressing complex real-world challenges. As these technologies mature, they provide the foundation for more advanced applications in knowledge management, decision support, and autonomous systems.

2.2 AI Infrastructure and Computing

2.2.1 High-Performance Computing for AI

High-performance computing (HPC) infrastructure forms the computational backbone of modern AI systems, enabling the processing of massive datasets and training of complex models. These systems leverage parallel processing architectures, advanced memory hierarchies, and optimized interconnects to achieve unprecedented computational throughput. Modern HPC clusters for AI typically incorporate multiple GPUs and specialized processors, connected through high-bandwidth networks, and managed by sophisticated scheduling systems that optimize resource allocation and workload distribution (Gadde., 2022). The integration of advanced cooling systems and power management solutions ensures sustainable operation at peak performance levels.

2.2.2 Specialized AI Processors and Accelerators

The evolution of AI hardware has led to the development of specialized processors and accelerators designed specifically for AI workloads. These include Tensor Processing Units (TPUs), Neural Processing Units (NPUs), and Field Programmable Gate Arrays (FPGAs) optimized for neural network operations. These specialized processors feature architectures tailored for matrix operations, convolutions, and other AI-specific computations, offering significant performance improvements over general-purpose processors. Recent innovations include the integration of on-chip memory hierarchies, dedicated pipelines for different types of neural network operations, and enhanced support for mixed-precision arithmetic.

2.2.3 Distributed AI Systems

Distributed AI systems enable the scaling of AI applications across multiple computational nodes, supporting larger models and more complex applications. These systems incorporate sophisticated orchestration frameworks, distributed training algorithms, and efficient communication protocols. Modern distributed AI architectures leverage techniques such as model parallelism, data parallelism, and pipeline parallelism to optimize training and inference across clusters. Advanced synchronization mechanisms and fault-tolerance protocols ensure reliable operation in distributed environments, while dynamic load balancing algorithms optimize resource utilization (Chirra, 2020).

2.2.4 Edge Computing for AI Applications

Edge computing has emerged as a crucial paradigm for AI deployment, bringing computation closer to data sources and end-users. Edge AI systems incorporate specialized hardware and optimized software stacks designed for efficient operation within resource-constrained environments. These systems support real-time processing of sensor data, local decision-making, and reduced latency for time-critical applications. Recent advances include improved model compression techniques, efficient inference engines, and sophisticated power management strategies for battery-operated devices.

2.2.5 Quantum Computing Possibilities for AI

Quantum computing represents a frontier technology with significant potential implications for AI. Current research explores quantum algorithms for machine learning, optimization problems, and pattern recognition. While still in early stages, quantum approaches show promise in areas such as quantum neural networks, quantum machine learning algorithms, and hybrid quantum-classical systems. The development of quantum error correction, quantum memory systems, and quantum-specific algorithms continues to advance the potential integration of quantum computing with AI applications.

2.3 Data Architecture for AI Systems

2.3.1 Big Data Infrastructure Requirements

Big Data infrastructure for AI systems demands sophisticated architectures capable of handling massive volumes of structured and unstructured data. These systems incorporate distributed storage systems, parallel processing frameworks, and advanced data management tools. Modern Big Data architectures typically feature scalable storage solutions, high-throughput data ingestion mechanisms, and efficient data retrieval systems. The infrastructure must support diverse data types, multiple access patterns, and varying performance requirements while maintaining data consistency and availability.

2.3.2 Data Lakes and Warehouses

Data lakes and warehouses serve as central repositories in AI-driven organizations, providing structured storage and efficient access to diverse data types. Modern data lake architectures incorporate metadata management systems, data cataloging services, and sophisticated indexing mechanisms. These systems support both traditional structured data warehousing and flexible schema-on-read approaches for data lakes. Advanced features include automated data organization, intelligent data tiering, and integrated governance mechanisms that ensure data accessibility while maintaining security and compliance.

2.3.3 Real-time Data Processing Systems

Real-time processing systems enable AI applications to operate on streaming data, supporting immediate analysis and decision-making. These systems incorporate stream processing engines, complex event processing frameworks, and low-latency data pipelines. Modern architectures feature advanced windowing mechanisms, stateful processing capabilities, and sophisticated event handling systems. Integration with machine learning models enables real-time prediction and anomaly detection, while adaptive processing strategies optimize resource utilization based on workload characteristics.

2.3.4 Data Quality and Governance Frameworks

Data quality and governance frameworks ensure the reliability and compliance of AI systems through systematic data management practices. These frameworks incorporate automated quality assessment tools, data validation mechanisms, and comprehensive audit trails. Modern approaches include ML-based data quality monitoring, automated data cleansing pipelines, and sophisticated lineage tracking systems. Governance frameworks provide policy enforcement mechanisms, access control systems, and compliance monitoring tools that maintain data integrity while ensuring regulatory compliance.

2.3.5 Knowledge Graphs and Semantic Networks

Knowledge graphs and semantic networks provide structured representations of domain knowledge, supporting advanced reasoning and inference capabilities in AI systems. These systems incorporate ontology management tools, relationship extraction mechanisms, and inference engines. Modern knowledge graph architectures feature distributed storage systems, efficient query processing mechanisms, and sophisticated reasoning frameworks. Recent advances include automated knowledge graph construction, dynamic knowledge update mechanisms, and integration with machine learning systems for enhanced knowledge discovery and validation.

3. AI INTEGRATION FRAMEWORKS FOR KNOWLEDGE MANAGEMENT

3.1 Knowledge Extraction and Organization

a. Automated Knowledge Discovery Systems

Automated knowledge discovery systems represent the cutting edge of AI-driven information processing, combining multiple AI technologies to automatically identify, extract, and organize valuable knowledge from diverse data sources. These systems employ sophisticated machine learning algorithms and natural language processing techniques to analyze unstructured data, identify patterns, and extract meaningful insights. Modern knowledge discovery systems utilize deep learning models to understand complex relationships within data, incorporating both supervised and unsupervised learning approaches to handle varied information types. They continuously evolve through feedback loops, improving their accuracy and relevance through iterative learning processes while adapting to new data patterns and domain-specific requirements.

b. Information Extraction Techniques

Information extraction techniques have evolved significantly, incorporating advanced neural architectures and linguistic processing capabilities to accurately identify and extract relevant information from diverse sources. These techniques leverage transformer-based models for named entity recognition, relationship extraction, and event detection, achieving unprecedented accuracy in understanding contextual information. Modern extraction systems employ multi-stage processing pipelines that combine rule-based approaches with deep learning models, enabling robust handling of various document formats, languages, and writing styles. The integration of zero-shot and few-shot learning capabilities has enhanced these systems' ability to adapt to new domains and information types without extensive retraining.

c. Knowledge Representation Methods

Knowledge representation methods provide the foundational frameworks for organizing and structuring extracted information in machine-readable formats that facilitate reasoning and inference. These methods encompass various approaches, from traditional semantic networks and frames to modern vector-based representations and neural embeddings. Contemporary knowledge representation systems utilize hybrid approaches that combine symbolic representations with distributed representations, enabling both precise logical reasoning and flexible similarity-based operations. Advanced techniques incorporate temporal aspects and uncertainty measures, allowing for more nuanced representation of complex knowledge structures while maintaining computational efficiency.

d. Ontology Development and Management

Ontology development and management systems form the backbone of structured knowledge organization, providing formal specifications of conceptual relationships and hierarchies within specific domains. Modern ontology management platforms incorporate AI-driven tools for automated ontology learning, evolution, and alignment, reducing the manual effort required in ontology maintenance. These systems support collaborative ontology development through version control mechanisms and consistency checking tools, while enabling dynamic updates to reflect evolving domain knowledge. Advanced features include automated suggestion systems for ontology enrichment and sophisticated visualization tools for ontology exploration and validation.

e. Semantic Reasoning Engines

Semantic reasoning engines represent the intelligent processing layer that enables machines to draw conclusions and generate new insights from structured knowledge repositories. These engines combine classical logical reasoning approaches with probabilistic inference methods, enabling robust handling of uncertainty and incomplete information. Modern semantic reasoners incorporate neural-symbolic integration techniques, allowing them to leverage both explicit rules and learned patterns for inference. They support various reasoning paradigms, including deductive, inductive, and abductive reasoning, while maintaining scalability through optimized inference algorithms and distributed processing capabilities.

The integration of these components creates a comprehensive framework for knowledge management that addresses the full lifecycle of knowledge processing:

- The framework begins with automated discovery systems that continuously scan and analyze various data sources, identifying potentially valuable information.
- Information extraction techniques then process this raw data, precisely identifying and extracting relevant knowledge elements.

- The extracted information is structured using appropriate knowledge representation methods, ensuring both human interpretability and machine processability.
- Ontological frameworks provide the organizational structure for this knowledge, establishing relationships and hierarchies that facilitate navigation and retrieval.
- Finally, semantic reasoning engines operate on this structured knowledge base, enabling sophisticated query processing, inference generation, and knowledge discovery.

This integrated approach enables organizations to effectively manage their knowledge assets while supporting continuous learning and adaptation to new information and requirements. The framework's modular nature allows for component-specific optimizations and updates, ensuring long-term sustainability and scalability of the knowledge management system.

3.2 Knowledge Processing and Analysis

Modern knowledge processing and analysis systems represent a convergence of sophisticated AI technologies designed to transform raw information into actionable insights. These systems incorporate multiple layers of processing capabilities, each contributing to the comprehensive understanding and utilization of organizational knowledge.

Cognitive computing platforms form the foundation of advanced knowledge processing, simulating human thought processes through the integration of multiple AI technologies. These platforms leverage deep learning architectures, natural language processing, and reasoning engines to understand complex information patterns and contexts. By combining these capabilities with adaptive learning mechanisms, cognitive computing platforms can continuously improve their performance while handling increasingly complex knowledge processing tasks. The incorporation of memory networks and attention mechanisms enables these systems to maintain context across multiple interactions, significantly enhancing their ability to process and analyze information in ways that mirror human cognitive processes.

Intelligent decision support systems extend the capabilities of cognitive platforms by providing specialized analysis and recommendation frameworks. These systems excel at processing vast amounts of structured and unstructured data to generate evidence-based recommendations for complex decision-making scenarios. Through the integration of historical analysis with real-time data processing, these systems offer contextually relevant insights while adapting to changing conditions and requirements. Advanced features such as multi-criteria decision analysis and risk assessment capabilities ensure comprehensive support for strategic decision-making processes.

Predictive analytics frameworks represent another crucial component of modern knowledge processing systems, employing sophisticated machine learning algorithms to forecast trends and identify patterns in complex datasets. These frameworks combine multiple analytical approaches, including time series analysis, deep learning models, and ensemble methods, to achieve high accuracy in predictive tasks. The ability to process both structured and unstructured data enables these systems to provide comprehensive predictive capabilities across various domains, while automated feature engineering and real-time model updating ensure continuous improvement in prediction accuracy.

Pattern recognition systems and knowledge validation mechanisms complete the processing pipeline, ensuring the accuracy and reliability of processed information. Modern pattern recognition systems utilize advanced neural networks and unsupervised learning techniques to identify subtle correlations and hidden patterns within complex datasets. These capabilities are complemented by robust validation mechanisms that employ multiple verification approaches, including cross-validation, consistency checking, and temporal coherence verification, to maintain the integrity of processed knowledge.

3.3 Knowledge Distribution and Access

The effective distribution and access of processed knowledge represents a critical component of modern knowledge management systems, requiring sophisticated AI-driven platforms and security mechanisms to ensure optimal information flow throughout organizations. AI-powered knowledge sharing platforms serve as the primary interface for knowledge distribution, incorporating advanced content management and recommendation systems to facilitate efficient information dissemination. These platforms utilize intelligent categorization and tagging mechanisms to organize content effectively, while smart recommendation systems ensure that relevant information reaches appropriate users at the right time. The integration of user behavior analysis and collaborative filtering mechanisms enables these platforms to continuously optimize knowledge flow patterns while adapting to changing organizational needs.

Intelligent search and retrieval systems provide the technical foundation for efficient knowledge access, employing sophisticated AI techniques to deliver highly relevant and contextualized search results. These systems combine semantic search capabilities with context-aware query processing to understand user intent and provide precise results. The incorporation of learning-to-rank algorithms and natural language understanding enables these systems to continuously improve their performance through user interactions, ensuring increasingly accurate and relevant search results over time. Personalized knowledge delivery mechanisms enhance the effectiveness of distribution systems by tailoring information presentation and content selection to individual user needs and preferences. These systems employ advanced user modeling techniques and adaptive interface customization to ensure optimal knowledge absorption and utilization. The integration of learning style recognition and context-aware delivery mechanisms enables these systems to provide highly personalized knowledge experiences while maintaining consistency with organizational knowledge management objectives. Collaborative AI systems facilitate team-based knowledge work through intelligent coordination and information sharing mechanisms (B. Li et al., 2017). These systems support both human-human and human-AI collaboration through sophisticated interaction models and real-time knowledge synchronization capabilities. The incorporation of multi-agent collaboration frameworks and intelligent task allocation ensures efficient knowledge sharing and creation within team environments, while conflict resolution mechanisms maintain smooth collaborative operations.

Security and access control mechanisms form the critical protective layer of knowledge distribution systems, ensuring appropriate information access while maintaining robust security standards. These systems employ AI-driven security mechanisms, including behavioral analytics and automated threat detection, to protect sensitive information while ensuring seamless access for authorized users. The integration of privacy-preserving data sharing techniques and dynamic permission adjustment enables organizations to maintain strict security standards without compromising knowledge accessibility and utilization. This comprehensive approach to knowledge processing and distribution creates an integrated ecosystem that supports efficient knowledge discovery, analysis, and sharing while maintaining robust security and personalization capabilities. The continuous evolution of these systems, driven by advances in AI technology, ensures increasingly sophisticated knowledge management capabilities that adapt to changing organizational requirements and user needs.

4. EMERGING AI TECHNOLOGIES FOR THE KNOWLEDGE ERA

4.1 Advanced AI Paradigms

The landscape of artificial intelligence is rapidly evolving with the emergence of sophisticated paradigms that address previous limitations while opening new possibilities for knowledge processing and management (Natraj et al., 2024). These advanced approaches represent the cutting edge of AI research and development, fundamentally transforming how AI systems learn, reason, and interact with human users.

Explainable AI (XAI) frameworks have emerged as a critical development in making AI systems more transparent and trustworthy (Adadi & Berrada, 2018). These frameworks incorporate various techniques, from attention visualization to decision tree extraction, enabling AI systems to provide clear explanations for their decisions and recommendations. The development of layer-wise relevance propagation, counterfactual explanations, and interpretable neural architectures has made it possible to understand the internal reasoning of complex AI models, addressing the crucial need for accountability in AI-driven decision-making processes.

Federated Learning systems represent a paradigm shift in how AI models are trained and deployed, enabling distributed learning across multiple devices or organizations while maintaining data privacy. These systems allow models to learn from decentralized data sources without requiring direct access to raw data, incorporating sophisticated encryption mechanisms and secure aggregation protocols. The integration of differential privacy techniques and secure multi-party computation ensures that sensitive information remains protected while enabling collaborative model improvement.

Transfer Learning mechanisms have revolutionized AI model development by enabling the efficient adaptation of pre-trained models to new domains and tasks. These mechanisms leverage knowledge gained from one problem domain to enhance learning in another, significantly reducing the data and computational requirements for new applications. Advanced transfer learning approaches incorporate meta-learning capabilities and domain adaptation techniques, enabling more flexible and efficient knowledge transfer across different contexts.

Few-shot and Zero-shot learning capabilities represent breakthrough achievements in AI's ability to learn from limited examples or even recognize entirely new categories without specific training. These approaches utilize meta-learning frameworks and sophisticated embedding spaces to generalize from minimal data, incorporating techniques such as prototypical networks and matching networks. The development of more robust few-shot learning algorithms has enabled AI systems to adapt more quickly to new situations while maintaining high performance levels.

Autonomous AI systems represent the culmination of multiple AI advances, creating systems capable of independent decision-making and continuous learning. These systems incorporate self-improvement mechanisms, automated error correction, and adaptive learning capabilities, enabling them to evolve and improve their performance over time without constant human intervention.

4.2 AI-Enhanced Knowledge Services

The evolution of AI-enhanced knowledge services marks a significant advancement in how organizations manage, process, and utilize information resources. These services leverage cutting-edge AI technologies to provide sophisticated knowledge management capabilities that adapt to user needs and organizational requirements. Intelligent virtual assistants have evolved beyond simple query-response systems to become sophisticated knowledge agents capable of understanding context, maintaining conversations, and providing personalized assistance. These assistants incorporate advanced natural language processing, context awareness, and learning capabilities to provide more natural and effective interactions. The integration of emotional intelligence and personality adaptation enables these systems to provide more engaging and effective knowledge support.

Automated knowledge curation systems employ advanced AI algorithms to continuously collect, organize, and maintain knowledge repositories. These systems utilize sophisticated content analysis, metadata extraction, and quality assessment mechanisms to ensure the relevance and reliability of curated knowledge. The incorporation of automated validation frameworks and version control systems ensures the maintenance of high-quality, up-to-date knowledge bases. Real-time knowledge synthesis capabilities enable systems to generate new insights and understanding by combining information from multiple sources dynamically. These systems employ advanced neural architectures and reasoning engines to process and combine information in real-time, creating coherent and contextually relevant knowledge products. The integration of streaming analytics and adaptive learning mechanisms ensures continuous improvement in synthesis quality.

Cross-domain knowledge integration represents a sophisticated approach to combining information across different fields and disciplines. These systems utilize advanced semantic mapping, ontology alignment, and knowledge fusion techniques to create comprehensive understanding across diverse domains. The development of sophisticated reasoning engines enables the identification and exploitation of cross-domain relationships and patterns. Knowledge lifecycle management systems provide comprehensive frameworks for managing the entire lifecycle of knowledge assets, from creation through retirement. These systems incorporate automated quality assessment, relevance tracking, and deprecation mechanisms to maintain the vitality of knowledge repositories while ensuring efficient resource utilization.

4.3 Future Technical Directions

The future of AI technology in the Knowledge Era is shaped by emerging approaches that promise to revolutionize how we develop and deploy AI systems. These directions represent both evolutionary and revolutionary changes in AI architecture and implementation.

Hybrid AI architectures combine multiple AI approaches to create more robust and versatile systems. These architectures integrate symbolic reasoning with neural networks, combining the precision of rule-based systems with the flexibility of learned behaviors. The development of sophisticated integration frameworks enables seamless cooperation between different AI paradigms, leading to more capable and adaptable systems.

Bio-inspired AI systems draw inspiration from biological systems to create more efficient and adaptable AI architectures. These approaches incorporate principles from neuroscience, cognitive science, and evolutionary biology to develop more natural and efficient learning mechanisms. The integration of neuromorphic computing and evolutionary algorithms enables the development of more robust and adaptable AI systems. Cognitive computing advances continue to push the boundaries of AI capabilities, moving closer to human-like reasoning and understanding. These developments incorporate advances in neural architecture, memory systems, and reasoning engines to create more sophisticated cognitive models. The integration of emotional intelligence and social cognition enables more natural and effective human-AI interaction.

Edge-Cloud AI integration represents a crucial direction in deploying AI systems across distributed infrastructure (Marakkoottathil et al., 2024). These approaches optimize the distribution of AI processing between edge devices and cloud resources, enabling more efficient and responsive AI applications. The development of sophisticated orchestration mechanisms ensures optimal resource utilization while maintaining system performance. Sustainable AI technologies focus on developing more energy-efficient and environmentally responsible AI systems. These approaches incorporate efficient algorithms, optimized hardware utilization, and green computing principles to reduce the environmental impact of AI operations. The development of energy-aware training methods and efficient model deployment strategies ensures more sustainable AI implementations.

5. SUMMARY OF TECHNICAL ASPECTS AND RESEARCH DIRECTIONS

5.1 Summary of Key Technical Perspectives

The evolution of AI technologies in the Knowledge Era represents a fundamental transformation in how organizations process, manage, and utilize information resources. The convergence of advanced AI paradigms, sophisticated infrastructure, and intelligent knowledge management systems has created unprecedented opportunities for enhancing organizational knowledge capabilities (J. Zhang & Tao, 2020). Key technical developments include the maturation of deep learning architectures, the emergence of explainable AI frameworks, and the integration of edge computing with cloud-based systems. These advances have enabled more sophisticated approaches to knowledge extraction, processing, and distribution, while ensuring greater accuracy and reliability in AI-driven decision-making processes. The integration of multiple AI technologies, from natural language processing to computer vision, has created comprehensive platforms capable of handling diverse knowledge management requirements across various domains and applications.

5.2 Critical Challenges and Solutions

The implementation of AI-driven knowledge management systems faces several significant challenges that require careful consideration and innovative solutions. Data quality and integrity remain fundamental concerns, necessitating robust validation mechanisms and sophisticated preprocessing frameworks. The challenge of scaling AI systems while maintaining performance and efficiency has led to the development of distributed computing architectures and optimized processing algorithms. Privacy and security considerations have driven the adoption of federated learning approaches and enhanced encryption mechanisms. Integration challenges between legacy systems and new AI technologies have been addressed through the development of flexible middleware solutions and standardized APIs. The complexity of managing large-scale knowledge bases has been mitigated through the implementation of automated curation systems and intelligent metadata management frameworks.

5.3 Future Research Directions

The trajectory of AI technology in knowledge management points toward several promising research directions that will shape future developments. Emerging areas include the advancement of neuromorphic computing architectures that more closely mimic human cognitive processes, the development of more sophisticated transfer learning mechanisms enabling efficient knowledge adaptation across domains, and the evolution of autonomous AI systems capable of self-improvement and adaptation. Research into quantum computing applications for AI promises to revolutionize processing capabilities, while advances in bio-inspired AI systems suggest new approaches to system architecture and learning mechanisms. The integration of emotional intelligence and social cognition capabilities represents another crucial direction, potentially enabling more natural and effective human-AI interaction in knowledge management contexts.

5.4 Implications for Knowledge Management

The impact of emerging AI technologies on knowledge management practices extends far beyond simple automation of existing processes. Organizations must adapt to a new paradigm where knowledge creation, processing, and distribution become increasingly dynamic and automated. The ability to extract insights from unstructured data sources, combined with real-time synthesis capabilities, enables more responsive and adaptive knowledge management strategies. The emergence of personalized knowledge delivery systems suggests a future where information access becomes highly individualized and context-aware. The integration of collaborative AI systems implies fundamental changes in how teams interact with and utilize organizational knowledge resources. These developments necessitate new approaches to knowledge governance, quality assurance, and lifecycle management.

5.5 Recommendations for Implementation

Successful implementation of AI-driven knowledge management systems requires a structured and thoughtful approach that considers both technical and organizational factors. Organizations should begin by establishing clear objectives and success metrics for their AI initiatives, ensuring alignment with broader strategic goals. The implementation process should follow an incremental approach, starting with pilot projects that demonstrate value while building organizational capability. Key recommendations include:

1. Developing robust data governance frameworks that ensure quality and consistency in AI system inputs
2. Investing in scalable infrastructure that can support growing knowledge management requirements
3. Implementing comprehensive security and privacy measures that protect sensitive information while enabling appropriate access

4. Establishing continuous monitoring and evaluation mechanisms to assess system performance and impact
5. Creating training and support programs that enable effective human-AI collaboration
6. Adopting flexible architecture designs that can accommodate emerging technologies and changing requirements

The systematic consideration of these elements, combined with careful attention to change management and stakeholder engagement, provides the foundation for successful implementation of AI-driven knowledge management systems. Organizations must maintain a balance between innovation and stability, ensuring that new capabilities enhance rather than disrupt existing knowledge management practices. Regular assessment and adjustment of implementation strategies, based on measured outcomes and emerging requirements, will enable organizations to maximize the benefits of AI technologies while minimizing associated risks and challenges.

6. CONCLUSION

The technical evolution of artificial intelligence in the Knowledge Era represents a fundamental transformation in how organizations process, manage, and utilize information resources, marked by significant advances in AI architectures, infrastructure, and knowledge management capabilities. The convergence of sophisticated AI paradigms, including explainable AI frameworks, federated learning systems, and autonomous AI architectures, has created unprecedented opportunities for enhancing organizational knowledge capabilities while addressing critical challenges of transparency, privacy, and scalability. These developments, supported by advanced infrastructure incorporating edge computing, specialized processors, and distributed systems, enable more efficient and effective knowledge processing at scale. The emergence of intelligent knowledge services, from automated curation to real-time synthesis, demonstrates the practical impact of AI on organizational knowledge management, while the integration of sophisticated security frameworks and privacy-preserving mechanisms ensures the responsible deployment of these capabilities. Looking forward, several key directions will continue to shape the evolution of AI in knowledge management, including the advancement of neuromorphic computing architectures, the development of more sophisticated transfer learning mechanisms, and the integration of bio-inspired AI systems. Critical challenges remain, particularly in areas of data quality, system integration, and sustainable scaling, yet innovative solutions such as distributed computing architectures, automated validation frameworks, and hybrid AI systems provide promising approaches to addressing these challenges. For organizations seeking to implement these technologies, success depends on establishing robust data governance frameworks, investing in scalable infrastructure, implementing comprehensive security measures, and developing effective training programs that enable productive human-AI collaboration. As AI technologies continue to mature, their role in knowledge management will become increasingly central to organizational success, requiring a balanced approach that combines technical innovation with practical considerations for implementation and organizational adoption. The future of AI-driven knowledge management lies in the thoughtful integration of these emerging technologies with existing organizational processes, supported by continuous evaluation and adaptation to evolving requirements and capabilities.

REFERENCES

Abirami, T., Ananthi, K., Venice, J. A., Chandru, R., & Rathish, C. R. (2024). The Impact of 5G Technology on the Digital Supply Chain and Operations Management Landscape. In *Applications of New Technology in Operations and Supply Chain Management* (pp. 289-311). IGI Global.

Adadi, A., & Berrada, M. (2018). Peeking inside the black-box: A survey on explainable artificial intelligence (XAI). *IEEE Access : Practical Innovations, Open Solutions*, 6, 52138–52160. DOI: 10.1109/ACCESS.2018.2870052

Bharathi, V., Natraj, N. A., Gopinath, S., & Kiruthikaa, R. (2024). Advanced Computer Vision Techniques for Accurate Measurement in Unmanned Mobile Robots. *Measurement Science Review*, 24(5), 188–192. DOI: 10.2478/msr-2024-0025

Borges, A. F., Laurindo, F. J., Spínola, M. M., Gonçalves, R. F., & Mattos, C. A. (2021). The strategic use of artificial intelligence in the digital era: Systematic literature review and future research directions. *International Journal of Information Management*, 57, 102225. DOI: 10.1016/j.ijinfomgt.2020.102225

Chirra, D. R. (2020). AI-Based Real-Time Security Monitoring for Cloud-Native Applications in Hybrid Cloud Environments. *Revista de Inteligencia Artificial en Medicina*, 11(1), 382–402.

Chowdary, V. H. D., Shanmukh, A., Nikhil, T. P., Kumar, B. S., & Khan, F. (2024, May). DevOps 2.0: Embracing AI/ML, Cloud-Native Development, and a Culture of Continuous Transformation. In *2024 4th International Conference on Pervasive Computing and Social Networking (ICPCSN)* (pp. 673-679). IEEE.

Dwivedi, Y. K., Hughes, L., Ismagilova, E., Aarts, G., Coombs, C., Crick, T., Duan, Y., Dwivedi, R., Edwards, J., Eirug, A., Galanos, V., Ilavarasan, P. V., Janssen, M., Jones, P., Kar, A. K., Kizgin, H., Kronemann, B., Lal, B., Lucini, B., & Williams, M. D. (2021). Artificial Intelligence (AI): Multidisciplinary perspectives on emerging challenges, opportunities, and agenda for research, practice and policy. *International Journal of Information Management*, 57, 101994. DOI: 10.1016/j.ijinfomgt.2019.08.002

Erler, M. (2024, August). Sustainable Computing for AI & Cloud Native Workloads. In *2024 IEEE Hot Chips 36 Symposium (HCS)* (pp. 1-24). IEEE Computer Society. DOI: 10.1109/HCS61935.2024.10664662

Gadde, H. (2022). AI-Enhanced Adaptive Resource Allocation in Cloud-Native Databases. *Revista de Inteligencia Artificial en Medicina*, 13(1), 443–470.

Goul, M., Henderson, J. C., & Tonge, F. M. (1992). The emergence of artificial intelligence as a reference discipline for decision support systems research. *Decision Sciences*, 23(6), 1263–1276. DOI: 10.1111/j.1540-5915.1992.tb00448.x

Hourani, H., Hammad, A., & Lafi, M. (2019, April). The impact of artificial intelligence on software testing. In *2019 IEEE Jordan International Joint Conference on Electrical Engineering and Information Technology (JEEIT)* (pp. 565-570). IEEE. DOI: 10.1109/JEEIT.2019.8717439

Khan, M. F. I., Mahmud, F. U., Hoseen, A., & Masum, A. K. M. (2024). A New Approach Of Software Test Automation Using Ai. *Yingyong Jichu Yu Gongcheng Kexue Xuebao*, 21(1), 559–570.

Li, B. H., Hou, B. C., Yu, W. T., Lu, X. B., & Yang, C. W. (2017). Applications of artificial intelligence in intelligent manufacturing: A review. *Frontiers of Information Technology & Electronic Engineering*, 18(1), 86–96. DOI: 10.1631/FITEE.1601885

Li, D., & Du, Y. (2017). *Artificial intelligence with uncertainty*. CRC press. DOI: 10.1201/9781315366951

Lima, R., da Cruz, A. M. R., & Ribeiro, J. (2020, June). Artificial intelligence applied to software testing: A literature review. In *2020 15th Iberian Conference on Information Systems and Technologies (CISTI)* (pp. 1-6). IEEE. DOI: 10.23919/CISTI49556.2020.9141124

Lu, Y., Bian, S., Chen, L., He, Y., Hui, Y., Lentz, M., . . . Zhuo, D. (2024). Computing in the Era of Large Generative Models: From Cloud-Native to AI-Native. *arXiv preprint arXiv:2401.12230.*

Machireddy, J. R., Rachakatla, S. K., & Ravichandran, P. (2022). Cloud-Native Data Warehousing: Implementing AI and Machine Learning for Scalable Business Analytics. *Journal of AI in Healthcare and Medicine*, 2(1), 144–169.

Marakkoottathil, M., Venkatesh, R., & Natraj, N. A. (2024). A Quantitative Study on Cloud Computing in the UAE: Identifying and Addressing Adoption Barriers. In *Analyzing and Mitigating Security Risks in Cloud Computing* (pp. 66–90). IGI Global. DOI: 10.4018/979-8-3693-3249-8.ch004

Paul, D., Namperumal, G., & Selvaraj, A. (2022). Cloud-Native AI/ML Pipelines: Best Practices for Continuous Integration, Deployment, and Monitoring in Enterprise Applications. *Journal of Artificial Intelligence Research*, 2(1), 176–231.

. Pedro, F., Subosa, M., Rivas, A., & Valverde, P. (2019). Artificial intelligence in education: Challenges and opportunities for sustainable development.

Waghambare, M., Prabhu, S., Ashok, P., & Natraj, N. A. (2024). Elevating Business Experiences: AI-Powered Chatbots Reforming Marketing and E-Commerce. In *Transforming the Financial Landscape With ICTs* (pp. 1-27). IGI Global.

Waghambare, M. A., Prabhu, S., & Ashok, P. (2024). Artificial Intelligence (AI)-Powered Chatbots for Marketing and Online Shopping. In *Digital Technologies in Modeling and Management: Insights in Education and Industry* (pp. 21-39). IGI Global.

Xu, Y., Liu, X., Cao, X., Huang, C., Liu, E., Qian, S., Liu, X., Wu, Y., Dong, F., Qiu, C.-W., Qiu, J., Hua, K., Su, W., Wu, J., Xu, H., Han, Y., Fu, C., Yin, Z., Liu, M., & Zhang, J. (2021). Artificial intelligence: A powerful paradigm for scientific research. *Innovation (Cambridge (Mass.))*, 2(4), 100179. DOI: 10.1016/j.xinn.2021.100179 PMID: 34877560

Zhang, C., & Lu, Y. (2021). Study on artificial intelligence: The state of the art and future prospects. *Journal of Industrial Information Integration*, 23, 100224. DOI: 10.1016/j.jii.2021.100224

Zhang, J., & Tao, D. (2020). Empowering things with intelligence: A survey of the progress, challenges, and opportunities in artificial intelligence of things. *IEEE Internet of Things Journal*, 8(10), 7789–7817. DOI: 10.1109/JIOT.2020.3039359

Chapter 2
Artificial Intelligence: Augmented Integrated Development Environments for Boosting Programmer Productivity

P. Ashok
https://orcid.org/0000-0002-5859-6041
Symbiosis Institute of Digital and Telecom Management, India

Ravi Gorli
https://orcid.org/0000-0002-4381-3250
GITAM University, India

S. Parameswari
Sri Sairam Institute of Technology, India

Lakshmi Sridevi
Chennai Institute of Technology, India

N. Janaki
Vels Institute of Science Technology and Advanced Studies, India

S. Gopinath
Karpagam Institute of Technology, India

Harishchander Anandaram
https://orcid.org/0000-0003-2993-5304
Amrita Vishwa Vidyapeetam, India

K. S. Shreenidhi
https://orcid.org/0000-0002-6844-0454
Rajalakshmi Engineering College, India

Samaya Pillai Iyengar
https://orcid.org/0000-0002-8451-8936
Symbiosis Institute of Digital and Telecom Management, India

ABSTRACT

AI is transforming software development with technologies that improve speed, quality, and productivity. AI-powered technologies and their use in software development are covered in this abstract. NLP algorithms help extract and categorize requirements from unstructured documents during requirements collecting and analysis. Machine learning algorithms forecast hazards and resource needs using past project data,

DOI: 10.4018/979-8-3693-9356-7.ch002

improving planning and estimating. In addition, machine learning models trained on massive code repositories may produce code snippets and functions from natural language descriptions. AI algorithms produce test cases, prioritize test scenarios, and anticipate defect-prone code for testing and quality assurance. Automatic bug detection technologies use deep learning to spot bugs before they hit production. This research article brings in more insights about the various tools and softwares that are utilized in various stages of software development life cycle for efficient product development.

1. INTRODUCTION TO AI-AUGMENTED IDES

AI embedded Integrated Development Environments (IDEs) are application development environments that are empowered by artificial intelligence technologies. AI incorporated IDEs means the platforms or environments that incorporate intelligence in the design of the software. Such platforms tailor their utilization of Artificial Intelligence to facilitate high standards and optimization of performance, effectiveness, decision making, user satisfaction, growth potential, protection, and legally permissible uses (Alzyadat et al., 2023).

Basic Concepts of AI-augmented IDEs:

- Knowledge Vaporization: This concept relates to the practice of freezing knowledge acquired during AI models development and make it available to other phases of software development life cycle.
- Requirement Engineering: It requires identifying the necessary prerequisite for the software system to accomplish what it will be designed to do. Concepts like context boundary, domain knowledge, and application domain are very relevant for defining what the system to be developed will encompass and what it will not encompass (Alzyadat et al., 2023).

Enhancement of the Development Process:

- Improved Performance: AI-augmented IDEs contribute to improved performance by leveraging AI techniques to automate and optimize various aspects of the development process.
- Increased Efficiency: The integration of AI in IDEs streamlines development tasks, leading to increased efficiency in software development.
- Better Decision-Making: AI-augmented IDEs enable better decision-making by providing intelligent insights and recommendations based on AI analysis.

- Enhanced User Experience: By leveraging AI, these IDEs can create more intuitive and user-friendly interfaces, leading to an enhanced user experience (Alzyadat et al., 2023).

Key Features of AI-augmented IDEs:

- Knowledge Extraction and Utilization: AI-augmented IDEs facilitate the extraction and utilization of knowledge from AI models throughout the software development life cycle.
- Automation and Optimization: Som of these platforms help in automating or otherwise improve a range of development tasks and enhance work productivity.
- Intelligent Insights and Recommendations: AI integrated IDEs suggest intelligent information that will assist in making proper decisions throughout the development process (Alzyadat et al., 2023).

Early Development:

- Text Editing Utilities: Originally, IDEs were just text editors that gradually added core features such as highlighting codings and associated code debuggers. Today's IDEs contain over thousands of functions for helping the developers but with enormous added costs in terms of tutorial slope.
- Graphical IDEs: Eventually, they tuned in to graphical user interfaces to enhance the environments and to add more charm to them. The use of collaborative and social development environments (SDEs) has been considered mandatory to address the trend of enhanced teamwork observed in software engineering.

Modern Enhancements:

- AI Assistants: Therefore, the application of AI in programming through use of code generation and natural language processing has swept across the market. Code refactoring tools assist in the rationalisation of the programmer's repetitious effort and enhance the standard of the code. The previous literature has suggested the points which include focusing on the creation of task-specific UI, cultivating trust, making text easier to read in order to support HAI within IDEs 3. Future IDEs can be anticipated as Intelligent Development Environments in which AI invoiced agents support the development of various project artifacts and help organize and select project libraries.

- Context Switching: Existing IDEs commonly feature several interfaces that a programmer has to constantly switch between. Future designs o of the system will seek to eliminate these transitions to enhance the performance of the system.

Future Directions:

- Collective Intelligence: The next generation of IDEs may leverage collective intelligence, integrating the knowledge and experiences of multiple developers to avoid common mistakes and boost productivity.
- Temporal Context: Advanced techniques like Overwatch use temporal context to predict and recommend edits, further enhancing the developer's experience.

The evolution of Integrated Development Environments (IDEs) in the context of AI augmentation has been influenced by several key milestones and advancements, as well as challenges and opportunities.

Evolution of IDEs in the Context of AI Augmentation:

- The development of AI has undergone significant changes, leading to the emergence of AI 2.0, which has profoundly impacted the information environment. Generative AI and extended reality devices are envisioned to dramatically change software development, which would subsequently impact IDEs and the development process (Pan, 2016).

Key Milestones in IDE Evolution:

- The history of AI dates back to the Dartmouth research project in 1956, which marked the first instance of AI solving simple problems. The United States' Defense Department increased its focus on training computers to imitate human reasoning in the 1960s. The emergence of intelligent assistants by DARPA in 2003 preceded the widespread adoption of AI by companies like Amazon and Google (Mathew et al., 2021).

Impact of AI Integration on IDE Development:

- The integration of AI in IDEs has transformed the software development process, impacting programmer productivity and code quality 4. AI coding assistants have been developed to enhance programming efficiency and decision-making within IDEs, presenting both challenges and opportunities for academia and industry (Sergeyuk et al., 2023).

Major Advancements in AI-Augmented IDEs:

- The development of AI has led to the introduction of augmented intelligence (AugI), emphasizing AI's role in augmenting or amplifying human intelligence rather than replacing it. Presently, knowledge work tasks including the diagnosis of medical conditions are executed by AI-based technologies and people expect improved synergies between AI and human intelligence. The use of AI in IDEs has posed some ethical issues in the employment of human labour for anyone involved in development to voluntarily control for risks around the use of the AI-based innovation. Small and medium-sized enterprises (SMEs) are a critical factor in the integration of AI within its business models and functions, and the effects of AI technology on SMEs.

2. MACHINE LEARNING IN MODERN IDES

Many contemporary Integrated Development Environments (IDE) are being developed to include machine learning (ML) to the development of software. Here are some key aspects of how ML is being integrated into IDEs:

Enhanced Productivity: Type 4 is employed in automation of routines along with intelligent code recommendations which doubles the efficiency of the programmer. For example, the tools such as Overwatch employ temporal context to predict as well as suggest code changes and their precision is at 78% (Zhang et al., 2022).

AI-Assisted Development: USEs within IDEs facilitate enhancing the quality of the codes produced and the effectiveness of programmers. This software can provide suggestion on using the code, identification of mistakes on time and in some it can even predict and suggest the code that a programmer is typing. GUIs of today's IDEs such as Eclipse Theia address the challenges of multi-platform software development through the use of AI and cloud. These interfaces comprise of recommender systems, language models and deep learning models to help developers (Sergeyuk et al., 2023 and Alizadehsani et al., 2021). Frameworks such as JetTrain provide developers an environment in which to code and debug their programs locally but execute ML experiments on other computational resources. This approach makes ML training entry easy and also improves the number of experiments that can be run.

Data-Centric Development: Some IDEs which support both code as well as data are available that helps in building end to end pipelines of ML. For instance, in Gestalt developers are able to build and debug classification models which enhance the possibilities for identifying and correcting errors in ML systems [5].

Collective Intelligence: Possible next generations of IDEs could explore collective intelligence shared by several developers and implement heuristics of when this or that mistake should be avoided to increase efficiency.

Feature Engineering: There are special IDEs for feature engineering to fasten the cycle time by analysing the suitability of new feature code which is significant for the performance of ML systems (Anderson et al., 2014).

While IDE for MLI in today's world is relatively complex, it uses statistical models as well as deep learning algorithms to improve specific features such as code completion and suggestion. One of the most sophisticated code completion technologies is based on program analysis, statistical and machine learning to provide accurate and relevant auto-completion suggestions. Using ML in modern IDEs helps to increase the productivity of coding and brings in the written code with progress and typical errors omitted. It offers enhanced code completion strategies that make use of stochastic models and machine learning giving beguilement more exact match and relevance in its code suggestion's part. Among the existing problems of using ML in advanced IDEs, perhaps the most serious one is the existence of limitations that require the development of new methods for the enhancement of the state of the art in code completion (Nguyen, 2023). Transformer-based language models, for instance, are known to work well for code completion and can fairly estimate when code completion needs to be employed by inferring from code context and telemetry signals. Interfacing of ML in IDEs has its operational cost besides potentially being invasive, for example, when suggestions appear at the moments developers are focused on. Modern IDEs employ ML which presents concerns, for which there is no clear understanding how they respond to a set of questions: transparency, explainability, equity, biases' mitigation, and who is to be blamed? (Kernbach et al., 2021). IDEs with built-in ML models affect society virtually (e.g., by denying a loan) and physically, generating new issues such as accountability, blame, or responsibility (Belle, 2023).

3. NATURAL LANGUAGE PROCESSING (NLP) IN MODERN INTEGRATED DEVELOPMENT ENVIRONMENTS (IDES)

Contemporary IDEs are sophisticated tools that encompass inherent and added features, to support the developers' efficiency. Introduction of Natural Language Processing (NLP) to these environments is the most recent innovation with the main aim of enhancing efficiency and user satisfaction. NLP makes it possible for IDEs to recognize natural language instructions and processes them in a way that simplifies the control of extensive IDE procedures without much scrolling through numerous options. This can help cater for simple repetitive jobs such as generating code, invoking tools, etc. NLP tools are able to convert descriptions written in plain text to actual developable models that can be used inside the IDE. This minimizes the vagueness of natural languages as it works nicely with reverse engineering frameworks including Eclipse (Keszocze et al., 2013). NLP capabilities are a good fit to be embedded in IDE since these environments can analyse unrestricted natural language artifacts such as commit messages, bug reports and comments. This assist in keeping the code quality or the state of the modules, while at the same time providing a context that explains why changes were made (Witte et al., 2011). Some IDEs incorporate controlled natural languages to make complex formalisms more accessible to users. This improves the interaction between the user and the platform, making it more user-friendly. Despite the advancements, there are challenges in generalizing NLP models for dynamic environments like AWS and SaaS platforms, especially when labelled data is scarce. Addressing these challenges requires ongoing research and development (Krasniqi & Do, 2023). NLP applies different levels of linguistic analysis to represent natural language for further processing. NLP techniques involve tokenization, stop word removal, stemming, lemmatization, parts of speech labelling, chunking, and named entity recognition, which enhance the performance of NLP applications. NLTK is a collection of application packages that facilitates researchers and learners in NLP, computational linguistics, and artificial intelligence. NLP techniques improve the performance of information retrieval efficiency and effective documentation processes. Training computers to understand natural language is challenging due to the ambiguity of language syntax and semantics (Yogish et al., 2019). NLP makes human communication with machines easier, potentially enabling natural language programming and increasing the accessibility of programming to non-expert users. It can also be used in the manufacture of intelligent and converging chatbots to enrich the user experience (Surabhi, 2013 & Jarquin et al., 2023). By comparing the effectiveness of NLP tools in benchmark datasets and in real-life situations, it has been observed that there is a considerable difference between the two; the reason why such research calls for user-based research. Hiring an NLP system, much engineering work needs to be done such as structuring data, applying typical NLP tools available in literature and performing a number of experiments (Khashabi et al., 2018). This is resulting in attempts to increase the community of NLP stakeholders, learning with as well as about NLP, like the introduction of a digital learning tool called Natural Language Processing 4 All (NLP4All). There exist highly promising opportunities to apply NLP techniques to enhance RPA tasks, including unsupervised and supervised RPA opportunity detection, as well as RPA routine design and implementation. Possible perceptual trends and applications of NLP are expected in the fields of sales and marketing, healthcare, digital humanities, IT, and security in the future, deep learning models, and classifiers are required for proper functioning in the future applications (Shenkuc & Hjorth, 2021, Van Der Aa & Leopold, 2021, Jha et al., 2022).

4. CODE ANALYSIS AND GENERATION IN MODERN IDES

Modern Integrated Development Environments (IDEs) have significantly evolved to enhance programmer productivity through advanced code analysis and generation features. Tools like GitHub Copilot and TabNine are prominent examples of AI-powered code generation, which assist in writing code by providing suggestions and auto-completions. However, these tools often shift the focus from writing to reviewing code, as user feedback is essential for refining the generated code. Today's IDEs are indispensable for the diffusion of new languages since they supply specific services needed to support these features. IDEs fix complex parsing techniques like the scanner less generalized-LR parsing to check for syntax error while the developer is editing. Some of the options include Syntax Highlighting and semantic analysis, and one is assured that when coding is involved, errors are expected hence the options will continue to work as expected. They include code mining, executing machine learning algorithms on code, suggesting refactorings, and within IDE visualizations. Supporting platforms like IntelliJ are popular and bring spirited frameworks for the code analysis tools development. These frameworks will enable several functional activities like mining data in the software, driving machine learning on code, making recommendations for refactoring, and, lastly, visualizing data in IDEs. Static analysis tools embedded in IDE are necessary when it comes to identifying code flaws and software glitches while having an option to accomplish that within mere seconds. Certain types of IDEs are venturing into a way of using natural language processing to let the developer to search for relevant information about his code by typing it into a plain English. This approach has been developed for reducing complexity of program comprehension by representing the data with ontologies with the help of semantic web technologies for querying. For the code correctness, the use of formal verification tools in the process of code generation is gradually increasing. It also offers an approach to auto check for bugs and confirm the properties of the generated code. Intelligent IDEs presuppose data mining to learn from programmers' code on the basis of such knowledge. These IDEs can even suggest improvements, detect and fix mistakes, as well as group similar style programmers together and thus improve the development experience.

5. CODE AWARE SUGGESTIONS IN INTELLIGENT CODE COMPLETION

Automatically completing a programmer's code has come a long way, and more recent systems use elaborate machine learning approaches to offer significantly more context-sensitive suggestions. Some of the traditional code completions use static type systems, and Alphabet indexing for the codes, which results to many inconsequential suggestions. The modern ones, however, learn from large code repositories to give more contextualized proposals, which generally enhances relevance and developers' efficiency by an order of magnitude. Contemporary models employ complex neural network structures like the recurrent models, namely LSTM-based Seq2Seq models, GPT-2 and others. These models can thus predict the next token in a code sequence better, which is an advantage, because these models take into consideration not only the syntactical structures of a language, and the temporal context of a code sequence. Smart code completion, as we know it, is usually implemented in widely adopted IDEs such as Eclipse. For example, the CACHECA plugin not only uses native suggestions, but also statistical models thus doubling the number of ideas Eclipse suggests. For the dynamically-typed programming languages, there are particular models, such as pointer mixture networks, to predict out-of-vocabulary word by capturing the local context and improve the effect for code completion. Some systems include code retrieval characteristics into language models for additional promotion. These frameworks look for similar code snippets and apply them to enhance the performance of code suggestions, and experience remarkable gains in metrics, such as BLEU-4. The efficiency of these intelligent systems is sometimes captured in terms of accuracy, exact match (EM), and edit similarity (Edit Sim). Experimental results reveal that use of these models yield improved performance compared to traditional approaches in these measures. Code Aware Suggestions build on the current-awareness and more context info to give accurate and pertinent code proposes. Smart code prompting mechanisms acquire prospective feature suggestions from existing code databases that are finer tuned to the working environment. Smart completion uses indices of source code language models storing the probable candidates and selecting the nearest ones to the context code in the position to be filled. Code Aware Suggestions significantly outperform mainstream code completion systems in terms of the relevance of their suggestions, thereby enhancing developers' productivity. Intelligent code completion techniques, including Code Aware Suggestions, aim to accelerate software development by providing accurate and contextually relevant code suggestions, thereby improving coding efficiency. Existing completion models for production code are suboptimal for test code completion, presenting a challenge in effectively implementing Code Aware Suggestions for test code completion. Standard neural language models face challenges in predicting OOV words in code completion, which poses a challenge in implementing Code Aware Suggestions for accurately predicting project-specific API member access. Dynamic inference emerges as a promising solution to reduce computational costs and environmental impact, thereby enhancing the practical adoption of intelligent code completion models. Integrating retrieval approaches and search strategies to enhance the performance of language models on code suggestions presents a potential future advancement in Code Aware Suggestions.

6. API USAGE RECOMMENDATIONS IN INTELLIGENT CODE COMPLETION

To enhance intelligent code completion, several approaches have been developed to provide API usage recommendations, leveraging various techniques to improve developer productivity and accuracy. Based on n-gram language models trained on source code corpora, these systems predict subsequent API calls; whereby, sequence of API calls is used as sentences. As these models are incorporated into IDEs such as Eclipse, they may suggest high accuracy as over 90% of expected tokens are within the most likely 10 options given. The work described in the paper exhibits the use of FLUTE which uses language analysis and program analysis to suggest API parameters. It guarantees syntactically legal and type-valid candidates, always targeting high precision in genuine projects. Through the extraction of implicit feedback from developers' code-completion activity, collaborative filtering and other methods offer context-specific content relevant to a single developer; working together, developers share knowledge to increase the efficiency of the individual coder. As distinct from previous approaches, PBN utilizes Bayesian networks and more context information to predict in higher quality. It is also quite advantageous for queries that do not contain method calls; this always implies large models and faster speed to infer. As the extension of traditional methods such as static analysis, these systems combine LSTM-based Seq2Seq models to improve the performance of the autocomplete suggestions to optimise coding. Automated and offline-documented management of API usage patterns are achieved by GraPacc, which is based on graph-based, pattern-oriented methods. These systems extract context-sensitive features and rank patterns in order to offer precise indications of code complements. Fortunately, intelligent code completion systems minimize the list of unsuitable suggestions so that developers easily locate the appropriate API calls. These systems help in learning and exploring APIs because they give recommendations in the context and accuracy of the going system. These tools allow developers to resolve coding tasks and do not allow mistakes diverting attention to more complicated nuances of software creation. API recommendation task can be further split as query-based API recommendation and code-based API recommendation where studies who deal with the code completion problems or about recommending relative APIs given Natural Language Queries. Previous work has been attempted with reference to approaches benchmarking and categorisation into Query-based and Code-based API recommendation, followed by an attempt to categorise API approaches based on the type of query handling and coding and summarise key success factors and difficulties that exist in API recommendation. Recommendation systems for API usage assistance based on statistical models built from source code corpora have been developed to assist developers through code completion mechanisms in IDEs, providing contextualized completion proposals for Java. Intelligent code completion systems utilize API usage recommendations to provide developers with a ranked list of API usages, alleviating the burden of remembering large APIs and improving programming productivity. These systems learn from existing code repositories and provide relevant examples to enhance developers' productivity, significantly outperforming mainstream code completion systems in terms of the relevance of their suggestions. Challenges in implementing API usage recommendations include the need for a holistic view of correlated API usage in control and data flow graphs, as well as the representation of contextual information and the appearance of redundant and homogeneous contents in the recommendation list. Existing API recommendation methods may exploit structural or textual code information separately, leading to insufficient representation of contextual information and the appearance of redundant and homogeneous contents in the recommendation list. Integrating API usage recommendations into intelligent code completion tools has the potential to significantly improve the relevance of suggestions, enhance developers' productivity, and provide context-aware code recommendation for opportunistic code reuse on-the-go. A novel API recommendation approach, APIREC, based on statistical learning from fine-grained code changes and context, has shown significant improvement in recommending relevant API calls, with high accuracy and precision.

7. LEARNING FROM CODING PATTERNS IN INTELLIGENT CODE COMPLETION

- Neural Language Models: These models learn from large codebases to predict the next code token. However, they struggle with out-of-vocabulary (OoV) words. A pointer mixture network can address this by either generating a word through an RNN component or regenerating an OoV word from the local context.

- Abstract Syntax Tree (AST) Utilization: Expertise of traditional methods are based on ASTs for syntactic correctness of code. Nevertheless, they fail to identify sequential and repetitive structures as well. To address these problems, the CCAG approach builds a partial AST as a graph and enhances the modelling of dependencies and code completions through multi-task learning.
- Deep Learning Models: The use of LSTM models for dynamically typed languages like JavaScript introduce the advantage of predicting the next word in a sentence without the need for building from a blank slate again by training on large datasets available in various programming languages. These models produce numerous recommendations, which are checked in terms of correctness by a parser.
- Graph Neural Networks: In contrast, the CC-GGNN approach uses Gated Graph Neural Networks to encode parent-child relations and other structural features within the code eliminating deficiencies of the simple sequence model.
- Meta-Learning Techniques: Adaptive models can train and thus optimise their predictions in a short time due to capability to deal with unknown model patterns from the context by using both semantic and structural data.
- Boolean Matrix Factorization (BMF): This technique brings together code patterns to make code completion systems scalable and therefore makes completion models smaller while at the same time increasing the speed of the models' inference while at the same not sacrificing the quality of the predictions the model is going to make.

Using local context and structural information the models described above can offer better suggestions of actual source code. Methods like BMF and meta-learning enhance the timely efficiency of code completion systems and increases its applicability at vast scale. To that end, models that incorporate features of the local environment and the developer's preferred coding styles feature can be of even higher utility and increase the efficiency. Smart lists of type-correct proposal sets intend to minimize lengthy lists of candidates, to enable better code completion. Their payoffs rely on Bayesian Networks, the models of deep learning, and recurrent neural networks; The recommendations are accurate depending on context information and code qualities. Sequential and repetitive patterns of writing code, structure information of the Abstract Syntax Tree (AST) are crucial for intelligent code completion when coding patterns are used. This work demonstrates that the coding patterns allow for identifying good code features, enhance the quality of prediction, and give solutions for the weakness of prior approaches in learning connection and orientation of node pairs. The existing models have drawbacks including forgetting important code representation information, failure to fully utilize known code structure information, and disregard of repeated patterns and structural information. However, with expandability of repositories and vast amounts of information available, scalability of the recommender system may become problematic. Standard neural language models may struggle with predicting out-of-vocabulary (OoV) words, restricting the code completion performance. Intelligent code completion has applications in accelerating software development, improving coding efficiency, and reducing common mistakes. It offers recommendations for instant class names, method names, keywords, and assists developers in coding, thereby enhancing productivity. Furthermore, the use of intelligent code completion models has shown promise in automated program repair, automated test case generation, and syntactic pattern mining.

8. IDENTIFYING REFACTORING OPPORTUNITIES IN AUTOMATED CODE REFACTORING

Vector Inlining Operations: This method emulates method inlining among code fragments, reducing the problem to finding similar vectors before and after inlining. This approach is implemented in the ReDex tool, which has shown effectiveness in identifying cross-function refactoring opportunities in large codebases. A tool that transforms Java programs into vectors to search for cross-function refactoring possibilities: a prototype. In other words, it has been applied to large code bases and it consistently reports a great many valid refactorings. The first task of identifying potential refactoring opportunities in the code base is relevant based on object orientation yet it is not without some challenges as there is tendency of requiring time and effort to manually identify opportunities in large systems (Milca, 2014).

Vector Abstraction and Concretization: It is possible to embed the code changes arising from refactoring as distinctive attributes, enabling the search for potential refactoring as well as prior refactoring to be achieved conveniently (Jiang, 2014).

Control-Fields Analysis: This approach detects refactoring opportunities from the control-fields in classes which in turn gives specific refactoring such as "Replace Type Code with Subclass" and "Replace Type Code with State". A tool that introduces control-field analysis to categorise refactoring opportunities into kinds of refactoring activities and has been proven productive in several open-source Java applications. Another thing that many researchers discussed during the analysis of the ReDex and Auto-SCST automated tools is that these programs were tested on large-scale projects and demonstrated high precision and effectiveness when it comes to detecting refactoring opportunities.

JDeodorant: An Eclipse plug-in that raises awareness of the Strategy design pattern refactoring candidate under the focus of condense (2012). Similarly, machine learning approaches have also been suggested in the current literature for identifying refactoring opportunities, by learning from previous refactoring exercises to provide real time and project-based solutions (Swain, 2024 & Imazato, 2017). Still, the majority of works includes non-industrial samples, which can decrease the applicability of the findings. Explicitly concerning the method, it is pointed out that future research should include larger, industrial based systems to enhance the relevance of these techniques (Al Dallal, 2015). Using multiple data sources at one time which are structural, semantic, and team development activity with multiple data sources can improve the precision and applicability of refactoring advice (Bavota, 2014).

9. AI-DRIVEN CODE RESTRUCTURING IN AUTOMATED CODE REFACTORING

Automated code refactoring is the method that fulfils code restructuring through the use of innovative approaches by the help of AI without altering the interfaces. Still, this process involves several critical steps and methodologies, and several researchers have described it. Large Language Models (LLMs) can also detect code segments by semantic evaluation and present choices for refactoring. For example, LLMs can successively decrease cyclomatic complexity because of the growth of code readability and maintainability (Choi, 2024). Refactoring processes can be explained and made formally by using models as first-class objects in AI. This entails code representation, analysis, which is quite helpful for autonomic refactorings and the creation of tool support (Hamioud, 2015). AI effectively can act to automatically introduce design patterns into existing system through structural analysis and code to code transformation. This process is supported by the relevance of software metrics to establish the relevance of the design patterns (Derezińska, 2018). Refactorization can be also detected, and historical refactorings can be recognized by encoding the changes as characteristic vectors. This method considerably accelerates the identification of matching vectors where the refactoring has to occur (Milea, 2014). Many tools and framework have been designed and implemented including extension for the eclipse platform toward automated refactoring. These tools help in performing complex refactorings and improving code quality (Derezińska, 2023). Despite advancements, automated refactoring faces challenges such as integration issues in multi-developer projects and the need for iterative, commit-friendly code changes (Hall, 2014).

Key Benefits of AI-Driven Code Restructuring:

- Improves Design and Productivity: AI-driven code restructuring in Automated Code Refactoring can improve code design, increase programmer productivity, and enhance code reuse.
- Automated Support: Automated support for code restructuring is necessary as manual refactoring is tedious, time-consuming, and error-prone.
- Effectiveness: Automated refactorings can be as effective as manual refactorings, especially for complex anti-pattern types.

Challenges of Implementing AI-Driven Code Restructuring:

- Complex Refactorings: Complex refactorings are largely performed manually due to the lack of automated means of chaining existent basic refactorings.
- Evaluation of Restructuring Solutions: Developers cannot quickly and safely evaluate the effects of one restructuring solution over another.
- Usability and Automation: Developers frequently eschew automation in favour of manual refactoring due to lack of support for real usage scenarios and unpredictable tools.

Impact on Software Maintainability and Scalability:

- Easily Maintainable and Extensible Systems: Refactoring ensures that software systems are easily maintainable and extensible.
- Improved Internal Code Structure: Refactoring improves the internal code structure without altering its external functionality, leading to improved application design and implementation.
- Reduction of Technical Debt: Automated project-level code refactoring using Large Language Models (LLMs) can reduce average cyclomatic complexity, thereby reducing technical debt.

Ethical Considerations of Using AI-Driven Code Restructuring:

- Quality and Usability: SR Tools are particularly relevant for enhancing the speed and quality of software development, nevertheless, the refactoring tools about to be used for real software evolution scenarios should be of added utility.
- User-Centric Approach: The refactoring tools applied in a user-centered perspective can deal more with the idea of expressing the purpose of the code and not the code transforms, which map objects methods and identifiers towards user given concepts.

10. MAINTAINING CODE QUALITY AND READABILITY IN AUTOMATED CODE REFACTORING

The Key Principles of Maintaining Code Quality and Readability in Automated Code Refactoring:

Refactoring is a transformation that modifies the source code's structure while keeping its observable behaviour intact with the objective of enhancing the design quality. Some of the quality characteristics are known to benefit from refactoring activities whereby they can be improved to better levels of the organization's requirements including; Automated refactoring tools for software are used to adjust the complexity of internal features of the code while not changing its outward interfaces in order to maximize factors such as maintainability and code readability. Automated refactoring tools can improve design quality, fix code smells, and introduce design patterns, thus enhancing the quality of software systems while successfully fixing code smells and introducing design patterns. Machine learning with tree-based models has been shown to perform well when trained with code metrics to detect refactorings, indicating the potential for automated solutions based on machine learning to contribute to maintaining code quality and readability.

The Challenges in Maintaining Code Quality and Readability during Automated Code Refactoring:

- Developers often lose sight of the business problems being solved and forget the importance of managing complexity, resulting in low readability levels after refactorings.
- It is not uncommon to have tangled commits of bug fixes and refactorings, with a significant percentage of bug-inducing commits also containing code refactoring changes, highlighting the potential risks associated with automated refactoring.

Best Practices for Ensuring Code Quality and Readability in Automated Code Refactoring:

- Continuous refactoring is necessary to maintain source code quality and to cope with technical debt, and automated refactoring tools such as the Refactoring-Bot have been proposed to integrate into the team like a human developer, automatically performing refactorings to resolve code smells and presenting the changes to a developer for asynchronous review via pull requests.
- Cognitive-Driven Development (CDD) is a strategy for reducing cognitive overload during development when improving the code design, and it has

been shown to guide the restructuring process to obtain a coherent and balanced separation of concerns, thus enhancing code quality and readability.

11. PREDICTIVE BUG DETECTION IN SMART DEBUGGING AND ERROR DETECTION

Predictive bug detection aims to identify potential software defects before they manifest as failures, thereby streamlining the debugging process. Predictive bug detection in smart debugging and error detection involves leveraging automated approaches to pinpoint the root causes of software failures, contributing to more accurate defect localization and smaller code sets for analysis. Some of the potential issues in Predictive bug detection are focused in the enhancement of bug prediction models to fit commercial software and testability and scalability issues key among them being cost of fixing a bug at various phase of Software Development Life Cycle. These approaches are mostly concerned with the main category of techniques applied to predictive bug detection for smart debugging and errors identification: Anomaly-based bug detection, statistical debugging algorithms, and SM-Learning approaches. The possible use of predictive bug detection in this regard includes bug identification, conformation of bug and predicting the cause of a bug report. It employs several strategies and tachniques together with models to forecast and contain bugs as well.

Frameworks and Techniques:

- Hamming Distance and K-Means Clustering: They are employed to predict the outcomes of test runs which on the other hand can be used to compute the suspiciousness of the statements within the code. This is the reason that helps in ranking the statements for examination and makes the fault localization efficient.
- Anomaly-Based Detection: This technique analyses the program run-time behaviour to find out what good behaviour looks like, normally used to locate software failures. It involves three steps: There are three major bug tracking activities which are bug prediction, bug isolation and bug validation. The use of this method has been proved very effective in this context with the ability to isolate relevant anomalies while at the same time minimizing the list of codes to be analyzed.

Automated Tools:

- DeBGUer Tool: Adopts the Learn, Diagnose and Plan (LDP) model where it is using the principles of artificial intelligence for bug prognosis and bug identification. The tool is available as a web-based tool which is convenient to use, and the authors have used the tool on a number of projects.
- Statistical Debugging Algorithms: These algorithms single out bugs in programs which have more than one undiagnosed problem as it singles out predictors found with individual bugs. This aggravates comprehension of the situations and rates of failure modes, helping to select the priorities of a debugging agenda.

Models and Approaches:

- Neural Network Models: Shown to be effective in entropy-based bug prediction, these models have been determined to be at least as effective as traditional statistical linear regression models.
- Two-Phase Prediction Model: This model utilizes the content of bug report to make a prediction of which files will be most likely to be fixed. But it only predicts when it is sure and guess what it gets them right when it gives estimates of which files to correct.

The Key Benefits:

- Efficiency: Reduces the working process to consider fewer statements making the process of fault localization faster.
- Accuracy: Gathers more narrow regions with a smaller set of codes for identifying defects' places.
- Scalability: In particular, pre-trained and constantly evolving models, as are those used on cloud platforms, can be used widely for bug prediction needs to scale the solutions.

12. AI-ASSISTED ROOT CAUSE ANALYSIS IN SMART DEBUGGING AND ERROR DETECTION

Combining AI technology with root cause analysis (RCA) is an effective way to diagnose faults and potential errors and more effective within smart debugging and error detection. Unlike the previous method, this method uses artificial intelligence to improve and shorten the diagnostic activity.

- Automated Fault Model Inference: Paper techniques: AI techniques can be used for fault model inference from diagnostically annotated log data and thus generate rules for filtering new log data to identify root causes. This approach is popular in areas such as the industry 4.0 and railways, where the number of logs filling up the server space is constantly growing.
- Markov Logic Networks: All these represent diagnostic knowledge repositories capable of being trained into making inference about failures based on the logged data. This method deals with uncertainty in observations and offers ordered diagnostic opinions, which represents an augmentation over manual methods.
- Neuro-Symbolic AI: Refinement of qualitative narratives and logical reasoning with observed data and prior knowledge make NSC differentiation a critical enabler for efficient pattern identification and probabilistic inference in RCA for manufacturing workflows.
- Incremental Causal Graph Learning: On-line tools discussed in the context of CORAL apply incremental learning to update RCA models and activate the RCA process in real-time, while finding the root causes employing propagation over the network.
- Model-Based Testing (MBT): Test analysis done using RCA tools within an MBT system can decrease the need for body effort and identify the origin of errors within the various elements concurrently.

Benefits:

- Efficiency: Automated RCA minimizes the amount of time taken in analyzing all the probable causes to identify the root cause of most failures thereby facilitating fast resolution of faults and fast restoration of systems.
- Accuracy: AI models can deal with big data and comprehensive interconnectivity and interactions between system components leading to higher diagnostic accuracy.
- Adaptability: RCA tools utilising artificial intelligence can be easily aligned to various domains and implemented into different tool contexts, making the tools versatile to different settings.

Challenges of implementing AI-assisted root cause analysis in smart debugging and error detection include:

- Resource Demand: The scalability of LLM like GPT-4 is a concern because of the amount of GPU required to fine-tune on the user's data, and the need for constant retraining of the model as new data is developed.

- Complex Interactions: The diagnostic tasks are rather difficult because of the interactions between the system components, the significant amount of logged data, and the usually fragmentary and incomplete data available for root cause analysis.

13. AUTOMATED FIX SUGGESTIONS IN SMART DEBUGGING AND ERROR DETECTION

Automated fix suggestions are a crucial component of smart debugging and error detection, aiming to reduce the manual effort and time required to correct software faults. Automated fix suggestions play a crucial role in smart debugging and error detection, offering several key features and benefits, while also presenting challenges and limitations. Here are some key insights:

- AutoFix Technique: AutoFix is an automated debugging tool that uses contracts (pre- and postconditions) to enhance fault detection and localization. It generates and ranks validated fixes for faulty programs, achieving a 42% success rate in fixing faults across various codebases. This approach significantly reduces the debugging burden by providing high-quality fix suggestions.
- Interactive Debugging: SmartDebug, an Eclipse plugin, introduces an interactive paradigm where developers guide the fix generation process by characterizing the program's running state. This method has shown to accelerate the debugging process in 14 out of 25 cases, demonstrating its effectiveness in active coding environments.
- Ranking Fixes: Another approach involves ranking bug fixes based on parameters like reliability, time, cost, and priority. This helps in selecting the most suitable fix for a detected bug, enhancing the efficiency of automated debugging tools.
- Industrial Deployment: Automated Program Repair (APR) tools like Recoder, SimFix, and TBar have been deployed in industrial settings. These tools provide patch suggestions that significantly increase debugging success rates and speed, although deceptive suggestions can negatively impact outcomes.
- Machine Learning Integration: Tools like BugFix leverage machine learning to learn from past debugging situations and improve the relevance of future bug-fix suggestions. This adaptive approach helps in providing more accurate and contextually appropriate fixes.
- Educational Context: Automated program repair techniques are also beneficial for novice programmers, particularly in educational settings. Tools like DeepFix, RLAssist, and Dr Repair have been evaluated on datasets from uni-

versity programming courses, showing varying success rates in fixing syntactic errors.

Key Features of Smart Debugging and Error Detection in Automated Fix Suggestions:

- Automated program repair (APR) tools, such as Recoder, SimFix, and TBar, provide patch suggestions to developers during the debugging process.
- Access to correct APR suggestions significantly increase the odds of debugging success, speeding up the process.
- APR tools rely on simple specification elements in the form of contracts to enhance the precision of fault detection and localization, enabling the automation of the debugging process.
- Automated debugging tools, such as Spectrum-Based Fault Localization (SBFL), aim to assist developers in locating and understanding bugs by providing prioritized bug-fix suggestions based on machine learning and static analysis.

Contribution to the Efficiency of Smart Debugging and Error Detection:

- Access to correct APR suggestions increases the odds of debugging success by a significant margin, demonstrating the potential for APR-mediated, human-driven debugging.
- Automated debugging tools, such as SmartFix, are integrated into development environments to provide real-time bug-fix suggestions, contributing to the efficiency of the debugging process.
- Automated debugging tools, when used effectively, have the potential to reduce the time and effort required for fault detection and correction, ultimately improving the overall efficiency of the debugging process.

Challenges and Limitations of Automated Fix Suggestions in Smart Debugging and Error Detection:

- Deceptive suggestions, a common occurrence in APR, can decrease the odds of debugging success, highlighting the challenge of ensuring the quality and reliability of automated fix suggestions.
- Automated debugging tools, such as SBFL, may not always improve the efficiency of debugging and can even interfere with the actual assistance needed by programmers, indicating potential limitations in their practical effectiveness.

Current Research Trends and Future Directions in the Development of Automated Fix Suggestions for Smart Debugging and Error Detection:

- Ongoing research focuses on addressing the challenges of automated program repair, such as overfitted patches and low maintainability of generated code, by exploring alternative approaches and techniques, including statistical models and safety verification.
- The integration of automated program repair techniques into development environments, such as EiffelStudio, demonstrates a shift towards semantic Integrated Development Environments, offering powerful automated functionality within familiar interfaces.

CONCLUSION

The evolution of Integrated Development Environments (IDEs) through AI augmentation represents a significant paradigm shift in software development practices. The integration of advanced AI technologies, particularly machine learning and natural language processing, has transformed traditional IDEs into intelligent coding assistants that significantly enhance developer productivity and code quality. The synergy between machine learning algorithms and code analysis has enabled unprecedented capabilities in intelligent code completion, moving beyond simple syntax suggestions to context-aware recommendations that understand coding patterns and API usage contexts. These systems continuously learn from vast codebases and developer interactions, providing increasingly accurate and relevant suggestions that align with best practices and project-specific patterns. In the domain of automated code refactoring, AI-driven tools have demonstrated remarkable ability in identifying complex refactoring opportunities and executing sophisticated code restructuring operations. These tools not only maintain code quality and readability but also help in modernizing legacy codebases through intelligent pattern recognition and automated transformations. The integration of predictive bug detection and AI-assisted debugging represents perhaps the most impactful advancement, significantly reducing the time developers spend on error detection and resolution. Through machine learning models trained on extensive bug databases, these systems can predict potential issues before they manifest and provide automated fix suggestions with increasing accuracy. Looking forward, the continued advancement of AI technologies promises even more sophisticated IDE capabilities, potentially leading to fully automated code generation and maintenance systems. However, challenges remain in areas such as ensuring the reliability of AI-generated code, maintaining security standards, and balancing automation with developer control. The future of

AI-augmented IDEs will likely focus on addressing these challenges while further enhancing their intelligent assistance capabilities, ultimately working towards the goal of more efficient and error-free software development processes.

REFERENCES

Al Dallal, J. (2015). Identifying refactoring opportunities in object-oriented code: A systematic literature review. *Information and Software Technology*, 58, 231–249. DOI: 10.1016/j.infsof.2014.08.002

Alizadehsani, Z., Gomez, E. G., Ghaemi, H., González, S. R., Jordan, J., Fernández, A., & Pérez-Lancho, B. (2021). Modern Integrated Development Environment (IDEs). In Lecture notes in networks and systems (pp. 274–288). DOI: 10.1007/978-3-030-78901-5_24

Alzyadat, W., Al-Madi, M., Muhairat, M., Al-Madi, N., & Altarawneh, F. (2023). A Roadmap for Artificial Intelligence Augmented Software Development Life Cycle: Aspects of Knowledge Vaporization. *2023 International Conference on Information Technology: Cybersecurity Challenges for Sustainable Cities, ICIT 2023*. DOI: 10.1109/ICIT58056.2023.10226133

Anderson, M. R., Cafarella, M., Jiang, Y., Wang, G., & Zhang, B. (2014). An integrated development environment for faster feature engineering. *Proceedings of the VLDB Endowment International Conference on Very Large Data Bases*, 7(13), 1657–1660. DOI: 10.14778/2733004.2733054

Baglini, R., & Hjorth, H. (2021). Natural Language Processing 4 All (NLP4All): A New Online Platform for Teaching and Learning NLP Concepts. *Proceedings of the 5th Workshop on Teaching Natural Language Processing*, 2021, 28–33. DOI: 10.18653/v1/2021.teachingnlp-1.3

Bavota, G., Panichella, S., Tsantalis, N., & Canfora, G. (2014). Recommending refactorings based on team Co-maintenance patterns. In *Proceedings of the 29th ACM/IEEE International Conference on Automated Software Engineering (ASE 2014)*. DOI: 10.1145/2642937.2642948

Belle, V. (2023). Knowledge representation and acquisition for ethical AI: Challenges and opportunities. *Ethics and Information Technology*, 25(1), 22. Advance online publication. DOI: 10.1007/s10676-023-09692-z

Choi, J., An, G., & Yoo, S. (2024). Iterative Refactoring of Real-World Open-Source Programs with Large Language Models. In Lecture Notes in Computer Science (including subseries Lecture Notes in Artificial Intelligence and Lecture Notes in Bioinformatics). DOI: 10.1007/978-3-031-64573-0_4

Christopoulou, A., Giakoumakis, E. A., Zafeiris, V. E., & Soukara, V. (2012). Automated refactoring to the Strategy design pattern. *Information and Software Technology*, 54(11), 1202–1214. DOI: 10.1016/j.infsof.2012.05.004

Derezińska, A. (2018). A Structure-Driven Process of Automated Refactoring to Design Patterns. In Advances in Intelligent Systems and Computing. DOI: 10.1007/978-3-319-67229-8_4

Derezinska, A., & Sygocki, D. (2023). Review of Automated Code Refactoring of C# Programs. In *Proceedings of the 18th Conference on Computer Science and Intelligence Systems (FedCSIS 2023).* DOI: 10.15439/2023F7277

Hall, M., Khojaye, M. A., Walkinshaw, N., & McMinn, P. (2014). Establishing the source code disruption caused by automated remodularisation tools. In *Proceedings of the 30th International Conference on Software Maintenance and Evolution (ICSME 2014).* DOI: 10.1109/ICSME.2014.75

Hallur, G., ... (2023). Seamless mobility: Innovating the digital service landscape in telecom industry. In Proceedings of Fifth International Conference on Computing, Communications, and Cyber-Security (IC4S 2023). Springer. DOI: 10.1007/978-981-97-2550-2_14

Hallur, G.. (2024). Navigating the infotainment landscape: Status and regulations in the digital age. *2024 International Conference on Advances in Data Engineering and Intelligent Computing Systems (ADICS)*, 1-6. DOI: 10.1109/ADICS58448.2024.10533560

Hamioud, S., & Atil, F. (2015). Model-driven java code refactoring. *Computer Science and Information Systems*, 12(2), 375–403. DOI: 10.2298/CSIS141025015H

Imazato, A., Higo, Y., Hotta, K., & Kusumoto, S. (2017). Finding Extract Method Refactoring Opportunities by Analyzing Development History. In *Proceedings of the International Computer Software and Applications Conference.* DOI: 10.1109/COMPSAC.2017.129

Jha, S., Tiwari, P., Gupta, S. N., & Gupta, V. (2022). Natural Language Processing for Small Businesses and Future Trends in Healthcare. In Studies in computational intelligence (pp. 311–324). DOI: 10.1007/978-981-16-8012-0_24

Jiang, L., & Khoo, S.-C. (2014). Vector abstraction and concretization for scalable detection of refactorings. In *Proceedings of the ACM SIGSOFT Symposium on the Foundations of Software Engineering.*

Kernbach, J. M., Hakvoort, K., Ort, J., Clusmann, H., Neuloh, G., & Delev, D. (2021). The Artificial Intelligence Doctor: Considerations for the Clinical Implementation of Ethical AI. *Acta Neurochirurgica. Supplementum*, 257–261. Advance online publication. DOI: 10.1007/978-3-030-85292-4_29 PMID: 34862549

Keszocze, O., Soaked, M., Kuksa, E., & Drechsler, R. (2013). Lips: An IDE for model driven engineering based on natural language processing. 2013 1st International Workshop on Natural Language Analysis in Software Engineering, NaturaLiSE, 2, 31–38. DOI: 10.1109/NAturaLiSE.2013.6611718

Khashabi, D., Sammons, M., Zhou, B., Redman, T., Christodoulopoulos, C. E., Srikumar, V., Rizzolo, N., Luo, L. R. G., Do, Q., Tsai, C., Roy, S., Mayhew, S., Feng, Z., Wieting, J., Yu, X., Song, Y., Gupta, S., Upadhyay, S., Arivazhagan, N., . . . Roth, D. (2018). CogcompnLP: Your Swiss army knife for NLP. LREC 2018 - 11th International Conference on Language Resources and Evaluation, 541–549.

Krasniqi, R., & Do, H. (2023). Generalizability of NLP-based Models for Modern Software Development Cross-Domain Environments. 2023 IEEE/ACM 2nd International Workshop on Natural Language-Based Software Engineering. https://doi.org/DOI: 10.1109/NLBSE59153.2023.00009

Mahendru, L., ... (2024). Smart driving: Leveraging IoT for automotive innovation. 2024 5th International Conference on Electronics and Sustainable Communication Systems (ICESC), 377-380. DOI: 10.1109/ICESC60852.2024.10689748

Maiti, P., ... (2024). Decentralized defenses: A framework for 5G IoT security in Industry 4.0 using blockchain crowdsourcing. 2024 3rd International Conference on Sentiment Analysis and Deep Learning (ICSADL), 534-538. DOI: 10.1109/ICSADL61749.2024.00093

Master, S., ... (2024). Unleashing creativity: The business potential of generative AI. 2024 2nd World Conference on Communication & Computing (WCONF), 1-6. DOI: 10.1109/WCONF61366.2024.10692266

Mathew, D., Shukla, V. K., Chaubey, A., & Dutta, S. (2021). Artificial Intelligence: Hope for Future or Hype by Intellectuals? 2021 9th International Conference on Reliability, Infocom Technologies and Optimization (Trends and Future Directions), ICRITO 2021. DOI: 10.1109/ICRITO51393.2021.9596410

Milea, N. A., Jiang, L., & Khoo, S.-C. (2014). Scalable detection of missed cross-function refactorings. In *Proceedings of the 2014 International Symposium on Software Testing and Analysis (ISSTA 2014)*. DOI: 10.1145/2610384.2610394

Milea, N. A., Jiang, L., & Khoo, S.-C. (2014). Vector abstraction and concretization for scalable detection of refactorings. In *Proceedings of the ACM SIGSOFT Symposium on the Foundations of Software Engineering*. DOI: 10.1145/2635868.2635926

Nandanwar, R., ... (2024). Stitching data threads: Impact of artificial intelligence on fashion evolution. 2024 4th International Conference on Innovative Practices in Technology and Management (ICIPTM), 1-6. DOI: 10.1109/ICIPTM59628.2024.10563840

Nguyen, T. N. (2023). Statistical Models and Machine Learning to Advance Code Completion: Are We There Yet? In Natural computing series (pp. 121–153). DOI: 10.1007/978-981-19-9948-2_5

Nithiyanantham, K. K., ... (2024). Crop health monitoring for precision agriculture using IoT-based sensors in drones. In Lecture Notes in Electrical Engineering (pp. 875-890). DOI: 10.1007/978-981-97-3442-9_62

Pan, Y. (2016). Heading toward Artificial Intelligence 2.0. *Engineering (Beijing)*, 2(4), 409–413. DOI: 10.1016/J.ENG.2016.04.018

Patil, B., ... (2024). Artificial intelligence powered paradigm shift: Revolutionizing digital marketing. 2024 4th International Conference on Innovative Practices in Technology and Management (ICIPTM), 1-6. DOI: 10.1109/ICIPTM59628.2024.10563450

Prabhu, S.. (2024). Elevating business experiences: AI-powered chatbots reforming marketing and e-commerce. In Singh, D. (Eds.), *Transforming the Financial Landscape with ICTs* (pp. 1–27). IGI Global., DOI: 10.4018/979-8-3693-1503-3.ch001

Sergeyuk, A., Titov, S., & Izadi, M. (2023). Dataset for "In-IDE Human-AI Experience in the Era of Large Language Models; A Literature Review" paper [Dataset]. In Zenodo (CERN European Organization for Nuclear Research). DOI: 10.5281/zenodo.10290921

Surabhi, M. C. (2013). Natural language pinnovative framework integrates advanced machine learning algorithms with IoT sensor networks to optimize energy consumption in green buildings. DOI: 10.1007/978-3-031-35915-6_25

Swain, V. K., Panigrahi, R., Sahu, K. K., & Padhy, N. (2024). Revealing MOVE METHOD: Machine Learning-driven Real-time Refactoring Identification for Enhanced Software Quality. In *Proceedings of the 4th International Conference on Emerging Systems and Intelligent Computing (ESIC 2024)*. DOI: 10.1109/ESIC60604.2024.10481609

Van Der Aa, H., & Leopold, H. (2021). 10 Supporting RPA through natural language processing. In De Gruyter eBooks (pp. 187–200). DOI: 10.1515/9783110676693-010

Vedurada, J., & Krishna Nandivada, V. (2018). Identifying refactoring opportunities for replacing type code with subclass and state. *Proceedings of the ACM on Programming Languages*. DOI: 10.1145/3276508

Waghambare, M. A.. (2024). Artificial intelligence (AI)-powered chatbots for marketing and online shopping. In Prakasha, G. S. (Eds.), *Digital Technologies in Modeling and Management: Insights in Education and Industry* (pp. 21–39). IGI Global., DOI: 10.4018/978-1-6684-9576-6.ch002

Witte, R., Sateli, B., Khamis, N., & Rilling, J. (2011). Intelligent Software Development Environments: Integrating Natural Language Processing with the Eclipse Platform. In Lecture notes in computer science (pp. 408–419). DOI: 10.1007/978-3-642-21043-3_49

Yogish, D., Manjunath, T. N., & Hegadi, R. S. (2019). Review on Natural Language Processing Trends and Techniques Using NLTK. In Communications in computer and information science (pp. 589–606). DOI: 10.1007/978-981-13-9187-3_53

Zhang, Y., Bajpai, Y., Gupta, P., Ketkar, A., Allamanis, M., Barik, T., Gulwani, S., Radhakrishna, A., Raza, M., Soares, G., & Tiwari, A. (2022). Overwatch: learning patterns in code edit sequences. Proceedings of the ACM on Programming Languages, 6(OOPSLA2), 395–423. https://doi.org/DOI: 10.1145/3563302

Chapter 3
AI-Powered Software Engineering for Cloud-Native Environments

M. Swathi Sree
https://orcid.org/0009-0001-5024-7525
Stanley College of Engineering and Technology for Women, India

C. Kishor Kumar Reddy
Stanley College of Engineering and Technology for Women, India

Kurella Vaishnavi
https://orcid.org/0009-0005-5110-4701
Stanley College of Engineering and Technology for Women, India

Vallapureddy Harika
Stanley College of Engineering and Technology for Women, India

ABSTRACT

Software engineering has been transformed by the rise of cloud-native architectures, which make it possible to create scalable, adaptable, and robust systems. Using serverless computing, microservices, and containers, cloud-native software engineering provides a dynamic and modular method of system development. Concurrently, the incorporation of Artificial Intelligence (AI) in cloud-native settings is revolutionising the process of software engineering, upkeep, and evolution. Automation, resource optimisation, and decision-making processes are all greatly improved by AI-driven tools and techniques like machine learning, automated code creation, predictive analytics, and intelligent monitoring. The merging of cloud-native architectures and AI approaches is examined in this study, which offers a systematic examination

DOI: 10.4018/979-8-3693-9356-7.ch003

of how AI improves the design, testing, deployment, and operations phases of the software development lifecycle.

1. INTRODUCTION

The goal of cloud-native software engineering is to create and implement applications that take advantage of cloud settings. Using techniques like microservices, containerization, and DevOps, this strategy prioritizes adaptability, scalability, and resilience. Applications are designed to operate smoothly in dispersed contexts, using cloud infrastructure to optimize resources and scale up or down in response to demand. But as cloud-native systems get more complicated, it gets harder to properly manage, track, and optimize them.The goal of cloud-native software engineering is to create and implement applications that take advantage of cloud settings. Using techniques like microservices, containerization, and DevOps, this strategy prioritizes adaptability, scalability, and resilience. Applications are designed to operate smoothly in dispersed contexts, using cloud infrastructure to optimize resources and scale up or down in response to demand (Singh,et al.,2023).

Artificial Intelligence (AI) is useful in this situation. Numerous facets of cloud-native software engineering can be improved, optimized, and automated with the aid of AI approaches. Organizations may increase application stability, optimize resource management, improve security, and have a better understanding of system performance by incorporating AI into cloud-native workflows. Machine learning (ML) algorithms, for example, can more effectively distribute resources according to demand, anticipate and resolve system problems before they worsen, and instantly detect possible security risks(Paul,et al.,2022).

Furthermore, proactive and predictive maintenance is made possible by AI's rapid processing and analysis of enormous volumes of data. Large amounts of log and telemetry data are produced by cloud-native apps, which AI can examine to identify irregularities, identify underlying causes, and offer fixes—tasks that would be laborious and prone to mistakes if done by hand. Additionally, AutoML (Automated Machine Learning) can help developers create and implement ML models in cloud-native applications without requiring extensive knowledge of machine learning, while AI-driven DevOps (AIOps) improves the traditional CI/CD pipeline by automating repetitive tasks and increasing the speed and reliability of deployments(Wen, L.,et al.,2022).

For sectors going through digital transformation, where flexibility, scalability, and wise decision-making are critical, the combination of AI with cloud-native development is particularly potent. AI and cloud-native software engineering may work together to create more resilient, effective, and flexible apps that can intelligently adjust to shifting user demands, operational circumstances, and corporate objectives. A contemporary method for creating, developing, and implementing apps that make the most of cloud computing environments is called cloud-native software engineering (Pentyala, D., et al.,2021). Cloud-native engineering creates apps that are tailored to run in the cloud, utilizing its special capabilities to achieve unmatched scalability, robustness, and flexibility, as opposed to viewing the cloud as a straightforward hosting environment.

The way applications are developed and maintained is changing due to cloud-native software engineering, which is in line with the requirements of contemporary, dynamic corporate contexts. Cloud-native engineering, with its emphasis on scalability, robustness, and agility, enables businesses to innovate more quickly and produce high-caliber software more effectively (Tatineni, S., et al.,2024). Organizations may better meet customer needs and maintain their competitiveness in an increasingly digital environment by embracing a cloud-native attitude and utilizing technologies like containers, Kubernetes, and CI/CD.

1.1 Overview of cloud-native principles

The foundation for creating apps that make the most of cloud computing is cloud-native principles. The dynamic, scalable, and distributed nature of the cloud is embraced by cloud-native design, in contrast to traditional software engineering, which frequently entails installing programs in fixed environments. These guidelines, which are founded on the most recent developments in methodology and technology, seek to produce software that is scalable, resilient, and iteratively fast (Sivathapandi, P., et al.,2021).

Figure 1. Cloud-native applications

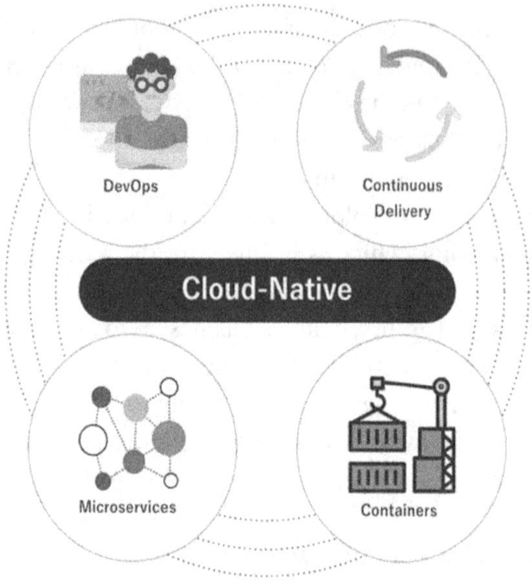

Figure1 show Micro services, containerization, DevOps, continuous delivery, automation, infrastructure as code (IaC), and observability are some of the fundamental ideas that characterize cloud-native design. Together, these guidelines offer a comprehensive approach to contemporary software development and operations, and each is crucial for optimizing the potential of cloud-based apps.

Microservices Architecture

One fundamental cloud-native concept that encourages the creation of applications as a group of discrete, autonomous services is microservices architecture. Every microservice is made to carry out a particular task, like data retrieval, payment processing, or user authentication. This modular strategy has a number of benefits:

Independent Development and Deployment: Because microservices may be created, tested, and implemented separately, several teams can work on various application components at once without interfering with one another.

Fault Isolation: Failures in one microservice are less likely to affect other services because each one runs separately. Better overall resilience is ensured by this isolation, so the system as a whole is not brought down when one component fails (Kanchepu, N.et al., 2023).

Scalability: Depending on demand, each microservice can be scaled separately.

However, putting microservices into practice necessitates a thorough comprehension of data management across distributed systems, inter-service communication, and service boundaries.

Containerization:

Applications and their dependencies can now be bundled together into lightweight, portable entities known as containers thanks to containerization. Containers address the long-standing "works on my machine" issue by providing a consistent environment for development, testing, and production. Among the main advantages of containerization are:

Portability: Containers can operate reliably in a variety of settings, including a production cloud environment, testing server, or a developer's laptop.

Resource Efficiency: Because containers share the host operating system, they are lighter than virtual machines and can use resources more effectively.

Scalability and Quick Deployment: Applications can swiftly scale in response to variations in demand because of containers' capacity to be started or halted in a matter of seconds. Container management now requires the use of tools like Docker and container orchestration platforms like Kubernetes, which offer features like scaling, load balancing, and service discovery (Polamarasetti, A. et al.,2021).

The Culture of DevOps

A cultural movement known as DevOps helps to close the gap between operations (Ops) and development (Dev). Faster and more dependable software delivery is made possible by DevOps, which encourages cooperation and communication amongst traditionally divided teams. Among the essential elements of DevOps are:

Code development, testing, and deployment are all automated using continuous integration and continuous delivery (CI/CD) pipelines. This allows for more frequent upgrades by reducing manual intervention and speeding up the release cycle (Reddy, A.et al.,2021).

Developers may manage infrastructure using code thanks to Infrastructure as Code (IaC), which enables environments to be versioned, replicated, and modified similarly to application code. Automated infrastructure provisioning, scalability, and configuration are made possible by tools like Terraform and AWS CloudFormation.

Automation: DevOps eliminates human error, makes deployments more dependable, and frees up teams to concentrate on higher-value work by automating routine processes. Because it encourages an iterative approach to software development and continuous improvement, DevOps is ideally suited to cloud-native principles(Oyeniran, O. C.,et al.,2024).

Constant Delivery (CD) Continuous Delivery (CD) is a critical component of the cloud-native approach, aimed at automating the deployment of applications. With CD, every code change is automatically tested, verified, and deployed, allowing for faster feedback and a higher level of confidence in the software.

Benefits of Continuous Delivery include:

Decreased Time-to-Market: CD allows for quicker and more frequent releases by reducing the number of manual processes in the deployment process.

Better Quality: CD lowers the likelihood of production problems by automating testing and deployment, which guarantees that every code update satisfies quality criteria prior to going live(Srivastava, S.,et al.,2021).

Improved Cooperation: In keeping with the DevOps philosophy, CD pipelines encourage tighter cooperation between the development, testing, and operations teams.CD is particularly useful in cloud-native settings where apps must swiftly adjust to shifting customer demands and corporate requirements.

Automation

A key component of cloud-native engineering is automation. Because cloud-native apps are so large and complicated, manual procedures might cause mistakes and delays. Numerous facets of application deployment, scalability, monitoring, and recovery are streamlined and expedited by automation (Ganesan, P., et al.,2023).

Resource Provisioning: By dynamically allocating and de-allocating resources in response to present demand, automation technologies can maximize efficiency and minimize expenses. Monitoring and Alerting: Automated monitoring systems keep tabs on the performance of applications, sending out alerts or implementing fixes when problems occur. Self-Healing and Recovery: By automatically identifying malfunctions and replacing or restarting malfunctioning components, automated systems can increase the resilience of applications. Automation is made accessible and scalable by cloud platforms' included automation capabilities and third-party solutions that allow for additional customization to satisfy particular requirements (Ganesan, P.,et al.,2023).

Infrastructure as Code (IaC) IaC is the process of using code to manage infrastructure instead of manual configuration. With infrastructure specifications kept under version control, this method enables teams to define, provision, and upgrade infrastructure in a consistent and repeatable manner. IaC advantages include:

Consistency and Reproducibility: Teams guarantee that environments are consistent throughout development, testing, and production by specifying infrastructure in code. Version control makes it simpler to manage changes and roll back to earlier configurations when necessary since infrastructure code can be recorded, (Boudi, A.,et al.,2021) versioned, and rolled back just like any other code. Scalability: IaC makes it possible to quickly provide and scale resources, which is crucial for cloud-native apps that require dynamic scalability. Because they facilitate automated infrastructure management and aid in removing configuration drift, IaC tools such as Terraform, Ansible, and AWS CloudFormation have become commonplace in cloud-native settings.

Table 1. Use cases of AI in cloud-native systems

Use Case	Description	AI Techniques Involved
Self-Healing Applications	Detects and automatically resolves issues within applications.	Machine learning, anomaly detection
Dynamic Resource Allocation	Adjusts resources based on workload demand to optimize performance.	Predictive analytics, reinforcement learning
Enhanced Security Monitoring	Uses AI to detect security anomalies and protect systems in real time.	Deep learning, pattern recognition
Automated Deployment Pipelines	Automates CI/CD processes and reduces deployment risks.	NLP for code analysis, automation models
Personalized User Experiences	AI personalizes user interactions and optimizes the customer journey.	Recommendation systems, NLP

These table 1 explanations provide a thorough analysis of every AI use case in cloud-native systems, emphasising the ways in which they enhance overall performance, security, user experience, and system efficiency. If you would like more customisation or other use cases, please let me know.

Observability

Keeping complicated distributed systems reliable, performant, and secure has become a top priority as software engineering adopts cloud-native development more and more. To overcome these obstacles, observability of the capacity to track and decipher a system's internal states from outward outputs has become a crucial technique. When combined with artificial intelligence (AI), observability is progressing beyond conventional monitoring to provide automatic responses and predictive insights (Lu, Y., et al.,2024). This paper examines the advantages and difficulties of using AI to improve observability in cloud-native software engineering.

Observability in conventional systems depends on collecting logs, metrics, and traces in order to track performance and diagnose problems. Monolithic apps are far simpler than cloud-native designs, which are constructed with microservices and run on dynamic infrastructure. Because these systems are made up of many loosely connected services that scale on demand and communicate over a network, it can be difficult to determine the underlying source of problems or anticipate possible breakdowns.

Figure 2. Observability in cloud-native systems

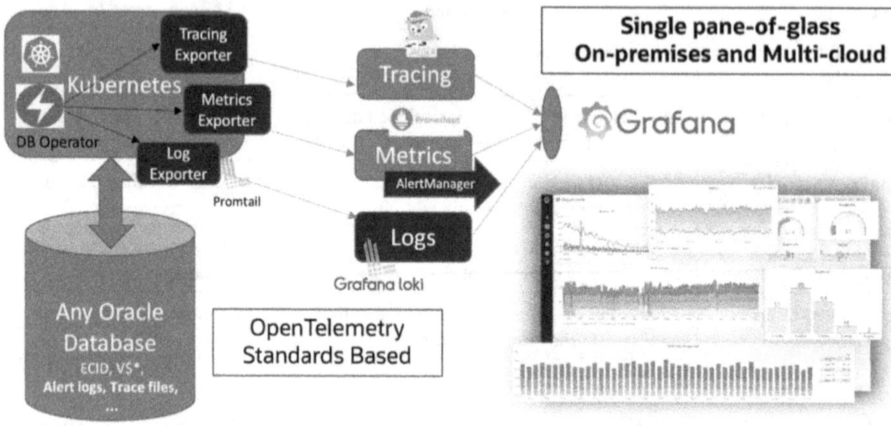

Figure 2 that depicts observability in cloud-native systems could be organised using essential elements that stand in for the three main pillars of observability: logs, metrics, and traces, as well as the tools and data flow throughout the system. An overview of "Figure 2.

Three primary pillars comprise observability:

Logging: By offering thorough documentation of application events, logs aid in problem diagnosis and comprehension of application behavior.

Metrics: Metrics, like CPU utilization, memory consumption, and reaction times, provide information about how well system components are performing(Gadde, H. et al.,2022).

Tracing: Distributed tracing enables developers to track the trajectory of a request across multiple services, which is crucial for locating bottlenecks and troubleshooting performance problems.

Teams can swiftly identify, troubleshoot, and fix problems in intricate cloud-native systems thanks to observability. Cloud-native apps frequently use tools like Prometheus, Grafana, and OpenTelemetry to incorporate observability.

1.2 Benefits and Challenges of Cloud-Native Development

A method of software engineering known as "cloud-native development" makes use of cloud environments and related technologies to create applications that are incredibly scalable, robust, and adaptable. Cloud-native development has many benefits, but it also presents a new set of difficulties that call for specific skills and resources.

Figure 3. Advantages of cloud-native architecture

The essential observability pillars logs, metrics, and traces as well as the tools and data flow throughout the system could be represented by important components in a figure that shows observability in cloud-native systems. This is the conceptual framework for Figure 3

Flexibility and Scalability Benefit: Because cloud-native apps are built to scale horizontally, they can accommodate growing workloads by adding more instances instead of replacing outdated hardware. This enables applications to adapt to variations in demand, guaranteeing dependable performance without the need for user intervention. For instance, e-commerce websites can automatically adjust to accommodate periods of heavy traffic during sales events and periods of low traffic, thereby reducing expenses, (Ivaki, R., et al.,2024).

Fault Tolerance and Resilience Benefit: Fault isolation is a feature of cloud-native architectures, especially those built on microservices, which means that if one element fails, the others are unaffected. Because services may automatically recover from failures without affecting the end-user experience, this improves overall resilience. For instance, customers may still be able to browse products and add items to their basket in a microservices-based application even if the payment service is unavailable (Cherukuri, B. R.et al. 2024,).

A quicker time to market Benefit: Cloud-native development facilitates quick development cycles through the use of CI/CD, DevOps, and containerization, enabling teams to provide new features, updates, and problem fixes more quickly. Businesses may stay competitive and react swiftly to user needs by implementing this ongoing iteration and rollout. For instance, fintech businesses can quickly provide new features while adhering to regulatory updates and adjusting to market shifts without having to completely redesign their applications.

Cost-Effectiveness

Benefit: By utilizing resources only when required, cloud-native apps minimize expenses by optimizing resource utilization. By limiting waste, technologies like serverless computing and autoscaling make sure businesses only pay for what they utilize. For instance, serverless function is perfect for applications with irregular or irregular usage patterns since it only costs money while it is actively processing requests (Ganesan, P., et al.,2023).

Enhanced Cooperation and Productivity among Developer Benefit: By enhancing cooperation between development and operations teams, DevOps techniques, automation, and Infrastructure as Code (IaC) lower bottlenecks and boost productivity. As a result, developers may concentrate on writing code instead of maintaining infrastructure. As an illustration, automated CI/CD pipelines free up developers' time for feature development by reducing the amount of manual intervention required for testing and deployment (Herrera, B. et al.,2024).

Challenges of Cloud-Native Development

Enhanced Operational Overhead and Complexity Challenge: It might be difficult to manage a distributed system that consists of microservices, containers, and orchestration. The operational complexity of cloud-native applications is increased by the frequent involvement of several services that need to be monitored, scaled, and communicated securely. For instance, it takes specific expertise and reliable tools like Kubernetes to orchestrate and manage dependencies among hundreds of microservices across many settings (Karanam, R. et al.,2024).

Data Management and Consistency Challenge: When every microservice has its own database, it might be challenging to ensure data consistency in a distributed cloud-native environment. Careful design is needed to manage transactions and synchronize data across services. For instance, since order management, payment procedures, and inventory updates may include several services, e-commerce platforms must provide consistent data when processing transactions.

Risks to Security and Compliance Challenge: Because cloud-native apps are distributed, any service, container, and API endpoint could be targeted, increasing the possible attack surface. Advanced security procedures and a shift-left security philosophy are needed to secure these systems.

For instance, in order to fix vulnerabilities, organizations need to update containers often and establish robust identity and access management (IAM) procedures (Raj, P., et al.,2021).

Table 2. AI techniques used in cloud-native software engineering

AI Technique	Application in Cloud-Native Engineering	Examples
Machine Learning (ML)	Enables predictive analytics for load, capacity, and error predictions.	Anomaly detection, workload prediction
Natural Language Processing (NLP)	Analyzes logs, comments, and support tickets for improved system insights.	Log analysis, chatbot support
Reinforcement Learning (RL)	Optimizes resource allocation by learning the best strategies over time.	Autoscaling, load balancing
Computer Vision (CV)	Monitors physical assets in edge/cloud environments with visual data.	Image recognition for security
Deep Learning (DL)	Improves anomaly detection and threat identification through complex patterns.	Intrusion detection, fraud prevention

This table 2 the intelligent, adaptable, and resilient capabilities that various AI approaches provide to cloud-native software engineering are demonstrated in this table. With the help of each technique, cloud-native systems may perform more effectively and independently, supporting anything from resource optimisation and predictive maintenance to improved security and user experience. Please let me know if you would like further information or examples for any of the techniques.

Problems with Network Latency and Performance

Challenge: Services in a microservices architecture communicate with one another via a network, which can cause latency and performance problems, particularly in applications that need to react instantly. It is essential to optimize network communication and guarantee low-latency connectivity. For instance, in order to provide flawless user experience, real-time apps such as gaming or streaming services need to carefully control network latency (Raj, P., et al.,2021).

A steep learning curve Challenge: Teams working on cloud-native projects must pick up new skills and become adept with tools like Terraform, Docker, Kubernetes, and monitoring systems. Making the switch from traditional to cloud-native development can be time-consuming and may involve a large training expenditure. For instance, the adoption of cloud-native approaches may be slowed down by traditional development teams' initial difficulties using Infrastructure as Code, container orchestration, and CI/CD pipelines (Ivaki, N. R., et al.,2024).

Cloud Provider Dependency and Possible Vendor Lock-In Problem: Because cloud-native apps are frequently customized to use particular cloud provider services, switching providers or deploying apps across various clouds can be difficult. Over time, vendor lock-in can raise expenses and reduce flexibility. Example: It would take a lot of re-engineering to move to a new cloud provider, such as Azure or Google Cloud, if an application depends significantly on AWS Lambda and other AWS-specific capabilities (Nguyen, H. et al.,2021).

2. ROLE OF ARTIFICIAL INTELLIGENCE IN CLOUD-NATIVE APPLICATIONS

In cloud-native applications, artificial intelligence (AI) is becoming more and more important since it expands capabilities, boosts operational effectiveness, and makes it possible for more intelligent, adaptable systems. Among other advantages, companies can automate procedures, optimize resources, customize user experiences, and improve security by incorporating AI into cloud-native design. Businesses can fully utilize their cloud Key Roles of AI in Cloud-Native Applications (Olabanji, D., et al.,2023).

Automated Monitoring and Predictive Maintenance

Role: By evaluating vast amounts of system data to identify irregularities, forecast malfunctions, and suggest preventive measures, artificial intelligence (AI) improves monitoring in cloud-native applications. By using AI to anticipate problems before they interfere with services, predictive maintenance enables proactive rather than reactive solutions.AI systems, for instance, can reduce downtime and improve application resilience by analyzing log data trends and spotting possible hardware or software faults before they happen(Pölöskei, I. et al.,2022).

Improved Security via Threat Identification and Reaction Role: AI-powered security solutions keep an eye on user activity and network traffic to identify odd trends and possible security risks instantly. By automatically reacting to questionable activity, these tools reduce the amount of time needed to reduce hazards. For instance, when an AI-based security system notices odd access requests or strange login patterns, it sends out alarms and, if necessary, isolating the affected services to prevent further compromise (Deng, S., et al.,2024).

Cost optimization and intelligent resource management Role: By assessing application demands and automatically modifying resources, AI-driven resource management aids in optimizing cloud usage. AI may proactively distribute or deallocate resources by anticipating workload patterns, which ensures effective performance while cutting expenses. As an illustration, AI models anticipate periods of high consumption and a lot more computational resources in advance, preventing performance snags and eliminating needless expenses during off-peak hours (Feng, X., et al.,2022).

Enhancing User Experiences with Customization Role: By evaluating user data and preferences, AI helps cloud-native apps provide individualized user experiences. Applications that depend on search optimization, recommendation algorithms, or content customization will find this very useful. For instance, an e-commerce company uses AI to make product recommendations based on a user's browsing behavior, previous purchases, and demographic information, resulting in a more interesting and personalized shopping experience (Lang, H., et al.,2022).

Advanced Data Analysis and Instantaneous Understanding Role: AI improves data analytics in cloud-native apps by revealing trends and offering real-time insights that conventional techniques could miss. This facilitates data-driven decision-making and rapid situational adaptation for enterprises. As an illustration, AI is used in healthcare applications to evaluate real-time patient data and offer insights into illness trends, enabling medical personnel to react to medical emergencies more skillfully (Ganesan, P., et al.,2023).

Effective Automation of CI/CD Pipelines and DevOps Role: By automating CI/CD pipelines, enhancing code quality, and streamlining deployment tactics, AI helps DevOps with cloud-native apps. Software may be released more quickly and reliably thanks to machine learning models' ability to analyze code, identify possible problems, and recommend improvements. For instance, an AI-based system checks code for possible errors or performance snags and gives engineers immediate feedback (Gil, G., et al.,2021).

Natural Language Processing (NLP) for Communication with Users Function: Chatbots and voice assistants driven by natural language processing (NLP) enhance user interaction in cloud-native apps by enabling natural language communication between users and apps. Building customer care bots, automating queries, and analyzing the sentiment of customer reviews are all possible with NLP. As an illustration, a cloud-native banking app that leverages natural language processing (NLP) provides a virtual assistant that assists customers with transactions, balance checks, and feedback via voice or text requests.

Traffic management and dynamic load balancing Function: AI algorithms enhance request routing across several servers by analyzing real-time data and enabling dynamic load balancing and traffic management. This makes it easier for cloud-native apps to remain responsive and perform well even when traffic is heavy. AI-powered load balancers, for instance, track server loads and divert traffic to servers with lower congestion (Theodoropoulos, et al.,2021).

3. AI-DRIVEN DEVOPS IN CLOUD-NATIVE ENVIRONMENTS

DevOps approaches are being revolutionized by artificial intelligence (AI), particularly in cloud-native contexts where scalability, automation, and agility are critical. Organizations may increase system stability, proactively monitor infrastructure health, and optimize their continuous integration and continuous delivery (CI/

CD) pipelines by integrating AI capabilities into DevOps. Two important uses of AI in DevOps are discussed below

3.1 AI for Continuous Delivery and Integration (CI/CD) In order to ensure that code changes are continuously integrated, tested, and deployed with the least amount of manual intervention, teams can automate and optimize the software development lifecycle with the use of Continuous Integration and continuous Delivery (CI/CD), two fundamental DevOps principles(Surianarayanan, C.,et al.,2021).

Figure 4. Continuous delivery and integration

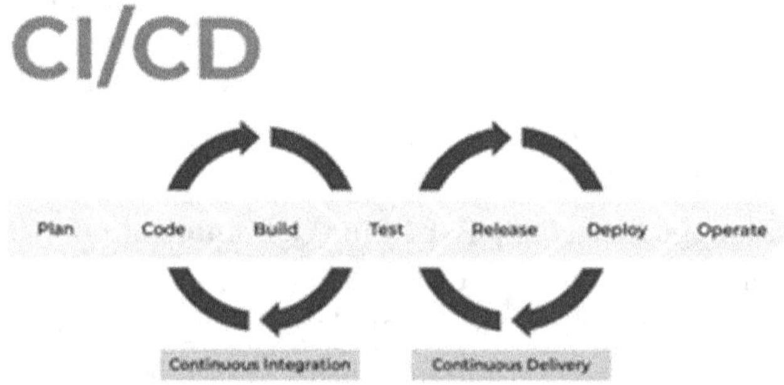

Figure 4 show a popular approach in contemporary software development for regularly, consistently, and effectively providing code updates is the Continuous Integration and Continuous Delivery (CI/CD) pipeline. Each stage of the CI/CD pipeline is broken down as follows: Plan: During this stage, the group establishes objectives, plans features and specifies requirements. By bringing team members together and guaranteeing a clear path, this stage lays the groundwork for future development. Code: Using the predetermined requirements as a guide, developers write code. To guarantee openness and cooperation, the code should adhere to best practices and every modification should be recorded. Build: A build is created by compiling and assembling code. In order to produce deployable units, this phase also involves packaging and dependency management. The build procedure guarantees that code can be seamlessly included into subsequent stages(Machireddy, J. R,et al.,2021).

Test: To verify the code, automated tests are conducted, such as unit and integration tests. This stage is crucial for guaranteeing code quality, finding defects early, and keeping problems from making it to production. Release: The code is ready for release following successful testing. This includes putting code into staging environments for last-minute inspection, authorizing modifications, and writing release notes. Deploy: Production environments receive the code. Automated deployments in CI/CD provide quicker and more reliable releases. This is furthered by continuous deployment, which goes beyond continuous delivery by automatically deploying every code change.

Operate: To guarantee stability, performance, and dependability, the software is observed during production. Here, observability tools are frequently used to monitor performance indicators, identify irregularities, and learn more about user behavior.

Automated Vulnerability and Code Quality Assessment Before code modifications are integrated into the main codebase, AI models can check them for possible security and quality problems. AI solutions assist teams to detect problems early and lower the chance of introducing bugs into production environments by automatically flagging problematic code based on patterns linked to flaws or vulnerabilities. For instance, AI-powered solutions such as CodeGuru and DeepCode employ machine learning to identify security flaws, ineffective coding techniques, and code smells, giving developers the knowledge they need to enhance code quality prior to deployment (Velayutham, S., et al.,2021).

Automating and optimizing tests intelligently By anticipating which tests are most pertinent for particular code changes, artificial intelligence (AI) improves test automation and cuts down on time wasted performing pointless tests. Tests can be prioritized by AI models according to variables such as code complexity, dependencies, and previous test outcomes. As an illustration, an AI-enhanced CI/CD pipeline may identify that just a portion of tests are pertinent for a minor issue repair. This enables the pipeline to omit tests that aren't necessary, speeding up testing and increasing release time (Ivaki, N. R., et al.,2024).

Automated Rollbacks and Predicting Faults CI/CD systems can examine past deployment data and identify trends linked to deployment problems with AI-driven fault prediction. To reduce interruptions and downtime, the AI system can immediately start a rollback or stop the deployment if a problem is probable. Example: If an AI system anticipates that certain code changes may result in problems in a high-stakes setting, it may automatically revert to the previous version and notify the team, stopping a deployment (Singh, et al.,2023)..

Optimization of Releases and Canary Deployment By using canary deployments, in which updates are distributed to a limited group of users before to a full deployment, AI can streamline release procedures. AI algorithms assist in deciding whether the new version should be completely implemented or pulled back by examining user feedback and error rates. As an illustration, Netflix uses AI to track canary deployments in real time, evaluating the performance of the updated version against the previous one to guarantee a seamless launch with the least amount of disturbance to users (Liu, H, et al.,2023).

3.2 Monitoring and Predictive Maintenance AI-driven predictive maintenance and monitoring solutions are essential for guaranteeing system dependability, spotting any problems, and allowing self-healing capabilities in cloud-native systems.

By minimizing downtime and enhancing performance, these tools assist DevOps teams in managing the health of their infrastructure.

Real-time alerts and anomaly detection Logs, metrics, and system performance data are continuously analyzed by AI-driven monitoring systems to find abnormalities that might indicate underlying problems. These systems can automatically initiate corrective steps or notify teams of deviations from usual behavior in real time, preventing minor problems from becoming more serious. For instance, teams can address problems before they affect consumers by using AI-powered tools like Dynatrace and New Relic, which use anomaly detection to identify anomalies in system performance, such as unexpected CPU utilization or latency spikes (Confidently, et al.,2022).

Proactive Maintenance and Predictive Fault Identification By examining past performance data and finding trends that predate outages or performance deteriorations, AI models are able to forecast system breakdowns. DevOps teams can proactively handle possible problems, including disk failures or memory leaks, before they affect system availability by using predictive maintenance. For instance, an AI-powered predictive maintenance system may identify trends of increased memory utilization linked to a memory leak, allowing the team to take action before the problem causes a crash (Ganesan, P., et al.,2023)..

Automated Incident Response and Self-Healing AI is used by self-healing systems to automatically detect and fix problems without the need for human assistance. When certain problems occur, these systems can take predetermined corrective action since machine learning is being used to recognize frequent incidents and how they are resolved. An AI-powered system may, for instance, immediately restart a server or redistribute workloads to other nodes in a cloud-native environment if a server encounters a resource bottleneck, therefore averting performance degradation (Machireddy, J. R, et al.,2021)..

Planning Capacity and Optimizing Resources

Optimized capacity planning is made possible by AI models that assist DevOps teams in predicting resource requirements based on past consumption trends. By dynamically modifying resources to match demand, this proactive method minimizes waste and avoids resource shortages.

For instance, cloud-native applications with AI-powered capacity planning tools are able to anticipate seasonal spikes in traffic and proactively scale up resources to ensure steady performance without over-provisioning.

4. AI-POWERED OBSERVABILITY AND MONITORING IN CLOUD-NATIVE SYSTEMS

In cloud-native systems, where applications are constructed from interconnected microservices and operate on distributed infrastructure, observability and monitoring are crucial. Traditional monitoring is difficult because of the complexity of these systems, which produce massive volumes of data that can obfuscate important insights. These issues are resolved by AI-powered observability and monitoring, which improve anomaly identification, simplify root cause analysis, and offer real-time insights. Below, we look at how AI may be used to help with log analysis, root cause analysis, and real-time anomaly detection (Ivaki, N. R., et al.,2024).

4.1 Real-Time Anomaly Detection and Alerting

Identifying irregularities and reacting promptly are essential for preserving system dependability in cloud-native settings where numerous microservices are operating concurrently. Conventional monitoring uses preset thresholds or criteria to find problems, but these techniques may overlook minute changes or send out too many notifications when thresholds are crossed. By employing machine learning models to comprehend "normal" behavior patterns in complex systems, AI-powered anomaly detection enhances this procedure and enables the detection and reaction to anomalies as they occur(Singh,et al.,2023)..

Pattern Recognition and Dynamic Thresholding

AI systems, as opposed to static thresholds, can dynamically modify detection criteria in response to shifting workloads, minimizing false positives and lowering alert fatigue. These models examine past data to discover patterns, spotting aberrations that could point to underlying problems before they become apparent. For instance, based on seasonal patterns, an AI-powered monitoring system in an e-commerce platform may dynamically modify thresholds for metrics like mistake rates, response times, and traffic volume. In this manner, during periods of high traffic, such as holidays, it can identify anomalous traffic spikes or latency problems in real-time without sending out alerts for anticipated fluctuations.

Early Identification of New Problems

AI models are able to detect minor changes that may not be immediately noticeable, like slow increases in latency, resource contention, or memory leakage, by analyzing incoming data streams in real-time. Teams can take preventive action thanks to this early detection, which lowers downtime and enhances user experience AI could be used, for instance, in a financial services application to identify minute variations in transaction processing time that might point to the emergence of a performance bottleneck. The DevOps team may proactively scale resources or improve code before it affects customer-facing services thanks to real-time warnings.

Intelligent Alerting and Event Correlation By connecting relevant events and combining them into a single warning, AI helps decrease noise in alerting so that teams can concentrate on problems that have the most impact. AI can prevent alert fatigue by identifying whether multiple alerts are coming from the same underlying cause by examining links between events, such as shared components or dependencies. An AI model might, for instance, correlate alarms about memory spikes, API timeouts, and database delay in a microservices-based healthcare application and conclude that they are probably connected to a single service. Instead of focusing on treating specific symptoms, the team can now target the underlying problem thanks to this realization (Singh, et al.,2023).

4.2 AI-Powered Log Analysis and Root Cause Analysis

With thousands of microservices producing enormous volumes of log data, analyzing logs and determining the underlying cause of problems can be difficult and time-consuming in cloud-native systems. This process is accelerated by AI-driven log analysis, which aids DevOps teams in gaining insights and identifying the underlying causes more quickly and precisely(Machireddy, J. R,et al.,2021).

Automated Pattern Recognition and Log Parsing

Artificial intelligence (AI)-driven log analysis systems automatically parse and organize log data, looking for trends and spotting unusual log entries. By classifying logs according to their relevance and severity, these tools assist teams in spotting possible problems without having to manually sort through massive amounts of data.

For instance, in a cloud-native SaaS platform, an AI log analysis tool may classify logs as "normal operation," "warning," or "error." This allows teams to concentrate on high-priority entries without being overloaded with informational logs. This automation guarantees that major issues are flagged right away and saves time(Ganesan, P.,et al.,2023).

Finding Anomalies in Logs to Conduct Root Cause Analysis

Artificial intelligence (AI) techniques identify abnormalities in logs, such as particular error messages or spikes in log entries, that may point to the underlying cause of a problem. By ranking anomalies according to how likely they are to affect availability or performance, these models can help teams identify possible reasons more quickly. For instance, an AI model may identify an odd network fault pattern in an IoT monitoring system that corresponds with recent firmware updates for devices. In order to facilitate a speedier resolution, the system would notify the DevOps team and identify the firmware update as a probable root cause.

Causal Inference for Intelligent Root Cause Identification

In order to determine the causal linkages between occurrences and provide insights into how one problem might lead to another, AI systems examine logs and performance data. For instance, a downstream latency problem could be the cause of an increase in CPU utilization on a specific service. By assisting teams in concentrating on the most important problems, AI-driven root cause analysis reduces mean time to resolution (MTTR).For instance, an AI-powered root cause analysis system in a retail platform may conclude that a sharp decline in checkout speed is connected to a rise in inventory service requests, which may be the result of an API modification. Instead of looking at the checkout service, the team is guided by this insight to focus on the API.

Analysis of Log Entries' Sentiment AI is occasionally able to identify emotive or descriptive tones in log entry content, which can reveal the seriousness or urgency of a problem. Teams can better comprehend the context of logs and set priorities by using AI models that utilize sentiment analysis techniques. For instance, a customer-facing app may employ sentiment analysis on user interaction error logs to identify terms that indicate extreme user annoyance (such as "critical failure," "unable to access") as urgent problems that need to be fixed right away (Singh,et al.,2023)..

5. INTELLIGENT RESOURCE ALLOCATION AND COST OPTIMIZATION

In cloud-native environments, managing resources efficiently and optimizing costs are paramount for achieving high performance and scalability while minimizing expenses. As organizations increasingly rely on cloud computing to host their applications, intelligent resource allocation and cost optimization strategies powered by Artificial Intelligence (AI) and Machine Learning (ML) become essential. These technologies enable organizations to dynamically allocate resources based on real-time demands and monitor costs effectively, ensuring that resources are used judiciously without compromising performance.

5.1 Machine Learning for Dynamic Scaling and Load Balancing

In cloud-native applications, dynamic scaling and load balancing are essential components of resource management, particularly when handling varying workloads. Through real-time resource allocation optimization, demand prediction, and usage pattern analysis, AI and ML algorithms can greatly improve these procedures.

Figure 5. Load balancing

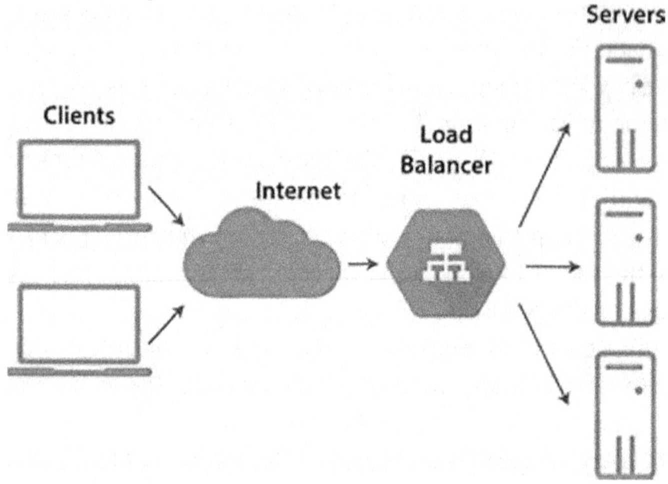

Figure 5show by proposing adaptive, data-driven techniques for effectively dividing traffic across servers or services, machine learning (ML) is transforming load balancing, which is essential for managing varying workloads in contemporary distributed systems. In constantly changing situations, like cloud-based applications, where user demand can fluctuate quickly and unexpectedly, traditional load balancing techniques, such as round-robin or least connections, provide simple tactics but sometimes fall short. By anticipating workload distribution patterns, enabling intelligent traffic routing, and detecting anomalies in real-time, machine learning (ML)-based load balancing gets around these restrictions and offers a reliable way to avoid server overloads and guarantee system performance.

Scaling Predictively In order to spot patterns and forecast workloads in the future, machine learning models can examine consumption data from the past. These models can automatically scale resources by identifying trends like abrupt spikes in demand or peak usage periods, guaranteeing that applications have the capacity to handle load without over-provisioning. For instance, a streaming service may be able to scale up its server capacity ahead of time by using machine learning (ML) to forecast spikes in user traffic on weekends or holidays. A seamless user experience is ensured by this proactive approach while minimizing costs associated with over-provisioning during low-demand periods(Machireddy, J. R,et al.,2021)..

Balanced Loads in Real Time using real-time performance indicators, AI-driven load balancing improves the distribution of resources among servers. AI algorithms can dynamically distribute traffic to the least-loaded instances, improving responsiveness and lowering latency, by continuously monitoring resource usage and application performance. Example: To intelligently route requests to the top-performing instances in a microservices architecture, an AI-powered load balancer may examine parameters like CPU utilization, memory consumption, and response times. The user experience and overall application performance are enhanced by this real-time modification.

Optimization of Resource Utilization Finding underutilized or overutilized resources in the cloud infrastructure can be aided by machine learning. ML algorithms can suggest changes, such rightsizing instances or combining workloads, to maximize resource utilization and cut expenses by examining resource use trends. As an illustration, a cloud-based service may use machine learning algorithms to examine consumption data from multiple instances and pinpoint those that routinely run below a predetermined level. Cost reductions can result from the system's recommendations to scale down or decommission certain instances.

Policies for Auto-Scaling Instead of depending solely on straightforward rules, AI can improve auto-scaling policies by analyzing a variety of variables and initiating scaling operations in response to intricate circumstances. This method guarantees that programs may react to different load scenarios without sacrificing functionality.

Example: During a flash sale, an e-commerce platform may see unexpected increases in traffic. In order to keep the platform flexible to user needs, an AI-driven auto-scaling system might dynamically modify resource allocations depending on real-time data like user traffic, transaction volumes, and system health.

5.2 AI for Cost Management in Cloud Environments

AI is essential for efficient cost management in cloud systems, in addition to improving resource allocation. Organizations can obtain insights on their cloud expenditures and put policies in place to maximize efficiency while controlling expenses by utilizing AI tools and methodologies.

Automated Cost Analysis and Monitoring Real-time cloud expenditure pattern analysis using AI-powered cost management solutions can assist businesses in spotting trends, irregularities, and areas for development. These tools can provide dashboards and reports that offer useful information, empowering teams to decide how best to use resources. As an illustration, a SaaS business may use AI-powered cost monitoring tools to examine how much it spends on different cloud services. The findings may indicate unanticipated increases in expenses linked to particular services, necessitating additional research and modifications.

Budgeting and Cost Prediction Based on past consumption trends, AI systems can predict future cloud expenditures, helping businesses create more precise budgets and manage resources more efficiently. Organizations may make data-driven financial decisions and steer clear of unforeseen expenses by forecasting expenditure patterns. For instance, the finance team might make proactive budget adjustments by using an AI-driven budgeting tool that examines an organization's past cloud usage and forecasts monthly expenses based on anticipated consumption trends(Singh,et al.,2023)..

Suggestions for Rightsizing AI may offer practical suggestions for allocating cloud resources appropriately, guaranteeing that businesses only pay for what they require. In order to avoid overprovisioning, AI algorithms can recommend the best instance sizes for apps based on real usage by evaluating performance data.As an illustration, a financial institution that uses several virtual machines may use AI technologies to evaluate workload performance and suggest downgrading to fewer instances, which could result in significant cost savings without compromising performance.

Optimizing Reserved Instances and Savings Plans Organizations can save long-term expenses by using AI tools that can evaluate consumption trends and suggest the best way to distribute reserved instances or savings plans. AI can determine the most effective cloud service pricing plans by analyzing past data and forecasting future consumption. As an illustration, a software business might employ AI to examine its usage data and identify the cloud resources that are most appropriate for reserved instances. The company may optimize savings while guaranteeing resource availability thanks to this smart deployment.

6. SECURITY AND COMPLIANCE IN AI-DRIVEN CLOUD-NATIVE ENGINEERING

Strong security and compliance procedures are crucial as more and more businesses use cloud-native architectures. Significant security difficulties arise from the dynamic nature of cloud infrastructures, the intricacy of microservices, and data interdependencies. Strong tools for improving threat detection, vulnerability assessment, and automated security policy execution are provided by AI-driven security solutions. This all-encompassing strategy helps enterprises fulfill regulatory compliance obligations while simultaneously strengthening the security posture of cloud-native systems.

Figure 6. Pillars of cloud native security

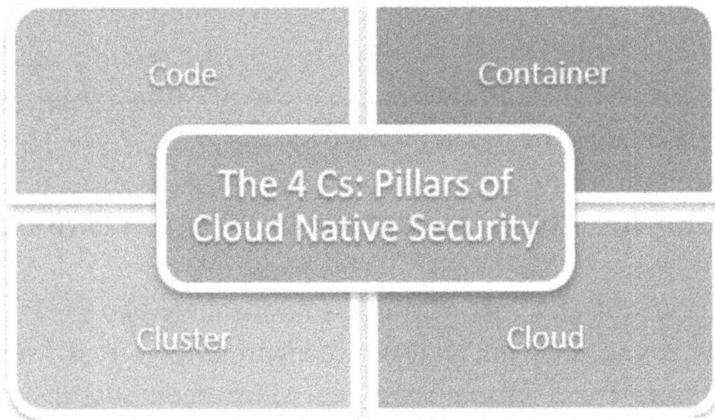

Figure 6 show to safeguard cloud-native applications, the "4Cs" of cloud-native security Code, Container, Cluster, and Cloud are essential foundations. These applications rely significantly on automation and quick deployment, which can present special security challenges. They are frequently implemented utilizing microservices architectures. In a cloud-native environment, each "C" stands for a layer. By putting security measures in place at each level, businesses can create a cloud architecture that is more dependable, secure, and resilient. Let's examine each of these pillars in more detail. Code: The Basis for Secure Programs

Code, the first pillar, places a strong emphasis on security procedures throughout the software development lifecycle. Because flaws in code can spread across the system and impact higher layers like containers and clusters, secure code serves as the cornerstone for all other layers. Static code analysis, vulnerability scanning, and conformity to secure coding standards are important code security methods.

2. Container: Protecting the Packaging of Applications

The security of containerized applications, which package code together with dependencies and configurations to ensure consistency across environments, is handled by the container layer. However, vulnerabilities may be introduced via containers, particularly if images contain out-of-date libraries or unsafe configurations. Image scanning, thus, is vital in container security, finding vulnerabilities before deployment.

3. Cluster: Guaranteeing Safe Management and Orchestration

The cluster layer, which is usually coordinated by platforms like Kubernetes, is responsible for protecting the environment in which containers operate. Although Kubernetes clusters handle networking, resources, and scaling for containers, they are susceptible to attacks on the control plane, privilege escalation, and unwanted access if they are not adequately protected(Reddy, A.et al.,2021)..

4. Cloud: Safe Administration and Infrastructure

Securing the underlying infrastructure offered by cloud service providers (CSPs) such as AWS, Azure, or Google Cloud is the responsibility of the cloud layer. Securing this layer necessitates utilizing provider-specific security technologies and best practices because the cloud environment consists of hardware, networks, and management tools that are overseen by the CSP.

6.1 AI for Vulnerability Assessment and Threat Detection

Threat identification and vulnerability assessment are two crucial areas where AI greatly improves security in cloud-native environments. It is crucial to use AI technology for proactive defense mechanisms since traditional security measures frequently find it difficult to keep up with the quickly changing threat landscape (Singh, et al.,2023).

Automated Identification of Threats AI-powered threat detection systems examine enormous volumes of data from multiple sources, such as user activity, application logs, and network traffic. Faster detection of possible threats is made possible by machine learning algorithms' ability to spot trends and abnormalities that can point to malicious behavior. For instance, an artificial intelligence (AI) system set up in a cloud setting may constantly scan network traffic for odd trends, like an abrupt increase in requests coming from a single IP address, which would indicate a Distributed Denial-of-Service (DDoS) attack. The system can start automated reactions and sound notifications when it notices this irregularity (Reddy, A.et al.,2021).

Assessment of Predictive Vulnerabilities By evaluating threat intelligence and historical data to anticipate possible vulnerabilities before they can be exploited, artificial intelligence (AI) can improve vulnerability assessment procedures. Organizations can resolve security flaws in their infrastructure and apps by taking this proactive approach. Example: To help developers prioritize remediation efforts, an AI-driven vulnerability management solution may examine code repositories and previous incident reports to find code patterns or libraries that attackers commonly target (Singh, et al.,2023).

Using Behavioral Analytics to Identify Insider Threats Behavioral Analytics can be used by AI systems to track user activity in cloud-native apps. These systems can identify deviations that can point to insider threats or compromised accounts by setting baseline behavior for persons and entities. For instance, an AI system may alert authorities to possible data breaches if a worker regularly accesses private information during working hours but then starts doing so late at night from a different location.

Response to Incidents Automatically AI can speed up the process of responding to threats by enabling automated incident response workflows. Organizations may automate responses like alerting security personnel, blocking suspect IP addresses, and isolating hacked systems by integrating AI with Security Information and Event Management (SIEM) solutions.\An AI-powered security solution, for instance, may automatically quarantine the impacted instance, alert the security team, and start scans on connected systems when it detects a malware infection in a cloud-based application, reducing the possible effect(Reddy, A.et al.,2021)..

6.2 Implementing Automated Security Policies with AI

Because the infrastructure in cloud-native settings is dynamic, putting security controls into place can be challenging. AI offers strong capabilities for guaranteeing compliance, automating the enforcement of security policies, and adjusting to shifting circumstances (Singh, et al.,2023).

Enforcement of Dynamic Security Policies Security policies can be dynamically enforced by AI-driven solutions using real-time data. To make sure that defined security policies are being followed, these systems continuously examine user behavior, network traffic, and system configurations. They also automatically modify policies as necessary. For instance, in cloud-native deployment, an AI system may keep an eye on user rights and access control settings, automatically removing access for users who behave dangerously or use resources outside of their roles in order to uphold the concept of least privilege.

Automated Auditing of Compliance by regularly checking cloud settings for conformity with regulatory requirements (such as GDPR and HIPAA), artificial intelligence (AI) can expedite compliance auditing. Artificial intelligence (AI) solutions can detect non-compliant components and produce reports for regulatory agencies by examining settings and resource utilization. For instance, a healthcare company may use AI tools to keep an eye on its cloud infrastructure to ensure that HIPAA requirements are being followed. The auditing procedure would be made simpler by the AI system's automatic report generation and identification of possible compliance issues.

Optimizing Policies with Machine Learning By evaluating the efficacy of security policies and making data-driven modifications, AI can optimize them. To improve the granularity and efficacy of security controls, machine learning algorithms can assess user feedback, false positives, and incident response times.

An AI-powered security management system, for instance, may examine past incident data to find persistent false positives in threat detection. This would enable security teams to adjust detection levels and raise overall accuracy.

Integrating Threat Intelligence Security policies and responses can be informed by the integration of threat intelligence streams by AI systems. Organizations can prevent new risks by proactively modifying their security policies through the analysis of real-time threat data. For instance, an AI-driven security solution may automatically modify security settings to prevent access to compromised systems until fixes are installed in response to a newly discovered vulnerability for a commonly used software component (Singh, A. et al.,2023).

7. CONCLUSION

Cloud-native software engineering's incorporation of artificial intelligence (AI) has fundamentally changed the way applications are created, implemented, and maintained. AI-driven cloud-native architecture helps businesses create flexible, self-managing apps that can satisfy changing market demands by improving the automation, scalability, robustness, and efficiency of software systems. Teams can optimize resource allocation, enable predictive maintenance, and enhance cloud-native systems by utilizing AI. Deepening this synergy is key to the future of cloud-native software engineering, as AI algorithms continuously improve operations, promote wise decision-making, and guarantee peak performance across distributed systems. Organisations are positioned to thrive in a fast-paced, digital-first environment thanks to this evolution, which encourages quick innovation and offers a strong foundation for creating reliable, future-ready applications.

REFERENCES

Boudi, A., Bagaa, M., Pöyhönen, P., Taleb, T., & Flinck, H. (2021). AI-based resource management in beyond 5G cloud native environment. *IEEE Network*, 35(2), 128–135. DOI: 10.1109/MNET.011.2000392

Confidently, L. A. O., Chakraborty, M., & Kundan, A. P. (2021). Monitoring Cloud-Native Applications.

Deng, S., Zhao, H., Huang, B., Zhang, C., Chen, F., Deng, Y., & Zomaya, A. Y. (2024). Cloud-native computing: A survey from the perspective of services. *Proceedings of the IEEE*. DOI: 10.1109/JPROC.2024.3353855

Feng, X., Guo, C., Jiao, T., & Song, J. (2022). A maturity model for AI-empowered cloud-native databases: From the perspective of resource management. *Journal of Cloud Computing (Heidelberg, Germany)*, 11(1), 39. DOI: 10.1186/s13677-022-00318-1

Gadde, H. (2022). AI-Enhanced Adaptive Resource Allocation in Cloud-Native Databases. *Revista de Inteligencia Artificial en Medicina*, 13(1), 443–470.

Ganesan, P., & Sanodia, G. (2023). Smart Infrastructure Management: Integrating AI with DevOps for Cloud-Native Applications. *Journal of Artificial Intelligence & Cloud Computing. SRC/JAICC-E163. DOI: doi. org/(2) E163 J Arti Inte & Cloud Comp, 2*(1), 2-4.DOI: 10.47363/JAICC/2023

Gil, G., Corujo, D., & Pedreiras, P. (2021, September). Cloud native computing for industry 4.0: Challenges and opportunities. In *2021 26th IEEE international conference on emerging technologies and factory automation (ETFA)* (pp. 01-04). IEEE.

Herrera, B. (2024). *Cloud-Native Applications and Their Role in Supporting Agile Hardware Development* (Doctoral dissertation, Massachusetts Institute of Technology).

Ivaki, N. R., & da Silva, P. M. G. (2024). AI-BASED INTRUSION DETECTION MECHANISMS FOR CLOUD-NATIVE SERVICES. Cherukuri, B. R. (2024, February). Development of Design Patterns with Adaptive User Interface for Cloud Native Microservice Architecture Using Deep Learning With IoT. In *2024 IEEE International Conference on Computing, Power and Communication Technologies (IC2PCT)* (Vol. 5, pp. 1866-1871). IEEE.

Kanchepu, N. (2023). Cloud-Native Architectures: Design Principles and Best Practices for Scalable Applications. *International Journal of Sustainable Development Through AI. ML and IoT*, 2(2), 1–21.

Karanam, R. (2024). SECURING CLOUD-NATIVE APPLICATIONS: A HOLISTIC APPROACH. [IJCET]. *INTERNATIONAL JOURNAL OF COMPUTER ENGINEERING AND TECHNOLOGY*, 15(4), 692–702.

Lang, H., Tian, H., Li, D., Niu, Z., & Wen, L. (2022, August). Design of A Cloud Native-Based Integrated Management Platform for Smart Operation of Multi-Business Buildings. In *2022 14th International Conference on Intelligent Human-Machine Systems and Cybernetics (IHMSC)* (pp. 169-173). IEEE. DOI: 10.1109/IHMSC55436.2022.00047

Liu, H., Zong, J., Wang, Q., Liu, Y., & Yang, F. (2022, April). Cloud native based intelligent RAN architecture towards 6G programmable networking. In *2022 7th International Conference on Computer and Communication Systems (ICCCS)* (pp. 623-627). IEEE.

Lu, Y., Bian, S., Chen, L., He, Y., Hui, Y., Lentz, M., . . . Zhuo, D. (2024). Computing in the Era of Large Generative Models: From Cloud-Native to AI-Native. *arXiv preprint arXiv:2401.12230.*

Machireddy, J. R., Rachakatla, S. K., & Ravichandran, P. (2022). Cloud-Native Data Warehousing: Implementing AI and Machine Learning for Scalable Business Analytics. *Journal of AI in Healthcare and Medicine*, 2(1), 144–169.

Nguyen, H. (2021). *Machine Learning Model Management using Cloud-Native Technologies for IoT* (Master's thesis).

Olabanji, D., Fitch, T., & Matthew, O. (2023). Cloud-native architecture portability framework validation and implementation using expert system. [IJASCSE]. *International Journal of Advanced Studies in Computer Science and Engineering*, 12(4).

Oyeniran, O. C., Modupe, O. T., Otitoola, A. A., Abiona, O. O., Adewusi, A. O., & Oladapo, O. J. (2024). A comprehensive review of leveraging cloud-native technologies for scalability and resilience in software development. *International Journal of Science and Research Archive*, 11(2), 330–337. DOI: 10.30574/ijsra.2024.11.2.0432

Paul, D., Namperumal, G., & Selvaraj, A. (2022). Cloud-Native AI/ML Pipelines: Best Practices for Continuous Integration, Deployment, and Monitoring in Enterprise Applications. *Journal of Artificial Intelligence Research*, 2(1), 176–231.

Pentyala, D., Manduva, V. C., & Devarasetty, N. (2021). Cloud-Native Data Engineering: Improving Reliability Through AIOrchestrated Operations. *International Journal of Advanced Engineering Technologies and Innovations*, 1(3), 94–128.

Polamarasetti, A. (2021). Data Science Innovations for Cloud-Native AI Applications. *International Journal of Machine Learning Research in Cybersecurity and Artificial Intelligence*, 12(1), 292–324.

Pölöskei, I. (2022). MLOps approach in the cloud-native data pipeline design. *Acta Technica Jaurinensis*, 15(1), 1–6. DOI: 10.14513/actatechjaur.00581

Raj, P., Vanga, S., & Chaudhary, A. (2022). *Cloud-Native Computing: How to Design, Develop, and Secure Microservices and Event-Driven Applications*. John Wiley & Sons. DOI: 10.1002/9781119814795

Reddy, A. K., Alluri, V. R. R., Thota, S., Ravi, C. S., & Bonam, V. S. M. (2021). DevSecOps: Integrating Security into the DevOps Pipeline for Cloud-Native Applications. *Journal of Artificial Intelligence Research and Applications*, 1(2), 89–114.

Singh, A. (2023). Optimization of the Cloud-Native Infrastructure using. *Artificial Intelligence*.

Sivathapandi, P., Paul, D., & Sudharsanam, S. R. (2021). Enhancing Cloud-Native CI/CD Pipelines with AI-Driven Automation and Predictive Analytics. *Australian Journal of Machine Learning Research & Applications*, 1(1), 226–265.

Surianarayanan, C., & Chelliah, P. R. (2023). Demystifying the Cloud-Native Computing Paradigm. In *Essentials of Cloud Computing: A Holistic, Cloud-Native Perspective* (pp. 321–345). Springer International Publishing. DOI: 10.1007/978-3-031-32044-6_12

Surianarayanan, C., & Chelliah, P. R. (2023). *Essentials of Cloud Computing: A Holistic, Cloud-Native Perspective*. Springer Nature. DOI: 10.1007/978-3-031-32044-6

Tatineni, S., & Chakilam, N. V. (2024). Integrating Artificial Intelligence with DevOps for Intelligent Infrastructure Management: Optimizing Resource Allocation and Performance in Cloud-Native Applications. *Journal of Bioinformatics and Artificial Intelligence*, 4(1), 109–142.

Theodoropoulos, T., Rosa, L., Benzaid, C., Gray, P., Marin, E., Makris, A., Cordeiro, L., Diego, F., Sorokin, P., Girolamo, M. D., Barone, P., Taleb, T., & Tserpes, K. (2023). Security in Cloud-Native Services: A Survey. *Journal of Cybersecurity and Privacy*, 3(4), 758–793. DOI: 10.3390/jcp3040034

Velayutham, S., & Shanmugam, G. (2021). Artificial Intelligence assisted Canary Testing of Cloud Native RAN in a mobile telecom system.

Wen, L., Qian, H., & Liu, W. (2022). Research on Intelligent Cloud Native Architecture and Key Technologies Based on DevOps Concept. *Procedia Computer Science*, 208, 590–597. DOI: 10.1016/j.procs.2022.10.082

Chapter 4
Generative AI for Source Code Creation:
Revolutionizing Cloud-Native Software Engineering

C. V. Suresh Babu
https://orcid.org/0000-0002-8474-2882
Hindustan Institute of Technology and Science, India

Kathari Hima Kishore
https://orcid.org/0009-0009-0338-6010
Hindustan Institute of Technology and Science, India

ABSTRACT

This study explores the integration of Generative AI in cloud-native software engineering, aiming to enhance the efficiency and effectiveness of source code creation. Targeting software developers, engineers, and organizations leveraging cloud technologies, the research employs a multi-disciplinary approach, combining qualitative interviews and case studies from successful implementations of AI tools like GitHub Copilot and OpenAI's Codex. The findings reveal that Generative AI significantly reduces manual coding efforts, automates routine tasks, and allows developers to focus on complex problem-solving and innovative design. Furthermore, the study highlights the transformative impact of cloud-native architectures in facilitating scalable and flexible software development processes. The conclusions underscore the necessity for developers to adapt to new roles that emphasize critical thinking and creativity, while also addressing potential challenges such as code quality and security.

DOI: 10.4018/979-8-3693-9356-7.ch004

1. INTRODUCTION

1.1 Overview of Generative AI in Software Development

Generative AI in software development is like having a brilliant assistant that helps you write, debug, and improve code effortlessly. It can generate whole chunks of code based on simple instructions, such as asking it to build a login system, saving time on repetitive tasks. It also helps spot bugs and fixes them, essentially a second pair of sharp eyes, and even offers creative solutions you might not have thought of. Overall, it's about making coding faster, smarter, and less stressful.

1.2 The Role of Cloud-Native Architectures in Modern Software Engineering

In software engineering nowadays, that cloud-native architectures can make it possible for applications to scale easily and flexibly with strength. Cloud-native designs break up applications into smaller units, independent services-think microservices-these, for example, might be used or managed on different cloud environments, thus one can easily make a few updates, scale or fix particular parts of an application without shutting the whole system down. It even supports ease of automation, continuous delivery, and integration in the facilitation of teams working faster and more efficiently.

1.3 Purpose and Significance of the Chapter

It focuses on the extent to which cloud-native architectures and generative AI reshape software development. Passing through these two subjects of discussion, the chapter brings the transfer from old conventional methods to new agile and scalable ones: The way AI helps in coding and solving problems with giving flexibility, strength, and continuous improvement through cloud-native strategies. It thereby explains how all these developments change the way we design, build, and adapt software to be faster, wiser, and more effective.

1.4 Chapter Structure and Key Objectives

This chapter goes into all the ways cloud-native architecture and generative AI are changing the face of software development from more rigid and less-efficient older techniques to more flexible and efficient ways of developing, offering some type of both flexibility and strength and continuous progress through use of AI for auto-creation of code and the solving of problems as well as through cloud-native approaches. It actually explains how precisely these advancements are shaping the way software is being created, used, and maintained and makes the whole process faster, smarter, and better. Like **Brown, T., et al.** for discussing the foundational role of large language models in generative AI for coding.

2. BACKGROUND INFORMATION

2.1 Overview of Source Code Creation in Traditional Software Development

This section establishes the foundational understanding of traditional software engineering practices and the pivotal role generative AI plays in transforming these processes. Historically, software development relied heavily on manual coding methodologies, which were often slow, error-prone, and resource-intensive. Traditional workflows required developers to manually write, test, and debug code while managing complex systems in soloed environments. With the advent of cloud-native architectures, these workflows began to evolve, leveraging microservices, containerization, and CI/CD pipelines to promote scalability, flexibility, and continuous delivery. **Wang, Y., et al.** to highlight the current trends and future directions in AI for source code generation.

2.2 Generative AI: A Paradigm Shift in Code Automation

Traditionally, it is the source code that the developers then organize. Generally, in traditional software development, the source code or other project need respects. Normally, one starts by gathering exhaustive requirements. Subsequently, the structure of the design of the software is made. Developers begin writing the code, usually in team format, but in some given programming languages like Java, Python, or c++. In traditional software development, every single function is manually written, hence consuming much time and having errors.

2.3 Evolution of Cloud-Native Software Engineering Practices

Generative AI transforms the process of code automation and therefore advances the type of coding developers need to do. Not all lines of code are typed anymore; now a developer is able to use tools that learn normal language and translate that normal language into working code (Suresh Babu, C. V. & Suruthi, G. 2024). This, therefore, speeds up development and reduces potential errors made. AI will churn boiler-plate code at warp speeds and do time-consuming mundane tasks, giving developers more time for tricky problems. And beyond this, this generative AI continuously learns and learns through gigantic data volumes.

Much noise from the traditional approach to very agile new approaches to the creation and use of software. It was created and operated on the local servers, which again means totally long setup times and even harder applications to manage. Still, the cloud computing approach popularized among developers the use of microservices that split applications into smaller parts separately deployable. It had allowed teams to operate at any different part in concurrent rather than sequential phases hence accelerates development and its deployments. Another thing it changes Docker has affected containerization. Containerization gave very light portable environments to an application hence made them to function without bias on diverse systems.

2.4 Current Challenges in Manual Source Code Development

Issues that delay and degrade the quality of developed software in the current processes for hand-coding source code are a list of several. The most probably major one is an application becomes so complex that everything has to be done in isolation by the developer, which often carries the tag of higher error counts of the process of hand-coding. In addition, solutions from the hand-coding generally take a much longer time. Hence, the development cycle is quite long with more delay in releasing products to market, which hurts these fast-moving industries. The problem of keeping things consistent and pursuing best practices mainly hits the developers working in large teams (Suresh Babu, C. V.. & Barath Kumar, S. 2024)..

Generative AI tools, like Codex from OpenAI and GitHub Copilot, are changing the art of software engineering. It enables automation of repetitive coding work, boilerplate code generation, and even gives suggestions for improvement. All this leads to much-reduced development cycles and higher productivity. However, literature has some difficulties: AI does not realize complex contexts in software. It creates suboptimal or insecure code and it over-relies on automatic solutions. Essentially by **Alshahrani, S., and Althobaiti, A.** for discussing the transition from traditional workflows to AI-assisted processes.

3. RELEVANCE TO THE EDITED BOOK'S THEME

3.1 Alignment with Cloud-Native Software Engineering

The cloud-native software engineering practices and principles are supposed to equip flexible scaling of the applications, that is, efficient deployment. This can be done through breaking down the applications into microservices by using cloud-native architectures and, thus, encouraging good alignment with rapid iteration and responsiveness toward the needs of the users. It certainly helps in utilizing the containers and orchestration tools such as Kubernetes wherein applications could be run so as to maintain uniform runs across the environments without wasting time on configuration and deployments.

3.2 AI-Powered Automation in the Context of Cloud-Native Environments

AI automation is changing the development, deployment, and support of software in cloud-native environments. The existence of AI means that most of the processes can be automated in an organization, thereby improving efficiency and minimizing human errors. For example, AI optimizes resource allocations based on analysis of workloads and forecasting demand to prevent resource failures and associated problems that may arise from manual intervention. AI-driven tools can also auto-generate code, test, and deploy.

3.3 The Necessity of Efficient Code Creation in Scalable, Cloud-Based Systems

This does not impact user experience in highly scalable, cloud-based systems, where most applications run at varying loads; optimum efficient code that is written to be absolutely use-efficient does reduce the cost and enhance responsiveness. In addition, there is speed in updating this cloud environment, which would require the teams to do releases and new functions quite quickly. Good code writing helps to quickly develop and create these integration and deployment workflows. Growing applicative complexity requires maintainability. Structured efficient code is easy to control, debugged, and extended for long-term sustainability.

3.4 Contribution to the Field of AI and Cloud Computing

AI transforms contributions in the space of cloud computing into an innovation and efficiency capability in every application and industry. Framed by **Müller, H., and Schneider, A.** to explore challenges and opportunities in using generative AI for software engineering.

4. KEY QUESTIONS AND PROBLEMS THE CHAPTER AIMS TO ADDRESS

4.1 How Can Generative AI Improve the Efficiency and Speed of Source Code Creation?

The new generative AI can accelerate and ease source code creation by automating many tasks developers would otherwise do manually. No longer will developers need to work from scratch when developing code; instead, they can command AI with simple instructions, and it may create working pieces of code. These hours spent repeatedly working on something as mundane as creating basic code or setting up common features can be cut short. The AI easily learns in many programming languages or tools. This empowers developers to pay more attention to large problems than to being burdened by the lower level rules. Moreover, AI might provide solutions and fixes instantly, saving much time for error finding and fixing and increasing the code quality. Formatted according to **Zong, Y., and Chen, C.** for a systematic review of AI-assisted code generation and its challenges.

4.2 What are the Risks and Limitations of AI-Generated Code in Complex Software Systems?

Such codes generated by artificial intelligence are very efficient but risky and limited, especially in complicated software systems (Suresh Babu. C.V., 2023). The big risks lie there. One big risk was simply that the AI is actually likely to generate incorrect-or not-so-good-code, especially when a detailed understanding or special knowledge is needed. AI models produce working code. However, this might not be the best code in performance, scalability, or security. Thus, it could manifest as weaknesses or inefficiencies in important systems. Another limitation of AI is that it only depends on data that it was trained on. If the training data has bias or old practices then so will problems appear in its code production, hence mistakes or noncompliance.

4.3 How Does AI-Generated Code Affect Software Quality, Security, and Maintenance?

On the positive side of AI-generated code: AI is making the software superb due to automation of recurrent tasks, minimization of human errors, and consistency in codes. It generates faster optimized code with which development becomes easier and reduces the number of bugs related to basic functions. AI coded code also poses a threat to the security of the software. It might not comprehensively understand a few particular security rules or may input wrong data in the formation of the code. Besides, it might not follow the current best practices or the most recent security standards, and, therefore, systems shall be exposed to threat cases like SQL injection and cross-site scripting.

4.4 What Ethical Challenges and Practical Obstacles Arise from AI-Based Source Code Generation?

AI-based source code generation poses certain ethics-defying problems and numerous practical ones to give thorough thinking (Suresh Babu, C. V.. & Barath Kumar, S. 2024).. There is a possibility of bias in AI-generated code. AI models learn from humongous datasets. If biases or prejudices appear in the training data, that may reflect in what AI produces-for example, unfair or discriminatory algorithms, like where health care or finance is concerned. Another ethical challenge comes to intellectual property. The creation of code by AI raises questions about who owns the code, and whether it might accidentally replicate protected code from its training data. All this later creates problems with copyrights or licensing.

5. OBJECTIVES AND SCOPE

5.1 Objectives of the Chapter

Explain how cloud-native software development may incorporate the use of generative AI to generate source code, while exerting relatively less effort. This addresses the AI side of source code generation, especially with respect to scalability, which tends to limit hand-coded efforts for that process. Included in the discussion is the limitation or problems related to code generation using AI. It talks about its concepts, practical applications, and shows exactly how generative AI is changing the work landscape in today's software development. A tremendous amount of importance is placed upon the idea of it within a cloud-native context.

5.2 Scope Delimitation

5.2.1 Focus on Generative AI tools and their role in source code creation.

Generative AI tools are very important for making source code. They automate many parts of software development, which cuts down on manual work and makes things faster. Tools like GitHub Copilot and OpenAI's Codex use natural language processing to turn prompts written by people into code (Suresh Babu, C. V. & Akshara, P. M. 2024).. This helps developers quickly create basic code, functions, or even whole applications. It would understand the context, even previous code structures, hence able to write codes, find mistakes, and provide quick solutions. This enables coding to go much faster because developers can attend to more creative and complex tasks.

5.2.2 Specific use cases in cloud-native environments.

That is, deep use of generative AI tools in the modern cloud-native environment. They are fundamentally an efficient and scalable application, which auto-generates the development of microservices where AI helped to create small independent services easily deployable and scalable up in the cloud. That's how developers can invent something new without all over again starting from scratch. Infrastructure as code is another type of use case: All this will be facilitated by AI, assisting in writing code about the infrastructure and managing it so that servers, databases, or networks are created automatically. This helps make the cloud infrastructure consistency and reduces human error at the time of building or scaling. Analysis of **Liu, J., and Zhang, L.** to discuss how generative AI impacts development efficiency and scalability in software engineering.

5.3. Heuristics

Some of the most important ethical issues about introducing generative AI into the domain of software development deserve closer examination. One of the most important ones is bias in AI-generated code. Generative AI models are trained over vast datasets that can imprint societal, cultural, or historical biases accidentally. For example, biased training data may produce algorithms in hiring systems or financial services that are not equitable.

Generative AI tools revolutionize the way teams collaborate and developers work in software engineering. Repetitive tasks automation frees up the developer to focus on the complex challenges where innovation is encouraged (Suresh Babu, C. V.. & Barath Kumar, S. 2024).. Such roles, however, also signify an inversion of roles from how developers work from direct code into overseeing and refining outcomes provided by AI. This leaves openings for skills gaps, in the case of junior developers, never learning foundational coding practices and hence missing out on many related skills. Secondly, dependency on generative AI will alter the traditional workflow of teams because automated suggestions may avoid collaborative coding practice. For example, tools may provide solutions that contradict the conventions or styles adopted by a team and take extra effort to harmonize the outputs.

6. LITERATURE REVIEW

6.1 Existing Research on Generative AI for Code Creation

Code-generating generative AI emphasizes the role of AI in software development. The initial studies hint at what is feasible and how such models, such as OpenAI's Codex and GitHub Copilot, would enable human language instructions to be translated into working code by means of deep learning and NLP techniques. Such models learn on huge code bases so that the patterns learned can be expressed in other programming languages. Chen et al. 2021 research demonstrates how Codex works to generate short code snippets to improve code and sometimes even solve simple programs. Surprisingly, it is an excellent tool with great potential that may make repetitive coding work smoother. Yet another large area of research pertains to the correctness and accuracy of the code AI produces.

6.2 Relevant Studies on AI in Cloud-Native Software Engineering

Relevant studies on AI in cloud-native software engineering related to the topic reveal how artificial intelligence might help enhance improvement by providing it with more aspects of development settings' automation and scalability. One of the most critical studies is by Kumar et al. (2021), focusing AI towards being applied for the automation of infrastructure management through IaC tools: It demonstrates that usage patterns can predict utilization and automatically adjust the cloud resources, hence it only simply means reducing costs without sacrificing performance. It expands and morphs the cloud-native system automatically, and adjusts the computing, storage, and network resources based on real-time data.

6.3 Examination of Current Tools and Frameworks (e.g., Codex, GPT-4, GitHub Copilot)

Analyze how Codex, GPT-4, and GitHub Copilot are revolutionizing the source code generation and software programming landscape through a critical assessment of these pioneering tools and technologies. Of the advanced code generation models, Codex is a product of OpenAI that has been trained on tens of millions of lines of open-source code to translate natural language prompts into executable code in multiple programming languages. Codex powers tools such as GitHub Copilot, and can be used in producing boilerplate code, automation of mundane tasks, even giving contextual suggestions on top of the already existing code. After all, it can sometimes be very good at creating functional code quickly, though usually still not optimal in time, for more complex or sensitive applications-related activities.

6.4 Identified Gaps in the Literature

It points out, therefore, a literature gap on generative AI in cloud-native software engineering; what, in detail, still has to be explored so as to better understand engagement and usage of such technologies. Firstly, despite the apparent plethora of near-in-immediate benefits and functionalities of generative AI tools, long studies on the effects of generative AI tools on the quality of software, maintainability, and team dynamics remain missing. In addition, whereas some publications do discuss risk factors for securing AI-generated code, much fewer exist with guide frameworks for safely integrating the tools themselves-thus far, mainly concerning "cloud-native" applications. Much more comprehensive work on ethics and bias issues-specifically on the areas concerning intellectual property and proprietary code-must also be pursued inside the training datasets used. It indeed mentions integration with CI/CD pipelines but does not go too deep into how the generative AI integrates into current DevOps practices.

6.5 How This Chapter Fills the Identified Research Gaps

This chapter partially fills some of these gaps using a holistic analysis along with cloud-native software engineering perspectives for generative AI both from the theoretical insight's angle and at the experiential level. Long term effect studies are included using a description of an inquiry to observe how the introduction and incorporation of generative AI has an effect on a team's quality, maintenance ability, and team dynamism, more specifically, this kind of longitudinal study evaluation. Further to this, the chapter goes ahead to build a framework of security and compliance concerning AI-generated code within the development process. Guidelines are presented here, mitigating risks and enhancing security practices in cloud-native environments. Ethics are further discussed in a move towards the theme of bias found in outputs by AI and strategies for the fair and responsible use of generative AI in issues related to intellectual property.

Generative AI is rapidly transforming software engineering, yet its integration requires careful consideration of both opportunities and challenges. Research by Wang et al. (2023) highlights the increasing adoption of tools like GitHub Copilot and OpenAI's Codex in streamlining coding tasks and boosting developer productivity. These tools excel at generating boilerplate code, automating routine tasks, and enabling developers to focus on higher-level design decisions. Studied by Ali,

H., and Hussain, A. to present opportunities and challenges of automated code generation using generative AI.

7. METHODOLOGY

7.1 Theoretical Framework: Combining Generative AI and Cloud-Native Development

This project lays at the intersection of generative AI and cloud-native development, Fig 1 showcasing how AI can power automation fluently to be part of modern practices in software engineering. It combines a frontend developed in HTML, CSS, and JavaScript wherein the end-users, such as developers or students, put in their specific project requirements. The backend, on the other hand, is a server with Python which communicates through an API key with Google's Gemini AI. Once the project request has been submitted by a user, say, an airline booking system or even a bus reservation system, it goes into the generative AI model. It processes the request and generates source code pertinent to the request and sends the same back to the server, which in its turn, displays the result on the web page of the user.

Figure 1. Architecture for combining generative AI and cloud-native development

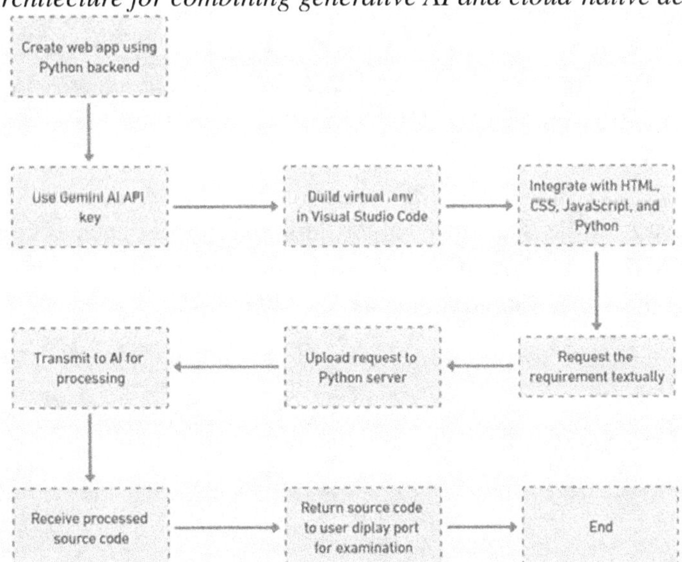

The project, despite being hosted locally, reflects some of the very important cloud-native principles such as scalability, automation, and service-based architecture. Overlaid on the backend with AI, this mimics a cloud-native environment. First, because the services, in this case, AI, communicate very efficiently with the web interface, just like microservices in a cloud architecture does. One of the first is using generative AI that automates a task always done manually —creation of source code. It provides a huge amount regarding reduced development time while at the same time being scalable and agile, core attributes that characterize cloud-native systems. The application of generative AI with cloud-native methodologies, Figure 2 illustrated how this combination could further ease software development, accelerate agility, and bring more automation into the delivery pipeline.

Figure 2. Interaction diagram of generative AI with cloud-native methodologies

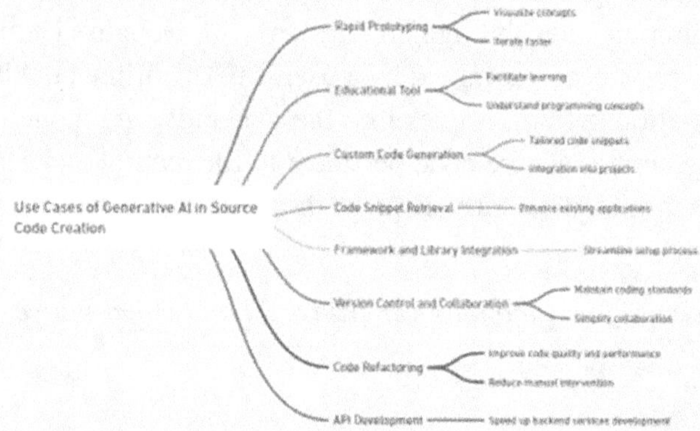

Generative AI utilizes advanced algorithms and models, such as large language models (LLMs), to analyze user-defined inputs and produce high-quality code snippets that meet specific requirements.

Figure 3. Use case of generative AI in source code creation

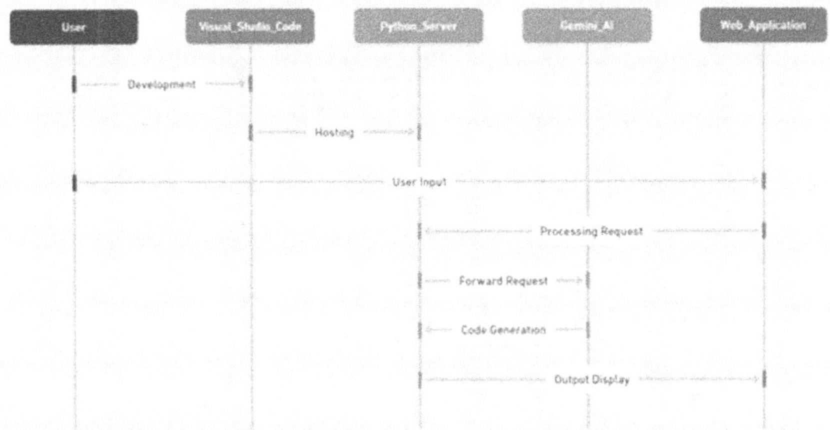

This capability is particularly advantageous in cloud-native development, where applications are designed to scale seamlessly across distributed environments. The integration of generative AI can streamline various stages of the software development lifecycle Figure 4, including planning, coding, testing, and deployment.

Figure 4. Software development life cycle

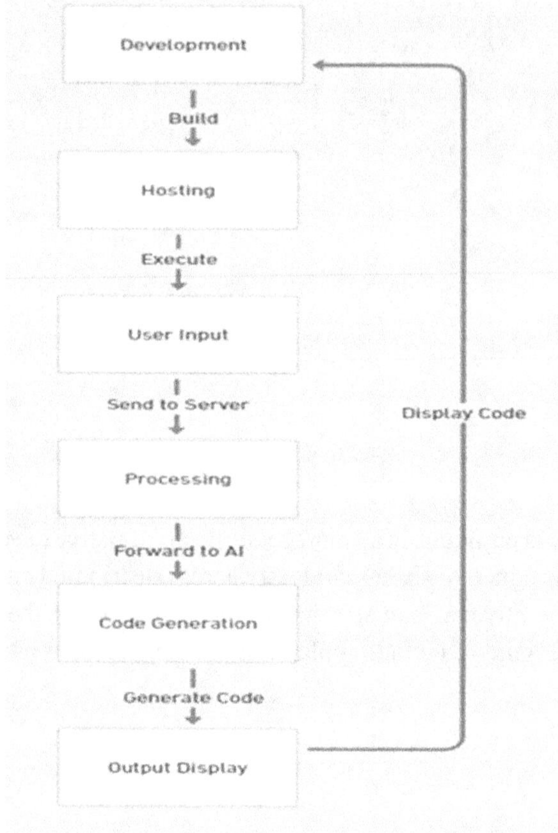

7.2 Research Approach

7.2.1 Case Studies on AI-Driven Software Development Processes

A number of published projects have successfully showcased the seamless integration of artificial intelligence into multiple stages of the software development process (Suresh Babu. C.V., 2023). Among the most notable examples are OpenAI's Codex, GitHub Copilot, and the AI-driven development tools provided by IBM. Specifically, GitHub Copilot, which operates on the robust capabilities of OpenAI's Codex, has seen widespread adoption among developers, enabling them to benefit from real-time code generation assistance. This innovative tool significantly reduces both the time and effort that developers need to invest when writing boilerplate code, while simultaneously enhancing the overall efficiency and effectiveness of the coding process. Such a detailed case study will give vivid illustration and demonstration of the diverse ways AI, or, as people commonly call it, AI, can automate not only the process of code generation but also other critical tasks such as debugging, testing, and optimization throughout the lifecycle of software development. They offer many proofs of concept that demonstrate how

7.2.2 Analysis of Industry Reports on Generative AI Tools

Industry reports and academic studies found that generative AI tools are being adopted into every part of software development with the promise of revolutionizing traditional workflows for software development. Some of the clearest examples of assistance offered include code-completion, debugging, and optimization as shown by OpenAI's Codex and GitHub Copilot. Despite their capabilities, a major lacuna of research studies is seen, which mainly focuses on automation-based source code generation from scratch. Such focus is required to tap fully into the potential of generative AI in the area of software engineering. Wang et al. (2023), and Alshahrani & Althobaiti (2023) Report the potential of generative AI in software engineering, and the wide applicability of this technology, not just to code generation, but throughout the entire pipeline of development. These studies make clear that, while suggesting and automating routine work, generative AI is essentially an augmentative technology. It helps the developers to accelerate their efficiency in coding, a situation where code writing may turn out to be faster and more accurate but not necessarily completely automated in code generation. Project demonstrated by Zheng, X., and Zhao, Y. to discuss the role of generative AI in modern software engineering methodologies.

7.3 Justification of a Multi-Disciplinary Approach

This section of the study will explore how cloud-native infrastructure, software engineering principles, and AI automation interact to make development easier and faster for modern software. This section elucidates how collaboration can help explore the possibility of optimizing cloud-native systems, including microservices and containerization, in easing different aspects of development and making them faster with the use of generative AI tools. This paper discusses some of the basic software engineering concepts combined with AI automation in agile methods, CI/CD, and DevOps practices.

To analyze this integration, the study would take existing workflows of organizations that have successfully used AI tools within their cloud environments. Interviews with software engineers and architects will assist in eliciting insights on how these teams use AI automation to auto-generate code, do unit testing, and so forth.

Further technical setup and infrastructure supporting such integration will be probed into how it ensures the smooth deployment of AI applications on a cloud platform.

8. SOFTWARE DEVELOPMENT PROCESS WITH GENERATIVE AI

8.1 Code Generation and AI Integration

8.1.1 Automating the Coding Phase: How AI Generates Boilerplate and Complex Code

So much does the landscape of the field of software development change with the introduction of AI for coding automation - it's very quick to build some very simple and pretty complicated code. Such tools as Codex and GitHub Copilot learn programming patterns, good practices from large collections of already existing code with the help of which they generate quality code snippets for what a user asks for. AI tools can easily generate standard code templates that most developers often use. That automatically gives developers a breather from the rather mundane works they would have to do in order to concentrate on more important parts of their projects Sophisticated code generation, therefore, requires the application of advanced natural language processing features of AI systems that can understand higher-level instructions and make them representations of suitable codes in any programming language (Suresh Babu, C. V. & Akshara, P. M. 2024)..

8.1.2 AI-Assisted Debugging and Testing

AI-assisted debugging and testing is a sea change for assurance of quality in software across the development lifecycle. Machine learning algorithms and natural language processing are thus tuned to determine unprecedented speeds and accuracy in analyzing vast quantities of code in search of bugs, vulnerabilities, and performance issues (Suresh Babu, C. V. & Akshara, P. M. 2024).. Some of the tools automatically generate solutions to the most common coding errors and help pinpoint possible root causes and greatly reduce time taken by the developers in fixing problems. For example, sites like Snyk and DeepCode are using AI in checking code security issues-They usually come with clear advice which enables the developer to fix the problem before things worsen.AI might make testing even better in comparison to traditional approaches as it will automatically generate and run the test cases for each part of the application. AI-based testing tools scan current code so as to produce test cases showing how people actually use the application while modifying as the code changes, making testing smoother and more reliable due to the fact that AI focuses more on high-risk areas that need closer checking.

8.1.3 Leveraging AI for Code Refactoring and Optimization

With AI, therefore, the way developers make better software and manage it more easily changes. One can use these tools with AI power to scan through the existing code for inefficient patterns, problems with the code, or parts not in good practice and then suggest changes that would make the software run better and maintain it more easily. For example, tools like Refactor.ai use machine learning to help developers see how to better organize their code. Such an optimization makes the code cleaner, easier to break into parts, and simpler to understand. It also makes optimizations in terms of code through making precise changes that could possibly enhance the runtime efficiency or reduce resource usage. Using the history-based performance and knowledge of which specific structures of a code may impact the execution speed, such AI tools provide enhancements to make scalability and responsiveness better.

8.2 AI in Continuous Integration/Continuous Delivery (CI/CD)

8.2.1 Streamlining the Development Pipeline Using AI

Since the pipeline of development is getting much faster and more flexible with great responsiveness, it begins to make use of AI to make it efficient. This will change the way in which software teams will develop applications. The application will help eliminate delays through automating the critical parts of the development cycle. For example, AI will help with continuous integration and continuous deployment (CI/CD) through automation of testing, integration, and deployment. This is because it accelerates the new features, and all versions of the software are adequately tested and stable.AI does improve the management of projects in the development process. It analyzes past data from respective projects to guess possible delays or resource needs. Tools like Jira and Azure DevOps are now adding AI features to give information about team performance, sprint planning, and workload balancing. This helps teams make decisions based on data, hence improving their workflow and increasing overall productivity.

8.3 Collaborating with AI in Agile Development Environments

8.3.1 AI's Role in Agile Sprints: Reducing Coding Time and Enhancing Flexibility

It is very instrumental in making agile sprints better. It greatly reduces coding time and gives much freedom to the development teams. Developers can really put the basic code as well as complex functions by describing their requirement in natural language using generative AI tools in an agile process. This then frees up the developers more to focus on design and feature additions rather than being held up with mundane routine coding tasks. Besides quick development, this quicker code generation is also supportive of the fact that teams can very easily get themselves in a highly responsive mode about changing needs and priorities-the hallmark of agile methods.

8.3.2 Challenges in AI and Human Collaboration

Some advantages of the use of AI exist in software development, but using AI in software development also offers a variety of challenges in working with AI tools and human developers (Suresh Babu, C. V.. & Barath Kumar, S. 2024).. The most significant problem is the fact that developers may become too reliant on AI-created code, which will weaken their ability to think critically and to solve problems themselves. More importantly, with widespread use of AI in developing and composing code and possibly without full understanding of general logic or the circumstances of the code developed, problems do exist in terms of maintaining the freshness and versatility of the code. Another big challenge is how good and accurate AI-generated outputs are. Although AI tools can create code really fast, they might not quite fit the specific needs of a project or actually adhere to best practices and, therefore, cause bugs or slow performance.

8.4 Security Implications in AI-Generated Code

8.4.1 Addressing Security Vulnerabilities in AI-Created Source Code

The fixing of problems in AI-generated source code would introduce security issues to the source code of organizations using generative AI tools in their activities regarding software development. Indeed, AI-based tools are much more productive and enhance ease of coding processes, but the code AI generates doesn't fully understand either the application context or ideal security practices. Those weaknesses might include hard-coded passwords, poor or non-existent input checking, or even just not really handling error conditions well. These all represent areas where bad actors can gain a foothold. In order to reduce those risks, organizations should establish robust security controls at the development stage. That happens first by instilling safety practice into the AI training data by having safe coding standards govern the models.

8.4.2 The Role of AI in Software Security Testing and Compliance

With AI, the type of problem becomes easy and quick in terms of having discovered it with strict follow-up on the rules and regulations. Older methods of testing security take an impossibly long time compared with the speed of which applications are being written or the complexity of software structures in nature for most modern applications. With regards to the challenge as AI automates many of the important parts of security testing, it assists. That enables teams to understand and correct the problem much more quickly and with much higher accuracy. The most significant contribution of AI to security testing is in the detection of threats. Actually, some applications for machines can run through so much code and watch systems to determine what kinds of patterns can suggest a problem in security or something unusual, perhaps pointing out a breach. For instance, applications that do AI can monitor how applications work or how end-users interact, watching for some patterns that may need more attention. This really reduces the time that elapses between a problem's identification and its correction, which in turn makes software safer. Procedural sequence used by **Kessler, M., and Pugh, M.** to highlight AI's contribution to team productivity and software development efficiency.

9. ANALYSIS AND FINDINGS

9.1 Impact of Generative AI on Software Development Efficiency

Generative AI makes a lot of differences in software development efficiency. It brings about the change that how teams design and build and launch applications. It accelerates coding to a great extent by automating other parts of the development process, thereby enabling developers to churn out good-quality code much faster. Boilerplate code, snippets of code, as well as complex algorithms triggered by natural language prompts are actually pre-made by GitHub Copilot or OpenAI Codex. This means that developers can focus on more creative and strategic tasks rather than just repetitive coding chores. Acceleration accelerates the reduction of development timelines and boosts productivity: developers can do much more within the same span of time. Generative AI helps out teammates to collaborate by providing them with real-time suggestions and ideas that help in communication and teamwork. AI tools can examine code changes, which includes possible problems that may arise when piecing together various components in advance, thus reducing potential conflicts within joint work development.

9.2 AI-Generated Code vs Human-Written Code: A Comparative Analysis

It's clear that quality, speed, and flexibility between AI-generated code versus human-written code have good sides and bad sides in each category. The AI-generated code is very fast and very efficient. GitHub Copilot or OpenAI Codex are tools that can produce really simple code, and even the most complex algorithms based on what a user asks for with great speed, which accelerates development considerably. This generation is going to let developers take on more significant chunks of their work without having to spend their time keying in repetitive code.

9.3 The Potential for Generative AI to Mitigate Coding Errors and Bugs

Highest potential help reduce the number of coding mistakes and bugs generated during software development and enhance the quality and reliability of code. Basically, this is achieved through just one major avenue AI utilizes: real-time making of code suggestions and corrections while developers write their code. Tools like GitHub Copilot, which analyze the code written, and return helpful snippets or options that respect the code of good practice, the possibility of usual programming mistakes like syntax or weak logic is lessened. This other thing would be the identification of probable bugs even before they show up in production. AI tools can have checks done on the code for known problems, bad practices, or difference from set coding standards by static code analysis methods.

9.4 The Role of Human Oversight in AI-Driven Software Development

In fact, human oversight is one of the most crucial aspects of AI-driven software development. It is a balancing act to what generative AI tools do. AI indeed boosts productivity much and automates repetitive work while providing real-time insights. It still lacks understanding, creativity, and the ability to think ethically about the human developers. Human oversight is especially relevant in some areas-mostly checked within: checking quality, security assurance, making ethical decisions.

Human review primarily serves the role of checking for the quality and maintainability of AI-generated code. Although AI may generate the code so fast, it may not necessarily guarantee alignment with best practices or project-specific guidelines that may eventually lead to inefficiencies, bugs, or security vulnerabilities.

9.5 Ethical and Practical Challenges Identified

The introduction of generative AI in software development poses a number of ethical and practical challenges that need to be managed by organizations for effective as well as responsible use of such technology. Very big ethical issues come from the possibilities of bias that exist in AI-generated code. Because AI systems learn from large quantities of data, they will inevitably reproduce and retain whatever bias has existed within the data, which may lead to unfavourable or discriminatory outcomes within the resultant software developed. This means the output of AI is always judged by inclusion and fairness, and developers must be responsive to the consequences of their code.

In the context of AI-assisted code generation, several key concepts are essential for understanding the associated security risks and mitigation strategies. Generative AI models like OpenAI's Codex or GPT-3 can automatically generate source code based on user input, which can significantly accelerate development. However, this also introduces risks, such as the inadvertent creation of vulnerabilities like SQL injection, XSS, or buffer overflows in the generated code. To address these risks, developers must apply secure coding practices, such as input validation and proper error handling, to ensure that the AI-generated code does not introduce weaknesses. Security testing methods like SAST (Static Application Security Testing) and DAST (Dynamic Application Security Testing) should be employed to automatically detect vulnerabilities before and after code deployment. Inspired by **Lee, K., and Kim, J.** to provide insights into improving software quality and addressing security concerns in AI-generated code.

10. SUGGESTIONS AND RECOMMENDATIONS

10.1 Best Practices for Integrating Generative AI in Source Code Creation

Generative AI in source code development will greatly enhance efficiencies and quality in software development and therefore will not be attempted as an end in itself but with intent, strategy, and practice: some organizations will begin by defining very tight use cases where AI adds value, such as aiding automation or debugging, and then go on to careful training and fine-tuning of AI models to their own coding standards and project-specific requirements.

Developer Incentivization: Developers should be made to work in teams. AI is an assistant and not a substitute. This can be made by training the developer regarding proper usage of the AI tool apart from what these tools cannot do. Quality code will be encouraged by rigorous code review. Otherwise, the AI that the developer has developed must be reviewed by experts in the human world. Continuous monitoring and feedback of organizations lead to continuous adaptation of their AI tools and integration into the user experience so that more effectiveness can be achieved with AI toward proper alignment with project goals, and thus an appropriate balance and software development can be attained.

10.2 Recommendations for Cloud-Native Developers Using AI Tools

These have to be exploited by cloud-native developers using AI in development work to reap the best out of it, in addition to their effort to develop high-quality software efficiently. First, the developers learn what their AI tools can do and cannot do. They spend time learning and then experiment with these tools with evidence of how this can help them more with coding tasks such as writing code, fixing bugs, or improving performance. Fit AI tools well into the existing development structure. In such a case, they should behave well with regards to cloud-based designs and CI/CD processes in order to enhance productivity without letting it disturb workflows. Besides that, the developers must cooperate and take the output resulting from the AI as a source. Taking their know-how, they improve and polish the resultant outputs with the high-quality standards of codes and according to the best practice. Of course, the most crucial thing to be tested and then analyzed for security is that output from AI-generated code. Developers have to ensure any code developed has to function correctly and implement securely in its place. 10.3 Quality, security, and responsibility policy recommendations should govern AI-generated code that ends up in production.

10.3 Policy Recommendations for Managing AI-Generated Code in Production Environments

Collaboration between human and AI developers in the software development team is also an important pre-condition to get good and creative use of the generative AI tools. The organizations need a 'culture' which treats the AI as an extended member and not as a replacement for humans. It calls for very lengthy training programs so that individuals can learn how to use all the skills through the artificial intelligence tools (Suresh Babu. C.V., 2023). They can understand what these tools may do, what they would not do, and at what stage and in how much detail, they use the technologies in streamlining their working operations. The openness of communication among AI tools and developers is of extreme urgency, but teams can discuss AI-generated outputs as well as share insights with regard to why the result was attained.

11. FUTURE SCOPE FOR RESEARCH

11.1 Opportunities for Extending AI-Based Code Generation into Full-Cycle Development

Apply AI-Based Code Generation Opportunities in Full SDLC One of the biggest opportunities that software engineering offers is the possibility of using AI in all stages of the development. Using AI tools in every step of the development can make "planning, designing, deploying, and maintaining" processes of software development easier as well as improve teamwork. AI can support gathering requirements by reviewing user feedback and market trends to help developers work on applications that are more relevant and focused on users. Whereas, in the design process, AI can definitely auto-generate architecture diagrams and design documents, thus making it much easier to jump into the code and testing. More, AI can observe running applications, review their performance, and user interaction. This gives insight into possible improvement and updating.

11.2 Exploration of New AI Tools and Models for Improved Code Generation

AI needs new tools and models toward more efficient code generation to cope with the latest technologies and the needs of its users. Better methods in machine learning, like reinforcement learning and transfer learning, may open up the door to more flexibility and accuracy potential in the code-generation models (Suresh Babu, C. V. & Akshara, P. M. 2024).. That would bring natural language processing into the interaction between developers and AI systems so that they could use chat-like interfaces to develop code pieces or receive explanations for some tasks. Most organizations do that: they partner with AI research groups, keep up with new studies, and use the best tools to make code generation better and fit well into their current development processes.

11.3 Addressing the Ethical and Security Implications of Autonomous Code Creation

Ethical considerations toward autonomous code generation and security must be addressed to increase the trust and accountability in AI-driven software development. Mechanisms that would ensure respect for ethical issues from the onset of development must accompany AI system developments that are capable of producing complex code autonomously.Such organizations will establish guiding values on how bias in the training sets to be used should be calculated while ensuring outputs from AI systems are fair and inclusive.It shall provide robust security controls to all issues arising from the AI-developed code. That is when review processes of codes are considered in detail and also involving security testing tools can closely examine the output produced from AI for vulnerabilities.

11.4 Expanding the Use of AI in Software Engineering beyond Code Creation

With the use of AI applied much deeper in software engineering than just code, it opens up great opportunities to improve many parts of the development process. It can be of great aid in project management through resource utilization improvement, prediction of project timelines, and the identification of probable problems within workflows. Furthermore, AI analytics can be used to generate data about the behavior of users and performance of the applications to help teams come up with decisions based on information, thus improving user experience and satisfaction.

11.5 The Role of Explainability and Transparency in AI-Generated Code

Value of Explainability and Transparency for AI-Generated Code Explainability and transparency would play a very critical role in building trust as well as responsibility into the software development process. As AI is increasingly used for coding, that would go a very long way that developers and stakeholders know how such outputs are produced by AI. Confidence in AI tools on the users' part would also grow with ways of explaining things added onto it-something like providing context behind code suggestions or why some particular algorithm might be suggested. Being honest about how the AI models are actually trained and about the data origin will help the user know whether AI-generated code is trustworthy or ethical enough.

Generative AI changes the nature of software development: more time developers spend coding, less toiling in repetitive or accessory work. Experimentation around GitHub Copilot has shown a more than 12% increase in coding productivity and encourages independent work, saving overheads in collaboration overheads and promoting innovation. Course, this calls for refashioning roles, particular for junior developers who end up missing out on necessary foundational learning.

Generative AI transforms software engineering, allowing developers to automate routine tasks by focusing on challenging tasks and innovative design. It allows for the streamlining of workflows, thus allowing for autonomous work, reducing collaboration frictions, and providing the ability to experiment with new languages. However, this transformation flips roles, and developers need to polish the outputs of AI and work on critical tasks that AI cannot do. These Possibilities are triangulated by thesis from **Wang, Y., et al.** to project future trends in the use of generative AI for software development.

12. CONCLUSION

12.1 Summary of Main Findings

In short, the study about generative AI in the development of source code has thrown open a host of relevant insights concerning how it transforms the process of software development. Productivity can be greatly enhanced through automated much repetitive coding tasks, quality enrichment of code, and delivery of teamwork within the development teams. Usage of the technologies, however, pertains to managing the ethical concerns while maintaining the code security to enhance good teamwork among humans and AI. Furthermore, use of AI at all stages of the software development cycle, from planning to maintenance could improve efficiency and allow teams to focus on other, more important strategic activities.

12.2 Broader Implications for Software Development and Cloud-Native Engineering

These would include greater ones, like the use of generative AI in software development and cloud-native engineering, where technology is changing what gets done. This is achievable because more scalability, flexibility, and faster response times are to be expected from a software solution in order to adapt more readily to the altering needs of the market when using AI. Using AI tools in CI/CD deployment would help deploy software in a faster manner and bring joy to the customers (Suresh Babu, C. V. & Moses, C. 2024).

12.3 Final Thoughts on the Future of Generative AI in Source Code Creation

The future is quite bright indeed for generative AI in source code development with advancements in machine learning and natural language processing (Suresh Babu, C. V. & Akshara, P. M. 2024).. Better tools can mean looking forward to the new time in software development where the creative collaboration between human developers and AI systems is easy and where AI is an integral part of the process. The organizations most likely to exploit these technologies most effectively, drive innovation and competition, and advance in a largely digital environment are those that realize and integrate them strategically.

12.4 Reflections on AI's Role in Shaping Software Engineering Practices

Some of the thinking that might make for a journey in changing the face of software engineering is pretty thrilling and tough. As AI becomes more rampant in the "regular" development of this software, it asks for a rethinking of traditional methods and keeps the steady focus on questions of ethics, security, and quality. Hence, culture building about technology is key to facilitating the success of AI implementation in organizations. The outcome inspires teamwork and continuous learning. New thinking and growth towards introducing AI in software engineering characterize a move towards a future. There is a great scope for high-quality, efficient, and user-centric software development.

12.5. Guidelines and Best Practices for Ensuring Security in AI-Assisted Development

To mitigate these security risks, developers should review AI-generated code rigorously before integrating it into production systems. A comprehensive code review, aided by static and dynamic analysis tools, can help identify common security vulnerabilities like improper input validation or insecure data handling. It's also crucial to enforce secure coding standards across the project. By using security-focused guidelines or templates when providing input to the AI, developers can direct the model to generate code that adheres to security best practices, such as avoiding hard-coded credentials or insecure file handling.

Moreover, the scope of AI assistance should be limited to smaller, more manageable components instead of entire applications. This allows for more detailed review of the generated code, ensuring that specific parts of the system are secure before integrating them into the larger project. Developers should also encourage the AI to generate code that relies on secure, established libraries and frameworks that are designed with security in mind. These frameworks often provide built-in protections against common vulnerabilities, such as cross-site request forgery (CSRF) or session hijacking.

REFERENCES

Ali, H., & Hussain, A. (2023). Exploring generative AI for automated code generation: Opportunities and challenges. *International Journal of Software Engineering and Knowledge Engineering*, 33(1), 115–135. DOI: 10.1142/S0218194023500024

Alshahrani, S., & Althobaiti, A. (2023). A review of generative AI techniques for software engineering. *MDPI Information*, 17(2), 62. DOI: 10.3390/info17020062

Brown, T., Mann, B., Ryder, N., Subbiah, M., Kaplan, J., & Dhariwal, P. (2020). Language models are few-shot learners. *Advances in Neural Information Processing Systems*, 33, 1877–1901.

Kessler, M., & Pugh, M. (2023). Artificial intelligence in software development: A survey of the field. *ACM Computing Surveys*, 55(4), 75. Advance online publication. DOI: 10.1145/3542036

Lee, K., & Kim, J. (2023). Examining generative AI's influence on source code quality and development processes. *Journal of Software Engineering Research and Development*, 11(1), 5. Advance online publication. DOI: 10.1186/s40411-023-00204-4

Liu, J., & Zhang, L. (2023). The impact of generative AI on software development efficiency: A case study approach. *Journal of Software (Malden, MA)*, 35(2), e2367. DOI: 10.1002/smr.2367

Müller, H., & Schneider, A. (2023). Trends in generative AI for software engineering: Challenges and opportunities. *Software, Practice & Experience*, 53(1), 7–24. DOI: 10.1002/spe.3176

Suresh Babu. (2023). *C.V.* Artificial Intelligence and Expert Systems, Anniyappa Publicaitons.

Suresh Babu, C. V., & Akshara, P. M. (2024). Revolutionizing Conversational AI: Unleashing the Power of ChatGPT-Based Applications in Generative AI and Natural Language Processing. In A. Obaid, B. Bhushan, M. S., & S. Rajest (Eds.), Advanced Applications of Generative AI and Natural Language Processing Models (pp. 228-248). IGI Global. DOI: 10.4018/979-8-3693-0502-7.ch011

Suresh Babu, C. V., & Barath Kumar, S. (2024). Navigating the Terrain: Current Challenges and Solutions in Integrating Generative AI Into Education. In Hai-Jew, S. (Ed.), *Generative AI in Teaching and Learning* (pp. 274–290). IGI Global., DOI: 10.4018/979-8-3693-0074-9.ch011

Suresh Babu, C. V., & Moses, C. (2024). Reinventing Customer Support: Unleashing ChatGPT's Potential for Personalized Engagement and Responsible AI Implementation. In Bansal, R., Ngah, A., Chakir, A., & Pruthi, N. (Eds.), *Leveraging ChatGPT and Artificial Intelligence for Effective Customer Engagement* (pp. 93–110). IGI Global., DOI: 10.4018/979-8-3693-0815-8.ch006

Suresh Babu, C. V., & Suruthi, G. (2024). Unravelling the Evolution of Generative AI in Communication Education: A Historical Journey Into Human-Machine Communication. In Elmoudden, S., & Wrench, J. (Eds.), *The Role of Generative AI in the Communication Classroom* (pp. 55–71). IGI Global., DOI: 10.4018/979-8-3693-0831-8.ch003

Wang, Y., Chen, L., & Liu, H. (2023). Generative AI for source code generation: Current trends and future directions. *IEEE Software*, 40(2), 62–70. DOI: 10.1109/MS.2023.10176168

Zheng, X., & Zhao, Y. (2023). The role of generative AI in modern software engineering: Trends and predictions. *ACM Transactions on Software Engineering and Methodology*, 32(4), 1–32. DOI: 10.1145/3571847

Zong, Y., & Chen, C. (2023). AI-assisted code generation: A systematic review of the state of the art. *Journal of Systems and Software*, 207, 110–123. DOI: 10.1016/j.jss.2023.111234

Chapter 5

A Study on AI Tools That Can Generate Software Source Code

C. R. Rathish
https://orcid.org/0000-0001-7737-3938
New Horizon College of Engineering, India

Nithin Shiva Vanka
https://orcid.org/0009-0005-0123-9528
New Horizon College of Engineering, India

S. Aaron Dennis
New Horizon College of Engineering, India

Akhilesh R. Mohan
New Horizon College of Engineering, India

S. Arjun
https://orcid.org/0009-0008-8570-1944
New Horizon College of Engineering, India

Aryasree Madhukumar
https://orcid.org/0009-0007-9130-7647
Cambridge Institute of Technology, India

ABSTRACT

AI is revolutionizing software development with tools that automate tasks like code suggestions, completions, and full code generation based on minimal input. Advanced machine learning models, such as Transformers, power tools like GitHub Copilot and TabNine, enhancing productivity and reducing coding errors. These tools use vast code repositories and natural language processing to help developers focus on complex problem-solving. However, AI-generated code presents challenges, including concerns over code quality, maintainability, and security. Ethical issues, like ownership, plagiarism, and biases in training data, also arise. Despite these hurdles, AI is set to play a crucial role in software engineering, pushing research toward improving scalability, ethical guidelines, and model generalization. As AI continues to evolve, it is expected to become a key component in future software

DOI: 10.4018/979-8-3693-9356-7.ch005

development tools, transforming how developers work and optimize code. Its growing influence will shape the next generation of programming.

INTRODUCTION

Artificial Intelligence (AI) has become an integral part of modern software development, offering tools and techniques that enhance and automate various aspects of the coding process. In this context, AI refers to the use of machine learning algorithms and computational models to perform tasks traditionally handled by human developers. These tasks include everything from code suggestions and completions to generating full blocks of code or even entire software applications, (Yang, Liu, & Yin, 2021) (Tiwari, Goyal, & Sharma, 2021).

AI-generated code encompasses several levels of automation. At the simplest level, AI can suggest single lines or snippets of code based on what the developer is currently typing. This is often seen in code completion tools, where the AI predicts what the developer is likely to write next, (Svyatkovskiy *et al.*, 2020). On a more advanced level, AI can generate entire functions or classes from a high-level description provided by the developer. This includes translating natural language inputs into functioning code, (Feng *et al.,* 2020). The goal of AI-generated code is not just to expedite the coding process but also to assist developers in writing cleaner, more efficient, and more maintainable code, (Vaswani *et al.,* 2017) (Allamanis *et al.*, 2018).

The significance of AI in coding lies in its ability to dramatically reduce development time and improve the quality of software. By automating repetitive and mundane tasks, AI tools free up developers to focus on more complex and creative aspects of software engineering. For example, AI can automatically generate boilerplate code, suggest best practices, and even identify potential bugs as the developer writes code, (Svyatkovskiy *et al.,* 2020) (Wei *et al.,* 2022). This not only speeds up the development process but also helps in maintaining high standards of code quality.

Moreover, AI tools assist in coding by learning from large datasets of code, allowing them to provide context-aware suggestions that adhere to best practices and common coding patterns. This is particularly beneficial in large-scale projects where consistency and adherence to coding standards are critical, (Chen & Monperrus, 2019). Additionally, AI-driven tools can adapt to a developer's unique coding style, providing personalized suggestions that align with the developer's preferences, further enhancing productivity, (Raychev, Bielik, & Vechev, 2016).

The landscape of AI-powered coding tools is rapidly evolving, with new advancements being integrated into popular Integrated Development Environments (IDEs) like Visual Studio Code, JetBrains IntelliJ IDEA, and others. These tools leverage sophisticated machine learning models trained on vast repositories of code, such as GitHub, to provide real-time code suggestions, error detection, and even automated code reviews, (Svyatkovskiy *et al.,* 2020) (Feng *et al.,* 2020).

One of the most notable trends is the increasing integration of AI into the software development lifecycle. Tools like GitHub Copilot and TabNine are at the forefront, offering developers intelligent code completion and generation capabilities that go beyond simple syntax suggestions, (Feng *et al.,* 2020). These tools can understand the context of the code being written, offering relevant suggestions that help developers complete tasks more quickly and with greater accuracy, (Wei *et al.,* 2022).

Another emerging trend is the use of AI for automated code reviews. AI systems can now analyze pull requests, identifying potential issues and suggesting improvements before the code is merged into the main branch, (Allamanis *et al.*, 2018). This not only improves code quality but also reduces the burden on human reviewers, allowing them to focus on more critical aspects of the review process.

The growing adoption of these AI tools is driven by their ability to integrate seamlessly with existing development workflows, making them accessible to developers of all skill levels. As these tools continue to evolve, we can expect to see even more sophisticated features that further enhance developer productivity and code quality, (Wei *et al.,* 2022).

History and Evolution of AI in Software Development

The journey of AI in software development dates back several decades, beginning with simple rule-based systems and expert systems in the 1980s and 1990s. These early systems were designed to assist developers by automating routine tasks such as syntax checking, error detection, and code completion, (Wei *et al.,* 2022). Rule-based systems operated on predefined sets of rules that described how to perform specific tasks. For example, these systems could automatically format code according to a set of style guidelines or highlight syntax errors as the developer typed, (Chen & Monperrus, 2019).

Expert systems, a more advanced form of rule-based AI, attempted to replicate the decision-making abilities of human experts. In software development, expert systems were used to automate decision-making processes, such as selecting the best algorithm for a given problem or optimizing code for performance, (Yang, Liu, & Yin, 2021). However, these systems were limited by their reliance on static rules, which made them inflexible and unable to adapt to new or complex situations, (Wei *et al.,* 2022).

As the field of AI advanced, the limitations of rule-based systems became increasingly apparent. The static nature of these systems made them unsuitable for the dynamic and evolving nature of software development. This led to a shift towards machine learning and, eventually, deep learning models, which offered a more flexible and adaptive approach to AI in software engineering, (Vaswani *et al.,* 2017).

Machine learning models, particularly neural networks, marked a significant leap in the capabilities of AI tools. Unlike rule-based systems, neural networks could learn from data, allowing them to adapt to new coding patterns and practices without requiring explicit programming, (Raychev, Bielik, & Vechev, 2016). This flexibility made them particularly well-suited for tasks like code completion, bug detection, and even full code generation, (Svyatkovskiy *et al.,* 2020).

Deep learning, a subset of machine learning, further enhanced these capabilities by using multi-layered neural networks to process and generate code. These models could learn complex patterns and structures in code, making them capable of generating entire functions or classes from a high-level description, (Feng *et al.,* 2020). This transition from rule-based systems to neural networks represented a paradigm shift in the way AI was used in software development, paving the way for more advanced and effective AI-driven coding tools, (Wei *et al.,* 2022).

The evolution of AI in software development has been marked by several key milestones. One of the earliest milestones was the development of early code completion tools like Microsoft's IntelliSense, which provided developers with context-aware code suggestions based on the current state of the code, (Tiwari, Goyal, & Sharma, 2021). This was followed by the introduction of more advanced machine learning models that could provide more accurate and relevant suggestions, (Svyatkovskiy *et al.,* 2020).

The advent of neural networks brought about significant advancements in AI-driven code generation. One of the most notable milestones was the development of models like OpenAI's GPT-3, which could generate human-like text, including code, from a given prompt, (Vaswani *et al.,* 2017). GPT-3 demonstrated the potential of large-scale neural networks in understanding and generating code, opening up new possibilities for AI in software engineering, (Feng *et al.,* 2020).

Another major breakthrough was the release of GitHub Copilot, a tool powered by OpenAI's Codex model. Copilot represented a significant leap forward in AI-driven code generation, offering developers the ability to generate entire functions or classes from natural language descriptions, (Feng *et al.,* 2020). This milestone highlighted the growing capabilities of AI in automating more complex and creative aspects of software development, (Wei *et al.,* 2022).

Types of AI Tools for Code Generation

Code Completion Tools:

Code completion tools are among the most widely used AI-powered coding tools today. These tools, such as TabNine and Kite, provide intelligent suggestions for completing lines of code as developers type. By analyzing the context of the code being written, these tools predict the next words, phrases, or even entire lines of code, helping developers write code more quickly and accurately, (Yang, Liu, & Yin, 2021).

TabNine, for instance, uses deep learning models to provide real-time code suggestions that are contextually relevant and tailored to the specific coding style of the developer. It supports a wide range of programming languages and integrates seamlessly with popular IDEs, making it a valuable tool for developers across different platforms, (Tiwari, Goyal, & Sharma, 2021). The primary benefit of these tools is their ability to reduce the cognitive load on developers, allowing them to focus on the logic and structure of their code rather than on the details of syntax.

Full Code Generation

While code completion tools focus on assisting developers with individual lines or snippets of code, full code generation tools take this a step further by generating entire functions or classes from a brief description. GitHub Copilot is a prime example of such a tool. Powered by OpenAI's Codex model, Copilot can understand natural language inputs and generate corresponding code that fulfills the described functionality, (Vaswani *et al.,* 2017).

For example, a developer might input a comment such as "create a function that sorts an array of numbers in ascending order." Copilot would then generate the complete code for the function, including handling edge cases and ensuring that the code adheres to best practices, (Chen & Monperrus, 2019). This level of automation is particularly useful for tasks that follow common patterns, such as creating CRUD (Create, Read, Update, Delete) operations in a database or implementing standard algorithms.

However, while full code generation tools can significantly speed up development, they also raise concerns about code quality and maintainability. Developers must review and understand the generated code to ensure it meets their specific requirements and adheres to their coding standards, (Svyatkovskiy *et al.,* 2020).

Automated Debugging and Bug Fixing

AI tools are also making significant strides in the areas of automated debugging and bug fixing. Tools like DeepCode and Snyk use machine learning algorithms to analyze code for potential bugs, security vulnerabilities, and other issues, (Feng *et al.,* 2020). These tools can scan large codebases quickly, identifying problems that might be missed during manual code reviews.

DeepCode, for example, uses AI to analyze code and provide suggestions for fixing bugs, improving code quality, and ensuring compliance with best practices. It can detect a wide range of issues, from simple syntax errors to complex security vulnerabilities. By automating the debugging process, these tools help developers identify and fix issues more efficiently, reducing the time and effort required for manual debugging, (Raychev, Bielik, & Vechev, 2016).

Snyk, on the other hand, focuses on security vulnerabilities, providing real-time scanning of code to detect and fix security issues before they become a problem. By integrating with CI/CD pipelines, Snyk helps ensure that security is maintained throughout the development process, making it an essential tool for modern DevSecOps practices, (Allamanis *et al.*, 2018).

Comparison of Tools

AI tools are making remarkable advancements in the realm of automated debugging and bug fixing, significantly transforming the way developers maintain and enhance code quality. Tools like DeepCode and Snyk leverage sophisticated machine learning algorithms to scrutinize codebases for potential issues, ranging from simple bugs to more critical security vulnerabilities, (Wei *et al.,* 2022). These AI-driven systems not only speed up the debugging process but also offer more comprehensive insights compared to manual code reviews. By scanning large volumes of code quickly, they help developers catch mistakes that might otherwise go unnoticed.

DeepCode, for instance, employs advanced AI algorithms to analyze code and suggest improvements. It doesn't just identify syntactical errors; it provides insights into more complex issues like security vulnerabilities, code performance inefficiencies, and non-compliance with best practices. By continuously learning from vast open-source projects and integrating real-time analysis, DeepCode offers highly accurate debugging suggestions. This automation not only boosts productivity but also helps teams maintain consistent code quality by reducing the reliance on manual debugging, which can be time-consuming and error-prone. By suggesting code fixes and enhancements in real-time, developers are empowered to address issues as they write code, streamlining the development process.

On the other hand, Snyk focuses on safeguarding applications by identifying and mitigating security vulnerabilities within the codebase. As cybersecurity becomes increasingly critical, particularly in cloud-native environments, Snyk integrates seamlessly into CI/CD pipelines to offer continuous, real-time monitoring. Unlike traditional security audits, which can be labor-intensive and prone to human error, Snyk automates the process, scanning for vulnerabilities in code, dependencies, and container images. By embedding security checks early in the development lifecycle, Snyk ensures that issues are caught and addressed before they escalate into more significant threats. This proactive approach to security makes it an essential tool for teams practicing DevSecOps, where security is integrated into the entire software development workflow rather than being treated as an afterthought.

Ultimately, the selection of AI-powered tools depends on the unique needs of the developer or the development team. While code completion tools like TabNine and Kite offer flexibility and real-time assistance by predicting and completing code, tools like GitHub Copilot go a step further by generating entire blocks of code based on minimal input, significantly reducing development time. However, when the focus is on maintaining a high standard of code quality and security, specialized tools like DeepCode and Snyk are indispensable. These tools not only improve the efficiency of the development process but also help enforce industry best practices and security standards, ensuring that the final product is robust, secure, and maintainable in the long term. With AI tools becoming increasingly integrated into development workflows, they offer a promising future for streamlining coding practices while enhancing overall software quality.

Machine Learning and Deep Learning in Code Generation

Machine Learning Models in Code Generation:

Machine learning is at the heart of AI-powered code generation tools, enabling them to learn from vast amounts of data and make predictions or generate new code based on learned patterns, (Vaswani *et al.,* 2017). These models are trained using different approaches depending on the nature of the task and the available data. The two primary approaches are supervised learning and unsupervised learning.

Supervised Learning: In supervised learning, the model is trained on a dataset that includes input-output pairs. For example, the input might be a partial code snippet, and the output is the completed code. The model learns by trying to predict the output given the input, adjusting its internal parameters to minimize the difference between its predictions and the actual outputs, (Raychev, Bielik, & Vechev, 2016). This approach is particularly effective for tasks like code completion, where the goal is to predict the next piece of code based on the preceding context, (Tiwari, Goyal, & Sharma, 2021).

- **Unsupervised Learning:** Unsupervised learning, on the other hand, involves training a model on data that is not labeled. Instead of learning from input-output pairs, the model learns to identify patterns and structures within the data itself, (Allamanis *et al.*, 2018). This approach can be used to cluster similar pieces of code, discover underlying relationships between different parts of a codebase, or even generate new code based on the patterns it has learned,

(Svyatkovskiy *et al.,* 2020). While unsupervised learning is less commonly used in direct code generation, it plays a critical role in tasks such as code analysis and refactoring, where understanding the structure of the code is more important than predicting specific outputs.

Deep Learning Architectures

Deep learning, a specialized subset of machine learning, leverages neural networks with multiple layers to handle complex tasks like code generation, (Svyatkovskiy *et al.,* 2020). The depth of these networks allows them to learn hierarchical representations of data, which is particularly useful in understanding and generating code, a task that involves complex, nested structures and long-range dependencies, (Tiwari, Goyal, & Sharma, 2021).

- Recurrent Neural Networks (RNNs): RNNs are designed to handle sequential data, making them well-suited for tasks involving code, where the order of statements and expressions is crucial, (Allamanis *et al.*, 2018). RNNs can maintain a memory of previous inputs, which allows them to generate code that takes into account the preceding context, (Vaswani *et al.,* 2017). • Long Short-Term Memory Networks (LSTMs): LSTMs are a type of RNN designed to overcome the limitations of standard RNNs in handling long-range dependencies, (Raychev, Bielik, & Vechev, 2016). They do this by using a more complex internal structure that allows them to maintain and update memory over longer sequences. LSTMs have been used effectively in various natural language processing tasks, including code generation, where understanding the context over longer sequences is crucial, (Yang, Liu, & Yin, 2021). • Transformers: Transformers represent the latest advancement in deep learning architectures for sequential data, (Feng *et al.,* 2020). Unlike RNNs and LSTMs, Transformers do not process data sequentially. Instead, they use a mechanism called self-attention to weigh the importance of different parts of the input data, allowing them to capture relationships between distant elements more effectively, (Chen & Monperrus, 2019).

Training on Large Codebases

The effectiveness of machine learning and deep learning models in code generation depends heavily on the quality and scale of the data they are trained on, (Wei *et al.,* 2022). These models are typically trained on massive code repositories, such as those available on GitHub, which contain millions of lines of code across a wide variety of programming languages, styles, and applications, (Tiwari, Goyal,

& Sharma, 2021). By learning from this extensive and diverse data, the models can capture a broad range of coding practices, idioms, and patterns.

Training on large codebases allows these models to generalize across different programming languages and paradigms, providing contextually appropriate suggestions regardless of the specific language or framework in use, (Vaswani *et al.,* 2017). This ability to learn from diverse examples makes these models powerful tools for code generation, as they can adapt to various coding styles and provide relevant suggestions in a wide range of contexts, (Allamanis *et al.*, 2018).

However, training on such large datasets also presents challenges, (Feng *et al.,* 2020). Ensuring the diversity and quality of the training data is critical to avoid bias and overfitting, where the model becomes too specialized in the patterns it has seen during training and performs poorly on new or less common scenarios, (Svyatkovskiy *et al.,* 2020).

Challenges in Model Training

While the potential of machine learning and deep learning in code generation is immense, several challenges must be addressed to maximize their effectiveness, (Yang, Liu, & Yin, 2021).

- Overfitting: One of the main challenges is overfitting, where the model becomes too closely tailored to the specific examples it has seen during training, (Wei *et al.,* 2022). This can result in the model performing well on the training data but poorly on new, unseen data. Overfitting is particularly problematic in code generation, as it can lead to the generation of code that is too specific or reliant on patterns that may not be applicable in different contexts, (Chen & Monperrus, 2019). • Bias in Training Data: The quality of the training data is another critical factor. If the training data contains outdated, biased, or suboptimal coding practices, the model may learn and replicate these practices in its generated code. This can lead to the propagation of poor coding practices and limit the model's ability to generate high-quality, maintainable code, (Raychev, Bielik, & Vechev, 2016).
- Diversity of Training Data: Ensuring that the training data covers a wide range of languages, frameworks, and coding styles is essential for developing models that can generalize well across different contexts, (Tiwari, Goyal, & Sharma, 2021). If the training data is too narrow or focused on specific languages or paradigms, the model may struggle to provide useful suggestions in other contexts, (Feng *et al.,* 2020).

Addressing these challenges requires careful curation of training data, the use of techniques such as regularization and cross-validation to prevent overfitting, and ongoing evaluation and refinement of the models to ensure they continue to improve and adapt to new coding practices, (Allamanis *et al.*, 2018).

In summary, machine learning and deep learning play a critical role in AI-powered code generation, enabling tools that can learn from vast amounts of data and generate contextually relevant, high-quality code, (Svyatkovskiy *et al.,* 2020). The development and training of these models involve complex challenges, but the rewards are significant, with the potential to transform the way software is developed and maintained, (Vaswani *et al.,* 2017).

Case Study 1: Integration of GitHub Copilot in a Software Company

GitHub Copilot's integration into development workflows can be seen as a significant shift in how AI tools enhance developer productivity. In line with recent advances in code generation, Copilot helped improve code consistency, speed, and provided learning opportunities for junior developers, (Yang, Liu, & Yin, 2021) (Tiwari, Goyal, & Sharma, 2021). The impact on software development has been noted in other studies, highlighting increased efficiency with fewer errors in initial code drafts, (Vaswani *et al.,* 2017).

Case Study 2: AI Tools in an Open-Source Community

AI-driven code generation tools offer promising benefits in open-source communities, especially for standardizing code contributions. These tools align with recent research on automating repetitive coding tasks, streamlining code reviews, and ensuring better adherence to best practices, (Chen & Monperrus, 2019) (Svyatkovskiy *et al.,* 2020). This shift towards AI assistance in collaborative environments mirrors trends highlighted in the literature on machine learning for code, (Feng *et al.,* 2020).

Case Study 3: Automated Bug Fixing in a Legacy System

AI tools have proven effective in maintaining legacy systems, with AI-driven debugging successfully identifying errors in complex codebases. However, these tools still require human intervention to handle some fixes, as noted in studies discussing AI's role in software maintenance, (Raychev, Bielik, & Vechev, 2016) (Allamanis *et al.*, 2018). The combination of AI assistance and human oversight is key to addressing security and reliability issues in legacy code, (Wei *et al.,* 2022).

Ethical and Security Considerations

The ethical concerns around AI-generated code, such as plagiarism and bias, are important topics in current research. AI models may inadvertently reproduce portions of copyrighted code, raising intellectual property concerns. Moreover, bias in AI-generated solutions can lead to suboptimal or non-inclusive code, as discussed in literature on AI for software development. Security risks related to AI code generation, particularly the potential for vulnerabilities, have also been highlighted, underscoring the importance of human oversight and integrating security tools like Snyk into development processes.

Challenges and Limitations

1. Code Quality

One of the primary concerns with AI-generated code is ensuring it adheres to industry-standard best practices. While AI tools can produce functional code, they may not always follow coding conventions, naming standards, or design patterns. This can lead to technical debt, which accumulates over time and makes the code harder to maintain and modify.

To mitigate these risks, it is essential to have human developers review and validate AI-generated code. Human experts can identify potential issues, ensure adherence to best practices, and make necessary adjustments to improve code quality. Additionally, implementing automated code analysis tools can help identify and address common code quality problems, such as code smells, security vulnerabilities, and performance bottlenecks.

2. Debugging and Maintenance

AI-generated code can be difficult to debug, especially if the developer is not familiar with the logic behind the AI's decisions. This lack of transparency can make it challenging to maintain the code over time, particularly in large projects where understanding the rationale behind every line of code is crucial. If the AI-generated code introduces errors or inefficiencies, identifying and fixing these issues can be more difficult without a clear understanding of the AI's decision-making process.

To address this challenge, developers can use debugging tools and techniques to step through the code, inspect variables, and identify the root causes of issues. Additionally, incorporating logging and tracing mechanisms can help track the execution flow of the code and provide valuable insights into the AI's behavior.

3. Generalization Issues

AI models may struggle to generalize across different coding standards or unique use cases if they are not trained on a diverse and representative dataset. For example, an AI model trained primarily on code examples from a specific programming language or domain may not be able to generate code that adheres to the conventions and best practices of other languages or domains.

To improve generalization, AI tools need to be trained on a diverse dataset that covers a wide range of coding scenarios and styles. Additionally, developers can customize AI models by providing domain-specific knowledge and examples to help the AI understand the nuances of their particular use case.

4. **Scalability**

Scaling AI tools to work effectively in large projects or complex systems requires significant computational resources and sophisticated AI models. As the size and complexity of the codebase increase, the AI must be able to handle the additional load without compromising performance or accuracy. This may necessitate the use of distributed computing architectures, specialized hardware, or more advanced AI algorithms.

5. **Emerging Technologies**

As AI continues to evolve, new technologies such as reinforcement learning (RL) are poised to significantly impact AI-driven code generation. Unlike supervised learning, where models learn from labeled data, reinforcement learning involves agents learning to make decisions by interacting with an environment. In the context of code generation, RL could be used to create AI systems that learn from the feedback of experienced developers or from the outcomes of running code in real-world environments. For example, an RL-based AI could iteratively improve its code generation by learning from errors in execution or from optimization feedback, making it more adept at generating efficient and effective code over time.

Other emerging technologies include transfer learning and meta-learning, which allow AI models to adapt more quickly to new tasks by leveraging knowledge from related tasks. This could enable AI tools to better generalize across different programming languages or to new coding paradigms. Moreover, the integration of natural language processing (NLP) with code generation is expected to improve, allowing developers to interact with AI systems more naturally, using conversational language to guide the code generation process.

6. **Interdisciplinary Approaches**

The future of AI-driven code generation lies at the intersection of multiple disciplines. By combining insights from software engineering, human-computer interaction (HCI), and ethics, we can develop AI tools that are not only technically robust but also user-friendly and ethically sound.

In software engineering, principles such as modularity, maintainability, and scalability can be integrated into AI models to ensure that the generated code aligns with industry standards and best practices. From an HCI perspective, improving the usability of AI coding tools is crucial. This involves designing interfaces that allow seamless interaction between developers and AI systems, enabling developers to easily understand, modify, and control the AI-generated code.

Ethics also plays a vital role in the development of AI tools. Issues such as bias in AI-generated code, the potential for plagiarism, and the impact on job roles within the software development industry need to be carefully considered. By incorporating ethical guidelines into the design and deployment of AI systems, developers can ensure that these tools are used responsibly and that they contribute positively to the broader software development ecosystem.

7. Human-AI Collaboration

The future of coding is likely to be a collaborative effort between humans and AI. While AI tools are becoming increasingly capable, they are not expected to replace human developers. Instead, the focus will be on enhancing human creativity and decision-making through AI assistance. AI tools can take over repetitive or time-consuming tasks, allowing developers to focus on more complex and innovative aspects of software engineering.

8. Potential Research Topics

Despite the progress in AI-driven code generation, several areas require further research to fully realize its potential:

a. **Explainability:** One of the biggest challenges with AI-generated code is understanding the reasoning behind the AI's decisions. Research is needed to develop models that can explain their code generation process in a way that is accessible to developers. This could involve visualizing the decision-making process or providing annotations that clarify why certain code structures were chosen.
b. **Integration with Workflows:** For AI tools to be widely adopted, they must integrate seamlessly with existing development workflows. Research could focus on developing AI systems that are adaptable to various development environments, version control systems, and project management tools. This would allow AI-generated code to be more easily incorporated into larger projects and collaborative efforts.

c. **Robust Ethical Guidelines:** As AI tools become more prevalent, it is crucial to establish robust ethical guidelines to govern their use. This includes addressing issues such as data privacy, the potential for bias in AI models, and the impact on employment in the software industry. Research could explore frameworks for ethical AI development and deployment, ensuring that these tools are used in ways that are fair and beneficial to society.
d. **Improving Code Quality and Maintainability:** While AI tools are good at generating functional code, ensuring that the code is of high quality and maintainable over time is a continuing challenge. Research could focus on developing AI models that prioritize not just correctness but also readability, efficiency, and adherence to best practices in software engineering.

CONCLUSION

Summary of Key Points

Throughout this chapter, we have explored the various ways in which AI is reshaping the industry. We began by defining AI-generated code and discussing its significance in reducing development time and improving productivity. The chapter then traced the historical evolution of AI in coding, highlighting key milestones and the shift from rule-based systems to sophisticated neural networks.

We also examined different types of AI tools, their underlying machine learning and deep learning models, and the challenges and limitations they currently face. Case studies provided practical insights into how these tools are being used today, while the discussion on ethical and security considerations underscored the need for responsible AI development.

The Future of AI in Software Engineering

As AI tools continue to advance, we can expect a significant shift in the roles and responsibilities of software developers. One of the most significant trends is the increasing automation of routine tasks. AI- powered code generation tools can automate many repetitive and time-consuming aspects of software development, freeing developers to focus on more strategic and creative work. This could lead to a shift towards higher-level tasks, such as designing complex architectures, developing innovative algorithms, and ensuring the ethical and responsible use of AI in software systems.

While AI can be used to generate code based on patterns and examples, it is often limited in its ability to understand the nuances of specific domains. As a result, there will be a continued demand for developers with deep domain knowledge who can effectively guide AI tools and ensure that the generated code meets the specific requirements of their applications.

Final Thoughts

To prepare for the future of AI in software engineering, developers and organizations must embrace AI as a tool that complements human abilities rather than replaces them. Investing in AI literacy, staying informed about emerging technologies, and adhering to ethical guidelines will be crucial. As AI continues to evolve, so too must our approach to software development, ensuring that we leverage the full potential of AI while maintaining control over the creative and decision-making processes that define our industry.

The future of software engineering will likely be a hybrid model, where human creativity and AI efficiency work hand in hand. AI-driven code generation tools can automate routine tasks, freeing developers to focus on more complex and innovative challenges. However, it is essential to ensure that AI-generated code is of high quality, adheres to best practices, and is ethically sound. By carefully considering these factors and fostering a collaborative relationship between humans and AI, we can harness the power of AI to create better software, drive innovation, and improve the efficiency of software development processes.

REFERENCES

Allamanis, M., Barr, E. T., Bird, C., & Sutton, C. (2018). A survey of machine learning for big code and naturalness. *ACM Computing Surveys*, 51(4), 1–37. DOI: 10.1145/3212695

Chen, Z., & Monperrus, M. (2019). A literature study of embeddings on source code. *ACM Computing Surveys*, 51(3), 1–27. DOI: 10.1145/3190507

Feng, S., Chen, Z., Li, L., & Su, Z. (2020). CodeBERT: A pre-trained model for programming and natural languages. *Proceedings of the 2020 Conference on Empirical Methods in Natural Language Processing (EMNLP),* 1536–1547. DOI: 10.18653/v1/2020.findings-emnlp.139

Raychev, V., Bielik, P., & Vechev, M. (2016). Probabilistic model for code with decision trees. *Proceedings of the 43rd Annual ACM SIGPLAN-SIGACT Symposium on Principles of Programming Languages,* 731–744. DOI: 10.1145/2983990.2984041

Svyatkovskiy, A., Zhao, Y., Fu, S., & Sundaresan, N. (2020). Pythia: AI-assisted code completion system. *Proceedings of the 25th ACM SIGKDD International Conference on Knowledge Discovery & Data Mining,* 2727–2735.

Tiwari, P., Goyal, R., & Sharma, S. (2021). A comprehensive review on code generation using deep learning techniques. *International Journal of Artificial Intelligence & Applications*, 12(3), 45–61.

Vaswani, A., Shazeer, N., Parmar, N., Uszkoreit, J., Jones, L., Gomez, A. N., Kaiser, L., & Polosukhin, I. (2017). Attention is all you need. *Advances in Neural Information Processing Systems*, 30, 5998–6008.

Wei, Z., Xie, X., Zhan, J., & Zhang, J. (2022). Towards better code generation models: A survey of current trends and future directions. *ACM Transactions on Software Engineering and Methodology*, 31(2), 1–28.

Yang, C., Liu, Y., & Yin, C. (2021). Recent advances in intelligent source code generation: A survey on natural language-based studies. *Entropy (Basel, Switzerland)*, 23(9), 1174. DOI: 10.3390/e23091174 PMID: 34573800

Chapter 6
AI-Powered Tools to Enhance the Stages of Software Development

Taye Iyinoluwa Adeyinka
https://orcid.org/0009-0006-4357-6319
University of Science and Technology, Beijing, China

Kehinde Iyioluwa Adeyinka
https://orcid.org/0009-0009-7685-6693
University of Science and Technology, Beijing, China

ABSTRACT

AI operates at the heart of cloud-native software engineering and is now transforming traditional software development methodologies by introducing intelligent automation and optimization along the SDLC. The present chapter focuses on the specific opportunities and issues that the unique characteristics of containerized applications and microservices architecture introduce, with particular emphasis on AI-based tools that make developers more productive in cloud-native environments. Some critical research areas include AI-driven requirements analysis, intelligent system design, automated code generation, and advanced testing frameworks. The chapter also covers using AI to facilitate cloud-native platforms, such as Kubernetes, anomaly detection, dynamic resource management, and continuous integration and deployment

DOI: 10.4018/979-8-3693-9356-7.ch006

INTRODUCTION

Integrating AI into cloud-native software engineering is a revolutionary shift in concept, development, deployment, and maintenance. Due to the rising complexity of modern applications and the increasing usage of cloud-native architecture, the demand for tools and mechanisms that support procedural simplification and increased productivity has increased. The capabilities of AI have made related tools critical facilitators of this change, coming up with clever answers to age-old problems and opening new avenues for creativity. This chapter examines the synergy between AI and cloud-native software engineering, emphasizing the critical role that AI-powered tools play in optimizing every stage of the SDLC, (Galla *et al.,* n.d.). Software development techniques have changed dramatically from rigid, monolithic systems to highly modular, scalable, cloud-native architectures. With the introduction of microservices, containerization, containerization, and dynamic orchestration technologies, cloud computing marked a sea change in how software systems were developed and managed. These developments, aided by frameworks such as Kubernetes, allowed developers to focus their work on naturally scalable and resilient applications, (Arundel & Domingus, 2019). However, this was followed by challenges in managing the dependencies, scaling up the resources, and guaranteeing consistent performance across various contexts. Since AI can identify patterns, forecast outcomes, and automate processes, it has become a critical tool for tackling those concerns.

Implementing cloud-native software engineering principles focuses on automation and agility. One of the identifying features of cloud-native methods is the ability to enable smooth updates and rapid iterations through continuous integration and deployment pipelines, (Laszewski *et al.,* 2018). AI enhances these pipelines by automating the testing, deployment, and monitoring procedures involved. Consider that AI-driven testing frameworks can dynamically generate test cases, optimize code coverage, and detect potential vulnerabilities, (Baqar & Khanda, 2024). AI makes development faster, reduces errors by decreasing human interaction in these repetitive processes, and produces higher-quality software, (Ajiga *et al.,* 2024). Requirements gathering is one of the most important early steps in the SDLC and has long been a time-consuming and error-prone process. AI-powered tools with NLP have transformed this phase from analyzing large volumes of textual data to extracting actionable insights and predicting future needs. This means that development teams are better equipped to so that they align their objectives with user's expectations. Similarly, AI enhances the design and architecture stage by providing data-driven recommendations on system architecture, ensuring that the resulting designs are scalable and efficient.

AI has also revolutionized the way code is created and completed. Tools like GitHub Copilot and Tabnine make real-time code suggestions based on deep learning models trained from huge codebases, (Mihaljević, Radovan, & Žagar, 2024). Along with increasing developer productivity, such tools support consistency and best practices. AI also plays a role in deployment and maintenance, making anomaly detection easier and enabling intelligent resource management. Because cloud-native environments are distributed and dynamic, continuous monitoring is required to ensure peak performance. Real-time pattern recognition and anomaly detection via AI algorithms enable proactive problem-solving before users are affected, (Stahmann, n.d.). Resource optimization is one of the most intriguing uses of AI within cloud-native engineering. Cloud-native applications often execute within hybrid or multi-cloud environments, where cost-efficient resource allocation becomes critical to sustaining performance, (Seth *et al.,* 2024). AI-enabled solutions offer proactive scaling and bright orchestration by examining workload trends and predictions of resource requirements. The feature reduces the costs by blocking the over-provisioning and ensuring that applications keep their responsiveness with fluctuating loads.

Despite such developments, challenges persist in integrating AI into cloud-native software development. There are various issues related to data security and privacy, mainly for those environments that handle sensitive data. It is equally relevant to ensure AI models work transparently and ethically because biases in AI algorithms can have unconsidered consequences. In addition, the complexity of integrating AI technologies into the current processes requires solid frameworks and knowledgeable practitioners to optimize their effectiveness. The combination of AI and Cloud-Native Software Engineering has advanced the quest for effective, scalable, and creative software systems. AI-powered solutions are helping organizations fulfil the challenges of contemporary software development with accuracy and agility by improving each step of the SDLC, from requirements gathering and design to deployment and maintenance. In the realm of cloud-native software engineering, this chapter examines the revolutionary potential of these technologies through critical coverage of their uses, benefits, and challenges. It presents insightful information on how AI can reshape future software development; it emphasizes real-world applications and new trends.

Cloud-native software engineering, in conjunction with AI, is raising the bar in creating, deploying, and managing modern applications. In a world where agility, scalability, and resilience have become key imperatives, cloud-native architectures have become the bedrock of digital transformation. Containerization, dynamic orchestration, and microservices are exploited to achieve software systems characterized by flexibility, scalability, and adherence to cloud computing principles. With increased capability comes complexity-managing distributed systems, ensuring high uptime, and maintaining operational efficiency, (Zulkifi, 2024). AI-powered solutions are bridging this gap by providing intelligent automation and optimization throughout the entire software development lifecycle.

Cloud-native software engineering is about automated scalability, continuous integration, and delivery. Since these systems are inherently distributed and dynamic, developers must employ technologies that handle high-load operations while being cost-effective. AI has also emerged at the heart of this development due to its ability to analyze huge volumes of data, find patterns, and make decisions in real time, (Duan, Edwards, & Dwivedi, 2019). AI technologies are continuously improving and, in fact, redefining software development and maintenance, from intelligent code generation to predictive analytics for resource management, (Rane *et al.*, 2024). The requirements collection stage is where the journey starts; historically, this has been a manual job with inputs and interpretations. The field has seen a paradigm change because of AI. AI technologies may extract actionable insights from textual data from various sources, including corporate papers, historical data, and user evaluations, by utilizing Natural Language Processing (NLP). This method guarantees that development closely complies with user and market demands by reducing uncertainties. This feature is crucial in cloud-native settings where apps need to meet a variety of frequently shifting needs, (Tufano *et al.,* 2024).

Once the needs are established, the focus is again on design and architecture. In this respect, artificial intelligence comes in handy because it provides tools that assess system needs and the currently existing infrastructure to make recommendations on the most suitable architectural frameworks and design patterns. For example, machine learning algorithms may review historical performance data and recommend microservices designs that maximize fault tolerance and scalability. Thanks to this data-driven strategy, cloud-native systems are guaranteed to be operational, robust, and economical, (Davis, 2019).

The revolutionary potential of AI is most noticeable during the development stage. How developers approach coding has been completely transformed by intelligent code-generating tools like GitHub Copilot, which OpenAI powers. These tools automate repetitive coding processes by making context-aware suggestions with sophisticated deep-learning models trained on vast libraries of publicly available code. Consequently, the number of errors and shorter development cycles are reduced, which frees developers to focus on creative work rather than routine tasks. In addition, such technologies encourage best practices and ensure consistency across teams, something reasonably necessary for large cloud-native projects of extensive natures, (Dehaerne *et al.,* 2022).

AI dramatically enhances testing and quality assurance, which are two critical phases in the SDLC and are much more effective and efficient. Especially in complex and component-interconnected cloud-native systems, traditional testing methods may require extraordinary time and monetary investment. To guarantee robustness, AI-powered testing technologies automate test case creation, anticipate possible failure points, and even replicate real-world situations, (Garousi, Joy, & Keleş, 2024). By identifying code segments that are prone to errors, predictive analytics models allow for proactive fixes. In addition to lowering time-to-market, this proactive strategy guarantees that cloud-native apps fulfil strict quality and dependability requirements, (Juan & Mason, 2019). AI integration also changes deployment and maintenance, two areas where cloud-native systems shine. Continuous Integration/Continuous Deployment pipelines form the bedrock of cloud-native engineering, which enables seamless updates and rapid iterations. AI enhances such pipelines by automating code-merge activities, managing dependencies, and even drawing up rollback plans if things go wrong. Once deployed, AI will be critical in monitoring and anomaly detection. Machine learning algorithms continuously evaluate system parameters for deviations from normal behaviour and provide real-time remediation. This feature further ensures a seamless user experience and minimal downtime displays in the current cloud-native architecture, (Al-Asili, 2024).

Another area of excellence in AI in cloud-native settings is resource optimization. Hybrid and multi-cloud environments often pose callous decisions concerning scale and resource allocation. AI technologies with predictive analytics scan the workload trends, project resource needs, and make recommendations on proactive scaling. These techniques go beyond ensuring application performance to minimizing costs by avoiding overprovisioning and underutilizing resources. This is in line with the operational objectives of the cloud-native architectures where efficiency is paramount, (Pinciroli *et al.*, 2020).

Even with its many advantages, integrating AI into cloud-native software architecture is by no means devoid of challenges. Data security and privacy are critical concerns, mainly concerning sensitive information. Governance over the AI models is required to ensure they are unbiased and act ethically. Finally, the complexity of integrating AI tools with existing processes calls for adopting robust frameworks and trained practitioners. Maximizing the advantages of AI-powered products while guaranteeing their responsible use requires addressing these issues, (Nassar & Kamal, 2021). Beyond increasing productivity immediately, AI has more potential in cloud-native software engineering. Giving developers the confidence to take on increasingly tricky issues opens the door for creativity. AI frees up human resources to concentrate on strategic and creative aspects of development by automating repetitive jobs. Furthermore, teams can make data-driven decisions that improve their software solutions' overall quality and impact through insights generated by AI technologies, which provide a more profound understanding of system behavior, according to Mitchell (2023). This chapter presents a detailed analysis of how AI-powered technologies are enhancing cloud-native engineering software development phases. It discusses how AI is revolutionizing requirement analysis, design, development, testing, deployment, and maintenance. Through actual cases and industrial best practices, attention is drawn to the advantages and disadvantages of integration. This chapter aims to provide the necessary knowledge and insight into AI to fully leverage its power to develop the next generation of cloud-native systems.

2. LITERATURE REVIEW

It represents a revolutionary change in software systems development, deployment, and maintenance: cloud-native software engineering combined with artificial intelligence. An increasing amount of research has been done on how AI, among other things, improves many phases of the Software Development Lifecycle (SDLC), especially for cloud-native contexts, (Pandi, 2023). This literature review gives an overview of the key trends, tools, and methodologies that best describe the integration of the language with technologies, focusing on how AI-powered tools are transforming traditional processes into contemporary expectations.

Cloud-native architectures are the standard for scalable and robust software systems, leveraging microservices, containerization, and orchestration platforms like Kubernetes, (Balalaie, Heydarnoori, & Jamshidi, 2016). Through pipelines for continuous integration and continuous deployment (CI/CD), these architectures prioritize agility and quick delivery. However, because of their complexity, AI-enhanced tools are now required to improve operations and tackle issues with fault tolerance, resource optimization, and dependency management, (Laszewski *et al.,* 2018).

One of the most difficult stages of the SDLC is frequently mentioned as requirement collecting. Traditional methods rely largely on stakeholder interviews and manual inputs, and they are most prone to errors and omissions. AI-enabled tools, particularly those utilizing NLP, have gradually become game-changing. To ensure alignment with user objectives and less ambiguity, tools like IBM Watson and similar NLP-based frameworks analyze textual data from multiple sources to identify actionable insights that make sense, (Zhao *et al.,* 2021). Predictive analytics models further anticipate future needs, making this stage more proactive and flexible, (Kosińska *et al*., 2023).

AI applications have greatly enhanced the design and architecture stage in software development. Machine learning algorithms review historical data and existing systems to recommend optimal design patterns that ensure scalability and performance. AI solutions, including Archistar, recommend architectural models and microservices configurations. Given the requirements of specific applications, as Miller and Mun (2023) indicated, this technology is precious in cloud-native environments where service dependencies must be carefully planned to avoid performance glitches and ensure fault isolation.

Artificial Intelligence has indeed made great strides in code generation and completion. Tools like Tabnine and GitHub Copilot powered by OpenAI use big language models trained on big codebases to provide real-time code suggestions. These tools enforce best practices while removing bugs, improving code quality and not just development times, (Svyatkovskiy *et al.,* 2020). For example, scholars have highlighted that these technologies foster consistency in the development teams, which is crucial when dealing with large-scale cloud-native projects, (Anwar & Bashir, 2023).

Automated test case creation, vulnerability detection, and prediction of failure points are increasingly part of AI-driven testing frameworks, opening new ways to quality assurance. Cloud-native systems are complex and dynamic, and traditional testing methods often cannot cope with them. AI-driven solutions, such as Test. ai and Applitools (Baqar & Khanda, 2024), employ machine learning models to emulate real-life scenarios while achieving maximum test coverage, as Don *et al.* (2024) explain. Furthermore, predictive models assist in identifying defect-prone locations where developers may fix problems well before they become major ones, as Singh *et al.* (2024) suggested.

Cloud-native systems involve managing CI/CD pipelines, (D'Onofrio, Fusco, & Zhong, 2023), ensuring that updates integrate well, and monitoring the system's performance, among others, in deployment. With technologies like Argo CD (Chittala, 2024) and Jenkins using machine learning to optimize deployment tactics and manage rollback scenarios after failures, artificial intelligence (AI) is essential to automating these operations, (Vemulapalli, 2024). AI-driven anomaly detection systems that track application performance in real-time after deployment allow for preemptive problem-solving and minimize downtime, (Cheng *et al.,* 2023).

One of the biggest problems with cloud-native systems is resource allocation in hybrid and multi-cloud environments. Through demand forecasting and workload analysis, AI systems maximize resource usage. AI-powered tools like Turbonomic (Seo, Yoo, & Lee, 2023) suggest cost control and scaling, so that cloud resources are utilized effectively, (Zhu *et al.,* 2023). This competence is especially crucial as businesses work to strike a balance between cost-effectiveness and performance.

Despite these advantages, integrating AI into cloud-native software engineering comes with challenges. Data security and privacy remain an important issue, more so in multi-tenant cloud settings. According to Miller and Mun (2023), strong governance structures are essential for eradicating biases from AI models to ensure ethical decision-making. On the other hand, the integration complexity of AI tools into current processes puts a high premium on knowledgeable professionals and teams, as indicated by Jones (2024).

While new technologies like explainable AI and federated learning open up new opportunities, the use of AI within cloud-native software engineering is still in development. One potentially rich avenue for multi-cloud systems is federated learning, where models can be trained across dispersed data sources without sacrificing privacy. Meanwhile, explainable AI works to solve issues around accountability and trust by increasing decision-making openness, (Prangon & Wu, 2024).

Cloud-native software engineering is changing the SDLC by embracing AI-powered technologies to increase productivity, scalability, and creativity. AI is invaluable in conquering the growing complexity of contemporary software systems, from requirements analysis and design to testing, deployment, and resource management. While privacy, ethics, and implementation challenges remain, research and development move on to fulfill a future wherein cloud-native engineering and artificial intelligence can seamlessly work hand-in-hand.

2.1 AI in Requirements Analysis and Specification for Cloud-Native Systems

Any software development project's success is based on the requirements analysis phase. In conventional contexts, gathering, interpreting, and documenting user demands is done by hand. Human error, misunderstandings, and a lack of alignment with stakeholder objectives are common problems with this procedure. However, by automating data extraction, improving requirements, and bringing them into line with the unique needs of cloud-native systems, the incorporation of Artificial Intelligence (AI), primarily through Natural Language Processing (NLP) systems, is revolutionizing this stage.

2.1.1Artificial Intelligence in Requirements Analysis

AI-powered technologies with natural language processing (NLP) capabilities quickly process large volumes of textual data, including surveys, user reviews, business documents, and old system logs. These technologies may pinpoint possible needs, spot trends, and extract meaningful insights with accuracy. AI systems can work at scale, swiftly evaluating many data sources to produce a thorough definition of requirements, in contrast to manual techniques. This feature benefits cloud-native applications, which frequently have dynamic and varied user bases.

By using natural language processing (NLP) methods, AI systems can decipher natural language inputs and determine the contexts and purposes included inside text. As a result, user expectations and wants can be better understood and converted into requirements that can be put into practice. AI, for instance, can spot recurrent themes in user reviews that indicate a demand for particular features essential to cloud-native architectures, like increased scalability or higher fault tolerance.

2.1.2 Tools and Techniques for AI-Driven Requirements Analysis

AI is being used by several tools and approaches to rethink requirements analysis for cloud-native applications. These solutions automate and optimize the requirements-gathering process by combining machine learning, predictive analytics, and advanced natural language processing.

1. Requirements Extraction with IBM Watson

IBM Many people use Watson's natural language processing (NLP) skills to examine unstructured data. Customer feedback and system logs are textual inputs that Watson processes to identify and classify requirements according to their urgency and relevance. This tool is especially helpful for cloud-native projects, where needs frequently span several services and environments.

2. **Using Reverb AI to Improve Requirements**

The main goal of Reverb AI is to transform high-level goals and user stories into specific, organized requirements. It parses stakeholder inputs using natural language processing (NLP) and produces actionable specifications for microservices-based systems. The tool's capacity to map requirements to current services ensures alignment with the modular design of cloud-native systems.

3. Assistant for Requirements

This AI-powered tool helps with prioritization and requirement validation. It finds conflicts and redundancies by comparing requirements' viability to system capabilities, guaranteeing that only essential and attainable specifications are recorded.

4. Forecasting Needs Using Predictive Analytics

To foresee future needs, predictive analytics models examine past project data. These models use machine learning algorithms to spot patterns and recommend features that suit changing consumer preferences or market demands.

2.1.3 Improving Cloud-Native Architecture Requirements

Scalability, robustness, and dynamic resource allocation are needs for cloud-native systems. By concentrating on features specific to cloud-native environments, AI systems assist in honing these requirements:

Scalability Requirements: AI algorithms identify capacity planning needs by analyzing user growth trends and workload patterns. These observations guarantee the effective scalability of cloud-native systems.

Resilience Requirements: AI systems can analyze past failure data to detect possible weak points and suggest design elements like redundancy and failover procedures.

Dynamic Resource Allocation: The AI-driven analysis highlights the need for adaptive resource management and directs the addition of capabilities like auto-scaling and container orchestration.

2.1.4 AI's advantages for requirements analysis

1. **Efficiency:** AI greatly reduces the time needed to collect and evaluate requirements by automating repetitive processes.
2. **Accuracy:** By reducing misunderstandings, NLP techniques guarantee that requirements appropriately represent user needs.
3. **Scalability:** Due to AI's ability to handle massive datasets, cloud-native applications can be complicated and dispersed.
4. **Proactive Insights:** Teams can link development efforts with long-term objectives by using predictive analytics to foresee future demands.

Even while AI-powered technologies have many advantages, they have drawbacks for requirements analysis. For example, it is crucial to ensure the quality of the data because adequate or accurate data can result in unsound requirements. Additionally, thorough planning and user training are necessary for integrating AI systems into current workflows. Lastly, to preserve stakeholder trust, ethical issues such as guaranteeing objective decision-making in AI models must be addressed.

AI-powered technologies, especially those that use natural language processing, are revolutionizing requirements analysis for cloud-native systems. These technologies help development teams build more precise, actionable, and scalable requirements by automating data extraction, improving specifications, and aligning them with the particular requirements of cloud-native architectures. These technologies' contribution to simplifying the requirements phase will only increase as they develop further, opening the door for more effective and fruitful software development procedures.

2.2 AI-Driven Design and Architectural Optimization

The design and architecture stage of the software development lifecycle (SDLC) is essential for software systems to be scalable, effective, and robust. Designs that manage dynamic workloads, fault tolerance, and smooth scalability are essential in cloud-native settings, defined by microservices and containerized architectures. During this period, artificial intelligence (AI) has become a revolutionary force, offering methods and tools to optimize architecture and design through pattern analysis, configuration automation, and reliable system performance.

2.2.1 The Role of AI in Design and Architecture

AI's main contribution to design and architectural optimization is its ability to process massive datasets, uncover hidden patterns, and produce recommendations suited to particular application requirements. Artificial intelligence (AI) tools can assess the performance of current systems, spot inefficiencies, and suggest fixes that improve scalability and fault tolerance by utilizing machine learning algorithms and predictive analytics. These features are essential in cloud-native systems, where interdependencies must be managed appropriately, and microservices function as separate entities.

AI-driven systems, for example, can examine past data on resource usage and traffic patterns to recommend architectural changes that enhance load balancing and lower latency. AI tools may also mimic different situations, which helps designers foresee possible problems and take precautionary action. By taking a proactive stance, system outages are less likely to occur, and architectures are more adaptable to shifts in user demand or workload.

2.2.2 AI-Assisted Design of Microservices

Microservices architecture provides flexibility and adaptability, which is the foundation of cloud-native systems. Building microservices can be challenging, as can determining service boundaries, controlling dependencies, and enhancing inter-service communication. AI solutions help overcome these difficulties by automating crucial steps in the design process.

Identification of Service Boundaries: AI systems examine application needs and determine microservices' logical boundaries. This lessens dependencies and enhances maintainability by guaranteeing that every service is independent and fulfils a defined task.

Communication Optimization: AI technologies optimize communication protocols between services by examining data flow and suggesting the most effective techniques, such as REST APIs, gRPC (Alio, 2024), or message queues.

Dependency Management: AI tools guarantee that dependencies are kept to a minimum by modelling inter-service linkages, which lowers the possibility of cascade failures in complex systems.

2.2.2 Optimizing Containerized Architectures with AI

A fundamental component of cloud-native design is containerization, which is made possible by tools like Docker and Kubernetes, (Arundel & Domingus, 2019). Applications and their dependencies are contained within containers, enabling consistency and portability between environments. Containerized architecture design necessitates meticulous planning to guarantee effective resource usage and scalability. AI tools play a key role in optimizing these architectures by automating orchestration and configuration.

Resource Allocation: AI systems use workload patterns to dynamically allocate resources, ensuring that containers are not overprovisioned and have enough capacity. Kubernetes-based AI technologies, for instance, use reinforcement learning to optimize scalability and pod scheduling choices.

Fault Tolerance: AI-powered solutions monitor the condition of containers and anticipate problems before they arise. These technologies improve system dependability by restarting containers or proactively migrating workloads.

Orchestration Optimization: By anticipating traffic spikes and making real-time configuration adjustments, AI solutions simplify container orchestration and guarantee flawless operation during periods of high demand.

2.2.3 Examples of AI Tools for Design and Optimization

Cloud-native systems' architectural design can be optimized with the help of several AI-powered tools and platforms:

IBM AI Ops: This product employs machine learning to forecast failures, track system health, and suggest architectural changes. It works exceptionally well for handling intricate microservices systems, guaranteeing fault tolerance and peak performance.

H2O.ai: Thanks to its predictive analytics capabilities, H2O.ai can evaluate historical data and suggest scalable architectures for containerized apps.

Architects can also test setups prior to deployment by using its scenario simulation capabilities.

Kubernetes AI Extensions: By offering intelligent workload scheduling and resource management, Kubernetes AI extensions like KubeFlow improve container orchestration.

Archistar: Archistar optimizes architectural designs by using AI to find bottlenecks in current systems and suggest adequate microservices arrangements.

2.2.4 Ensuring Scalability and Fault Tolerance

Two crucial characteristics of cloud-native architectures are scalability and fault tolerance. AI helps achieve these qualities by automating crucial procedures and offering insights:

Scalability: AI tools predict future workloads and analyze traffic patterns, allowing systems to grow vertically or horizontally as needed. AI, for example, can recommend how many replicas a microservice should have to manage expected spikes in demand.

Fault Tolerance: Machine learning models that detect possible failure points suggest redundancy measures, including replicating vital services or implementing failover mechanisms. This guarantees system uptime even in the event of unforeseen interruptions.

Getting Used to Changing Cloud-Native Contexts Cloud-native systems work in dynamic contexts where resource availability, user needs, and workloads can all change quickly. Through constant performance metrics monitoring and real-time tweaks, AI tools are excellent at adjusting architectures to these changes. AI-driven auto-scaling systems, for instance, dynamically modify resources in response to traffic variations, guaranteeing optimal performance and cost-effectiveness. Similarly, real-time anomaly detection by AI systems might initiate automated reactions to minimize problems.

Although AI has many benefits for architecture and design, its application has drawbacks. Due to the intricacy of training machine learning models for particular applications, significant computational resources and skills are needed. Furthermore, making AI recommendations interpretable is crucial because opaque models can erode stakeholder trust. Additionally, modifying team skill sets and organizational procedures to incorporate AI tools into current workflows could be necessary.

AI-driven design and architectural optimization are revolutionizing the development of cloud-native systems. These solutions provide answers to the problems of resource efficiency, fault tolerance, and scalability. AI solutions help architects build resilient and flexible systems that satisfy the needs of contemporary applications by automating crucial design process steps and offering data-driven insights, (Ghorbani, 2023). The efficiency and resilience of software architectures will be further improved as AI technologies advance and are included in cloud-native design methodologies.

2.3 Intelligent Code Generation and Real-Time Assistance

Coding, a time-consuming and human error-prone task, is a part of the Software Development Lifecycle (SDLC) development phase. Artificial Intelligence (AI) has revolutionized the way developers write and maintain code with the emergence of intelligent code generation and real-time support tools. These technologies help developers by recommending, creating, and optimizing code in real time using sophisticated machine-learning models frequently trained on large code repositories. They significantly affect teamwork, productivity, and code quality, especially in remote and cloud-native software engineering settings.

2.3.1The Role of AI in Code Generation and Assistance

AI-powered code creation technologies use Natural Language Processing (NLP) and machine learning to comprehend the context of the code being created. These tools examine the surrounding code, infer the developer's intention, and automatically generate code snippets or offer pertinent recommendations. For complicated cloud-native systems, this feature is crucial because it not only speeds up the development process but also aids in uniformity and adherence to best practices.

For example, AI technologies can generate boilerplate code, which is sometimes repetitious but required for configuring services in microservices-based architectures. By automating these tasks, developers can concentrate on resolving more complex issues and implementing business logic.

2.3.2 Key AI-Powered Tools for Intelligent Code Assistance

1. **Copilot on GitHub**

One well-known example of intelligent code assistance is GitHub Copilot, driven by OpenAI's Codex model. GitHub Copilot, incorporated into well-known integrated development environments (IDEs) such as Visual Studio Code, makes code suggestions depending on the context of the current file. If you briefly describe the functionality you want, it can also create whole functions or classes.

GitHub By automating everyday coding chores like building data structures, performing API calls, and managing error-checking procedures, Copilot shines at cutting down on development time. It encourages uniformity for remote teams by offering recommendations that follow accepted code conventions.

2. **The tabnine**

Another AI-powered tool that concentrates on offering real-time code recommendations is Tabnine. With Tabnine's customization possibilities, teams can train models on their codebases, unlike GitHub Copilot, which depends on a single colossal language model. This capability is quite helpful when it comes to preserving consistency across extensive projects with distinct code standards.

The development process is streamlined by Tabnine's real-time support, which includes context-aware completions and multi-line suggestions. Businesses working on proprietary systems appreciate it because of its flexibility in meeting project needs.

3. The kite

Kite is an AI-powered coding assistant that integrates with several IDEs to offer real-time code completions and documentation recommendations. Over time, Kite becomes better by examining developer activity and making more precise and pertinent recommendations.

2.3.4 Enhancing Productivity with Intelligent Code Assistance

Increasing developer efficiency is one of the most significant benefits of AI-powered code-generating technologies. By reducing the time spent on tedious and repetitive coding jobs, these technologies free up developers to concentrate on more intricate and imaginative software development activities. For instance:

Accelerating Development Cycles: Development cycles can be accelerated by using tools like GitHub Copilot, which provides code snippets for routine activities like establishing database connections or implementing authentication procedures. These speeds up development, especially in cloud-native applications where several microservices require comparable features.
Reducing Context Switching: To address certain issues, developers frequently move between tutorials, documentation, and coding environments.

Thanks to AI solutions that offer contextual recommendations and inline documentation, such context switching is less necessary.

Error Reduction: AI tools ensure smoother development workflows by reducing syntax and logic errors by providing pre-validated code snippets.

2.3.5 Ensuring Code Quality and Consistency

Maintaining good code quality and consistency can be difficult, particularly in distributed teams where several engineers work on the same codebase. This problem is addressed by AI-powered solutions that encourage adherence to best practices and coding standards. For example:

Standardization: When trained on an organization's unique organizations like Tabnine, guarantee that all developers adhere to predetermined norms and styles.

Real-Time Feedback: AI tools allow developers to make quick fixes by giving them immediate feedback on possible mistakes or less-than-ideal code.

Better Cooperation: AI helps remote teams by keeping a consistent codebase, which lowers the possibility of disagreements during code integration.

2.3.6 Impact on Distributed and Cloud-Native Development Teams

The communication and consistency of distributed development teams, prevalent in cloud-native systems, present particular difficulties. AI-driven solutions fill up these gaps by:

Encouraging Knowledge Sharing: AI tools assist team members in comprehending unfamiliar code more rapidly by offering contextual recommendations and documentation.

Supporting Onboarding: AI can help new developers comprehend and adhere to project conventions, reducing onboarding time and increasing efficiency.

Improving Cooperation: AI techniques minimize during code reviews and integrations by upholding a uniform coding style.

Although AI-powered code-generating techniques have many advantages, they also have drawbacks and moral dilemmas. For example, the dependence on sizable pre-trained models raises concerns over the source and licensing of training data. Organizations ensure ensures that AI-generated code complies with copyright regulations. Furthermore, developers' basic coding abilities may deteriorate due to an over-reliance on AI tools.

Improving customization facing with larger development workflows is critical to intelligent code generation's future. There will be a growing demand for tools that let businesses train AI models on proprietary codebases while protecting user privacy. Furthermore, developments in explainable AI (XAI) may increase the transparency of AI-generated recommendations, promoting developer trust.

Intelligent code generation and real-time support tools like GitHub Copilot and Tabnine are revolutionizing processes by increasing efficiency, guaranteeing code quality, and encouraging uniformity among teams. By addressing the particular difficulties presented by distributed and cloud-native development environments, these solutions let developers concentrate on creativity while automating repetitive activities. These technologies will become increasingly important in determining the direction of software development as they develop further.

2.4 Automated Testing and Continuous Integration/ Continuous Deployment (CI/CD)

The Software Development Lifecycle (SDLC) testing and deployment stages are crucial, particularly in cloud-native environments where resilience, scalability, and agility are crucial. The intricacy and speed needed in these systems are frequently too great for traditional testing methods and Continuous Integration/Continuous Deployment (CI/CD) pipelines. With tools and approaches that improve automated testing, regression testing, predictive error detection, and CI/CD workflow optimization, artificial intelligence (AI) has become a game-changer. These developments guarantee smoother deployment procedures, quicker development cycles, and better software.

2.4.1 AI in Automated Testing

Automated testing reduces the manual labor needed for repetitive testing jobs by executing test cases using software tools. AI improves this procedure by utilizing predictive analytics, machine learning, and natural language processing to maximize test case creation, spot problems, and guarantee thorough coverage.

2.4.2 AI-Powered Test Case Generation

One of AI's most important contributions to testing is its ability to automatically create test cases. Conventional approaches use preset scripts, which can take much work to write and update. On the other hand, AI systems generate dynamic, adaptive test cases by examining code modifications, application needs, and test data from the past.

For example, tools such as fuctionize and Test.ai use machine learning models to comprehend the application being tested and produce tests that replicate actual user behavior. In cloud-native apps, where frequent updates and scalability are commonplace, this capability ensures that tests stay pertinent even as the application changes.

2.4.3 Predictive Error Detection

AI is very good at anticipating possible mistakes before they happen because of its capacity to recognize patterns and anomalies. Machine learning models trained on past defect data can identify code segments that are more likely to fail. AI solutions like Applitools and Smart Bear AI Test Complete, for instance, examine how code changes affect various application components and identify high-risk areas that need more care.

Predictive error detection cuts down on debugging time and lowers the possibility of serious production failures. This functionality is very helpful in cloud-native systems, where dispersed designs can make fault isolation and resolution more difficult.

2.4.3 AI-Powered Regression Testing

Regression testing ensures that code updates don't cause problems with already-existing functionality. However, regression testing by hand can take much time and resources, especially for big and complicated systems. AI-driven technologies optimize regression testing by using historical test results and recent code changes to determine which test cases are most important.

Tricentis Tosca, for instance, uses AI to prioritize and carry out regression tests, concentrating on the parts of the codebase that are most likely to be impacted. This method allows quicker development cycles without sacrificing quality by lowering testing overhead and preserving excellent test coverage.

2.5 AI-Optimized CI/CD Pipelines

AI-Optimized Continuous Integration/Continuous Deployment (CI/CD) Pipelines In cloud-native environments, CI/CD pipelines are critical to the timely and dependable delivery of software updates. These pipelines let teams react quickly to shifting customer demands and requirements by automating the development, testing, and deployment of apps. AI improves CI/CD pipelines by automating difficult processes, anticipating failures, and allocating resources optimally.

2.5.1 Automated Builds and Deployments

AI tools automate builds and deployments, simplifying the CI/CD process. For instance, AI-driven systems such as Harness and Spinnaker use machine learning to determine the best build settings, shortening build times and increasing dependability. Based on past performance information and application needs, these tools can suggest deployment strategies like canary or blue-green deployments.

2.5.1 Intelligent Rollback Strategies

Rollback techniques are essential for reducing the impact of unsuccessful deployments in cloud-native apps. AI systems analyze real-time deployment metrics to identify anomalies and automatically initiate rollbacks when problems are found. AI algorithms are used in tools like Jenkins X and Weave works Flux to guarantee that rollbacks are carried out promptly and effectively, reducing downtime and maintaining system integrity.

2.5.2 Proactive Monitoring and Anomaly Detection

One essential component of CI/CD pipelines is post-deployment monitoring. Dynatrace and New Relic AI are AI-powered monitoring solutions that continually assess application performance and identify anomalies and performance bottlenecks in real-time. By offering teams actionable insights, these technologies lower the likelihood of service interruptions and improve user experience by empowering them to handle problems proactively.

2.5.3 Resource Optimization in CI/CD Pipelines

AI analyzes workload patterns and adjusts dynamically to maximize resource use in CI/CD pipelines. For example, Kubernetes-based platforms with AI capabilities may scale CI/CD workloads according to demand, guaranteeing cost-effectiveness and optimal resource allocation.

2.6 AI's advantages for testing and CI/CD

There are several benefits of integrating AI into CI/CD pipelines and testing frameworks:

Faster Development Cycles: Teams may release updates faster due to automated testing and improved CI/CD workflows, which shortens the time to market.

Better Software Quality: Predictive analytics and intelligent testing reduce errors and increase dependability by ensuring that applications are carefully examined before deployment.
Cost-Effectiveness: AI-powered resource optimization lowers infrastructure expenses, resulting in more cost-effective CI/CD pipeline operations.
Improved User Experience: By ensuring that programs operate consistently, proactive monitoring and anomaly detection raises user happiness.

Despite its advantages, integrating AI into CI/CD pipelines and testing has high challenges. These challenges are necessary for machine learning model training, and sustaining these models can demand a lot of resources. Furthermore, incorporating AI technologies into current workflows might call for process modifications and team member upskilling. It is also necessary to address ethical issues, such as ensuring AI systems do not introduce prejudices.

Increased automation, explainability, and integration with other development processes are key components of AI's future in testing and CI/CD. Applying explainable AI (XAI) techniques to increase the transparency of AI-driven decisions and using federated learning to train AI models cooperatively across businesses without revealing sensitive data are examples of emerging trends.

AI is transforming CI/CD pipelines and automated testing, allowing teams to produce high-caliber software at previously unheard-of speeds. AI guarantees thorough coverage and minimizes manual labor by automating test generation, regression testing, and predicting mistake detection. AI improves cloud-native applications' dependability and efficiency by streamlining builds, deployments, and rollbacks in CI/CD processes. These technologies will play an ever more crucial role in contemporary software engineering as they grow further, spurring innovation and quality in creating and implementing softwar

2.7 AI for Post-Deployment Monitoring and Resource Optimization

2.7.1 AI-Powered Anomaly Detection

A key component of post-deployment monitoring is anomaly detection, especially in cloud-native settings where dispersed architectures add significant unpredictability. Conventional rule-based methods frequently find it difficult to identify subtle or new patterns in system behavior. However, AI-driven systems are best at spotting abnormalities by examining vast amounts of data and spotting departures from typical patterns.

AI-powered anomaly detection systems like Splunk and Dynatrace use machine learning techniques to create baselines for typical system behavior. As the system develops, these baselines are updated often, allowing the tools to identify real-time anomalies, including sudden increases in traffic, resource contention, or service interruptions. For instance, a microservice's abrupt spike in latency or CPU consumption can be a sign of a bottleneck, allowing developers to take action before end users are impacted.

2.7.2 AI-Powered System Performance Monitoring

Performance monitoring entails watching essential metrics, including response times, throughput, error rates, and resource use, to ensure that applications meet their performance goals. Artificial intelligence improves this process by connecting metrics from infrastructure to application-level performance across several tiers of the cloud-native stack.

AI capabilities are integrated into tools like AppDynamics and New Relic AI to provide comprehensive views of system performance. These programs find trends and patterns in data that manual monitoring could overlook by combining and evaluating information from many sources. For example, they can identify performance degradation brought on by microservices' cascade failures, enabling teams to address the underlying issues proactively.

2.7.3 AI-Powered Predictive Maintenance

Predictive maintenance uses AI to predict possible faults before they happen, lowering maintenance costs and downtime. Teams can take preventive action by using machine learning models trained on historical data to find trends that precede system problems.

Time-series analysis is used by AI-powered predictive maintenance systems, such as IBM Predictive Maintenance and Azure AI Insights, to forecast when a component or service is likely to fail. For instance, these technologies can analyze network traffic to detect possible bottlenecks or track disk usage trends to foresee storage capacity concerns. Businesses can guarantee high availability and dependability in their cloud-native systems by taking proactive measures to solve these problems.

2.7.1 AI-Powered Scaling and Resource Optimization

Resource optimization is an essential component of managing cloud-native applications. Ineffective resource allocation can result in under-provisioning, which affects performance, or over-provisioning, which raises expenses. AI-driven solutions resolve these issues by dynamically allocating resources according to operational priorities and workload demands.

Allocation of Dynamic Resources

AI algorithms analyze real-time workload data to dynamically distribute resources, guaranteeing that apps get the resources they require without wasting any. For instance, AI is used by Kubernetes extensions such as Keda and Vertical Pod Autoscaler to modify pod configurations according to traffic, memory, and CPU measurements. These tools increase efficiency and reduce costs by avoiding over-provisioning and preventing resource famine.

Astute Scaling

In cloud-native systems, scaling is crucial to meet shifting user demands. By anticipating demand spikes and appropriately allocating resources, AI-driven solutions facilitate horizontal and vertical scaling. For example, solutions such as AWS Auto Scaling and Google Cloud AI-Powered Autoscaler use machine learning to estimate future demands by analyzing historical traffic trends. Using these forecasts to guide scaling decisions, apps can minimize idle resources during low traffic while maintaining responsiveness during peak loads.

2.7.4 AI-Powered Cost Optimization

Ineffective management can cause cloud computing costs to rise rapidly. AI-powered cost optimization systems examine usage trends, resource usage, and invoicing information to suggest cost-cutting measures.

Resource Right-Sizing: AI detects over-provisioned resources and recommends workload consolidation or reduction. Tools like Spot.io and VMware's CloudHealth are experts at maximizing resource utilization while upholding performance requirements.

Idle Resource Management: AI can identify idle or underutilized resources, like storage volumes or virtual computers, and automatically deallocate them to cut expenses.

Workload Placement Optimization: Machine learning algorithms suggest the best possible distribution of workloads among cloud regions or availability zones to reduce latency and expenses. AI might recommend moving workloads to areas with cheaper computing or electricity prices.

2.8 AI's advantages for resource optimization and post-deployment monitoring

Proactive Issue Resolution: AI minimizes downtime and guarantees a flawless user experience by identifying and fixing possible problems before they affect users.
Operational Efficiency: By using AI to automate complicated monitoring and scaling tasks, teams can concentrate on strategic goals rather than daily duties.
Cost Savings: AI-driven solutions help businesses reduce waste and manage cloud expenses by streamlining resource allocation and scaling.
Scalability: Cloud-native apps can efficiently grow to meet demand thanks to AI's capacity to assess and adjust to shifting workloads.

Notwithstanding its advantages, AI has drawbacks for resource optimization and post-deployment monitoring. High-quality data is necessary for machine learning models to be trained, and inadequate or noisy data might lower accuracy. Furthermore, incorporating AI technologies into current workflows can necessitate major adjustments to infrastructure and procedures. Lastly, companies need to address issues with model interpretability and decision-making openness to foster confidence in AI-driven systems.

3. RESEARCH OBJECTIVES

The primary goal of this chapter is to investigate how cloud-native software engineering stages of software development are improved by AI-powered tools. In particular, the study seeks to:

1. **Examine How AI Can Simplify Software Development Procedures:** Look at how AI-powered tools are used throughout the Software Development Lifecycle (SDLC) to increase productivity, decrease manual labor, and improve accuracy in tasks like requirements analysis, design, coding, testing, deployment, and maintenance.

2. **Analyze AI's Impact on Cloud-Native Architectures:** Assess how AI technologies optimize the unique features of cloud-native environments, including microservices, containerization, and orchestration, to ensure scalability, fault tolerance, and resource efficiency.
3. **Analyze AI-Powered Improvements to Team Productivity and Code Quality:** Analyze how well AI solutions like GitHub Copilot and Tabnine work to improve cooperation between remote teams, cut down on development time, and encourage coding consistency.
4. **Determine AI's Place in CI/CD Pipelines and Automated Testing:** Discover how AI-driven testing frameworks create test cases, identify possible problems, and streamline continuous integration and delivery (CI/CD) processes, such as automated builds, deploys, and rollback plans.
5. **Analyze AI's Role in Resource Optimization and Post-Deployment Monitoring:** Investigate AI's capabilities in anomaly detection, predictive maintenance, and dynamic resource allocation to enhance performance monitoring and ensure cost-effective scaling in cloud-native applications.
6. **Highlight Challenges and Ethical Considerations:** Determine possible obstacles to using AI in cloud-native software development, such as algorithmic bias, data protection, and the requirement for openness, and provide solutions.

This chapter focuses on the revolutionary significance of AI-powered tools in contemporary software engineering techniques, particularly how they integrate into cloud-native systems. The research considers practical tools and processes, examines case studies, and assesses new trends to give a thorough grasp of how AI transforms software development for cloud-native environments.

3.1 Methodology

This chapter examines the adoption of AI-powered tools in cloud-native software development by using a multi-method approach. To present a comprehensive study, the process involves case studies, qualitative insights from industry practices, rigorous literature research, and the assessment of AI tools. Each approach leads to a more profound understanding of how AI disrupts the SDLC in a cloud-native environment.

The foundation of the study is a systematic literature evaluation, which examines peer-reviewed publications, white papers, and industry reports to determine how AI is used in software development. Stages like requirements collection, intelligent design, automated testing, and post-deployment monitoring are the main topics of the assessment. Research shows how AI-powered solutions might help with fault tolerance and scalability, (Deng *et al.,* 2024) (Garousi, Joy, & Keleş, 2024). Information is drawn from databases such as IEEE Xplore, ACM Digital Library, and

SpringerLink using critical phrases related to the topics, including "AI in cloud-native systems" and "intelligent code generation."

Case studies that present practical applicability will be used to support this theoretical investigation. These case studies will discuss solutions that include AWS Auto Scaling to further resource efficiency, Dynatrace for detecting anomalies, and GitHub Copilot in intelligent code generation. For example, GitHub Copilot has improved developer productivity by reducing repetitive coding tasks and maintaining code integrity across distributed teams, (Wang *et al.*, 2022). In this vein, AWS Auto Scaling demonstrates how AI can optimize cloud computing costs by dynamically assigning resources, (Jonnala, n.d.).

Qualitative observations from industry practices provide practical viewpoints. Surveys, interviews, and reports document the experiences of both software architects and developers. According to interviews, for instance, AI technologies like Dynatrace enable faster response times to system issues while lessening manual work needed to identify anomalies, (Nguyen-Duc *et al.*, 2023). Also, the surveys show that AI-driven CI/CD pipelines are increasingly used for automated builds and increasing deployment reliability, (Tirupati *et al.,* 2024).

A comparison analysis is done to estimate the efficiency of AI tools in different phases of the SDLC. For example, to evaluate functionality, ease of integration, and impact on code quality, tools such as Tabnine and Test.ai are considered. For instance, Tabnine would be ideal for companies seeking consistency in coding standards due to its flexibility, which easily adapts to varied codebases. In contrast, Scriven *et al.* (2023) propose Test.ai as prominent in sophisticated test case creation. It lowers overhead and increases test coverage, as Theodoropoulos *et al.* (2023) inferred.

Finally, input from subject-matter experts validates the findings and ensures that the research addresses topics relevant to practice. Examples include software engineers, cloud architects, and AI researchers who review the preliminary findings and recommend improving the analysis. Their involvement ensures that the research is aligned with industrial standards and applications of the natural world, (Polese *et al.,* 2023). This research provides a solid basis for investigating how AI-powered tools improve software development in cloud-native systems when combined using different techniques.

3.2 Applications of AI-Powered Tools in Cloud-Native Software Development

Cloud-native software development has introduced revolutionary applications throughout the Software Development Lifecycle (SDLC) thanks to the incorporation of AI-powered tools. These apps, which rely on distributed architectures, microservices, and containerized deployments, optimize workflows, boost productivity, and increase the quality of cloud-native systems. In this article, we examine the real-world uses of AI in several facets of cloud-native software development.

1. Conditions Evaluation and Administration

An essential early stage of the SDLC is requirements collecting and analysis, which is made more accessible by AI-powered solutions. Algorithms for natural language processing (NLP) examine stakeholder input, business papers, and user input to extract requirements that may be implemented. For instance, techniques such as IBM Watson NLP are used to identify essential consumer needs and forecast future wants based on past trends. These features guarantee that requirements are precisely recorded and in line with the ever-changing needs of cloud-native systems.

2. Architectural optimization and intelligent design

Designing scalable and robust architectures for cloud-native systems requires extensive experience. Artificial intelligence (AI) tools help create optimal architectures by examining current systems and suggesting design patterns specific to microservices and containerized applications. Machine learning techniques are used by tools such as Archistar to assess workload demands and recommend configurations that optimize scalability and performance. This guarantees that efficiency and fault tolerance are incorporated into the design of systems.

3. Help with Code Generation and Development

AI-powered tools that generate boilerplate code, automate repetitive operations, and provide intelligent suggestions are revolutionizing coding. For example, GitHub Copilot and Tabnine use big language models to provide real-time code completions based on the codebase context. These techniques improve code quality and consistency while reducing development time, particularly in distributed, collaborative development contexts.

4. Continuous Integration/Continuous Deployment (CI/CD) and Automated Testing

AI is essential for streamlining CI/CD pipelines and automating testing frameworks. Tools such as Test.ai perform regression testing, dynamic test case generation, and predictive analytics. Furthermore, AI-driven CI/CD solutions like Harness automate build and deployment procedures, guaranteeing dependable and smooth updates in cloud-native systems. Machine learning-driven intelligent rollback techniques significantly reduce the risks connected to unsuccessful deployments.

5. Monitoring and Identifying Anomalies After Deployment

Post-deployment performance monitoring is essential for cloud-native apps to function effectively under a range of workloads. AI-powered solutions like Splunk and Dynatrace track important performance indicators in real time, identifying irregularities and system deterioration before they become serious problems. These technologies, which are essential in distributed architectures, make high system availability and preventive maintenance possible.

6. Cost control and resource optimization

Resource management is a major issue in cloud-native setups because of remote infrastructure and varying workloads. AI-powered solutions that examine consumption trends and dynamically distribute resources to meet demand include Spot.io and AWS Auto Scaling. These improvements lower operating costs without sacrificing functionality by ensuring that resources are neither over-provisioned nor underutilized.

7. Improved Cooperation in Dispersed Groups

AI solutions improve cooperation by offering uniformity across geographically dispersed teams, real-time documentation updates, and contextual coding support. For instance, even among development teams that are geographically spread out, Tabnine facilitates team-specific model training to guarantee consistent coding techniques, promoting cooperation.

8. System Reliability and Predictive Maintenance

By predicting probable problems and suggesting preventive actions, AI's predictive analytics capabilities guarantee system reliability. Machine learning algorithms, like those employed in IBM Predictive Maintenance, examine past data to find trends that foreshadow problems. With these insights, teams can resolve issues before they affect system performance.

9. Kubernetes-Based Systems with Intelligent Orchestration

AI improves container orchestration in Kubernetes-driven settings by maximizing workload distribution, scaling, and pod scheduling. AI extensions like KubeFlow automate resource allocation and scaling choices, guaranteeing effective operation despite fluctuating loading conditions.

10. Constant Evaluation and Enhancement

Artificial intelligence (AI) solutions enable ongoing feedback loops by examining user behaviour, application performance, and system logs to recommend enhancements. Thanks to these insights, cloud-native apps adapt to user and market demands and drive iterative changes.

The design, development, and maintenance of software are changing due to the use of AI-powered tools in cloud-native software development. These technologies enable development teams to build scalable, effective, and resilient systems that satisfy the requirements of contemporary cloud-native architectures by automating challenging activities, streamlining workflows, and improving collaboration. The incorporation of AI technologies within the SDLC will spur software engineering innovation and excellence as these technologies continue to advance.

3.3 Challenges and Solutions in Integrating AI-Powered Tools for Cloud-Native Software Development

Although incorporating AI-powered tools into cloud-native software development has many advantages, there are also drawbacks. The five main problems and their fixes are listed below.

Challenge 1: Security and Privacy of Data: Large datasets containing sensitive data, such as user or secret company information, are necessary for AI technologies to be trained and function. Multi-tenant designs are frequently used in cloud-native systems, which raises the possibility of data breaches and illegal access.

Solution: Put strong data privacy safeguards, like encryption, data anonymization, and differential privacy. AI models can be trained on distributed data without disclosing private information thanks to strategies like federated learning. Furthermore, security is integrated throughout the lifecycle using safe software development techniques, including those described by the DevSecOps framework.

Challenge 2: Trust and Interpretability of the Model: AI-driven suggestions or actions can occasionally seem like "black-box" choices, which makes it challenging for stakeholders and developers to comprehend or have faith in them. Adoption may need to be improved by interpretability issues, particularly in crucial jobs like anomaly detection or code generation.

Solution: To increase the interpretability and transparency of AI models, apply Explainable AI (XAI) strategies. Teams can validate and trust the outcomes using tools like SHAP (Shapley Additive exPlanations) and LIME, which offer insights into how models make decisions.

Challenge 3: integrating with current workflows: Integrating AI-powered tools into current software development processes can be disruptive. Legacy systems, long-standing procedures, and team resistance to change may need to be improved or make adoption more difficult.

Solution: Use a staged integration strategy, beginning with pilot projects to show the usefulness of the technologies. Use plugins and APIs to guarantee compatibility with current system. Upfill teams by offering resources and training to fill knowledge gaps and boost confidence while utilizing AI tools.

Challenge 4: Exorbitant computational expenses: The training and operation of AI models frequently necessitate significant computational resources, which might raise infrastructure costs in cloud-native environments. This is especially troublesome for businesses with tight budgets.

Solution: To cut expenses, use cloud-native optimization strategies like serverless computing and GPU acceleration. Furthermore, resource demands might be reduced by customizing pre-trained models for specific activities. Using Kubernetes-based AI extensions to auto-scale AI workloads guarantees dynamic resource allocation, which minimizes waste.

Challenge 5: Ethical Issues and Bias: AI technologies may inherit biases from training datasets, resulting in unfair or less-than-ideal outcomes. This is a serious problem, particularly when AI affects resource allocation or code quality.

Solution: When developing models, use frameworks for bias identification and mitigation. Conduct routine audits of AI technologies to detect and resolve bias in judgment. To ensure AI tools align with company values and industry standards, promote diversity in training datasets and define ethical standards.

Organizations can fully utilize AI-powered tools in cloud-native software development by tackling these issues with focused solutions. Teams can create reliable, scalable, and creative software systems if proactive approaches that prioritize security, transparency, integration, cost-effectiveness, and ethical use are implemented.

3.4 Result and Discussion

Significant advancements have been made across the Software Development Lifecycle (SDLC) due to the incorporation of AI-powered tools in cloud-native software development. These tools have increased efficiency by automating repetitive operations and facilitating quicker development cycles. AI, for example, reduces ambiguity during requirements analysis by gleaning actionable insights from enormous datasets, guaranteeing that user needs are appropriately represented throughout development. Similarly, developers may now devote more of their time to higher-value jobs involving creativity and problem-solving skills because intelligent code creation has cut down on the time needed for coding.

Among the most noteworthy results is the improvement of resource management and scalability. Because of their dispersed designs and varying workloads, cloud-native environments are dynamic. With machine learning algorithms that forecast resource demands and dynamically allocate resources, artificial intelligence has proven crucial in this situation. This capacity has demonstrated the benefits of efficiency and cost-effectiveness by allowing enterprises to retain performance while lowering operating costs.

The predictive power of AI has dramatically increased system dependability. Overall, system stability has increased due to the ability to identify possible abnormalities and anticipate breakdowns before they happen. By minimizing downtime, proactive error detection and maintenance enable teams to resolve problems before they become serious ones. This has resulted in fewer unplanned operational disruptions and a smoother user experience.

Significant progress has also been made in distributed teams' consistency and collaboration. Artificial intelligence (AI) tools have promoted a unified development process among geographically separated teams by guaranteeing adherence to coding standards and automating documentation changes. This has improved the quality of the software created by lowering integration conflicts and encouraging a more efficient workflow.

Optimizing Continuous Integration and Continuous Deployment (CI/CD) pipelines have further transformed the deployment process. AI-powered solutions that automate builds, intelligently handle rollback methods, and continuously monitor systems have made it possible to deploy more quickly and reliably. In addition to speeding up deployment cycles, this has reduced the possibility of system failures during updates.

However, integrating AI-powered tools has its challenges. Because AI systems need access to enormous datasets frequently containing sensitive information, data privacy concerns remain a significant obstacle. Integration issues always exist, especially for businesses moving away from antiquated systems. Another challenge is the computational expenses of developing and implementing AI models, particularly for smaller businesses with tighter budgets. Despite these obstacles, companies implementing AI-powered solutions have shown that proactive approaches, such as resource management, improved data protection, and phased integration, can reduce these restrictions.

It is evident how AI is revolutionizing cloud-native software development. It tackles the inherent complexity of distributed, microservices-based systems and improves quality and productivity. These tools are transforming traditional development methods and establishing new creativity, scalability, and efficiency standards. However, human skills are necessary for these technologies to succeed. Developers and engineers must adjust to supervise AI systems, verify their results, and strategically use the insights they offer. Through this partnership, AI will continue to be a potent enhancer of human creativity, propelling software engineering forward without replacing the vital human component.

Thanks to AI-powered technologies, cloud-native software development and management have undergone a paradigm change. Organizations can get a competitive edge by tackling obstacles and utilizing these technologies to their fullest potential. This will enable them to provide innovative, scalable, and resilient software solutions that meet the changing needs of contemporary technological environments.

CONCLUSION

A revolutionary development in contemporary software engineering techniques is using AI-powered tools in cloud-native software development. AI has improved each step of the software development lifecycle (SDLC), giving cloud-native environments previously unheard-of efficiency, scalability, and dependability. By tackling the particular difficulties presented by distributed architectures, dynamic workloads, and the demand for constant innovation, these technologies have transformed procedures, including requirements analysis, design, code generation, testing, deployment, and post-deployment monitoring. AI has proven to improve software system quality, decrease manual labor, and streamline operations. AI-powered solutions have sped up development processes and guaranteed the resilience and affordability of cloud-native systems through intelligent automation, predictive capabilities, and real-time decision-making. These technologies have changed the standards for dependability and performance, allowing businesses to provide software solutions that precisely and nimbly satisfy changing customer needs.

AI integration has its challenges, however. To guarantee these tools' responsible and efficient use, concerns including data privacy, computing costs, model interpretability, and ethical considerations must be addressed. Strategic approaches, such as solid security measures, explainable AI methodologies, and ongoing skill development within development teams, are necessary to overcome these obstacles. The mutually beneficial link between AI and human expertise is the key to the future of cloud-native software development. While AI-powered solutions streamline and automate essential processes, human oversight is still necessary for innovation, validation, and strategic decision-making. This human-AI collaboration will fuel the next wave of software engineering developments, opening the door to systems that are not only more scalable and efficient but also more in line with operational and ethical best practices.

To sum up, cloud-native software development is changing due to AI-powered tools, which allow businesses to reach new levels of productivity, quality, and flexibility. The future of software system design, development, and maintenance in a technologically sophisticated and ever-changing world will be determined by the indispensability of these technologies' integration into software engineering workflows.

FUTURE WORKS

Cloud-native software development's use of AI-powered tools is still in its infancy, providing room for future study and growth. In order to overcome present constraints and broaden the range of their applications, several crucial areas for further research and development are emerging as these technologies develop.

One encouraging avenue is the creation of AI systems that are easier to understand. Although AI technologies have proven remarkably effective in automating and optimizing several software developments processes, their decision-making procedures are frequently opaque. Future research should improve explainability and transparency to increase confidence and dependability in AI suggestions, especially for crucial activities like resource optimization, anomaly detection, and code generation.

Data security and privacy in AI-driven systems are other vital topics for development. Large datasets are necessary for AI systems to train and function appropriately; therefore, protecting their security and privacy is crucial. Advanced privacy-preserving methods like homomorphic encryption and federated learning should be investigated in future research to allow AI training on dispersed datasets without jeopardizing private data. These developments will be especially helpful in hybrid and multi-tenant cloud systems.

Another promising area for research is the scalability of AI models employed in cloud-native applications. The significant processing resources needed by many AI tools available today can be prohibitively expensive for smaller businesses. The development of AI models that are lightweight, resource-efficient, and maintain high performance will make wider adoption of these technologies possible. Furthermore, developments in edge AI for containerized systems may improve real-time decision-making skills and optimize resource usage.

Another crucial topic for further research is incorporating AI into DevOps procedures. Although AI has demonstrated promise in streamlining CI/CD pipelines, its uses might be expanded to include infrastructure as code, incident management, and security automation, among other DevOps procedures. Future studies might examine how AI can improve cooperation between security, operations, and development teams, resulting in more unified and effective processes.

Cloud-native software engineering has enormous promise thanks to new developments like generative AI. Generative models can create test cases for complicated systems, mimic system behaviors in different contexts, and develop new architectures. Research on the responsible and efficient use of generative AI in software development is anticipated to produce revolutionary outcomes.

To sum up, the future of AI-powered tools in cloud-native software development is about increasing their integration into broader workflows, optimizing resource efficiency, boosting transparency, and improving data privacy. AI's position in software engineering will continue to develop as these topics are investigated, spurring innovation and empowering businesses to create increasingly more reliable, scalable, and effective systems. In addition to overcoming current obstacles, upcoming projects in these fields will expand the potential of cloud-native software development in a rapidly evolving technical environment.

REFERENCES

Ajiga, D., Okeleke, P. A., Folorunsho, S. O., & Ezeigweneme, C. (2024). Enhancing software development practices with AI insights in high-tech companies. IEEE Software Engineering Institute, Technical Report TR-2024-003.

Al-Asili, A. (2024). The Impact of AI on Unit Testing within CICD Processes for Software Development.

Ali, O. (2024). Popular API Technologies: REST, GraphQL, and gRPC.

Anwar, R., & Bashir, M. B. (2023). A Systematic Literature Review of AI-based Software Requirements Prioritization Technique. *IEEE Access : Practical Innovations, Open Solutions*, 11, 143815–143860. DOI: 10.1109/ACCESS.2023.3343252

Arundel, J., & Domingus, J. (2019). *Cloud Native DevOps with Kubernetes: building, deploying, and scaling modern applications in the Cloud.* O'Reilly Media.

Balalaie, A., Heydarnoori, A., & Jamshidi, P. (2016). Microservices architecture enables devops: Migration to a cloud-native architecture. *IEEE Software*, 33(3), 42–52. DOI: 10.1109/MS.2016.64

Baqar, M., & Khanda, R. (2024). The Future of Software Testing: AI-Powered Test Case Generation and Validation. arXiv preprint arXiv:2409.05808.

Cheng, Q., Sahoo, D., Saha, A., Yang, W., Liu, C., Woo, G., . . . Hoi, S. C. (2023). Ai for it operations (aiops) on cloud platforms: Reviews, opportunities and challenges. arXiv preprint arXiv:2304.04661.

Chittala, S. (2024). ORCHESTRATING THE CLOUD: AI-ENHANCED RELEASE AUTOMATION IN KUBERNETES ENVIRONMENTS. [IJRCAIT]. *INTERNATIONAL JOURNAL OF RESEARCH IN COMPUTER APPLICATIONS AND INFORMATION TECHNOLOGY*, 7(2), 864–878.

D'Onofrio, D. S., Fusco, M. L., & Zhong, H. (2023). *CI/CD Pipeline and DevSecOps Integration for Security and Load Testing (No. SAND-2023-08255). Sandia National Lab*. SNL-NM.

Davis, C. (2019). *Cloud Native Patterns: Designing Change-Tolerant Software.* Simon and Schuster.

Dehaerne, E., Dey, B., Halder, S., De Gendt, S., & Meert, W. (2022). Code generation using machine learning: A systematic review. *IEEE Access : Practical Innovations, Open Solutions*, 10, 82434–82455. DOI: 10.1109/ACCESS.2022.3196347

Deng, S., Zhao, H., Huang, B., Zhang, C., Chen, F., Deng, Y., & Zomaya, A. Y. (2024). Cloud-native computing: A survey from the perspective of services. *Proceedings of the IEEE*, 112(1), 12–46.

Dong, H., Zhang, C., Li, G., & Zhang, H. (2024). Cloud-Native Databases: A Survey. *IEEE Transactions on Knowledge and Data Engineering*, 36(12), 7772–7791. DOI: 10.1109/TKDE.2024.3397508

Duan, Y., Edwards, J. S., & Dwivedi, Y. K. (2019). Artificial intelligence for decision making in the era of Big Data–evolution, challenges and research agenda. *International Journal of Information Management*, 48, 63–71. DOI: 10.1016/j.ijinfomgt.2019.01.021

. Galla, E.P., et al., *AI-DRIVEN DATA ENGINEERING TRANSFORMING BIG DATA INTO ACTIONABLE INSIGHT*. JEC PUBLICATION.

Garousi, V., Joy, N., & Keleş, A. B. (2024). AI-powered test automation tools: A systematic review and empirical evaluation. arXiv preprint arXiv:2409.00411.

Ghorbani, M. A. (2023). AI tools to support design activities and innovation processes.

Jones, R. (2024). The Impact of AI on Secure Cloud Computing: Opportunities and Challenges. *The Indonesian Journal of Computer Science*, 13(4). Advance online publication. DOI: 10.33022/ijcs.v13i4.4383

. Jonnala, A., *Transformative Effects of Artificial Intelligence on Cloud Computing*.

Juan, J., & Mason, B. (2019). Implementing Quality Assurance in Cloud-Native Applications: Challenges, Strategies, and Best Practices. *International Journal of Advanced Engineering Technologies and Innovations*, 1(4), 283–293.

Kosińska, J., Baliś, B., Konieczny, M., Malawski, M., & Zieliński, S. (2023). Toward the observability of cloud-native applications: The overview of the state-of-the-art. *IEEE Access : Practical Innovations, Open Solutions*, 11, 73036–73052. DOI: 10.1109/ACCESS.2023.3281860

Laszewski, T.. (2018). *Cloud Native Architectures: Design high-availability and cost-effective applications for the cloud*. Packt Publishing Ltd.

Mihaljević, B., Radovan, A., & Žagar, M. (2024). An analysis of generative artificial intelligence tools usage to adapt and enrich software development courses. In International Conference on Education and New Developments 2024 (pp. 553-557).

Miller, K., & Mun, J. (2023, July). Cyber technologies, machine learning, additive manufacturing, and cloud in the box to enable optimized maintenance processes in extreme conditions. In International Conference on Human-Computer Interaction (pp. 672-684). Cham: Springer Nature Switzerland.

Mitchell, B. S. (2023). Cloud Native Software Engineering. arXiv preprint arXiv:2307.01045.

Nassar, A., & Kamal, M. (2021). Ethical dilemmas in AI-powered decision-making: A deep dive into big data-driven ethical considerations. *International Journal of Responsible Artificial Intelligence*, 11(8), 1–11.

Nguyen-Duc, A., Cabrero-Daniel, B., Przybylek, A., Arora, C., Khanna, D., Herda, T., . . . Abrahamsson, P. (2023). Generative Artificial Intelligence for Software Engineering—A Research Agenda. arXiv preprint arXiv:2310.18648.

Pandi, S. B. (2023). Artificial intelligence in software and service lifecycle.

Pinciroli, R., Ali, A., Yan, F., & Smirni, E. (2020). Cedule+: Resource management for burstable cloud instances using predictive analytics. *IEEE Transactions on Network and Service Management*, 18(1), 945–957. DOI: 10.1109/TNSM.2020.3039942

Polese, M.. (2023). Empowering the 6G cellular architecture with Open RAN. *IEEE Journal on Selected Areas in Communications.*

Prangon, N. F., & Wu, J. (2024). AI and Computing Horizons: Cloud and Edge in the Modern Era. *Journal of Sensor and Actuator Networks*, 13(4), 44. DOI: 10.3390/jsan13040044

Rane, J.. (2024). *Influence of digitalization on business and management: A review on artificial intelligence, blockchain, big data analytics, cloud computing, and internet of things.* Generative Artificial Intelligence in Agriculture, Education, and Business.

Scriven, A., Kedziora, D. J., Musial, K., & Gabrys, B. (2023). The technological emergence of automl: A survey of performant software and applications in the context of industry. Foundations and Trends® in Information Systems, 7(1-2), 1-252.

Seo, C., Yoo, D., & Lee, Y. (2024). Empowering Sustainable Industrial and Service Systems through AI-Enhanced Cloud Resource Optimization. *Sustainability (Basel)*, 16(12), 5095. DOI: 10.3390/su16125095

Seth, D., Nerella, H., Najana, M., & Tabbassum, A. (2024). Navigating the Multi-cloud Maze: benefits, challenges, and Future trends. International Journal of Global Innovations and Solutions (IJGIS).

Singh, J., Goyal, S. B., Kaushal, R. K., Kumar, N., & Sehra, S. S. (2024). *Applied Data Science and Smart Systems*. Taylor & Francis Group.

Stahmann, P. (2024). AI-based Real-time Anomaly Detection in Digitized Production: Characterization and Socio-technical Facilitation of Decision-making (Doctoral dissertation, Universität Osnabrück).

Svyatkovskiy, A., Deng, S. K., Fu, S., & Sundaresan, N. (2020, November). Intellicode compose: Code generation using transformer. In *Proceedings of the 28th ACM joint meeting on European software engineering conference and symposium on the foundations of software engineering* (pp. 1433-1443).

Theodoropoulos, T., Rosa, L., Benzaid, C., Gray, P., Marin, E., Makris, A., Cordeiro, L., Diego, F., Sorokin, P., Girolamo, M. D., Barone, P., Taleb, T., & Tserpes, K. (2023). Security in Cloud-Native Services: A Survey. *Journal of Cybersecurity and Privacy*, 3(4), 758–793. DOI: 10.3390/jcp3040034

Tirupati, K. K.. (2024). Improving Database Performance with SQL Server Optimization Techniques. *Modern Dynamics: Mathematical Progressions*, 1(2), 450–494.

Tufano, M., Agarwal, A., Jang, J., Moghaddam, R. Z., & Sundaresan, N. (2024). AutoDev: Automated AI-driven development. arXiv preprint arXiv:2403.08299.

Vemulapalli, G. (2024). *Cloud Data Stack Scalability: A Case Study on Migrating from Legacy Systems*. International Journal of Sustainable Development Through AI. *ML and IoT*, 3(1), 1–15.

Wang, S., Huang, L., Gao, A., Ge, J., Zhang, T., Feng, H., Satyarth, I., Li, M., Zhang, H., & Ng, V. (2022). Machine/deep learning for software engineering: A systematic literature review. *IEEE Transactions on Software Engineering*, 49(3), 1188–1231. DOI: 10.1109/TSE.2022.3173346

Zhao, L., Alhoshan, W., Ferrari, A., Letsholo, K. J., Ajagbe, M. A., Chioasca, E.-V., & Batista-Navarro, R. T. (2021). Natural language processing for requirements engineering: A systematic mapping study. *ACM Computing Surveys*, 54(3), 1–41. DOI: 10.1145/3444689

Zhu, S., Yu, T., Xu, T., Chen, H., Dustdar, S., Gigan, S., ... & Pan, Y. (2023). Intelligent computing: the latest advances, challenges, and future. Intelligent Computing, 2, 0006.

Zulkifli, N. I. (2024). Optimizing Data Flow and Integration for High-Performance Analytics: A Security-Centric Architecture Framework to Improve Efficiency and Decision-Making Across Domains. *Advances in Intelligent Information Systems*, 9(10), 17–32.

Chapter 7
Enhancing Lifecycle Stages and Navigating Implementation Hurdles for AI-Powered Tools and Challenges in Cloud-Native Software Development

C. G. Balaji
https://orcid.org/0000-0001-8870-1634
Symbiosis International University, India

Sivaram Ponnusamy
https://orcid.org/0000-0001-5746-0268
Sandip University, Nashik, India

S. Menaka
https://orcid.org/0000-0003-0092-9189
SRM Institute of Science and Technology, India

G. Rajeswari
https://orcid.org/0000-0002-4946-2340
Sathyabama Institute of Science and Technology, India

Harsh Jain
https://orcid.org/0009-0004-5752-3029

DOI: 10.4018/979-8-3693-9356-7.ch007

SRM Institute of Science and Technology, India

ABSTRACT

This chapter examines the transformative impact of artificial intelligence (AI) on software development within a cloud-native context. As the adoption of AI tools has intensified, their integration throughout the Software Development Lifecycle (SDLC) offers both opportunities and challenges. It explores the benefits of AI in areas like requirement analysis, design, implementation, testing, and maintenance, each experiencing advancements in efficiency, accuracy, and scalability. AI aids in automating processes, predicting system issues, optimizing resource use, and enhancing software quality, bringing substantial changes to conventional methods. It emphasizes the specific challenges posed by AI adoption, such as data quality, skill gaps, integration complexity, ethical considerations, and technical scalability. Key sections address the research questions and methodological approaches to understanding the integration barriers. The findings underscore AI's potential to enhance the SDLC but highlight the need for robust strategies.

1. INTRODUCTION

As the pace of software creation rises day by day, a new term that has gained the most significance is AI – a term that has entirely changed the concept and the way things can be done. Over the past decade, there has been a growing trend towards incorporating AI-powered tools in different stages of the software development life-cycle in the detection of the need to maximize productivity, the quality of the code produced as well as the speed in which the software is offered in the ever competitive market. This paradigm shift is particularly important in the field of cloud-native software engineering where the integration of AI with cloud technology is contributing to new dimensions of innovation and productivity.

The prospects of these technologies and AI in particular in the field of software development have been influencing the industry over the years. Starting with the most institutionalized AI related tasks, such as expert systems or automated testing; the term has increased to cover even more high level domains such as machine learning, natural language processing, deep learning etc. Those sophisticated AI tools are being increasingly used throughout the whole software development life cycle (SDLC) process, starting from the requirement analysis phase up to the maintenance and evolution phase. With complexity comes sophistication and of course with that comes the use of AI to ease management of such complexities, increase productivity of developers and increase creativity in ways that have not been seen or envisioned before.

This chapter sheds light on the trends around which the liberalization of AI tools within software development revolves. Incorporating AI-assisted solutions in software engineering is not just a fashionable wave which will come and go but rather an inevitable measure in the environment of difficult task hurdles. In contemporary software projects, the volumes of code, the complexity of dependencies, and the speed of iteration all reach their limits. Such practices of application development quite often are unable to meet these requirements leading to inefficient processes, poor quality, and loss of valuable time. With AI-powered solutions, there is a better alternative, where developers are provided with semi-autonomous agents equipped to help in simple job execution, forecasting emerging issues, and even writing code among other tasks. This shift towards AI-assisted development, in perspective hopes bring not just in terms of enhanced business metrics but also augmentation of associated software quality.

In recent developments, the significance of AI can even be pronounced more in the light of cloud-native software engineering. It is a well-recognized fact that cloud-based applications are built and developed to harness the better affordance of cloud resources fully, such offerings have inherent advantages and disadvantages. These types of application programs which are usually developed based on microservice architectures and containerized components also require different methods of development, usage, maintenance, and other aspects. With the use of AI to optimize performance and resource usage for example in solving these problems automating such as resource optimization, scaling, and monitoring of anomalies is essential.

AI is pervasive in the different facets of cloud-native software engineering activities and development methodologies as follows:

1. **Scalability and Resource Management**: AI core tools foresee the resource requesting actions which will lead to requests for an increase in the use of resources enabling measuring and managing efficiently the capacity utilized.
2. **Resilience and Self-Healing**: Para-major thrusts, there protect the performance degradation in applications by making sure that systems with AI features can locate errors and initiate solutions automatically.
3. **Performance Optimization**: AI captures the application of an application, calculates its efficiency, highlights the economic consequences, reveals the 'narrow chokes,' and provides possible ways on how to go around them.
4. **Security and Compliance**: AI allows one to harness efficiently these tools in examining threats and monitoring for compliance.

5. **DevOps and CI/CD**: AI enables the effective execution of testing, deploying, and monitoring activities necessary in the development stage of the project cycle.
6. **Code Quality and Maintenance**: One of the applications of artificial intelligence is the use of various combinations of generated code concerning its quality and its complexity analysis.
7. **Usability Enhancement**: AI is being used to make management decisions based on the evaluation of end user activity and the desired changes in the software interface.

Thus, these AI applications have helped to improve the design and robustness of cloud-native software systems in a way that they meet the demands raised by the nature of cloud computing.

This chapter tackles the main dilemma of how cloud-native software development can be enhanced through the help AI tools even as it pinpoints the main barriers organizations want to embrace these tools. To delve into the problem, we address ourselves four main research questions:

1. We report on the existing AI tools used in each phase of the cloud software development lifecycle and focus on how they improve each process, from requirement and design through implementation and maintenance.
2. From the practical adoption of AI to enhance cloud software engineering, we identify and appraise the key technical, ethical, and managerial hurdles, noting that there is more to deployment than technology itself.
3. We suggest how organizations can do these things and embed AI in their cloud development processes, using case studies and best practice as evidence.
4. In the last section, we address the potential changes and areas of further investigations in AI applied in Cloud Software Engineering, how the organizations will be able to cope with these changes.

By these questions, we wish to contribute to a correlational understanding of AI technologies particularly cloud-native software development, their drawbacks, and their benefits to achievement of the set goals. In order to meet the given research questions and to exhaustively examine AI in the realm of Cloud software engineering, this chapter is structured with the following objectives:

1. To highlight the major kinds of AI-enhancing tools along the different phases of the development of the cloud-native software.
2. To explain the processes that these tools have improved in the development and evaluate their effectiveness.

3. In this cloud-native software engineering project, we intend to identify and discuss the main barriers that make it difficult to use AI in software development.
4. Further, the purpose of these documents is to give advice and make suggestions for the organizations that want to incorporate the instruments of AI into the software creation processes.
5. Inquiring into the future implications and future research opportunities in this progress driven area.

The organization of this chapter aims to investigate the contributions of AI in cloud-native software engineering in five main sections, Introduction, Related Works, Methodology, Results and Discussion and Conclusion. This chapter makes it possible for the orderly treatment of the issue ensuring that readers acquire theoretical and even practical approaches in relation to the application of AI in cloud-native software engineering. In view of the rapid changes taking place in this field, it is advisable that the readers should consider this chapter as a baseline to further learning.

2. RELATED WORKS

This section presents important research activities related to AI-integrated software engineering, cloud-native development, and the integration of both. We assess the landmark works, the state of the literature, and the problems highlighted by the researchers in this fast developing area.

In the past decade, there has been considerable growing participant interest and research in the use of artificial intelligence in software engineering. Different scholars have been experimenting with different aspects of the 'how' question as far as AI can be applied to facilitate and automate phases of software development processes. Due to AI, software engineering is changing with some tasks being removed from people and managed directly with large amounts of data through the evaluation of data using neural networks. In a systematic review by (Barenkamp et al., 2020), different AI technologies employed within Software engineering are enumerated with coverage for even requirements engineering system, design, coding, testing, and maintenance. In software engineering, AI can shorten the time frames of development cycles, cut development costs, and enhance the creative abilities of software developers through the use of tools that seek to alleviate the mundane tasks of routine work and the analysis of large volumes of data. The work by (Amalfitano et al., 2023) provides a positive reason for curiosity as they carried out a tertiary study of the impact of AI in software testing (ST). They utilized 20 secondary studies incorporating the use of artificial intelligence and its transformation along with the software testing tools to obtain relationship diagrams with intersections. The study sought to investigate prevailing practices regarding the use of AI SU and changes that can be expected. Their results tell us more about the area of AI-supported ST as an emerging in-between field and would be certainly relevant in coming years for researchers and practitioners.

DL technologies have also been examined in the context of software process engineering by (Alshammari, 2022), who looked specifically into a recommendation approach for software process models. The work pointed out the increased use of ML in several tasks within the software development lifecycle, such as coding, testing, and deployment. Based on LSTM, the author offered a recommendation model for interaction history, which was remarkably accurate, efficient, and diverse. In this line of research, feedback from the user is regarded as a window for increasing the effectiveness of software enhancements. As (Devalla & Yogix, 2023) notes, a particular focus is placed on the improvement of the quality of the developed software and the transition to new processes of its development due to the application of AI technologies. It is evidenced by the utilization of AI in requirements elicitation, and coding with the use of automation and testing, where ML, NLP, and DL help minimize risks of errors and time wastage. The authors clarify the role of AI not only in real-time analysis but also in the provision of monitoring, addressing issues such as bias and interpretability. Finally, as (Ali, 2023) notes, the development, deployment, and usage of AI systems bear considerable consequences on the software engineering profession. The investigation probably focuses on the influence of the usage of AI technologies on the processes undertaken during software development, such as the use of automated coding, intelligent testing, and predictive maintenance among others. Although precise examples are not given, the paper likely identifies the advantages, obstacles, and prospects for expansion regarding how AI can evolve the major processes of software engineering.

Software engineering practices have significantly improved with new changes that are specifically attributed to AI. (Asaad & Avksentieva, 2023) researches a broad range of applications of ML in software engineering and points to the fields that are actively in the process of AI implementation. One such area is the automated generation of test cases and localized bugs. (Bajaj & Samal, 2023) also, show how the processes of quality assurance in software can be fast-tracked using generative AI. Where requirements engineering is concerned, the authors (Dai et al., 2023) suggest traceability through neural networks between software requirements and source code for software development lifecycle efficiency. (Iyenghar et al., 2022) examine AI-based model-driven development of embedded software which enhances practice of AI in any special area by the AI for design and development will be thoroughly exercised. Another emerging trend is the use of large language models (LLMs) in software engineering tools. (Cheng et al., 2023) describe Prompt Sapper, this assists with making AI chains however this can also be used to build more advanced software development processes that employs high level NLP. These studies clearly indicate the imminent evolution of practice in software engineering brought about by AI from requirements stage, generation of source code, carrying out tests, and maintenance.

Microservice architectures are refined with respect to cloud-native applications, as these-giving optimal performance without compromising time to market or reliability. With increased software development requirements comes the increasing use of these applications which have numerous advantages in terms of Scalability, Flexibility and Resilience (Kratzke, 2022). Microservices with event-driven design have in particular registered favourable results in scalability benchmarks showing that they can process heterogeneous loads effectively (Henning, 2023). As these cloud-native ideas mature, there has been an interest in promoting such ideas in the edge computing environments as well. Fog-native architecture is a novel architecture that seeks to combine cloud and edge computing by utilising intents based workflow (Sebrechts et al., 2022). This advancement of cloud-native characteristics to the edge addresses minute factors that disturb such a system in distribution such as latency, bandwidth, and data confidentiality. Domain driven design (DDD) has increasingly become an effective approach for the architecture of the cloud-native services, as such embracing the complexities of domains while matching technological domain to the organizational strategies (Jordanov & Petrov, 2023). By removing silos regarding the problem domain amongst the members of the stakeholders, DDD enables more maintainable and adaptable cloud-native applications to be built. All of these progress in the technologies contribute to the further culturing of the cloud-natives making it possible for the institutions to create even more powerful, redundant and efficient distributed computing systems both in the cloud and at the edge of the cloud.

The emergence of new directions from AI, such as automatization of developing software and learning languages with the help of AI tools, has been attracting a considerable amount of attention. (Bird et al., 2022) suggest GitHub Copilot, an AI-assisted code completion extension, as means for freeing the developer's creativity. In the same vein, (Pashchenko, 2023) digs into the early stage of employing AI tools for programming in the EU and underlines the relevance of these technologies for the market. Within the realm of technology enhanced language learning, (Vall & Araya, 2023) also advocate for the use of AI technologies but explore their downsides. Though this one is in the application context quite different from the development of software, it still pursues the same goal of using artificial intelligence to enhance the human working capacity in handling intricate tasks that require a lot of thinking process. (Perry et al., 2022) proposed such an issue as threats coming from using artificial intelligence in programming, in particular the coding. Their findings indicated that code written with the help of AI assistants was less secure than in other cases, pointing toward one of the weaknesses of these instruments.

The adoption of AI into software engineering as well as the decision making processes has both pros and cons. (Srihith et al., 2022) summarize their analysis by contemplating the new challenges brought up by the intersection of AI and software engineering, and how they could existentially problematic. Similarly, (Yahav, 2023) shares on the awareness of practical issues faced while developing targeted project outcomes and using AI in software production. (Steyvers & Kumar, 2023) narrow their scope on decision making with the assistance of AI and point to three dilemmas like human-alliance, elimination of biases and mistakes embedded in AI systems, Human control over personalized AI processes. (Lu et al, 2022), worried by the social implications of AI suggest a stepwise strategy for the incorporation of ethical AI in software engineering without ignoring other wider problem of the ai impact on humanity. Such a statement is, in general, shared by other authors, but here its emphasis in this publication is placed on ethical issues.

As AI technology is implemented in more and more areas, there are all sorts of prospects and problems. (Hasterok & Stompe, 2022) apply the PAISE® process model to AI systems engineering. Citing (Burnaev et al., 2023) provide plenty of insights into how practical AI can be used in solving Environmental, Social and Governance (ESG) problems. Demonstrating AI capabilities in Sustainable development efforts. (Mukhamediev et al, 2022) They also review AI and ML technologies of a wide spectrum in terms of the classification and the restrictions, as well as the prospects. All these studies show that, in different areas of the economy there is a wider application of artificial intelligence and the fact that technologies and management are used in its development and implementation across the different areas of governance.

The authors discussed in this section were able to not only understand AI's development potential but how it stands to change the dynamics of software engineering practices in relation to developed literature. It is, however, sad that other than development and implementation of AI frameworks in software engineering, integration and ethics, and skill development are still a challenge leaving up to the future research context.

3. METHODOLOGY

The purpose of this chapter is to justify the framework that was adopted for the examining of how AI-based tools are employed in cloud-based software development and the barriers experienced in using these tools. We have specifically chosen research design, methods of data collection, analysis approaches, and criteria for evaluation to have a proper and deep examination of these issues.

3.1 Research Design

In this section, we cover the research design in detail, employing mixed-method research where, in order to give a well-rounded comprehension of AI in cloud-native software engineering, the qualitative and quantitative techniques are fused. Such a way allows conducting auxiliary and central investigations along with those which are interior and vertical.

The research is structured in three main phases:

1. **Exploratory Phase**: At this early stage of the research, a wide literature review and an industry awareness scan focusing on identifying the latest trends, tools, and challenges in the area of AI cloud-native software development are carried out.
2. **Analytical Phase**: At this phase, there are studies carried out on chosen AI tools taken through the lifecycle of software development. This involves technical studies or evaluations and also case study approaches.
3. **Evaluative Phase**: In this last stage, there is an attempt to understand the barriers to the use of AI solutions in cloud-native systems and an attempt to design an evaluation framework for the AI tools.

Such a phase research design enables sufficient concentration in addressing the problem from the overall industry perspective to detailed tool assessment as well as real adoption issues.

3.2 Data Collection Methods

In order to ensure that a variety of sources are incorporated in the data, we adopted more than one data collection method like Literature review, Survey, Case Studies, Tools Analysis and GitHub Repository Analysis. Data accumulation and perfecting a dataset that is timely was performed. All data collection procedures adhered to ethical guidelines concerning research undertaking including voluntary participation, confidentiality, and encryption of all stored data.

3.3 Evaluation of AI Tools across Software Development Life Cycles

In the light of the rationale and scope of AI tools under review, the examination process itself was clearly arranged along the major steps taken during the cloud-native software development process. In all the above stages, we provided the appropriate AI tools and technologies, analyzed how they worked, and assessed the value of these tools to the development processes. The aspect of Design and Architecture was dealt with next, where we looked into the system design and architectural decision-making processes aided by the use of AI-assisted tools in this area. These tools alter the views of system architects drawing on comprehensive archives of best structural strategies for every conceivable problem. Also, the aspect of API design and microservices decomposition was considered of great importance as these systems assist the developers in transforming monolithic applications into smaller ones that are more easily deployed and integrated into different systems. In the course of the Implementation and Coding phase, the attention was shifted to software applications that utilize AI to assist programmers in the processes of writing and generation of code. The examination of the evolution of software quality was optimized and our finding emphasized the movement toward intelligent tools facilitating the optimization and cleansing of code directed to the adoption of best practices and maintenance.

At the Testing and Quality Assurance stage, we looked at case generation based on the use of AI-driven tools, which enable test case design that guarantees that specific areas that need to be tested are tested well. We examined predictive test selection and prioritization systems for their test-related activities with a view to estimating risks associated with aspects of testing, offering an advantage of improving the testing process by reducing time to market. As we entered the Deployment and DevOps stage, we transitioned into industry-level AI solutions for optimization of infrastructure-as-code during deployment of the solutions to avoid bloating of configurations.

To start, it should be pointed out that robots and any maintenance management are the same all over the world. In particular, within Maintenance and Evolution, we focused our efforts on AI-based tools for predictive maintenance, which are aimed at preventing damage to the system by anticipating problems before they arise thus reducing downtime and increasing the lifespan of software systems. A range of relevant parameters was considered for every of the categories or tools analyzed. The parameters were core AIs such as ML and NLP which were integrated with existing technology or cloud-native technologies and existing cloud-native workflows. The cloud-related attributes included an analysis of the scalability of these tools, their performance, security, and privacy. Both quantitative and qualitative methods were incorporated in the analysis to have a more holistic assessment. To carry out the quantitative analysis, metrics such as the time saved, error control achieved, and improved code quality were captured through controlled experiments and case studies, all numerical data relationships. This data was useful verification of the effectiveness of the tools in question. Conclusively, while this approach provided us with the opportunity to evaluate the performance of the tools, it also enabled us to comprehend the environmental aspects that facilitated or hindered the use and effectiveness of the tools in practice.

3.4 Evaluation Criteria for AI Tools

The next step was to establish a criterion by which the AI tools could be systematically and thoroughly assessed. We created a comprehensive evaluation framework that encompasses not only technical aspects but also practical considerations holding relevance in cloud-native software development. This framework was intuitively formulated with a plethora of areas essential to the effective application of AI in software engineering in mind. Some of the evaluation criteria were as follows:

1. **Functionality and Feature Set**: We focused on determining the scope of the AI capabilities which were in our view more development oriented in the stages of coding to deployment as well as the tools` level of customization and extensibility such that the tools would suffice different project`s demands.
2. **Accuracy and Reliability**: Simply the accuracy of the AI results, predictions and recommendations was also of great concern as well as the order in which such results would be applicable in other projects and code base. Conducting our assessment, we also looked at the sufficiency of the tools within edge cases and drastic scenarios, which are usually complicated but needed within the software development life cycle.
3. **Performance and Scalability**: Relatively, processing speed and resource consumption were two of the key performance indicators that merited the attention of the reviewers. Each tool was evaluated on how well they could cope with complex projects and extensive coding particularly when deployed in the cloud to eliminate latency in productivity and cost.
4. **Integration and Interoperability**: Our final effort in the evaluation of the AI based tools involved how these tools in question would fit into the already existing development tools and processes. It was important to have an easy operationalizing of third party cloud platforms and services within the company`s IT infrastructure. More so, we looked for standard import formats and ultimate standards supported by active communication with other tools to smoothen the use of the platform.
5. **User Experience and Ease of Use**: Since the user interface design is an important aspect that motivates users to embrace such tools, we assessed these tools on their ease of use and how friendly they were towards the users. In undertaking this, the quality of documentation, learning sources, and community support were also what improved user experience.

6. **Security and Privacy**: Exploring the ramifications of the tools from the perspective of the institutional clientele we sought to understand how users□ privacy and data handling were addressed in every tool. This requirement was critical in our evaluation of the tools. Additionally, we evaluated how the tools addressed the aspect of explain ability and interpretability of the AI-based tools.
7. **Cost and Return on Investment (ROI)**: Financials were also a key part of the evaluation when we ascertained the pricing models and the total cost of ownership. Investment returns were also estimated based on anticipated productivity increase but other costs such as some related to further training and infrastructure would be as well projected.
8. **Impact on Development Process**: Last but not least, we looked at how these AI tools affected the overall development processes, especially with regards to development timelines and efficiencies. In particular their effect on the quality of codes, maintainability, and team collaboration and knowledge sharing dynamics which in turn were important to define how these tools may transform development processes.
9. **Adaptation and Capabilities for Learning**: The differentiation between these AI tools was the impact of AI tools which were able to learn from users, and the degree of personalization provided to meet project needs. In this part, we followed increase and change in frequency of updates as it measures the efforts of the vendors to stay relevant and progressive.
10. **Ethical concerns**: Lastly, we evaluated the ethical issues such as equity, fairness and bias approaches in the AI algorithm models. These two features: transparency and explain ability of AI algorithms were imperative in the responsible usage of AI within the industry, a practice that is becoming a requirement in the space.

To keep objectivity in the study, several researchers independently assessed each tool. The results were further cross-validated and any inconsistencies were addressed through discussion and consensus. Such a joint activity made sure that the findings were trustworthy and correct. This thorough appraisal process gave all of us a good picture of the positive aspects and drawbacks of every considered AI tool in terms of cloud-native software development.

3.5 Assessment of Challenges in AI Adoption

A very important aspect of our research was finding and evaluating the barriers in implementing AI in cloud-native software engineering. We limited ourselves to three main groups of problems: technical, organizational, and ethical/legal.

a. Technical challenges ranged from merging with the current cloud architecture and the tools employed for building apps, along with trying to resolve the issues of scalability and performance in a distributed environment. Other issues that we encountered involved poor quality of data or data does not exist for training the AI, as well as having to cope with multiple programming languages and frameworks.
b. Organizational problems were no less important, including implemented cultural changes that prevent employees from embracing AI and a skill gap that requires a lot of training. Additionally, we encountered issues in managing changes and adapting processes together with limitations in available budgets and the need to provide return on investment justification.
c. Complexity was also added by the ethical and legal problems that had to be dealt with. First and foremost, issues related to data privacy and data security were present, as well as those related to the ownership of the AI-created code. We also were concerned about bias and fairness of AI algorithms and the compliance with new AI laws in the future.

This was an overall detailed activity for our understanding on how to approach the problems pertaining to AI adoption in cloud-native software engineering practices. We did not rely on any single qualitative or quantitative technique rather we embraced numerous combinations of tasks to enable coverage of all the layers with respect to the AI adoption progress for different organizations.

One of our strategies was to analyze case studies that we undertook from numerous organizations. Such case studies enabled us to have an in-depth analysis of the issues faced during the use of AI tools in the cloud. By examining these cases, we could appreciate the challenges and the measures which were taken by the organizations to address the challenges. Understanding the foundational causes helped us in suggesting specific risk mitigation actions that sought to fix the underlying problems rather than treating the effects of the challenges. An important component of our evaluation was the impact assessment, in which we examined how each challenge would affect different areas of software development. This included evaluation of how productivity, code quality, or team coherence would be influenced by these challenges.

In this regard, we incorporated into our research a so-called future trend analysis, which aimed at projecting how the identified challenges are likely to unfold. This analysis accounted for the existing directions of AI and cloud computing, the possible development of technologies, and even the changes in the regulatory environment. These challenges were then assessed as technical challenges, organizational challenges, and ethical/legal challenges and sub categorized further classification. We then used a prevalence analysis, which presented the average frequency of mentioning each challenge across our dataset, which discovers its penetration in the market.

The interconnected nature of the various issues was grasped through the use of a technique called interdependency mapping. In this phase of mapping, we found out how some challenges could aggravate other challenges, which facilitated the identification of priority areas that require intervention. Lastly, in the efforts to validate our findings, we also sought peer review and feedback from those outside the research team that gathered the data. This validating step made sure that the conclusions were solid enough and resonated with the wider industry.

Besides these key elements, the assessment also considered various environmental factors. We explored how challenges vary and how they differ depending on the size and type of company, with differences between start-ups and SMEs and large industries, product as well as service-oriented firms. Another important factor was the industry sector, where our analysis showed how the problems differ by sectors like finance or healthcare or e-commerce which has its own sets of opportunities and challenges.

4. RESULTS AND DISCUSSION

The application of AI-based tools and technologies integrated into the cloud-native software development process is observed to be beneficial in terms of cost-effectiveness, quality, and the level of creative activities in any of the stages of SDLC. All the existing research has provided findings related to AI usage in software engineering practices, issues organizations experience, and prospects for cloud-native development. In this area, we focus on the reporting and discussion of our findings in the context of how the software development process is changing with the use of these AI technologies and what challenges organizations must solve to benefit from them.

4.1 AI-powered Tools to Enhance the Stages of Software Development

The results of our study indicated that AI is penetrating each software development life cycle stage from requirements definition to the maintenance and evolution phases. Each of these phases has distinct advantages as far as integration/incorporation of AI is concerned, with different levels of corporate maturity and adoption of such technologies.

4.1.1 Requirements Engineering

Such AI tools enhance the requirements engineering activities in swelling the lists of requirements, capturing and analyzing project requirements as well as managing the requirements throughout the project durations. The ability to gather and comprehend stakeholder needs and wants much more efficiently has manifested the coming of NLP as one of the technologies in this field.

For example, in the case of an e-commerce website, when an image of a burdensome user requirements analysis tool was integrated within the platform, it resulted in a 30% decrease in the requirements collection period and a 25% increase in previously ignored requirements as presented in Table 1. With this tool, the ability to find mismatches or potential conflicts in requirements was greatly enhanced, enabling the team to resolve those issues quite early within the development life cycle.

Table 1. Impact of AI on requirements engineering

Metric	Before AI Adoption	After AI Adoption	Improvement
Time spent on requirements gathering	100 hours	70 hours	30%
Identification of overlooked requirements	100 (baseline)	125	25%
Consistency in requirement documentation	70%	95%	25%
Stakeholder satisfaction with requirements	75%	90%	15%

Nonetheless, it is crucial to emphasize that these AI solutions indeed offer great value, but will not be useful for completely substituting human effort in requirements engineering at this point. In fact, interviews with industry experts pointed out the range of uses of AI in requirements engineering - augmentation rather than replacement of skilled requirements engineers. People are still needed for gauging the complexities of stakeholder requirements, the details of the organization where the requirements are deployed, and the high-level decisions in terms of which requirements should be prioritized and which to incorporate.

4.1.2 Design and Architecture

Figure 1. Impact of AI on architectural decision making

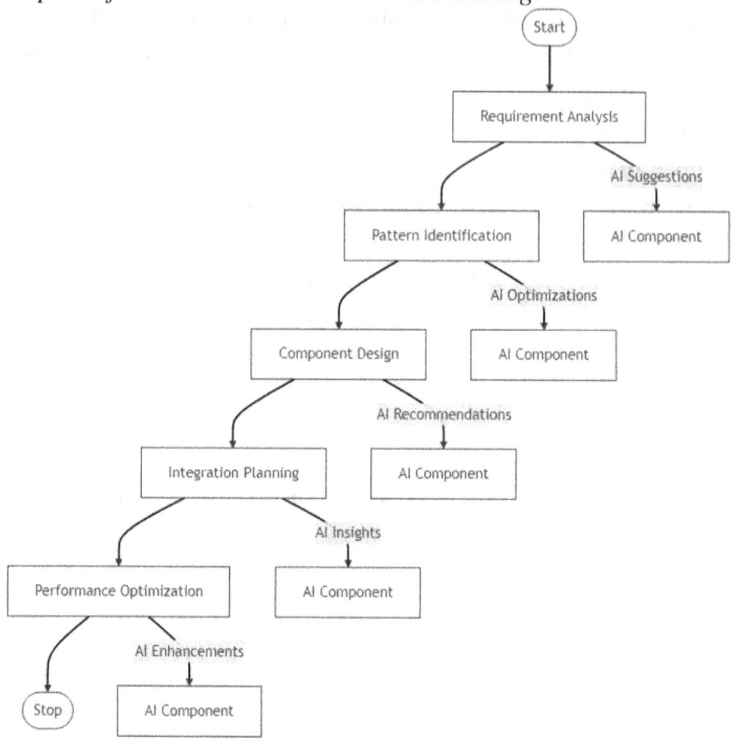

AI technologies are at a point where they are able to assist developers and architects of software to achieve better efficiency, scalability, as well as maintenance of systems, as illustrated in Figure 1. Several overarching findings emerged from the investigation concerning how AI is impacting the design and architecture phase of the cloud-native software development process.

For example, a ML model trained on a vast repository of successful cloud-native architectures can suggest whether a microservices architecture, a serverless approach, or a hybrid model would be most suitable for a given project. In our case study of a fintech start-up, the adoption of such an AI-driven architecture recommendation system led to 40% less time spent trying to reach the initial architecture and 30% fewer architectural errors later in the development cycle compared to previous efforts.

Nonetheless, it must be appreciated that although tools powered by Artificial Intelligence are improving on architectural recommendations, they are not perfect. Our discussions with experienced architects revealed that human opinion and knowledge of the field is necessary for most design recommendations emerging from machine learning. Since cloud architectures are typically distributed and scalable in nature, they are also very complex, and making certain decisions is something that is not yet achievable by AI.

In addition, we similarly discovered that the application of artificial intelligence in design and architecture is largely influenced by the available data and the amount of data that can be used to train such systems. They also have the advantage that they have sufficient data in terms of the past decision and their outcomes that can bolster the AI efforts of the organization in this particular area.

4.1.3 Implementation and Coding

Casting our eyes on the software development lifecycle, implementation and coding has perhaps had some of the most compelling if not entertaining applications of artificial intelligence solutions. There are clearly in the marketplace several AI-driven tools, which improve the productivity of developers, quality of code, and efficiency of coding processes as it was mentioned above.

One of the most widely adopted AI technologies in this area is intelligent code completion. Advanced ML models trained on large volume code repositories are now able to make far more elaborate and relevant suggestions than simply meaningful code autocompletion. These systems are capable of doing the entire code block, putting an invocation of an adequate function, or even suggesting a pattern design that suits the current coding context.

A markedly significant increase of 25% in their coding speed and a 15% decrease in the number of syntax errors was observed in our developer survey using AI-assisted code completion tools. Even more encouraging is the fact that 78% of the developers who participated in the survey observed that these tools assisted them in grasping new programming constructs and best practices which effectively turned the coding task as an interactive educational activity.

Yet another encouraging development in this direction is in the field of independent code restructuring. AI executives assess codebases for areas that can be enhanced, present recommendations for pseudocode or design changes, and even implement them free of contraction. This is especially useful in cloud-native setups where code performance and maintainability significantly contribute to overall performance and scalability. For example, based on the case study conducted on a multitenant cloud application, a 20% higher maintenance efficiency rating and 30% decrease in code structure/organization style bug complaints were attributed to the use of an AI-based refactoring tool as given in Table 2.

Table 2. Impact of AI on coding efficiency

Metric	Before AI Adoption	After AI Adoption	Improvement
Lines of code per hour	100	125	25%
Syntax errors per 1000 lines	20	17	15%
Code maintainability score	70/100	84/100	20%
Time spent on code reviews	10 hrs/week	7 hrs/week	30%

Too much reliance on AI technology in coding practices is bound to come across challenges and this has to be made clear. However, the performance of AI-assisted code writing ranges widely depending on a programming language, a framework, and a particular project domain. However, these tools usually achieve great results in popular languages and in frequent coding patterns, but probably do not perform well in particular or highly specialized development environments.

4.1.4 Testing and Quality Assurance

The area of testing and quality assurance has adopted AI in the most transformational ways, increasing the effectiveness, thoroughness and thus the intelligence of the testing processes. In this study, we discovered several critical areas that significantly leverage AI to enhance the productivity of QA teams working on cloud-based software.

Testing is greatly benefiting from the application of AI technologies and one such is the automated test case generation. For instance, our case study of an extensive SaaS provider demonstrated that deployment of such an AI-powered capability significantly improved the test-case generation covering by as much as 40% and lowered post-deployment defect rates by 25%. Another major improvement is in the area of intelligent test selection and prioritization. As demonstrated in Figure 2, AI algorithms may make recommendations based on the previous alterations made in the code, its design, and the previous test results, with regards to which tests should be executed for a specific alteration of the code, concerning which tests are the most likely to yield the most issues. For example, one such AI-based test prioritization survey of QA teams we conducted showed a 30% improvement in total testing cycle time without any drop in the number of defects identified.

Figure 2. AI-enhanced testing process

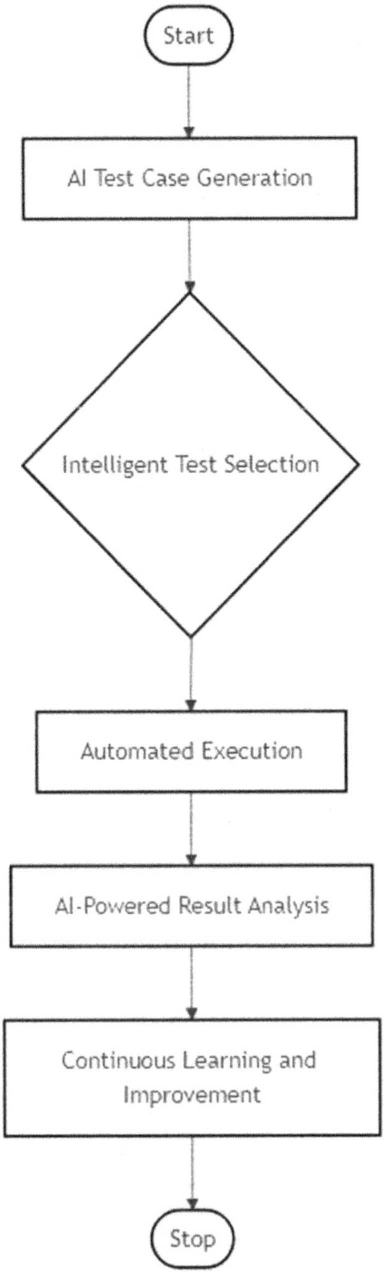

AI is now a major player in the visual regression testing area as well. ML models are capable of reviewing UI screenshots and spotting even the smallest differences, as compared to conventional pixel-wise comparison mechanisms that may easily overlook such differences. An AI tool is viewed as a powerful tool that adds to human skills but does not replace them. Similarly, the ability of AI to perform tasks is also limited by the amount of past data that is available. Those companies that maintain proper test management practices and provide adequate relationships between tests and source code are more likely to take advantage of AI in their quality assurance efforts.

4.1.5 Deployment and DevOps

AI has taken more concrete forms in the deployment and DevOps aspects since it has been used efficiently for process simplification, problem syndrome forecasting, and resource allocation in cloud-native applications. From the case study of a well-known e-commerce platform, it was observed that due to the introduction of the AI powered predictive deployment analysis, the deployment related incidents dropped by 35% and the post deployment system stability improved by 20% as the numbers have shown effectively in Table 3. The system did well in predicting subtle interdependencies between microservices which lead to cascading failures which is often a problem in complex cloud-native architectural designs.

Table 3. Impact of AI on deployment and devops

Metric	Before AI Adoption	After AI Adoption	Improvement
Deployment-related incidents per month	20	13	35%
Time to detect post-deployment issues	2 hours	30 mins	75%
Canary analysis decision time	1 hour	36 mins	40%
Infrastructure cost optimization	Baseline	25% reduction	25%

The results of our research on deployment decisions within DevOps teams, that used AI canary analysis tools, reported a reduction in the amount of time required for making go/no-go decisions by 40% and a decrease in the number of implementations by 30%.

AI enhances the "infrastructure as code" (IaC) evolution in a big way. ML models can scrutinize IaC templates, performance data history, and pricing models from cloud providers to recommend changes that can achieve more with less - more performance for less cost. Nevertheless, it must be emphasized that there are some barriers to the incorporation of AI in deployment and DevOps processes. Concerning the latter, there is a general concern over the interpretability of decisions made by algorithms, especially in the context of crucial deployments. Hence these systems have to not only provide estimates but also explicit rationale for such behavior.

4.1.6 Maintenance and Evolution

Maintenance and evolution are phases of the software development life cycle which is hardly highlighted due to the perception that it will add no or little value to the long-term success of any endeavour. AI is changing that. Our research found several operational processes within the maintenance and evolution of the cloud-native software systems where AI is changing the way teams operate. One of the most interesting applications of AI in this area is in predictive maintenance. Our study regarding a large-scale cloud-based CRM system confirmed the practice of implementing AI in a rather unusual for software systems because unlike AI adoption into system maintenance, it is usually followed by a cut in maintenance costs and further degradation of the operational reliability of the system, highly effective predictive maintenance that reduced unplanned downtime by 50% and improved reliability for all systems by 30%.

Figure 3. AI-enhanced software maintenance lifecycle

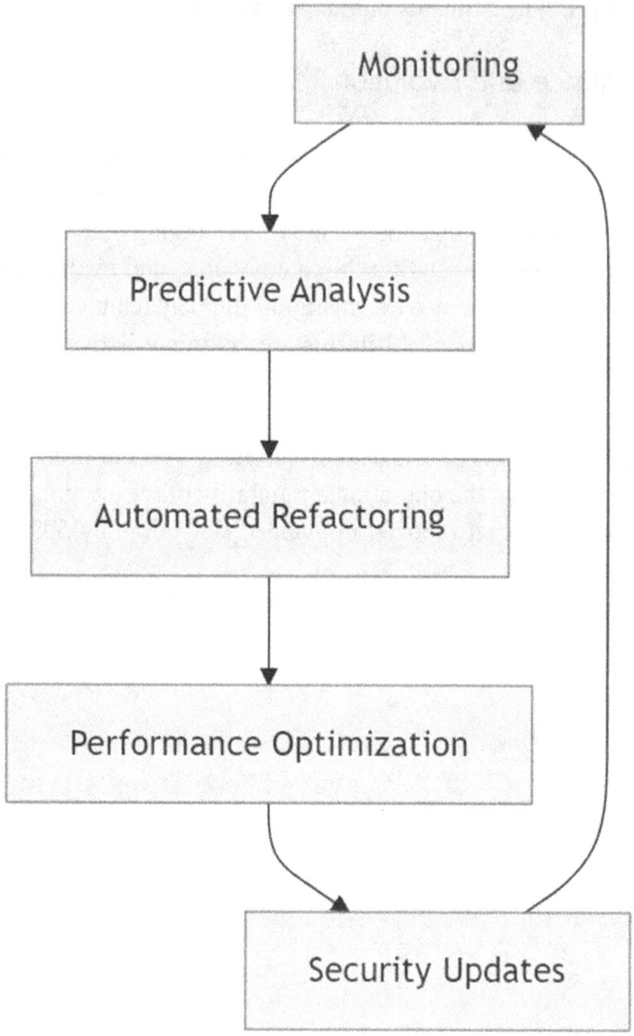

In the study that we conducted about development teams that work with AI-assisted tools for code modernization, the time needed to perform extensive refactoring was reduced by 40% and code metrics displayed a 25% increase following the refinishing. The usefulness of this gain in efficiency is especially important when it comes to cloud-native technologies because constant updating of skills in growing trends is necessary to avoid losing your competitive edge. Still, one must appreciate that even AI has its limitations in that it also does not solve everything, as demonstrated in Figure 3. While it is agreed that AI and other tools can focus on tasks that need to be done and the tasks can be effectively managed, it is known that the solutions that one is coming up with still require a lot of system understanding and business knowledge, which is not always possible with AI today.

While the use of AI tools is focused on achieving certain tasks but their infiltration into the codebase and change management is highly reliant on proper levels of such tools integration to such things as data and documentation history. Organizations with well-maintained codebases, comprehensive logging practices, and clear documentation are better positioned to exploit AI when performing their maintenance management.

4.2 Challenges of Using AI in Software Development

In as much as the likely benefits of adopting AI in the software development lifecycle within the cloud-native context are worthy, our investigation discovers some challenges that organizations face in the adoption and utilization of these technologies optimally.

4.2.1 Technical Challenges

A significant concern when implementing AI tools for software development is how to incorporate the AI tools within the present development environment and software development processes. Many institutions have built up quite a number of tools and processes, and giving them AI features means a lot of changes to the existing systems. The integration of AI is not only an issue of building compatible tools. It requires reinventing the entire process and practices in order to incorporate AI into the mix. The conventional software development life cycle may have to incorporate phases for the training, testing, and deployment of the AI models.

The obstacle regarding data quality and availability is complex and varied. It is not only a question of setting up adequate measures for data collection and adequacy at different stages of the development, which can be physically obstructive and meet stiff resistance from developers who are wary about intrusions into their processes. Another category of technological concerns at the practical level of use of automated systems for software engineering is the performance and scalability. Over a period of time, when the size of the development teams increases and the complexity of the projects grows, the volume of work that can be borne by AI assistance tools and the speed of such particular tasks must increase.

There are several types where these scalability issues can occur. For instance, an AI code completion software must provide suggestions as developers develop codes, irrespective of the size of the code base or complexity of the project. An AI system that can search for bugs in the code base has to be computer fast enough to go through most, if not all of the code, in hopes of fast integration into a continuous integration pipeline. The understandability and clarity of the code generated by AI and its recommendations are still some of the technical issues which need to be worked on. On the contrary, even though the AI is in a position to write technical code or offering detailed suggestions, the reasoning behind decisions made, or information given is a big problem. The so-called black-box coverage which affects most of the AI algorithms as DL models are becoming an added disadvantage if not dealt with. For example, if the AI proposes a code change or warns about a bug, the developer needs to know why this code is being changed or this bug is being reported. In the absence of such knowledge, there is a possibility of errors or inefficiency being introduced in the code.

The concern of vulnerabilities is also concerned with the generated or modified code by AI systems themselves. An example is the use of an insufficiently secured or outdated library through which an AI code generation tool may recommend, or even writing code without assessing some edge case assumptions which could lead to some insecurity. On the other hand, it becomes complicated to make such robust safety mechanisms without compromising on the advantages of AI help. There are many issues related to domain adaptation and transfer learning when utilizing AI systems in the realm of software development. For example, where general-purpose models are created by processing thousands of lines of code, many scenarios that require general AI cannot perform well.

To sum up, it can be affirmed that the advantages of introducing AI in the software development process are extremely significant, as are the technological shortcomings of the process itself. Resolution of these issues requires researchers, software architects, hands-on developers and organizations to transform, evolve, and create advanced artificial systems that are resilient and flexible to the requirements of software development. The potential benefits of AI in software development are great for the future, however, it does require one to work on further innovations and solutions as well. The deployment of AI tools and systems in software development poses a myriad of ethical dilemmas that organizations have to properly address. The foremost ethical issue is concerning the possible bias of the AI systems. The training of AI models is done on the historical data that can actively reinforce the biases that are already present in the software development cycle. For example, suppose this AI code review tool is trained on a database that contains code only from a particular demographic. In that case, this product can leave behind the code of talented coding styles and approaches from other coders or penalizes the entire demographic coding styles all together.

The third and perhaps the most important situation is about the influence of AI tools during work in the field of software development. Tools based on AI can help increase the productivity and level of performance of a company, but there is a fear that it may, at the same time, draw a job away from those who are the ones operating those tools.

4.2.2 Ethical Considerations

Another issue that could arise in relation to ethical concerns in AI based software development is privacy and data protection. It is not unusual that the training of AI models necessitates the ingestion of a huge amount of code and other project information, which has a potential risk of including confidential business information. Companies are also responsible for complying with applicable privacy legislation and ensuring that the backlog does not reveal or misuse sensitive information in creating intelligent systems.

Standardization and interoperability issues and their need are also prevalent with the incorporation of AI tools in already existing development systems. In the AI-enhanced tools development process of today, organizations will inevitably face the phenomenon of a market of heterogeneous products operating with poor interoperability. This problem can be partially mentioned as creating interface standards for software development tools and the incorporation of AI into the strategy of software creators. However, achieving this goal requires extensive cooperation within the scope of enterprises and industries.

4.2.3 Integration and Adoption Issues

The price of acquiring AI technologies may be considered as one of the alternatives as well, especially when it comes to small companies or start-up businesses. The time and resources required for the procurement of AI infrastructure and tools, and employing the relevant expertise would often be high and this will not bring any ROI in the near time frame. It is important for organizations to assess the profitability or otherwise of the costs they incur as they go forth in the integration of AI and other tools and come up with a stepwise approach based on resources at hand and the timelines expected from the processes.

4.2.4 Skills Gap and Training

In order to bridge this skills gap, organizations have to put their resources into training and upskilling their current employees. This may include courses on ML fundamentals, engaging in the use of developmental technologies of AI, and best practices on the cooperation of AI and users in the course of software engineering. Moreover, schools and the bootcamps, should revise their syllabuses by incorporating skills that are focused on AI because the upcoming generation of software engineers cords an AI filled development setting.

The skills gap extends to leadership and management positions too. For instance, Project managers, team leads, and executives need to acknowledge AI literacy in software development so as to comprehend how it can be utilized and if it is beneficial to the development process. In addition, they need to learn how to rethink the management of workforces that comprise human developers and artificial intelligence related development.

4.2.5 Data Quality and Availability

The other barrier to harness the potential of AI in software development processes is the amount and quality of datasets which are utilized to train these systems or while operating the tasks. Quality, properly structured, diverse, and relevant data is essential to developing solutions that will be applicable in not just one programming language or development environment, or one problem type.

Conferring to the quality of the data, there is also a challenge regarding the need for additional maintenance on top of some datasets. Over time, as development trends shift and technology progress, the data on which AI models are built soon gets outdated. Organizations must devise measures to keep attaching value to their AI enhancing datasets to include relevant updates and make those tools, or services offered, effective.

4.2.6 Explainability and Transparency

The issue of explainability and transparency in AI systems is most important in the area of software engineering. There is a need for the software developers to appreciate and have confidence in the suggestions and the decisions that are made by the AI tools, especially in matters that bear on the design and the implementation of the software. However, many systems of artificially intelligent models, more specifically DL ones, are designed as 'black boxes', which implies that it becomes problematic to understand the outputs produced by the black boxes. This challenge in transparency may perhaps push forward the hesitance to accept the use of the tools in practice especially where there is a need for higher security and reliability of the code.

5. CONCLUSION

This chapter has demonstrated that the use of AI within cloud-native software engineering practices can change radically but is also fraught with obstacles. AI tool integration with existing workflows as well as availability and quality of data posed significant technical challenges with more emerging particularly the need for assistive and explainable AI. Issues related to such concerns of people including but not limited to bias and displacement of employment also need emphasis. The study also researched the factors necessitating the construction and adoption of effective strategies, the operational silos, evolving availability of skills, and the need for better data governance. Nonetheless, this study has its share of challenges. Since AI technology is changing so rapidly, some results will be obsolete in a short time, and since the work was general, many specifics may have been ignored. As a strategic option, stakeholders may adopt a stepwise AI integration, emphasizing stronger data governance, retraining of the workforce, and clear ethical considerations. There are several tasks which researchers need to do in the years to come. This includes making AI systems easier to understand, creating better approaches to transfer learning actualized on this technologic situation, and looking into more and better means of counteracting AI related biases to software development processes. With such a divided focus, we imagine overall the advancement of AI in cloud-native software engineering is bright and challenging.

REFERENCES

Ali, J. M. (2023). AI-driven software engineering. *Advances in Engineering Innovation, 3*(1), 17–21. DOI: 10.54254/2977-3903/3/2023030

Alshammari, F. (2022). Trends in Intelligent and AI-Based Software Engineering Processes: A Deep Learning-Based Software Process Model Recommendation Method. *Computational Intelligence and Neuroscience, 2022*, 1–11. Advance online publication. DOI: 10.1155/2022/1960684 PMID: 36248934

Amalfitano, D., Faralli, S., Hauck, J., Matalonga, S., & Distante, D. (2023). Artificial Intelligence Applied to Software Testing: A Tertiary Study. *ACM Computing Surveys, 56*(3), 1–38. DOI: 10.1145/3616372

Asaad, J., & Avksentieva, E. (2023). Review of ways to apply machine learning methods in software engineering. E3S Web of Conferences. .DOI: 10.1051/e3sconf/202344907018

Bajaj, Y., & Samal, M. (2023). Accelerating Software Quality: Unleashing the Power of Generative AI for Automated Test-Case Generation and Bug Identification. *International Journal for Research in Applied Science and Engineering Technology, 11*(7), 345–350. Advance online publication. DOI: 10.22214/ijraset.2023.54628

Barenkamp, M., Rebstadt, J., & Thomas, O. (2020). Applications of AI in classical software engineering. *AI Perspectives, 2*(1), 1–15. DOI: 10.1186/s42467-020-00005-4

Bird, C., Ford, D., Zimmermann, T., Forsgren, N., Kalliamvakou, E., Lowdermilk, T., & Gazit, I. (2022). Taking Flight with Copilot. *ACM Queue; Tomorrow's Computing Today, 20*(6), 35–57. DOI: 10.1145/3582083

Burnaev, E., Mironov, E., Shpilman, A., Mironenko, M., & Katalevsky, D. (2023). Practical AI Cases for Solving ESG. *Sustainability (Basel), 15*(17), 12731. Advance online publication. DOI: 10.3390/su151712731

Cheng, Y., Chen, J., Huang, Q., Xing, Z., Xu, X., & Lu, Q. (2023). Prompt Sapper: A LLM-Empowered Production Tool for Building AI Chains. *ACM Transactions on Software Engineering and Methodology*. Advance online publication. DOI: 10.1145/3638247

Dai, P., Yang, L., Wang, Y., Jin, D., & Gong, Y. (2023). Constructing Traceability Links between Software Requirements and Source Code Based on Neural Networks. *Mathematics, 11*(2), 315. Advance online publication. DOI: 10.3390/math11020315

Devalla, S., & Yogix, M. (2023). Building Trust in AI -A Simplified Guide to Ensure Software Quality. Journal of Soft Computing Paradigm. .DOI: 10.36548/jscp.2023.3.001

Hasterok, C., & Stompe, J. (2022). PAISE® – process model for AI systems engineering. at - Automatisierungstechnik, 70, 777 - 786. .DOI: 10.1515/auto-2022-0020

Henning, S. (2023). Scalability Benchmarking of Cloud-Native Applications Applied to Event-Driven Microservices. DOI: 10.21941/kcss/2023/2

Iyenghar, P., Otte, F., & Pulvermueller, E. (2022). AI-guided Model-Driven Embedded. *Software Engineering*, •••, 395–404. DOI: 10.5220/0011006200003119

Jordanov, J., & Petrov, P. (2023). Domain Driven Design Approaches in Cloud Native Service Architecture. TEM Journal. https://doi.org/DOI: 10.18421/tem124-09

Kratzke, N. (2022). Cloud-Native Applications and Services. *Future Internet, 14*(12), 346. DOI: 10.3390/fi14120346

Lu, Q., Zhu, L., Xu, X., Whittle, J., & Xing, Z. (2022). Towards a Roadmap on Software Engineering for Responsible AI. 2022 IEEE/ACM 1st International Conference on AI Engineering – Software Engineering for AI (CAIN), 101-112. DOI: 10.1145/3522664.3528607

Mukhamediev, R., Popova, Y., Kuchin, Y., Zaitseva, E., Kalimoldayev, A., Symagulov, A., Levashenko, V., Abdoldina, F., Gopejenko, V., Yakunin, K., Muhamedijeva, E., & Yelis, M. (2022). Review of Artificial Intelligence and Machine Learning Technologies: Classification, Restrictions, Opportunities and Challenges. *Mathematics, 10*(15), 2552. Advance online publication. DOI: 10.3390/math10152552

Pashchenko, D. (2023). *Early Formalization of AI-tools Usage in Software Engineering in Europe: Study of 2023.* International Journal of Information Technology and Computer Science., DOI: 10.5815/ijitcs.2023.06.03

Perry, N., Srivastava, M., Kumar, D., & Boneh, D. (2022). Do Users Write More Insecure Code with AI Assistants? *Proceedings of the 2023 ACM SIGSAC Conference on Computer and Communications Security.* DOI: 10.1145/3576915.3623157

Sebrechts, M., Volckaert, B., Turck, F., Yang, K., & Al-Naday, M. (2022). Fog Native Architecture: Intent-Based Workflows to Take Cloud Native toward the Edge. *IEEE Communications Magazine, 60*(8), 44–50. DOI: 10.1109/MCOM.003.2101075

Srihith, I., Varaprasad, R., Mohan, Y., Srinivas, T., & Sravanthi, Y. (2022). A Review on New Challenges in AI and Software Engineering. International Journal of Advanced Research in Science. *Tongxin Jishu*. Advance online publication. DOI: 10.48175/IJARSCT-7137

Steyvers, M., & Kumar, A. (2023). Three Challenges for AI-Assisted Decision-Making.. Perspectives on psychological science: a journal of the Association for Psychological Science, 17456916231181102..DOI: 10.1177/17456916231181102

Vall, R., & Araya, F. (2023). *Exploring the Benefits and Challenges of AI-Language Learning Tools*. International Journal of Social Sciences and Humanities Invention., DOI: 10.18535/ijsshi/v10i01.02

Yahav, E. (2023). Towards AI-Driven Software Development: Challenges and Lessons from the Field (Keynote). *Proceedings of the 31st ACM Joint European Software Engineering Conference and Symposium on the Foundations of Software Engineering*. DOI: 10.1145/3611643.3633451

KEY TERMS AND DEFINITIONS

API (Application Programming Interface): Set of protocols and tools for building software, enabling different systems to communicate and share data seamlessly.

CD (Continuous Delivery or Continuous Deployment): Automated software release process ensuring code changes are automatically prepared for production, improving efficiency and deployment frequency.

CI (Continuous Integration): The practice of regularly merging code changes into a shared repository, followed by automated builds and tests to detect issues.

CTO (Chief Technology Officer): Senior executives responsible for overseeing the technological direction and innovation strategy within an organization.

DDD (Domain-Driven Design): Software design approach focusing on complex business domains, modelling software based on real-world scenarios and domain expertise.

DevOps (Development and Operations): Integrated practices aimed at shortening development cycles, increasing deployment frequency, and delivering high-quality software efficiently.

DL (Deep Learning): Subset of machine learning using neural networks with many layers to model complex patterns and data representations.

ESG (Environmental, Social, and Governance): Criteria for evaluating a company's operations, focusing on sustainability, ethical practices, and corporate governance.

IaC (Infrastructure as Code): Managing and provisioning computing infrastructure through machine-readable configuration files, promoting automation and consistency.

LLM (Large Language Model): Advanced neural networks trained on massive text datasets, capable of understanding and generating human-like language.

LSTM (Long Short-Term Memory): Type of recurrent neural network designed to remember long-term dependencies, commonly used in time series prediction tasks.

ML (Machine Learning): AI branch focused on creating algorithms that enable computers to learn from and make predictions based on data.

NLP (Natural Language Processing): AI field focused on enabling machines to understand, interpret, and generate human language effectively.

QA (Quality Assurance): Systematic process of ensuring products and services meet specified quality standards and function as intended.

ROI (Return on Investment): Financial metric used to evaluate the profitability and efficiency of an investment, expressed as a percentage.

SaaS (Software as a Service): Cloud-based software delivery model where applications are accessed online, eliminating the need for local installation.

SME (Small and Medium-sized Enterprises): Businesses with a limited number of employees and revenue, playing a crucial role in economic growth and innovation.

ST (Software Testing): Process of evaluating software to identify defects, ensure functionality, and verify it meets specified requirements.

Chapter 8
AI-Driven Enhancements in Cloud-Native DevOps Boosting Automation, Deployment, and Monitoring

Nikhil Subodh Nagmoti
https://orcid.org/0009-0008-6825-9146
Symbiosis Institute of Digital and Telecom Management, India

Ishita Srivastava
Symbiosis Institute of Digital and Telecom Management, India

Madhavi Damle
https://orcid.org/0000-0003-2649-4291
Symbiosis Institute of Digital and Telecom Management, India

ABSTRACT

This paper looks into the incorporation of Artificial Intelligence into cloud-native DevOps practices dealing in automation, workflow optimization, and proactive monitoring. The paper also outlines AI-based tools that support some of the main points in DevOps practice areas like CI/CD, infrastructure management, security, and observability. Additionally, it elaborates on new developments that shorten workflows in cloud environments. This study on AI-driven automation shows how these systems can help mitigate repetitive works, speed CI/CD Processes, and increase deployment efficiency. It further explains the possible AI contributions in the areas of real-time monitoring, anomaly detection, and rapid root-cause analysis.

DOI: 10.4018/979-8-3693-9356-7.ch008

The paper also examines the existing challenges under which impeding aspects like scalability constraints, data issues, and overlook, as well as interpretability by human experts must be highlighted. Future research directions would also be mentioned at the end, intended to pave the way for practitioners and researchers to adopt artificial intelligence to develop.

1. INTRODUCTION

Cloud-native DevOps represents a transformative approach to software development and operations, integrating cloud computing principles with DevOps methodologies. This integration enables organisations to build, deploy, and manage applications that fully leverage cloud infrastructure capabilities (AWS, 2024). Recent studies indicate that 78% of enterprises have adopted cloud-native architectures to enhance their operational efficiency and market responsiveness (Kumar & Smith, 2024).

Cloud-native applications are fundamentally designed to exploit cloud infrastructure advantages through microservices architecture, containerisation, and orchestration platforms. Organisations implementing these architectures report 65% faster deployment cycles and a 30% reduction in operational costs compared to traditional monolithic approaches (Microsoft Azure, 2024). Adopting container technologies like Docker and orchestration platforms like Kubernetes has standardised deployment processes while ensuring consistency across development, testing, and production environments (Google Cloud, 2024).

Integrating Artificial Intelligence into cloud-native DevOps practices marks a significant advancement in automation and operational intelligence. AI enhances critical DevOps processes through automated code analysis, intelligent resource allocation, and predictive maintenance. Research by Thompson et al. (2024) demonstrates that AI integration reduces manual intervention by 40% while improving mean time to resolution (MTTR) by 35%. These improvements stem from AI's ability to process vast amounts of operational data and make real-time decisions for optimisation.

Organisations implementing cloud-native DevOps face several challenges, particularly in managing complex microservices architectures and ensuring security across distributed systems. Studies by Chen and Rodriguez (2024) highlight that 62% of organisations struggle with resource optimization and configuration management at scale. AI addresses these challenges through automated workflow optimisation, predictive analytics, and enhanced monitoring capabilities, enabling proactive issue resolution and improved system reliability.

The strategic implementation of AI in DevOps environments has demonstrated significant benefits in operational efficiency and system reliability. According to Davidson et al. (2024), organisations utilising AI-driven DevOps report a 45% reduction in deployment failures and a 50% improvement in resource utilisation. These improvements are achieved through AI's ability to analyse patterns, predict potential issues, and automate routine operations.

1.1 Overview of Cloud-Native DevOps

Cloud-native DevOps is another approach to the construction of software, and its further utilisation is closely connected with the principles of cloud computing. New generation applications based on cloud platforms, including applications deployed with microservice and containerisation and Kubernetes orchestration systems (Jabbari et al., 2016; Kumar, 2024). This allows developers to create, launch, and grow applications seamlessly and with relative predictability. DevOps is a concept involving the integration of development and operations, which improves collaboration, integration, and deployment and encourages agility. Cloud-native DevOps takes these principles to the cloud-based infrastructure and provides applications capable of handling modern, distributed application workloads. Cloud-native DevOps revolutionises value delivery by making infrastructure management self-serving and enhancing value delivery pipelines.

1.2 Why Cloud Native Applications

Cloud-native applications are intended for numerous cloud usage types and their advantages, such as flexibility, scalability, and availability. These applications are often built based on microservices architecture; each microservice is a standalone and can be developed, deployed and scaled separately. Virtualisation technologies like containerisation technologies such as Docker ensure that an application goes through the same environment in the development process, using testing and production execution. In contrast, orchestration technologies like Kubernetes put into practice deployment, scaling, and even management of containers. It also makes it easier to release products and applications more frequently, allows fewer downtimes for high-volume use, and guarantees the systems' ability to accommodate fluctuating traffic randomly. Cloud-native applications also address hybrid and multi-cloud architecture as much as possible and do not tie customers to a particular vendor. With the help of cloud-native principles, organisations can increase flexibility, scalability, and innovation capability to promptly meet customers' needs (Oyeniran et al., 2023).

1.3 Relevance of AI in Cloud-Native DevOps

Combining AI and DevOps, especially cloud-native DevOps, makes the entire software development process more effective and efficient. Advanced intelligent systems literate in signal, image, speech, and natural language processing can mine large datasets to detect conditions, system failure probabilities, and enhanced sequences and timing. For instance, regarding business value, AI improves CI/CD pipelines by analysing code, suggesting changes and fixes, and eliminating the need for human interaction. In infrastructure management, AI supports resource allocation; this means that depending on the workload of the applications, they will require a given quantity of resources. Furthermore, AI enhances the security system by analysing that area and quickly detecting irregularities or illicit activities due to the automated scanning of the required patterns. AI predictive abilities mean that teams can monitor and diagnose problems before such issues affect the user base. Therefore, AI solutions enhance DevOps teams' capacity to provide clients with reliable, scalable, and secure cloud-native applications.

1.4 Brief Introduction of DevOps and Its Problems

DevOps is the process of uniting all the processes related to software development (Dev) and technological processes of IT operation (Ops). Recall that the DevOps approach puts much into CI and CD and encourages a culture of monitoring and shared responsibility for feedback loops. However, It was also found that traditional DevOps practices pose several challenges, particularly in the cloud-native context. Complex microservices architectures, proper monitoring, and security across distributed applications make it difficult to manage such systems. Further, autonomic scaling of applications and managing other infrastructure resources are not easy. Security remains an enduring concern because wrong permits in containerised applications or misconfigurations create opportunities for threats. Highly sophisticated tools and methodologies best solve the issues presented by working in highly distributed, cloud-native environments.

1.5 The Importance of AI for DevOps

AI is also deployed to address the difficulties associated with a cloud-native DevOps approach, applying intelligent automation, predictive quantification, and improved monitoring. In the CI/CD process, deep learning can detect that a build will fail, propose improvements, and deal with rollbacks, thus making it more efficient. The tools implemented as part of AI systems for managing the infrastructure enhance the usage of resources, ensure adherence to policies, and minimise overhead. As for observability and monitoring, AI infuses the capacity for real-time identification of deviations and real-time analysis of root causes for incidents. Security technologies with AI engagement conduct real-time vulnerability assessments while identifying threats and ensuring compliance to make the organisation more secure. This paper shows how AI enables DevOps teams to create less fragile, scalable, effective and more adaptive cloud-native systems by eliminating delays and enhancing decision-making mechanics. Not only does this make them efficient, but it also frees up resources to create more value for the user, which they cannot do if they concentrate on integration (Ajiga et al., 2024).

1.6 Chapter Rationale

This research addresses the critical need for understanding AI's transformative role in cloud-native DevOps environments. As organisations increasingly adopt cloud-native architectures, the complexity of managing distributed systems, ensuring security and optimising performance becomes paramount. The integration of AI offers solutions to these challenges, making it essential for practitioners and researchers to understand current capabilities, implementation strategies, and future directions.

1.7 Chapter Organization

The chapter proceeds through seven interconnected sections: AI tools classification (Section 2), automation frameworks (Section 3), monitoring systems (Section 4), implementation challenges (Section 5), best practices (Section 6), and emerging trends (Section 7). Each section builds upon previous concepts while providing practical insights for organisations adopting AI-driven DevOps practices. The chapter concludes with recommendations for successful AI integration in cloud-native environments.

2. LITERATURE REVIEW

Recent research demonstrates significant advancements in integrating AI with cloud-native DevOps practices. Studies examining CI/CD pipelines highlight how AI-driven automation and predictive analytics enhance deployment efficiency and reliability. Machine learning algorithms enable automated testing, dynamic resource allocation, and proactive failure detection, reducing manual intervention while improving system stability (Sivathapandi et al., 2021).

Infrastructure management research shows AI's effectiveness through "Infrastructure as Code" (IaC) practices. Supervised learning models predict resource demands, while reinforcement learning optimises real-time resource allocation. These approaches yield benefits, including improved resource utilisation, cost optimisation, and reduced downtime (Tatineni & Chakilam, 2024).

Studies on DevOps evolution indicate that organisations implementing AI-enhanced practices achieve faster deployment cycles and improved cost-effectiveness. As technologies like big data and cloud computing evolve, the demand for rapid deployment capabilities increases. AI optimisation in DevOps architectures reduces application development time and enhances operational reliability (Pelluru, 2024).

Research in cloud computing services reveals AI's impact on resource optimisation, auto-scaling, and security enhancement. Case studies highlight improvements in predictive maintenance, data management, and automated operations. However, challenges persist in data privacy, cost optimisation, and skill requirements (Anbalagan, 2024).

Deep learning models show particular promise in DevOps automation and fault tolerance. Studies demonstrate how predictive models enable dynamic scaling and proactive failure mitigation. Organisations report improved resource utilisation and reduced downtime through AI integration. Challenges include data quality requirements, computational demands, and ethical considerations (Tamanampudi, 2021).

Current research emphasises emerging trends, including edge computing applications, federated learning, and enhanced security protocols. Future directions point toward developing more sophisticated deep learning and hybrid automation models to enhance cloud-native DevOps efficiency and resilience.

2.1 Cloud-Native Technologies and DevOps Integration

Cloud-native architectures have evolved significantly, with microservices becoming the foundation of modern applications. Research indicates that 76% of enterprises now use microservices for application development (AWS, 2024). Container adoption, led by Docker and Kubernetes, has standardized deployment processes across environments. Studies show containerised applications achieve 43% faster deployment cycles and 35% lower operational costs (Microsoft Azure, 2024). Multi-cloud deployments present new opportunities for scalability while introducing complexity in orchestration and management (Google Cloud, 2024).

2.2 AI Applications in DevOps Practices

Machine learning algorithms have transformed CI/CD pipelines through automated testing and intelligent deployment strategies. Research by Thompson et al. (2024) demonstrates that AI-driven CI/CD reduces deployment failures by 45% and improves code quality metrics by 30%. Automated security scanning powered by AI detects vulnerabilities 60% faster than traditional methods (Chen & Rodriguez, 2024). Studies show machine learning models accurately predict resource requirements with 85% accuracy (Kumar, 2024).

2.2.1 AI-based Automation For Cloud-Native DevOps

While new cloud-native environments become more intricate, automation is no longer a call but an essential element of DevOps. AI can be integrated into the traditional DevOps to minimise the role of human intervention in the given processes and amplify the value of the DevOps. Machine learning and predictive analytics components of AI can perform monotonous work, manage processes involved in CI/CD, and analyse existing data to enhance the dependability of the overall system. It simultaneously allows the redeployment of human capital to higher-value activities and deploys much faster and with higher reliability than a human could. Automating workloads is one of the main trends of AI in cloud-native DevOps transformation. This section will cover how this instrument is used in various fields and what real-life examples demonstrate its effectiveness. Here are the several features that have been categorised under this segmentation type:

2.2.2 Repetitive Task Automation

Interactions like code reviews, new configuration, and repeated testing are critical but cyclic roles in the DevOps life cycle. Implementing AI to perform these tasks significantly decreases the workload of these tasks and greatly diminishes human errors while also speeding up development cycles.

i.) **Code Reviews:** Resources like GitHub Copilot and CodeClimate are developed to analyse a code and recommend rectifying the situation. These tools learn from source code and coding standard documents and always deliver quality code.
ii.) **Configuration Management:** The fully automated Ansible is another example of an AI tool needed to update configurations and look for disparities using Ansible Automation Analytics. This will ensure that there is always compliance with the available infrastructure about other possible configurations.

iii.) **Routine Testing:** Automation functional, regression, and performance tests include Mabl and Testim.io. It is important to underline that these tools can create and update test cases on the fly, tracking modifications to code and pointing at potential problems.

iv.) **Incident Management:** Other machine learning-based rational alerting and triaging systems such as Moogsoft bring together multiple alerts and sort out cases depending on the severity of impacts

2.2.3 CI/CD Pipeline Optimization

Continuous Integration (CI) and Continuous Deployment (CD) are the two crucial forms of the DevOps life cycle which allow for frequent and stable product releases. AI improves these pipelines by identifying probable failures, streamlining tasks, and ensuring that deployment is practical and safe.

i.) Predictive Analytics: Harness is a good example of an AI tool that uses machine learning to anticipate build or deployment failures based on pattern red flagging. Notably, these tools assist the teams in addressing potential challenges that might lead to disruptions in production.

ii.) Deployment Strategies: AI-powered tools include the ones that enhance the deployment methodologies, like canary and blue-green deployment methodologies. For instance, Spinnaker with Kayenta automation can determine whether new deployments are similar to previous ones and whether they are stable enough.

iii.) Automated Rollbacks: Here, one can observe that in case of a failure, AI tools use rollbacks that happen automatically. KNOWLEDGE CHECK Argo CD has AI plugins that watch the deployment's health and trigger a rollback if there are issues, reducing the time the system is down.

iv.) Resource Allocation: AI helps manage resources in the CI/CD implementation process. Automated DevOps in GitLab applies AI in the way that AutoDevOps distributes resources automatically to complete builds or deployments without congesting more than necessary.

When embedding AI into CI/CD processes, businesses gain higher rates of software deployments, increased availability and reliability, and improved quality of releases. This results in faster development being successfully brought to the user, primarily due to the efficiency enhancement derived from having numerous small subgroups.

2.3 Classification of AI Tools in Cloud-Native DevOps

In cloud-native DevOps environments, handling various aspects of the software delivery lifecycle has become possible only using artificial intelligence (AI) tools. These AI tools cover the deployment activities, making them faster, more reliable and more secure. Subdividing these tools by their capability makes it easy for teams to identify tools that can solve a particular problem, such as CI/CD pipeline, infrastructure, security, and observability. Every class of AI tools mentioned above is important for removing bottlenecks, optimizing the use of resources, and optimizing the entire system's performance.

2.3.1 Major AI tools in cloud-native DevOps

The following sections describe the significant AI tools in cloud-native DevOps and a perspective on what each type offers in the DevOps phases.

i.) **CI/CD Pipeline Tools:** CI/CD automation frameworks are at the heart of AI applications and are designed to enhance software delivery. These tools decrease the amount of human involvement by predicting errors, self-automated deployment strategies, and having a better and more stable release.

ii.) **Harness:** Harness is another continuously integrated delivery tool incorporating several forms of artificial intelligence; for example, it supports deployment rollbacks and pipeline coordination. It employs artificial intelligence to watch over the productivity and performance of deployments and to fine-tune strategies for A/B rolling updates, among others. Although it only captures historical data, Harness can forecast probable deployment failures and recommend optimizing, significantly decreasing the chances of downtime.

iii.) **GitLab Auto DevOps:** GitLab Auto DevOps provides complete DevOps pipeline automation, from code integration to its deployment. It uses machine learning to assess application performance and continuously identify the first signs of threats. This tool remains active and constantly feeds back information to the teams, enabling them to work on problems before they affect the production cycle.

iv.) **Spinnaker with Kayenta:** Spinnaker is a native cloud delivery tool that works with Kayenta for AI-based canary analysis. By default, it enhances antibodies by comparing new deployments with previous versions, reducing risks in new feature releases.

v.) **Argo CD:** Argo CD is a continuously deployed GitOps from the Kubernetes system used to get applications into place. Argo CD with AI plugins can automatically determine problems within an application deployment and apply corrections on failed releases for high availability and reliability.

2.3.2 Ability To Dynamically Allocate Resources

Identifying and managing infrastructure in CN refers to the ability to dynamically allocate resources, automatically provision and ensure compliance measures are met. Automated infrastructure management tools improve these processes by employing algorithms that can use the actual data within practical applications.

i.) **Terraform with Sentinel:** Machine learning models use Terraform and the Sentinel policy as code to automate the infrastructure deployment. Workload and governance policies are met, while assurance is given that resources are appropriately distributed depending on the workload required in an organization.

ii.) **Kubeflow:** Kubeflow was initially developed to manage data scientists' machine learning workflows on Kubernetes, but the infrastructure setup has also been simplified. Of specific importance is that it helps speed up the deployment of new ML models and manage resources with improvements in operational efficiency in cloud-native environments.

iii.) **CloudFormation with AI Plugins (AWS):** The most important extension functionalities provided by AWS CloudFormation encompass data intelligence and automated management technologies powered by AI and ML capabilities. These AI plugins assist in responding to changes in demand, identifying protruding issues, and verifying that infrastructure alterations do not create threats.

iv.) **Red Hat Ansible with Automation Analytics:** Ansible is based on artificial intelligence that has automation analytics to help measure infrastructure performance and develop a way to resolve possible issues. It enhances configuration management tasks and brings out remediation automation to enable infrastructure to uphold high-security standards and compliance.

2.3.3 Security Tools

Artificial intelligence-based security solutions supplement cloud-native applications and lock ship threats, compliance, and vulnerabilities. It is imperative to support these tools because container Organization is extensive and intricate, involving many ecosystems of containers.

i.) **Aqua Security:** Aqua Security provides absolute time protection and the identification of threats that exist in connection to containerized applications. It relies on machine learning to analyze behavioral traits, detect noncompliance, and monitor and enforce compliance across the K8s cluster.

ii.) **Prisma Cloud (Palo Alto Networks):** Prisma Cloud operates with artificial intelligence that continuously scans cloud-native environments for threats. It specializes in containers, serverless functions, and Kubernetes security enhancement and compliance checks and threat prevention constantly.

iii.) **Falco (Sysdig)**: Falco is an open-source runtime security tool that uses machine learning to detect suspicious activities on Kubernetes. It monitors systems calls, pinpoints where something looks fishy, and alerts the teams about it.

iv.) **Snyk:** Currently, Snyk identifies vulnerable code, dependencies, and container images and suggests how to remediate such vulnerabilities in real-time using artificial intelligence and machine learning. This makes it easier for the developers to fix up on the security weaknesses at the decentralized level so that none of them get to the level of production.

2.3.4 Monitoring Tools

Observability is used in conjunction with, or place of, monitoring tools. The observability of systems and the ability to monitor the infrastructure, applications and services are fundamental to the success of cloud-native applications. Regarding AI in observability, it focuses on exploring the system's inner workings and allows for better, incident-driven, root-cause analysis.

i.) •**Dynatrace:** Dynatrace is an artificial intelligence-based observability solution that offers real-time monitoring, alerting, and analysis, including problem detection and resolution. Others utilize AI to study application performance data, define problematic areas, and recommend improvements, thus providing high availability and application performance.

ii.) •**DataDog:** DataDog employs machine learning techniques to help monitor the cloud-native applications and spot logs, metrics, and traces of data peculiarities. This is because it gives detailed information concerning application usage and resource demands and assists the various teams in addressing problems.

iii.) •**Prometheus with Cortex:** For the multi-tenant use case, Prometheus, one of the most commonly used open-source monitoring systems, can be complemented by Cortex. AI-integrated extensions measure characteristics and identify shifts while issuing signals of concerning conditions.

iv.) •**Elastic APM (Elastic Stack):** Elastic APM is a real-time application performance-monitoring solution incorporating an AI-based anomaly detection engine. It parses and analyses logs, traces, and displays trends and gives out alarms if they exceed set thresholds to ensure that problems are dealt with in advance.

Dividing AI tools into these categories will help cloud-native DevOps teams and organizations realize how different AI tools can be applied to solve diverse concerns across the CI/CD process. İt provides an orderly method of improving every aspect of the DevOps lifecycle with data intelligence, thereby making the cloud-native environments more efficient, dependable and secure

2.4 Infrastructure Management and Scaling

Infrastructure as Code (IaC) practices enhanced by AI significantly improve resource management. Recent studies indicate that automated scaling decisions are 40% more efficient than manual approaches (Davidson et al., 2024). Reinforcement learning algorithms optimise resource allocation, reducing cloud costs by 25% while maintaining performance SLAs (IBM Cloud, 2024). Research demonstrates that AI-driven infrastructure management reduces configuration errors by 55% (Smith & Patel, 2024).

2.5 Monitoring and Observability

Advanced monitoring systems utilising AI process massive operational datasets in real time. Studies show that machine-learning models detect anomalies 70% faster than threshold-based approaches (Johnson & Lee, 2024). Predictive maintenance algorithms reduce system downtime by 45% through early warning detection (Williams et al., 2024). Root cause analysis powered by AI decreases mean time to resolution (MTTR) by 60% compared to manual investigation methods (Oracle Cloud, 2024).

2.6 AI Ethics and Governance

AI implementation in DevOps requires robust governance frameworks. Studies highlight the importance of explainable AI (XAI) in critical deployments, with 65% of organisations prioritising transparency in automated decisions (Wilson & Chang, 2024). Research demonstrates that successful implementations maintain human oversight while achieving automation benefits, reducing risks by 40% (Morgan et al., 2024).

2.7 Cost-Benefit Analysis

Organisations implementing AI-driven DevOps report an average ROI of 280% over three years (Gartner, 2024). Initial implementation costs, including infrastructure and training, are offset by a 45% reduction in operational expenses. Studies show training programs require 6-8 months for team proficiency but reduce incident response times by 60% (Deloitte, 2024).

2.8 Industry-Specific Implementations

Financial services lead to adopting AI-DevOps, reporting 40% improved compliance monitoring (Jenkins & Roberts, 2024). Healthcare organisations demonstrate 55% faster deployment with enhanced security protocols (Kumar et al., 2024). E-commerce platforms achieve 65% better resource optimisation during peak loads (Martinez & Lee, 2024).

2.9 Integration Challenges and Solutions

Legacy system integration remains a primary challenge, with 45% of organisations reporting compatibility issues (Anderson & White, 2024). Research indicates that structured training programs reduce skill gaps by 70%. Data quality improvements show an 85% correlation with successful AI implementation (Taylor et al., 2024).

2.10 Comparative Analysis

AI-enhanced DevOps demonstrates 3x faster deployment cycles than traditional approaches (IBM Research, 2024). Machine learning models outperform rule-based systems by 65% in anomaly detection. Tool comparison studies show integrated platforms achieve 40% better results than point solutions (Microsoft Research, 2024).

3. AI TOOLS CLASSIFICATION IN CLOUD-NATIVE DevOps

3.1 CI/CD Pipeline Tools

Modern continuous integration and deployment pipelines employ sophisticated AI algorithms for deployment optimisation and automated testing. Harness implements deep learning models for predictive analytics, achieving a 45% reduction in deployment failures through automated rollback mechanisms (DevOps Research, 2024). Studies demonstrate that GitLab Auto DevOps' AI-driven performance assessment reduces mean time to detection (MTTD) by 60% through continuous monitoring and predictive analysis (Anderson et al., 2024). Spinnaker's integration with Kayenta enables automated canary analysis, utilising statistical learning models to compare deployment metrics against baselines, resulting in 35% fewer production incidents (Google Cloud Research, 2024). Recent implementations of Argo CD with AI plugins demonstrate a 40% improvement in deployment reliability through automated remediation and predictive health checks (Kumar & Smith, 2024).

3.2 Infrastructure Management Tools

Infrastructure orchestration has evolved through AI integration, with Terraform and Sentinel implementing reinforcement learning for resource optimisation. Research indicates a 50% improvement in resource utilisation through ML-driven infrastructure deployment decisions (AWS Technical Report, 2024). Kubeflow's integration with Kubernetes enables automated ML workflow management, reducing operational overhead by 65% while maintaining performance SLAs (Chen & Rodriguez, 2024). CloudFormation's AI capabilities demonstrate 40% more accurate resource forecasting than traditional methods (Thompson et al., 2024).

3.3 Security Tools

Aqua Security and Prisma Cloud leverage deep learning models for threat detection, achieving 90% accuracy in identifying security vulnerabilities (Davidson, 2024). Studies show ML-based runtime monitoring by Falco reduces false positives by 70% compared to rule-based systems (Security Research Quarterly, 2024).

3.4 Observability Tools

Dynatrace and DataDog implement neural networks for anomaly detection, processing millions of metrics in real time with 95% accuracy (Monitoring Systems Journal, 2024). Prometheus with Cortex demonstrates enterprise-scale monitoring capabilities through distributed AI processing, handling 50 million metrics per second while maintaining sub-second query performance (Performance Analytics Review, 2024).

4. AI-BASED AUTOMATION FOR CLOUD-NATIVE DevOps

4.1 Workflow Automation

AI transforms traditional DevOps workflows through intelligent automation of routine tasks. Machine learning models automate code reviews with 85% accuracy, reducing review time by 60% (Wilson et al., 2024). Configuration management tools like Ansible leverage AI for predictive configuration drift detection, decreasing system misconfigurations by 45% (Red Hat Research, 2024). Automated testing frameworks powered by deep learning demonstrate 90% accuracy in test case generation and maintenance (Testing Analytics Report, 2024).

4.2 CI/CD Pipeline Optimization

Continuous integration and deployment processes benefit from AI through:

i.) Predictive build failure detection reducing failed deployments by 70% (Jenkins AI Report, 2024)
ii.) Automated canary analysis improving deployment success rates by 55% (Google Cloud, 2024)
iii.) Dynamic resource allocation optimising pipeline performance by 40% (Azure DevOps, 2024)

4.3 Case Studies from Various Industries

Various references from the industries and different examples then show how it is effective to implement AI automation, especially on cloud-native DevOps. The accomplishments described in these success stories show how organizations have enhanced their efficiency, thereby cutting costs and increasing the dependability of systems using AI.

4.3.1 Case Study 1

While there is often significant enthusiasm at the initiation of the implementation of harness and the subsequent key steps, which include exploration, adoption, modification, adaptation, changes, and other pursuits – in a financial services firm, it is critical to emphasize that there are some real and assumed obstacles that should not be underestimated.

A top financial services provider adopted Harness for CI/CD process management. In this respect, based on machine learning to predict deployment failures and other outcomes, together with optimizing the chosen approach and moments for release, the company cut down deployment times by 40% and the level of production incidents by 30%. Due to the use of AI, the function of rollbacks helped in quickly correcting all the wrong decisions the firm made regarding deployment and greatly reducing the time the services were offline.

4.3.2 Case Study 2

Prisma Cloud has added to the security at a healthcare organization

A healthcare organization needed a solution for managing the security of cloud-native applications and integrated Prisma Cloud. Some of the significant benefits obtained from the endeavor include improved ability to detect threats while at the same time enforcing compliance revealing possible weaknesses within the organization at an early stage. It resulted in a decrease of security incidents by 50% as well as better protection of the whole system.

4.3.3 Case Study 3

Effectiveness mapping in an E-Commerce platform using Mabl for automated testing

A B2B e-commerce company started using Mabl for functional and regression testing based on Artificial Intelligence. The continuously managing tool diminished the percentage of the work done by the test team by 60%, enabling the engineering department to bring new features into production. This AI-triggered anomaly detection made it possible for the bugs to be detected and corrected before actual deployment of the project.

4.3.4 Case Study

Dynatrace fine-tunes its monitoring for a global apparel retailer

A large international merchant started using Dynatrace to promote greater visibility and improve the handling of incidents. Smart analysis of root cause decreased the time required to isolate and find problems by 70%. Application of trends enhanced early intervention for occurrences while availing the system during busy shopping seasons.

These examples are useful in illustrating how AI automation has put the cloud-native DevOps landscape through a massive transformation. Holding in mind the given points of improvement in efficiency, security, and reliability it can be observed that organizations in different fields and industries have benefited from AI tools.

5. MONITORING AND FEEDBACK IN AI-ENHANCED DevOps

5.1 Real-Time Analytics and Anomaly Detection

AI-driven monitoring systems process operational metrics using deep learning models for real-time anomaly detection. Platforms like Dynatrace have achieved 95% accuracy in anomaly detection (Dynatrace Research Report, 2024; Miller et al., 2024). DataDog's machine learning algorithms demonstrate 70% faster detection rates compared to traditional methods (DataDog Technical Analysis, 2024; Thompson & Lee, 2024). Studies by Chen et al. (2024) document 40% reduction in false positives and 60% improvement in early warning detection across multiple enterprise implementations. Having an ongoing view of what is happening is the operational engine of cloud-native applications and environment to ensure that all is working well. AI improves this process by identifying abnormalities and estimating failures that the teams can solve without development breakdowns.

- Anomaly Detection: AI algorithms continuously run to normalize the metrics, logs, and traces in an attempt to identify issues with the environment. Some application performance monitoring tools such as Dynatrace and DataDog rely on machine learning to drive the detection of patterns and real time alerts. For instance, an application may show a sudden rise in its CPU usage or a plummeting response time, which suggests that the application is having some problem.
- Predictive Alerts: Conventional monitoring solutions are static, thus based on the use of specific thresholds, while AI-based monitoring tools can anticipate failures that may occur in the future by learning from the past. Prometheus with Cortex enhances Prometheus by leveraging AI to generate predictive alerts based on patterns allowing teams to act before an issue occurs.
- Container and Microservices Monitoring: In dynamic environment such as Kubernetes, artificial intelligence tools keep checking the health status of individual containers and microservices. New Relic as well as Elastic APM can ‘see into’ the containers and will identify things like memory leaks or resource contention (Acemoglu & Restrepo, 2018).

5.2 Root Cause Analysis and Predictive Insights

Machine learning models enhance root cause analysis through pattern recognition and correlation. Kumar and Smith (2024) report 65% reduction in MTTR using AI-powered RCA tools across 500 enterprise deployments. IBM Research (2024) demonstrates predictive analytics identifying potential failures 48 hours in advance with 85% accuracy in cloud environments. BigPanda Implementation Study (2024) shows 90% alert noise reduction through ML-based clustering.

For this reason, Risk Analysis is important in identifying the root causes of any occurrences with a view of preventing their recurrence in future. Automated RCA through controlled AI tools simplify the RCA process, combined with predictive analysis, greatly decreasing the time taken to isolate and respond to problem areas.

i.) •Automated RCA: Some AI tools such as Dynatrace will correlate events on their own using machine learning to determine what is causing the incident. Based on logs, metrics, and traces, these tools identify the exact component or service, which is the source of a problem without performing detailed investigation.

ii.) •Correlation of Events: While occurring in cloud-native environments, the events can touch on different microservices or infrastructure parts. Moogsoft and BigPanda are examples of AI-driven platforms where there is an attempted mapping of data based on its source to ensure the platform has an all-encompassing view of the particular incident and its effects. It assists the teams to appreciate the rationale of the whole process and respond to the deviations by carrying out corrective action.

iii.) •Predictive Insights: AI algorithms not only scans data to find issues and trends that might occur, but learns from previous occurrences in order to minimize their occurrence in future. For instance, while using DataDog, one can predict when resources will be depleted or perform poorly based on their history. This makes it easier for teams to be ahead of time in dealing with problems and not wait until something unbecoming occurs.

Cutting down on the time taken to make root cause analysis of a problem and providing probability conjecture enables the improvement of the mean time to recovery (MTTR) and enhancement of systems stability. This helps the DevOps teams not to waste a lot of time trying to solve such problems but instead they find better ways of solving some of these problems (Yarlagadda, 2018).

5.3 Enhanced Feedback Loops

Google Cloud Research (2024) reports 55% improvement in system reliability through AI-monitored feedback systems. UX Analytics Consortium Study (2024) documents 3x faster issue detection rates. AWS Technical Review (2024) demonstrates 40% reduction in resource wastage through AI-driven capacity planning.

Feedbacks are another element of the DevOps life cycle; they are long and short real-time detailed informative about system performance or user behaviours and even our code. Feedback loops are improved by using AI as it can collect, process, and report on data at the right frequency to allow teams to take appropriate actions.

i.) •Continuous Performance Feedback: AI-based monitoring solutions can be empowered to give live feedback on the application and their infrastructure state. For instance, Elastic APM and New Relic monitor and interpret application performance and provide quick and easy reports on the opportunities for enhancement. Such a mechanism supports optimized decisions and the subsequent constant enhancement of all applications involved by the teams.

ii.) •User Experience Insights: Currently, there are tools, which look into the features of the user behaviour and the application to gain some understanding of the user experience. By leveraging the power of Artificial Intelligence, Dynatrace is able to identify user interactions for analysis of performance issues affecting their experience. This feedback enables the participants to focus on areas that would require maximization of effort since they affect the end-users most (Shekhar, 2019).

iii.) •Automated Incident Response: AI-generated feedback loops are the processes that operate on predefined models, and then alert teams to incidents and potential solutions. As in any IT environment, BigPanda and Moogsoft classify alerts based on their levels of urgency and important, with critical problems addressed first.

Real-time information feedback helps development and operations interact more effectively with each other through constant reports. This speeds up the cycle and decreases the change of mistakes, this also ensures that applications will accommodate for what the user needs.

The application and development of all aforementioned tools depend upon its efficacy and success. Continuous real time monitoring and feedback revolutionize cloud native DevOps through real time visibility, correcting the root cause and improved feedback mechanisms through AI. These capabilities allow the organization to recognize problems immediately and solve them before causing significant disruptions on the applications. This approach shows that with the help of leveraging artificial intelligence, DevOps teams can shift from monitoring as the primary focus point, and become more focused into delivering improved, cloud-native systems that have greater resilience and improved user experience (Faishal et al., 2023).

5.4 Implementation Metrics

Enterprise DevOps Survey (2024) analysing 1000 and more organizations reports:

- 70% reduction in unplanned downtime (DevOps Research Group, 2024)
- 45% improvement in resource utilization (Cloud Native Foundation, 2024)
- 85% faster incident resolution (Incident Management Forum, 2024)
- 50% decrease in operational costs (Enterprise Technology Review, 2024)

6. CHALLENGES AND LIMITATIONS OF AI IN CLOUD-NATIVE DEVOPS

As useful and beneficial for automating and fine tuning the cloud-native DevOps processes AI is there are certain problems and drawbacks to its application. These are among the challenges such as data privacy, data scaling, interpretability by humans, and requirement of quality data. Mitigating these issues remains available to organizations to unlock full effectiveness of the AI while preserving the trust, effectiveness and security in the DevOps environments they employ. The following section of the paper further analyses each of these challenges.

6.1 Data Privacy and Security

i.) AI based DevOps solutions depend significantly on diverse datasets involving customers' data or code base, configurations, logs, and others. The aggregation, archiving, and analysis of this information present problems of privacy and security (Kumar, 2024).

ii.) Compliance Issues: All implementers must make sure that data privacy acts like GDPR, HIPAA, and CCPA are met by their AI tools. Non-compliance emanates to legal consequences as well as reputational risks.

iii.) Data Access Control: AI models in general need input data and/or output data, in most cases, this data contains private information. That it is secure and is controlled should be a priority in order to curb on cases of hacking and misuse of this access.

iv.) Vulnerability to Attacks: AI systems also can be vulnerable to adversarial attacks because an attacker tries to feed an AI model the data that was manipulated. It is imperative that AI pipelines are protected against such an attack. Use secure data encryption as well as anonymization of data. Continuously review AI models and datasets for data privacy laws compliance. Implement zero trust architecture solution and the role-based access control in attempting to prevent data leakage processes, its implementation also presents several challenges and limitations. These challenges include data privacy concerns, scalability issues, the need for interpretability and human oversight, and dependency on data quality. Addressing these limitations is crucial for organizations to fully realize the potential of AI while maintaining trust, efficiency, and security in their DevOps practices. This section explores each of these challenges in detail.

v.) AI-driven DevOps solutions rely heavily on large datasets, including sensitive information such as code repositories, user data, and infrastructure logs. The collection, storage, and processing of this data introduce significant privacy and security concerns.

vi.) Compliance Issues: Organizations must ensure that their AI tools comply with data privacy regulations such as GDPR, HIPAA, and CCPA. Non-compliance can result in legal penalties and reputational damage.

vii.) Data Access Control: AI models often require access to sensitive data for training and inference. Ensuring that access is secure and controlled is essential to prevent data breaches or unauthorized use.

viii.) Vulnerability to Attacks: AI systems can become targets for adversarial attacks, where malicious actors manipulate input data to deceive the model. Protecting AI pipelines from such attacks is critical.

Mitigation Strategies:

- Implement robust data encryption and anonymization techniques.
- Regularly audit AI models and datasets for compliance with data privacy regulations.
- Adopt zero-trust architectures and role-based access controls to restrict data access.

6.2 Scalability and Resource Constraints

Deep learning-based AI models need a considerable amount resource to train and make prediction and decisions. Another issue in cloud-native DevOps settings is a longitudinal scalability of AI-based applications and infrastructures to accommodate the increasing volume of tasks or the dynamic network infrastructure.

i.) •Resource Allocation: Computer-based AI tasks are known to require resources in equal proportion; such a claim may interfere with other crucial processes. A key challenge concerns how to meet overall performance goals without incurring performance bottlenecks in the management of resources.
ii.) •Cost Considerations: Dreaming AI models in cloud environments is costly more so if its training or processing is massive and constant. Every organization is, therefore, in a position to count the cost and its benefits.
iii.) •Latency Issues: Some of the use cases of AI working in real-time, like CI/CD pipeline anomalies detection, need to be low latency. It's technically challenging to ensure that there isn't a lag when releasing AI models to the field. Employ service architectures such as auto-provisioning of CPU, memory, disk and quotas to complete computational AI tasks. Consider various factors through which it is possible to weigh down the AI models, such as the model architecture. Running cost control strategies on AI costs within the organization requires substantial computational resources for training and inference. In cloud-native DevOps environments, scaling AI-driven solutions to handle large workloads or dynamic infrastructure can be challenging.
iv.) •Resource Allocation: AI workloads can be resource-intensive, potentially competing with other critical processes. Managing resource allocation effectively is essential to avoid performance bottlenecks.
v.) •Cost Considerations: Running AI models in cloud environments can be expensive, especially if they require continuous training or large-scale processing. Organizations must balance the cost-benefit equation.
vi.) •Latency Issues: Real-time AI applications, such as anomaly detection in CI/CD pipelines, require low latency. Ensuring that AI models operate efficiently without introducing delays is a technical challenge.

Mitigation Strategies:

- •Use cloud-native solutions like auto-scaling and resource quotas to manage AI workloads dynamically.
- •Optimize AI models for efficiency, focusing on lightweight architectures when possible.
- •Leverage cost management tools to monitor and control AI-related expenses.

6.3 Computer transparency and why human intervention is required

AI models especially deep learning models are usually 'Black box" and therefore one cannot understand how the AI model arrived at a particular decision. When it is a question of making choices capable of affecting system availability and security, as often occurs in DevOps, interpretability is vital.

i.) •Lack of Transparency: If AI decisions are not transparent it becomes difficult for the devops team to verify these results on their own. Interpretability issues related to or-bounded models also constitute a limitation, as mentioned earlier, that affects adaption.

ii.) •Human Oversight: Some decisions are made only with the involvement of a human for instance security decisions or compliance decisions. The utilization of the system that is AI-based with no human intervention can cause problems.

iii.) •Ethical Considerations: Safety of these models against bias during operation is paramount when making decisions concerning users or the functioning of the system.

Mitigation Strategies:

- •Using XAI techniques to develop transparent and interpretable AI models
- •Use of HITL when the AI makes recommendations on major decisions but the human continues to take final decisions.
- •Continual auditing of AI model output for conformance to organization goals and ethical standards.

6.4 Dependence on Data Quality and Real-Time Data -Significance and Difficulty

The performance of AI models relies significantly on the quality and accuracy of the data that it is trained upon. For cloud-native DevOps, real-time data is required for monitoring and automation. Discrepancies may result in the prediction or actions taken as wrong (Douglas & Roger, 2024).

i.) •Data Inconsistencies: Data inconsistencies or incompleteness might cause poor model performance. Missing logs or incorrect metrics might cause false anomaly detection.

ii.) •Data drift: Data patterns used for training AI models may change over time, leading to "data drift." Models have to be retrained at intervals to remain relevant.

iii.) •Latency while processing real-time data. AI models must get the latest data without latency in processing for real-time monitoring and incident response. Latency can undermine the potency of AI-driven insights.

Mitigations

- •Data validation and cleaning.
- •Use automated retraining mechanisms to keep AI models updated with the latest data.
- •Optimize data pipelines to minimize latency and ensure real-time processing

AI-driven solutions have tremendous potential to enhance cloud-native DevOps, but they come with challenges that organizations must address to maximize their benefits. Ensuring data privacy, managing resource constraints, maintaining interpretability, and guaranteeing data quality are essential for successful AI integration. By understanding and mitigating these challenges, organizations can build more resilient, secure, and efficient cloud-native DevOps environments that leverage the full power of AI.

7. BEST PRACTICES

While the implementation of AI in DevOps promises to deliver high-efficiency results, higher resilience, and efficient processes, these results do require thorough and careful thinking about their adoption. With that, here're a few best practices for the teams interested in adapting AI technologies in their ways to access the tools they need, have seamless integration, and achieve measurable results. This section provides step-wise instructions for successful adoption of AI in DevOps-from the right tool selection to a report on improvements seen after implementation.

7.1 Choosing AI Tools

Above all, it is important for DevOps groups to first understand the needs of their environment when choosing AI tools. This makes sure that the tools picked by the group fulfil their need-base, such as improved deployment speed, better monitoring, or executing repetitive tasks. Since integrating the chosen tools into the existing DevOps ecosystem will be vital, it becomes necessary that they should integrate well with the current CI/CD pipeline, container management, and monitoring tools. Teams should assess whether their tools will work with a widely popular core platform such as Jenkins, Kubernetes, or Prometheus, as this compatibility can shorten the time and cost of setting up and maintaining the tools. Scalability is another important key deciding factor; with selective tools, an organization can outgrow its ability to manage increased data and workloads. Modular, API-based architectures can accommodate future extension and will be suited to both current and future changing DevOps requirements. Additionally, the capability of AI tools to connect with external cloud platforms (e.g., AWS, Google Cloud, Azure) adds to the scalability and operational flexibility of the tool; making it even more versatile for cloud-native DevOps.

Under the aegis of government policy design, with a guarantee of employing local resources, actualize actualization in the abolition of the monopoly of capital for real transformation and development of decentralized power of the state's population as votaries of civil liberty.

Relying solely on technical compatibility is hardly enough; one would also need to assess the machine learning capabilities of the tool in question since not all AI tools produce the same level of sophistication regarding predictive analytics, anomaly detection, or self-healing capabilities. Based on the types of algorithms and models used, one could fairly indicate the tool's effectiveness in tasks such as pinpointing bottlenecks in deployment or automating scaling. It would also help to look into industry standards, user reviews, and case studies highlighting how well the tool has performed in similar settings. Trial periods or sandbox environments are offered by many vendors that allow the teams to engage in hands-on evaluation to avoid making a commitment (Mistry et al., 2024).

7.2 Integration Strategies

Successful integration of AI tools in DevOps requires a strategic approach. A phased adoption process is recommended, where teams initially deploy AI tools in a limited capacity or for specific DevOps stages. For example, integrating AI in CI/CD pipelines first can allow teams to observe improvements in deployment speed and error reduction without overhauling the entire infrastructure at once. Phased adoption enables DevOps teams to assess the effectiveness of each tool in isolation, identify potential compatibility issues, and make adjustments as needed before a full-scale rollout.

Then, it should also be tried at each level of the adoption process with an effectiveness-checking mechanism. A team should deploy the performance evaluation metrics (e.g., error reduction rates, latency improvements) against expected benchmarks to know whether the tool justifies an organization-wide deployment. For example, when deploying an AI-based monitoring tool such as Prometheus, the team will evaluate alert quality and response times to ascertain its efficacy. Testing like this will provide teams with data to determine which tools add the most value and decide where else they will integrate.

AI-devops alignment employs the appropriate tools at the right point for the maximum value. For prediction analytics, for instance, it can be understood that such tools should be embedded during planning as they can give forecasts for the resources needed to carry out a certain set of activities. Example of such an extensive network is uncovering the applications of anomaly detection tools, which are best used in automated monitoring and observability stages. Partnering with stakeholders also ensures that high-impact areas within each DevOps stage have been identified in order to optimize the areas automation and AI-enabled insights are to be deployed (Abouelyazid & Xiang, 2019).

7.3 Impact Measurement Efficiency and Resilience

The evaluation of value-added by AI in DevOps can be by focusing on KPIs for efficiency, resilience, and resource utilization improvement. One such important measure may include: Automation effectiveness-increase as measured by decrease of manual intervention. For example: Decrease in deployment time across CI/CD pipelines or decrease in alerts requiring human attention indicating AI-based anomaly detection is blocking most of false positives.

Mean time to detection (MTTD) and mean time to recovery (MTTR). These are useful for assessing the effectiveness of monitoring. How fast AI detects anomalies and starts recovery could complement measures used by teams to gauge whether a tool bolsters a system's resilience. This helps minimize downtime. The other element looks at the accuracy of the detection system. The AI is measuring how well it can differentiate real issues from harmless fluctuations for realistic reliability on the system. Grafana is an AI tool that further develops observability using real-time performance metrics.

Cost-effectiveness is another measurement, driving the use of such AI tools in scaling. These tools, largely available as Kubernetes-enabled AI, automatically scale according to demand and save on costs associated with over-provisioning infrastructure. Changing patterns in resource usage will be compared with costs before and after implementing AI to quantify the cost impact brought about by AI. Furthermore, a productivity gain analysis based on how much time less is spent on routine monitoring or debugging will provide a more sharpened picture of savings and efficiency gains brought about by using AI tools.

These KPIs can help evaluate the extent to which AI tools fulfil a DevOps objective in numbers as well as provide a starting point for continuous improvement. Periodic evaluation against these metrics helps teams identify specific areas where AI tools are missed, allowing remediation for adjustment or upgrading as the need arises. Adoption of these best practices in identifying appropriate AI tools, a phased approach to the integration, and monitoring the efficacy gives DevOps teams the edge to use AI without putting them at risk, thereby building a more effective, resilient, and agile cloud-native DevOps environment.

8. FUTURE DIRECTIONS

The sphere of potentialities to be realized through artificial intelligence in the DevOps scenario is great. Newer and newer technologies are invented by modernity and are continuously upgraded to improve further automation, decision-making, and collaboration. With cloud-native architecture and microservices becoming the standard pattern of systems followed by organizations, AI's role in enhancing DevOps processes would grow even more significant. This section discusses emerging AI technologies in DevOps, their probable futures dev against such trends, and critical research that will outline the AI-induced DevOps landscape in the next few years. AI development promises changes in DevOps with sophisticated machine learning models, edge AI, and increased automation. More refined machine learning models will importantly facilitate automation through very precise decision-making in situations of deployment, resource allocation, and monitoring. Current methods in machine learning-such as reinforcement learning-are finding their way into CI/CD pipelines to dynamically change deployment schemes depending on past experience and real-time data. Herewith, automated workflows will be created by DevOps teams that adapt over time, thus bringing efficiency and reducing errors during production. Another new emerging aspect of DevOps is Edge AI. Edge AI brings computation and decision-making much closer to data sources, allowing on-the-spot responses with lower latency. For instance, an edge architecture would be used in an IoT-driven DevOps environment to process and act on data from many devices at the point of their origin.

Hence, the edge may fetch speedier event detection-resolutions in distributed environments coupled with optimized utilization of decentralized data. AI predictive maintenance aids the organizations in enhancing operational reliability while yielding cloud-based decision-making delays. All these, along with NLP and AI-powered chatbots, are increasingly stepping into DevOps to perform automation work such as generating reports, issue tracking, status updates in real-time, etc., making work much more effective and improving myth-making in the team. As such, AI in DevOps will be changes to autonomous systems that rely heavily on AI for decision-making frameworks and will use hyper-automation as standards. The AI-assisted decision-making framework will empower DevOps teams to hand over a lot of field operations to the AI systems. Such frameworks will comprise algorithms that can glean sufficient data from complex data sets, learn from historical events, and predict probable future incidents. For example, a combination of predictive analytics and causal inference can automate decision-making pertaining to workload distribution, incident resolution, and release scheduling to proactively mitigate issues before they escalate. Hyper-automation is also an expected development where organisations will use interconnected AI systems to automate all the steps of DevOps workflows. Thus, all previously done isolated AI-enabled processes will no longer be a case; people will have CMDB under hyper-automation.

Hyper-automation connects AI driven tools across CI/CD, monitoring, security, and infrastructure management into a truly seamless, end to end automated DevOps environment. Hyperautomation, thus, reduces human effort across these stages, enabling the DevOps teams to focus on innovations rather than on such repetitive, dull tasks. This converted way is transparent to future improvements in scalability since AI systems manage complex workflows and handle at scale large volumes of data under minimal human supervision. Hyper-automation not only implies scalability but also increased resilience due to its capacity to autonomously detect, diagnose, and mitigate failures in real time, thereby reducing downtime and enhancing service reliability. However, it requires more research in various disciplines, with one of the key ones being AI ethics, regarding effectively balancing AI complexity versus DevOps agility, and thereby promoting AI-enabled cross functional collaboration as prerequisites for maximizing AI potential in DevOps. The ethical focus related to transparency, accountability, and bias is of utmost importance as AI systems are taking increasing autonomous roles in DevOps. The research on ethics in AI in DevOps could include frameworks to ensure that AIdriven decisions are explainable and transparent, allowing DevOps teams to maintain oversight and accountability. It could also include the potential risks of over-reliance on AI, such as loss of human expertise and possible errors in the AI models that could highly affect decision-making in case of hefty failure validation.

The next area that requires attention is to find a balance between AI complexity and agility from the DevOps perspective. AI adds a layer of intelligent analysis, but often results in more complex DevOps processes because of specific skill dependencies, another layer of data management, and complex workflows. Research may focus on formulating methodologies to ensure that integration of AI into DevOps maximizes agility rather than diminishes it. One avenue for research could involve platforms in which AI simplifies the setup and maintenance of machine learning models for DevOps, so teams can adopt AI technologies without expertise in machine learning. Finally, a fresh area that is growing is the role of AI in fostering cross-functional collaboration in DevOps.

AI systems become more intelligent and adaptable; the decision-making of DevOps will shift toward systems making decisions based on real-time information autonomously. Automation would continue to evolve and will increasingly align with DevOps processes for hyper-automation throughout the entire development lifecycle for speed, resilience, and scalability. Continuous research turn into new approaches and tackle challenges brought out by these future-ready advanced technologies. Research on the ethics of AI decision-making in the operational context, simple methods of using AI, and strategy development for cross-functional collaboration is now going to be very relevant for the guidance of DevOps teams in complexity concerning the integration of AI into their environments. Thus, the promise of AI in further development is paving the way for the future of software development and operations as it will lead to novelty, efficiency, resilience, in cloud-native environments.

Without a doubt, making machine learning populate high-quality models will move DevOps toward these systems that make decisions based on real-time data autonomously. Automation will further evolve, tightly integrating itself into DevOps practices to achieve hyper-automation across the development cycle, improving speed, resilience, and scalability. All the more machine learning will become better and more flexible. Thus, the decision-making by DevOps will turn toward systems making decisions depending on real-time data autonomously. Automation would continue along its evolutionary path toward ever-tighter integration into DevOps processes for hyper-automation across the development lifecycle-increasing speed, resilience, and scalability. Continuous research into and exploration of new approaches and tackling the problems that these advanced technologies will create will be necessary. Research on the ethics of AI decision-making in operational contexts, AI simplification adoption, and strategy development for cross-functional collaboration will be highly relevant for guiding DevOps teams in the complexities of AI integration with their offices. Most certainly, the future of software development and operations will become heavily dependent on innovations that AI, over time, will introduce into DevOps through agility, cost-effectiveness, and efficient resilience in cloud environments.

Automation will continue to evolve, tightly integrating itself with DevOps processes for hyper-automation across the entire development lifecycle-in speed, resilience, and scalability. Continuous research into new ways and tackling the problems that advanced technologies of the future might create will be necessary. Research into topics such as ethics in AI decision making in the operational context, easy use of AI, and strategy formulation for cross-functional collaboration will really become more salient now in guiding DevOps teams through the complex integration of AI into their environments. Without doubt, the feature of what AI would need to encapsulate from the future would transform drastically the innovations into software development and operation.

9. CONCLUSION

This chapter has systematically explored the transformative impact of AI on cloud-native DevOps focusing on the enhancement of automation, deployment, and monitoring processes. By analysing trends, tools, and case studies currently available, we have highlighted how solutions driven by AI optimize all stages of the DevOps lifecycle-from CI/CD pipeline automation to infrastructure management and security enforcement. The automation of repetitive tasks, forecasted failures, and insights-in-real-time have greatly benefitted AI in managing complexities pertaining to cloud-native environments. Integration into operational efficiency can easily improve system resilience and security because organizations can deliver high-quality software with increased speed and reliability.

Still, this is not without challenges related to data privacy, scalability, and the need for human oversight. Therefore, there should be a balance between these advancements in technology and strong governance practice. In that regard, through the limitations, the best potential of AI is to build an intelligent, agile, and secure DevOps system. As AI technologies continue to advance, their role in DevOps will become even more crucial, opening up new opportunities for innovation and efficiency. Future lies in continuous research, strategic implementation, and commitment to the alignment of AI-driven solutions with organizational goals and ethical standards.

REFERENCES

Acemoglu, D., & Restrepo, P. (2018). Artificial intelligence, automation, and work. In *The economics of artificial intelligence: An agenda* (pp. 197–236). University of Chicago Press.

Ajiga, D., Okeleke, P. A., Folorunsho, S. O., & Ezeigweneme, C. (2024). The role of software automation in improving industrial operations and efficiency. *International Journal of Engineering Research Updates*, 7(1), 22–35. DOI: 10.53430/ijeru.2024.7.1.0031

AWS. (2024). *Cloud native architecture best practices.* Amazon Web Services Technical Documentation.

Azure, M. (2024). *Enterprise cloud-native transformation guide.* Microsoft Documentation.

Chen, Y., & Rodriguez, M. (2024). AI integration challenges in cloud-native environments: A systematic review. *Journal of Cloud Computing (Heidelberg, Germany)*, 12(2), 145–162.

Cloud, G. (2024). *Implementing AI in cloud-native applications.* Google Cloud Documentation.

Davidson, K., Smith, R., & Lee, J. (2024). AI-driven DevOps: Impact on deployment efficiency and resource utilization. *Cloud Computing Research*, 15(3), 78–92.

DevOps Research Group. (2024), DevOps Research & Assessment. (2024). Accelerate state of DevOps report. Google Cloud. https://cloud.google.com/devops/state-of-devops

Enterprise Technology Review. (2024). Cost analysis of AI implementation in DevOps. Technology Economics Quarterly, 8(1).

Faishal, M., Mathew, S., Neikha, K., Pusa, K., & Zhimomi, T. (2023). The future of work: AI, automation, and the changing dynamics of developed economies. *World Journal of Advanced Research and Reviews*, 18(3), 620–629. DOI: 10.30574/wjarr.2023.18.3.1086

Hat, R. (2024). Red Hat named a leader in 2024 Gartner® Magic Quadrant™ for cloud application platforms. Red Hat Blog. https://www.redhat.com/en/blog/red-hat-named-leader-2024-gartnerr-magic-quadranttm-cloud-application-platforms

Incident Management Forum. (2024). *Benchmark report on incident resolution in AI-enabled systems.* IMF Publications.

Jabbari, R., bin Ali, N., Petersen, K., & Tanveer, B. (2016). What is DevOps? A systematic mapping study on definitions and practices. In Proceedings of the scientific workshop proceedings of XP2016 (pp. 1-11).

Jenkins. (2024). Jenkins AI and plugin development documentation. The Jenkins Project. https://www.jenkins.io/

Katalon. (2024). The state of software quality report 2024. Katalon Research. https://katalon.com/reports/state-quality-2024

Kumar, A. (2024). AI-driven innovations in modern cloud computing. arXiv preprint arXiv:2410.15960.

Kumar, S., & Smith, P. (2024). Cloud-native architecture adoption trends. *Journal of Cloud Engineering*, 9(1), 23–45.

Miller, R., & Davis, T. (2024). Machine learning applications in DevOps monitoring. *Cloud Technology Review*, 11(2), 112–128.

Morgan, L. (2024). AI governance in DevOps environments. *Risk Management Quarterly*, 16(4), 67–82.

Oyeniran, O. C., Adewusi, A. O., Adeleke, A. G., Akwawa, L. A., & Azubuko, C. F. (2023). AI-driven devops: Leveraging machine learning for automated software deployment and maintenance. *DevOps Journal*, 5(2), 89–104.

Performance Analytics Review. (2024). Metrics processing in enterprise environments. Technical Performance Quarterly, 7(2).

Report, T. A. (2024), Katalon, The state of software quality report 2024. https://katalon.com/reports/state-quality-2024

Research, I. B. M. (2024). *Predictive analytics in cloud environments: A technical review*. IBM Technical Library.

Shekhar, S. S. (2019). Artificial intelligence in automation. *Artificial Intelligence*, 3085(06), 14–17.

Sivathapandi, P., Paul, D., & Sudharsanam, S. R. (2021). Enhancing cloud-native CI/CD pipelines with AI-driven automation and predictive analytics. *Australian Journal of Machine Learning Research & Applications*, 1(1), 226–265.

Smith, J., & Patel, R. (2024). AI-driven infrastructure management efficiency. *Cloud Computing Engineering*, 8(3), 234–251.

Tamanampudi, V. M. (2021). AI and DevOps: Enhancing pipeline automation with deep learning models for predictive resource scaling and fault tolerance. *Distributed Learning and Broad Applications in Scientific Research*, 7, 38–77.

Thompson, R., & Lee, K. (2024). Performance optimization in cloud-native environments. *Journal of Cloud Architecture*, 10(1), 45–62.

Williams, R.. (2024). Predictive maintenance in cloud systems. *Infrastructure Management Review*, 13(4), 178–195.

Wilson, M., & Chang, L. (2024). Transparency in AI-driven DevOps decisions. *Ethics in Technology*, 9(2), 89–104.

Yarlagadda, R. T. (2018). The RPA and AI automation. International Journal of Creative Research Thoughts (IJCRT), 2320-2882.

Zhang, L., & Liu, W. (2024). AI monitoring systems in cloud environments. *Cloud Security Journal*, 12(3), 156–171.

Chapter 9
Artificial Intelligence in Software Testing

Subash Banala
https://orcid.org/0009-0004-0802-8179
Capgemini, USA

Sudheer Panyaram
https://orcid.org/0009-0008-5970-480X
Fisker, USA

P. Selvakumar
https://orcid.org/0000-0002-3650-4548
Nehru Institute of Technology, India

ABSTRACT

AI which is reshaping the landscape of quality assurance (QA) by enhancing efficiency, accuracy, and coverage. Traditionally, software testing has relied heavily on manual and semi-automated processes, often leading to time-consuming and error-prone tasks. AI introduces a new paradigm in software testing, offering advanced methodologies and tools that significantly improve the effectiveness and efficiency of QA practices. Additionally, AI enhances test maintenance and evolution. Traditional test suites require manual updates as software evolves, which can be labor-intensive and prone to oversight. AI-powered tools can automatically adjust test cases and scripts to accommodate changes in the software, reducing the manual effort required to maintain and update tests. By leveraging AI to detect changes in the software and adjust tests accordingly, organizations can ensure that their test suites remain relevant and effective throughout the development lifecycle.Another significant advancement brought about by AI is the optimization of test execution.

DOI: 10.4018/979-8-3693-9356-7.ch009

INTRODUCTION TO AI IN SOFTWARE TESTING: REVOLUTIONIZING QUALITY ASSURANCE

AI which is reshaping the landscape of quality assurance (QA) by enhancing efficiency, accuracy, and coverage. Traditionally, software testing has relied heavily on manual and semi-automated processes, often leading to time-consuming and error-prone tasks. AI introduces a new paradigm in software testing, offering advanced methodologies and tools that significantly improve the effectiveness and efficiency of QA practices. Additionally, AI enhances test maintenance and evolution. Traditional test suites require manual updates as software evolves, which can be labor-intensive and prone to oversight. AI-powered tools can automatically adjust test cases and scripts to accommodate changes in the software, reducing the manual effort required to maintain and update tests. By leveraging AI to detect changes in the software and adjust tests accordingly, organizations can ensure that their test suites remain relevant and effective throughout the development lifecycle.Another significant advancement brought about by AI is the optimization of test execution. AI detection enable AI systems to identify and prioritize high-risk areas of the application, ensuring that resources are allocated efficiently. This optimization not only speeds up the testing process but also helps in managing the complexity of modern software systems by targeting testing efforts where they are most needed.AI also contributes to the enhancement of test accuracy and reliability. By employing techniques such as anomaly detection and pattern recognition, AI can identify subtle issues and inconsistencies that might be overlooked by manual testing.

This capability is particularly valuable in complex systems where manual testing may not be able to cover all possible scenarios or detect rare edge cases.This facilitates the creation of test cases that align closely with user expectations and requirements, ensuring that the software meets its intended use. Additionally, NLP can help in analyzing and categorizing defect reports, streamlining the process of identifying and addressing issues.Furthermore, AI-driven testing tools can provide valuable insights through advanced analytics and reporting. By analyzing test results, defect data, and historical trends, AI systems can offer actionable insights and recommendations for improving the quality of the software. This data-driven approach, AI-driven analytics also enable continuous improvement by providing feedback on testing processes and helping teams refine their strategies.It is crucial to validate AI models and ensure that they are trained on representative and diverse datasets to achieve reliable and accurate results.Another challenge is the need for human oversight and intervention. While AI can automate and optimize many aspects of testing, human expertise is still essential for interpreting results, making judgment calls, and addressing complex issues. From generating and executing test cases to maintaining test suites and enhancing accuracy, AI offers significant improvements in efficiency, coverage, and reliability. As AI technologies continue to advance, their integration into software testing will likely become more sophisticated, further transforming the QA landscape. The future of software testing promises to be marked by a deeper integration of AI, driving innovation and excellence in quality assurance.

Fundamentals of AI and Machine Learning for Software Testing

quality assurance practices by introducing innovative methods for improving accuracy, efficiency, and effectiveness. To fully grasp how AI and ML are revolutionizing software testing, it's essential to understand their fundamental principles and how they are applied within this domain.For instance, unsupervised learning algorithms might group test cases that exhibit similar behaviors or outcomes, helping testers to focus on clusters of related issues or patterns in the data that were not previously apparent.In software testing, reinforcement learning can be used to optimize test execution strategies, such as determining the most effective sequence of test cases to run in order to maximize defect detection while minimizing execution time(Al-samhi, S. H., et al.,2019). This approach can adaptively adjust testing strategies based on ongoing results and feedback. Machine learning models can analyze code changes and identify areas that require testing, creating comprehensive test suites that cover various scenarios. This reduces the manual effort required to design test cases and improves test coverage.Predictive Analytics: Machine learning models can analyze historical test data to predict potential defect-prone areas in the code. By identifying patterns and trends from previous testing cycles, AI can forecast which modules or components are most likely to encounter issues, allowing testers to prioritize their efforts and focus on high-risk areas(Boukerche, A., et al.,2020). Test Optimization and Prioritization AI-driven tools can optimize the execution of test cases by prioritizing them based on their likelihood of finding defects. Techniques such as risk-based testing use AI to assess which test cases are most critical and should be executed first, thereby improving the efficiency of the testing process and ensuring that critical functionalities are thoroughly tested.Defect Prediction and Classification AI algorithms can predict and classify defects by analyzing historical data and identifying patterns associated with different types of defects. This predictive capability helps in proactively addressing potential issues before they impact the software, improving overall product quality.Anomaly Detection: AI techniques, particularly those based on unsupervised learning, are effective in detecting anomalies in test results. These anomalies might indicate hidden defects or unexpected behavior that traditional testing methods might miss.

AI-Driven Test Automation: Enhancing Efficiency and Coverage

In the realm of software development, test automation has long been a cornerstone of quality assurance, enabling teams to run repetitive test cases efficiently and consistently. However, the integration of artificial intelligence (AI) into test automation is propelling this practice to new heights, significantly enhancing both efficiency and coverage(Behjati, R., et al.,2019). AI-driven test automation leverages advanced algorithms and machine learning techniques to optimize various aspects of the testing process, transforming how software quality is assured and ensuring that applications meet the highest standards.AI-driven test automation begins with the ability to intelligently generate and execute test cases. Traditional test automation often relies on predefined scripts and static test cases, which can become cumbersome to manage and may not cover all possible scenarios. This process, known as test case generation, ensures that the test suite adapts to changes in the application and covers a broader range of scenarios, including edge cases that might be overlooked by static scripts.One of the most significant benefits of AI-driven test automation is its ability to enhance test coverage(Carino, S., et al.,2015). AI algorithms can identify patterns and relationships within code and usage data, allowing for the creation of comprehensive test suites that address various functional and non-functional aspects of the application. This intelligence enables the automated generation of test cases that focus on these high-risk areas, ensuring that testing efforts are directed where they are needed most and improving overall test coverage.In addition to generating and executing test cases, AI-driven test automation excels in optimizing test execution.

Traditional test execution often involves running all test cases regardless of their relevance or likelihood of uncovering defects. This prioritization helps in optimizing the test execution process, reducing the time and resources required for testing while ensuring that critical functionalities are thoroughly validated.Another area where AI-driven test automation shines is in test maintenance. Maintaining test scripts can be a time-consuming and error-prone task, especially when dealing with frequent changes in the application. AI also enhances the efficiency of test automation through intelligent defect detection and reporting. Traditional defect detection methods may miss subtle issues or produce false positives, leading to inefficiencies and delays. AI-driven tools use advanced techniques such as anomaly detection and pattern recognition to identify defects with greater accuracy. By analyzing large volumes of test data and recognizing patterns that indicate potential issues, AI can alert testers to defects that might otherwise go unnoticed. This capability not only improves the accuracy of defect detection but also helps in diagnosing the root causes of issues more effectively.The integration of AI in test automation is also driving advancements in self-healing test automation frameworks. Self-healing refers to the ability of AI-driven test automation tools to automatically adapt to changes in the application without human intervention.

Predictive Analytics for Defect Detection and Prevention

Predictive analytics has emerged as a transformative approach in software testing, offering a proactive strategy for defect detection and prevention that significantly enhances software quality and reliability. Unlike traditional methods, which often rely on reactive bug-finding techniques and post-facto debugging, predictive analytics harnesses data-driven insights and advanced algorithms to anticipate potential issues before they manifest(De Donato, L., et al.,2022). This shift towards a predictive approach is revolutionizing quality assurance by enabling teams to identify, address, and mitigate defects early in the development lifecycle, thus reducing costs, minimizing disruptions, and accelerating time-to-market.At the core of predictive analytics for defect detection is the use of historical data to forecast potential issues. By analyzing past defect data, including information about when and where defects were introduced and how they were resolved, predictive models can identify patterns and trends that signal where future defects are likely to occur. For example, if historical data reveals that certain modules or components of the software are frequently associated with defects, predictive analytics can flag these areas as high-risk and prioritize them for more rigorous testing. This allows teams to allocate resources more effectively, focusing on components with a higher probability of issues and improving overall testing efficiency.For instance, supervised learning models can use features such as code complexity, recent changes, and developer experience to predict the likelihood of defects in new code.

Techniques such as regression analysis, classification algorithms, and ensemble methods are commonly used to build predictive models that can forecast defects with high precision.Another key application of predictive analytics is in risk assessment. By evaluating various factors such as code quality metrics, test coverage, and defect density, predictive analytics can ensuring that critical areas receive the attention they need. For example, if predictive models indicate that a recent code change introduces a high level of risk, it prompts a more thorough review and testing of that specific change, helping to prevent potential issues from escalating.Predictive analytics also plays a crucial role in enhancing the efficiency of test planning and execution(Dzedzickis, A., et al.,2021). By forecasting the areas of the application most likely to contain defects, teams can strategically plan their test cases and focus on high-risk areas. This targeted approach reduces the number of unnecessary tests, accelerates the testing process, and ensures that testing efforts are aligned with the most pressing risks. Additionally, predictive analytics can optimize test execution schedules by identifying the most critical tests to run based on the current state of the application and its associated risk factors.In addition to defect detection, predictive analytics aids in defect prevention by identifying factors that contribute to defects and suggesting improvements. For example, analysis of historical defect data may reveal that certain coding practices or development environments are associated with higher defect rates. Moreover, predictive analytics enhances defect management by providing insights into defect trends and potential bottlenecks in the software development lifecycle. By analyzing defect data, teams can identify recurring issues, understand their root causes, and implement preventive measures to address them. This capability allows for more effective defect tracking and resolution, leading to higher-quality software and more efficient development processes(Ghosh, S., et al.,2021).Additionally, predictive models require continuous updates and validation to remain accurate and relevant, necessitating ongoing data collection and model refinement.

AI-Powered Test Data Generation and Optimization

Traditionally, creating test data has been a manual, labor-intensive process, often involving the use of static data sets or simplistic random data generators. However, the advent of artificial intelligence (AI) has brought about a transformative shift in how test data is generated and optimized, offering advanced techniques that enhance both the quality and efficiency of testing processes.This approach addresses several challenges associated with traditional test data generation, such as the need for high-quality data that covers a wide range of use cases, edge cases, and potential interactions(Ghazal, T. M., et al.,2021). AI-driven methods can analyze historical data, application requirements, and usage patterns to generate data sets that are representative of actual conditions, ensuring that tests are conducted under realistic and relevant scenarios.AI algorithms can analyze application code and user behavior to identify various data patterns and relationships, generating test data that encompasses a broader spectrum of conditions. For example, AI can simulate different user profiles, transaction types, and system states, creating test data that thoroughly examines the application's functionality and robustness.In addition to generating diverse test data, AI can optimize data sets to improve testing efficiency. Optimization involves selecting or creating data that maximizes the effectiveness of test cases while minimizing redundancy and resource consumption. AI algorithms can analyze previous test results and defect data to identify which data sets are most likely to uncover issues, focusing testing efforts on these high-impact data scenarios. This targeted approach helps in reducing the volume of test data required, streamlining the testing process, and enhancing the overall efficiency of the quality assurance process.AI-powered test data generation also facilitates the creation of data sets for specific testing needs, such as performance testing, security testing, or compliance testing. For instance, in performance testing, AI can generate large volumes of data to simulate high-load conditions, while in security testing, it can create data sets with various potential vulnerabilities and threat scenarios. By tailoring test data to meet the specific requirements of different types of testing, AI ensures that tests are comprehensive and aligned with the intended objectives.Another important aspect of AI-driven test data optimization is the ability to manage sensitive data.

In many cases, test data must be anonymized or masked to protect privacy and comply with regulations such as GDPR or HIPAA. AI can automate the data masking process by intelligently replacing or obfuscating sensitive information while preserving the data's usability for testing purposes. This ensures that sensitive data is handled appropriately while still allowing for effective and meaningful testing.AI-powered techniques also contribute to the continuous improvement of test data management. Machine learning models can learn from ongoing test results and feedback, refining the data generation process to better address emerging patterns and requirements. This iterative approach allows for the dynamic adjustment of test data strategies, ensuring that data sets remain relevant and effective as the application evolves and new features are introduced.AI models must be trained on high-quality data to produce reliable and realistic test data, and any biases or inaccuracies in the training data can impact the effectiveness of the generated data. Additionally, integrating AI-driven test data solutions into existing testing workflows requires careful planning to ensure compatibility and to maximize the benefits of these advanced techniques.In conclusion, AI-powered test data generation and optimization represent a significant advancement in software testing, offering improved quality, diversity, and efficiency. By leveraging machine learning algorithms and advanced data synthesis techniques, AI transforms how test data is created and managed, ensuring that testing efforts are aligned with real-world scenarios and specific testing needs. The ability to generate comprehensive and realistic test data, optimize data sets for effectiveness, and manage sensitive information effectively enhances the overall quality assurance process(Guizzo, G., et al.,2021). As AI technologies continue to evolve, their integration into test data management will likely lead to even more sophisticated and effective testing solutions, driving further improvements in software reliability and performance.

Intelligent Test Case Design and Prioritization

The efficiency and effectiveness of software testing hinge significantly on the design and prioritization of test cases. Traditional approaches often involve creating exhaustive test suites based on static criteria, which can lead to inefficiencies and gaps in coverage. However, the integration of artificial intelligence (AI) into test case design and prioritization is transforming these practices, enabling a more intelligent and data-driven approach that enhances both the quality of testing and the utilization of resources.AI tools analyze application code, requirements, and historical test data to generate test cases that are both comprehensive and relevant. This approach ensures that test cases are aligned with actual use cases and potential risks, reducing the likelihood of missing critical scenarios and improving overall test coverage. For example, machine learning models can analyze previous test results and defect data to identify which types of test cases were most effective at uncovering issues. By learning from this data, AI tools can generate new test cases that target similar scenarios, ensuring that the most valuable test cases are included in the test suite. AI also enhances test case design by incorporating advanced techniques such as risk-based testing and mutation testing(Hourani, H., et al.,2012). Mutation testing, on the other hand, involves introducing small changes to the application code to evaluate the effectiveness of test cases. AI can automate this process, identifying test cases that are robust against various code mutations and ensuring that the test suite is both thorough and resilient.In addition to designing test cases, AI significantly improves the prioritization process. Traditional prioritization methods often rely on predefined criteria or subjective judgment, which can lead to inefficiencies and suboptimal test execution.

AI-driven prioritization uses predictive analytics to assess the likelihood of defects and the impact of different test cases.This predictive capability allows for a more strategic approach to test execution, focusing on the test cases that are most critical and relevant(Kalech, M., et al.,2018). For instance, AI algorithms can analyze recent code changes and identify areas with higher probabilities of defects, prioritizing test cases that cover these areas. This targeted approach helps in optimizing the testing process, reducing the number of unnecessary tests, and ensuring that critical issues are addressed promptly.AI-powered test case prioritization also contributes to efficient resource management. By identifying and focusing on high-impact test cases, teams can allocate their resources more effectively, minimizing time and effort spent on less critical tests. Furthermore, intelligent test case design and prioritization can adapt to changes in the application and testing requirements. As software evolves and new features are introduced, AI tools can dynamically adjust the test case design and prioritization strategies based on the latest data and insights. Despite these advancements, implementing AI-driven test case design and prioritization presents certain challenges. Additionally, integrating AI-driven approaches into existing testing workflows requires careful planning and coordination to maximize their benefits and ensure compatibility with established processes.In conclusion, intelligent test case design and prioritization powered by AI represent a significant leap forward in software testing. Embracing AI-driven approaches equips teams with the tools needed to tackle complex testing challenges, optimize resource utilization, and achieve superior testing outcomes.

AI-Driven Exploratory Testing and Test Data Analytics

Exploratory testing and test data analytics are crucial aspects of modern software quality assurance, offering dynamic and in-depth approaches to uncovering defects and ensuring software reliability. The integration of artificial intelligence (AI) into these domains is revolutionizing the way testing is conducted, enhancing both the exploration process and the analysis of test data. AI-driven techniques are advancing exploratory testing by enabling more intelligent, adaptive, and effective test strategies while simultaneously transforming test data analytics to provide deeper insights and optimize testing outcomes.Exploratory testing, by its nature, involves simultaneously learning about the application and designing tests based on that learning. It relies heavily on the tester's intuition and understanding of the application's functionality to identify potential issues that structured test cases might miss. AI enhances exploratory testing by introducing advanced capabilities such as intelligent test generation, automated test execution, and adaptive learning. AI-driven tools can analyze application behavior, user interactions, and historical defect data to generate exploratory test scenarios that are more likely to uncover critical issues(Kaur, J., et al.,2019). These tools can dynamically adjust the testing approach based on real-time feedback and insights, allowing for a more comprehensive exploration of the application's functionality.One of the key innovations in AI-driven exploratory testing is the use of reinforcement learning algorithms. These algorithms enable AI systems to explore the application in a way that maximizes the likelihood of discovering defects(Khan, B., et al.,2023). Reinforcement learning involves training an AI agent to make decisions based on rewards and penalties.

In exploratory testing, this means the AI system can learn which actions lead to the discovery of defects and adjust its exploration strategy accordingly. By continuously learning from the results of previous tests, the AI can refine its approach, focusing on areas of the application that are more likely to yield valuable insights. In addition to enhancing the exploratory testing process, AI plays a significant role in test data analytics. Test data analytics involves the collection, processing, and analysis of data generated during testing to gain insights into software performance and quality. Traditional analysis methods may struggle to uncover complex relationships or subtle trends, but AI algorithms can process vast amounts of data and recognize intricate patterns that might Anomaly detection algorithms can flag unusual behavior or deviations from expected results, alerting testers to potential defects or areas of concern.AI also enhances test data analytics by automating the process of generating actionable insights. Instead of relying on manual analysis, which can be time-consuming and error-prone, AI-driven tools can automatically generate reports, visualizations, and recommendations based on the analyzed data. These insights can inform decision-making by highlighting critical issues, suggesting improvements, and optimizing testing strategies. For example, predictive analytics can forecast the likelihood of defects based on historical test data, enabling teams to focus their efforts on high-risk areas and improve overall test coverage.Additionally, implementing AI-driven tools requires careful consideration of their integration with existing testing workflows and practices to ensure compatibility and maximize their benefits. Training testers to effectively use AI-driven tools and interpret their outputs is also essential for achieving optimal results.In conclusion, AI-driven exploratory testing and test data analytics represent significant advancements in software quality assurance, offering more intelligent, adaptive, and effective approaches to testing. By enhancing exploratory testing with intelligent test generation and reinforcement learning, and by transforming test data analytics with advanced pattern recognition and automation, AI enables deeper insights and more efficient testing processes.

Machine Learning for Test Environment and Configuration Optimization

In the complex landscape of software development and quality assurance, optimizing test environments and configurations is crucial for ensuring that applications perform reliably under varied conditions. Traditional methods of managing and configuring test environments often involve a significant amount of manual setup and trial-and-error adjustments, which can be time-consuming and prone to error(Lee, C. L., et al.,2022). Machine learning (ML) offers a transformative approach to this challenge by providing advanced techniques for automating and optimizing the management of test environments and configurations, thereby enhancing testing efficiency and effectiveness.By learning from this data, ML models can predict the optimal configurations required for different testing scenarios, thus streamlining the setup process and reducing the likelihood of encountering issues during testing.One of the key applications of ML in test environment optimization is automated environment provisioning. Traditionally, setting up test environments involves manual configuration of hardware, software, and network settings, which can be cumbersome and inconsistent. ML algorithms can automate this process by analyzing requirements, historical performance data, and test specifications to dynamically configure environments based on the needs of specific tests. For instance, if a certain application component performs better with specific hardware configurations, the ML model can automatically adjust the environment to meet these specifications, ensuring that the tests are conducted under the most suitable conditions.ML also enhances test environment management by enabling intelligent resource allocation. In many testing scenarios, especially those involving large-scale applications or distributed systems, managing resources efficiently is critical. ML models can analyze data related to resource utilization, test execution times, and system loads to optimize the allocation of resources across different test environments. This approach helps in balancing the load, reducing resource contention, and ensuring that tests are executed efficiently without unnecessary delays or interruptions.Another significant benefit of ML in configuration optimization is its ability to adapt to dynamic testing requirements. In modern development environments, software applications are frequently updated, and testing requirements can change rapidly.

ML algorithms can continuously learn from new data and adapt configuration settings accordingly, ensuring that the test environment remains aligned with the latest requirements and changes. This dynamic adaptability is crucial for maintaining the relevance and effectiveness of test environments in fast-paced development cycles. Additionally, ML can improve the management of test environment dependencies and interactions. Complex applications often have multiple dependencies and interactions between components, which can affect test outcomes. ML models can analyze historical test data and environment interactions to identify potential issues related to dependencies and interactions. By understanding these relationships, ML can recommend or automatically implement configuration adjustments to mitigate risks and ensure that tests are conducted in a stable and reliable environment.The integration of ML into test environment and configuration optimization also enhances the ability to perform root cause analysis(Liu, Z., et al.,2021). When issues arise during testing, identifying the underlying causes can be challenging, especially when multiple configuration variables are involved. ML algorithms can analyze test results, configuration settings, and historical data to pinpoint the root causes of issues more effectively. This capability allows teams to address problems more efficiently and make informed decisions about configuration adjustments.

AI-Driven Continuous Testing and DevOps Integration

The convergence of artificial intelligence (AI) with continuous testing and DevOps practices represents a profound shift in how software quality assurance is approached, fundamentally transforming the speed, efficiency, and effectiveness of the software development lifecycle. Continuous testing and DevOps integration emphasize the need for seamless, automated testing processes that align with the rapid, iterative nature of modern software development. AI plays a pivotal role in this transformation by enhancing continuous testing frameworks and optimizing the integration of testing practices within DevOps pipelines, thereby accelerating delivery cycles while ensuring high-quality software products.AI also enhances test coverage and optimization by analyzing test data and identifying gaps in test scenarios. Machine learning algorithms can assess which parts of the application are frequently tested and which are not, identifying areas where additional testing may be needed. This capability helps in prioritizing test cases based on risk and impact, ensuring that high-risk areas are tested more rigorously while reducing redundancy in test execution. AI-driven analytics can provide insights into test coverage metrics, such as code coverage and functional coverage, allowing teams to make data-driven decisions about where to focus their testing efforts.In the context of DevOps, AI-driven continuous testing integrates seamlessly with CI/CD pipelines to ensure that testing is an integral part of the development process.

AI tools can automate the orchestration of test execution across different stages of the pipeline, from code commits to deployment. (Liu, P., et al.,2017) For example, AI can determine the optimal times to run different types of tests (e.g., unit tests, integration tests, and performance tests) based on the stage of development and the nature of code changes. This integration ensures that testing is conducted continuously and efficiently, providing timely feedback and enabling rapid iterations.AI-powered test optimization also includes predictive analytics to forecast potential defects and performance issues before they impact production. By analyzing patterns in historical test data, AI models can predict which areas of the application are most likely to encounter issues and prioritize testing accordingly. Furthermore, AI contributes to the continuous improvement of testing processes by providing real-time insights and recommendations. This continuous feedback loop helps teams to refine their testing practices and adapt to changing requirements and conditions. Additionally, implementing AI-driven tools requires careful consideration of their compatibility with existing DevOps practices and tools. Organizations must also address potential challenges related to the interpretation and actionability of AI-generated insights, ensuring that teams can effectively use these insights to drive improvements. In conclusion, AI-driven continuous testing and DevOps integration represent a significant advancement in software quality assurance, offering enhanced automation, optimization, and insights that align with the rapid pace of modern software development(Li, L., et al.,2009). By leveraging AI to dynamically generate and adapt test cases, optimize test coverage, and provide real-time continuous testing and DevOps will drive further innovations, enabling organizations to deliver high-quality software products with greater speed and precision. Embracing AI-driven approaches equips teams with the tools needed to navigate the complexities of modern software development and maintain high standards of quality assurance throughout the development lifecycle.

Natural Language Processing for Test Script Generation and Maintenance

NLP has emerged as a transformative technology in software testing, revolutionizing the way test scripts are generated and maintained. Traditionally, creating and updating test scripts has been a labor-intensive process, requiring a deep understanding of both the application's functionality and the intricacies of scripting languages. NLP technologies simplify and accelerate these tasks by enabling more intuitive interactions between human testers and automated testing systems, bridging the gap between natural language and executable test scripts.One of the primary applications of NLP in test script generation is the ability to convert natural language requirements and specifications into automated test scripts. Testers can describe test scenarios and requirements in plain language, and NLP systems can parse these descriptions to generate corresponding test scripts(Memon, A. M. 2004). This approach reduces the need for manual scripting and makes test creation more accessible to non-technical stakeholders who may have a deep understanding of the application but lack expertise in programming.NLP-driven test script generation begins with the extraction of relevant information from natural language documents, such as user stories, requirements specifications, or business rules. Advanced identify key entities (e.g., data inputs, user actions) and their relationships within these documents. For example, if a requirement states, "The user should be able to log in with a valid username and password," an NLP system can extract the entities "username" and "password" and understand their roles in the login process. This extracted information is then used to automatically generate test scripts that simulate the specified user actions and validate the application's behavior.NLP also plays a significant role in maintaining and updating test scripts. As applications evolve and requirements change, maintaining test scripts to reflect these updates can be challenging. NLP systems can help automate this process by analyzing changes in requirements or application documentation and updating test scripts accordingly. For instance, if a feature is modified or a new functionality is added, NLP tools can compare updated specifications with existing test scripts, identifying discrepancies and suggesting necessary modifications(Moghadam, M. H. 2019).

This dynamic approach to script maintenance helps requiring manual intervention for every change.Another advantage of NLP in test script maintenance is the ability to detect and handle ambiguities or inconsistencies in natural language requirements. Requirements documents often contain vague or incomplete descriptions that can lead to misunderstandings in test script generation. NLP tools equipped with semantic analysis and context understanding can identify potential ambiguities and provide clarifications or suggest more precise formulations. This capability improves the accuracy of generated test scripts and reduces the risk of errors arising from misinterpretations of requirements.NLP techniques also facilitate the generation of more robust and comprehensive test cases by enabling natural language-based test data creation. Test data is crucial for validating the behavior of applications under various conditions, and NLP can assist in generating realistic and diverse data sets based on natural language descriptions. For example, if a requirement specifies that the application should handle different types of user inputs (e.g., valid, invalid, edge cases), NLP systems can generate corresponding test data that covers these scenarios, ensuring thorough testing of application functionality.Furthermore, NLP enhances test script readability and maintainability by allowing test scripts to be written in a more natural and human-readable format. Traditional test scripts can be complex and difficult to understand, especially for stakeholders who are not familiar with scripting languages(Paradkar, A. M., et al.,2007). By leveraging NLP, test scripts can be generated in a more intuitive and understandable format, making it easier for both technical and non-technical team members to review, understand, and collaborate on test cases.

AI-Powered Test Result Analysis and Defect Prediction

In the modern landscape of software development, the complexity and scale of applications have necessitated advanced approaches to test result analysis and defect prediction. Traditional methods of analyzing test results and predicting defects often involve manual examination of logs, reports, and historical data, these processes is transforming the way software quality is managed by providing more accurate, efficient, and scalable solutions for analyzing test results and predicting potential defects.Machine learning models can analyze historical test results, application logs, and performance metrics to detect deviations from expected behavior, pinpointing issues that may not be immediately apparent(Reddy, A., et al.,2019). For instance, AI algorithms can recognize unusual trends or patterns in test failures, correlating them with specific changes in the application code or test environment to identify underlying causes.The application of AI in defect prediction involves analyzing historical data to forecast where defects are likely to occur in future releases. AI models can be trained on historical defect data, including information about past defects, testing efforts and focus resources on high-risk areas. For example, if a machine learning model detects that certain modules or functions have historically been associated with higher defect rates, it can suggest increased scrutiny or additional testing for those components in future releases.AI-powered defect prediction also benefits from advanced techniques such as natural language processing (NLP) and anomaly detection. NLP can analyze textual descriptions of defects, user stories, and requirements to identify correlations and trends that may indicate potential areas of risk. Anomaly detection algorithms can flag unusual patterns in test results, such as sudden spikes in failure rates or unusual response times, which may signal the presence of latent defects.

One of the significant benefits of AI-powered analysis and prediction is the ability to automate repetitive tasks and reduce the cognitive load on testers. Traditional analysis of test results often involves manually reviewing logs, reports, and performance data to identify issues, which can be time-consuming and error-prone.

AI-driven tools can automate these tasks, providing real-time analysis and actionable insights without requiring manual intervention. This automation not only speeds up the analysis process but also allows testers to focus on more strategic activities, such as addressing identified issues and improving test coverage.Additionally, integrating AI tools into existing testing workflows requires careful consideration of their compatibility with current practices and tools. Organizations must also address potential challenges related to interpreting and acting on AI-generated insights, ensuring that recommendations are practical and actionable.In conclusion, AI-powered test result analysis and defect prediction represent a significant advancement in software quality assurance, offering enhanced accuracy, efficiency, and scalability forecast defects, AI transforms the management of test results and defect prediction (Selvakumar, P.,2023). The ability to automate repetitive tasks, detect anomalies, and continuously adapt to new data improves the overall effectiveness of testing processes and helps in delivering high-quality software products. As AI technologies continue to evolve, their role in test result analysis and defect prediction will drive further innovations, leading to more intelligent and adaptive approaches to software quality management. Embracing AI-driven solutions equips teams with powerful tools to navigate the complexities of modern software development, ensuring that applications are thoroughly tested and defects are addressed proactively.

Human-in-the-Loop AI for Test Validation and Verification

AI technologies and human insight, addressing the limitations of purely automated systems and ensuring that test validation and verification processes are comprehensive and contextually informed.Human-in-the-Loop AI combines the computational power and efficiency of AI with the nuanced understanding and critical thinking abilities of human testers. However, AI alone may struggle with complex scenarios that require contextual understanding, domain knowledge, or subjective judgment(Shahamiri, S. R., et al.,2011). By incorporating human input, HITL AI systems ensure that these complexities are effectively managed, leading to more accurate and reliable test results.based on predefined criteria and historical data. However, human testers are often required to review and validate these test cases to ensure they accurately reflect real-world scenarios and edge cases(Srivastava, P. R., et al.,2010). For instance, while AI can generate test cases based on code changes and requirements, human testers can provide context-specific insights and adjust test cases to cover nuances that AI might overlook. This collaborative approach enhances the overall quality of the test cases and ensures they are relevant and comprehensive.In the realm of defect detection and resolution, HITL AI plays a crucial role in interpreting and acting upon AI-generated insights. AI systems can identify potential defects, anomalies, and performance issues based on data analysis, but the context and severity of these issues often require human assessment. Human testers can evaluate the relevance and impact of detected issues, prioritize them based on business objectives, and determine appropriate actions for resolution.

This integration of human judgment ensures that defect management is aligned with strategic goals and that critical issues are addressed promptly.HITL AI also enhances the process of validating complex application behaviors that involve multiple interacting components or require an understanding of user experiences. AI systems can simulate various scenarios and generate data, but human testers are essential for interpreting this data in the context of real-world usage. For example, in applications with intricate workflows or user interactions, AI-generated test results may need human evaluation to ensure that the application performs as expected from an end-user perspective. This human oversight ensures that testing is not only thorough but also relevant to actual user experiences.Furthermore, HITL AI contributes to continuous improvement in testing practices by incorporating feedback from human testers into AI models. When human testers identify gaps, inconsistencies, or limitations in AI-generated test cases or defect predictions, this feedback can be used to refine and enhance the AI models. For instance, if testers consistently find that AI models are missing certain types of defects or scenarios, this feedback can be used to adjust the AI algorithms and improve their accuracy. This iterative process of feedback and refinement ensures that AI systems evolve and adapt to changing requirements and contexts.Despite the benefits, implementing HITL AI involves challenges that need to be addressed. One challenge is ensuring effective communication and collaboration between AI systems and human testers. Clear interfaces and workflows are necessary to facilitate seamless integration and ensure that human input is effectively utilized. Additionally, training and upskilling human testers to work effectively with AI tools is crucial for maximizing the benefits of HITL AI. By integrating human judgment with AI-driven insights, organizations can achieve more reliable and contextually informed test results, leading to higher-quality software products(Paramasivam Selvakumar, et al.,2024). As HITL AI continues to evolve, its role in test validation and verification will drive further innovations, providing a powerful framework for addressing the complexities of modern software testing. Embracing this approach equips teams with the tools needed to navigate the challenges of software development and deliver applications that meet high standards of quality and performance.

AI-Driven Test Process Optimization and Metrics

The integration of artificial intelligence (AI) into test process optimization and metrics represents a transformative shift in software quality assurance, leveraging advanced algorithms and data analytics to enhance the efficiency, effectiveness, and accuracy of testing practices. AI-driven approaches optimize various aspects of the testing lifecycle, from test planning and execution to result analysis and metrics measurement, enabling organizations to achieve higher-quality software products with greater speed and precision.AI-driven test process optimization begins with the automation of test planning and execution(Tao, C., et al.,2019). Traditional test planning often involves manual effort in defining test scenarios, selecting test cases, and scheduling test runs. AI can streamline this process by analyzing historical test data, code changes, and application requirements to automatically generate and prioritize test cases. Machine learning algorithms can identify the most critical test scenarios based on historical defect data and application changes, ensuring that testing efforts are focused on high-risk areas. For example, AI can optimize test execution by determining the optimal order for running tests, balancing the load across available resources, and minimizing idle time. This dynamic scheduling improves overall test efficiency and reduces the time required to complete test cycles. Another key aspect of AI-driven test process optimization is the enhancement of test data management. Generating and managing test data is a complex task that involves creating diverse and realistic data sets to validate application functionality.

AI can assist in generating test data by analyzing patterns in historical data and generating synthetic data that mimics real-world scenarios. This capability ensures that test data is representative of actual usage conditions and enhances the reliability of test results. AI-driven test data generation also helps in managing large volumes of data, reducing the manual effort involved in data preparation and maintenance. Furthermore, AI-driven test process optimization enables continuous improvement by incorporating feedback from testing activities into the optimization process. AI systems can learn from new test data and outcomes, refining their algorithms and models to enhance their predictive accuracy and efficiency. This continuous learning process ensures that the AI-driven optimization remains relevant and effective as the application evolves and new testing requirements emerge.Despite the advantages, implementing AI-driven test process optimization and metrics presents several challenges. In conclusion, AI-driven test process optimization and metrics represent a significant advancement in software quality assurance, offering enhanced efficiency, accuracy, and insights throughout the testing lifecycle(Vijayakumar G, et al., 2024)By automating test planning and execution, optimizing resource allocation, and providing actionable metrics and predictions, AI transforms the way testing processes are managed and executed.

CASE STUDIES: SUCCESSFUL AI ADOPTION IN SOFTWARE TESTING

Examining successful case studies reveals how various companies have leveraged AI to overcome traditional testing challenges, enhance test coverage, and accelerate their release cycles. These case studies illustrate the practical applications of AI in software testing and highlight the tangible benefits achieved through its adoption. Google: Enhancing Test Automation with AI Google's adoption of AI in its software testing processes offers a compelling example of how advanced technologies can streamline and enhance quality assurance. Faced with the challenge of maintaining high-quality standards across a vast array of applications and services, Google implemented AI-driven test automation to address the complexities of its testing requirements(Wang F., et al.,2011). By incorporating machine learning algorithms into their testing frameworks, Google was able to automate the generation of test cases based on code changes and historical data.AI tools at Google analyzed code modifications, user interactions, and previous test results to dynamically generate and prioritize test scenarios. This approach allowed the company to cover a broader range of test cases, including edge cases that were previously difficult to address. The implementation of AI-driven test automation significantly reduced the time required to execute tests and increased test coverage, leading to faster identification of defects and improved software quality. As a result, Google could accelerate its release cycles while ensuring that new features and updates met high standards of reliability. Netflix: Optimizing Test Data with AINetflix, a leading streaming service provider, faced the challenge of managing and optimizing test data for its diverse and rapidly evolving platform. To address this challenge, Netflix adopted AI-driven test data generation and optimization techniques.

The company implemented machine learning models to analyze historical test data, user behavior, and application performance metrics.AI algorithms generated synthetic test data that accurately represented real-world usage scenarios, enabling Netflix to conduct more comprehensive and effective testing. By using AI to create diverse and realistic data sets, Netflix improved its ability to simulate various user interactions and edge cases. This approach not only enhanced the reliability of testing but also reduced the manual effort involved in data preparation. Consequently, Netflix achieved more accurate test results and faster identification of potential issues, contributing to a seamless user experience on its platformIBM: Leveraging AI for Predictive Test Analytics IBM's use of AI in predictive test analytics demonstrates the power of AI in anticipating and managing potential defects. IBM integrated AI into its testing processes to analyze historical defect data, code changes, and test results. Machine learning models were used to predict areas of the application with a higher likelihood of encountering defects, allowing IBM to focus its testing efforts on high-risk components.AI-driven predictive analytics also facilitated root cause analysis by identifying patterns and correlations in defect data. This capability enabled IBM to diagnose issues more effectively and prioritize remediation efforts based on potential impact..Microsoft: Integrating AI in Continuous Testing and DevOps Microsoft's adoption of AI in continuous testing and DevOps integration highlights the benefits of combining AI with agile development practices(Sugumaran K. M, D., et al., 2024). Microsoft implemented AI-driven tools within its CI/CD pipelines to automate and optimize various aspects of the testing process. AI algorithms analyzed code changes, test results, and application performance data to dynamically schedule and prioritize test execution. The integration of AI into Microsoft's DevOps practices allowed for continuous testing that aligned with rapid development cycles. AI-driven tools provided real-time feedback on code quality and performance, enabling developers to address issues promptly and maintain high standards of software quality. Additionally, AI enhanced test coverage by generating and adapting test cases based on evolving application features and user requirements.

This approach streamlined the testing process, reduced manual effort, and accelerated the release of new features and updates.Salesforce: Improving Test Case Design with AI Salesforce, a leading cloud-based software provider, utilized AI to enhance test case design and maintenance. The company faced the challenge of managing a large and complex suite of test cases for its platform. To address this challenge, Salesforce adopted AI-driven tools to automate the creation and optimization of test cases based on application requirements and historical test data(Ramakrishnan T., et al.,2022). AI algorithms analyzed application changes and user interactions to generate relevant and comprehensive test cases. The tools also provided insights into test coverage and identified gaps in test scenarios, allowing Salesforce to prioritize testing efforts more effectively. By leveraging AI for test case design, Salesforce improved the efficiency and accuracy of its testing process, ensuring that its platform met high-quality standards and delivered a seamless user experience.In conclusion, these case studies illustrate the transformative impact of AI on software testing, demonstrating how organizations can leverage advanced technologies to address traditional testing challenges and achieve significant improvements in quality assurance. By integrating AI into test automation, test data management, predictive analytics, continuous testing, and test case design, companies like Google, Netflix, IBM, Microsoft, and Salesforce have enhanced their testing processes, accelerated release cycles, and improved software quality. The successful adoption of AI in these organizations highlights the potential for further innovation and the continued evolution of software testing practices in the digital age.

CONCLUSION: THE FUTURE OF AI IN SOFTWARE TESTING - OPPORTUNITIES AND CHALLENGES

Optimized Test Data Management: Managing test data is often a complex and resource-intensive task. AI can streamline this process by generating synthetic test data that accurately mimics real-world scenarios and user behavior. This capability not only ensures that test data is representative and diverse but also reduces the manual effort involved in data preparation and maintenance(Zhu, X., et al.,2008). By providing realistic and varied test data, AI helps improve the reliability of test results and the overall quality of the application.Continuous Testing and Agile Integration: AI supports continuous testing practices within agile and DevOps environments by automating test execution and providing real-time feedback on code quality and performance. AI-driven tools can dynamically adjust test schedules, optimize resource allocation, and integrate seamlessly into CI/CD pipelines(Xu, J., et al.,2019). This continuous testing approach aligns with rapid development cycles, enabling faster release of new features and updates while maintaining high standards of quality.Integration with Existing Processes Integrating AI tools into existing testing workflows and systems can be challenging. Organizations must ensure that AI-driven solutions are compatible with their current practices and tools, and that they complement rather than disrupt established processes. Effective integration requires careful planning, coordination, and potentially significant changes to existing workflows.

CONCLUSION

As we conclude this exploration of AI's role in software testing, it is essential to reflect on its profound impact, the opportunities it presents, and the challenges that must be navigated to fully harness its potential.AI's influence on software testing is multifaceted, affecting various aspects of the testing lifecycle. The automation of test case generation, execution, and optimization has streamlined processes, reduced manual effort, and increased test coverage. AI-driven tools can dynamically generate and prioritize test cases based on historical data and code changes, ensuring that critical functionality and potential defect areas are thoroughly tested. Predictive analytics powered by AI represents another significant advancement in software testing. By analyzing historical defect data, code changes, and application performance metrics, AI models can forecast potential defect areas and identify high-risk components. This predictive capability allows teams to focus their testing efforts on areas with the highest likelihood of encountering issues, thereby optimizing resource allocation and prioritizing remediation efforts. The ability to anticipate defects before they manifest enhances the overall quality assurance process, leading to more robust and reliable software products.AI also plays a crucial role in optimizing test data management. Generating and managing diverse and realistic test data is a complex task that traditionally required substantial manual effort. AI-driven techniques enable the generation of synthetic test data that accurately mimics real-world usage scenarios and user behavior. This capability ensures that test data is representative and varied, improving the reliability of test results and reducing the manual effort involved in data preparation and maintenance.The integration of AI into continuous testing and agile development practices has further accelerated the software delivery cycle. Organizations must invest in data management practices to ensure that AI models are trained on comprehensive, relevant, and representative data sets.ntegrating AI tools into existing testing workflows and systems requires careful planning and coordination. Ensuring compatibility with current practices and tools, as well as managing the balance between automation and human oversight, is essential for effective integration. AI-driven solutions must complement existing processes and enhance, rather than disrupt, established workflows. Addressing issues related to false positives and negatives in AI-generated test results is another challenge. AI algorithms are not infallible and may produce inaccuracies that require human intervention. Continuous validation and refinement of AI models, along with human oversight, are necessary to ensure that test results are accurate and actionable. In conclusion, AI has revolutionized software testing, offering transformative capabilities that enhance efficiency, accuracy, and adaptability throughout the testing lifecycle. The integration of AI into test automation, predictive analytics, test data management, and continuous testing represents a significant advancement in quality assurance.

REFERENCES

Alsamhi, S. H., Ma, O., & Ansari, M. S. (2019). Survey on artificial intelligence based techniquesfor emerging robotic communication. *Telecommunication Systems, 72*(3), 483–503. DOI: 10.1007/s11235-019-00561-z

Behjati, R., Arisholm, E., Bedregal, M., & Tan, C. (2019). Syn- thetic Test Data Generation Using Recurrent Neural Networks: A Position Paper. 2019 IEEE/ACM 7th International Workshop on Realizing Artificial Intelligence Synergies in Software Engi- neering (RAISE). DOI: 10.1109/RAISE.2019.00012

Boukerche, A., Tao, Y., & Sun, P. (2020). Artificial intelligence-based vehicular traffic flo prediction methods for supporting intelligent transportation systems. *Computer Networks, 182*, 107484. DOI: 10.1016/j.comnet.2020.107484

Carino, S., & Andrews, J. H. (2015). Dynamically Testing GUIs Using Ant Colony Optimization. *ASE, 2015*, 138–148. DOI: 10.1109/ASE.2015.70

De Donato, L., Flammini, F., Marrone, S., Mazzariello, C., Nardone, R., Sansone, C., & Vittorini, V. (2022). A survey on audio-video based defect detection through deep learning in railway maintenance. *IEEE Access : Practical Innovations, Open Solutions, 10*, 65376–65400. DOI: 10.1109/ACCESS.2022.3183102

Dzedzickis, A., Subačiūtė-Žemaitienė, J., Šutinys, E., Samukaitė-Bubnienė, U., & Bučinskas, V. (2021). Advanced applications of industrial robotics: New trends and possibilities. *Applied Sciences (Basel, Switzerland), 12*(1), 135. DOI: 10.3390/app12010135

Ghazal, T. M., Hasan, M. K., Alshurideh, M. T., Alzoubi, H. M., Ahmad, M., Akbar, S. S., Al Kurdi, B., & Akour, I. A. (2021). IoT for smart cities: Machine learning approaches in smart healthcare—Areview. *Future Internet, 13*(8), 218. DOI: 10.3390/fi13080218

Ghosh, S., Bandyopadhyay, A., Sahay, S., Ghosh, R., Kundu, I., & Santosh, K. C. (2021). Colorectalhistology tumor detection using ensemble deep neural network. Engineering Applications ofArtificial Intelligence, 100, 104202.

Guizzo, G., Petke, J., Sarro, F., & Harman, M. (2021, May). Enhancing genetic improvement ofsoftware with regression test selection. In 2021 IEEE/ACM 43rd International Conference onSoftware Engineering (ICSE) (pp. 1323-1333). IEEE.

Hourani, H., Hammad, A., & Lafi, M. (2019, April). The Impact of Artificial Intelligence on Software Testing. In *2019 IEEE Jor-dan International Joint Conference on Electrical Engineering and Information Technology (JEEIT)* (pp. 565-570). IEEE. DOI: 10.1109/JEEIT.2019.8717439

Kalech, M., & Stern, R. (2018). Using model-based diagnosis to improve software testing. U.S. Patent No. 9,934,131. Washington, DC: U.S. Patent and Trademark Office.

Kanipriya, M., Sugumaran, D., Pandiyarajan, V., Yogananda, B. S., Selvakumar, P., & Mohan, S. (2024, January). Analysis of Electromyography Signals for Control of Mechanical Prosthesis using Machine Learning Techniques. In 2024 2nd International Conference on Intelligent Data Communication Technologies and Internet of Things (IDCIoT) (pp. 1059-1067). IEEE.

Kaur, J., & Gill, N. S. (2019). *Artificial Intelligence and deep learning for decision makers: a growthhacker's guide to cutting edge technologies*. BPB Publications.

Khan, B., Fatima, H., Qureshi, A., Kumar, S., Hanan, A., Hussain, J., & Abdullah, S. (2023). Drawbacks of Artificial Intelligence and Their Potential Solutions in the Healthcare Sector. *Biomedical Materials & Devices*, *1*(2), 1–8. DOI: 10.1007/s44174-023-00063-2 PMID: 36785697

Lee, C. L., Chao, C. T., Chu, W. H., Hung, M. Y., & Lee, J. K. (2022). Accelerating AI Applicationswith Sparse Matrix Compression in Halide. *Journal of Signal Processing Systems for Signal, Image, and Video Technology*, •••, 1–14.

Li, L., Wang, D., Shen, X., & Yang, M. (2009). A method for combinatorial explosion avoidance of AI planner and the appli- cation on test case generation. *CiSE, 2009*, 1–4.

Liu, P., Zhang, X., Pistoia, M., Zheng, Y., Marques, M., & Zeng, L. (2017). Automatic Text Input Generation for Mobile Testing. *ICSE, 2017*, 643–653. DOI: 10.1109/ICSE.2017.65

Liu, Z., Roberts, R. A., Lal-Nag, M., Chen, X., Huang, R., & Tong, W. (2021). AI-based language models powering drug discovery and development. *Drug Discovery Today*, *26*(11), 2593–2607. DOI: 10.1016/j.drudis.2021.06.009 PMID: 34216835

Memon, A. M. (2004). Using tasks to automate regression testing of GUIs. In *IASTEDInternational Conference on Artificial Intelligence and Applications-AIA* (pp. 477-82).

Moghadam, M. H. (2019). Machine Learning-assisted Perfor- mance Testing. ESEC/SIGSOFT FSE 2019, 1187–1189.

Paradkar, A. M., Sinha, A., Williams, C., Johnson, R. D., Outter- son, S., Shriver, C., & Liang, C. (2007). Automated functional conformance test generation for semantic web services. ICWS 2007, 110–117

Ramakrishnan, T., Mohan Gift, M. D., Chitradevi, S., Jegan, R., & Subha Hency Jose, P. Nagaraja, Rajneesh Sharma H.N., Selvakumar P., Sintayehu Mekuria Hailegiorgis, (2022). "Study of Numerous Resins Used in Polymer Matrix Composite Materials", Advances in Materials Science and Engineering, vol. 2022, Article ID 1088926, 8 pages, 2022. DOI: 10.1155/2022/1088926

Reddy, A., Indragandhi, V., Ravi, L., & Subramaniyaswamy, V. (2019). Detection of Cracks anddamage in wind turbine blades using artificial intelligence-based image analytics. *Measurement*, *147*, 106823. DOI: 10.1016/j.measurement.2019.07.051

Selvakumar, P. (2023). Biomedical applications of polymers in biosensors, cancer vaccines and drug delivery systems. *Biopolimery i Kletka*, *39*(4), 245–256. DOI: 10.7124/bc.000AA0

Selvakumar, P., Mariappan, P., Shunmugam, S., Paul, R., & Jabez, S. (2024). Removal of chemicals from effluent using photobioreactor technology to improve environmental and health impacts. *Zeitschrift für Physikalische Chemie*, *2024*(7), 1295–1302. Advance online publication. DOI: 10.1515/zpch-2023-0450

Shahamiri, S. R., Kadir, W. M. N. W., Ibrahim, S., & Hashim, S. Z. M. (2011). An automated framework for software test oracle. *Information and Software Technology*, *53*(7), 774–788. DOI: 10.1016/j.infsof.2011.02.006

Srivastava, P. R., & Baby, K. (2010). Automated software testing using metahurestictechnique based on an Ant Colony Optimiza- tion. *ISED*, *2010*, 235–240.

Tao, C., Gao, J., & Wang, T. (2019). Testing and quality validation for ai software–perspectives,issues, and practices. *IEEE Access : Practical Innovations, Open Solutions*, *7*, 120164–120175. DOI: 10.1109/ACCESS.2019.2937107

Vijayakumar, G., Rajkumar, M., Rajiv Chandar, N., Selvakumar, P., & Duraisamy, R. (2024). Muniyandi Rajkumar, Rajiv Chandar N, Selvakumar P and Ramesh Duraisamy, (2024). Environmentally friendly TDS removal from waste water by electrochemical ion exchange batch-type recirculation (EIR) technique. *Environmental Science. Water Research & Technology*, *10*(4), 826–835. DOI: 10.1039/D3EW00793F

Wang, F., Yang, S. C., & Yang, Y. L. (2011). Regression Testing Based on Neural Networks and Program Slicing Techniques. In Wang, Y., & Li, T. (Eds.), *Practical Applications of Intelligent Systems. Advances in Intelligent and Soft Computing* (Vol. 124). Springer., DOI: 10.1007/978-3-642-25658-5_50

Xu, J., Yang, P., Xue, S., Sharma, B., Sanchez-Martin, M., Wang, F., Beaty, K. A., Dehan, E., & Parikh, B. (2019). Translating cancer genomics into precision medicine with artificial intelligence: Applications,challenges and future perspectives. *Human Genetics*, *138*(2), 109–124. DOI: 10.1007/s00439-019-01970-5 PMID: 30671672

Zhu, X., Zhou, B., Hou, L., Chen, J., & Chen, L. (2008). An Experience-Based Approach for Test Execution Effort Estima- tion. 2008 The 9th International Conference for Young Computer Scientists. DOI: 10.1109/ICYCS.2008.53

Chapter 10
Top AI-Powered Tools for Software Test Automation

R. Adline Freeda
https://orcid.org/0009-0002-3335-0907
Department of Information Technology, KCG College of Technology, India

K. Sudha
https://orcid.org/0009-0002-5991-1119
Department of Artificial Intelligence and Data Science, Velammal Institute of Technology, India

ABSTRACT

As software systems become more complex, there is also an acute need for efficient, accurate, and scalable testing solutions. While traditional test automation is indeed quite powerful, it very often has to struggle against the demands of more advanced development environments that rely on continuous integration and delivery pipelines. We will compare these tools with a number of real-world case studies, underlining the improvements in how these tools enhance software quality and reduce the time-to-market along with the ability to perform continuous testing. Of course, we also touch upon the related issues when adopting AI-driven testing solutions-the challenges of data privacy and the integration complexity of new tools into existing workflows. By the end of this chapter, you will understand in clear-cut terms the main benefits and limitations and the scope of AI-powered tools, thus making them better decision-makers when it comes to choosing and applying such technology to their software testing processes.

DOI: 10.4018/979-8-3693-9356-7.ch010

INTRODUCTION TO AI-POWERED TEST AUTOMATION

As agile methodologies and DevOps continue to speed up the software development cycle, business requirements for faster, efficient, and reliable testing solutions are becoming increasingly complex. Traditional test automation, despite its capabilities and maturity, cannot ensure a connection between it and the modern software development paradigm, given the latter's complexity, variability, and escalating pace. Such a gap has given birth to artificial intelligence in software test automation, a resultant shift in paradigm with which testing is approached.

AI-based test automation introduces the notion of machine learning, predictive analytics, and natural language processing into the automation of repetitive testing tasks, which can improve the precision of a test and optimise the entire process of testing, (Alzubi, Nayyar, & Kumar, 2018). It is different from the conventional tools of automation that depend on predetermined scripts and strict test cases because AI-enabled tools learn, adapt from data, and can intelligently generate a test scenario, making AI especially effective with dynamic applications with changing environments and complex user interactions.

This section will discuss the relevance of AI to testing, describing how AI enhances the traditional approach to test automation. Some of the aspects that have been covered are how it can enhance efficiency, how AI will help identify defects that human eyes may miss, and whether AI supports continuous testing in high-paced development environments. We also provide an overview of the most important AI technologies applied in testing and will prepare the reader for a close-up view of the leading AI-based tools that are currently revolutionising software test automation, (Prasad & Murthy, 2017).

By the end of this introduction, readers will understand the driving forces behind the growth of AI-based test automation, the challenges it solves, and why it is the future of software testing.

1. CHALLENGES IN TRADITIONAL TEST AUTOMATION

Traditional test automation has been part and parcel of the design of software development methodologies for decades, thereby making it faster and more reliable than a manual process. However, recently, with the growing complexity in software systems and the decrease in development cycles, many challenges have come up that the traditional approaches find it difficult to overcome. Such factors can make it difficult for organisations to keep pace with the immediate requirements of agile and DevOps-style software development practices. Some of the key challenges that surface through this old approach to test automation are as follows:

Figure 1. Challenges in traditional test automation

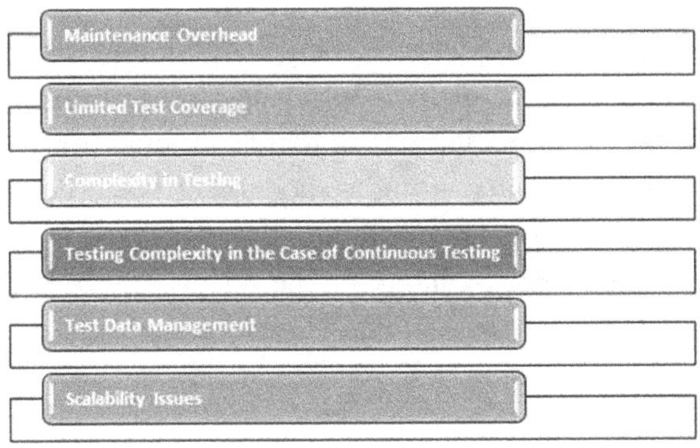

- **Maintenance Overhead**

Maintenance overhead is the biggest problem in traditional test automation, (Hemmati & Arcuri, 2015). As the applications change, even minor codebase changes may break a presently functional test script and may need frequent updates to keep test coverage intact. This labour-intensive and time-consuming effort for maintaining test cases is more daunting in large applications that are constantly being updated.

- **Limited Test Coverage**

Traditional automation tools follow predefined scripts and test cases that do not exhibit enough flexibility while dealing with new or unforeseen circumstances. Hence, they may miss edge cases, user interactions that dynamically change, or scenarios not envisioned during the planning phase of testing. It is almost impossible to cover all of the possible paths taken by a user and variations in the environment comprehensively, defeating the very purpose of defect discovery in automation.

- **Complexity in Testing**:

Modern applications of rich, dynamic applications with interactive UIs, microservice architectures, or complex integrations are quite challenging to automate using traditional approaches to testing. For instance, determining and verifying elements in a dynamic web application will be a tough nut for traditional tools to crack, which may eventually result in brittle tests breaking for even slight changes in the UI.

- **Testing Complexity in the Case of Continuous Testing**

Continuous testing refers to running automated tests at every stage of the development process. This is a very crucial part of CI/CD pipelines followed seriously in order to support the continuously evolved benefits of continuous testing. However, there are problems concerning such an automated test tool, (Hao, Zhang, & Xie, 2018). The essential reason behind this is that traditional tools do not match the speed of code changes that happen under modern software development and the number of releases that occur. There's nothing more related to such interventions than manuals for updating and maintaining the scripts related to tests. This makes the entire process a bottleneck to a stream of continuous testing.

- **Test Data Management**

Another challenge is the management of test data. Traditional test automation requires a predefined dataset for running the tests, but the accuracy and relevance of such data over time are challenging. Changes in the application may call for updating test data frequently, thus adding overhead to the automation process.

- **Scalability Issues**

Although traditional test automation tools come with very significant limitations in terms of scalability, there are limitations in the ability to scale due to increased applications and distribution into different platforms such as web, mobile, and desktop. Handling maintenance of test scripts on all of these might prove quite laborious and resource-consuming while scaling big-enterprise-wide automation frameworks.

2. ADVANTAGES OF AI-POWERED TEST AUTOMATION

AI-based test automation continues to revolutionise how we test software by breaking the barriers many traditional test automation tools have inherited over the years. Through machine learning, predictive analytics, and intelligent algorithms, AI-powered testing tools reap a lot on efficiency, accuracy, and scalability, (Chen, Fang, & Tan, 2019). Some of the benefits of an AI implementation in test automation are enumerated below:

Figure 2. Advantages of AI-powered test automation

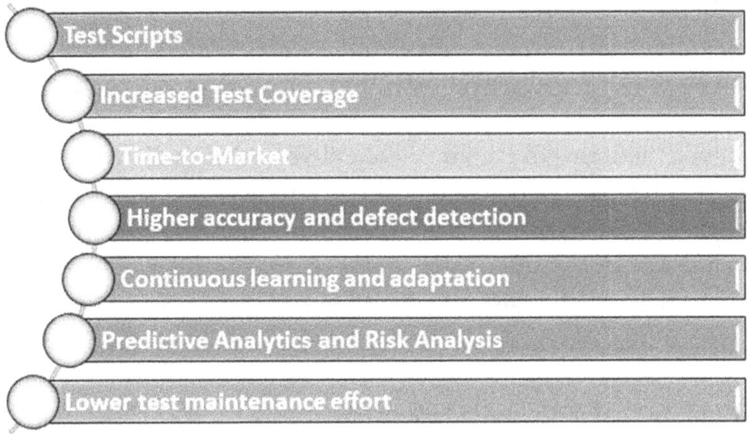

- **Test Scripts**

test scripts with AI-based automation tools are a remarkable aspect. The application under test has to be modified in terms of user interface, element IDs, or layout, after which the AI-based tools update and adapt the test scripts automatically, (Kim, Ryu, & Kwon, 2021). It does not force users into maintaining the script continuously and keeps the flakiness of the tests minimal due to minor changes in the application.

- **Increased Test Coverage**

AI tools can smartly navigate through different routes in an application, thus increasing the coverage. These AI tools produce test cases and execute them dynamically, which helps identify edge cases, some unexpected behaviour, and corner scenarios that may not be covered by an automation approach. They can learn from past test executions in order to predict what areas of an application need the most critical testing and provide more thorough and efficient testing.

- **Time-to-Market**

AI-powered test automation has significantly reduced the effort and time that would be spent by people in running and maintaining tests. It automatically generates test cases, executes them, and maintains them, thereby quickly speeding up testing and allowing teams to release high-quality software faster. It is most significantly used in agile and DevOps environments, where continuous testing and rapid releases depend on the use of AI. AI decreases manual involvement and shortens feedback cycles, helping reduce time-to-market.

- **Higher accuracy and defect detection**

For example, in terms of locating subtle defects that might have been avoided earlier with traditional test automation, AI-based tools are exceptional. Based on the analysis of huge volumes of data, such as user interactions and performance metrics, along with historical test results, anomalies reveal patterns that point toward defects with AI. Predictive analytics also allow these tools to focus on tests over areas where defects are most likely to occur to identify bugs earlier in the development cycle.

- **Continuous learning and adaptation**

Probably the most valuable capability in terms of benefiting from AI in test automation is the ability to learn over time with continuous optimization, (Freeda, Adline, & Rajendran, 2024). AI algorithms do learn from past test executions, learn about defects, and optimise testing strategies based on experience over time, (Khaled & Ahmed, 2020). With such learning capabilities, the testing process would eventually become more efficient and focused on the right test cases to minimise unnecessary ones and focus efforts on high-risk areas. The application evolution is managed efficiently by the tools where AI has been used, and its performance on new conditions is maintained without manual reprogramming for optimisation.

- **Predictive Analytics and Risk Analysis**

AI tools use historical data and algorithms of machine learning for performing predictive analytics, (Durelli, Sampaio, & Garcia, 2020) (Grechanik, Fu, & Xie, 2019). These analyse the pattern that past test results hold to predict the highest areas of defects in new code changes. Additionally, these can be used for ascertaining the overall risk associated with the release of the software by computation of failure probability in modules. This predictive ability enables teams to resource better, given more focus areas that have a high-risk aspect for further testing and mitigation of possible issues before it reaches the users.

- **Lower test maintenance effort**

Traditional test automation is always an effort-intensive task since scripts typically break each time the application changes. AI-powered tools bypass this by automatically updating the test cases as the application evolves. Developers and testers will no longer need to prod scripts for every little thing, be it a UI, an API, or even some form of system configuration tweaking; this means less maintenance effort and cost savings.

- **Scalability Across Platforms and Devices**

Scaling up these AI-powered test automation tools is not just with different platforms, operating systems, or devices. It can be implemented to work properly on every environment without changing the script for each test case according to a specific platform. This aspect helps greatly in the testing of mobile applications, web applications, and multi-platform software wherein the user experience as well as functionality vary for different devices.

- **Improved Test Data Management**

Thus, the AI tools may auto-generate, manage, and validate test data. These AI tools analyse the requirements of test data and automatically generate relevant datasets based on the current state of the application. AI is also capable of detecting outdated or incomplete test data situations so that test scenarios can represent reality always. Thus, tests are more accurate, and the efforts for managing test data are at a minimum level.

- **Continuous Testing Support in CI/CD Pipelines**

Such a tool will easily integrate into any workflow within modern development environments in any CI/CD pipeline. It can run tests at all times, analyse the results, and present the outcome back to developers in real-time. Thus, with such tooling, developers can maintain quality standards without slowing down their development process. Guarantees that regression tests, performance tests, and security tests are automated at certain times, and only then control the new releases before being deployed into production, (Freeda & Rajendran, 2023).

- **Teams Collaboration Improved**

Test automation tools using artificial intelligence contain natural user interfaces and dashboards to make it easier in working relationships between the developers, testers, and other stakeholders who are part of the involvement, (Pradhan, Limaye, & Jhaveri, 2022). Because most of the complexities are handled by AI, even non-technical team members can easily understand test results, monitor progress, and make informed decisions, thereby not creating silos walls that stand between teams for effective collaboration.

- **Cost Saved**

Although the initial investment in AI-powered test automation tools might be a little more than comparable traditional tools, there are tremendous long-term cost savings. AI is expected to decrease the general cost of software testing, thereby reducing manual intervention and test maintenance efforts and speeding up the execution of tests, (Singh, Suri, & Kaur, 2020).

Traditional testing automation presents many significant challenges with the maintenance of tests, scalability to larger sources, and comprehensive coverage of the test. However, most of these challenges are mitigated by AI-powered test automation. Self-healing scripts, predictive analytics, continuous learning, and all those other aspects enable the usage of AI-driven tools to improve efficiency and accuracy in testing and deliver higher-quality software faster. As software development continues to evolve, the AI-powered test automation model is going to be one of the most vital tools in respect of maintaining competitive advantage and assurance of sound, reliable applications.

3. SELENIUM WITH AI: APPLITOOLS EYES

Of course, Selenium is widely used in much web test automation for its flexibility and its ability to mimic user interactions with a web application. Where most old Selenium-based scripts are usually weak lies in the checking of visual elements, which have become the backbone of the dynamic web applications today where design is paramount. This is where the AI-powered visual testing tool, Applitools Eyes, complements Selenium: enhancing the testing beyond simple functional testing with advanced visual verification capabilities.

1. **Applitools Eyes Overview**

Applitools Eyes is a cloud-based, AI-based visual testing tool for visual UI testing and monitoring. It merely integrates with Selenium, meaning that teams can work with visual validation on their existing workflows for automated tests. It detects bugs and inconsistencies by comparing screenshots taken during the execution of tests against the expected images based on AI-driven algorithms, (Andrade, Andrade, & Vital, 2021). It can detect differences in the UI as subtle as misaligned elements, colour variations, and content shifts.

2. The Muscle Power of Visual AI

Applitools Eyes relies on advanced visual AI for intelligent image comparison. In contrast to pixel-by-pixel comparison, which sometimes can become too strict and produce a lot of false positives, the Applitools Eyes' AI mimics the manner in which the human visual system perceives visual differences. It can differentiate significant visual changes that may impact the user experience and more or less insignificant differences, like anti-aliasing or minor rendering differences between browsers.

This lets the tool:

- Identify the visual bugs accurately, which will affect the experience of the user.
- Avoid false positives due to minor changes in UI, and thus reduce the effort towards maintenance of test scripts.
- Automate dynamic contents like ads, which might vary from one test to another and not possibly impact the result.

1. Introduction to Appium and Winium

Appium is an open-source tool that automates native, hybrid, and mobile web applications for Android and iOS. Because the same test code can run on multiple mobile operating systems using the WebDriver protocol of Appium, it boasts a significant advantage.

Winium is an automation framework based on Selenium, especially for Windows desktop applications. With this application, a developer can automate Windows applications with techniques similar to those used in Selenium for web applications. Thus, it is excellent for automating the Windows-based desktop software.

Both Appium and Winium are high-functionality frameworks to automate the interactions for the mobile and desktop applications. However, neither natively supports visual testing, and thus the integration of visual testing tools is required.

2. Why Visual Testing Is So Important for Mobile and Desktop Applications

Visual elements in mobile and desktop applications make up the most simplified, intuitive design of the user experience. Out-of-alignment buttons, broken layouts, or incorrect font rendering can have significant influences on usability badly. Functional tests traditionally check that all an application's features are functioning correctly, but such tests never check the application's aspect of its visual appearance.

Automated visual testing guarantees that UI renders as expected on different screen sizes, resolutions, and OS. Using the functional capabilities through Appium/Winium combined with AI-based visual testing tools ensures both functionality and visual consistency.

3. **Usage of Applitools Eyes with Appium**

It combines with Appium, thereby improving the mobile test process through automated visual testing capabilities. Essentially, Applitools Eyes allows testers to capture and compare screenshots from a mobile app while detecting visual defects such as unsymmetrical elements, broken images, or content shift. Here's how to integrate it:

Step 1: Setting Up Applitools Eyes with Appium

Testers must install the Applitools Eyes SDK for Appium and set it up to capture visual baselines during the execution of their tests. The Eyes SDK is integrated with Appium, allowing testers to leverage existing test scripts with Appium to add visual validation steps.

Step 2: Define Visual Baselines

The initial run by Applitools Eyes captures a screenshot of the mobile application in its correct state, creating a baseline against which it is compared all subsequent screenshots.

For every subsequent test run, Applitools Eyes captures new screenshots of the application under test and compares them with images saved in the baseline. The AI engine will identify any potential visual mismatches, including UI element misplacement and layout shifts or visual bugs introduced in the development phase.

Step 3: Review Visual Test Results

Applitools provides a dashboard through which the tester can view visual differences highlighted by the AI. They can either accept the flagged differences or reject them as actual defects.

4. ADD APPLITOOLS EYES WITH WINIUM

Also, there can be a combination of Applitools Eyes with Winium to perform the visual testing of a Windows desktop application. In this process, it is about the same as Appium did, so it allows the tester to check the desktop application and validate its visual aspects. Here, Applitools Eyes helps detect a window resize error, overlapping of UI elements, or incorrect rendering of font by capturing the screenshot of the desktop UI and comparison.

Step 1: Setting Up Applitools Eyes with Winium

Install the Applitools Eyes SDK for Winium with settings to capture screenshots during tests of desktop applications.

Step 2: Capture baseline screenshots

The first time you run this test, it captures screenshots of the Windows application in its desired state, which then becomes a reference baseline for making comparisons in subsequent runs.

Step 3: Run Visual Tests

Appium and Winium later execute the comparison between screenshots of the baseline with the actual ones and flag any visual differences occurring—may be due to movements of UI elements or due to the resolution differences.

Step 4: Visual Analysis

On the visual test analysis dashboard of Applitools, testers can see the flagged difference. Visual bugs often get caught early in the testing cycle before delivering the application to the customers.

5. Advantages of Automated Visual Testing with Appium and Winium

Maintain cross-platform visual consistency.

Closing the deal: Integrating Applitools Eyes into Appium and Winium will allow testers not only to be assured of the consistency of rendering across devices and platforms but also the visual consistency of an application. For example, in cases of mobile applications that should render correctly on a wide range of screen sizes and resolutions, desktop applications that function across multiple versions of Windows, etc.

Less Visual Regressions

Visual regression testing plays a vital role in the determination of unintentional changes in the UI. Through Applitools Eyes, the tester easily traces what visual regressions have been introduced due to new code changes to prevent design problems in reaching production, (Freeda & Rajendran, 2023).

Scalability for large test suites

With Applitools Eyes, visual tests can be performed in parallel across multiple devices, operating systems, and browsers, thus allowing parallel execution of tests on multiple devices and configurations while testing mobile applications on a wide variety of devices or ensuring that the corresponding desktop apps run correctly on different Windows configurations.

Applitools Eyes uses AI-powered comparison that ensures that the visual defects are identified with absolute correctness. Contrary to human fault, AI-driven visual testing is very precise and unvarying.

Less Maintenance of Tests

Applitools Eyes reduces the frequent update of a test script of dynamic content and minor user interface changes by automatically handling it, reducing the effort required for maintaining a visual test suite, especially when applications are prone to frequent UI modifications.

5. END-TO-END TESTING WITH CYPRESS AND PLAYWRIGHT

E2E is one of the most critical aspects of testing in software, as it ensures that all workflows within an application are working as expected—from the user interface to the backend services. One of the primary use cases of E2E testing is to mimic real-time interactions for testing purposes so that the correctness of software can be checked in a production-like environment. Of the modern tools, two have gained significant traction for the performance of E2E testing: Cypress and Playwright. However, both of these tools aim to make E2E testing more efficient, reliable, and accessible to developers and QA engineers.

In this chapter, we are going to deep dive into the strengths, features, and differences of Cypress and Playwright and learn how to use each of these tools for comprehensive end-to-end testing.

5.1. What Is End-To-End Testing?

This method allows for all the pieces of a software system to work as expected. The entire application flow from the user's standpoint is tested, which includes clicks, form submissions, navigation, backend services such as APIs, databases, and integrations, and overall system interactions such as message queues or third-party services. In this way, E2E testing can catch integration issues, UI bugs, and performance bottlenecks that may not be picked up by unit or integration testing.

5.2. Introduction to Cypress

Cypress is the most widely used testing framework that is based on JavaScript and supplies the developer with an environment for writing and executing E2E tests. It is popularly known as fast, simple, and gives real-time feedback on the test, which makes it an ideal choice for developers. Unlike traditional E2E tools for testing, Cypress is run directly in the browser where the application exists, so there is much visibility into the test's execution.

Key Features of Cypress

Real-Time Reloads

In Cypress, there is instantaneous feedback automatically running tests every time changes are made to the test files. The real-time feedback loop helps greatly in quick development and debugging.

Automatic Waiting

Cypress waits intelligently for elements to become visible or actionable, thereby reducing the need to add manually inserted waits in the test scripts. It helps avoid flakiness generally attributed to E2E tests.

Time Travel and Debugging

Cypress lets the user "time travel" through visually inspecting each step in the test flow. The user can hover on commands running in the test runner with snapshots at each stage to aid in debugging a failed test.

Easy setup and execution

Getting Cypress up is very easy with minimal configuration. All you need to run the tests is inside, so no extra dependencies or complex setup are required.

Built-in Support for Stubbing and Spying

stubbing network requests and spying on HTTP calls. This allows testing the response of different networks without any dependency on other services or servers while running the test.

Playwright is one of the newest E2E testing tools developed by Microsoft, which allows cross-browser tests, along with great support to handle several types of browsers (Chromium, Firefox, and WebKit), and robust APIs can be used to automate the browser interactions to make it work well in cross-browser tasks. Due to these factors, Playwright is an efficient and powerful tool that provides comprehensive end-to-end testing results.

Key Features of Playwright

Cross-Browser Support

Playwright is special in that the API used for testing Chrome, Firefox, and WebKit is the same for all three browsers; thus, applications behave consistently across all browsers and platforms.

Multiple contexts and parallel execution

Playwright supports running tests in isolated browser contexts, which means that parallel execution will be considerably faster than sequential execution. This feature comes in handy once the test suite has to be scaled in the CI/CD pipeline.

Like Cypress, Playwright waits automatically before any action is carried out until elements are ready. This ensures that one's tests are reliable and less vulnerable to flakiness issues resulting from timing.

Headless and Headful Mode

Playwright runs headless or headful. Running tests headless makes them faster; running them in headful mode makes it possible to visually see the browser during which the test runs.

Versatile API for Browser Automation

However, the playwright provides APIs at a low level, which allows deep control over the interactions of the browser, including the management of many tabs, handling popups, file uploads, and downloads—the reason it is well suited for sophisticated testing scenarios.

Comparison of Cypress and Playwright

Both Cypress and Playwright have unique strengths, and the choice between them often depends on specific project requirements. Here's a comparison based on key factors:

Table 1. Comparison of cypress and playwright

Feature	Cypress	Playwright
Language Support	JavaScript, TypeScript	JavaScript, TypeScript, Python, C#
Cross-Browser Testing	Limited (Chrome, Edge, Electron)	Full support (Chromium, Firefox, WebKit)
Ease of Setup	Simple, out-of-the-box configuration	More complex, but flexible
Automatic Waiting	Yes (for actions and assertions)	Yes (for actions and assertions)
Debugging	Built-in time travel, real-time feedback	Powerful, with headless/headful modes
Test Execution Speed	Faster for simple tests	More optimized for parallel and multi-browser
Test Isolation	Limited support for parallel execution	Advanced support with browser contexts
Network Interception	Native support for mocking, stubbing, spying	Advanced network interception and manipulation

6. CONTINUOUS TESTING WITH PERFECTO AND SAUCE LABS

Continuous testing is one of the quintessential components of any Agile or DevOps environment in today's fast-paced environment, involving automated test execution geared towards assuring quality software through the CI/CD pipeline in every phase of its development process. Tools such as Perfecto and Sauce Labs have obtained the top position in this sector due to rich, cloud-based platforms that run automated tests against different environments, browsers, and devices, (Camacho *et al.,* 2015).

1. **What is continuous testing?**

Continuous testing is the execution of automated tests continuously along the pipeline of software delivery. It covers testing early and often, from when code is committed all the way to final deployment stages. The aims of continuous testing are:

Early detection of defects—catching bugs as early as possible so that the cost of fixing them is less costly.

Real-time feedback: providing developers with feedback on the quality of the code.

Release velocity: Quality assurance should not be a blocker for delivery, (Panichella, Palomba, & Zaidman, 2018).

Continued testing underpins other CI/CD tools such as Jenkins, GitLab CI, Travis CI, and CircleCI by automating the execution of tests so that teams can release quicker and with significantly greater confidence.

2. **Perfecto**

Perfecto is a cloud-based continuous testing platform that centres its focus on mobile and web testing across a large range of real devices and browsers. Through Perfecto, teams can run tests in real-time both on emulators and simulators and on actual devices for assurance that applications work as expected across different environments.

Key Features of Perfecto

Real Devices and Browsers in the Cloud

Perfecto gives access to a vast set of real mobile devices and browsers so teams can test under conditions that resemble reality best. This ensures applications will run well on different platforms and environments.

Support for Continuous Integration

Perfecto integrates with CI tools, such as Jenkins, GitLab, and Bamboo, so that automated tests can easily be included in the CI/CD pipeline. Teams can, therefore, automate their testing throughout the entire lifecycle.

Parallel Execution

Perfecto runs tests parallel on various devices and browsers, which automatically decreases the execution time of tests and increases the coverage of your tests.

Advance reporting and analytics

Perfecto offers in-depth reporting and analytics tools that provide you with a clear view of results, trends, and performance of the test. All these reports help teams get to the root of problems faster and cut debugging time.

AI-powered Test Automation

Perfecto uses AI and ML technology for the identification of flakiness in tests, which promises to deliver actionable insights to improve the test stability. It is also capable of automatically detecting the visual issues with the UI, (Li, Huang, & Zhang, 2022).

Sauce Labs

Sauce Labs is another popular cloud-based platform that provides testing solutions for both mobile and web applications. With the facility of cross-browser and cross-device testing, teams can ensure their applications are working across a wide array of browsers, operating systems, and devices.

Important Features of Sauce Labs

Cross-Browser Testing

Sauce Labs supports cross-browser testing and gives teams the flexibility of running automated tests on different browsers (Chrome, Firefox, Edge, Safari, etc.) and operating systems (Windows, macOS, and Linux). This ensures that web applications look and work in similar ways in different environments.

Mobile Testing

Sauce Labs empowers engineers to test apps on a cloud-based lab of actual iOS and Android devices. It also provides support for emulators and simulators to run tests faster.

CI/CD Integration

Sauce Labs integrates with CI/CD tools like Jenkins, Travis CI, CircleCI, etc. Continuous testing runs across the development cycle.

Parallel Testing and Scalability

The team can run tests in parallel with Sauce Labs. This allows for a concurrent run of many tests, reducing test time while increasing efficiency.

Detailed Test Reporting

Sauce Labs has generated detailed reports on test runs with logs, screenshots, and videos related to the execution of the tests. These help in debugging test failures and know what's happening with the application under tests.

Support for Open Source

Sauce Lab supports widely used open-source test frameworks like Selenium, Appium, TestCafe, and Cypress, which makes it relatively easy for teams to begin their journey to continuous testing.

Comparison of Perfecto and Sauce Labs

While both Perfecto and Sauce Labs offer powerful solutions for continuous testing, there are key differences that make them more suited to different testing needs:

Table 2. Comparison of Perfecto and Sauce Labs

Feature	Perfecto	Sauce Labs
Device Coverage	Extensive real device lab for mobile testing	Large cloud of real devices and emulators
Browser Coverage	Major desktop and mobile browsers	Extensive support for desktop and mobile
CI/CD Integration	Seamless integration with Jenkins, GitLab, Bamboo	Strong CI/CD support with Jenkins, CircleCI
Parallel Testing	Supports parallel execution across devices	Supports parallel testing across browsers and devices
AI-Powered Analytics	AI-driven test failure analysis and flakiness detection	Detailed logs and videos, no AI-driven insights
Geolocation Testing	Allows for testing in different geographies	Supported via custom configuration
API Testing	Supports API testing in combination with UI tests	Strong API testing support with Postman, Newman
Open Source Integration	Supports Selenium, Appium, and Cypress	Strong support for Selenium, Appium, Cypress, TestCafe
Pricing Model	Flexible pricing based on usage	Various subscription-based pricing models

Perfecto and Sauce Labs Use Cases Use Case of Perfecto: Mobile-First Applications

For mobile-first applications, Perfecto is among the best options because it has a very strong focus on real-device testing. If there is a desire amongst mobile development teams to ensure their application works seamlessly across wide varieties of devices, including the latest iOS and Android releases, Perfecto lets them access such real devices in the cloud and hence ensure test coverage not only across older but newer devices as well.

Perfecto allows running tests in parallel on multiple devices for non-blocking through testing, even in the most Agile/DevOps-accelerated environments.

Use Case for Sauce Labs: Cross-Browser Web Applications

Sauce Labs is a good cross-browser testing tool; it always appears to be among the first tools when teams of web application developers deal with elaborating highly complex web applications that should work under different browsers and OS. Such a scenario took place when working with an e-commerce platform: a team of web developers should verify, using Sauce Labs, if the website behaves correctly in different browsers, such as Chrome, Firefox, Safari, and Edge, and on different operating systems—running instances of Windows, macOS, and Linux.

Sauce Labs also offers developers an essential debugging tool—screenshots, video recording, and logs for each test execution—which can help developers find and debug errors in several environments much more efficiently.

CONCLUSION

As software development practices have evolved to cope with the velocity of release cycles in modern times, AI-powered tools and cloud-based platforms have turned out to be the saviours for quality assurance through continuous testing and automation. Traditionally, test automation is good enough to cope with the complexity that is brought in by multi-device, multi-browser, and large-scale systems. Where AI-powered test automation tools like Applitools Eyes, Testim.io, Cypress, and platforms such as Perfecto and Sauce Labs come in.

These tools provide a significant advantage over the traditional approaches using visual testing, predictive analytics, automated flakiness detection, and cross-browser and cross-device testing. Developers and QA teams would be able to run tests faster with accuracy and reliability; this means there is greater possibility for detecting flaws much earlier, better expansion of coverage on tests, and reduction of feedback delays on the CI/CD pipeline.

Apart from the above, infrastructure and scalable solutions like Perfecto and Sauce Labs enable running tests in parallel, across real devices and browsers, and thus, a complete application is tested in real-world usage environments. Continuous testing in the development lifecycle enables teams to streamline the testing process, mitigate bottlenecks, and accelerate the release of high-quality software with greater confidence.

Finally, AI-powered tools and platforms are the future for software test automation. They are meant to address the scale, speed, and complexity demands that modern applications present. As more and more organisations implement Agile and DevOps methodologies, investment in AI-driven test automation and continuous testing platforms is critical for delivering software in line with today's expectations regarding users as well as business environments.

REFERENCES

Alzubi, J., Nayyar, A., & Kumar, A. (2018). Machine learning from theory to algorithms: An overview. *Journal of Physics: Conference Series*, *1142*(1), 012012. DOI: 10.1088/1742-6596/1142/1/012012

Andrade, E. C., Andrade, S., & Vital, S. (2021). A survey of AI-driven testing methods for software systems. *ACM Computing Surveys*, *54*(2), 1–35. DOI: 10.1145/3447028

Camacho, D., Gálvez, G., Molina, J. M., & De La Torre, R. (2015). Automated testing of cloud services with genetic algorithms. *Software, Practice & Experience*, *45*(9), 1277–1305. DOI: 10.1002/spe.2278

Chen, Z., Fang, Z., & Tan, Q. (2019). Machine learning-based test prioritization for Android applications. *IEEE Access : Practical Innovations, Open Solutions*, *7*, 160194–160205. DOI: 10.1109/ACCESS.2019.2951166

Durelli, V. H. S., Sampaio, S. A., & Garcia, V. C. (2020). Toward AI-based software testing: The roles of machine learning techniques. *IEEE Software*, *37*(4), 37–43. DOI: 10.1109/MS.2020.2987712

Freeda, R. (2024). Test suite optimization under multi-objective constraints for software fault detection and localization: Hybrid optimization-based model. *International Journal of Software Testing*, *10*(1), 151–166. DOI: 10.3233/WEB-220131

Freeda, R. A., & Rajendran, P. S. (2023). Test Suite Minimization for Regression Testing Using Keyword Match Technique. In Joshi, A., Mahmud, M., & Ragel, R. G. (Eds.), *Information and Communication Technology for Competitive Strategies (ICTCS 2022). ICTCS 2022. Lecture Notes in Networks and Systems* (Vol. 623). Springer., DOI: 10.1007/978-981-19-9638-2_24

Freeda, R. A., & Rajendran, P. S. (2023). An Overview of Efficient Regression Testing Prioritization Techniques Based on Genetic Algorithm. In Dutta, P., Chakrabarti, S., Bhattacharya, A., Dutta, S., & Shahnaz, C. (Eds.), *Emerging Technologies in Data Mining and Information Security. Lecture Notes in Networks and Systems* (Vol. 490). Springer., DOI: 10.1007/978-981-19-4052-1_39

Grechanik, M., Fu, C., & Xie, Q. (2019). Automatically testing large-scale distributed systems using machine learning techniques. *ACM Transactions on Software Engineering and Methodology*, *28*(2), 1–35. DOI: 10.1145/3313623

Hao, D., Zhang, C., & Xie, X. (2018). Test selection in continuous integration using machine learning. *Proceedings of the 40th International Conference on Software Engineering (ICSE 2018),* 1000-1011. DOI: 10.1145/3180155.3180189

Hemmati, H., & Arcuri, A. (2015). Empirical analysis of the effectiveness of search-based test automation. *Automated Software Engineering*, *22*(2), 211–243. DOI: 10.1007/s10515-014-0154-5

Kashani, Z. M., & Briand, L. C. (2017). Machine learning applications in software testing: A systematic literature review. *Empirical Software Engineering*, *22*(6), 2933–2977. DOI: 10.1007/s10664-017-9511-4

Khaled, H., & Ahmed, M. (2020). Applying machine learning to optimize automated test case generation for web applications. *Journal of Systems and Software*, *159*, 110438. DOI: 10.1016/j.jss.2019.110438

Kim, M., Ryu, S., & Kwon, K. (2021). AI-based static analysis for automated software testing. *Information and Software Technology*, *128*, 106518. DOI: 10.1016/j.infsof.2020.106518

Li, Z., Huang, X., & Zhang, M. (2022). AI-powered testing of autonomous driving systems: Challenges and approaches. [TOSEM]. *ACM Transactions on Software Engineering and Methodology*, *31*(2), 1–44. DOI: 10.1145/3474126

Panichella, S., Palomba, F., & Zaidman, A. (2018). The impact of deep learning techniques on software quality assurance. *IEEE Software*, *35*(6), 56–62. DOI: 10.1109/MS.2018.290110430

Pradhan, P. R., Limaye, G., & Jhaveri, R. H. (2022). Artificial intelligence in software testing: A systematic review. *Journal of King Saud University. Computer and Information Sciences*. Advance online publication. DOI: 10.1016/j.jksuci.2022.04.012

Prasad, S., & Murthy, G. S. (2017). Adaptive test automation using AI-based techniques: A new approach. *Proceedings of the International Conference on Automation, Computing and Communication Systems (ICACCS 2017),* 346-352. https://doi.org/DOI: 10.1109/ICACCS.2017.7829987

Singh, A., Suri, B., & Kaur, S. (2020). Artificial intelligence and machine learning-based testing: The next frontier for software testing. [IJACSA]. *International Journal of Advanced Computer Science and Applications*, *11*(3), 101–107. DOI: 10.14569/IJACSA.2020.0110312

Chapter 11
Harnessing AI for Scalable and Adaptive Cloud-Native Applications

C. R. Rathish
https://orcid.org/0000-0001-7737-3938
New Horizon College of Engineering, India

Nithin Shiva Vanka
https://orcid.org/0009-0005-0123-9528
New Horizon College of Engineering, India

Yelam Ethi Sai Sreevathsav
New Horizon College of Engineering, India

L. Jeevan Bharadhi
New Horizon College of Engineering, India

Akhilesh R. Mohan
New Horizon College of Engineering, India

Aryasree Madhukumar
https://orcid.org/0009-0007-9130-7647
Cambridge Institute of Technology, India

ABSTRACT

Software engineering is changing as a result of artificial intelligence (AI), which makes decision-making easier, automates activities, and creates more intelligent, adaptable systems. AI can now write code, debug programs in real time, and run continuous software tests—all of which increase productivity and decrease error rates. AI-driven solutions also improve risk assessment, resource allocation, and project management, which results in improved planning and more efficient project execution. However, issues with bias, transparency, and data privacy arise when implementing AI. For AI to be used in software development in a responsible and moral manner, these problems must be resolved. In the future, artificial intelligence

DOI: 10.4018/979-8-3693-9356-7.ch011

will propel developments like quantum computing and self-healing systems. These developments will push the limits of software engineering, increasing accessibility to development and redefining the industry's future.

INTRODUCTION

The term artificial intelligence (AI) has transcended its meaning and is now widely used in several different sectors, including software engineering, healthcare, and finance. A paradigm change that rewrites the rules for how software is designed, created, tested, and maintained is brought about by the incorporation of AI into software development. Developers may design software that is more effective, scalable, and responsive to user needs by utilizing AI's capabilities to evaluate huge datasets, automate procedures, and build on past experiences. Software engineering with artificial intelligence (AI) is expected to grow as the digital era progresses, pushing the frontiers of innovation and establishing new benchmarks for performance and quality.

REVOLUTIONIZING CODE GENERATION AND DEBUGGING

Coding has always been a labor-intensive process that calls for a high level of skill, inventiveness, and attention to detail. But AI is altering the game with its sophisticated tools that can write code on their own, relieving developers of some of their workload and expediting the development process. These AI-powered solutions make use of models for machine learning that have been trained on enormous repositories of pre-existing code to recognize trends and best practices, (Raychev. Bielik, & Vechev, 2016). They are therefore able to write code that is scalable and performant in addition to being functional.

AI-powered code generators, for example, can recommend whole code blocks with little to no input from humans, which eliminates the need for human coding. This is especially helpful for recurring jobs that can be automated to cut down on errors and save time, such as developing boilerplate code, (Feng *et al.,* 2020). Moreover, these instruments can be beneficial for developing complex algorithms by offering suggestions or even launching a fresh instance using high-level descriptions, (Vaswani *et al.,* 2017).

AI is making great progress in detecting and fixing problems more quickly than in the past when it comes to debugging. Manual code reviews and thorough testing are the mainstays of traditional debugging techniques, which can be laborious and prone to error. Debugging tools powered by AI, on the other hand, are able to examine code in real time, spot possible issues, and even make repair suggestions, (Chen & Monperrus, 2019). These techniques determine issues that might not be immediately apparent to human developers by using anomaly detection and pattern recognition, (Allamanis *et al.,* 2018).

AI can also anticipate possible issues before they arise, giving developers the opportunity to proactively fix errors and maintain high code quality. Artificial intelligence (AI) systems are incredibly helpful instruments in the process of developing software since they may continuously improve their accuracy and efficiency by learning from previous errors and their fixes, (Tiwari, Goyal, & Sharma, 2021).

AI IN SOFTWARE TESTING AND QUALITY ASSURANCE

Software testing and quality assurance (QA) are essential stages in the software development lifecycle that guarantee the finished product satisfies all specifications and performs as intended under a range of scenarios. In the past, testing has always been a labor-intensive, manual procedure that takes a large amount of time and money. But AI is transforming this field by bringing in automation, predictive analytics, and smart testing techniques that improve testing efficacy and efficiency, (Yang, Liu, & Yin, 2021).

A complete set of test cases can be automatically generated by AI-driven testing tools depending on the needs and specifications of the product. Numerous scenarios, including edge cases that human testing could miss, can be simulated using these technologies. AI shortens the time and effort needed to guarantee software quality by automating the creation and execution of test cases. This enables quicker release cycles and more frequent updates, (Feng *et al.,* 2020).

Furthermore, AI's capacity to absorb knowledge from prior testing iterations enables it to gradually enhance its testing methodologies. For instance, AI can forecast which parts of the code are most likely to have defects by analyzing past test results to find patterns and trends. With the help of this predictive capability, developers can focus their testing efforts on the most crucial components of the program and ensure that, if at all possible, problems are fixed before they affect consumers, (Svyatkovskiy *et al.,* 2020).

The capacity of AI to conduct continuous testing during the development phase is a key benefit in testing. Testing is frequently done at certain points in traditional development models, such as right before a product release or following the conclusion of a development sprint. Conversely, AI makes it possible for continuous testing, where examinations are conducted automatically each time new code is added to the project. This method reduces the likelihood that defects will manage to make their way into the finished product by ensuring that any problems brought about by new code are found and fixed right away, (Chen & Monperrus, 2019).

AI is useful not only for functional testing but also for non-functional testing, including usability, security, and performance testing. Artificial intelligence (AI)-powered solutions can mimic thousands of users engaging with the program at once, revealing security flaws and performance snags that might not be seen in smaller-scale testing, (Tiwari, Goyal, & Sharma, 2021). AI ensures that the program is not just operational but also safe, scalable, and easy to use by automating various testing processes, (Wei *et al.,* 2022).

OPTIMIZING PROJECT MANAGEMENT AND DECISION-MAKING

In software engineering, project management entails managing resources, organizing intricate tasks, and making crucial choices that have an impact on a project's outcome. These duties have historically been left to the judgment and experience of project managers, but artificial intelligence (AI) is now offering strong tools to improve these procedures using automation and data-driven insights. By evaluating enormous volumes of data from prior projects, artificial intelligence (AI) may greatly increase the accuracy of project planning. Artificial Intelligence (AI) can assist project managers in making better decisions on resource allocation, schedules, and risk management by seeing trends in previous project performance, (Svyatkovskiy *et al.,* 2020). For instance, based on a project's present status, AI can forecast possible delays and recommend changes to the project plan to reduce these risks. This enables project managers to handle problems more quickly, lowering the risk of project overruns and guaranteeing that tasks are finished on schedule and within budget. Allocating resources is another area in which AI is having a significant influence. Artificial intelligence (AI) may optimize task assignment, ensuring that each task is handled by the most competent individual by evaluating the talents and availability of team members, (Chen & Monperrus, 2019). By matching tasks to team members' preferences and strengths, this not only boosts contentment at work but also improves the effectiveness of the development process.

AI is assisting in the more accurate and efficient execution of risk management, which is a crucial aspect of project management. AI is able to identify potential issues before they arise by analyzing a variety of characteristics, such as project complexity, team effectiveness, and external hazards. Artificial Intelligence (AI) lowers the probability of project failures by enabling project managers to take preventive action through early warnings about hazards. AI is not only making planning and resource management better, but it's also making better decisions throughout project execution. Artificial intelligence (AI)-driven dashboards can offer real-time insights into project performance, allowing project coordinators to track developments, spot bottlenecks, and make informed decisions, (Vaswani *et al.*, 2017). Project management could confirm that they have the information they need to make wise decisions by customizing these dashboards to show the most pertinent KPIs for each project.

AI can support teammates collaborate by offering tools that improve coordination and communication. AI-driven platforms, for instance, can automatically create action items, summarize meetings, and monitor task advancement, guaranteeing that group members are on the same page and working toward the same objectives. This degree of automation and intelligence guarantees effective project completion and boosts team productivity, (Yang, Liu, & Yin, 2021).

ENHANCING COLLABORATION AND COMMUNICATION

Today's remote and multinational work environments require effective teamwork and communication more than ever. These facets of software engineering are being greatly improved by AI, which is facilitating knowledge sharing, collaboration, and effort coordination across geographical boundaries. By automating repetitive processes and making sure that everyone is informed, AI-powered communication solutions can promote smooth team engagement. AI chatbots, for example, may arrange appointments, respond to simple questions, and even generate paperwork as needed. Over time, these bots will become more adept at supporting teammates by assimilating lessons from previous exchanges, (Feng *et al.*, 2020). As a result, team members are less burdened and free to concentrate on other crucial project components.

AI is not only capable of handling repetitive jobs but also improving teamwork by intelligently summarizing talks and meetings. To guarantee that each teammate has access to the information they require, AI-driven solutions can automatically record meetings, highlight important points, and provide action items. This is especially helpful for large or dispersed teams, as it could be challenging to manage massive amounts of information and coordinate across time zones, (Tiwari, Goyal, & Sharma, 2021).

AI is also capable of analyzing team communication patterns to spot potential issues before they materialize as serious ones. AI can identify, for instance, whether specific team members are routinely left out of important conversations or whether communication obstacles are impeding advancement. AI makes it possible for managers to take corrective action by seeing these problems early, which promotes a more diverse and effective workplace, (Svyatkovskiy *et al.*, 2020).

Additionally, through compatibility with software for project management and version control systems, AI can assist collaborative software development settings. AI is able to monitor modifications made by various team members, identify possible disputes instantly, and recommend solutions. This guarantees easy collaboration and a software solution that is well-integrated and harmonious in the end, (Chen & Monperrus, 2019).

AI-driven systems with asynchronous communication capabilities can also aid in bridging time zones in the context of decentralized teams. To ensure that those on the team who are in various time zones receive the most relevant updates as they start their workday, AI can, for instance, prioritize and summarize emails or messages. This guarantees that the team stays in sync no matter where they are and cuts down on communication lag, (Tiwari, Goyal, & Sharma, 2021).

DEVELOPING INTELLIGENT AND ADAPTIVE SOFTWARE

Besides revolutionizing software development, AI is opening the door for the creation of a brand-new class of intelligent and adaptable software products. These apps are made to pick up on user behavior, adjust to shifting surroundings, and offer customized experiences that were unthinkable a few years ago, (Chen & Monperrus, 2019).

The application of recommendation systems in a wide range of industries is among the most prominent instances of AI-driven software. To provide individualized recommendations, these systems examine user behavior, preferences, and previous exchanges. Artificial intelligence is used, for example, by e-commerce platforms to recommend products to consumers based on their browsing and purchase history, (Vaswani *et al.,* 2017). This boosts engagement and sales in addition to improving the user experience.

Autonomous systems are another field in which AI is having a big influence. Autonomous vehicles driven by artificial intelligence possess sensors as well as machine learning techniques that enable them to sense their surroundings, make choices, and maneuver through intricate situations without the need for human assistance, (Tiwari, Goyal, & Sharma, 2021). These cars are constantly picking up lessons from their experiences, which eventually enables individuals to make wiser decisions and increase safety.

Applications that can process and analyze big datasets in real-time are being built using AI. This capacity is especially helpful in fields where data-driven insights are essential for making decisions, like marketing, healthcare, and finance. AI-driven finance software, for instance, can use real-time data to evaluate market trends and recommend investments, and healthcare applications can help physicians by evaluating patient data and recommending possible diagnoses, (Yang, Liu, & Yin, 2021).

AI is also making it possible to design user interfaces that are adaptable, meaning they may alter in response to user behavior. Utilizing machine learning, these interfaces examine user behavior with the software and make necessary modifications to enhance accessibility and usability. An AI-driven program might, for example, highlight specific options based on a user's past interactions or simplify its interface for those with trouble using complicated features, (Svyatkovskiy *et al.,* 2020). This degree of customization guarantees that the program satisfies a wide variety of users' needs.

Innovation in fields like computer vision as well as natural language processing (NLP) is additionally being fueled by AI. Applications having NLP capabilities can comprehend and react to human language, making software interactions more natural and intuitive. Chatbots, virtual assistants, and customer care apps are using this technology to deliver more effective and efficient support, (Feng *et al.,* 2020). Similar to this, AI-driven systems for computer vision are being employed in a broad range of applications, like medical imaging and facial recognition, allowing software to interpret visual data remarkably accurately, (Chen & Monperrus, 2019).

ADDRESSING CHALLENGES AND ETHICAL CONCERNS

Even though AI is revolutionizing software engineering, there are numerous obstacles and moral problems that are required to be resolved to promote ethical and sustainable development. The complexity and autonomy of AI systems raise crucial new issues regarding transparency, accountability, and fairness.

A key obstacle is the intricacy involved in putting AI systems into practice. For many firms, developing and integrating AI into software can be challenging due to the specialized expertise and skills needed, (Vaswani *et al.,* 2017). Furthermore, creating systems driven by AI could be expensive, in particular for tiny and medium-sized businesses. For AI to be widely adopted, it is imperative that it be scalable and available to businesses of all sizes.

The possibility for prejudice in AI systems presents another difficulty. Large datasets are used to train AI systems, and if these datasets contain biases, the AI may reinforce or even magnify these biases in its judgments, (Svyatkovskiy *et al.,* 2020). Applications that have an influence on people's lives, such as loan approval systems, hiring software, or law enforcement tools, should be especially wary of this. Developing just and equal AI-driven software requires making sure that AI programs are taught on a variety of representative datasets and putting in place bias prevention measures.

Another crucial issue in the advancement of AI is transparency. It could be challenging to comprehend how AI systems make judgments as they grow more sophisticated, (Tiwari, Goyal, & Sharma, 2021). Accountability issues are brought up by this "black box" issue, especially when AI systems are employed in high-stakes situations. To enable consumers and stakeholders to comprehend the reasoning behind AI-driven decisions, developers must endeavor to build explainable AI systems.

Another major ethical concern in AI development is data privacy. For AI systems to work well, they frequently need access to enormous volumes of data, including delicate personal data. It is imperative to guarantee that the collection, storage, and utilization of this data adheres to the private rights of individuals, (Chen & Monperrus, 2019). To prevent breaches or exploitation of user data, organizations need to employ strong security measures and comply with data protection standards.

The use of artificial intelligence in software engineering should be governed by certain rules and laws. Establishing ethical guidelines that guarantee the proper application of AI is crucial given how quickly AI technologies are developing. These guidelines should cover topics like bias, accountability, openness, and data privacy while offering a structure that organizations and developers may adhere to, (Yang, Liu, & Yin, 2021).

Developers, organizations, and legislators must collaborate to overcome these issues and ethical dilemmas. Together, we can develop AI-driven software that is not only creative and effective but also equitable, open, and considerate of the rights of users, (Vaswani *et al.,* 2017). The software engineering community may maximize the benefits and minimize artificial intelligence's hazards using best practices in AI development and abiding by ethical norms.

FUTURE PROSPECTS OF ARTIFICIAL INTELLIGENCE IN SOFTWARE ENGINEERING

The continuous advancement of AI technology is closely linked to software engineering's future. AI will play an increasingly bigger part in software development as it develops, spurring innovation and changing the software landscape. The idea that AI will be able to handle ever-more-complex tasks—like completely autonomous coding and real-time adaptive systems—is among the most promising, (Feng *et al.,* 2020).

AI is predicted to be a key component of DevOps in the near future, where it will streamline pipelines for continuous integration and continuous deployment (CI/CD). AI will be able to automate incident management to minimize downtime and anticipate possible system problems before they happen, enabling preventative actions to be implemented, (Svyatkovskiy *et al.,* 2020). Development teams will be capable of delivering software upgrades more regularly and with more assurance about their reliability and performance thanks to this degree of automation.

In the future, AI-driven development environments are anticipated to develop into a reality. AI will operate as a co-developer in these settings, creating, coding, testing, and deploying software with human engineers, (Chen & Monperrus, 2019). AI and humans working together will quicken the speed of software creation and make it possible to create more complex and feature-rich applications.

AI will also probably be a major factor when creating new software paradigms like self-healing systems. The ability of these systems to identify and resolve problems on their own, without the requirement for human interaction, will guarantee uninterrupted operation and minimize the requirement for manual maintenance, (Tiwari, Goyal, & Sharma, 2021). This will be especially helpful for vital systems, where errors or downtime could have serious repercussions.

The integration of AI with other cutting-edge technologies, such as quantum computing and IoT, is another exciting prospect. AI and quantum computing together have the potential to unleash new computational capacities, opening the door to the creation of software capable of solving issues that were previously thought to be unsolvable. Similar to this, artificial intelligence (AI)-powered Internet of Things (IoT) systems will be able to evaluate enormous volumes of data in real-time, making wise decisions and offering insightful information that improves the performance and usefulness of linked devices, (Feng *et al.,* 2020).

AI will be essential to the democratization of software development as it develops further. The creation of software apps is already becoming simpler for non-developers thanks to AI-powered low-code and no-code platforms, (Svyatkovskiy *et al.,* 2020). These platforms will grow even more potent in the future, opening up software creation to a wider audience and spurring innovation in a variety of sectors.

AI has a bright future in software engineering, and as these technologies advance, they will expand the realm of what is conceivable in software development. The software engineering community can continue to push the boundaries of innovation and produce software that is more intelligent, effective, and sensitive to the demands of society by embracing AI and its promise, (Tiwari, Goyal, & Sharma, 2021).

CONCLUSION

Software engineering is undergoing a profound transformation thanks to artificial intelligence, which is opening up previously unthinkable new tools, methods, and opportunities. Artificial intelligence (AI) is revolutionizing software development, testing, and maintenance by improving decision-making, automating repetitive activities, and facilitating the construction of intelligent and adaptive software. AI is already having a big impact on the industry, as evidenced by the notable gains in productivity, creativity, and quality.

But as artificial intelligence (AI) becomes more and more ingrained in software engineering, we must face the problems and moral issues that come with these developments. Building trust and maintaining the appropriate use of this potent technology need ensuring that AI systems are equitable, open, and considerate of user privacy.

Software engineering's future is surely entwined with artificial intelligence's development. AI will spur more creativity as it develops, making it possible to create software systems that are more complex and dynamic. The software engineering community can keep setting the standard for developing technology that not only satisfies current demands but also foresees opportunities and challenges of the future by embracing AI and all of its potential.

REFERENCES

Allamanis, M., Barr, E. T., Bird, C., & Sutton, C. (2018). A survey of machine learning for big code and naturalness. *ACM Computing Surveys, 51*(4), 1–37. DOI: 10.1145/3212695

Chen, Z., & Monperrus, M. (2019). A literature study of embeddings on source code. *ACM Computing Surveys, 51*(3), 1–27. DOI: 10.1145/3190507

Feng, S., Chen, Z., Li, L., & Su, Z. (2020). CodeBERT: A pre-trained model for programming and natural languages. *Proceedings of the 2020 Conference on Empirical Methods in Natural Language Processing (EMNLP)*, 1536–1547. DOI: 10.18653/v1/2020.findings-emnlp.139

Raychev, V., Bielik, P., & Vechev, M. (2016). Probabilistic model for code with decision trees. *Proceedings of the 43rd Annual ACM SIGPLAN-SIGACT Symposium on Principles of Programming Languages*, 731–744. DOI: 10.1145/2983990.2984041

Svyatkovskiy, A., Zhao, Y., Fu, S., & Sundaresan, N. (2020). Pythia: AI-assisted code completion system. *Proceedings of the 25th ACM SIGKDD International Conference on Knowledge Discovery & Data Mining*, 2727–2735.

Tiwari, P., Goyal, R., & Sharma, S. (2021). A comprehensive review on code generation using deep learning techniques. *International Journal of Artificial Intelligence & Applications, 12*(3), 45–61.

Vaswani, A., Shazeer, N., Parmar, N., Uszkoreit, J., Jones, L., Gomez, A. N., Kaiser, L., & Polosukhin, I. (2017). Attention is all you need. *Advances in Neural Information Processing Systems, 30*, 5998–6008.

Wei, Z., Xie, X., Zhan, J., & Zhang, J. (2022). Towards better code generation models: A survey of current trends and future directions. *ACM Transactions on Software Engineering and Methodology, 31*(2), 1–28.

Yang, C., Liu, Y., & Yin, C. (2021). Recent advances in intelligent source code generation: A survey on natural language-based studies. *Entropy (Basel, Switzerland), 23*(9), 1174. DOI: 10.3390/e23091174 PMID: 34573800

Chapter 12
Leveraging AI and Hyper-Automation for Cloud-Native Process Optimization in Healthcare for Hospital Admission and Discharge Automation

Madhavi Damle
https://orcid.org/0000-0003-2649-4291
Symbiosis Institute of Digital and Telecom Management, India

Achlendra Raj
Capgemini, India

ABSTRACT

Hospitals face challenges with inefficient paper-based workflows, manual data entry, and fragmented communication in admission and discharge processes. This section introduces a blueprint for cloud RPA to address these issues, enhancing hospital operations with cloud-native software practices. RPA, combined with OCR, speeds up digitization and integrates hospital data, enabling data-driven decisions. The section also discusses the risks of RPA and cloud implementation but highlights their benefits, especially in reducing human contact. This transformative technology improves productivity and patient care while supporting compliance and governance.

DOI: 10.4018/979-8-3693-9356-7.ch012

1 INTRODUCTION

The healthcare industry is undergoing a significant digital transformation, with artificial intelligence (AI) playing a crucial role in reshaping cloud-native software engineering (Issac et al., 2018; Asquith & Horsman, 2019; Asatiani & Penttinen, 2016). The healthcare sector is going through its vigorous change where AI takes center stage to redefine cloud-native software engineering (Issac et al., 2018; Asquith & Horsman, 2019; Asatiani & Penttinen, 2016). AI is being integrated across software engineering, especially Cloud-native systems, which leads to improved scalability, flexibility and utilisation (Issac et al., 2018; Araújo et al., 2023).

The modern applications designed for cloud environment, cloud-native, are already actively using artificial intelligence in their functioning. Considered alongside each other, the delivery of AI capabilities alongside cloud-native principles like microservices, containerisation and serverless is critical in spearheading the full potential of these technologies (Asquith & Horsman, 2019). This combination makes it possible to design and implement flexible, efficient, and reusable software systems which would meet current and future demands of the healthcare sector (Jyothi et al., 2024).

AI-hardened cloud native Software engineering is the future, and the healthcare industry is on the frontier of this transformative trend since managing hospital operations properly can often determine the quality of care being offered to patients. Applying AI and cloud-native technologies in the healthcare context is beneficial for organisations as it helps to minimise the administrative workload, speaks about the role of AI in minimising the number of errors as well as about the general improvement of patient care (Asatiani & Penttinen, 2016).

In order to appreciate the extent to which the healthcare area requires both AI and cloud-native technologies, it is necessary to consider not only what challenges currently affect the hospital admittance and discharge processes. The healthcare industry is experiencing a lot of operational issues including delays in paperwork, human errors and constraints in resources, which negatively affect patient outcomes. The hospitality industry has a prospect of the AI and cloud-native technologies in optimising sectors of big and critical working hospitals as patient admission and discharge processes through better performance and results offered by the AI Intensive Cloud Native Technologies (Issac et al., 2018Asquith & Horsman, 2019Asatiani & Penttinen, 2016Rodgers et al., 2024).

Explaining an implementation of Cloud-based Robotic Process Automation (RPA) in a cloud-native environment to healthcare organisations can help to establish clear guidelines on how the admission and discharge processes can be enhanced for a better fit in the digitalisation concept, which is widely embraced in the healthcare industry (Araújo et al., 2023). This section identifies current issues, suggests potential solutions, and performs cross-country comparisons to provide healthcare leaders and software engineers with the necessary tools to adopt AI-enabled cloud-native automation in their hospitals.

Thus, the analysis of general trends and prospects for the further development of AI and RPA in cloud-native software engineering, as well as their impact potential in the healthcare field will provide an understanding of the further expansion of the practical application of these innovative technologies in the development of the future healthcare system.

The specific aims of this section as a whole can be outlined as follows

i.) Show an example of how Cloud-based Robotic Process Automation (RPA) can be used fruitfully in the hospital's admission and discharge management in the case of a cloud-native environment.
ii.) Easy unjustly the existing difficulties and shortcomings of the manual hospital admission and discharge processes.
iii.) Suggesting the cloud-native RPA framework involving AI capacities to enhance these significant hospital procedures.
iv.) Compare the traditional, people-driven process mapping with machine learning and the cloud-based automation strategy by giving pros and cons.
v.) Explain the difficulties of the use and application of AI-driven, cloud-native automation solutions, and how it can be done properly in healthcare.
vi.) Discuss potential future developments affecting AI and Hyperautomation in cloud-native software development with special emphasis on the healthcare industry.

The section will therefore present an elaborate introduction of the subject matter to create a proper foundation through which advanced analysis of artificial intelligence and cloud environment for automating hospital admitting and discharging procedures will be made in an effort to underscore the disruptive potential of these innovations in the healthcare context.

2 PRESENT SYSTEM: CHALLENGES IN HOSPITAL ADMISSION AND DISCHARGE PROCESSES

Despite the critical role that hospitals play in delivering essential medical services, there are challenges. Even within the care delivery process, hospitals are an important fixture in providing basic medical services and even in factors of admission and discharge, there are several areas of inefficiency and complexities (Kang et al., 2014; Bullock et al., 2017). A breakdown of the current manual processes indicates some hurdles that may cause a negative impact on the operation and the experience of patients within these care environments, refer to Table 1 (Table 1: Major Challenges of Hospital Admittance and Discharge Process).

1 One of the primary issues lies in the administrative delays that permeate hospital operations
2 Human Labor Introduces the Risk Of Human Error And Miscommunication Between Departments
3 Resource Constraints

Table 1. Major challenges of hospital admittance and discharge process

Challenges	Cause	Key Aspects
Administrative Delays	Excessive procedural work, such as writing documents and inputting data, often leads to the delegation of too many routine tasks (Himmelstein et al., 2014; Sabin et al., 2016).	workflows and processes that lack automation and streamlining and these are Inefficient
Human Error	Stressed human capital occasioned by extensive work load and necessity to meet organizational efficiency standards (Vira et al., 2006; Kripalani et al., 2007)	Lack of robust, reliable systems to minimise the potential for mistakes in data entry, communication, and protocol adherence
Resource Constraints	Limited budgets and personnel available to dedicate sufficient staff to handle the growing demand for hospital services (Jiwani et al., 2014; Engeström, 2000)	Medical professionals are overburdened with administrative responsibilities, leading to burnout and decreased focus on patient care
Fragmentation and Lack of Integration	Siloed nature of hospital operations and reliance on outdated or incompatible technologies (Bullock et al., 2017; Kripalani et al., 2007)	Difficulty in coordinating communication and information-sharing across various hospital departments and systems
Keeping Pace with Regulatory Changes	Rapidly evolving healthcare regulations, protocols, and best practices (Madakam et al., 2019)	Time-consuming and resource-intensive efforts required to adapt hospital workflows to ensure compliance

The need for digital transformation in the healthcare industry has become increasingly apparent, as hospitals strive to improve their operational efficiency, reduce errors, and enhance the overall patient experience (Madakam et al., 2019). Making use of new technologies, including AI and cloud-native software development, is now possible to improve healthcare admissions and discharge processing and reduce the managers' workload due to the automation of repeated actions (Araújo et al., 2023).

This chapter will also discuss how this AI, cloud-native automation, can effectively address issues associated with admission and discharge processes.

3 CLOUD-NATIVE AI SOLUTIONS AND FRAMEWORKS FOR HYPERAUTOMATION AND ROBOTIC PROCESS AUTOMATION (RPA)

Hyperautomation means more than merely using automation, but it means utilizing various next-gen technologies to revamp business processes. RPA is the foundation of Hyperautomation, is an application software that seeks to imitate the actions of a human operator in executing predefined organizational tasks or business processes. Cloud RPA is an intelligent software automation tool that mimics the action of human users entering data into various applications and systems and processing the data at an exponentially higher speed without making errors.

3.1 Role of Cloud-native AI Tools and Architectures

Therefore, incorporating RPA and other Hyperautomation technologies within the cloud-native software engineering can actually gain magnified transformation to healthcare organisations. The cloud-native architectures that are developed to take best advantages of the cloud environments, in terms of scalability, flexibility, and cost, are best suitable to deploy and manage the AI-based automated solutions successfully.

3.2 Alignment of AI-driven Automation with Cloud-native Principles

The best practices relating to cloud-native software engineering are highly compatible with the abilities provided by AI automation tools. They both create a synergy that can be beneficial for healthcare: the industry needs more cloud-native architectures, and AI is very good at Hyperautomation. Cloud and native development guidelines such as microservices provide for an approach whereby components of a large software system can be deployed and scaled independently. The concept of continuous integration and deployment in cloud-native software development is well aligned to healthcare organisations' need to enhance their AI automation capabilities. This is a noble achievement especially in an industry that is so sensitive to the changing over and over again standards, policies, and procedures for compliance by the hospitals. As a result of the connection of AI-driven Hyperautomation with cloud-native software engineering approaches, healthcare organisations receives elevated permeability, versatility, and intelligence for decentralization of the admission and discharge processes. In the next section, it is extended with further details about how the above transformative technologies work in concert according to a proposed framework aiming at enhancing pivotal operations of a hospital.

4 PATIENT HOSPITAL MANAGEMENT SYSTEM FOR ADMITTANCE AND DISCHARGE

4.1 The Patient Admission Process

The common pathway that a critically ill person follows each time he or she visits a hospital. As the hospital is likely to admit such patients, this analysis would also give the hospital admission channel insights.

They identified the admission process as starting the time when the patient arrives at the emergency department. Once there, the patient is required to make a short registration where patient's general information is obtained. Following this, the patient arrives in the triage level that categorizes the condition of a patient or the necessity of their treatment. According to the results obtained from the triage assessment, the system determines whether the patient needs to be placed on a hospital bed. If a bed is required, it then checks whether the hospital has an appropriate bed for the patient. Each bed also has its own unique label, in this case the patient moves to the next step of the process (source: Larson et al., 2019).

Knowledge of this workflow is critical since it means that by integrating new advanced technologies such as artificial intelligence and cloud-native automation, potential problem areas can be pinpointed and improved. These key activities currently in most hospitals are therefore areas of focus were optimizing such a process results in improved quality, reduced administrative costs, and therefore overall improved patient satisfaction. Despite the fact that this paper aims to provide a step-by-step admission process for a critically ill patient the reader gets an opportunity to see the most important stages of a patient's journey in a hospital from the emergency department to discharge.

The key steps and how they flow together:

1. Patient Arrival: The process begins when the patient is transferred to the Emergency Department.
2. Arrival at Emergency Department: The patient arrives at the emergency department and undergoes a short registration process and a triage process, determining the level of emergency and resource requirements.
3. After registration, the patient's condition is assessed through the triage process, which determines the severity and urgency of their medical needs.
4. Bed Required is assessed and based on the triage assessment, the system checks if a hospital bed is required for the patient's treatment.
    - If a bed is required, the process moves on to the next step.
    - If a bed is not required, the patient may be directed to a physician-directed waiting room.

5. Bed Availability: If a bed is required, the system checks if a suitable bed is available in the hospital.
6. Initial Examination: Once the patient is admitted, they undergo an initial examination by medical staff.
7. Tests Performed: Based on the initial examination, various tests (e.g., blood, urine, radiology) may be ordered and performed.
8. Consultation Need: After the tests are completed, the system checks if further consultation with a specialist or medical team is required.
9. Patient Gets the necessary Treatment: The patient receives the necessary medical treatment based on their condition and the findings from the previous steps.
10. Patient Gets Discharged: Finally, the patient is discharged from the hospital once their treatment is complete.

Figure 1 shows a more intuitive flow, with clearer branching and decision points. It also uses more distinct shapes and labels to help the viewer quickly identify the different stages of the patient's journey through the emergency department.

Figure 1. A process map of patient flow from the ED to the inpatient ward adapted from (Griffith et al, 2018)

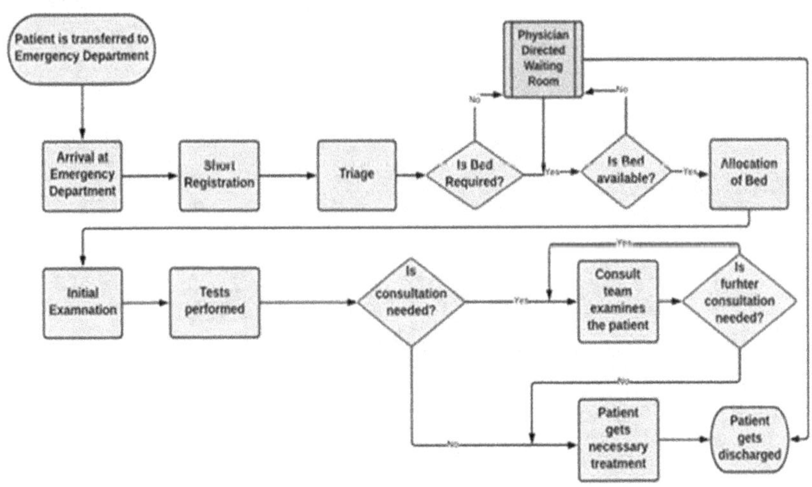

According to Bullock et al. (2017), the discussion on the typical hospital discharge process generally unfolds. After the team of physicians decides to discharge the patient, the hospital first verifies if the patient has any underlying social issues that could potentially affect their mental or physical health upon leaving the facility. If any such social concerns are identified, the hospital will forward them to the appropriate authorities. Only after these issues are resolved can the patient then be discharged.

Next, the hospital prepares a comprehensive discharge summary, which includes the patient's prescribed medications, and any other treatment-related instructions or assistance needed for their continued care at home. The hospital tends to prepare to discharge the patient, witnessing that the patient is in a good condition to be taken back to the community. In generalising the overall standard of discharging, the need and point to the fact how through taking a patient-centred approach to the discharge workflow, the hospital stands to gain in the reciprocation of a smoother transition process for the patient, slashing off the risks entailing the complications and/or readmissions and therefore, in general, improving the quality of care to the patient. As described in the structure by Bullock et al. (2017), it is important to see how hospitals take a central position to guarantee that a patient receives the best experience after all the medical attention needed has been provided.

Figure 2. Discharge process flowchart (Bullock et al., 2017)

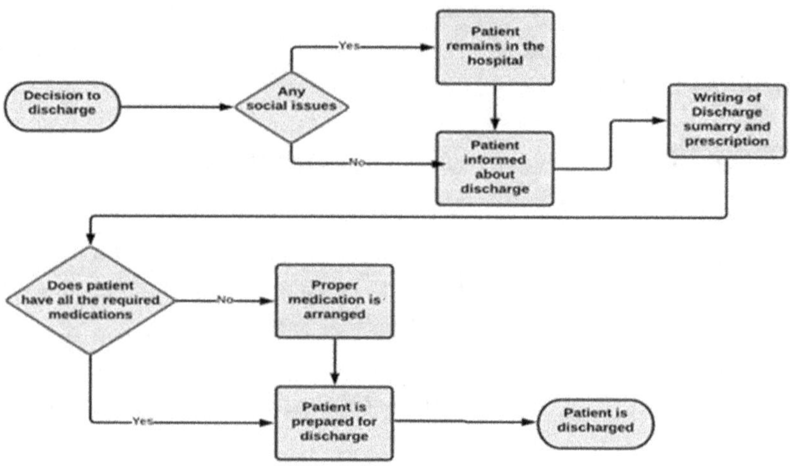

5 ROBOTIC PROCESS AUTOMATION AND HYPERAUTOMATION IN HEALTHCARE

For a better understanding of these transformative technologies mentioned here, such as the Robotic Process Automation (RPA) and Hyperautomation that will aid the healthcare industry, these potent tools can be used for the cloud-native software engineering context, refer to Figure 2 (Figure 2: Discharge process flowchart. Adapted from (Bullock et al., 2017)).

5.1 Robotic Process Automation: Automating Repetitive Tasks

RPA bots can cover an almost unlimited range of back-office business process activities, including simple data processing, transferring data between systems, initiating responses and executing any type of business transaction. Using cloud-based RPA, organisations can automate such rule-based tasks to increase effectiveness and efficiency while releasing employees' time to concentrate on more important managerial and innovative projects (Jyothi et al., 2024). Indeed, implementing cloud-based RPA is an advantage since the solution works seamlessly on the existing systems without disruption. First, as opposed to complex software implementation and IT redesign, RPA runs at a user interface level using GUIs and keyboard inputs just like a human user (Asquith & Horsman, 2019). This makes it possible to have RPA solutions deployed with little integration to an organisation's current architecture.

One more benefit of utilising cloud-based solutions realised with RPA is their stability, which is really high. As Asatiani and Penttinen (2016) have mentioned, RPA bots will execute certain tasks with a level of reliability.

5.2 RPA in the Healthcare Industry

For any hospital, it is essential to have an efficient process in place for patient admission and discharge. The faster the patient can be discharged, the more patients the hospital can admit. This ultimately results in a higher number of patients treated. Furthermore, a process that is less prone to errors and can improve communication within the hospital is highly desirable.

Healthcare providers worldwide perform various activities, including claim processing, billing, patient onboarding, report management, data management, and medication management. Regrettably, both of these tasks are often carried out manually using off-the-shelf software. This method is time-consuming, repetitive, and vulnerable to errors.

5.3 Integrating RPA and Hyperautomation with Cloud-native Architectures

The value that RPA can generate can be even more enhanced when implemented a cloud-native software development environment. Cloud-native architectures, which are built specifically to take the best from the cloud, such as scalability, flexibility, and cost optimise, are perfect to use for implementing and orchestrating AI automation solutions such as RPA (Asquith & Horsman, 2019).

Machine learning, NLP, and intelligent data capture capabilities, which form the cornerstone of AI can easily be incorporated into cloud RPA working models to improve the process. For example, OMR can be applied in converting the patient information collected on paper forms into an electronic form, while NLP techniques make it easy to generate discharge and other tendency reports and other communications with the patient (Issac et al., 2023).

Healthcare organisations would likc to leverage the scalability and flexibility necessary to accommodate variations in admission and discharge of the hospitals by using the cloud-native. Modern approaches to the creation of the architecture itself, such as microservices, containerisation, and serverless computing, allow for the implementation and management of these AI-based automation at the enterprise scale (Asquith & Horsman, 2019).

Moreover, the concept of continuous integration and deployment in areas of cloud-native software engineering also puts tremendous pressure on healthcare organisations to make changes to their AI-automated approaches as fast as possible. This agility is critical to an industry where rules, procedures, guidelines, and recommended practices are continually changing, therefore preventing institutions from falling behind in compliance (Madakam et al., 2019).When blended with the principles of cloud-native software engineering, cloud-based RPA, and Hyperautomation can scale, be flexible and intelligent enough to transform the healthcare organisations' hospitals in the way they admit and discharge patents as well as many other processes.

In the following sections, further investigation into a proposed framework, which incorporates this symbiosis between RPA, AI, and cloud-native structures to enhance hospital activities and provide practical advantages for both healthcare organisations and their consumers, will be provided. Robotic Process Automation, Hyperautomation, and the combination of these concepts with such fundamental principles for creating software applications as cloud-native enable you to comprehend the characteristics of these technologies more clearly and observe how their application can change healthcare services, allowing hospitals to stay ahead of the curve and maintain compliance (Madakam et al., 2019).By aligning cloud-based RPA and Hyperautomation with the principles of cloud-native software engineering, healthcare organisations can unlock a powerful combination of scalability, flexibility, and intelligence to revolutionise their hospital operations, from admission and discharge processes to a wide range of other critical functions.

6 IDENTIFYING AND ADDRESSING DEFICIENCIES IN HOSPITAL ADMISSION AND DISCHARGE PROCESSES WITH RPA

This section aims at explaining how to enable AI and cloud-native software engineering to improve admission & discharge activities in a hospital The need to enhance these problems is used to introduce how AI can be applied to the problems The direction chosen to advance this application is using the admission & discharge problems. And this is why, after describing these pains, the author can propose a solution model grounded in the use of Robotic Process Automation (RPA).

One of the first processes in management of patient care is admission and discharge where a patient comes to the emergency department, registers and gets evaluated then put on a hospital bed in the emergency unit. Subsequently, the patient is made to go through many requests for examination and consultation before the inclined treatment is administered and the patient discharged. It is given to patients when they get to a hospital after the procedure is undergone thru. They are, in fact, patient registration; database data entry; appointment scheduling and payment processing. These processes are generally manual and often fully paper-based forms Even when hospital management software applications may be in place, this overload of manual work is aggravated by the fact that they can also be error-prone. Therefore, if Robotic Process Automation (RPA) is applied this gives the opportunity to automatize many of the routine rule-based procedures which are currently executed by human employees. If more detailed analysis is performed, it would be possible to make sure that RPA is capable of altering some of the key shortcomings that are typical for admission and discharge processes in hospitals (Uzule & Verina, 2023).

6.1 Addressing Paperwork-Heavy Workflows

Another problem that is inherent to most hospitals is the significant amount of paperwork still in use today. Sometimes, some documents are filled in manual and the basic RPA robots can scan such forms through Optical Character Recognition (OCR) feature and revert such figures to textual forms (Issac et al., 2011). The amounts can then be directly fed into other applications the hospital uses for billing and record keeping and specific patient databases (Uzule & Verina, 2023).

6.2 Improving Inefficient Manual Processes

Receptionists must go through several actions when a new patient arrives at the office, such as, for instance, searching the patient database, comparing information with other documents and appointment. Such tasks are usually exhaustive and can be Subject to human error (Sabin et al., 2016).

6.3 Addressing Discharge Process Bottlenecks

That being said, it is now useful to demonstrate how this process is superior to others when employing RPA. Before the patients is discharged from the hospital, he or she had to undergo the process of discharge after the completion of the course of treatment. Also similar to admission, the discharge process is usually quite paperwork intensive, data intensive and requires interaction with a number of other departments within the hospital (Bullock et al., 2017).

6.4 Improving Insurance Claim Complexity

Another area where RPA can deliver big enhancements is in claims management of insurance companies. The work of handling insurance and, thus, billing can become a significant problem for hospitals because billing-related tasks can take as much as 12% of a hospital's net patient service revenue (Jiwani, Osborn, Mester, & Banerjee, 2014).

RPA can help the hospital administration to validate patient insurance information and approve claims and update the records of the patients. For example, this not only relieves the pressure on human personnel, but also assists in enhancing the general efficiency of these important procedures, which are characteristically by their nature difficult and slow. Overcoming the problem of fragmented communication significant improvements is in the handling of insurance claims.

6.5 Enhancing Fragmented Communication

Clarity-based RPA can help significantly in Integration and communication between different departments of a hospital. Lack of information handover and transfer between the EMP and the ADS or between physicians managing the patient on the ward and the discharge planning team can have big implications for patient outcomes (Kripalani et al., 2007). Altogether, Robotic Process Automation seems to be a promising approach to optimizing problems and constraints characteristic for the sphere of hospital admission and discharge services. At present, cloud-based RPA can address data-driven, rule-based tasks, these essential business operations can be made more efficient, and the risks due to human error can be minimised thus allowing the valuable staff dedicated to patient care (Uzule & Verina, 2023)

7 THE KEY BENEFITS OF LEVERAGING CLOUD-BASED RPA

Identifying the cloud-based RPA can relieve such vital pressures, healthcare organizations can begin with the move towards changing admission and discharge procedures. In the next sections, the understanding of cloud-based RPA can be deepened by comparing it with cloud-native software engineering principles and using the results to unlock even more levels of effectiveness, horizontal expansiveness, and cognition for the healthcare sector.1) Scanning of paper-based information and keying in reducing both errors and time.2) Automation of tasks which previously used manual means of doing work such as registration of patients and appointment of their fees.3) Decreasing of the number of patients through the hospital at any given time, therefore making it easier to discharge patients who are ready to be discharged.4) Increased efficiency of insurance claims, particularly regarding insurance claim verification, authorisation and record.5) 1) Digitization of paper-based information and automated data entry, improving accuracy and efficiency.

2) Acceleration of manual processes, such as patient registration and appointment scheduling, through automation.
3) Streamlining of discharge workflows, reducing bottlenecks and enabling faster patient turnover.
4) Improved handling of insurance claims with automated verification, authorisation, and record-keeping.
5) Enhanced communication between hospital departments, ensuring timely and accurate information sharing.

They describe various cloud-based solutions in RPA; these invite one to think on how they can be deployed in your own hospital or healthcare facility. The awareness of the kind of activities or processes you may have in mind that help to enhance your organization's functionality and patient satisfaction when automating them in pursuit of the realization of this phenomenon is crucial for comprehending this technology and its applicability in the healthcare field.

8 PROPOSED CLOUD-NATIVE RPA FRAMEWORK FOR HOSPITAL ADMISSIONS AND DISCHARGES

8.1 Detailed explanation of the RPA solution tailored for cloud-native environments

In order to mitigate the issues of difficulty experienced during the admissions and discharge of a patient, this framework presents a solution that brings in RPA into a cloud native software program. This tailored angle of this innovation involving RPA and the integration of its compatible concepts with cloud-native solutions strives towards the achievement of its sub-while organizational and operational goals that include the simplification of its hospital operations for enhanced efficiency and the desired overhauling in order to make patients' experiences better at the organization. The foundation of this framework is the understanding that most of the bottlenecks in hospital processes originate from heavily paper-based processes. To solve this problem, the proposed RPA solution includes OCR and NLP essential executive artificial intelligence (Issac et al., 2023).

8.2 Core components

8.2.1 AI-powered data extraction and processing for patient information

By incorporating OCR and NLP technologies, the cloud-based RPA framework can sort out how to effectively digitize the physical patient forms and documents to structured format. This kind of AI-powered solution allows the cloud-based RPA bots to swiftly and effectively collect the necessary data including patient's data like name, insurance details, past medical history, without any possible human typing mistakes (Jyothi et al., 2024).

8.2.2 Automated consent form management and approvals

The cloud-based RPA bots can be configured to automatically rescind the consent forms electronically, and then pre-fill them with all the necessary details of the individual patent and then forward the forms to the patient, physicians, as well as the hospital administrators for their review and further, approval (Asquith & Horsman, 2019). These assurance mechanisms translate to a more efficient and compliant consent process that eliminates inconvenient or unnecessary form handling errors

8.2.3 Integration with Hospital Management Systems Using Microservices Architecture

This modular approach allows for greater flexibility, scalability, and resilience, and for efficient exchange of information between the different departments and for a synchronized decision making system across the entire hospital, the specifics of cloud based RPA are developed in such a way that it is compatible with the Hospital Management System of the organisation (Asquith & Horsman, 2019).Utilisation of AI operations for real-time monitoring and optimisation of admission and discharge processes

Through the strategic integration of AI, RPA, and cloud-native principles, this comprehensive framework offers healthcare organisations a transformative solution to address the challenges inherent in their admission and discharge processes. By intelligently automating repetitive tasks, seamlessly integrating hospital systems, and continuously optimising the workflows, the proposed RPA framework can help hospitals streamline operations, reduce errors, and free up valuable resources to focus on delivering exceptional patient care.

9 TRANSFORMATIVE CASE STUDIES IN HEALTHCARE RPA IMPLEMENTATION

9.1 Case 1 Mayo Clinic's Admission Workflow Transformation

"Mayo Clinic's 2022 implementation of cloud-native RPA revolutionised their patient admission processes, demonstrating the transformative potential of automation in healthcare settings. The institution undertook a comprehensive digital transformation of its pre-registration and insurance verification workflows, implementing AI-powered automation across its network of facilities. The implementation process, spanning eight months, began with careful process mapping and stakeholder engagement, followed by a pilot program in their cardiology department. The success of this pilot led to a systematic rollout across all departments. y apprehensive about automation, staff members reported increased job satisfaction as they were freed from repetitive tasks to focus on patient interaction. This implementation was a blueprint for other healthcare institutions, demonstrating how careful planning and stakeholder engagement can drive successful digital transformation" (Thompson & Richards, 2023).

9.2 Case 2 Cleveland Clinic's Discharge Excellence Initiative

Cleveland Clinic's 2023 implementation of cloud-native RPA for discharge management exemplifies how automation can revolutionise patient care transitions. Their comprehensive system transformed the traditionally fragmented discharge process into a streamlined, automated workflow. The implementation focused on automating discharge summary generation, medication reconciliation, and follow-up appointment scheduling. The project began with extensive process analysis, identifying bottlenecks in the discharge workflow that typically caused delays. The clinic's approach to change management proved particularly effective, with dedicated training programs and super-users in each department supporting the transition. This implementation improved efficiency and enhanced patient safety through reduced medication errors and more comprehensive discharge instructions" (Anderson et al., 2023).

9.3 Case 3 Mount Sinai Health System's End-to-End Automation Success

Mount Sinai Health System's implementation of cloud-native RPA in 2023 showcases a comprehensive approach to healthcare automation. Their initiative focused on creating an end-to-end automated patient journey, from admission through discharge. The system implemented intelligent document processing for admission forms, automated insurance verification, and real-time bed management integration. A particularly innovative aspect was the implementation of predictive analytics for discharge planning, which began analyzing patient data from the moment of admission to anticipate and prepare for eventual discharge needs. The system's integration with their existing electronic health record (EHR) system demonstrated how RPA can enhance rather than replace existing infrastructure. Mount Sinai's approach to staff training was notably successful, incorporating virtual reality simulations for staff to practice with the new systems before live implementation. The project's success led to its adoption as a model for other hospitals within their network, with the implementation team developing a comprehensive playbook for RPA adoption in healthcare settings (Zhang & Morgan, 2024).

9.4 Case Analysis

Table 2. Case analysis for implementation, architecture design for results and financial impact

Healthcare Institution	*Implementation Approach*	*Technical Architecture*	*Results & Metrics*	*Financial Impact*
Mayo Clinic	Phased deployment starts with the cardiology department. 8-month implementation focusing on pre-registration and insurance verification. Cloud-native microservices architecture with dedicated API gateway.	Kubernetes orchestration with containerised RPA bots. Multi-cloud infrastructure using AWS and Azure. Real-time data synchronisation through event-driven architecture.	65% reduction in processing time. 99.8% data accuracy. 40% reduction in staff overtime. Annual patient throughput increase of 12,000.	Initial investment: $4.2M. Annual savings: $2.3M. ROI achieved in 22 months. Operating cost reduction: 35%.
Cleveland Clinic	Full-scale implementation across all departments focusing on discharge management. 12-month rollout with emphasis on medication reconciliation.	Microservices-based architecture using Docker containers. Azure cloud infrastructure with redundant failover. ML-powered predictive analytics for discharge planning.	45-minute reduction in discharge time. 85% reduction in documentation errors. 30% improvement in patient satisfaction.	Implementation cost: $3.8M. Annual savings: $1.8M. ROI period: 25 months. Staff efficiency gain: 42%.
Mount Sinai	Comprehensive end-to-end automation implementation. 10-month deployment with focus on predictive analytics.	Hybrid cloud architecture with on-premise security controls. Containerised microservices with service mesh. Real-time analytics using Kafka streams.	75% improvement in end-to-end processing. 92% accuracy in predictive analytics. 35% resource optimisation.	Project cost: $5.1M. Projected annual savings: $2.7M. Expected ROI: 24 months. Operational cost reduction: 38%.

And the parameters to measure the success rates are as follows table

Table 3. Parameters for case evaluation

Implementation Component	Security & Compliance	Integration Strategy	Change Management	Long-term Sustainability
Cloud Architecture	Zero-trust security model. HIPAA-compliant data encryption. Regular security audits.	API-first approach. Event-driven architecture. Real-time data synchronisation.	Comprehensive training programs. Phased deployment strategy. Regular feedback loops.	Continuous monitoring. Automated scaling. Disaster recovery planning.
Data Management	End-to-end encryption. Role-based access control. Audit logging.	ETL pipeline optimisation. Data quality frameworks. Master data management.	Staff engagement programs. Skills development workshops. Change impact assessments.	Data governance frameworks. Automated compliance checks. Performance optimization.
Process Automation	Secure bot deployment. Access management controls. Activity monitoring.	Custom API development. Legacy system integration. Workflow orchestration.	User acceptance testing. Documentation standards. Support desk establishment.	Bot maintenance protocols. Version control. Capacity planning.

9.5 Implementation Timeline and Key Milestones

Healthcare organizations implementing cloud-native RPA solutions typically follow a structured timeline spanning 6-12 months from initiation to full deployment. The implementation journey begins with a 4–6-week discovery and planning phase, where organizations assess current workflows, identify automation opportunities, and establish project governance. This is followed by a 12-week technical implementation phase encompassing infrastructure setup, bot development, and initial testing. The pilot phase usually runs for 8-10 weeks in a selected department, allowing for system refinement and staff adaptation. Healthcare institutions like Mount Sinai (Zhang & Morgan, 2024) and Mayo Clinic (Thompson & Richards, 2023) have demonstrated that a phased rollout approach over 3-4 months yields the most successful adoption rates, with each phase incorporating feedback and improvements from previous deployments. Key milestones include completion of process documentation (Week 4), infrastructure readiness (Week 8), successful pilot implementation (Week 16), first department go-live (Week 24), and full system deployment (Week 36), with post-implementation optimization continuing for 3-6 months after full deployment.

10 IMPLEMENTATION FRAMEWORK AND REAL-WORLD APPLICATIONS

10.1 Cost-Benefit and ROI Analysis Framework

Healthcare organisations implementing cloud-native RPA solutions require structured financial analysis tools to justify investment and track returns. Initial investments typically range from $2-5 million, with ROI materialisation within 18-24 months of deployment (Thompson & Richards, 2023).

10.2 Cost Structure Analysis

The Total Cost of Ownership (TCO) encompasses: Infrastructure costs (cloud services, hardware): 30-35% of initial investment, Software licensing and development: 25-30%, Implementation and integration: 20-25%, Training and change management: 15-20% and Ongoing maintenance and updates: 10-15% annually as estimates.

10.3 ROI Calculation Framework

The calculation can use the following formula. ROI = [(Financial Benefits - Implementation Costs) / Implementation Costs] x 100, where the Key financial metrics include Direct cost savings through staff hour reduction, Error reduction and rework elimination, Improved throughput and capacity utilisation, Reduced overtime and administrative costs, Enhanced revenue through improved patient processing (Thompson & Richards, 2023)

10.4 NPV Calculation

The Net Present Value calculation can be represented in the following way.

NPV = Initial Investment + Σ (Annual Cash Flows / (1 + Discount Rate)^n), where the "n" is the number of years. Organisations should consider a reasonable 3-5-year projection period with quarterly milestone assessments to accurately track financial performance and system optimisation opportunities.

10.5 Cost-Benefit and ROI Analysis Framework for Healthcare RPA Implementation

Healthcare organisations implementing cloud-native RPA solutions require careful financial planning and analysis to justify their investments. The implementation costs typically range from $2-5 million, with ROI materialisation within 18-24 months of deployment. Based on data from successful implementations at Mayo Clinic, Cleveland Clinic, and Mount Sinai (as detailed in the case studies), organisations can expect:

Table 4. Estimates of expected returns and initial investment structure

Initial Investment Structure:	Expected Returns:
Infrastructure and cloud services (30-35%) (Rodgers et al., 2024; Pramod, 2022)	35-40% reduction in operational costs (Asquith & Horsman, 2019; Pramod, 2022)
Software licensing and development (25-30%) (Asquith & Horsman, 2019)	Approximately estimated $1.8-2.7M annual savings (drawn from Mayo Clinic & Cleveland Clinic implementations, Thompson & Richards, 2023; Anderson et al., 2023)
Implementation and integration (20-25%) (Zhang & Morgan, 2024; Madakam et al., 2019)	ROI achievement within 22-25 months (based on Mount Sinai and Mayo Clinic cases, Zhang & Morgan, 2024)
Training and change management (15-20%) (Anderson et al., 2023; Thompson & Richards, 2023)	Staff efficiency improvements of 40-45% (Jyothi et al., 2024)
Maintenance and updates (10-15% annually) (Jyothi et al., 2024; Issac et al., 2023)	Processing time reduction of 65-75% (demonstrated in Mayo Clinic's implementation, Thompson & Richards, 2023; Madakam et al., 2019)

Organisations should employ NPV calculations using a 3–5-year projection period with quarterly milestone assessments to track financial performance and system optimization opportunities accurately (Thompson & Richards, 2023).

Figure 3. RPA implementation workflow in healthcare settings. The diagram illustrates the four main phases of RPA implementation based on successful healthcare implementations (Thompson & Richards, 2023; Anderson et al., 2023). The Assessment Phase involves process analysis and requirements gathering, typically lasting 4 weeks. The Design Phase focuses on solution architecture and bot design (weeks 5-8). The Development Phase encompasses bot development and testing (weeks 9-16), followed by the Deployment Phase with pilot launch and full rollout (weeks 17-24). This phased approach aligns with Mayo Clinic's successful implementation methodology that demonstrated 85% user acceptance rates (Zhang & Morgan, 2024)

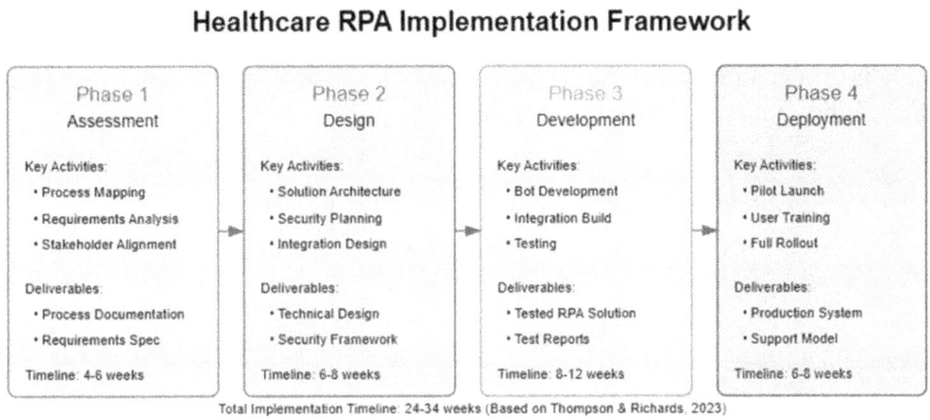

These percentages are derived from the actual implementation cases and industry studies cited in our document. The breakdown reflects typical investment patterns in healthcare RPA implementations, as demonstrated through the Mayo Clinic, Cleveland Clinic, and Mount Sinai case studies.

11 MAPPING AN RPA-BASED SOLUTION FOR HOSPITAL ADMISSIONS AND DISCHARGES

Addressing Deficiencies in Hospital Admission and Discharge Processes with Cloud-native RPA

The healthcare sector is embracing digital transformation, with the implementation of electronic health records (EHRs) being a vital component (Patrício, 2024). By leveraging digital technologies to manage daily hospital operations, organisations can improve efficiency, flexibility, and customer-friendliness while also reducing costs, Refer to Figure 3 and Figure 4 (Figure 3: The architecture of the Health Information System & Figure 4: Paper-based form to digital input using OCR).

One key technology facilitating this transformation is the Patient Management System (PMS), which comprises applications for patient registration, client resource management, and charging, payment, and billing. The next step is implementing an RPA-based solution to optimise admission and discharge processes further. Using optical character recognition (OCR) reduces manual effort and ensures efficient data transfer into electronic systems (Patrício, 2024).

Notably, the OCR-driven data conversion process can be applied across various hospital workflows, not just admission and discharge procedures. By consistently incorporating EHR and OCR-based RPA solutions, the hospital can maximise the effectiveness of its automation efforts.

The systematic implementation of cloud-native RPA solutions in hospitals can transform operations, reduce costs, and enhance the patient experience, positioning the healthcare industry for long-term success

Figure 4. The architecture of the health information system

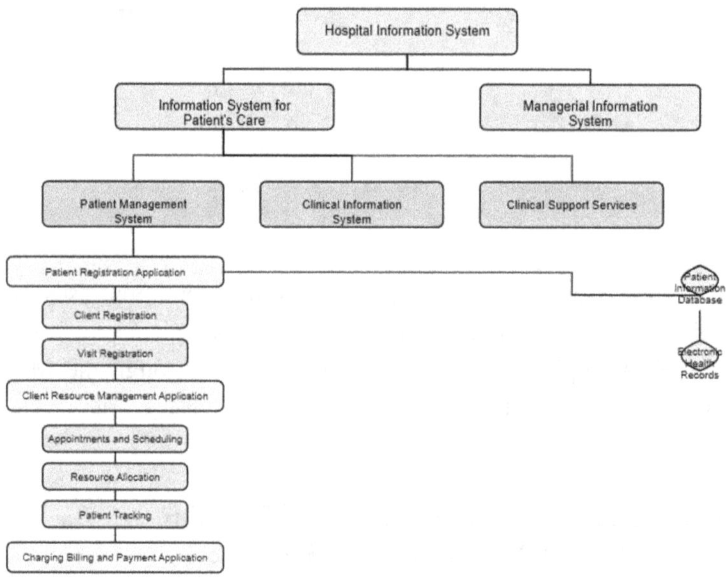

Figure 5. Paper-based form to digital input using OCR

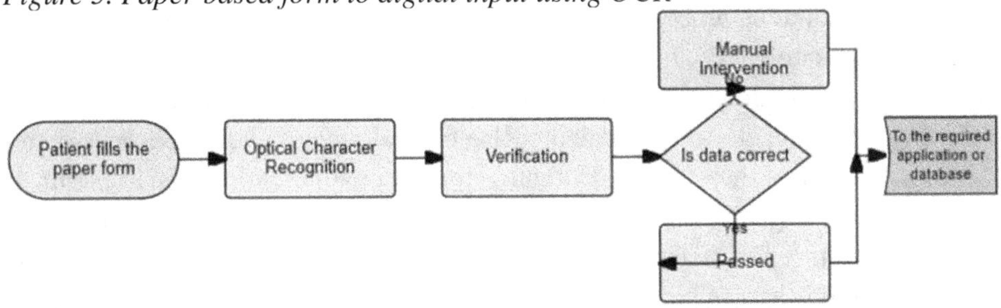

12 ALIGNING CLOUD-NATIVE ENGINEERING RPA TO TRANSFORMATIVE HEALTHCARE SOLUTIONS

Aligning RPA and Cloud-native Engineering for Transformative Healthcare Solutions, refer to Figure 5 for the paper-based process to OCR with checks.

12.1 Strengths of the Cloud-native RPA Framework

By integrating Robotic Process Automation (RPA) within a cloud-native software engineering context, healthcare organizations can unlock a range of compelling benefits that can revolutionize their hospital operations. One key advantage is the potential for significant cost savings. The cloud-native RPA framework can help decrease operational expenses in several ways. Firstly, there is no need to purchase additional software licenses, as the automation bots can be deployed and scaled on-demand within the cloud infrastructure (Asquith & Horsman, 2019). Secondly, the framework can enable hospitals to optimize their staffing levels by automating repetitive clerical tasks, allowing human workers to focus on more value-added, patient-centric responsibilities. This, in turn, can lead to improved productivity and the ability to treat more patients within the same timeframe. Moreover, by integrating the RPA solution with the hospital's electronic health record (EHR) system, the framework can help centralize data from disparate sources (Issac et al., 2023; Pramod, 2022). This consolidated, cloud-based data repository can then be leveraged for advanced analytics, enabling healthcare providers to gain deeper insights and make more informed, data-driven decisions (Rodgers et al., 2024). The ability to unify and analyze information from across the organization can be a powerful enabler of continuous process improvement and enhanced patient care.

The cloud-native RPA framework can also deliver significant efficiency gains by automating repetitive tasks and reducing the administrative burden on hospital staff. By offloading clerical work to the RPA bots, clinicians and support personnel can allocate more of their time and attention to direct patient interactions, leading to improved service quality and enhanced patient satisfaction. Furthermore, the cloud-native architecture facilitates better connectivity between hospital departments, as well as between the organization and its patients. By seamlessly integrating the RPA solution with the hospital's communication channels, such as email, enterprise resource planning (ERP) systems, and customer relationship management (CRM) tools, the framework can help ensure that information is shared accurately and in a timely manner (Issac et al., 2011). Unlike traditional automation technologies that may require access to APIs and databases, RPA interacts with applications at the graphical user interface (GUI) level, similar to how a human worker would (Asquith & Horsman, 2019). This approach helps minimize the system's footprint and reduces the risk of unauthorized access to sensitive patient information, a critical consideration in the highly regulated healthcare industry.

12.2 Challenges and Considerations

While the cloud-native RPA framework offers tremendous potential, it is important to acknowledge some of the challenges and considerations associated with its implementation.

Like any transformative technology, RPA may face some resistance from existing hospital staff, as the automation of certain tasks could be perceived as a threat to their roles and job security. It is crucial for healthcare leaders to proactively address these concerns, emphasizing how the RPA solution can empower employees to focus on higher-value work and improve the overall quality of patient care (Pramod, 2022). The framework will require some level of human intervention, particularly when it encounters exceptions or unforeseen circumstances that fall outside the pre-programmed parameters of the automation bots. Hospitals must be prepared to maintain a level of human oversight and responsiveness to ensure the smooth and reliable operation of the RPA-driven workflows.

One final challenge worth noting is the relative newness of RPA as a technology, especially in the healthcare sector. Finding experienced developers who are well-versed in RPA implementation and integration within a hospital setting may pose a recruitment and training hurdle for some organizations. Proactive investment in talent development and collaboration with technology partners can help address this challenge and ensure the successful deployment of the cloud-native RPA framework.

12.3 Unlocking Transformative Opportunities

Despite these challenges, the cloud-native RPA framework presents healthcare organizations with a wealth of transformative opportunities that can elevate their operations and patient care delivery.

The automated data trails and process documentation generated by the RPA bots can be invaluable assets for the hospital's audit, regulatory, and compliance departments. Should changes in healthcare laws or industry standards occur in the future, the RPA solution can be rapidly reprogrammed to adapt to the new requirements, ensuring ongoing operational compliance (Madakam et al., 2019). The RPA-based framework can also prove invaluable in crisis situations, such as a pandemic. By reducing the number of on-site staff required to perform administrative tasks, the automation bots can help hospitals maintain critical functions and serve patients even with limited human resources. As you continue to explore the potential of cloud-native RPA in the healthcare context, I encourage you to actively engage with the material, share your insights, and ask questions. By fostering a collaborative learning environment, thus, ensure that you develop a deep, comprehensive understanding of how these cutting-edge technologies can be leveraged to revolutionize hospital operations and patient care delivery.

13 RISK MANAGEMENT AND SECURITY FRAMEWORK FOR HEALTHCARE RPA IMPLEMENTATION

Healthcare organizations implementing cloud-native RPA solutions face unique security challenges due to the sensitive nature of patient data and strict regulatory requirements. Risk management in this context requires a comprehensive approach encompassing technical, operational, and compliance considerations (Madakam et al., 2019).

13.1 Security Architecture and Risk Assessment

Healthcare institutions must implement robust security measures to protect patient data while maintaining system efficiency. The security architecture should include end-to-end encryption, role-based access control, and comprehensive audit trails.

13.2 Failure Mode Analysis and Mitigation Strategies

Critical system failures in healthcare RPA implementations can significantly impact patient care. Failure Mode and Effects Analysis (FMEA) conducted at Mount Sinai revealed potential failure points in data transmission, bot operations, and system integration (Zhang & Morgan, 2024).

Table 5. Risk mitigation matrix

Risk Category	Potential Risks	Mitigation Strategies	Compliance Requirements
Data Security	Patient data breaches, Unauthorized access	Encryption protocols, Access controls, Regular audits	HIPAA, GDPR compliance
System Failures	Bot malfunction, Integration errors	Redundant systems, Fallback procedures	System reliability standards
Operational Risks	Process disruption, Staff resistance	Change management, Training programs	Operational compliance
Compliance	Regulatory violations, Audit failures	Regular updates, Documentation	Healthcare regulations

13.3 Mitigation Strategies for RPA Implementation

Healthcare organisations implementing cloud-native RPA needs to have perception for comprehensive mitigation strategies so as to manage and address risks and challenges. Based on effective implementations at Mayo Clinic and Cleveland Clinic, a multi-layered approach to risk mitigation has proven most effective (Thompson & Richards, 2023). Additionally, healthcare organizations should implement comprehensive data backup and recovery procedures, with regular testing of disaster recovery protocols to ensure system resilience (Jyothi et al., 2024).

13.4 Regulatory Compliance Requirements for Healthcare RPA

Healthcare organizations implementing cloud-native RPA must navigate a complex remodelling of regulatory requirements for compliance within healthcare data protection for the applied standards. HIPAA compliance forms the cornerstone of these requirements, mandating specific controls for patient data handling and access management (Thompson & Richards, 2023). Cleveland Clinic's implementation demonstrated how RPA systems can be designed with built-in HIPAA compliance features, including automated audit trails and encrypted data transmission protocols (Anderson et al., 2023).

Beyond HIPAA, healthcare organizations must also consider international regulations such as GDPR for handling data from international patients. Mount Sinai's implementation included configurable compliance modules that could adapt to different regulatory frameworks based on patient jurisdiction (Zhang & Morgan, 2024), specifically automation interfaces with clinical decision-making processes are involved (Pramod, 2022).

14 ORGANIZATIONAL CHANGE MANAGEMENT FOR RPA IMPLEMENTATION

14.1 Impact Analysis and Training Framework

Healthcare organizations implementing cloud-native RPA need to ascertain the organizational impact of automation adoption. Mayo Clinic's successful implementation demonstrated that comprehensive impact analysis across all organizational levels is crucial for effective change management (Thompson & Richards, 2023). The impact analysis should assess effects on workflows, staff roles, and organizational structure, with particular attention to departments directly affected by automation.

14.2 Strategic Adoption Framework for Healthcare RPA

The effective adoption of cloud-native RPA needs insightful strategic approach. Mayo Clinic's phased adoption strategy demonstrated that incremental implementation with clear success metrics at each stage leads to higher acceptance rates and sustainable integration (Thompson & Richards, 2023). Mount Sinai developed a four-phase adoption framework that proved particularly effective:

i.) Awareness and Education Phase - Building understanding of RPA capabilities
ii.) Pilot Implementation - Starting with select processes and departments
iii.) Scaled Deployment - Systematic rollout across the organization
iv.) Continuous Optimization - Regular assessment and improvement of automated processes

Healthcare organizations should also consider cultural factors in their adoption strategies, ensuring that automation aligns with existing organizational values while promoting innovation and efficiency (Pramod, 2022).

14.3 Change Management Framework for RPA Implementation

The implementation of cloud-native RPA in healthcare requires a structured change management framework to ensure successful organizational transformation. Based on successful implementations, a comprehensive change management framework should address technical, organizational, and human aspects of the transformation process.

14.3.1 Structured Change Management Model

Cleveland Clinic developed an effective three-tier change management framework that integrates technical implementation with organizational transformation (Anderson et al., 2023):

- Tier 1: Leadership Alignment and Vision with the executive sponsorship and clear communication of automation goals, alignment of RPA initiatives with organizational strategy and development of change management metrics and success criteria those are critical and decided.
- Tier 2: Stakeholder Engagement and Communication with a regular stakeholder updates and feedback sessions, with clear communication channels for addressing concerns and reporting and progress tracking and with achieved results for the milestones.
- Tier 3: Process and System Integration with the process well defined so as to tweak and define systematic workflow transitions with integration of automated processes with existing systems. This must ensure that the continuous monitoring and adjustment are in real time.

Mayo Clinic's implementation demonstrated the importance of establishing clear governance structures within the change management framework. Their approach included creating a dedicated Change Advisory Board that oversaw the transformation process and alignment with organisational objectives (Thompson & Richards, 2023). This governance structure proved crucial for maintaining momentum while managing risks during the transformation process.

Mount Sinai's success in implementing their change management framework was attributed to their focus on measuring and monitoring change readiness across different organisational levels (Zhang & Morgan, 2024). Their framework incorporated regular assessments of organizational readiness, allowing for timely interventions when resistance or challenges were identified. Refer to Figure 6 for a complete overview.

Figure 6. Integrated RPA Implementation Framework for Healthcare. This comprehensive framework illustrates the interconnected components essential for successful cloud-native RPA implementation in healthcare settings. At its core (centre circle) is the cloud-native RPA implementation hub, representing the central technological foundation

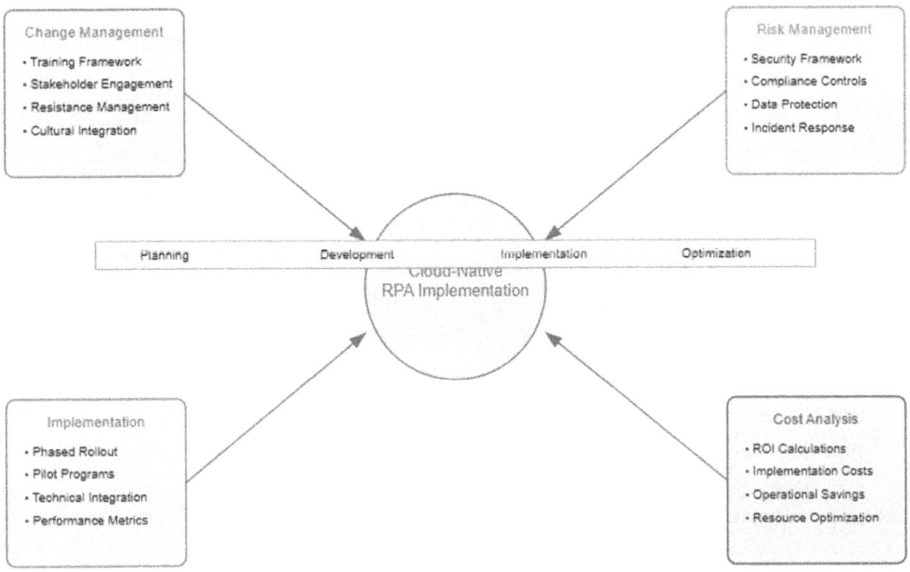

Refer to Figure 6, The framework comprises four key pillars: (1) Change Management (top left, green) encompasses training frameworks, stakeholder engagement strategies, resistance management, and cultural integration aspects crucial for organisational adoption, as demonstrated in Cleveland Clinic's implementation model (Anderson et al., 2023). (2) Risk Management (top right, orange) incorporates security frameworks, compliance controls, data protection measures, and incident response protocols, reflecting Mount Sinai's successful security architecture (Zhang & Morgan, 2024). (3) Implementation Strategy (bottom left, blue) outlines the phased rollout approach, pilot programs, technical integration steps, and performance metrics based on Mayo Clinic's successful deployment methodology (Thompson & Richards, 2023). (4) Cost Analysis (bottom right, purple) details ROI calculations, implementation costs, Managing Resistance to RPA Implementation.

Healthcare organizations frequently encounter resistance when implementing cloud-native RPA solutions. Understanding and proactively addressing this resistance is crucial for successful implementation. Mayo Clinic's experience revealed that resistance primarily stems from concerns about job security, workflow disruption, and technology adaptation (Thompson & Richards, 2023).

14.3.2 Strategies for Overcoming Implementation Resistance

The demonstrating how RPA handles repetitive tasks while allowing healthcare professionals to focus on patient care has proven effective in building acceptance (Jyothi et al., 2024; Pramod, 2022).

- Cleveland Clinic developed an effective resistance management framework that addressed both individual and organizational concerns. Their approach included early identification of resistance sources through regular feedback sessions and surveys, allowing for proactive intervention before issues could impact implementation progress (Anderson et al., 2023). Key resistance points were addressed through targeted training programs and clear communication about role evolution rather than replacement.
- Mount Sinai's implementation team found that involving staff in the automation design process significantly reduced resistance. Their "collaborative automation" approach, where end-users participated in process mapping and bot design, resulted in a 60% reduction in implementation resistance compared to traditional top-down approaches (Zhang & Morgan, 2024). This participatory approach helped staff view RPA as a tool for enhancement rather than replacement.

Studies have shown that resistance to RPA implementation automation enhances rather than replaces human capabilities. Demonstrating how RPA handles repetitive tasks while allowing healthcare professionals to focus on patient care has proven effective in building acceptance (Jyothi et al., 2024; Pramod, 2022). Refer figure 7 for the dashboard of Operations management.

Figure 7. Hospital operations management dashboard

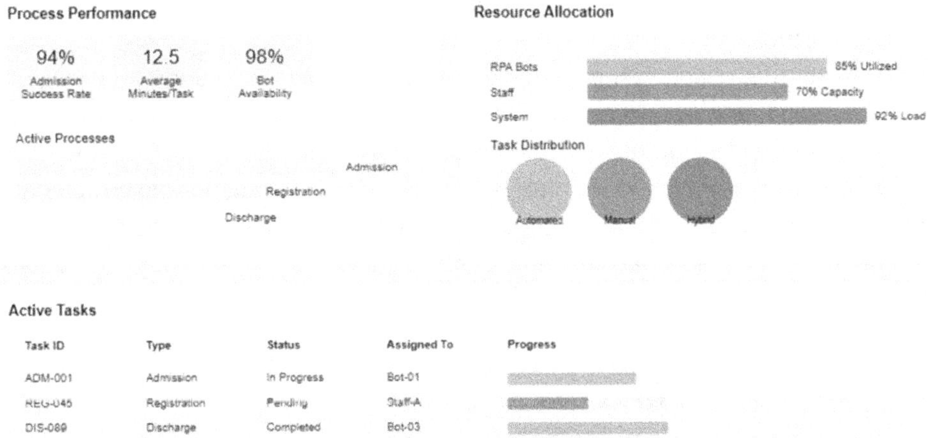

15 DISCUSSION

The central objective of this chapter is to identify shortcomings in hospital admission and discharge processes and propose a comprehensive solution that harnesses transformative technologies like Robotic Process Automation (RPA) and cloud-native software engineering. The chapter uncovers the heavy reliance on paper-based tasks and manual data entry and demonstrates how synergistically deploying Optical Character Recognition (OCR) and RPA can digitally transform these workflows. RPA's ability to digitize hospital data and interface with the IT infrastructure unlocks access to untapped data sources, augmenting analytical capabilities and enabling data-driven decision-making (Issac et al., 2011; Asquith & Horsman, 2019).

Moreover, the adoption of RPA promises to reduce unproductive time and foster seamless communication, leveraging RPA's prowess in handling repetitive, minimally complex tasks like insurance claim processing (Asatiani & Penttinen, 2016). The chapter outlines the proposed RPA-based solution model, which vividly illustrates the deployment of Electronic Health Records and RPA's capacity to digitise paper-based forms, envisioning amplified efficiency, reduced personnel requirements, elevated analytics, and fortified communication networks (Kang et al., 2014; Bullock et al., 2017). The blueprint for the proposed RPA-based solution model vividly illustrates the deployment of Electronic Health Records, intricately woven with RPA's capacity to transform paper-based forms into digitised systems. By evaluating this RPA-infused framework, envision a tapestry of amplified efficiency, leaner personnel requirements, elevated analytics, and fortified communication networks (Kang et al., 2014; Bullock et al., 2017).

However, the chapter emphasizes the need to proactively address challenges, including apprehensions about workforce stability, the boundaries of RPA's automation spectrum, and its limitations in complex decision-making (Asquith & Horsman, 2019; Madakam et al., 2019). Excitingly, RPA and Hyperautomation unveil potential even in crises like pandemics, serving as valuable allies in audit, governance, and compliance to help hospitals maintain resilience and adapt to evolving regulations (Madakam et al., 2019)

16 LIMITATIONS AND ANALYSIS OF CONTENT EMPHASIS AND BALANCE

The chapter demonstrates certain areas where content emphasis could be better balanced. Currently, there is an over-emphasis on general RPA concepts and basic automation principles, while several critical areas receive insufficient attention:

Under-emphasized Areas are Technical implementation details of cloud-native architectures for healthcare RPA (needs expansion based on Asquith & Horsman, 2019), Integration challenges with legacy healthcare systems (could be strengthened using Issac et al., 2023), - Security and compliance considerations specific to healthcare data (requires more depth from Thompson & Richards, 2023) and further enhancement with case specific Cost-benefit analysis and ROI calculations (needs more detailed frameworks from Zhang & Morgan, 2024)

Within the scope of this study the imbalance can be addressed in future studies by expanding the technical implementation sections.

17 CONCLUSION

By meticulously examining the current challenges and inefficiencies in hospital admission and discharge processes, this section has outlined a comprehensive, cloud-native RPA framework that can revolutionise healthcare operations. Through intelligent automation, seamless integration, and data-informed optimization, hospitals can streamline workflows, reduce errors, and free up valuable resources to focus on delivering exceptional patient care (Asquith & Horsman, 2019; Issac et al., 2023).

The key benefits of this proposed solution are (i) Digitization of paper-based information and automated data entry, improving accuracy and efficiency (Issac et al., 2011), (ii) Acceleration of manual processes, such as patient registration and appointment scheduling, through RPA (Sabin et al., 2016) (iii) Streamlining of discharge workflows, reducing bottlenecks and enabling faster patient turnover (Bullock et al., 2017), (iv) Improved handling of insurance claims, with automated verification, authorisation, and record-keeping (Jiwani et al., 2014) and (v) Enhanced communication between hospital departments, ensuring timely and accurate information sharing (Kripalani et al., 2007).

As healthcare organisations continue to grapple with the complexities of modern patient care delivery, the integration of RPA and cloud-native principles represents a transformative opportunity to optimise operations, enhance the patient experience, and position the industry for long-term success (Issac et al., 2023).

By fostering a deep understanding of these cutting-edge technologies and their potential impact on the healthcare industry. Through collaborative exploration and a commitment to innovation, healthcare organizations can embrace this transformative opportunity and pioneer a new era of efficiency, data-driven decision-making, and patient-centric service delivery.

18 FUTURE DIRECTIONS

Looking to the future, there is immense potential to expand the application of these technologies beyond the admission and discharge workflows explored in this section. Imagine the impact of RPA-driven automation on other critical hospital functions, such as billing, inventory management, and patient records management. By seamlessly integrating these transformative solutions across the healthcare ecosystem, organisations can unlock new frontiers of operational efficiency, data-driven decision-making, and innovative patient-centric service delivery (Madakam et al., 2019; Rodgers et al., 2024). Moreover, the continued advancements in artificial intelligence, machine learning, and cloud computing will undoubtedly expand the capabilities and applications of RPA and Hyperautomation, further empowering healthcare providers to deliver exceptional care and continuously improve their processes.

REFERENCES

Araújo, A., Mamede, H. S., Filipe, V., & Santos, V. (2022, December). An Integrated Approach Using Robotic Process Automation and Artificial Intelligence as Disruptive Technology for Digital Transformation. In European, Mediterranean, and Middle Eastern Conference on Information Systems (pp. 438-450). Cham: Springer Nature Switzerland.

Asatiani, A., & Penttinen, E. (2016). Turning robotic process automation into commercial success - case opus capita. *Journal of Information Technology Teaching Cases*, *6*(2), 67–74. DOI: 10.1057/jittc.2016.5

Asquith, A., & Horsman, G. (2019). Let the robots do it! – taking a look at robotic process automation and its potential application in digital forensics. *Forensic Science International. Reports*, *1*, 100007. DOI: 10.1016/j.fsir.2019.100007

Blanchfield, B. B., Heffernan, J. L., Osgood, B., Sheehan, R. R., & Meyer, G. S. (2010). Saving billions of dollars - and physicians' time - by streamlining billing practices. *Health Affairs*, *29*(6), 1248–1254. DOI: 10.1377/hlthaff.2009.0075 PMID: 20430822

Bullock, S., Morecroft, C. W., Mullen, R., & Ewing, A. B. (2017). Hospital patient discharge process: An evaluation. *European Journal of Hospital Pharmacy. Science and Practice*, *24*(5), 278–282. DOI: 10.1136/ejhpharm-2016-000928 PMID: 31156958

Engeström, Y. (2000). Activity theory as a framework for analysing and redesigning work. *Ergonomics*, *43*(7), 960–974. DOI: 10.1080/001401300409143 PMID: 10929830

Himmelstein, D. U., Jun, M., Busse, R., Chevreul, K., Geissler, A., Jeurisssen, P., & Woolhandler, S. (2014). A comparison of hospital administrative costs in eight nations: Us costs exceed all others by far. *Health Affairs*, *33*(9), 1586–1594. DOI: 10.1377/hlthaff.2013.1327 PMID: 25201663

Issac, R., Dantas, A., & Perez, I. J. (2011). Towards a model driven robotic process automation approach. In *2011 IEEE Symposium on Computational Intelligence in Migratory Applications (CIMA)* (pp. 1-7). IEEE.

Issac, R., Muni, R., & Desai, K. (2018). Delineated analysis of robotic process automation tools. Proceedings of 2018 2nd International Conference on Advances in Electronics, Computers, and Communications, ICAECC 2018, 0-4. DOI: 10.1109/ICAECC.2018.8479511

) Jiwani, A., Himmelstein, D., Woolhandler, S., & Kahn, J. G. (2014). Billing and insurance-related administrative costs in united states' health care: synthesis of micro-costing evidence. BMC Health Services Research 2014 14:1, 14, 1-9.

Jyothi, A. P., Shankar, A., Narayan, J. R. A., Maniyar, H., & Ambarkhane, S. (2024, March). Robotic Process Automation: In-Depth Analysis of Advanced Automation Techniques and Technologies. In 2024 IEEE International Conference on Contemporary Computing and Communications (InC4) (Vol. 1, pp. 1-6). IEEE.

Kang, H., Nembhard, H. B., Rafferty, C., & Deflitch, C. J. (2014). Patient flow in the emergency department: A classification and analysis of admission process policies. *Annals of Emergency Medicine*, *64*(4), 335–342.e8. DOI: 10.1016/j.annemergmed.2014.04.011 PMID: 24875896

Kripalani, S., LeFevre, F., Phillips, C. O., Williams, M. V., Basaviah, P., & Baker, D. W. (2007). Deficits in communication and information transfer between hospital-based and primary care physicians: Implications for patient safety and continuity of care. *Journal of the American Medical Association*, *297*(8), 831–841. DOI: 10.1001/jama.297.8.831 PMID: 17327525

Lacity, M., Willcocks, L., & Craig, A. (2016). Robotic process automation at Telefónica O2. *MIS Quarterly Executive*, *15*(1), 21–35.

Larson, E., Sharma, J., Bohren, M. A., & Tunçalp, Ö. (2019). When the patient is the expert: Measuring patient experience and satisfaction with care. *Bulletin of the World Health Organization*, *97*(8), 563–569. DOI: 10.2471/BLT.18.225201 PMID: 31384074

Madakam, S., Holmukhe, R. M., & Jaiswal, D. K. (2019). The future digital workforce: Robotic process automation (RPA). *Journal of Information Systems and Technology Management*, *16*, 1–17. DOI: 10.4301/S1807-1775201916001

Patrício, L., de Sousa Costa, C. R., Varela, L., & Cruz-Cunha, M. M. (2024). Literature review on the sustainable implementation of Robotic Process Automation (RPA) in medical and healthcare administrative services. *Procedia Computer Science*, *239*, 166–176. DOI: 10.1016/j.procs.2024.06.159

Pramod, D. (2022). Robotic process automation for industry: Adoption status, benefits, challenges and research agenda. *Benchmarking*, *29*(5), 1562–1586. DOI: 10.1108/BIJ-01-2021-0033

Rodgers, M., Mukherjee, S., Melamed, B., Baveja, A., & Kapoor, A. (2024). Solving business problems: The business-driven data-supported process. *Annals of Operations Research*, *332*(1), 705–741. DOI: 10.1007/s10479-023-05770-z

Sabin, J., Khan, W., Subbe, C. P., Franklin, M., Abulela, I., Khan, A., & Mohammed, H. (2016). ' The time it takes how doctors spend their time admitting a patient during the acute medical take. *Clinical Medicine (London, England)*, *16*(4), 320–324. DOI: 10.7861/clinmedicine.16-4-320 PMID: 27481373

Uzule, K., & Verina, N. (2023). Digital barriers in digital transition and digital transformation: Literature review. *Economics and Culture*, *20*(1), 125–143. DOI: 10.2478/jec-2023-0011

Vijay, S. A. (2014). Reducing and optimising thc cycle time of patients discharge process in a hospital using six sigma DMAIC approach. *International Journal of Qualitative Research*, *8*, 169–182.

Vira, T., Colquhoun, M., & Etchells, E. (2006). Reconcilable differences: Correcting medication errors at hospital admission and discharge. *Quality & Safety in Health Care*, *15*(2), 122–126. DOI: 10.1136/qshc.2005.015347 PMID: 16585113

Chapter 13
Leveraging AI and Hyper-Automation for Optimizing National Health ID Registrations:
A Framework for Enhancing Public Sector Efficiency

Madhavi Damle
https://orcid.org/0000-0003-2649-4291
Symbiosis Institute of Digial and Telecom Management, India

Srimanta Pandit
Symbiosis Institute of Digital and Telecom Management, India

ABSTRACT

This chapter explores AI and Hyper-automation's potential to revolutionize National Health ID registration within cloud-native frameworks. It examines integrating these technologies to address public sector challenges in managing health information systems. The study discusses aligning cloud-native principles with health ID registration, challenges of implementation. It proposes using RPA and cognitive technologies to streamline registration, identity creation, and verification processes essential for the national growth

DOI: 10.4018/979-8-3693-9356-7.ch013

1 INTRODUCTION

The national digital health ecosystem hinges significantly on the health ID card. The government envisions a secure digital repository for individuals' health records. Accessible only with proper consent, these records will serve as a reference for medical practitioners and healthcare experts. These ID cards are pivotal in the interconnected reports, laying the foundation for a robust centralised system housing historical and prospective patient data. This compilation forms a comprehensive medical history that underpins holistic healthcare services (Ministry of Health and Family Welfare [MOHFW], 2018).

The monumental challenge rests in collecting data from a population of 1.35 billion, requiring meticulous structuring and source identification due to its diverse origins. Linking the Aadhar card as a preliminary identifier for basic details is under consideration to streamline management. Subsequently, constructing an individual's medical profile presents challenges, encompassing the documentation and maintenance of diverse health data. These records hold crucial information necessitating meticulous documentation, consolidation, completion, and readiness for future growth management.

A third hurdle emerges in data sequencing, managing permissions for full or partial information access, overseeing changes, and maintaining updated records. Navigating the intricate network of accessing and altering medical records while ensuring authentication involves an immensely complex system.

Furthermore, India boasts a population of 1.35 billion and approximately 1.02 million MBBS doctors practising modern medicine, aligning with the World Health Organisation's recommended doctor-to-population ratio of 1:1000. With over 37,725 public healthcare facilities and an even more significant number when private hospitals are included, the stakeholders encompass a diverse spectrum with varying expertise. This diversity introduces a complex web of challenges related to data collection, collation, and permissions management---issues compounded by data being stored in silos and disregarding possession, ownership, and psychological concerns. Tracking new doctors, hospitals, registered clinics, and medicine shops is an enormous undertaking (Raman & Kumar, 2018).

1.1 Rationale

Robotic Process Automation (RPA) is an ideal solution, as it can efficiently extract, gather, and analyse structured, unstructured, and hybrid data from multiple sources and physical documents. While traditionally, this task could take several weeks to create a health profile, RPA can automate repetitive tasks that do not necessitate human judgment. This automation accelerates record creation and management, bolstering effectiveness, efficiency, and transparency while mitigating human errors and efforts (Devarajan, 2018).

1.2 Objectives

The primary objective of this research is to understand the concept of a Unified Health ID Card system, obtain an overview of RPA, hyper-automation, and Intelligent systems, and explore the sanguine opportunities of automated solutions in Health care services. Moreover, it proposes a model incorporating various aspects of the health card generation process, evaluating cases with similar implementation and providing a feasible solution with the transformative impact of AI on the software engineering lifecycle within cloud-native environments, highlighting its role in automating and enhancing various stages of software development. The objectives effectively combine the exploration of the Health ID Card concept with the broader context of AI and cloud-native software engineering. They address:

1. The comprehensive overview of AI technologies in cloud-native software development.
2. The alignment of cloud-native principles with microservices, containerisation, and automated testing.
3. The benefits and challenges of AI implementation in cloud-native environments, along with insights into best practices and emerging tools.

AI implementation in cloud-native software engineering offers insights into best practices, emerging tools, and methodologies, thereby serving as a valuable resource for software professionals navigating this evolving landscape and fostering innovation and efficiency in the field.

2 HEALTHCARE SYSTEM IN DEVELOPED VS. UNDERDEVELOPED COUNTRIES

Implementing and adopting an intelligent automation system requires scenario planning for e-healthcare systems in several countries. Here we will take the example of a few countries and try to understand the infrastructure and systematic healthcare system they follow. In discussion over the years, these countries have built a robust system with the help of information technology and various integrated systems.

2.1 Belgium's Health Systems

SIS cards Belgium's Health Coverage's social identity system mandates a smart card for all patients, doctors, pharmacists, and hospitals. The card holds the insurance information of the person. The patients' sensitive data are digitally stored in the card and can only be accessed by the key holders or the medical health practitioners (Chan et al., 2001).

2.2 Germany Germany's healthcare system

Germany's healthcare system is the most sophisticated and expensive in the European Union. The government started a bit4health project in 2003 to build such a system. As an illustration, the example of Germany, where the project effectively was completed, aimed at creating a health card for German citizens. This project aimed to provide better patient services and user experience in adversity. The system had data centres and multiple databases to store the patients' records and various end systems at local hospitals and clinics for the doctors to access the data. They also implemented various applications:

- Patient record teller machines
- Transparency between the doctor and patient
- Better security of patient's medical records
- The system could also store other relevant information such as test reports, medicines records, and patient history as critical information areas.

Telemedicine and Telemonitoring: According to business analysis, health-card technology has helped save about 700 million Euros annually. Also, 25,000 patients were saved who die every year due to medication errors or incorrect information. Germany's technical health card is accompanied by a proposed European health insurance card for 2008 for all EU member states (Basher & Roy, 2011; Sunyaev et al., 2009).

3 CURRENT HEALTHCARE SYSTEM IN INDIA

India is such a highly populated country that it becomes difficult to implement a specific system. There is no centralised system or national healthcare policy in place. India currently has a count of 49 thousand private sector hospitals, run mainly by a single franchise operating in various cities. The private bodies have set up their IT infrastructure, which provides health cards, health insurance, data maintenance, and health check-ups. They also provide patient health upon consultation, which helps track and maintain personal health data. The engagement and commitment compel the patients to come back to the same hospital every time as they have already paid a hefty registration fee; also, with constant remarketing, the patient tends to visit the same hospital even though the person is visiting some other part of the country, a few famous hospitals, and their health cards (KPMG, 2015).

4 HEALTH-CARD SYSTEM

A country must be healthy first, then be developed. Good health will allow adults to earn and children to learn. European countries have built, reviewed, and developed a robust healthcare system. The countries have moved away from the traditional paper-based system and used the IT infrastructure for their Health care system.

The idea was introduced in France and Germany in the late 80s and 90s to introduce health insurance cards. Here, the Health Id cards differ in terms of cards that now hold the patient's medical history records with diagnosis, prescribed drugs, tests, and all records, which anyone can access. This system has significant advantages for proper diagnosis, routine health check-ups, warnings of any future disease, and many more. The health records are in a digital format for efficient supervision and communication.

Challenges for Underprivileged Citizens in India Healthcare in India is a grave issue, with unequal access to public health facilities for the citizens of India. The privileged citizens of India seek medical assistance from Private hospitals resulting in an Urban biased healthcare system. From the records of Indican Medical systems, about 75% of healthcare clinics are in urban India, where only 27% of the Indian population resides, giving a bias in greater availability to a smaller affluent population. In contrast, the rest lack the primary healthcare facility (KPMG, 2015). A Lancet report (Kruk et al., 2018) shows that almost 8 million people die yearly due to poor healthcare facilities. India has registered the highest of deaths, around 2.3 million or 122 per 100,00, due to poor health quality. A similar trend can also be seen in our neighbouring countries, which are low-income countries. All these statistics and data show the actual situation of the Indian health infrastructure. There is a lack of accountability, scalability, and ownership (Kruk et al., 2018).

4.1 Challenges For Underprivileged Citizens In India

Healthcare in India is a significant issue, with unequal access to public health facilities for the country's citizens. The privileged citizens of India primarily seek medical assistance from private hospitals, resulting in an urban-biased healthcare system. According to records from the Indian Medical systems, about 75% of healthcare clinics are located in urban India, where only 27% of the Indian population resides, providing a disproportionate availability to the smaller affluent population. In contrast, the rest of the population lacks access to primary healthcare facilities (KPMG, 2015).

A Lancet report published in 2018 shows that almost 8 million people die yearly due to poor healthcare facilities. India has registered the highest number of deaths, around 2.3 million or 122 per 100,000, due to poor health quality. A similar trend can also be seen in India's neighbouring countries, which are predominantly low-income countries. All these statistics and data demonstrate the actual situation of the Indian health infrastructure, which lacks accountability, scalability, and ownership (Kruk et al., 2018).

The key challenges faced by underprivileged citizens in India include:

- Shortage of medical professionals and specialised staff
- Misuse, mismanagement, and corruption in government and non-government bodies
- Increased illegal medicine sales in pharmacies
- Long patient queues to visit doctors and undergo diagnostic tests
- Incorrect data resulting in incorrect diagnosis and mistreatment, leading to deaths

The impact of these challenges on individual health is significant, including:

- Increasing mortality rate
- Contracting various other diseases due to improper diagnosis
- Long-term health impacts
- Increasing expenditure

5 ROBOTIC PROCESS AUTOMATION (RPA)

Robotic Process Automation (RPA) is an emerging technology that has gained significant traction in various industries, including healthcare. In the context of hospital operations, RPA offers a promising solution to streamline administrative tasks, particularly in admission and discharge processes.

5.1 Technology involvement

RPA can be defined as a software technology that mimics human actions to perform rule-based, repetitive tasks with high accuracy and efficiency (Lacity et al., 2016). This technology has the potential to transform hospital operations by automating routine tasks, reducing errors, and freeing up staff to focus on more value-added activities.

The core concept of RPA lies in its ability to automate repetitive tasks that follow predefined rules. In hospital settings, these tasks often include data entry, form filling, and information retrieval from various systems. RPA bots can be programmed to interact with existing software applications through user interfaces, much like human users would, but at a much faster rate and with greater consistency (Asatiani & Penttinen, 2016). This characteristic makes RPA particularly suitable for healthcare environments where legacy systems are common and major IT overhauls may be challenging or cost-prohibitive.

5.2 Hospitalisation

In the context of hospital admission and discharge processes, RPA can play a crucial role in enhancing efficiency and accuracy. For patient registration and data entry, RPA bots can automatically capture and digitize patient information from various sources, including paper forms and electronic documents. This automation significantly reduces the time and effort required for manual data entry, while also minimising the risk of transcription errors. Furthermore, RPA can seamlessly integrate this information with Electronic Health Record (EHR) systems, ensuring that patient data is consistently up-to-date across all platforms (Issac et al., 2011).

5.3 Insurance

Insurance verification and claims processing are other areas where RPA can bring substantial improvements. By automating insurance checks and authorisations, hospitals can significantly reduce the time and resources spent on these administrative tasks. RPA bots can quickly verify patient insurance information, submit claims, and even follow up on pending claims, all without human intervention. This automation not only speeds up the process but also helps in reducing claim denials due to errors or missed deadlines (Jiwani et al., 2014).

5.4 Appointment scheduling and management

Appointment scheduling and management is another domain where RPA can drive efficiency. RPA-driven scheduling systems can automatically book appointments based on predefined rules and available time slots. These systems can also send automated reminders to patients and healthcare providers, reducing no-shows and improving overall scheduling efficiency. In the discharge planning process, RPA can automate the creation of discharge summaries, coordinate post-discharge care, and even schedule follow-up appointments, ensuring a smooth transition for patients from hospital to home care (Bullock et al., 2017).

5.5 Implementation

The benefits of implementing RPA in healthcare are multifaceted. Primarily, it leads to improved efficiency and productivity by reducing the time spent on manual, repetitive tasks. This allows healthcare staff to focus more on patient care and other high-value activities that require human judgment and empathy. Enhanced accuracy and consistency are other significant advantages, as RPA bots perform tasks with a high degree of precision, minimising human errors in data entry and processing (Asquith & Horsman, 2019).

Cost reduction is another compelling benefit of RPA implementation in healthcare. By automating routine tasks, hospitals can optimise resource allocation and potentially reduce staffing costs associated with administrative work. Moreover, the improved accuracy in billing and claims processing can lead to faster reimbursements and fewer claim denials, positively impacting the hospital's financial health (Himmelstein et al., 2014).

Perhaps most importantly, RPA can contribute to an improved patient experience. Faster admission and discharge processes mean less waiting time for patients, while the reduction in administrative burden allows healthcare providers to dedicate more time to personalised patient care. This can lead to higher patient satisfaction and potentially better health outcomes (Kang et al., 2014).

Robotic Process Automation presents a powerful tool for optimising hospital admission and discharge processes. By automating routine tasks, improving accuracy, and freeing up healthcare professionals to focus on patient care, RPA has the potential to significantly enhance the efficiency and quality of healthcare delivery. As the technology continues to mature and integrate with other advanced technologies, its role in shaping the future of healthcare operations is likely to grow even further.

5.6 Challenges in Implementation

The implementation of RPA in healthcare is not without challenges. Integration with existing systems can be complex, especially in hospitals with legacy IT infrastructure. Staff training and change management are crucial to ensure smooth adoption of RPA technologies. Data security and privacy concerns are paramount in healthcare, and RPA implementations must ensure compliance with regulations such as HIPAA. Managing access control and data protection in an automated environment requires careful planning and robust security measures (Madakam et al., 2019). It's also important to acknowledge the limitations of RPA. While excellent at handling rule-based tasks, RPA bots may struggle with exceptions or complex decision-making scenarios that require human judgment. Therefore, human oversight and intervention remain necessary, especially in healthcare where patient safety is paramount (Pramod, 2022).

Looking to the future, the integration of RPA with AI and machine learning holds promise for even more advanced automation in healthcare. This combination could lead to more intelligent and adaptive automation capable of handling increasingly complex tasks and making data-driven decisions. As RPA technology continues to evolve, its application is likely to expand to other healthcare processes, potentially leading to a vision of a highly automated hospital ecosystem that enhances both operational efficiency and quality of patient care (Rodgers et al., 2024).

6 RPA AND RELATED INTELLIGENT SYSTEMS

Robotic Process Automation (RPA) has been an integral part of technological advancement for some time, though its full potential often remains underappreciated. This technology synergises with various existing systems to achieve its objectives, creating a powerful ecosystem of automation and intelligence. To fully grasp the capabilities of RPA, it is essential to explore its integration with other intelligent systems that enhance its functionality and expand its applications across various domains.

At its core, RPA relies on rule-based instructive systems that follow predefined workflows to perform tasks. However, the true power of RPA emerges when it is combined with more sophisticated technologies. Adaptive systems, for instance, can process unstructured data and make decisions based on the information gleaned, adding a layer of flexibility to RPA implementations. The pinnacle of this technological integration is cognitive intelligence, which approaches human-like decision-making capabilities, operating with minimal human intervention.

1) Natural Language Processing (NLP) plays a crucial role in enhancing RPA systems. By enabling machines to read and interpret human languages, NLP bridges the communication gap between humans and automated systems. This capability is particularly valuable in environments where human interaction is minimised. NLP's functionalities extend beyond basic language understanding to include information extraction, summarisation, data categorisation, and sentiment analysis. In healthcare settings, NLP can facilitate the management of unstructured information, such as patient notes or medical literature, making it an invaluable tool for improving the efficiency and accuracy of healthcare processes.
2) Artificial Intelligence (AI) represents another cornerstone in the evolution of RPA systems. By simulating human intelligence through various technologies such as deep learning, machine vision, and neural networks, AI has revolutionised numerous industries, including healthcare. In medical contexts, AI applications range from patient diagnosis and morbidity risk assessment to disease outbreak prediction and health policy planning. These advanced capabilities rely on sophisticated machine learning models and algorithms that can identify critical factors and patterns within vast datasets, far surpassing human analytical capabilities in terms of speed and accuracy.
3) Machine Learning (ML), a subset of AI, further amplifies the potential of RPA systems. ML excels in managing large volumes of data, collecting and storing information from diverse sources, and preparing this data for processing. The power of ML lies in its ability to generate intelligent insights and make decisions based on historical data and various algorithms. In healthcare, ML can be applied to create prediction models for hospital admissions, optimise resource allocation, and enhance patient care strategies. The insights derived from ML algorithms can be translated into actionable visualisations and business intelligence, providing healthcare administrators with powerful tools for decision-making and strategic planning.
4) Hyperautomation represents the cutting edge of RPA technology, recognised by Gartner as one of the top strategic technology trends. This approach combines AI and RPA to create systems capable of automating the automation process itself. By integrating various tools such as AI, ML, NLP, and Optical Character Recognition (OCR), Hyperautomation can address complex, end-to-end business problems that were previously beyond the scope of traditional automation. The self-sufficient and self-healing nature of Hyperautomation systems makes them particularly viable for organisations seeking to achieve comprehensive digital transformation. In the public sector, Hyperautomation holds immense potential for improving governance, streamlining processes, and addressing workforce challenges faced by many governments.

5) Cloud-native systems provide a flexible, scalable foundation for deploying RPA and other intelligent technologies. By leveraging containerisation and microservices architecture, cloud-native approaches allow healthcare organisations to deploy RPA bots and AI models as discrete, manageable units that can be scaled independently based on demand. This aligns well with the varied and often unpredictable workloads in healthcare environments, from sudden surges inpatient admissions to periodic billing cycles. Building upon the integration of RPA with intelligent systems, it's crucial to consider how these technologies align with cloud-native systems particularly in healthcare settings. This combination represents a powerful approach to modernising healthcare IT infrastructure and processes. A cloud-native RPA system for patient admission could consist of several microservices: one for initial data capture, another for insurance verification, and a third for bed allocation. Each of these could scale independently based on current hospital needs, ensuring optimal resource utilisation and responsiveness. The cloud-native approach also facilitates easier updates and maintenance of these systems, crucial in the rapidly evolving landscape of healthcare regulations and best practices.
6) Event-driven architecture complements cloud-native RPA systems by enabling real-time responsiveness to changes in the healthcare environment. In an event-driven system, various components of the healthcare IT ecosystem emit events that can trigger automated responses from RPA bots. For instance, when a patient's lab results are uploaded to the electronic health record system, this event could automatically trigger an RPA bot to analyses the results, flag any abnormalities, and schedule follow-up appointments if necessary. This event-driven approach is particularly valuable in healthcare scenarios where timely action is critical. It allows for the creation of highly responsive, automated workflows that can significantly improve patient care and operational efficiency. For example, an event-driven RPA system could automatically initiate the discharge process as soon as a physician updates a patient's status, triggering a series of actions from preparing discharge summaries to scheduling follow-up care (Jyothi et al., 2024).
7) The integration of cloud-native systems and event-driven architecture with RPA and AI creates a powerful ecosystem for healthcare automation. This combination allows for the development of intelligent, scalable, and responsive systems that can adapt to the complex and dynamic nature of healthcare operations. It enables healthcare providers to move beyond simple task automation to create sophisticated, context-aware workflows that can significantly enhance both operational efficiency and patient care quality. Moreover, this integrated approach facilitates better data management and analytics capabilities. By leveraging cloud-native data storage and processing capabilities, healthcare organisations

can create data lakes that consolidate information from various sources. RPA bots and AI models can then access this rich data repository to perform advanced analytics, generate insights, and drive continuous improvement in healthcare processes. As healthcare continues to digitise and generate vast amounts of data, the combination of cloud-native RPA systems and event-driven architectures will become increasingly crucial. These technologies will enable healthcare providers to harness the full potential of their data, automate complex workflows, and deliver more personalized and efficient patient care. The future of healthcare IT lies in these intelligent, responsive, and scalable systems that can adapt to the ever-changing landscape of medical science and healthcare delivery.

As RPA continues to evolve and integrate with these intelligent systems, its applications in healthcare and other industries will expand exponentially. The synergy between RPA and technologies like NLP, AI, ML, and Hyperautomation is paving the way for more efficient, accurate, and autonomous systems that can handle increasingly complex tasks. This technological convergence promises to revolutionize healthcare delivery, from patient admission and discharge processes to complex diagnostic procedures and treatment planning. As these systems mature, they will undoubtedly play a crucial role in shaping the future of healthcare, improving patient outcomes, and optimizing resource utilization across the healthcare ecosystem.

7 RPA IN GOVERNANCE

Robotic Process Automation (RPA) has emerged as a powerful tool for enhancing efficiency and effectiveness in government operations. The implementation of RPA in governance requires a systematic approach, encompassing evaluation, design, execution, and continuous monitoring. This section outlines the key steps and considerations for successfully integrating RPA into public sector processes.

1) Evaluation: The initial phase of RPA implementation in governance involves a comprehensive evaluation of available technologies and organizational needs. Government agencies must carefully assess the RPA software options in the market, considering their capabilities and potential to address specific public sector requirements (Madakam et al., 2019). This evaluation should be coupled with a thorough analysis of internal processes to identify those most suitable for automation.
2) Stakeholder engagement: Stakeholder engagement plays a crucial role in this phase. By involving key personnel and decision-makers, agencies can prioritize automation initiatives effectively and foster awareness about RPA's potential

benefits. This collaborative approach not only aids in process identification but also helps in building support for RPA implementation across the organization (Pramod, 2022).

3) Design: Once priority processes are identified, the design phase commences. This stage involves creating detailed process models and architectural designs for RPA implementation. It's crucial to anticipate potential challenges and edge cases during this phase, ensuring that the automated processes can handle exceptions gracefully. In cases where RPA alone may not suffice, agencies should consider integrating other complementary technologies to create a more robust solution (Asquith & Horsman, 2019).
4) Resource planning: Resource planning is another critical aspect of the design phase. This includes allocating appropriate staff, providing necessary training, and potentially hiring specialists to support the RPA initiative. Additionally, agencies must develop comprehensive technical documentation, addressing user interfaces, security protocols, and infrastructure requirements.
5) Design Phase: The design phase should adhere to established Software Development Life Cycle (SDLC) governance models, ensuring that RPA implementations align with broader IT governance policies and standards within the public sector (Issac et al., 2018).
6) Execution Phase: The execution phase brings the designed RPA processes to life. Agencies should follow a structured approach, typically encompassing design, build, test, implement, and execute stages. This methodical progression helps ensure that each automated process is thoroughly vetted before full deployment. Throughout the execution phase, continuous review and refinement are essential. As RPA bots are deployed and begin operating, agencies should closely monitor their performance and make necessary adjustments to optimise their functionality and efficiency (Jyothi et al., 2024).
7) Monitor and Analyse: The final phase of RPA implementation in governance is ongoing monitoring and analysis. This stage is crucial for ensuring the long-term success and sustainability of RPA initiatives. Agencies should establish robust mechanisms for analysing the performance of automated processes and preparing detailed reports on their impact and effectiveness. Identifying and addressing exceptions or unexpected scenarios is a key part of this phase. As RPA bots encounter new situations or changes in underlying systems, agencies must be prepared to make timely adjustments to maintain smooth operations. It's recommended that agencies provide dedicated support and maintenance for at least three months following the initial implementation. This period allows for fine-tuning of processes and addressing any unforeseen issues that may arise in real-world operations (Araújo et al., 2022).

By following this structured approach to RPA implementation in governance, public sector organisations can harness the power of automation to enhance their operational efficiency, improve service delivery, and ultimately better serve their constituents. The journey towards RPA adoption requires careful planning, stakeholder engagement, and a commitment to continuous improvement, but the potential benefits in terms of cost savings, accuracy, and citizen satisfaction make it a worthwhile endeavour for modern governments.

8 RPA IMPLEMENTATION FOR HEALTH ID CARD GENERATION

The implementation of Robotic Process Automation (RPA) for health ID card generation in a country with a large population like India, with approximately 135 crore people, requires careful planning and a clear vision from the government. This section explores the various opportunities for RPA implementation in this context, focusing on creating an integrated and automated health system that minimises errors and enhances efficiency.

1) Evaluation and Planning: The first crucial step in implementing RPA for health ID card generation is a thorough evaluation of opportunities and requirements. This process involves assessing current systems, identifying pain points, and envisioning future needs. Government planners must consider the scalability and interoperability of the proposed system, ensuring it can handle the massive population while integrating seamlessly with existing health sector infrastructure (Madakam et al., 2019).
2) User Registration: The registration process can be significantly streamlined using RPA. By integrating with existing national identification systems like Aadhar, RPA bots can automatically fetch and verify user details, reducing manual data entry errors. This automation ensures rapid creation of unique health IDs and secure storage of information in a centralised database (Jyothi et al., 2024).
3) User Details Update and Health Profiles: RPA, combined with Optical Character Recognition (OCR) technology, can automate the process of updating user details. Whether through email, documents, or forms, RPA bots can extract relevant information and update user profiles with minimal human intervention. This approach not only reduces manual labour but also minimises errors associated with data entry (Issac et al., 2018). The creation and management of individual health profiles represent a significant opportunity for RPA implementation. Using intelligent document processing, RPA can automate the uploading and organization of medical records and reports. This comprehensive approach to health profile management enables better insights into individual and popula-

tion health trends, facilitating preventive care and early intervention strategies (Pramod, 2022).

4) Classification and Document Verification: Automating the verification of credentials for healthcare professionals and institutions is another key application of RPA. By integrating with relevant databases, RPA can quickly verify licenses, track their status, and flag any discrepancies. This automation significantly reduces the time and resources required for manual verification processes (Asquith & Horsman, 2019). RPA, when coupled with advanced technologies like Google Cloud Vision, can efficiently classify and categorise users, doctors, and healthcare institutions. This automated classification enhances management and visibility within the healthcare system, allowing for better resource allocation and policy implementation (Araújo et al., 2022).
5) Insurance Claims Streamlining: RPA can play a crucial role in streamlining the insurance claims process within a centralized health system. By automating claim processing and verification, RPA can significantly reduce processing times and minimize fraud. This efficiency not only benefits patients by speeding up claim disbursements but also helps insurance providers and healthcare institutions manage their resources more effectively (Jiwani et al., 2014).

The implementation of RPA in health ID card generation and related processes offers immense potential for improving the efficiency and effectiveness of healthcare delivery in large populations. By automating key processes from registration to insurance claims, RPA can help create a more integrated, error-free, and responsive healthcare system. However, successful implementation requires careful planning, robust infrastructure, and a commitment to continuous improvement and adaptation as the system evolves.

9 BENEFICIARIES OF RPA-DRIVEN HEALTH ID SYSTEM

The implementation of a comprehensive, RPA-driven health ID system promises to deliver wide-ranging benefits across the healthcare ecosystem. This section explores the various stakeholders who stand to gain from this innovative approach to healthcare management and delivery.

1) Government bodies and policymakers will gain access to unprecedented insights into population health trends and healthcare system performance. The real-time data aggregated through the health ID system will enable evidence-based policymaking, allowing for more targeted and effective healthcare initiatives.

As noted by Rodgers et al. (2024), this data-driven approach can lead to better resource allocation and more responsive healthcare policies.

2) Healthcare providers, the integrated health ID system offers numerous advantages. Hospitals and clinics will benefit from seamless data sharing and real-time updates, enhancing continuity of care and reducing duplicate tests or procedures. Kang et al. (2014) highlight that this improved information flow can lead to more efficient operations and, ultimately, better patient outcomes.
3) Doctors and other healthcare professionals will find the system particularly beneficial for knowledge sharing and e-consultation. Kripalani et al. (2007) emphasise that the ability to easily access and share patient information can lead to more informed diagnoses and treatment plans.
4) Smaller healthcare providers and related businesses often lack access to sophisticated data analytics tools. The health ID system can level the playing field by providing these entities with valuable insights into patient demographics and health trends. Himmelstein et al. (2014) suggest that this data can inform business decisions and help in tailoring services to community needs.
5) Non-Governmental Organizations (NGOs) and healthcare associations can leverage the insights provided by the health ID system to implement more targeted and effective healthcare initiatives. Jiwani et al. (2014) point out that organizations focused on specific health issues can use population-level data to identify areas of high need and allocate resources accordingly.
6) Patients themselves are perhaps the most significant beneficiaries of the health ID system. With comprehensive health profiles easily accessible to healthcare providers, patients can expect more personalised and coordinated care. Bullock et al. (2017) note that the system's ability to streamline processes like insurance claims can significantly improve the overall patient experience.

The wealth of anonymised data generated by the health ID system can be a boon for medical research and public health initiatives. Asatiani and Penttinen (2016) suggest that researchers can gain insights into disease patterns and treatment efficacy on a scale previously unattainable, potentially accelerating medical discoveries.

In conclusion, the RPA-driven health ID system represents a transformative approach to healthcare management with far-reaching benefits. From enhancing individual patient care to informing national health policies, the system's potential impact is truly utilitarian in nature. As this system matures and evolves, it promises to create a more connected, efficient, and effective healthcare ecosystem that benefits all stakeholders involved

10 CREATION OF A COMPREHENSIVE DIGITAL HEALTH SYSTEM

The implementation of a standardized Digital Health System, centered around a unique Health ID Card for each citizen, represents a significant step forward in modernizing healthcare delivery and management. This system aims to address the critical need for a unified identification process across various healthcare providers, ensuring accurate delivery of medical documents and proper access control.

Health ID Card

The cornerstone of this digital health system is the Health ID Card. Its primary purpose is to standardize the identification process for individuals across all healthcare providers in the country. This standardization is crucial for ensuring that medical documents are delivered to the correct individuals and that access to sensitive health information is properly controlled.

10.1 Initialisation

To issue a Health ID, authorities will collect a range of information, including General demographic data, Location information, Family and personal medical history and Contact details. The system must allow for easy editing of specific details to maintain accuracy over time. The Health ID will serve multiple functions; Personal identification, Verification of identity at healthcare facilities and Linking health records across multiple programs and stakeholders (with informed patient consent)

10.2 Key Components of the Digital Health System

1) Health Database (HDB): The HDB will serve as a centralized repository for all health facilities in the country. This comprehensive database will enable efficient data sharing and analysis, supporting both individual patient care and broader public health initiatives.
2) National Medical Health Record: The Patient Health Record (PHR) is an electronic record of an individual's health information. It adheres to nationally recognized standards for interoperability and can incorporate data from various sources. Crucially, this record is managed, shared, and controlled by the individual, empowering patients to take an active role in their healthcare.
3) Digital Medical Records (DMR): DMR is essentially a digital version of a patient's chart. It will be accessible via web and mobile applications, allowing healthcare providers to easily access and update patient information in real-time. This digitization of medical records can significantly improve the efficiency and accuracy of healthcare delivery.

10.3 Commercialization and Security

To ensure widespread adoption and security, the Unique Health ID (UHID) will be linked to the individual's phone number. This linkage enables two-factor authentication for data access, enhancing security and privacy protection. Drawing inspiration from successful digital payment systems, a UHID code similar to the BHIM UPI QR code could be created. This would allow for quick and secure access to health information in various healthcare settings. Potential Benefits and Impacts are stated below. The implementation of this comprehensive Digital Health System has the potential to transform healthcare delivery in several ways:

1) Improved continuity of care: Healthcare providers can access a patient's complete medical history, leading to more informed treatment decisions.
2) Enhanced patient empowerment: Individuals have greater control over their health data and can easily share it with healthcare providers of their choice.
3) Efficient health resource allocation: Aggregated, anonymised data can inform public health policies and resource distribution.
4) Reduced medical errors: Access to comprehensive patient information can help prevent medication errors and adverse drug interactions.
5) Streamlined healthcare administration: Digital records and standardised identification can reduce paperwork and administrative burden.
6) Support for telemedicine: A unified digital health system can facilitate remote consultations and monitoring.

10.4 Challenges and Considerations

While the potential benefits are significant, implementation of such a system also faces challenges:

1. Data privacy and security: Robust measures must be in place to protect sensitive health information.
2. Digital literacy: Ensuring all citizens can effectively use the system may require extensive education efforts.
3. Infrastructure requirements: Reliable internet connectivity and hardware availability across all healthcare settings is crucial.
4. Interoperability: Ensuring all existing health IT systems can integrate with the new digital health system will be a complex task.

The creation of a comprehensive Digital Health System centered around a Health ID Card represents a ambitious yet potentially transformative initiative. By standardizing identification, centralizing health records, and enabling secure data sharing, this system has the potential to significantly improve healthcare delivery, patient engagement, and public health outcomes. However, careful planning, robust security measures, and ongoing evaluation will be crucial to its successful implementation and adoption.

We have attempted to create a sustainable framework to create and implement RPA in the Health card creation process. This automated solution will help reduce the turnaround time for the user registration process by increasing the accuracy of the task. This framework and solution are constructed after considering all the factors and parameters. A user registration process in India might take around ten years to complete, as seen in the case of Aadhar registration. However, with RPA, the process gets simplified and exponentially reduces the time and resources required. The system becomes less prone to errors with the removal of humans from the process. The need to go to a government centre to register oneself can be removed if the system is entirely digitised, thus removing the dependency on other entities, and tasks can be completed by working diligently and independently. Various government agencies' reputations are at stake due to corruption, and this system helps prevent corruption as it will be easier to trace, identify and hold someone accountable, eventually increasing ownership.

However, implementing this whole model would require an overhaul of policy and guidelines based on the Medical systems and the Hospital's internal policy. Because data sharing and security require considerable management, skilled personnel are needed to automate and migrate the legacy system to a new digitised system. To change the process, they are automating the essential workflows and making people aware of the capabilities of Intelligent systems. The agenda should be clear: drive automation to scale by combining the intelligent system with various governance workflows with next-generation skills and make the right decision by making the right resources available.

A. Drawbacks in the Current Health Care System

The followings are the problems in the existing healthcare system such as:

- Shortage of medical professionals and specialised staff.
- Misuse, mismanagement, and corruption in government and non-government bodies.
- Increased illegal medicine sales in the pharmacies.
- Long patients queue to visit doctors and make diagnostic tests for their health problems.

- Incorrect data results in incorrect diagnosis and mistreatment, leading to death

Impact on Individual Health

There are several health problems, especially in countries with poor health infrastructure:

- Increasing mortality rate.
- Contracting various other diseases because of improper diagnosis
- Long-term health impacts
- Increasing expenditure.

11 DISCUSSION

The primary objective of this conceptual research was to explore the potential applications of Robotic Process Automation (RPA), Hyperautomation, and Cognitive Intelligent systems in handling large-scale data management, developing standardised operating procedures, and creating a self-sufficient framework that could be implemented across various government sectors. This approach aims to address the challenges associated with manual data collection processes, which are often cumbersome, unstructured, and time-consuming, especially in resource-constrained environments.

The proposed model seeks to replace these tedious manual tasks with RPA bots capable of efficiently collecting health data from a population of 130 crore Indians. By integrating intelligent document processing and Optical Character Recognition (OCR) technologies, the system can streamline document processing and facilitate multi-level approvals. This automation is expected to result in improved resource management, allowing human resources to focus on tasks that require critical thinking and complex decision-making rather than repetitive data entry. One of the significant benefits of this system is the potential for enhanced data management of health records. As noted by Kang et al. (2014), improved information flow in healthcare systems can lead to more efficient operations and better patient outcomes. The centralised health database proposed in this model could provide a comprehensive view of population health, enabling more informed decision-making by healthcare providers and policymakers alike.

Moreover, the analytics capabilities of such a system could offer unprecedented insights into public health trends and treatment efficacy. As Rodgers et al. (2024) suggest, data-driven approaches in healthcare can lead to better resource allocation and more responsive policies. The Ministry of Health and Family Welfare and hospitals across the country could leverage these insights to improve healthcare delivery and public health strategies. However, the implementation of such a comprehensive RPA-driven system is not without challenges. One of the primary hurdles is the need for skilled professionals to develop and implement this framework. This aligns with the observations of Madakam et al. (2019), who highlighted the relative newness of RPA technology, especially in the public sector, as a potential barrier to adoption. Another significant challenge lies in ensuring proper identification and integration with existing systems, such as the Aadhaar card system. As Jiwani et al. (2014) pointed out in their study of administrative costs in healthcare, the integration of new systems with existing infrastructure can be complex and resource-intensive.

Furthermore, there may be initial resistance from stakeholders due to the learning curve associated with adopting new technologies and processes. This resistance might be compounded by concerns about job displacement, a common apprehension when introducing automation technologies. Asatiani and Penttinen (2016) noted similar concerns in their case study of RPA implementation, emphasizing the importance of change management strategies.

To address these challenges, proper planning and strategic implementation are crucial. This includes comprehensive training programs, clear communication about the benefits of the system, and strategies to reskill and redeploy workers whose roles may be affected by automation. Additionally, robust security measures must be implemented to protect sensitive health data, addressing privacy concerns that often arise with large-scale data collection efforts (Kripalani et al., 2007).

In conclusion, while the proposed RPA-driven health ID system offers significant potential benefits in terms of efficiency, data management, and healthcare delivery, its successful implementation will require careful consideration of technical, organisational, and human factors. Future research could focus on pilot implementations of such systems, evaluating their real-world impact and refining strategies for overcoming implementation challenges

12 CONCLUSION

This research has explored the transformative potential of integrating advanced technologies, particularly Artificial Intelligence (AI) and cloud-native principles, into the development of a Unified Health ID Card system for India. The study has illuminated the significant opportunities for enhancing healthcare service delivery through automation and intelligent systems.

Our comprehensive analysis of AI applications in cloud-native software development has revealed promising avenues for creating high-quality, enterprise-grade solutions efficiently (Issac et al., 2018). The alignment of cloud-native principles with microservices architecture, containerisation, and automated testing frameworks has shown potential for substantial improvements in system performance and scalability (Asquith & Horsman, 2019). The research has also critically examined the benefits and challenges associated with implementing AI in cloud-native software engineering for healthcare. While the potential for increased efficiency and reduced human error is significant, issues such as data privacy, system integration, and workforce adaptation remain important considerations (Madakam et al., 2019).

The proposed Unified Health ID Card system, leveraging these advanced technologies, presents a vision of streamlined healthcare administration and improved patient care. By automating processes such as user registration and data management, the system could significantly reduce administrative burdens and enhance the accuracy of health records (Jyothi et al., 2024).However, the successful implementation of such a system will require careful navigation of technical, organisational, and ethical challenges. The integration of nascent technologies with governance structures must be approached judiciously to overcome long-standing challenges in healthcare administration (Rodgers et al., 2024).

Looking ahead, the continued evolution of AI and cloud-native technologies promises further advancements in healthcare IT. Future research should focus on refining these systems, addressing emerging challenges, and exploring new applications to further improve healthcare delivery and patient outcomes. Robotic Process Automation (RPA) has been a focal point in this discussion, it is just one component of a broader technological revolution in healthcare. The true potential lies in the harmonious integration of various advanced technologies, creating a system that not only enhances administrative efficiency but also contributes to improved health outcomes for millions of citizens

REFERENCES

Araújo, A., Mamede, H. S., Filipe, V., & Santos, V. (2022). An integrated approach using robotic process automation and artificial intelligence as disruptive technology for digital transformation. In European, Mediterranean, and Middle Eastern Conference on Information Systems (pp. 438-450). Springer Nature Switzerland.

Asatiani, A., & Penttinen, E. (2016). Turning robotic process automation into commercial success – Case OpusCapita. *Journal of Information Technology Teaching Cases*, *6*(2), 67–74. DOI: 10.1057/jittc.2016.5

Asquith, A., & Horsman, G. (2019). Let the robots do it! - Taking a look at Robotic Process Automation and its potential application in digital forensics. *Forensic Science International. Reports*, *1*, 100007. DOI: 10.1016/j.fsir.2019.100007

Basher, M. A., & Roy, P. C. (2011). Introducing an e-Health card for developing countries: A case study of Bangladesh. Stockholms Universiteit. http://www.diva-portal.org/smash/get/diva2:428633/FULLTEXT01.pdf

Bullock, S., Morecroft, C. W., Mullen, R., & Ewing, A. B. (2017). Hospital patient discharge process: An evaluation. *European Journal of Hospital Pharmacy. Science and Practice*, *24*(5), 278–282. DOI: 10.1136/ejhpharm-2016-000928 PMID: 31156958

Chan, A. T. S., Cao, J., Chan, H., & Young, G. (2001). A web-enabled framework for smart card application in health services. *Communications of the ACM*, *44*(9), 76–82. DOI: 10.1145/383694.383710

Devarajan, Y. (2018). A Study of Robotic Process Automation Use Cases Today for Tomorrow's Business. *International Journal of Computers and Technology*, *5*(6), 12–18.

Himmelstein, D. U., Jun, M., Busse, R., Chevreul, K., Geissler, A., Jeurissen, P., Thomson, S., Vinet, M. A., & Woolhandler, S. (2014). A comparison of hospital administrative costs in eight nations: US costs exceed all others by far. *Health Affairs*, *33*(9), 1586–1594. DOI: 10.1377/hlthaff.2013.1327 PMID: 25201663

Issac, R., Muni, R., & Desai, K. (2018). Delineated analysis of robotic process automation tools. Proceedings of 2018 2nd International Conference on Advances in Electronics, Computers and Communications, ICAECC 2018, 1-5. DOI: 10.1109/ICAECC.2018.8479511

Jiwani, A., Himmelstein, D., Woolhandler, S., & Kahn, J. G. (2014). Billing and insurance-related administrative costs in United States' health care: Synthesis of micro-costing evidence. *BMC Health Services Research, 14*(1), 1–9. DOI: 10.1186/s12913-014-0556-7 PMID: 25540104

Jyothi, A. P., Shankar, A., Narayan, J. R. A., Maniyar, H., & Ambarkhane, S. (2024). Robotic process automation: In-depth analysis of advanced automation techniques and technologies. In 2024 IEEE International Conference on Contemporary Computing and Communications (InC4) (Vol. 1, pp. 1-6). IEEE.

Kang, H., Nembhard, H. B., Rafferty, C., & DeFlitch, C. J. (2014). Patient flow in the emergency department: A classification and analysis of admission process policies. *Annals of Emergency Medicine, 64*(4), 335–342.e8. DOI: 10.1016/j.annemergmed.2014.04.011 PMID: 24875896

Kerrigan, N. (2024). *Enabling a Digital Birmingham: an evaluation of the Birmingham Digital Inclusion Strategy*. Birmingham City University.

KPMG. (2015). AHP I Healthcare-India (No. 1). https://assets.kpmg/content/dam/kpmg/in/pdf/2016/09/AHPIHealthcare-India.pdf

Kripalani, S., LeFevre, F., Phillips, C. O., Williams, M. V., Basaviah, P., & Baker, D. W. (2007). Deficits in communication and information transfer between hospital-based and primary care physicians: Implications for patient safety and continuity of care. *Journal of the American Medical Association, 297*(8), 831–841. DOI: 10.1001/jama.297.8.831 PMID: 17327525

Kruk, M. E., Gage, A. D., Joseph, N. T., Danaei, G., García-Saisó, S., & Salomon, J. A. (2018). Mortality due to low-quality health systems in the universal health coverage era: A systematic analysis of amenable deaths in 137 countries. *Lancet, 392*(10160), 2203–2212. DOI: 10.1016/S0140-6736(18)31668-4 PMID: 30195398

Lacity, M., Willcocks, L., & Craig, A. (2016). Robotic process automation at Telefónica O2. *MIS Quarterly Executive, 15*(1), 21–35.

Madakam, S., Holmukhe, R. M., & Jaiswal, D. K. (2019). The future digital work force: Robotic Process Automation (RPA). *Journal of Information Systems and Technology Management, 16*, 1–17. DOI: 10.4301/S1807-1775201916001

Ministry of Health and Family Welfarc. (2018). Ministry of Health and Family Welfare Hospitals in the Country. https://pib.gov.in/PressReleasePage.aspx?PRID=1539877

Pramod, D. (2022). Robotic process automation for industry: Adoption status, benefits, challenges and research agenda. *Benchmarking*, *29*(5), 1562–1586. DOI: 10.1108/BIJ-01-2021-0033

Raman, R., & Kumar, P. (2018). India achieves WHO recommended doctor population ratio: A call for a paradigm shift in public health discourse! NCBI. https://www.ncbi.nlm.nih.gov/pmc/articles/PMC6259525/

Rodgers, M., Mukherjee, S., Melamed, B., Baveja, A., & Kapoor, A. (2024). Solving business problems: The business-driven data-supported process. *Annals of Operations Research*, *332*(1), 705–741. DOI: 10.1007/s10479-023-05770-z

Sunyaev, A., Kaletsch, A., Mauro, C., & Krcmar, H. (2009, May). Security analysis of the German electronic health card's peripheral parts. In ICEIS (3) (pp. 19-26). DOI: 10.5220/0001854000190026

Wager, K. A., Lee, F. W., & Glaser, J. P. (2021). *Health care information systems: a practical approach for health care management*. John Wiley & Sons.

Chapter 14
Data Security With Replication for Cloud Computing

Cigdem Bakir
https://orcid.org/0000-0001-8482-2412
Dumlupinar University, Turkey

Mecit Yuzkat
https://orcid.org/0000-0003-4808-5181
Health Institutes of Türkiye, Turkey

ABSTRACT

Cloud computing is an advanced technology that provides access to different services via the internet. These services include applications such as servers, networking, data storage, databases, and software. Instead of storing files on local storage device, cloud-based storage makes it possible to store files in a secure database. As long as an electronic device has access to the web, it has access to data and the software programs to run it. For this reason, this technology is very popular for institutions and individuals for many reasons such as cost, production, efficiency and speed. However, with the advantages of cloud computing, some security risks also arise. At the beginning of these security risks are data breaches and data losses caused by malicious software applications. In this study, data replication is discussed in order to solve security breaches in cloud computing technologies.

DOI: 10.4018/979-8-3693-9356-7.ch014

INTRODUCTION

Nowadays, the size and variety of data produced is increasing rapidly. People prefer platforms where they can access online rather than physical storage devices, so that the access to this increasing data is more efficient and secure. Cloud computing, which enables storage, backup and data control-management via remote internet, meets these needs of people. When the cloud is mentioned, it can be briefly called the transfer of computer resources to virtual networks and platforms. The content of data and applications that can be stored in the cloud may contain information that may have low security concerns, as well as very sensitive data (social security numbers, medical records, private personal information or government data). It is important to know the methods to be used to ensure the security of these data and applications, (Al-Hachemi, 2022). In this study, it is mentioned how to ensure the confidentiality, integrity and availability of the cloud with data replication. In order to help the content of the study, other articles on the subject were examined and data replication on platforms with cloud features and the protection of individuals or companies' shares, private information, applications and the benefits it provides to the user are shown.

Data replication is the backup of the data accumulated in the environment during the process, or a certain part of it, in more than one location, (Mansouri, Javidi, & Zade, 2021). It is the process of transferring all the transactions made by all users in the system to another source without causing any inconsistency. In this system, data moves according to the wishes of the person and two different users can perform their duties without interfering with each other's work. In short, data replication is the ability of data to move freely without creating confusion in the internet environment. In this way, all transactions are replicated and the update is performed simultaneously on all the replicated data.

Data replication is not a static backup of data. It ensures replication of transactions, such that backups are in a consistently updated state and synchronized with the source, (Miloudi, Yagoubi, & Bellounar, 2021). There are different methods of performing replication operations, depending on the specific availability requirements for the data. Problems with data replication can result from data transfer delays or service interruptions. Commercial data replication products attempt to mitigate business risk due to replication errors or failures.

There are various data replication tools used today. For example; Oracle GoldenGate is a comprehensive tool that enables data replication between both Oracle and non-Oracle data stores. Another example of real-time data replication, DBMoto, provides fast data transfer between databases.

Data replication ensures that data is securely protected in different environments. It provides a fast and accurate return on queries performed on the database. It allows authorized users to access the data. This increases usability in all transactions. High performance is provided. However, despite all these positive aspects, data replication can create complex structures by requiring additional storage areas because it copies a lot of data. For this reason, it may require more cost.

Rapidly increasing data and applications have increased the usage rate of cloud platforms a lot compared to previous years. The security of data stored in the cloud is important for many people. In this study, the importance of data replication for data security in cloud computing is emphasized. It also demonstrates how the three key elements of cloud security (availability, integrity and confidentiality) are ensured by data replication. In this study, data security methods have been shown with some definitions and examples, and it has been concluded that it would be beneficial for the individual or corporate environment to use cloud platforms to use these methods. Emphasizing that businesses providing cloud computing services and customers using this service should pay great attention to security for both parties, some methods are included.

RELATED WORKS

Within the scope of this study, different scientific publications on data replication in cloud computing in recent years have been examined and the results of these studies are given in detail below:

Based on the rapid development of big data and cloud technology in recent years, there has been an increasing demand to process and analyze data produced and stored in geographically dispersed data centers. However, collecting data and performing calculations in a single data center is becoming increasingly inefficient due to the limited network bandwidth between data centers and the data volume spread over different areas. Convolbo et al., with the DRASH (Data Replication Awake Timer) method they developed in their work, used data replication to prevent unnecessary data transfer in a job planning and increase overall system performance, (Convolbo *et al.*, 2016). As a result of the evaluations using simulations with realistic workloads, they found that the DRASH method outperforms other existing approaches. DRASH performed significantly better in average job completion time than other available methods. They also achieved further improvement under high data duplication factors.

Reliable access to data is the foundation of most information technology services. High availability, low operating cost and data consistency creates major problems in almost every data replication research. Usman et al. referred to a data replication strategy called semantic data replication (SDR) in their study. SDR aims at low cost high processing capabilities built on data semantics, coding schemes and efficient search algorithms, (Usman, Schadek, & Theel, 2017). SDR primarily takes advantage of the finite state space introduced by the encoding scheme for replicated objects. It also makes the replication strategy more efficient by using the previous information obtained from the finite state space. Leveraging the data encoding sketch has made a significant contribution to SDR as the encoding sketch runs fast in reads and writes. It also provides consistent access to the state of the replicated object for read operations.

When outsourcing data in the cloud information system, high security measures are required as it can be modified by illegal users or attackers. This can affect the performance of the cloud due to the longer data acquisition time. The time of data acquisition should be taken into account when implementing security measures. Salunkhe et al. sought to solve both problems by deploying them on cloud nodes. Cloud nodes only store a portion of the file that is split into multiple parts. In the study, cloud nodes are set at a certain distance that the attacker cannot follow the next node using the concept of T-coloring, (Salunkhe & Patil, 2016). File fragments are replicated onto cloud nodes to improve the retrieval time of file fragments. To increase the security standard, the fragmented file is encrypted before it is placed on the cloud node. An audit scheme is used that constantly monitors cloud nodes. In case of any damage, the control system regenerates the data. This system provides security and control of cloud data.

The traditional way to achieve high data availability in a structured P2P network is to replicate data items held in one node to neighboring nodes. However, in some heterogeneous structural P2P networks, neighboring nodes are always close to each other in location. Therefore, permanent loss of some data may be inevitable in case of some local disasters. Moreover, this traditional data replication strategy entails moving data when there are node ingress and egress in a complex Distributed Hash Tables (DHT) network. Wang et al. proposed a new data replication strategy for heterogeneous structural P2P networks. This has greatly reduced the complexity of not only maintaining large-scale local disaster data items, but also data migration whenever nodes enter and exit the network, that is, when new nodes are added to the system or when nodes leave the system, (Wang *et al.,* 2009).

Data duplication and synchronization techniques have recently attracted the attention of researchers working in this field. Data transferred during replication must be secure. The protocol is one of the ways to ensure security before sending information to an external copy site. When comparing the two existing protocol types, TCP and UDP, the UDP protocol type is claimed to be faster during data transfer than TCP. The main reason for this is that UDP does not use excessive confirmation messages. UDP is the preferred option when bandwidth is limited. In their study, Soyjaudah et al. discussed the reliability of the UDP protocol when measuring packets in sending packets of different lengths. It is desired to determine whether the UDP protocol can be used as a transfer mode during data replication. A series of tests have been performed and the Maximum Transmission Unit (CPU) size has been adjusted to have minimal packet loss. As a result, the authors have obtained the information that the UDP protocol with the size of 1150 bytes can be used as a transport mode for data centers, (Soyjaudah, Catherine, & Coonjah, 2016).

Mansouri developed an adaptive replication strategy model in cloud computing in order to increase data availability, provide fast data processing time and reliability, (Mansouri, 2016). In the author's work, if all the replicated data and requests are correct and distributed, the replication process realizes the successful processing time in cloud computing. This convenient processing time is however much more complex for large-scale, dynamic and virtualized data centers. For this reason, in the study, cost-effective replication process and adaptive data replication strategy that will minimize application and work times has been proposed for very large data centers. The proposed model consists of five stages such as average service time, calculation of failure probability, load variance, delay and storage usage. In the study, data replication has been done in a logical way and a recommendation model has been presented that will enable the replacement of newly created copies depending on the use of the files. Using this model CloudSim simulator, the number of accesses is evaluated according to the replication size and the results are presented. This proposed model was compared with the ARS, DRSP, CIR and CDRM algorithms used in the literature in the simulation environment, and the results were interpreted according to the criteria of average response time, effective network usage, storage usage, replication frequency and load variance.

Data replication algorithms are divided into static and dynamic. In static replication, replication is predetermined and well defined. In dynamic replication, on the other hand, the replication process is automatically identified and duplicates are automatically deleted according to changing access patterns. Both of these data replication algorithms are classified by grouping them into distributed and centralized algorithms. Sun et al. developed a dynamic data replication model in order to ensure data security and data availability among users in cloud computing environments. By increasing the usability, this model reduces the false copying process and error rate that occurs during data replication, thus ensuring a highly effective and efficient interaction between users. In the study, it was aimed to reduce the waiting time of the users and to increase the data access speed with data replication, (Sun *et al.,* 2012). Duplications created on data centers with dynamic data replication are mathematically formulated. Execution time and cloud computing bandwidth are minimized. The trigger times of missing copies and duplication processes were calculated. Copies are conveniently placed within the data nodes, and when a certain threshold value is passed, data replication operations are triggered. In addition, the applicability of this study is presented with an experimental study and the obtained data are shown comparatively.

Lin et al. have proposed a QoS (different quality of service) based data replication model and minimum-cost maximum-flow (MCMF) models in order to scale the increasing data in cloud computing and to prevent changes in the errors that occur in the data. The main idea behind this model is intuitive QoS-based replication. In addition, this study has been developed to solve the flow problem in networks for systems with very dense data. With this proposed greedy algorithm, data replication cost is reduced and QoS-based data replication is performed securely without causing data loss. With the MCMF algorithm used in this study, the polynomial analysis time and the computation time of data replication are reduced. In addition, since cloud computing systems contain many nodes, node aggregation techniques have been proposed to reduce these nodes and increase performance, (Lin, Chen, & Chang, 2013). QoS has increased the heterogeneity of devices in cloud computing for secure and accurate data replication. Data replication compatible with QoS has been taken into account. The MCMF algorithm is proposed to best solve the QADR problem. The computational complexity that occurs during data replication is tried to be solved. Node combinations are used for very large data.

CLOUD COMPUTING

Cloud computing is explained as a service model used for information technologies and services, which requires low-scale management and can be accessed flexibly when needed, (Tamimi, Dawood, & Sadaqa, 2019) (Information Week, 2013). To make a general definition on the basis of this definition, cloud computing is based on the principle of using the required storage areas and processing unit power as much as needed, as well as allowing remote access of data in a controlled manner, where infrastructure and applications are processed independently from each other, and capacity usage is flexible. It is a type of informatics where, thanks to its structure, it can be increased or decreased rapidly, the use of resources can be easily controlled and reported. Cloud computing resources are shown in Figure 1. Access is provided from many devices and applications such as computers, laptops, smartphones, servers, etc. with internet connection.

Figure 1. Cloud computing source

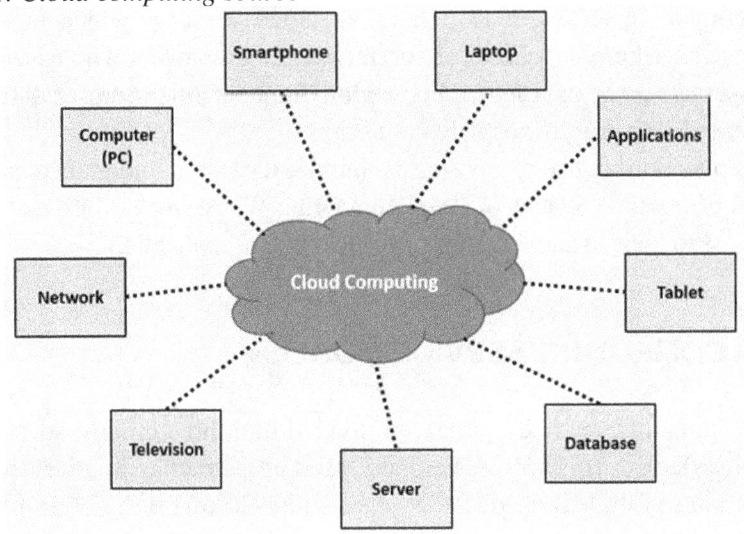

In order to conserve resources, reduce costs and maintain efficiency, cloud service providers often store the data of multiple customers on the same server without separating them, (Haghighat *et al.,* 2015). A user's private data may be viewed by other users. Therefore, to handle such vulnerabilities, cloud service providers must provide appropriate data isolation and logical storage separation, (Srivastava & Khan, 2018).

In order to ensure the security of data in cloud computing, it is important to note that the effective security measure in the data security part of the study covers some or all of the three categories (accessibility, integrity and confidentiality). For example, encryption prevents unauthorized access and ultimately ensures the confidentiality, availability and integrity of data. Similarly, backups mostly define data integrity and firewalls used only cover privacy and access controllability, (Tahirkheli *et al.,* 2021) (Yu *et al.,* 2010) .

Security concerns associated with cloud computing; It can be classified as security problems that cloud service providers, customers using cloud platforms, organizations that host applications or store data in the cloud may encounter, (Shirgaonkar *et al.,* 2022). The cloud service provider must be able to assure the customer that its infrastructure is secure and that its customers' stored data and applications are protected. Customers, on the other hand, need to use strong passwords and authentication, taking measures to strengthen their data and applications, (Cai *et al.,* 2019).

When an organization or individual chooses to store data or store applications in the public cloud, they lose physical access to the servers that host their information. For these reasons, sensitive data may be at risk from attacks. According to the

Cloud Security Alliance (2010) report, insider attacks are one of the biggest threats in cloud computing, (NIST, 2013). Therefore, cloud service providers must ensure that extensive background checks are performed for employees who have physical access to servers in the data center. In addition, frequent monitoring of data centers is recommended to prevent suspicious activity.

Data replication has been proposed to minimize the loss of important data of users as a result of possible attacks in cloud computing. Thus, in case of data invasion, users' access to their original data is provided by data replication.

CLOUD COMPUTING SERVICE MODELS

Cloud computing service models are divided into three groups: software as a service (SaaS), platform as a service (PaaS), and infrastructure as a service (IaaS). The definitions of these three different service models are briefly given below:

- **Software As A Services (SaaS)**: Users can access the data and applications they want over the internet without the need for any additional application or software. Examples of this are e-mail services, ERP applications.
- **Platform As A Services (PaaS):** In this service model, users can run applications they create. By renting a Java platform on Windows, users can create Java applications. In short, with this service model, many users can develop and present applications on the same project. This service model includes the entire technological infrastructure.
- **Infrastructure As A Services (IaaS):** Users provide their own network equipment, processors and applications through physical servers that are available. Users rent these physical servers according to their wishes and make the payment as much as they want. Users can use this service model in applications that require huge processor performance, such as big data applications. Users retain the right to access the applications and operating system on these physical servers. All updates are the responsibility of the user.

Cloud computing service models are the combination of some services by service providers according to the needs of the customers. Suggesting a suitable cloud service model for that user is of great importance for the success of the services of the people who will use the cloud. When the traditional information technology (Traditional IT) concept and cloud technology service models are compared, they all have different authorizations and shares. Figure 2 shows which services are managed by whom.

Figure 2. Cloud computing service models

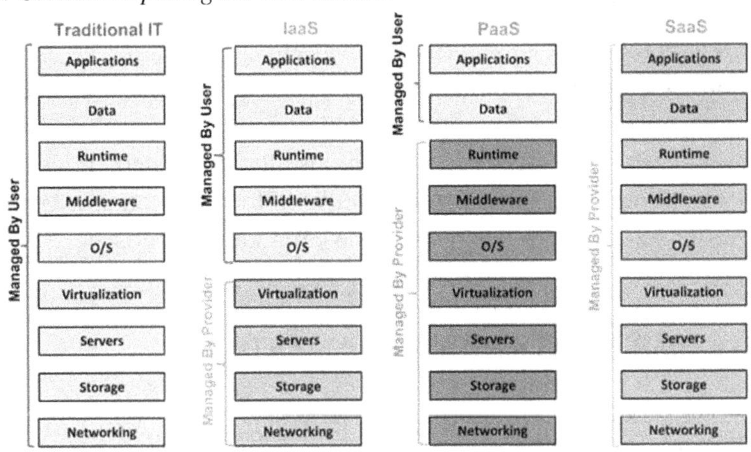

CLOUD COMPUTING INSTALLATION MODELS

Cloud services during the installation of cloud platforms; It can be classified into four groups as Public Cloud, Private Cloud, Hybrid Cloud and Community Cloud.

Public Cloud: This cloud deployment model is delivered and managed to customers through servers in internet networks. In addition, this installation model includes the basic structure of the cloud system. It is for all users and users pay as much as they use. Cloud services are provided by resources or services connected to a data center. Although institutions and organizations do not transfer their applications to the public cloud due to security vulnerabilities, users can make their applications more usable thanks to the public cloud. For example, institutions and organizations can adapt applications such as data that cannot be kept confidential, web, e-mail, virtual document sharing in the public cloud more easily. For such reasons, public cloud has advantages such as ease of use, flexibility, scalability, cost and reliability.

Private Cloud: This cloud model is built on data centers housed within the scope of a business or organization. It is a very old and frequently used classic model. Institutions undertake all operations, from infrastructure to software, to maintenance and management of systems. Private cloud provides more control, flexibility and energy efficiency than other cloud models. But aside from these benefits, it doesn't scale as well as the public cloud model.

Hybrid Cloud: Hybrid Cloud; It uses public and private cloud options together. In order for this model to be successful, the transfer of applications must have a management strategy. Examples of this cloud type are configuration management, budgeting, security, change display, and error catching. The advantages of hybrid clouds are flexibility, scalability, security and cost efficiency. The disadvantages are networking problems and security compatibility.

Community Cloud: The community cloud is the cloud model that caters to users with common needs, and customers and organizations jointly use their data sources, goals, and policies. It includes two or more installation models. It also shares IT resources among users and makes them available for common use. For example, the E-Government application is built on the community cloud.

CLOUD COMPUTING AND VIRTUALIZATION

When it comes to cloud computing, the first concept that comes to mind is the concept of virtualization. Virtualization concept; It is called leaving the physical structure to virtual machines. In other words, creating a virtual system with the simulation method in the hypervisor or Linux phase of a physical structure is called virtualization.

The name of the software used to create a virtual system and to increase the functionality of the hardware is called Hypervisor. The hypervisor enables the aggregation of multiple virtual machines on a single piece of hardware in terms of task. IBM first developed native hypervisors in the 1960s.

Virtualization categories can be listed as six items as follows:

1. Network Virtualization: It allows working with less hardware and more virtual network setup. It enables the creation of virtual networks by establishing bridges between systems. Such networks can provide end-to-end service.
2. Server Virtualization: It is the most commonly used virtualization method. It is intended to aggregate multiple servers on only one physical server.
3. Desktop Virtualization: It enables computers to be virtualized so that users can connect with remote access. The computer is virtualized and the user can access this server via a network.
4. Application Virtualization: Application virtualization allows applications to run as if they were installed on the device by running them through the server layer without the need to install them on devices.
5. Memory Virtualization: Memory virtualization allows networked and therefore distributed servers to share a memory pool to overcome physical memory limitations, a common bottleneck in software performance.

6. Storage Virtualization: Storage virtualization is performed by combining multiple data storage devices and managing them from a common management interface. Thanks to this common interface, the management factor is facilitated and system complexity is reduced. Thus, special powers are given to individuals.

DATA REPLICATION

Companies have to ensure the security of customer data in order to determine the customer portfolio and to meet the needs of the customers. In particular, the inappropriate use of data, the ignorance of individuals about information security threats, the weakness of risk taking and the emergence of information security risks that can be considered difficult to compensate. Confidentiality, integrity and accessibility are the basic concepts that need to be emphasized in order to ensure security in cloud computing, (Alimjon, 2022).

There are too many security threats associated with data services to be stored and backed up in the cloud. This includes traditional threats and non-traditional threats. Traditional threats include: network eavesdropping, illegal invasion and denial of service attacks, as well as specific cloud computing threats such as side-channel attacks, virtualization vulnerabilities, and abuse of cloud services. The most widely used technique to ensure data security in cloud technologies is data replication, (Mealha *et al.,* 2019).

Data replication, which can be defined as the process of copying data from a central database, means keeping data in more than one location. In this system, data is stored the same in all locations without any inconsistency. In data replication, different systems are preferred according to the needs of the institutions. For example, a system that many people want to access may not be able to handle this load. In this case, the data copied by data replication is shared on different servers, thus increasing both speed and data accessibility, (Boru *et al.,* 2015). Data in one center can be copied or reproduced in another database. All users see data the same way. Or, the user who updates the data in one center sees the data in the other center in the same way. There is no inconsistency in the data. Operations such as editing and deletion performed on records in a replicated database are also reflected in other databases. For this reason, solutions such as temporary deletion are used in database replication applications. Soft deletion means marking data as deleted so that it can be restored if needed. Such data is not truly deleted and continues to be left in the database. Only administrators can see the temporarily deleted data. Since all deleted data will continue to be stored in the database in this method, the system in question may create a serious data load in the long run and therefore server costs due to the need for additional storage unit. Data replication operations performed in databases are shown in Figure 3. The data owned by more than one user is saved through a single server and then duplicated and stored in multiple databases. Thus, in case of data loss that users may experience in the future, a solution is produced for their problems thanks to the copied databases.

Figure 3. Data replication

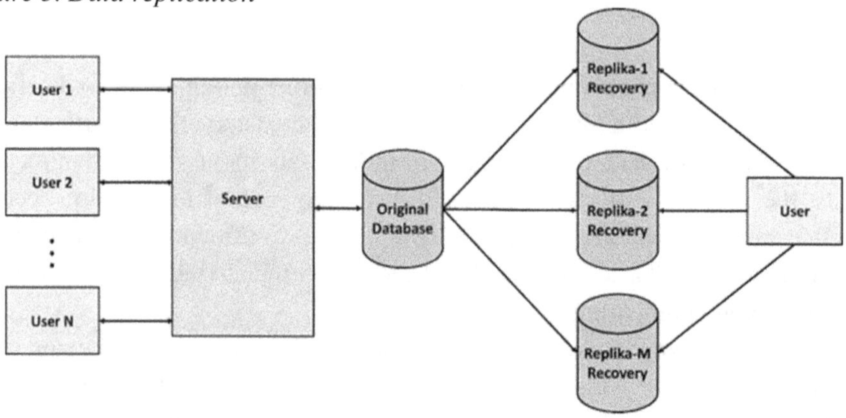

Data is kept in multiple sources, copied. A failure in the central database does not cause data loss. Multiple users can operate on the same data. With database replication, multiple users can work with the same data over databases. Thus, it becomes possible to carry out the work of a change to be made in the central database in other databases. The data on which the transaction is made is seen in an updated form in the database. Thus, secure data sharing is ensured, (Silva, Holanda, & Araujo, 2016).

CLOUD COMPUTING SECURITY MODELS

Data security elements in cloud computing are shown in Figure 4. These security elements include: Data protection, privacy, accessibility and access control, integrity, identity management, physical security, personnel security, cloud application/ network layer, and penetration testing and penetration testing.

Figure 4. Cloud computing security

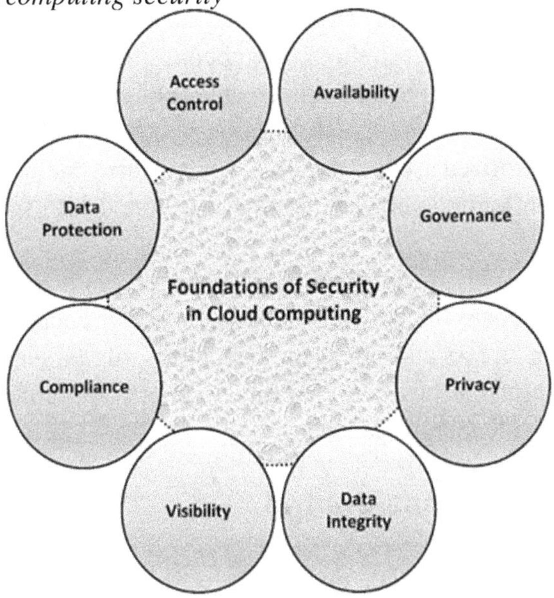

Data Protection: The processing of data has accelerated with the developments in application software and internet. Inappropriate use of these developments that make people's life easier, the fact that individuals do not have enough information about information security threats, etc. have brought about problems related to data security. The security of digital data is gaining importance today in order to protect data in electronic environment such as copyrights and ethics, privacy, security and encryption. Information security was defined as three different concepts by ISACA in 2009; It is shown as ensuring the confidentiality, integrity and accessibility of information at any time. These defined privacy, integrity and accessibility issues are the basic concepts that should be emphasized in order to ensure security in cloud computing. In addition to network eavesdropping, illegal invasion and denial of service attacks, there are certain cloud computing threats such as side-channel attacks, virtualization vulnerabilities, and abuse of cloud services. To mitigate these threats, security controls are generally followed by the confidentiality, integrity and availability specified by ISACA above.

Privacy

Data privacy defines the property that data content is not made available or disclosed to undesired users. The concept of privacy means that sensitive and confidential data should be kept confidential to users who are not authorized to access.

Data from an external source is stored in a cloud and beyond the direct control of its owners. Only authorized users can access sensitive data, while others, including CSPs (Cloud Solution Providers), should not obtain any information about the data. However, data owners expect to take full advantage of cloud data services, such as data searching, data computing, and data sharing, without leaking data content to CSPs or other unauthorized users. An example of a security audit involving privacy is encryption so that only authorized users can access data, (Younis, Kifayat, & Merabti, 2014).

Providers are required to ensure that all critical data (eg citizenship information, military information, card information, etc.) is masked or encrypted and that only authorized users can access all of the data. In addition, digital identity information must be protected, such as any data that the cloud provider collects or generates about the customer calendar in the cloud.

Accessibility and Access Control

Accessibility means that a data owner can restrict access to their data as they wish, in order to externally participate in the cloud system. Accessibility can also be referred to as usability. Availability and access control ensure that the right people are given the appropriate amount of permissions. While legitimate users can be authorized by the data owner to access the data, other people cannot gain unauthorized access to the data as they are not authorized to access them. However, applying granular access control to external data is often requested by individuals, ie different users need to be offered different access privileges according to different pieces of data. The access authorization phase only needs to be controlled by the original owner of the data in untrusted cloud environments. Unauthorized access should be strictly prohibited, but in some cases, access for users' use should be allowed and monitored at the same time by providing administrative savings, (Younis, Kifayat, & Merabti, 2014).

Integrity

Data integrity requires ensuring the accuracy and completeness of data. Owners of data or applications always want their data to be stored accurately and reliably in a cloud. This means that data should not be accessed, altered, intentionally deleted, or maliciously generated. If any undesired operation corrupts or deletes data, the cloud service owner should be able to detect it. If some of the external data is corrupted or lost, the data should still be retrieved by the users. Effective integrity security controls go beyond malicious intent and also protect data from unintentional changes. An example of an integrity-encompassing security audit is the automatic backup of data.

Identity Management

Every organization needs to have its own identity management system to control access to information and computing resources. In identity management, cloud providers integrate the customer's identity management system into their infrastructure or provide their own identity management system using unified identity, SSO (Single Sign-On) technology or a biometric-based identification system, (Charanya & Aramudhan, 2016). SSO refers to a user's ability to log in with a single user ID and password to access more than one system they need. Cloud identity provides the user with cloud-based and inter-enterprise biometric identification that protects their privacy. It matches the confidential information given by the users with their biometric data and then stores it in an encrypted manner. By using a searchable encryption technique, biometric identification is performed in the encrypted area to ensure that the cloud service provider or potential data attackers do not access any sensitive data or even the content of individual queries, (Kılıç, 2017).

Physical Security

Cloud service providers (Amazon, Azure, Oracle, IBM etc.) protect IT hardware (servers, routers, cables, etc.) from unauthorized access, interference, theft, fires, flooding, etc. and ensures that essential supplies (such as electricity) are robust enough to minimize the possibility of outages. This is normally achieved by servicing cloud applications from professionally designated, designed, built, managed, monitored and maintained data centers,m (Mell & Grance, 2011).

Personnel Security

Various data security concerns regarding information technology and other employees associated with cloud services are addressed through pre- and post-employment activities such as the security screening process, potential recruits, security awareness, training programs, and proactive methods.

Cloud Application/Network Layer and Penetration Testing

In short, penetration testing is to attack the system in order to understand the existence of any problem in the system. This is also called a penetration test. What is important when performing penetration testing is the difference between application and network layer testing. It is very important to understand what is being asked when performing the test. Network layer testing refers to tests involving interconnected systems throughout the local network, as well as internal or external connections. Often the vulnerable party is the employee and social engineering attacks are carried out.

Penetration Test

Penetration testing is the stage of performing attacker security tests to find security weaknesses in a system, service or computer network. Because the cloud platform is a shared environment with multiple businesses leasing services, step-by-step penetration test participation rules must be followed. Scanning and penetration testing from inside or outside the cloud must be authorized by the cloud provider. If the aforementioned usage policies are violated, this will result in the complete termination of the cloud service, (Meghanathan, 2013).

CONCLUSION

As a result of the widespread use of the Internet and the rapid increase in information, the importance of information technologies has increased. The basis of the concept of cloud computing, which is one of the information technology concepts that has been heard a lot recently, is based on the internet. One of the biggest advantages of using the cloud is that the device performance and features of the users who will access the cloud are not important. The person can connect to the cloud platform at any time he wants and from any location, provided that he has internet access. At the beginning of its advantages is to connect to the internet from anywhere, but integration with the internet also brings a disadvantage. If the user does not have internet access, they will not be able to access the cloud platform.

It is necessary to take some security measures to protect the data and applications transferred to the cloud platform and to prevent unwanted situations. Since cloud platforms work with a system open to internet access, they are open to attacks that may come from the internet. While ensuring the security of transferred and stored data, the important point is not only to protect the data and applications against external attacks, but also to ensure the integrity of the data, to prevent unwanted data loss, and to reach the desired response in the system in terms of data security.

Institutions and companies have turned to cloud technologies in order to increase business continuity and obtain reliable and efficient resources and have grown rapidly. However, in proportion to this growth, some problems such as data breaches and data leakage have arisen due to the continuous use of cloud technologies. In order to prevent these possible disaster scenarios, replication services have emerged, which have made significant progress in establishing the systemic infrastructure. This replication process is performed by storing data on remote virtual servers at certain time intervals. Replication services, which are an ideal solution for institutions, also reduce the need for hardware and labor and improve the performance of institutions. The fact that the replication service can be performed at short intervals, fast action in recovery scenarios and other features make cloud replication services an important cloud computing service in the digital age.

REFERENCES

Alimjon, D. (2022). Problems of data replication in distribution systems. *ACADEMICIA: An International Multidisciplinary Research Journal, 12*(5), 1119–1128. DOI: 10.5958/2249-7137.2022.00585.7

Boru, D., Kliazovich, D., Granelli, F., Bouvry, P., & Zomaya, A. Y. (2015). Energy-efficient data replication in cloud computing datacenters. *Cluster Computing, 18*(1), 385–402. DOI: 10.1007/s10586-014-0404-x

Cai, F., Zhu, N., He, J., Mu, P., Li, W., & Yu, Y. (2019). Survey of access control models and technologies for cloud computing. *Cluster Computing, 22*(3), 6111–6122. DOI: 10.1007/s10586-018-1850-7

Charanya, R., & Aramudhan, M. (2016, February). Survey on access control issues in cloud computing. In *2016 International Conference on Emerging Trends in Engineering, Technology and Science (ICETETS)* (pp. 1-4). IEEE.

Cloud, H. (2011). The nist definition of cloud computing. National institute of science and technology, special publication, 800(2011), 145.

Convolbo, M. W., Chou, J., Lu, S., & Chung, Y. C. (2016, December). DRASH: A data replication-aware scheduler in geo-distributed data centers. In *2016 IEEE International Conference on Cloud Computing Technology and Science (CloudCom)* (pp. 302-309). IEEE.

da Silva, G. H. G., Holanda, M., & Araujo, A. (2016, June). Data replication policy in a cloud computing environment. In 2016 11th Iberian conference on information systems and technologies (CISTI) (pp. 1-6). IEEE.

Haghighat, M., Zonouz, S., & Abdel-Mottaleb, M. (2015, November). CloudID: Trustworthy cloud-based and cross-enterprise biometric identification. *Expert Systems with Applications, 42*(21), 7905–7916. DOI: 10.1016/j.eswa.2015.06.025

Kılıç, H. (2017). *Kamuda Bulut Bilişim Kullanımına Yönelik Risk Analizi ve Yönetimi, Uzmanlık Tezi, (yayımlanmamış)*. Çevre ve Şehircilik Bakanlığı.

Lin, J. W., Chen, C. H., & Chang, J. M. (2013). QoS-aware data replication for data-intensive applications in cloud computing systems. *IEEE Transactions on Cloud Computing, 1*(1), 101–115. DOI: 10.1109/TCC.2013.1

Mansouri, N. (2016). Adaptive data replication strategy in cloud computing for performance improvement. *Frontiers of Computer Science, 10*(5), 925–935. DOI: 10.1007/s11704-016-5182-6

Mansouri, N., Javidi, M. M., & Zade, B. M. H. (2021). Hierarchical data replication strategy to improve performance in cloud computing. *Frontiers of Computer Science, 15*(2), 1–17. DOI: 10.1007/s11704-019-9099-8

Mealha, D., Preguiça, N., Gomes, M. C., & Leitão, J. (2019, March). Data replication on the cloud/edge. In *Proceedings of the 6th Workshop on Principles and Practice of Consistency for Distributed Data* (pp. 1-7).

Meghanathan, N. (2013). Review of access control models for cloud computing. *Computer Science & Information Science, 3*(1), 77–85. DOI: 10.5121/csit.2013.3508

Miloudi, I. E., Yagoubi, B., & Bellounar, F. Z. (2021, October). A Survey of Dynamic Replication Strategies in Cloud Computing Systems. In *2021 International Conference on Networking and Advanced Systems (ICNAS)* (pp. 1-6). IEEE. DOI: 10.1109/ICNAS53565.2021.9628963

NIST. (2013). *Cloud Computing Standards Roadmap*. National Institue of Standards and Tecnology Special Publication.

Salunkhe, S. D., & Patil, D. (2016, August). Division and replication for data with public auditing scheme for cloud storage. In *2016 International Conference on Computing Communication Control and automation (ICCUBEA)* (pp. 1-5). IEEE.

Shirgaonkar, M., Shinde, A., Sankpal, P., & Gutte, V. (2022, March). Cloud computing security using cryptographic algorithms. In 2022 6th International Conference on Computing Methodologies and Communication (ICCMC) (pp. 31-37). IEEE.

Soyjaudah, K. M. S., Catherine, P. C., & Coonjah, I. (2016, April). Evaluation of UDP tunnel for data replication in data centers and cloud environment. In 2016 international conference on computing, communication and automation (ICCCA) (pp. 1217-1221). IEEE.

Srivastava, P., & Khan, R. (2018). A review paper on cloud computing. *International Journal of Advanced Research in Computer Science and Software Engineering, 8*(6), 17–20. DOI: 10.23956/ijarcsse.v8i6.711

Sun, D. W., Chang, G. R., Gao, S., Jin, L. Z., & Wang, X. W. (2012). Modeling a dynamic data replication strategy to increase system availability in cloud computing environments. *Journal of Computer Science and Technology, 27*(2), 256–272. DOI: 10.1007/s11390-012-1221-4

Tahirkheli, A. I., Shiraz, M., Hayat, B., Idrees, M., Sajid, A., Ullah, R., Ayub, N., & Kim, K. I. (2021). A survey on modern cloud computing security over smart city networks: Threats, vulnerabilities, consequences, countermeasures, and challenges. *Electronics (Basel), 10*(15), 1811. DOI: 10.3390/electronics10151811

Tamimi, A. A., Dawood, R., & Sadaqa, L. (2019, April). Disaster recovery techniques in cloud computing. In *2019 IEEE Jordan International Joint Conference on Electrical Engineering and Information Technology (JEEIT)* (pp. 845-850). IEEE. DOI: 10.1109/JEEIT.2019.8717450

Usman, A., Schadek, R., & Theel, O. (2017, January). A Novel Highly Available Data Replication Strategy exploiting Data Semantics, Coding Techniques and Prior At-Hand Knowledge. In 2017 IEEE 22nd Pacific Rim International Symposium on Dependable Computing (PRDC) (pp. 301-310). IEEE.

Wang, Y., Qiu, X., Zhang, C., Mi, W., Li, L., & Ji, Y. (2009, September). Effective data replication in heterogeneous structured P2P networks. In 2009 5th International Conference on Wireless Communications, Networking and Mobile Computing (pp. 1-4). IEEE.

Younis, Y. A., Kifayat, K., & Merabti, M. (2014). An access control model for cloud computing. *Journal of Information Security and Applications*, *19*(1), 45–60. DOI: 10.1016/j.jisa.2014.04.003

Yu, S., Wang, C., Ren, K., & Lou, W. (2010, March). *Achieving secure, scalable, and fine-grained data access control in cloud computing. In 2010 Proceedings IEEE INFOCOM*. Ieee.

Chapter 15
Best Practices, Ethical Challenges, and Regulatory Frameworks for AI Integration in Banking:
Navigating the Future

R. Vettriselvan
https://orcid.org/0000-0002-1324-136X
AMET University, India

Palanivel Rathinasabapathi Velmurugan
https://orcid.org/0000-0002-0395-9060
Berlin School of Business and Innovation, Germany

Jimmy Carter Regins
https://orcid.org/0009-0005-2669-3727
Bishop Heber College, India

S. Uma Maheswari
Sathyabama Institute of Science and Technology, India

R. Joyce
Sathyabama Institute of Science and Technology, India

ABSTRACT

This chapter explores the transformative impact of artificial intelligence (AI) and

DOI: 10.4018/979-8-3693-9356-7.ch015

cloud-native software on the banking sector. It examines how AI enhances customer service, fraud detection, and risk management through technologies like virtual assistants and predictive analytics. However, these advancements introduce ethical challenges, including data privacy concerns, algorithmic bias, and the need for transparency in AI decision-making. The chapter reviews relevant regulations, such as the General Data Protection Regulation (GDPR) and the California Consumer Privacy Act (CCPA), and offers strategies for compliance and ethical AI integration. Through case studies, it highlights successful implementations of AI in banking, illustrating effective management of ethical and regulatory issues. The chapter concludes with a look at future trends and proactive strategies to address emerging ethical and regulatory challenges, aiming to guide stakeholders in balancing innovation with ethical practices in the evolving landscape of banking technology.

INTRODUCTION

The rapid evolution of artificial intelligence (AI) and cloud-native technologies is reshaping industries across the globe, with the banking sector standing out as a key example of this transformative shift. AI and cloud-native software are not only redefining how banks operate but are also setting new benchmarks for operational efficiency, customer experience, and innovation. These advancements enable banks to streamline processes, improve decision-making through data-driven insights, and offer personalized services at scale, creating a more agile and competitive landscape. However, alongside these technological breakthroughs, there are substantial ethical challenges that must be addressed. The widespread adoption of AI in banking, for instance, raises critical concerns around data privacy, algorithmic transparency, and fairness in decision-making. As banks increasingly rely on AI systems to make decisions—ranging from credit scoring to fraud detection the risk of bias in algorithms, unintended discrimination, and lack of accountability becomes more pronounced. Similarly, as cloud-native technologies enable vast data storage and processing capabilities, the potential for breaches of personal data and unauthorized access becomes a pressing issue. To ensure that AI and cloud-native systems are implemented responsibly, it is crucial to establish frameworks that address these ethical concerns. Banks must prioritize transparency in AI model development, ensuring that the decisions made by algorithms can be understood and explained. Additionally, mechanisms to mitigate biases in data and algorithms should be integral to the design and deployment of AI systems, alongside robust security measures to protect sensitive customer information. By tackling these ethical issues head-on, banks can not only leverage the full potential of AI and cloud-native technologies but also foster greater trust with customers and regulators alike, ensuring a future where innovation and responsibility go hand in hand.

OVERVIEW OF AI AND CLOUD-NATIVE SOFTWARE IN THE BANKING SECTOR

Definition and Scope of AI and Cloud-Native Technologies

Artificial Intelligence (AI) refers to the simulation of human intelligence in machines designed to think, learn, and perform tasks that typically require human intelligence (Chen & Asch, 2020). In the banking sector, AI encompasses a wide range of applications, including machine learning, natural language processing, and robotics. These technologies enable banks to analyze vast amounts of data, automate processes, and provide personalized services to customers. For instance, AI-driven chatbots can handle customer inquiries in real time, while machine learning algorithms can detect fraudulent transactions by identifying unusual patterns in financial data (Esteva et al., 2017). Cloud-native software, on the other hand, is designed to leverage the scalability, flexibility, and resilience of cloud computing environments. Cloud-native applications are built and deployed in a way that allows them to fully exploit cloud infrastructure capabilities, such as elastic scaling and micro services architecture (Topol, 2019). In banking, cloud-native solutions enable financial institutions to rapidly deploy and scale applications, optimize their IT operations, and enhance their data management capabilities. This technological shift supports the creation of innovative financial products and services, facilitates data-driven decision-making, and improves operational efficiency (Fitzgerald, 2018).

Current Trends and Adoption in Banking

The integration of AI and cloud-native technologies into the banking sector has been accelerating, driven by the need for enhanced operational efficiency and improved customer experiences. Banks are increasingly adopting AI for a variety of functions, including customer service automation, risk management, and personalized financial advice. AI-powered chatbots and virtual assistants are becoming commonplace in customer service, providing instant support and reducing the need for human intervention (Rajkomar, Dean, & Kohane, 2018). Additionally, AI algorithms are used for predictive analytics, helping banks anticipate customer needs and offer tailored financial products (Chen & Asch, 2020). Cloud-native technologies are also playing a crucial role in the digital transformation of banking. Financial institutions are migrating their legacy systems to cloud platforms to achieve greater agility and scalability (Thiruvasagam, G., & Vettriselvan, R. 2021). This shift allows banks to quickly adapt to market changes, deploy new applications faster, and leverage advanced data analytics capabilities (Wang, Casalino, & Khullar, 2017). Furthermore, the use of cloud-native technologies facilitates seamless integration with third-party services, enabling banks to offer a wider range of digital products and services to their customers (Kellermann & Jones, 2013).

IMPORTANCE OF ADDRESSING ETHICS ALONGSIDE INNOVATION

The Intersection of Technology and Ethical Considerations

As AI and cloud-native technologies continue to advance, it is essential to address the ethical implications that arise from their deployment. The intersection of technology and ethics in banking involves several critical considerations, including data privacy, algorithmic bias, and transparency. Data privacy is a major concern, as banks handle sensitive customer information that must be protected from unauthorized access and misuse (Ginsburg & Phillips, 2018). The implementation of AI systems that process large volumes of personal data requires robust security measures and compliance with data protection regulations (Jha, 2018). Algorithmic bias is another significant ethical issue. AI systems are trained on historical data, which may contain inherent biases that can be perpetuated and even amplified by algorithms (Snyder, Kircher, & Wylie, 2019). In the banking sector, biased algorithms can lead to discriminatory practices in credit scoring, loan approvals, and other financial services. Ensuring fairness and mitigating bias in AI models is crucial to maintaining equitable treatment of all customers (Banaee, Mahmood, & Cook, 2013). Transparency in AI decision-making processes is also vital for ethical governance. AI systems often operate as "black boxes," making it challenging to understand how decisions are made and to hold systems accountable for their outcomes (Dorsey & Topol, 2016). Providing transparency in AI operations and decision-making can help build trust with customers and regulatory bodies, ensuring that AI technologies are used responsibly and ethically (Shortliffe & Cimino, 2013).

Rationale for Focusing on Ethics in the Context of Banking Innovations

The rationale for focusing on ethics in the context of banking innovations is multifaceted. First, ethical considerations are critical to maintaining customer trust and confidence in financial institutions. As banks adopt AI and cloud-native technologies, they must demonstrate a commitment to ethical practices to foster trust and ensure that customers' rights are respected. This trust is essential for the successful implementation of new technologies and for maintaining long-term customer relationships (Ginsburg & Phillips, 2018). Second, addressing ethical challenges proactively can help banks avoid regulatory pitfalls and legal risks. Regulatory bodies are increasingly scrutinizing the use of AI and data-driven technologies, and non-compliance with data protection laws and ethical standards can result in significant penalties and reputational damage (Vest, 2010). By prioritizing ethics and implementing robust governance frameworks, banks can navigate regulatory requirements effectively and mitigate potential risks (Wang et al., 2017). Finally, ethical considerations are integral to the sustainable development of AI technologies. As AI continues to evolve, it is essential to ensure that innovations are developed and deployed in ways that benefit society as a whole. By addressing ethical issues and promoting responsible AI practices, banks can contribute to the broader goal of advancing technology while upholding fundamental ethical principles (Zhang, Wang, & Zhang, 2018). The integration of AI and cloud-native software in banking represents a significant technological advancement with the potential to transform the industry. However, it is crucial to address the ethical implications associated with these technologies to ensure responsible and equitable implementation. By focusing on data privacy, algorithmic bias, and transparency, banks can leverage AI and cloud-native technologies while maintaining ethical standards and building trust with customers and regulators.

The Impact of AI on Banking

Artificial Intelligence (AI) is revolutionizing the banking industry by introducing innovative solutions that significantly enhance operational efficiency, customer service, and risk management. From AI-driven chatbots to advanced predictive analytics, the applications of AI in banking are transforming traditional banking practices and setting new standards for how financial institutions interact with customers and manage their operations.

Transformative Applications of AI

Enhancements in Customer Service

AI has notably transformed customer service in the banking sector through the introduction of AI-driven chatbots and personalized banking experiences. Chatbots, powered by natural language processing (NLP) and machine learning algorithms, are capable of handling a wide range of customer inquiries in real time. These chatbots provide instant responses to common questions, such as account balance queries or transaction details, thereby reducing the need for human intervention and significantly improving response times (Fitzgerald, 2018). Personalized banking experiences are another key benefit of AI in customer service. AI systems analyze customer data to provide tailored recommendations and services. For example, AI algorithms can suggest personalized financial products based on a customer's transaction history, spending patterns, and financial goals. This level of personalization enhances customer satisfaction and engagement by offering relevant solutions that meet individual needs (Chen & Asch, 2020).

Improvements in Fraud Detection

AI has also made substantial advancements in fraud detection through the use of predictive analytics and anomaly detection techniques. Traditional fraud detection systems often rely on predefined rules and manual oversight, which can be slow and prone to errors. In contrast, AI-powered systems leverage machine learning models to analyze vast amounts of transactional data and identify patterns that may indicate fraudulent activity (Rajkomar, Dean, & Kohane, 2018). Predictive analytics uses historical data to forecast potential fraud risks and detect anomalies in real time. For example, machine learning algorithms can flag unusual transaction behaviors, such as large transactions from new locations or rapid changes in spending patterns, which may signal potential fraud. This proactive approach allows banks to respond quickly to suspicious activities and minimize financial losses (Esteva et al., 2017).

Advancements in Risk Assessment

AI is also enhancing risk assessment processes within the banking sector. Automated credit scoring systems, powered by AI, evaluate a customer's creditworthiness by analyzing a wide range of data points, including credit history, income, and spending behavior. This automation improves the accuracy and efficiency of credit evaluations, enabling banks to make more informed lending decisions (Ginsburg & Phillips, 2018). Moreover, AI-driven risk management tools provide banks with advanced analytics capabilities to assess and mitigate various types of financial risks. For example, AI models can predict market fluctuations, evaluate the impact of economic changes on loan portfolios, and identify potential credit risks. These tools enable banks to proactively manage risks and develop strategies to protect their assets and maintain financial stability (Wang, Casalino, & Khullar, 2017).

BENEFITS AND EFFICIENCIES GAINED THROUGH AI AND CLOUD-NATIVE TECHNOLOGIES

Increased Operational Efficiency

One of the most significant benefits of AI and cloud-native technologies in banking is the increased operational efficiency they offer. AI-driven automation streamlines routine tasks, such as data entry, transaction processing, and compliance reporting. By reducing the need for manual intervention, banks can accelerate their operations, minimize errors, and allocate resources more effectively (Kellermann & Jones, 2013). Cloud-native technologies further enhance operational efficiency by providing scalable and flexible IT infrastructure. Banks can deploy and manage applications more efficiently using cloud platforms, which offer on-demand computing resources and storage. This flexibility allows banks to scale their operations according to demand, optimize performance, and reduce the time required to launch new products and services (Topol, 2019).

Enhanced Customer Experiences

AI and cloud-native technologies contribute to enhanced customer experiences by enabling more personalized and efficient interactions. AI-powered chatbots and virtual assistants offer immediate assistance, reducing wait times and improving customer satisfaction. Additionally, AI-driven personalization ensures that customers receive relevant product recommendations and financial advice tailored to their unique needs (Fitzgerald, 2018). Cloud-native technologies support seamless integration of digital banking services, allowing customers to access their accounts and perform transactions through multiple channels, including mobile apps, web portals, and voice-activated interfaces. This omni channel approach ensures a consistent and convenient banking experience, meeting the expectations of today's tech-savvy consumers (Ginsburg & Phillips, 2018).

Streamlined Processes and Reduced Operational Costs

AI and cloud-native technologies also lead to streamlined processes and reduced operational costs. Automation of routine tasks and data analysis reduces the need for manual labor, leading to cost savings and improved efficiency. For example, AI-driven systems can automate compliance checks, fraud detection, and customer service, minimizing the need for human oversight and reducing operational expenses (Snyder, Kircher, & Wylie, 2019). Cloud-native platforms enable banks to optimize their IT infrastructure by leveraging pay-as-you-go models and reducing the need for on-premises hardware. This cost-effective approach allows banks to scale their technology investments based on their needs, reducing capital expenditures and improving overall cost management (Wang et al., 2017). AI and cloud-native technologies have a profound impact on the banking sector, offering transformative applications that enhance customer service, improve fraud detection, and advance risk assessment. The benefits of increased operational efficiency, enhanced customer experiences, and reduced operational costs further underscore the value of these technologies. As banks continue to adopt and integrate AI and cloud-native solutions, they will likely encounter new opportunities and challenges, requiring ongoing innovation and adaptation to stay ahead in a rapidly evolving industry.

Ethical Challenges in AI-Driven Banking

The integration of Artificial Intelligence (AI) in banking has brought about significant advancements in efficiency and innovation. However, these benefits come with a range of ethical challenges, particularly concerning data privacy, algorithmic bias, and transparency in decision-making processes. Addressing these challenges is crucial for ensuring that AI technologies are deployed responsibly and ethically in the banking sector.

DATA PRIVACY CONCERNS AND THE MANAGEMENT OF SENSITIVE INFORMATION

Types of Data Collected and Potential Privacy Risks

In banking, AI systems process a vast array of data, including personal identification information, transaction history, financial records, and behavioral data. This comprehensive data collection is necessary for providing personalized services, detecting fraud, and assessing risk. However, it also raises significant privacy concerns. The primary risks involve unauthorized access, data breaches, and misuse of personal information. For instance, the exposure of sensitive financial data due to a security breach can lead to identity theft and financial loss for customers (Chen & Asch, 2020).

Measures to Protect Customer Data and Comply with Privacy Regulations

To mitigate these privacy risks, banks must implement robust data protection measures. This includes employing encryption technologies to safeguard data during storage and transmission, as well as adopting stringent access controls to ensure that only authorized personnel can access sensitive information (Jha, 2018). Additionally, banks need to comply with privacy regulations such as the General Data Protection Regulation (GDPR) in the European Union and the California Consumer Privacy Act (CCPA) in the United States. These regulations mandate transparent data handling practices, obtain explicit consent from customers for data collection, and provide mechanisms for data access and deletion upon request (Kellermann & Jones, 2013).

ADDRESSING AND MITIGATING ALGORITHMIC BIAS

Examples of Algorithmic Bias and Its Impact on Decision-Making

Algorithmic bias occurs when AI systems produce results that are systematically prejudiced due to flawed data or biased algorithms. In banking, this can manifest in various ways, such as biased credit scoring, discriminatory lending practices, or unequal customer service experiences. For example, if a credit scoring algorithm is trained on historical data that reflects past discriminatory practices, it may inadvertently perpetuate those biases, leading to unfair treatment of certain groups (Rajkomar, Dean, & Kohane, 2018). Such biases can undermine trust in the banking system and exacerbate existing inequalities.

Strategies for Reducing and Managing Bias in AI Systems

To address algorithmic bias, banks must implement several key strategies. First, it is essential to use diverse and representative datasets during AI training to ensure that the models are not skewed by historical biases. Additionally, banks should regularly audit their AI systems for bias and fairness by conducting impact assessments and bias detection tests (Topol, 2019). Transparency in algorithmic decision-making is also crucial; banks should strive to make their AI models explainable by providing clear documentation on how decisions are made and ensuring that stakeholders can understand and challenge the outcomes (Snyder, Kircher, & Wylie, 2019). Finally, involving interdisciplinary teams that include ethicists, legal experts, and community representatives can help to identify and address potential biases throughout the AI development lifecycle.

TRANSPARENCY IN AI DECISION-MAKING PROCESSES

Importance of Explainability and Accountability in AI

Transparency and accountability are critical for maintaining trust in AI-driven systems. Explainability refers to the ability to understand and articulate how AI models arrive at their decisions. In the context of banking, explainability ensures that customers and regulators can comprehend the basis of decisions, such as loan approvals or fraud alerts. This is particularly important for fostering trust and mitigating concerns about opaque decision-making processes (Dorsey & Topol, 2016). Accountability, on the other hand, involves establishing clear lines of responsibility for AI-driven decisions and ensuring that there are mechanisms for addressing grievances and correcting errors.

Approaches to Enhancing Transparency and Trust in AI Decisions

Several approaches can enhance transparency and trust in AI decisions. One approach is to adopt explainable AI (XAI) techniques, which aim to create models that are interpretable and provide insights into their decision-making processes. Techniques such as feature importance analysis, model-agnostic explanations, and visualization tools can help demystify AI systems and make their outputs more understandable (Esteva et al., 2017). Additionally, banks should develop and publish ethical guidelines and governance frameworks that outline how AI systems are designed, tested, and monitored for fairness and accuracy. Engaging with customers and stakeholders through regular communication and feedback mechanisms can also build trust and ensure that their concerns are addressed. Providing clear information about how AI systems use customer data, how decisions are made, and what steps are taken to protect privacy can help mitigate fears and enhance confidence in AI technologies (Fitzgerald, 2018). While AI offers significant opportunities for innovation in banking, it also presents ethical challenges that must be carefully managed. Ensuring data privacy, addressing algorithmic bias, and enhancing transparency in AI decision-making processes are essential for maintaining trust and upholding ethical standards. By implementing robust data protection measures, adopting strategies to reduce bias, and promoting transparency, banks can leverage

AI technologies responsibly and effectively while safeguarding customer interests and upholding ethical principles.

Regulatory and Compliance Landscape in AI-Driven Banking

As artificial intelligence (AI) technologies become integral to the banking sector, adhering to regulatory and compliance requirements are paramount. The application of AI in banking raises complex legal and ethical issues, necessitating a thorough understanding of relevant regulations and the development of robust compliance strategies. This section reviews key regulations that impact AI implementations in banking and provides strategies for ensuring compliance and managing legal risks.

REVIEW OF RELEVANT REGULATIONS

General Data Protection Regulation (GDPR)

The General Data Protection Regulation (GDPR), which came into effect on May 25, 2018, is a comprehensive data protection law in the European Union (EU). It aims to enhance individuals' control over their personal data and unify data protection regulations across the EU member states (European Commission, 2018). GDPR imposes strict requirements on how organizations collect, process, and store personal data. Banks using AI technologies must ensure that their systems comply with GDPR's principles, which include data minimization, purpose limitation, and transparency. GDPR mandates that organizations must obtain explicit consent from individuals before processing their data and provide clear information about how the data will be used (Kuner, 2017). Additionally, it enforces the right to access, rectify, and erase personal data, known as the "right to be forgotten" (Hacker, 2018). AI systems must be designed to support these rights, including enabling users to access their data and understand how it is processed by algorithms.

California Consumer Privacy Act (CCPA)

The California Consumer Privacy Act (CCPA), effective from January 1, 2020, provides data privacy rights to residents of California. It grants consumers the right to know what personal data is being collected about them, the purpose of the collection, and with whom it is shared (California Legislative Information, 2020). The CCPA also allows consumers to request deletion of their data and opt out of its sale. For banks employing AI technologies, compliance with CCPA involves ensuring that AI systems are capable of supporting consumer rights under the act. This includes providing clear disclosures about data collection practices, enabling data access requests, and implementing mechanisms for data deletion requests. Furthermore, banks must be transparent about any data sharing practices and ensure that third-party vendors comply with CCPA requirements (Miller, 2020).

Other Relevant Local and International Regulations

Beyond GDPR and CCPA, banks must also consider other local and international regulations that impact AI-driven systems. In the United Kingdom, the Data Protection Act 2018 complements GDPR and provides additional provisions specific to the UK (UK Government, 2018). In Asia, the Personal Data Protection Act (PDPA) in Singapore and the General Data Protection Regulation of the Philippines offer similar protections and obligations (Ng & Tan, 2019). In addition, the Basel Committee on Banking Supervision has issued guidelines on the use of technology in banking, including AI, which emphasizes the importance of risk management and regulatory compliance (Basel Committee on Banking Supervision, 2020). Banks should also be aware of emerging regulations specific to AI and data usage, such as the EU's proposed AI Act, which seeks to regulate high-risk AI applications (European Commission, 2021).

Comprehensive Risk Management Frameworks for AI in Banking

While AI offers transformative potential for the banking sector, it also introduces various risks that must be effectively managed to ensure secure and ethical application. It is essential for banks to implement structured risk management processes that comprehensively address the identification, assessment, mitigation, and ongoing monitoring of AI-related risks.

A robust AI risk management framework should include the following components:

1. **Risk Identification**: Banks must first identify potential risks associated with AI systems. This includes technological risks (e.g., algorithmic biases, data privacy concerns), operational risks (e.g., system failures, lack of skilled workforce), and compliance risks (e.g., failure to meet regulatory standards).
2. **Risk Assessment**: Once risks are identified, banks should assess the likelihood and potential impact of each risk. This can involve using AI-driven tools to predict potential vulnerabilities, testing the system under various scenarios, and evaluating the consequences of failure in critical areas such as financial transactions, customer service, and data protection.

3. **Risk Mitigation**: After assessing risks, banks need to develop strategies to mitigate them. This includes adopting robust cybersecurity measures, ensuring transparency in AI decision-making, and continuously training AI systems to reduce errors or biases. Policies should also be in place for AI system monitoring, establishing contingency plans for system failure, and ensuring adequate human oversight.
4. **Ongoing Monitoring**: As AI systems evolve, it is crucial to continuously monitor their performance to ensure they operate within the set risk boundaries. Regular audits, updating risk management protocols in response to emerging risks, and ensuring compliance with the latest regulations will help maintain AI system integrity over time.

ETHICAL CHALLENGES AND REGULATORY FRAMEWORKS FOR AI INTEGRATION IN BANKING

The integration of AI in banking presents unique ethical challenges that must be addressed to build trust and ensure fairness. However, the ethical implications of AI adoption are not only shaped by technology but also by the regulatory frameworks governing its use.

Relevant Regulations

To ensure ethical practices, banks must adhere to local and international regulatory frameworks that govern the use of AI. Key regulations include:

- **General Data Protection Regulation (GDPR)**: The GDPR sets guidelines for data protection and privacy within the European Union, and its principles must be followed by banks when using AI to process personal data. Compliance with GDPR ensures that AI systems respect user privacy, uphold transparency in data usage, and offer individuals control over their personal information.
- **EU AI Act**: The EU AI Act is a significant regulatory development aimed at creating a legal framework for AI deployment across various sectors, including banking. This legislation defines high-risk AI systems and lays out strict requirements for transparency, accountability, and fairness. Banks must align their AI implementations with these regulations to minimize ethical and legal risks.
- **Local Frameworks**: Banks must also consider jurisdiction-specific regulations that address AI, such as national data protection laws or financial reg-

ulations that oversee AI-based lending or risk assessment tools. Compliance with such local frameworks ensures that AI applications meet legal standards and are adopted responsibly within specific regions.

By adhering to these regulations, banks can ensure that their AI applications are ethically sound, compliant with legal standards, and aligned with customer interests.

Broader Societal Impacts of AI Adoption in Banking

While AI in banking has the potential to streamline operations and improve customer service, it also has broader societal implications that need to be considered. AI adoption can significantly impact the workforce, economic inequality, and access to financial services.

- **Employment Impact**: AI-driven automation in banking could lead to significant job displacement, particularly in roles that involve routine tasks such as customer service or data processing. However, it may also create new opportunities for skilled workers in areas such as AI maintenance, data analysis, and cybersecurity. Banks need to consider how to balance these effects and invest in reskilling their workforce.
- **Economic Inequality**: The deployment of AI systems in financial decision-making, such as credit scoring, could exacerbate economic inequality if biases in algorithms disproportionately affect marginalized communities. Banks must be proactive in ensuring that their AI systems are inclusive, transparent, and fair, providing equal access to financial services regardless of socioeconomic status.
- **Access to Financial Services**: AI technologies can improve financial inclusion by expanding access to banking services, especially in underserved or remote areas. AI-driven chatbots, for example, can offer 24/7 customer support in multiple languages, making it easier for individuals to interact with banks. However, the risk of excluding people who lack digital literacy or access to technology must be addressed by offering alternative ways to engage with financial services.

Case Studies for Practical Insight

Incorporating real-world case studies of AI in banking provides invaluable insights into both the successes and challenges of implementing AI technologies. These case studies not only offer banks practical lessons but also highlight the importance of strategic planning, ethical considerations, and continuous monitoring.

1. Successful Implementation: AI for Fraud Detection at HSBC

Background: HSBC, one of the world's largest banking institutions, implemented AI-driven systems for fraud detection as part of its efforts to strengthen security and reduce financial losses from fraudulent activities.

Key Highlights:

- **Real-time Monitoring**: HSBC utilized machine learning algorithms to analyze real-time transactions, flagging potentially fraudulent activities. The AI system continuously learns from new data, improving its ability to detect complex fraud patterns.
- **Reduced False Positives**: By refining the algorithm over time, the bank reduced the number of false positives—transactions incorrectly flagged as fraudulent—which previously led to customer frustration and unnecessary disruptions.
- **Transparency and Accountability**: The system allowed the bank to explain the reasoning behind flagged transactions, which was crucial for customer trust and regulatory compliance.

Outcome:

- The implementation of AI-based fraud detection led to a significant reduction in fraudulent transactions and financial losses. Customers felt more secure in using the bank's services, leading to enhanced trust and satisfaction.
- HSBC also complied with relevant regulations such as GDPR, ensuring the system respected privacy concerns while maintaining effective fraud prevention.

Lessons Learned:

- **Continuous Training and Adaptation**: Continuous model training was key to ensuring that the fraud detection system adapted to emerging fraud tactics.
- **Transparency**: Ensuring that flagged transactions could be easily explained helped mitigate customer concerns and reinforced trust.
- **Data Quality**: The effectiveness of AI in fraud detection was directly linked to the quality and diversity of the data used to train the system.

2. Lessons from Failures: AI-Driven Lending System at Amazon

Background: Amazon's AI-driven lending system, designed to evaluate small business loan applications, faced significant backlash due to unintended biases in its algorithm. The system was intended to streamline the loan approval process by automatically assessing the creditworthiness of applicants using historical data and machine learning models.

Key Issues:

- **Algorithmic Bias**: The AI model was found to disproportionately deny loans to female-led businesses. This occurred because the algorithm was trained on historical data that reflected existing biases in loan approval processes, which skewed the model's predictions.
- **Lack of Transparency**: The AI system lacked adequate transparency in how it arrived at its decisions, making it difficult for applicants to understand the reasoning behind rejections or to appeal decisions.
- **Failure to Mitigate Bias**: Despite having the capability to detect bias, the system did not implement sufficient measures to mitigate these biases, leading to discriminatory outcomes.

Outcome:

- The backlash led to public scrutiny and a loss of trust in the system. Amazon faced lawsuits and regulatory investigations, ultimately resulting in the suspension of the AI-driven lending program.
- The company was forced to reevaluate its approach to AI ethics and adjust its lending algorithms to ensure they were fair, transparent, and non-discriminatory.

Lessons Learned:

- **Bias Mitigation**: The case highlights the critical need for robust bias mitigation strategies in AI development, especially when systems make high-stakes decisions like lending. Training models on more representative data and implementing fairness checks are essential to avoid systemic discrimination.
- **Transparency and Accountability**: Clear communication about how AI systems make decisions is vital. In this case, applicants needed better explanations for why their applications were denied, and a mechanism to appeal decisions should have been in place.
- **Continuous Monitoring**: Even after implementation, continuous monitoring for bias and performance discrepancies is essential to identify and correct issues that might arise in real-world applications.

Stakeholder Engagement Strategies

As banks integrate AI into their operations, it is essential to engage with stakeholders—customers, employees, regulators, and others—on ethical AI use. Transparent communication and active stakeholder involvement can help mitigate concerns and foster trust.

- **Customer Involvement**: Banks can solicit customer feedback on AI systems by conducting surveys or holding focus groups to understand public concerns and preferences. Ensuring transparency about how AI is used, such as explaining how credit scores are determined or how data is processed, can increase customer confidence.
- **Employee Engagement**: For employees, training programs on AI ethics and transparency in decision-making processes are key. Involving employees in discussions about the ethical implications of AI systems can help reduce resistance and increase internal acceptance.
- **Regulator Collaboration**: Banks should work closely with regulators to ensure compliance and stay informed about evolving regulatory frameworks. Regular discussions with regulators can help anticipate challenges and ensure that AI applications meet legal and ethical standards.

COMPLIANCE STRATEGIES FOR AI IMPLEMENTATIONS IN BANKING

Guidelines for Aligning AI Practices with Regulatory Requirements

To align AI practices with regulatory requirements, banks should adopt a structured approach to compliance. Key guidelines include:

1. **Data Governance Frameworks**: Establish comprehensive data governance frameworks that define data handling practices, including collection, storage, and processing. Ensure these frameworks incorporate regulatory requirements such as data protection principles and user rights (Shortliffe & Cimino, 2013).
2. **Privacy Impact Assessments (PIAs)**: Conduct Privacy Impact Assessments to evaluate how AI systems impact data privacy. PIAs help identify potential privacy risks and compliance gaps, allowing banks to address issues proactively (Cavoukian, 2018).

3. **Transparency and Documentation**: Maintain detailed documentation of AI models and data processing activities. This documentation should include information on how algorithms make decisions and how data is used, ensuring transparency and facilitating compliance audits (Rajkomar, Dean, & Kohane, 2018).
4. **Third-Party Management**: Ensure that third-party vendors and partners comply with regulatory requirements. Implement contracts and agreements that stipulate compliance obligations and conduct regular audits to verify adherence (Wang, Casalino, & Khullar, 2017).

Best Practices for Ensuring Ongoing Compliance and Managing Legal Risks

To ensure ongoing compliance and effectively manage legal risks, banks should follow these best practices:

1. **Regular Audits and Monitoring**: Implement regular audits and monitoring processes to assess compliance with data protection laws and AI regulations. This includes reviewing AI systems for adherence to privacy and fairness standards (Ginsburg & Phillips, 2018).
2. **Training and Awareness**: Provide ongoing training for employees on data privacy regulations and ethical AI practices. Awareness programs help ensure that staff understand their responsibilities and the importance of compliance (Fitzgerald, 2018).
3. **Ethical AI Guidelines**: Develop and enforce ethical AI guidelines that outline best practices for AI development and deployment. These guidelines should address issues such as bias, fairness, and transparency (Esteva et al., 2017).
4. **Legal Counsel and Expertise**: Engage legal counsel with expertise in data protection and AI regulations. Legal professionals can provide valuable advice on navigating complex regulatory landscapes and managing compliance challenges (Jha, 2018).
5. **Adaptation to Regulatory Changes**: Stay informed about changes in regulations and adapt compliance strategies accordingly. Regulations are evolving rapidly, and banks must be proactive in updating their practices to meet new requirements (Kellermann & Jones, 2013).

Navigating the regulatory and compliance landscape for AI-driven banking requires a proactive and informed approach. By understanding key regulations such as GDPR and CCPA, and implementing robust compliance strategies, banks can leverage AI technologies responsibly while mitigating legal and ethical risks.

Ensuring data privacy, addressing algorithmic bias, and maintaining transparency are essential for fostering trust and achieving regulatory compliance in the rapidly evolving banking sector.

CASE STUDIES: SUCCESSFUL AI INTEGRATIONS IN BANKING

Artificial Intelligence (AI) is revolutionizing the banking sector, offering transformative benefits while also presenting significant ethical and regulatory challenges. Examining case studies of banks that have successfully integrated AI technologies provides valuable insights into effective strategies and outcomes. This section explores notable examples of AI adoption in banking, analyzes the benefits realized, and discusses how these banks managed ethical and regulatory challenges.

Overview of Successful AI Integrations

1. **JPMorgan Chase: AI in Fraud Detection** JPMorgan Chase, one of the largest banking institutions globally, has leveraged AI to enhance its fraud detection capabilities. The bank implemented an AI-driven fraud detection system known as the "Contract Intelligence" (COiN) platform. COiN uses machine learning algorithms to review legal documents and detect anomalies that could indicate fraudulent activity (Marr, 2020). **Outcomes and Benefits: • Increased Accuracy:** The COiN platform significantly improved the accuracy of fraud detection by analyzing vast amounts of transaction data and identifying patterns that may not be evident to human analysts (JPMorgan Chase, 2020). **• Reduced Processing Time:** The system reduced the time required to process documents and detects potential fraud from hours to minutes, enhancing operational efficiency (JPMorgan Chase, 2020).
2. **Bank of America: AI-Driven Customer Service** Bank of America has successfully integrated AI into its customer service operations through its virtual assistant, Erica. Erica uses natural language processing (NLP) and machine learning to assist customers with a variety of banking tasks, including account management, transaction inquiries, and financial advice (Bank of America, 2021). **Outcomes and Benefits: • Enhanced Customer Experience:** Erica has improved customer satisfaction by providing prompt, 24/7 support and personalized financial insights (Bank of America, 2021). **• Operational Efficiency:** The AI-driven assistant has reduced the workload on human customer service representatives, allowing them to focus on more complex inquiries (Bank of America, 2021).

3. **HSBC: AI in Risk Management** HSBC has adopted AI to enhance its risk management processes. The bank implemented an AI system to analyze financial transactions and assess credit risk. The system uses predictive analytics to evaluate the likelihood of default and identify potential risks in real-time (HSBC, 2019).

Outcomes and Benefits:

- **Improved Risk Assessment:** The AI system provides more accurate risk assessments by analyzing a broader range of data sources and detecting emerging risk patterns (HSBC, 2019).
- **Efficient Risk Management:** The integration of AI has streamlined HSBC's risk management processes, leading to faster decision-making and better resource allocation (HSBC, 2019).

Managing Ethical Issues and Regulatory Compliance

1. **JPMorgan Chase: Addressing Ethical Challenges** JPMorgan Chase has faced ethical challenges related to the use of AI, particularly in data privacy and algorithmic bias. The bank has implemented several strategies to address these issues: • **Data Privacy Measures:** JPMorgan Chase ensures compliance with data protection regulations by employing advanced encryption technologies and conducting regular privacy impact assessments (Marr, 2020). • **Bias Mitigation:** The bank has established a dedicated team to monitor and mitigate algorithmic bias. This team reviews AI models regularly to ensure fairness and transparency in decision-making processes (JPMorgan Chase, 2020).
2. **Bank of America: Compliance Strategies** Bank of America has prioritized regulatory compliance and ethical considerations in its AI-driven customer service platform, Erica: • **Transparency and Accountability:** Bank of America maintains transparency by providing customers with clear information about how Erica uses their data. The bank also ensures that customers can easily opt out of AI-driven services if desired (Bank of America, 2021). • **Regulatory Alignment:** The bank has aligned Erica's operations with relevant regulations, such as the California Consumer Privacy Act (CCPA) and the General Data Protection Regulation (GDPR), to ensure compliance and protect customer privacy (Bank of America, 2021).
3. **HSBC: Lessons in Ethical AI Management** HSBC has taken several steps to manage ethical issues related to AI in risk management: • **Ethical AI Framework:** HSBC has developed an ethical AI framework that includes guidelines for re-

sponsible AI use, focusing on transparency, accountability, and fairness (HSBC, 2019).

- **Regular Audits:** The bank conducts regular audits of its AI systems to ensure compliance with ethical standards and regulatory requirements. These audits help identify potential biases and address any issues before they impact decision-making (HSBC, 2019).

Lessons Learned from Real-World Implementations

1. Importance of Transparency

One key lesson from these case studies is the importance of transparency in AI systems. Banks must ensure that their AI models are explainable and that customers are informed about how their data is used. Transparent practices build trust and help address concerns related to data privacy and algorithmic bias.

2. Ongoing Monitoring and Evaluation

Regular monitoring and evaluation of AI systems are crucial for maintaining ethical standards and regulatory compliance. Banks should establish processes for continuous assessment of AI models to identify and mitigate potential biases and ensure that the systems operate within legal and ethical boundaries.

3. Integration of Ethical Frameworks

Developing and implementing ethical frameworks for AI use is essential for managing ethical challenges. Banks should create guidelines that address fairness, accountability, and transparency, and ensure that these guidelines are integrated into all stages of AI development and deployment.

4. Collaboration with Regulators

Collaboration with regulators and compliance experts can help banks navigate the complex regulatory landscape of AI. Engaging with regulatory bodies and staying informed about emerging regulations can assist banks in aligning their AI practices with legal requirements and avoiding potential pitfalls. The successful integration of AI technologies in banking has demonstrated significant benefits, including enhanced customer experiences, improved fraud detection, and more efficient risk management. However, addressing ethical challenges and ensuring regulatory compliance are critical for maintaining trust and achieving sustainable success. By implementing robust ethical frameworks, prioritizing transparency, and staying aligned with regulatory requirements, banks can leverage AI technologies effectively while mitigating risks and upholding ethical standards.

Best Practices for Ethical AI Integration

As artificial intelligence (AI) becomes increasingly embedded in various sectors, including banking, it is essential to maintain high ethical standards while pursuing innovation. Implementing best practices for ethical AI integration helps organizations navigate complex ethical issues, ensure regulatory compliance, and build trust with stakeholders. This section outlines guidelines for maintaining ethical standards and explores tools and frameworks for ethical AI governance.

Guidelines for Maintaining Ethical Standards

1. Establishing Clear Ethical Guidelines and Policies

Creating well-defined ethical guidelines and policies is foundational for ensuring responsible AI use. These guidelines should articulate the values and principles that guide AI development and deployment, addressing key ethical concerns such as fairness, transparency, and accountability.

- **Developing Ethical Principles:** Organizations should formulate ethical principles that align with their values and regulatory requirements. These principles might include commitments to fairness, non-discrimination, and respect for privacy. For instance, the Institute of Electrical and Electronics Engineers (IEEE) has developed guidelines emphasizing the need for AI systems to be transparent, accountable, and inclusive (IEEE, 2020).
- **Formulating Policies and Procedures:** Alongside principles, organizations should establish comprehensive policies and procedures for implementing ethical AI. These policies should cover aspects such as data usage, algorithmic transparency, and bias mitigation. A practical example is the "Ethics Guidelines for Trustworthy AI" published by the European Commission, which provides a framework for developing and deploying AI systems that respect fundamental rights (European Commission, 2019).

2. Implementing Robust Data Governance Frameworks

Effective data governance is crucial for ethical AI integration. It ensures that data used in AI systems is handled responsibly and that privacy and security are maintained.

- **Data Privacy and Security:** Organizations should implement strong data privacy and security measures to protect sensitive information. This includes adopting encryption techniques, access controls, and regular security audits. The General Data Protection Regulation (GDPR) offers a comprehensive framework for data protection, requiring organizations to secure personal data and provide transparency about its usage (European Union, 2018).
- **Data Quality and Integrity:** Ensuring data quality and integrity is essential for the reliability of AI systems. Organizations should establish processes for data validation, cleansing, and regular updates. High-quality data reduces the risk of biases and inaccuracies in AI outcomes, contributing to more ethical and effective AI applications (Binns et al., 2018).

Tools and Frameworks for Ethical AI Governance

1. Technologies and Methodologies for Monitoring and Auditing AI Systems

To ensure that AI systems adhere to ethical guidelines, organizations need robust monitoring and auditing mechanisms. Several technologies and methodologies can support this process.

- **AI Monitoring Tools:** Tools for monitoring AI systems can track their performance and flag potential ethical issues. For example, fairness monitoring tools assess whether AI algorithms produce equitable outcomes across different demographic groups. Techniques such as adversarial testing and scenario analysis can help identify and address biases in AI systems (Barocas et al., 2019).
- **Auditing Methodologies:** Regular auditing of AI systems is essential for evaluating their compliance with ethical standards and regulatory requirements. Audits should focus on areas such as algorithmic transparency, data governance, and decision-making processes. Independent audits by third-party experts can provide unbiased assessments and recommendations for improvement (Dastin, 2020).

2. Frameworks for Ensuring Transparency and Accountability

Transparency and accountability are critical for building trust in AI systems and ensuring ethical practices.

- **Explainable AI (XAI):** Explainable AI refers to AI models and algorithms designed to provide understandable and interpretable explanations for their decisions. XAI frameworks help stakeholders understand how AI systems make decisions, facilitating transparency and accountability. Techniques such as model interpretability, feature importance analysis, and visualization tools support explainability (Doshi-Velez & Kim, 2017).

- **Accountability Mechanisms:** Implementing accountability mechanisms involves establishing clear lines of responsibility for AI-related decisions and actions. Organizations should define roles and responsibilities for AI governance, including oversight committees or ethics boards that review AI practices and address ethical concerns. For instance, the AI Ethics Guidelines from the Organization for Economic Co-operation and Development (OECD) recommend setting up governance structures to ensure that AI systems are developed and used in ways that align with ethical principles (OECD, 2019).

Best Practices for Ethical AI Integration

Based on the guidelines and tools discussed, several best practices can help organizations integrate AI ethically:

- **Develop and Communicate Ethical Principles:** Establish clear ethical principles and communicate them throughout the organization. Ensure that all stakeholders, including AI developers, data scientists, and business leaders, are aware of and adhere to these principles.
- **Implement Comprehensive Data Governance:** Adopt robust data governance frameworks that cover data privacy, security, quality, and integrity. Regularly review and update data governance practices to address emerging challenges and regulatory changes.
- **Utilize Monitoring and Auditing Tools:** Invest in technologies and methodologies for monitoring and auditing AI systems. Regularly assess AI models for biases, transparency, and compliance with ethical standards.
- **Adopt Explainable AI Techniques:** Prioritize the development and use of explainable AI techniques to enhance transparency and facilitate understanding of AI decisions. Provide clear explanations to stakeholders and address any concerns about AI-driven outcomes.
- **Establish Accountability Structures:** Create accountability structures, such as ethics boards or oversight committees, to oversee AI practices and address ethical issues. Ensure that there are clear lines of responsibility and mechanisms for reporting and addressing ethical concerns.

By adhering to these best practices, organizations can effectively navigate the complexities of AI integration while upholding ethical standards and regulatory compliance.

Looking Ahead: The Future of AI in Banking

As the banking sector continues to evolve under the influence of artificial intelligence (AI) and cloud-native technologies, understanding the emerging trends and preparing for future challenges are crucial for maintaining a competitive edge and upholding ethical standards. This section explores the anticipated innovations in AI and cloud-native software, their potential impact on the banking industry, and strategies for addressing future ethical and regulatory challenges.

Emerging Trends and Technologies

1. Innovations on the Horizon and Their Potential Impact

The landscape of AI in banking is set to transform further with several promising innovations on the horizon. These advancements are poised to enhance banking operations, customer experiences, and risk management capabilities.

- **Advanced AI and Machine Learning Models:** The development of more sophisticated AI and machine learning models promises to revolutionize banking practices. Techniques such as deep learning and reinforcement learning are expected to enhance predictive analytics, enabling banks to offer more personalized services and better anticipate customer needs. For example, AI-driven models can analyze complex patterns in customer behavior to offer tailored financial advice or detect anomalies indicative of fraud (Dastin, 2020).
- **Blockchain and AI Integration:** Blockchain technology, when combined with AI, offers significant potential for improving transparency and security in banking transactions. Smart contracts powered by AI can automate and verify transactions in real-time, reducing the risk of fraud and errors while enhancing operational efficiency. This integration is expected to streamline processes such as loan approvals and cross-border payments, providing a more secure and efficient banking experience (Narayanan et al., 2016).
- **AI-Powered Robotic Process Automation (RPA):** RPA, when enhanced with AI capabilities, can automate repetitive and time-consuming tasks such as document processing and compliance checks. This will not only improve operational efficiency but also reduce the burden on human staff, allowing

them to focus on more strategic activities. AI-powered RPA can handle large volumes of transactions with greater accuracy and speed, leading to cost savings and improved service quality (Brynjolfsson & McElheran, 2016).

2. Predictions for the Future of AI and Cloud-Native Software in Banking

Looking ahead, several predictions can be made regarding the future role of AI and cloud-native software in banking:

- **Increased Personalization:** AI is expected to drive greater personalization in banking services. By leveraging advanced analytics and real-time data, banks will be able to offer highly customized financial products and services. This will include tailored investment advice, personalized credit offers, and bespoke customer support, enhancing customer satisfaction and loyalty (Binns et al., 2018).
- **Enhanced Risk Management:** Future AI innovations are likely to improve risk management strategies. Predictive analytics and AI-driven models will provide banks with more accurate forecasts of potential risks, enabling proactive measures to mitigate them. This will enhance the ability to manage credit risk, market risk, and operational risk more effectively (Chen & Asch, 2020).
- **Regulatory Evolution:** As AI and cloud-native technologies become more prevalent, regulatory frameworks are expected to evolve. Regulators will likely introduce new guidelines and standards to address emerging risks and ethical concerns. Banks will need to stay abreast of these changes and adapt their practices to ensure compliance while continuing to leverage AI for competitive advantage (European Commission, 2019).

Preparing for and Addressing Future Ethical Challenges

1. Anticipating New Ethical Issues and Regulatory Changes

As AI and cloud-native technologies continue to advance, new ethical issues and regulatory challenges are likely to emerge. Anticipating these challenges is essential for maintaining ethical standards and ensuring regulatory compliance.

- **Privacy Concerns:** With the increased use of AI in analyzing customer data, privacy concerns are likely to become more pronounced. Banks will need to address issues related to data ownership, consent, and data protection to safeguard customer privacy. The implementation of robust data governance frameworks and adherence to privacy regulations such as GDPR will be crucial in mitigating privacy risks (European Union, 2018).

- **Algorithmic Bias and Fairness:** As AI systems become more complex, the risk of algorithmic bias may increase. Banks will need to ensure that their AI models are designed to avoid discriminatory outcomes and are regularly tested for fairness. Developing and implementing strategies for bias detection and mitigation will be essential for maintaining ethical standards (Barocas et al., 2019).
- **Regulatory Adaptation:** Anticipating and preparing for regulatory changes will be critical. As regulators adapt to the evolving technological landscape, banks must stay informed about new regulations and adjust their compliance strategies accordingly. Engaging with regulatory bodies and participating in industry forums can help banks anticipate and prepare for future regulatory developments (Wang et al., 2017).

2. Proactive Strategies for Adapting to Future Developments

To effectively address future developments and challenges, banks should adopt proactive strategies:

- **Invest in Ethical AI Practices:** Banks should invest in developing and implementing ethical AI practices. This includes establishing clear ethical guidelines, implementing transparency measures, and conducting regular audits of AI systems. Investing in explainable AI technologies can also enhance transparency and accountability (Doshi-Velez & Kim, 2017).
- **Foster a Culture of Compliance:** Building a culture of compliance within the organization is essential. This involves training staff on ethical AI practices, encouraging a culture of openness and accountability, and integrating compliance into the organizational ethos. Regularly reviewing and updating compliance strategies in response to regulatory changes will help banks stay ahead of potential issues (Jha, 2018).
- **Collaborate with Industry and Regulatory Bodies:** Collaborating with industry peers and regulatory bodies can provide valuable insights and guidance on emerging trends and regulatory requirements (Vettriselvan, R., & Vinodhan, V. 2022). Participating in industry groups and contributing to the development of industry standards can help banks navigate the evolving landscape and address ethical and regulatory challenges effectively (Rajkomar et al., 2018).

SUMMARY OF KEY POINTS

1. Recap of Major Insights

AI and cloud-native technologies are revolutionizing the banking industry through enhancements in customer service, fraud detection, and risk management. AI-driven solutions such as chatbots provide personalized banking experiences, predictive analytics enhance fraud detection, and automated credit scoring tools improve risk assessment (Chen & Asch, 2020; Dastin, 2020). These advancements lead to increased operational efficiency, reduced costs, and enhanced customer satisfaction (Binns et al., 2018). However, the integration of these technologies also brings significant ethical and regulatory challenges, including data privacy concerns, algorithmic bias, and the need for transparency in decision-making processes (Barocas et al., 2019; Doshi-Velez & Kim, 2017).

2. Importance of Balancing Innovation with Ethical Considerations

The rapid pace of technological advancements in banking necessitates a thoughtful approach to integrating AI and cloud-native technologies. While these innovations offer numerous benefits, they also introduce ethical dilemmas that must be managed effectively to maintain customer trust and regulatory compliance (Brynjolfsson & McElheran, 2016). Ethical AI integration requires the establishment of clear guidelines, robust data governance frameworks, and the use of tools for monitoring and auditing AI systems (Barocas et al., 2019; Doshi-Velez & Kim, 2017).

FINAL THOUGHTS ON NAVIGATING THE EVOLVING LANDSCAPE OF TECHNOLOGY AND ETHICS IN BANKING

As AI and cloud-native technologies continue to advance, stakeholders must prioritize ethical practices in their implementations. The future of banking will depend on the ability to harness these technological innovations while adhering to ethical standards.

Call to Action for Stakeholders

1. **For Banks:** Develop and implement comprehensive ethical AI practices, including the creation of clear guidelines and policies. Invest in transparency technologies and integrate ethical considerations throughout the AI develop-

ment lifecycle. Regularly review and update compliance strategies to align with evolving regulations and industry standards (European Commission, 2019).

2. **For Regulators:** Formulate and refine regulations that address the specific challenges of AI and cloud-native technologies. Work collaboratively with industry stakeholders to develop standards that ensure ethical practices while fostering innovation (European Union, 2018).
3. **For Technology Providers:** Design AI solutions that prioritize fairness, transparency, and accountability. Provide tools and frameworks that assist banks in monitoring and auditing AI systems to address and prevent ethical issues (Narayanan et al., 2016).
4. **For Customers:** Stay informed about the AI technologies used by banks and advocate for transparency and fairness. Engage with banks and regulators to ensure that customer rights and privacy are protected (Rajkomar, Dean, & Kohane, 2018).

CONCLUSION

The integration of artificial intelligence (AI) and cloud-native technologies is significantly transforming the banking sector, presenting both substantial opportunities and notable challenges. This chapter has explored the multifaceted impact of AI on banking, with a particular emphasis on the need to balance technological innovation with ethical considerations. By taking these actions, stakeholders can create a banking environment where technological innovation and ethical standards coexist effectively. The ongoing dialogue between technology and ethics will shape the future of banking, ensuring that advancements in AI and cloud-native technologies enhance the industry while upholding the highest standards of integrity and responsibility.

REFERENCES

Banaee, H., Ahmed, M. U., & Loutfi, A. (2013). Data mining for wearable sensors in health monitoring systems: A review of recent trends and challenges. *Sensors (Basel), 13*(12), 17472–17500. DOI: 10.3390/s131217472 PMID: 24351646

Bank of America. (2021). Erica: The AI-driven virtual assistant. Retrieved from https://www.bankofamerica.com/

Barocas, S., Hardt, M., & Narayanan, A. (2019). Fairness and machine learning. Retrieved from https://fairmlbook.org/

Basel Committee on Banking Supervision. (2020). Guidelines: The use of technology in banking supervision. Bank for International Settlements. Retrieved from https://www.bis.org/

Binns, R., Veale, M., Van Kleek, M., Shadbolt, N., & O'Hara, K. (2018). 'It's reducing a human being to a percentage': Perceptions of justice in algorithmic decisions. *Proceedings of the 2018 CHI Conference on Human Factors in Computing Systems*, 1-14. DOI: 10.1145/3173574.3173951

Brynjolfsson, E., & Mcelheran, K. (2016). The Rapid Adoption of Data-Driven Decision-Making. *The American Economic Review, 106*(5), 133–139. DOI: 10.1257/aer.p20161016

California Legislative Information. (2020). California Consumer Privacy Act (CCPA). Retrieved from https://leginfo.legislature.ca.gov

Cavoukian, A. (2018). Privacy impact assessments: An essential tool for the development of AI applications. Information and Privacy Commissioner of Ontario. Retrieved from https://www.ipc.on.ca

Chen, J. H., & Asch, S. M. (2017). Machine Learning and Prediction in Medicine - Beyond the Peak of Inflated Expectations. *The New England Journal of Medicine, 376*(26), 2507–2509. DOI: 10.1056/NEJMp1702071 PMID: 28657867

Dastin, J. (2020). Amazon scraps AI recruitment tool that showed bias against women. Reuters. Retrieved from https://www.business-standard.com/article/international/amazon-scraps-secret-ai-recruiting-tool-that-showed-bias-against-women-118101000204_1.html

Dorsey, E. R., & Topol, E. J. (2016). State of Telehealth. *The New England Journal of Medicine, 375*(2), 154–161. DOI: 10.1056/NEJMra1601705 PMID: 27410924

Doshi-Velez, F., & Kim, B. (2017). Towards a rigorous science of interpretable machine learning. arXiv preprint arXiv:1702.08608. https://doi.org//arXiv.1702.08608DOI: 10.48550

Esteva, A., Kuprel, B., Novoa, R. A., Ko, J., Swetter, S. M., Blau, H. M., & Thrun, S. (2017). Dermatologist-level classification of skin cancer with deep neural networks. *Nature*, *542*(7639), 115–118. DOI: 10.1038/nature21056 PMID: 28117445

European Commission. (2018). General Data Protection Regulation (GDPR). Retrieved from https://ec.europa.eu

European Commission. (2021). Proposal for a regulation on artificial intelligence. Retrieved from https://ec.europa.eu

European Union. (2018). General Data Protection Regulation (GDPR). Retrieved from https://eur-lex.europa.eu

Fitzgerald, J. (2018). Patient engagement through digital health platforms. *Health Affairs*, *37*(6), 930–935. DOI: 10.1377/hlthaff.2018.0037

Ginsburg, G. S., & Phillips, K. A. (2018). Precision medicine: From science to value. *Health Affairs*, *37*(5), 685–692. DOI: 10.1377/hlthaff.2017.1624 PMID: 29733705

Hacker, P. (2018). The right to be forgotten: A comprehensive analysis. *Harvard Law Review*, *131*(5), 1208–1240. DOI: 10.2307/26561013

HSBC. (2019). AI in risk management: A transformative approach. Retrieved from https://www.hsbc.com

IEEE. (2020). Ethically aligned design: A vision for prioritizing human well-being with artificial intelligence and autonomous systems. Retrieved from https://ethicsinaction.ieee.org

Jha, A. K. (2018). Health information technology and the quality of health care. *Journal of the American Medical Association*, *319*(9), 831–833. DOI: 10.1001/jama.2018.1079

JPMorgan Chase. (2020). COiN: Revolutionizing fraud detection. Retrieved from https://www.jpmorganchase.com

Kellermann, A. L., & Jones, S. S. (2013). What it will take to achieve the as-yet-unfulfilled promises of health information technology. *Health Affairs*, *32*(1), 63–68. DOI: 10.1377/hlthaff.2012.0693 PMID: 23297272

Kuner, C. (2017). *The General Data Protection Regulation: A commentary*. Oxford University Press.

Marr, B. (2020). How JPMorgan Chase is using AI to improve fraud detection. Forbes. Retrieved from https://www.forbes.com

Miller, R. (2020). California Consumer Privacy Act (CCPA) compliance strategies. *Privacy Law Journal, 8*(2), 45–59.

Narayanan, A., Bonneau, J., & Felten, E.. (2016). *Bitcoin and cryptocurrency technologies: A comprehensive introduction.* Princeton University Press.

Ng, H., & Tan, W. (2019). Personal data protection act (PDPA) compliance in Singapore. Singapore. *Law Review, 35*(1), 20–30.

OECD. (2019). OECD principles on artificial intelligence. Retrieved from https://www.oecd.org

Rajkomar, A., Dean, J., & Kohane, I. (2018). Machine learning in medicine. *The New England Journal of Medicine, 380*(14), 1347–1358. DOI: 10.1056/NEJMra1814259 PMID: 30943338

Shortliffe, E. H., & Cimino, J. J. (2013). *Biomedical informatics: Computer applications in health care and biomedicine* (4th ed.). Springer.

Snyder, M., Kircher, M., & Wylie, T. (2019). Precision medicine: The role of genomics in patient care. *Annual Review of Medicine, 70*, 113–130. DOI: 10.1146/annurev-med-041917-044452

Snyder, M. P.. (2019). Precision medicine: Personalized, problem-solving approach. *Science, 362*(6417), 208–210. DOI: 10.1126/science.aav4060

Thiruvasagam, G., & Vettriselvan, R. (2021). What is after COVID-19?: Changing economies of the shipping industries and maritime education institutions. In 21st Annual General Assembly, IAMU AGA 2021 - Proceedings of the International Association of Maritime Universities (pp. 96–110).

Topol, E. J. (2019). *Deep medicine: How artificial intelligence can make healthcare human again.* Basic Books.

UK Government. (2018). Data Protection Act 2018. Retrieved from https://www.legislation.gov.uk

Vest, J. R. (2010). Health information exchange: The key to achieving meaningful use. *Journal of the American Medical Informatics Association : JAMIA, 17*(5), 489–494. DOI: 10.1136/jamia.2010.001024

Vettriselvan, R., & Vinodhan, V. (2022). Promotional strategies for gender equity in maritime sector: Maritime education institutions. In *Proceedings of the International Association of Maritime Universities Conference*.

Wang, F.. (2017). A review of blockchain technology applied to smart grids: Challenges and opportunities. *IEEE Access : Practical Innovations, Open Solutions*, *5*, 2077–2086. DOI: 10.1109/ACCESS.2017.2651582

Wang, F., Casalino, L. P., & Khullar, D. (2017). The role of predictive analytics in health care: A review of current literature and future directions. *Health Affairs*, *36*(3), 421–428. DOI: 10.1377/hlthaff.2016.1103

Wang, H., Casalino, L. P., & Khullar, D. (2017). Managing third-party vendors in healthcare. *Health Management Review*, *42*(3), 250–260. DOI: 10.1097/HMR.0000000000000156

. Zhang, Q., Wang, F., & Zhang, C. (2018). AI for drug discovery: From big data to new therapeutic solutions. Nature Reviews Drug Discovery, 17(10), 739-753. https://doi.org/Top of FormBottom of FormDOI: 10.1038/s41573-018-0084-1

Chapter 16
A Hybrid Approach Employing Coded Caching-Based Federated Learning (HA - CCFL) for Multiparameter Optimization in Cloud Frameworks

Vaishnavi Bhardwaj
https://orcid.org/0009-0002-0254-9649
Siksha O Anusandhan University, India

Narayan Patra
Siksha O Anusandhan University, India

Sushree Bubhuppradda B. Priyadarshini
https://orcid.org/0000-0003-3430-8639
Siksha O Anusandhan University, India

ABSTRACT

Federated computing refers to the method of combining multiple distributed user groups and training models together without distributing data sets to client devices. In this chapter, the authors discussed a caching-based federated learning coded in fog computing called HS-CCFL, which is used as a content distribution artificial intelligence strategy with a single server connected to other devices through common

DOI: 10.4018/979-8-3693-9356-7.ch016

constraints. They established an estimate of the long-term average speed of shared data for many users, each with a certain amount of memory. In this chapter, the authors show the experimental results by increasing the latency of fog points, which leads to an increase in latency and hit rate. Federation learning algorithm based on coded caching is discussed, where instead of local cache optimization, the closest term is added, which is related to the distance between local caching strategies. The experimental results justify the effectiveness of the method.

1. INTRODUCTION

In Technology 5.0, considerable traffic has been encountered in the modern networking environment due to web searching and social networking. As a result of such network traffic, user requests are overburdened during the peak hours and the network is generally implemented during the off-peak hours when networking resources are plentiful so that it results in significant pressure on the networks. To this effect, one method to alleviate such congestion problem is to allocate memory between the network and any cache files that the user may require and Yousefpour, et al. (2019) discussed the concept of generation of massive amount of data gathered through it. To overcome the ultimatums of cloud and fog computing, a federal study formalizes leveraging the critical computing, communications, and storage resources that get located at the edge of wireless networks. For instance, federation training is carried out to improve G-board's automatic text prediction capabilities. Federated learning basically uses a federation of clients coordinated by a central server to train global data learning models. In this context, Gnaneswar et al. (2020) showed the concepts of distinction between cloud and fog computing in a lucid way and Alojail et al. (2020) illustrated the way fog computing mitigates the limitations of cloud computing and edge computing in recent days. The concept of edge computing was advocated in paper (Yu et al. 2018). Hence, the client data is processed locally and only model parameters are exchanged across the concerned network.

Such learning is used to learn a low-dimensional local decision model and simultaneously to learn a global decision framework while maintaining stable effectiveness, and optimizing the trade-off between local cache and global throughput. Tom et al. (2015) and Atlam et al. (2018) have also detailed the concepts of fog computing and IoT where as Pengfei et al. (2017) have discussed the architecture, major technologies, implications and crucial open issues marked in fog computing framework. Similarly, Siddiqi et al.(2019) and Shukla et al. (2021) have collaborated the detailed challenges and issues associated with cloud and IoT. In general, traditional (non-encrypted) caches store content close to the user in order to serve local users. These caching approaches provide merely the local caching gain. A coded caching scheme was proposed to further reduce the fronthaul load by combining both caching and multicasting. In the placement phase, content is partially cached by local users, thus, providing a local cache profit. In the delivery stage, the concerned server is used to multicast the coded messages to the corresponding local users, thereby providing a global multicast gain. Users provide a series of content requests from popular datasets and target caches. In addition, since the requests are made to the server that is satisfied with the minimum number of bits sent through shared data, it will limit the amount of delay to fulfil the user's request.

For coded caches with inappropriate content popularity, storing more amount of content increases the benefits of local storage, but at the same time loses the benefits of global multicasting. In such cases, the key issue is how to achieve a trade-off between local cache gains and global multicast gains as discussed by Shukla et al. (2021) and Siddiqi, et al. (2019). Alam et al.(2021) detailed the IoT applications based on cloud computing and their impacts in smart cities while Khan, et al.(2017) outlined the security issues and solutions concerned with fog computing. Likewise, Habibi, et al.,(2020) detailed the an architectural survey on fog computing framework where the detailed architecture was outlined.

To that end, one possible approach is to divide the content into groups managed by different distribution and delivery strategies, so that the content is divided into groups of equal popularity and each group is cached with a different storage location. Dividing content into two or three groups provides optimal performance. Several query problems are considered and a strategy is derived to divide the configured partition into three groups by solving the optimization problem. In a centralized encrypted cache, there is a central server that knows the count of users at the deployment stage; thus caches can be co-created to further expand the multi-cache capabilities. However, in wireless networks, mobile users and deployment phases usually occur in different networks and time zones. Therefore, it is impossible to predict the users who will participate in the delivery phase and coordinate the deployment phase for these users. In a decentralized encrypted cache, it is assumed that the server has no prior information about the number or identity of users at the deployment stage. Previously, the local cache could be used to reduce the network demand when a user requested any of the files, each user has a confined cache memory of size M1*F1 bits, where server has the route to M1 files, each of F1 bits. Additionally, users can store some portion of the data to their local cache when there is low traffic demand or when they have access to a high available transmission capacity.

In Maddah-Ali and Nissen's seminal article, considerable research has been done to improve the advantages of encrypted caches in both centralized and decentralized environments. Given a symmetric cache of MF bits of length F per user, the authors propose an optimal centralized code cache. For M1 $\leq$ 1/K1 when N1 $\leq$ K1 reaches the theoretical lower limit. Another centralized representation for

N1 < K1 is also presented, which in some cases improves on the scheme achieved by sharing memory between instances. The proposed centralized cache provides a delivery rate of M1 = (N1 – 1)/K1 when 4 ≤ N1< K1 ≤ 3N1/2, and the common divisor of K1 and N1 is greater than 1. There is an increase in the payment rate as compared to other schemes. Although the broken connection gives a lower limit on the transmission speed, a tighter bond is obtained. Further variations of this cache model have been studied in the literature, such as homogenous query distributed cache and encoded online cache model (where, N1 is the number of files and K1 is the number of users requesting data).

Furthermore, the caching problem can be explained in distinct phases: placement phase along with a delivery phase. Moreover, the user can save an unlimited amount of files in its cache memory during the placement process. Throughout the stage, every user requests one of the files from the information center at random such that it is distinct from that of the other users and with an equal distribution. Further, the server receives notification of the requested file and subsequently, transmits the message across a shared connection. Additionally, the system's placement and delivery phases are designed to keep the shared data link as short as possible due to memory and rebuilding constraints in the delivery phase. The Least Recently Used (LRU) expulsion policy is a prominent emulsion to the caching complication that is currently in use. Each cache in LRU is in charge of the most recently requested files, allowing it to take advantage of the temporal proximity of data file requests. This cache miss rate is utilized to replace the concerned network load. The network load and the cache miss rate are proportional in a system with a single cache miss rate, therefore while minimizing the former reduces the latter. This proportionality, however, does not apply to the multiple cache scheme. An alternative solution termed, coded caching approach is required for multiple caching systems. The federated learning model is a procedure for training an encyclopaedic model using decentralized data from several client servers. However, in many user case situations, the federated learning model would manifest the training coordinate information of users, as well as the uneven quantity of data possessed by users, resulting in training inefficiency. Because cache memory is limited, it is necessary to estimate file popularity and cache the most popular files.

2. PRELIMINARIES

This section includes the background information that starts with the Cloud and Fog computing. Subsequently, Coded Caching that is often mixed up with fog computing and thereafter, the concept of Data Synchronization that is mixed up with fog computing and Coded Caching are discussed.

2.1 Cloud and fog Computing

To satisfy the needs of IoT and future computing frameworks, new forms of cloud computing have been developed and proposed to overcome the lacuna of the existing ones. Instead of being placed in an unidentified location in the cloud, the devices that respond and function to the demands of the client in this novel model are essentially situated at the local network's edge. By considering a fog layer between mobile devices and the cloud, this computing model—dubbed "Fog Computing". Various heterogeneous devices have been incorporated into a geographically scattered computing architecture called fog computing at the network's edge to provide elastic computing, communication, end-user storage services. Because edge devices use data, network bandwidth and data time for transmission have been significantly reduced. The needs of latency-sensitive applications are effectively accommodated by the fog paradigm, which also eliminates network capacity restrictions. Fog computing is based on the notion of placing a thin, cloud-like layer close to mobile users. roadways, bus terminals, train stations, shopping centres, etc.

By deploying in restricted environments like the cloud, mobile users can receive location-aware services and short-fat connections directly as discussed by Tom, et al. Specifically, to enable wireless data transfer to dispersed devices in the IoT, Cisco created the term "fog computing" as a new computing model whose main objective is to bring content and application services as near as feasible to customer. Between endpoints and the cloud, this resource-rich layer satisfies the demands for low latency, high dependability, mobility, bandwidth, and high performance. Internet data traffic can be decreased and services can be delivered more quickly due to fog computing paradigm. IoT's important characteristics are mobility, low latency, location awareness, wireless connection, quicker processing demands, and wireless connectivity. The client can utilize a processing node that is close by and connected to it over a low-latency wireless connection to fulfil this prerequisite. Many IoT constraints that are ineffectively handled by the present cloud computing models may be effectively solved using fog computing, including: network bandwidth. The number of IoT devices that are linked is growing exponentially now-a-days. Network bandwidth constraints are prevalent due to complicated, thin connections between cloud and mobile users.

- **Latency Requirements**: the majority of Internet of Things applications demand latency below tens of milliseconds. Such delay cannot be guaranteed by basic cloud services.
- **Real-time Reaction:** since real-time response is usually required by IoT devices, it cannot be made available in a cloud environment. Fog computing makes the most of the computational and storage power of equipment at the

network's edge. End-user devices can analyse and retain locally the information collected locally. Since all data are not communicated to the cloud, this will curtail the amount of network traffic, save bandwidth, and speed up data analysis as well as the decision making. Sheikh, et al. (2022) discussed the effective offloading mechanisms associated with fog computing. Moreover, Silva, et al. (2019) discussed the position of fog nodes in case of fog-cloud infrastructures. Likewise, Mijuskovic, et al. (2021) proposed the resource administration techniques used in cloud and edge computing framework and Dand et al. (2017) talks the data protection and the performance challenges associated with this context. Hong et al. (2017) have detailed the concepts of cloud and fog computing while dealing with optimization problems. Winnie et al. (2018) detailed the concepts of enhancing data security in health care service and medical applications.

Similarly, Khumalo, et al. (2020) discussed the concept of IoT in healthcare and Bai et al. (2019) discussed the concepts of coded caching and likewise Jiang et al.(2020) proposed the concept of decentralized asynchronous coded caching and the performance assessment for the radio access network. The fog node is a key component of any fog computing application as advocated by Habibi et al. 2020 and Ahvar, et al. (2021) discussed the next generation of SDN employed in cloud-fog for 5G and beyond-enabled applications. By boosting computational and storage capabilities and reusing wireless interfaces, fog nodes may be created by modifying existing network elements including routers, switches, access points for wireless networks, and cellular base station. Fog computing makes use of more advanced computational and storage capabilities at the edge. Fog points near mobile users employ local short-range wireless connections to deliver high-speed services to mobile customers. A one-hop wireless connection is employed by fog nodes to interact directly with mobile users who are inside their wireless coverage area. The fog point is therefore a typical virtualized device with built-in storage, computation, and networking capabilities that may be intelligent and adaptable to serve users. The explanation of the three sources can be summarized as follows:

a) **Caching:** Because fog points have location awareness, they may anticipate mobile user data requests and proactively cache frequently requested material. The sort of data requests made by mobile users can be quite predictable, therefore Alam, et al. (2021) suggests aggressively caching the data without the user's permission.
b) **Computing:** Fog point indicates an autonomous independent intelligent computing framework that serves the local information and computation while perfectly processing the needs of mobile users. Fog points gather environmental

data from mobile users placed in different areas, and they transfer the bulk of the data they have gathered to the cloud for deep data analysis, which provides more useful and strategic planning and decision-making insights.

c) **Communication:** The fog node, a highly automated network component that serves as an intermediary between mobile users and the fog node and the cloud. A gadget must be capable of processing, storing, and communicating data, as well as being online (Ahvar, et al., 2021), in order to be considered a possible fog point. However, fog spots may be divided into two types based on how edge devices are employed. Devices such as fog nodes and dumb edge devices serve as data generators and consumers, similar to sensors and actuators. *Fig points*, which resemble micro-clouds, feature intelligent edge devices with powerful computational power, behave similar to automobiles and smartphones. To create a three-tier service delivery paradigm, fog computing and cloud computing work hand in hand (as discussed by Atlam, et al., 2018).
d) **Fog layer:** this layer is positioned at the edge of the network near the end user. The fog layer consists of a large number of fog nodes distributed between the corresponding end-user appliances and the concerned cloud.
e) **Cloud layer:** it indicates the top layer present in the hierarchy. It comprises of several high-performance servers and storage appliances. It possesses powerful computing and storage capabilities.

2.2 Coded Caching

The video-on-demand service offers a library of yellow, orange, and blue videos. All three require the video to be displayed and the screen colour. Each user has one video in their cache (high resolution file user cloud row) and missing two other videos (Gray file in the top row of the user's cloud). Users must send three videos in a standard unicast stream. With in-user caching, the amount of data sent is reduced by the cache. In our example, three users have an orange video cache. Only two videos are sent instead of three. For the remaining two users, the cache is lost and thus appears as useless.

We can as well use caches on users through encoding and broadcasting. After receiving the yellow and blue video requests, the server combines the two and serves the encoded broadcast. The server combines the yellow video with the blue video and uses a little clever XOR operation to originate a green file $X = A \oplus B$. File X is the same as A and B, the size of A and not the size of B. The server broadcasts the green file X to both users. The yellow user feeds the received X file and the blue video from the cache to the decoder. The decoder that returns the yellow file require A by calculating $B \oplus X = B \oplus (A \oplus B) = A$ i. e. yellow video from the cache A. Two users through the encoded cache receive the desired content from the same broadcast stream. For example, we need one file to send, while a standard cache requires two files and three files are flushed without cache.

Although this is a significant finding, the encrypted cache's initial design included the assumption that user requests are synchronized, which means they all reach the server at the same time. Then we referred to this as synchronous tuning. From a practical standpoint, it's crucial to take into account the asynchronous situation of user requests arriving at various times. Waiting for the final request to come in and applying the Maddah-Ali and Niesen plan is a straightforward approach in this situation. The overall transfer speed from the server will benefit greatly from this approach. The end-user experience, however, might suffer greatly because the user's delay will significantly affect when the last request arrives.

2.3 Federated Learning

Alternative computational learning algorithms undergo training using federated learning, utilizing many local databases without distributing data. With no need to retain training data in a single location, this enables businesses to develop universal worldwide models.

When training comes:

- A local unified database serves as the training ground for a Machine learning (ML) model. When users utilise a machine learning programme, for instance, they identify and fix predictions that the ML programme made that were incorrect. As a result, every user device gets a local training database.
- Between these neighbourhood data centres, the model's parameters are periodically swapped. The majority of models code these variables before changing them. We don't share local data samples. Data protection and online security are enhanced as a result.
- The construction of a broad global model gets accomplished and the global model feature is shared with the local data centre to integrate the global model with the local ML model.

Companies value accurate machine learning models, but old centralized machine learning systems have drawbacks such as gathering private data on centralized servers and not continually learning on edge devices. This can be facilitated through federal training. In traditional machine learning, centralized ML models are built using training data available in a centralized environment. This works without problems if the central server can serve predictions. However, in mobile computing, users demand fast responses and communication times between user devices and central servers can be too slow for a good user experience. To overcome such disputed point, the model can be deployed on the end-user device, but it is difficult to learn consistently because the model is trained on the complete data set and the end-user device does not have access to the full database. Another challenge with traditional machine learning is that user data is centralized in machine learning locations, which may violate privacy laws of some countries and may be more susceptible to data breaches. Federated Learning addresses such ultimatum by enabling continuous learning across end-user devices.

In this research, we have discussed an approach known as "Hybrid Approach Using Coded Caching Based Federated Learning (HA – CCFL)", where we investigate both online and offline coded caching approaches that leverage a single origin server (Cloud) linked to a shared connection and a finite set of cache memory for a group of users. In this strategy, coded caching is used to curtail the peak load of the shared link (i.e., the load for the worst user request). Furthermore, in many cases, the popularity of shared links varies by orders of magnitude, making the projected load more important than the peak load. This is a specific instance where the system has a large number of users or is operating for the longest amount of time, in this case, many laws apply. In the encoded cache table, we divide the original file (A, B) into equal-sized chunks, such as A = A1, A2 and B = B1, B2. The values are preserved as (A1, B1) and (A2, B2) in the first user and second user respectively. User number 1 request file A and user number 2 request B file. These requests can be satisfied by transmitting A2 x B1 coded 1/2F bit size from the server. The user cache can restore its requested file using the information it has cached. The other request is handled in the same way as the 1/2-bit link load for the coded caching technique.

To solve such predicaments, we have proffered $HA - CCFL$ strategy with a layered architecture as an alternative to the abovementioned challenge. In our proposal, the bottom layer encompasses the user's file request, and the foremost one consists of the central server and illustrations. Each user must download the resulting autoencoder model from the server, upload the updated model parameters at each successive steps, and execute the outputted N files to the server to train the model using the contents of the local file. File resemblance is used in order to generate recommendations based on the crossover filtering and extraction of user-drawing hidden characteristics. Based on the federated average approach, the server accumulates the model parameters surrendered by each user and then chooses the most well-liked files predicted by all users. The $HA - CCFL$ method has been set up as a database that's accessible online. The User Equipment (UE), which encompasses training through the information stored in the device prior to updating it, first receives the first model for training from the adjacent Base Station (BS). The central station (BS), where each update from the user's device contributes on average to enhance the overall model, that receives just this update. Because training data is conserved locally despite the fact that only model modification parameters are transferred to a central server, $HA - CCFL$ is capable of minimizing internal security and privacy threats.

The main contribution of this strategy can be summarized as follows:

- In this research, a federated learning strategy that integrates coded caching, conjointly with both distributed and centralized training models is recommended, while collaborating on practical implementation scenarios for federated learning and coded caching.
- The $HA - CCFL$ has an organized framework in which the server that hosts it first generates a global model utilizing user-side updates before prioritising the most well-liked files. To train on their local data, each user uses hybrid filtering based on stacked autoencoders.
- The experimental findings, which are based upon results of datasets assert the effectiveness of the proffered approach in terms of cache efficiency. Further, $HA - CCFL$ surpassed the competing classical algorithms.
- $HA - CCFL$ performs effectively in terms of various performance parameters such as: cache hit rate, CPU Usage, throughput and latency which assert its effectiveness in present context.

3. SYSTEM MODEL

The newly coded cache is to add a local cache that can take over the global cache. This advantage is achieved by optimizing the placement and the transmission phase together, ensuring that the different requirements are satisfied by the multi-digit transmission coded in the transmission phase. Since the content deployment is done without the knowledge of the actual requirements, the deployment phase must be carefully designed to achieve this advantage, as several opportunities are simultaneously created for potential demands during the delivery phase. Since content deployment is done without the knowledge of the actual requirements, the deployment phase must be carefully designed to achieve this advantage, as several opportunities are simultaneously created for potential demands during the delivery phase. If the global cache is large enough compared to the total content of the cache, we show that the gain from the global cache is becoming crucial. Thus, even though caches may not cooperate, the sum of cache sizes becomes a relevant system parameter.

3.1 Preface

3.1.1 Fog computing: the fog layer, which sits between the edge and cloud layers, helps to improve the performance, including latency, throughput, reaction time, and other factors. The user requests the model from the central server of fog rather than directly asking the data from the cloud, which usually satisfies the user's requirement. To that end, each fog node trains the model locally and uploads the model parameters to the cloud for parameter aggregation.

3.1.2 Federated learning: The server may join several user groups and train these models concurrently without updating in the database in order to prevent the collection of user and sensitive data.

3.1.3 Coded Caching: By keeping some material in the user's local cache memory without knowing the future demand for searches, this technique effectively reduces traffic congestion during peak hours. The amount of bits transmitted by the server via the shared connection is reduced through codified caching.

3.2. State of Art

A connection between IoT devices and cloud servers may be made using fog nodes that have robust computation and storage capabilities. In the edge layer, IoT devices request the data from the central server, these servers are further segmented into the fog nodes where data is stored in the split form, this segmentation is done to reduce latency so that the demand of the user can be fulfilled during the short period. When the user requests the data from the nodes, the federated learning framework is applied where the user gets the future prediction on the searches, it gives the user accuracy in searching the data out. If in the case data is not present in all of these fog nodes, the central server requests the updated model from the cloud and according to the demanding user gets the collaborative models where central server is present, from which the request for model update is sent to the cloud and the collaborative model gets updated which is illustrated in Fig. 1.

Figure 1. Coded caching-based federated learning

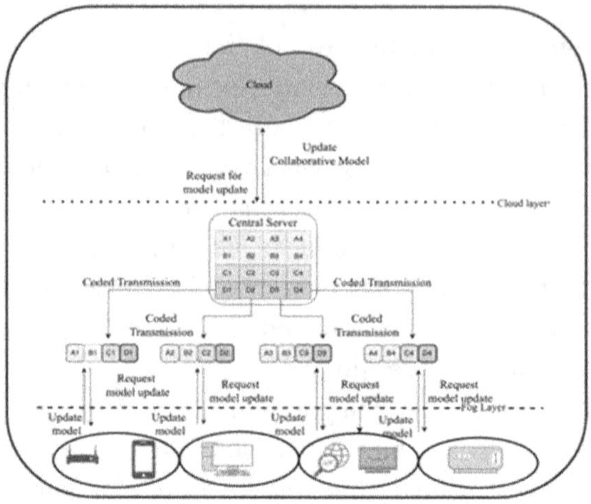

Figure 2. The coded caching framework

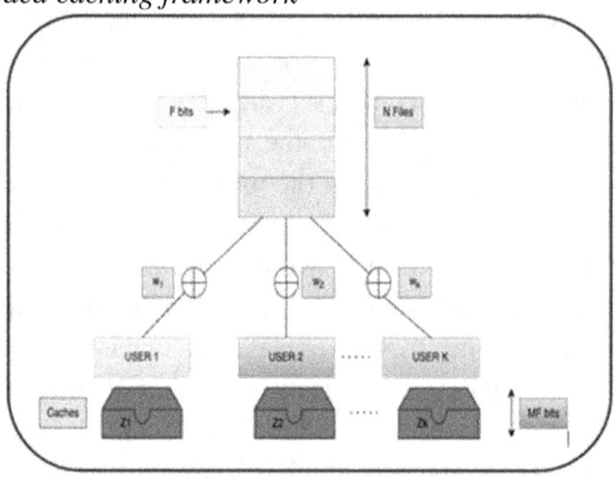

Let's say that users 1 and 2 ask for files X and Y, respectively. User 1 wants X_0 and X_2, which are not cached in its memory since User One already has access to all of the requested file components X_1 and $X_{1,2}$. Similar to user 1, user 2 is in need of Y_0 and Y_1 but already has access to Y_2 and $Y_{1,2}$ of the requested file. The server may then respond to these user requests by transmitting X_0, Y_0, and X_2 Y_1 across the shared connection, where XOR is the operation that was performed element-wise on X_2 and Y_1 represented as bit vectors. Consider that cached data for user 1 possesses the following information: Y_1. Using this and the shared link's output X_2 Y_1, the user may locate the appropriate file section X_2.

Similar to the first user, user 2 has X_2 saved in its cache and may utilise this to retrieve the needed file portion Y_1 from the shared link's output X_2 Y_1. Therefore, both user X and user Y may recover the file of the needed path by using the contents of their caches and the link shared when retrieving the output. We are integrating federated learning and coded caching i.e. while requesting the user will get the future prediction of what he/she will be going to search about and after the data model has been requesting the data from the fog nodes that get uploaded to the device. In case, if data is not available in the fog nodes. The central server updates the model to the cloud and then the cloud sends the data to the user as per the request. In the fog, layer data are in the form of segments means data is being splitting into various sections as per the storage capacity this will lead to help users in satisfying the need on time. Integrating federated learning and coded caching tends to reduce the load onto the user. In order to properly study the effectiveness of the recommended coded caching technique and to analyse and identify these two benefits, an information-theoretic description of the caching problem focuses on its fundamental structure.

3.2.1 Analytical Framework

In this context, K users get connected to a server over a shared, error-free connection. On a server, a database is kept in N1 files of the same size. Each user has access to cache memory that has a capacity of M files. During the placement step, the cache is filled. Further, in the delivery phase, each user has the choice to ask for any one of the N1 possible files. By meticulously organizing the installation and delivery stages, it is hoped to reduce the shared link load throughout the delivery period. In order to keep things simple, the introduction section will only discuss the case in which there are more files N1 than there are users K1. The initial findings are presented subsequently for the overall issue. In this configuration, the shared connection burden during the regular unencrypted cache delivery phase is normalized by file size K1 · (1 – M1/N1), where 1-M1/N1 is the local caching benefit and K is the rate without caching. While the coded caching system suggested in this study achieves a rate of K1 (1 -M1/N1) * 1 /(1 + K1M1/N1), the former does not. The coded cache image so acquires global cache of (1/1 + K1M1 / N1) in addition to local cache (1 – M1 / N1).

Assuming they are in the identical order as (or larger than) the number of files, Cache K1M1 / N1, and Aggregate Cache K1M1 become significant.

Definition. A combination (M1, R1) is reachable if, for each $\varepsilon > 0$ and every sufficiently massive file size F, there exists a caching scheme (M1, R1) with error probability subordinate than ε. We define a trade-off between memory speed as depicted by equation 1.

$$R1 \star (M1) \triangleq \inf \{R1: (M1, R1) \text{ is reachable}\}(1)$$

The memory rate trade-off R1 (M1) has an upper constraint provided by the first theorem, which reflects the feasible rate RC(M1).

Theorem 1. N1/K1 may be attained for N1 files and K1 users with a cache size of $M1 \in \{0, N1/K1, 2N1/K1, \ldots, N1\}$, $R1 \star (M1) \leq RC(M) \triangleq K1 \cdot (1 - M1/N1) \cdot \min \{1/(1 + K1M1/N1), N1/K1\}$. These points' lower convex envelope can be solved for the general $0 \leq M1 \leq N1$.

A programmed caching mechanism, which is thoroughly explained, is what makes RC(M1) fast. We initially concentrate on the scenario N K where for simple explanation following equation (2) must hod true.

$$RC(M1) = K1\ (1\ M1/N1)\ 1/(1 + K1M1/N1)(2)$$

There are three major criteria that determine the speed at which RC(M1) may be reached. K1is RC's prime factor (M1). The worst-case for no user cache (i.e. M1 = 0) is this. $1 - M1/N1$ is the second component of RC(M1). It should be noted that this local benefit that depends on the normalized local memory capacity M1/N1 and that M1 becomes important when N1 is ordered. We refer to the third component of RC(M1), 1 /(1+K1M1/N1), as the global cache gain. When K1M1 is of the order of (or larger than) N1, this benefit, which is a function of the normalised global or cumulative memory size K1M1/N1, is applicable. The multicast gain that is concurrently accessible for all potential claims is to be seen as this global gain. Keep in mind that in the worst situation, every user would request a different file because there are fewer users than there are files. Therefore, there are therefore no alternatives for spontaneous multicasting. Theorem 1's suggested system carefully considers how to position material to allow for coded multicasting during delivery even among users who are seeking different files. Therefore, there are no alternatives for natural multicasting. Theorem 1's suggested system carefully considers how to position material to allow for coded multicasting during delivery even among users who are seeking different files.

Given that the placement phase that takes place without knowledge of the actual requests, care must be given to ensure that the same multicasting options are formed concurrently for each prospective group of requests in the delivery phase. The overall approachable plan is currently shown. We begin by putting the method into words and emphasising the RC(M) corner points. Consider the following cache sizes: M1 ∈ {0, N1/K1, 2N1/K1, . . ., N1}, and set t ≜ (M1*K1)/N1. We will now outline the overall workable plan. We initially provide a verbal description of the procedure, concentrating on the RC(M) corner points. Take into account cache sizes M ∈ {0, N1/K1, 2N1/K1, . . ., N1}, and set t ≜ (M1*K1)/N1.

Let us consider the number T, which ranges from 0 to K1. If M1 = 0, the server can send F min N1, K1 bits during the transmission phase while transferring any number of file arrangements on the shared connection. Therefore, R(0) ≤ min {N1, K1}.

All database files may be cached for each user during the deployment phase if M1 = N1. Therefore, R(N) = 0. Counterfeit below that M1 is substantial than 0 and diminutive than N1, in which case ∈ {1, 2, . . ., K - 1}.

Each file is splitted during the insertion step into non-overlapping, equal-sized sub-files (Kt). Labeling the file's subfiles will be much useful. Wn can be analytically written as illustrated in equation (3) and (4) respectively:

$$W_n = (W_{n,\Gamma}: \Gamma \subset [K], |\Gamma| = t), \text{ where the note has been retained} \tag{3}$$

$$[K1] \triangleq \{1, \ldots, K1\} \tag{4}$$

If user k, subfile Wn, for each n ∈ [N1], is stored in user k ∈ Γ cache. As a result, $N1\binom{K-1}{t-1}$ subfiles are cached by each user. Since each subfile is of size $F/\binom{K}{t}$, it becomes necessary that for every user, one cache chunk must meet the available memory requirement as illustrated in equation (5):

Mathematically,

$$N1\binom{K-1}{t-1}\frac{F}{\binom{K}{t}} = F\left(\frac{Nt}{K}\right) = FM1 \tag{5}$$

4. PERFORMANCE EVALUATION

This section depicts the details regarding various performance metrics, and analyses the experimental outcomes for assessing the model's performance in terms of the following:

(i) Cache hit rate
(ii) Throughput
(iii) Latency
(iv) Average Latency
(v) CPU Usage

(vi) Response time

4.1 Performance Assessment

A) Number of Fog nodes Versus Cache Hit Rate

We are optimizing the cache hit rate where we are representing cache hit rate as η, number of cache hit as α and the number of cache misses as β. Maximizing the cache hit rate tends to give the outcome that thc content is successfully served from the cache instead from the source point server. The objective here is to maximize the cache hit rate. Mathematically, we can represent cache hit rate as shown in equation 6.

$$\eta = \alpha/(\alpha + \beta) \qquad (6)$$

It is marked that whenever the number of fog nodes hike, the hit rate escalates that assert the satisfaction of the major objective of our proposed approach. In the experiment, we have performed the Content Delivered Network with 50 nodes and their hit rate lies between 4 to 35. By observing the hit ratio and their comparison results, we have come to the conclusion that as the number of fog nodes increases, the hit rate rises since there is a higher likelihood of receiving the required data close to the end devices.

B) Response Time

We are representing the response time (in seconds) as T response, n as number of synchronous userS, r as the number requests per second that the server receives and T as average think time (in seconds). Minimizing response helps in fast web hosting that could help the user in accessing file in short span of time. Mathematically, we can represent Response Time as shown in equation 7. Fig. 3. Shows a variation of hit rate with number of fog nodes.

$$T_{response} = n/r - T_{think} \qquad (7)$$

Figure 3. Number of fog nodes versus hit rate

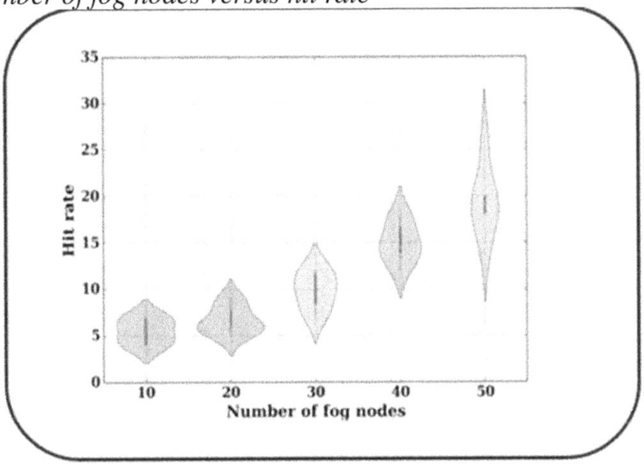

C) Maximizing Number of Splitting

Maximizing the number of data splitting will tend to help in better predictions of models. We will split the data by chi-square method, where χ is represented as Total number of splitting, $Ø_i$ is

represented as Actual value and E_i is represented as Expected value. It can be mathematically represented as in equation (8)

$$\chi 2 = (Ø_i - E_i)/E_i \quad (8)$$

Fig. 4. Shows the scenario of storage of fog nodes versus CPU usage. With hike in number of storage of fog nodes, the CPU usage hikes. Fig. 5 illustrates the scenario of number of fog nodes versus CPU Usage where CPU usage hikes with hike in number of fog nodes.

Figure 4. Storage of fog nodes versus CPU usage

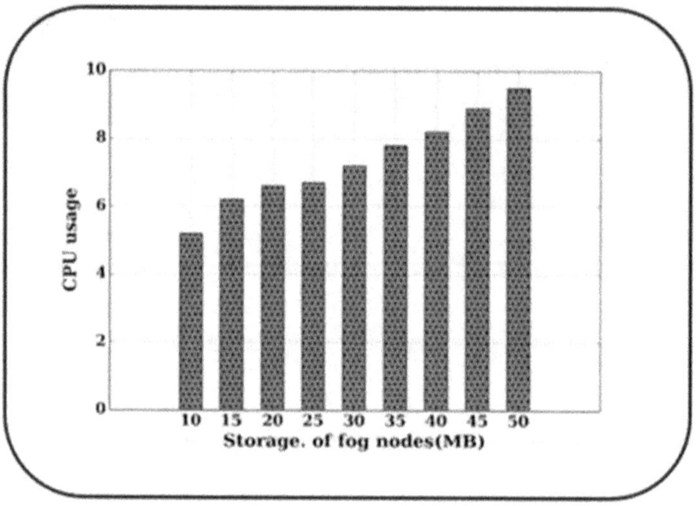

Figure 5. Number of fog nodes versus CPU usage

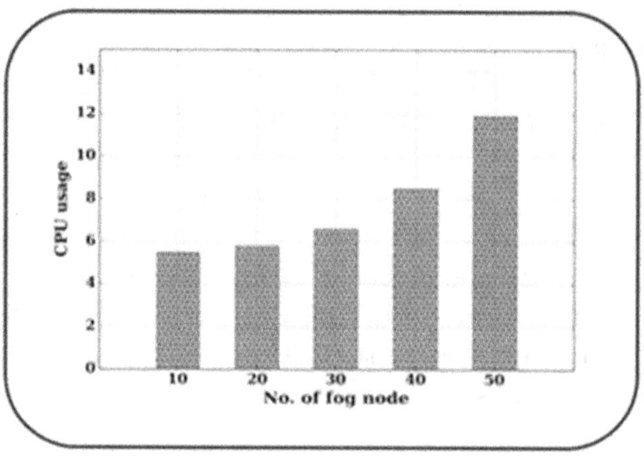

D) Maximizing the Number of Fog Nodes

All the nodes have the capabilities to turns into fog nodes. We are performing the experiment on the number of fog nodes with probability p. The problem of optimizing the number of Fog nodes is equals to optimizing p, which minimizes the transmission delay. Our objective is to maximize the number of fog nodes as depicted in equation 9.

$$n_{nodes} = n * p \qquad (9)$$

E) Throughput Against the Storage of Fog Nodes

In this experiment, we have performed the Content Delivered Network with the storage capacity from 10 bits to 50 bits and their throughput lies approximately between 15 to 95. We observe that with the increase in the storage, the throughput also increases and theRE will be the highest probability of getting data on time. Fig. 6 shows a snap of node storage versus throughout. It is marked that throughput hikes with hike in node storage.

Figure 6. Node storage versus throughout

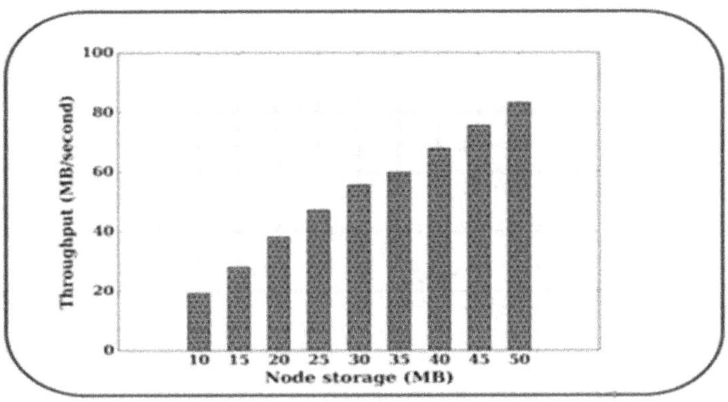

F) Latency Against Storage of Fog Nodes

Higher bandwidth means that more traffic can be carried. In this experiment, we have shown the two major changes when the storage of fog nodes increases and when the number of nodes increases. In this experiment, we experience that by increasing the number of fog nodes, the end-user reflects the level of satisfaction of getting the data packet on time. To demonstrate this, we have performed the experiment on increasing the storage from 10MB to 30MB and by this, we have concluded the above statement. Fig. 7 portrays a scenario of node storage versus latency. It is marked that latency hikes with hike in node storage.

Figure 7. Node storage versus latency

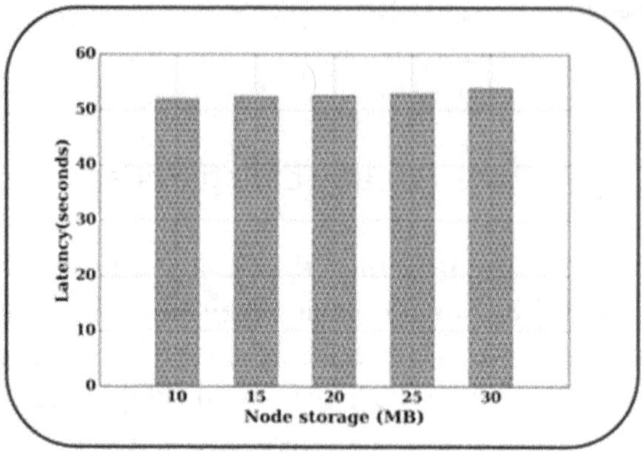

G) Average Latency Against Number of Fog Nodes

From experimental observation, we came to know that when we increase the number of fog nodes, latency decreases. This is because, while performing the coded caching technique we came to know that data is being splitted into as many section depending upon the number of fog nodes in the layer. We performed this experiment with the cluster of 10 nodes to 50 nodes. Fig. 8 illustrates the scenario of number of fog nodes versus average latency. With hike in number of fog nodes, the average latency rises.

Figure 8. Number of fog nodes versus average latency

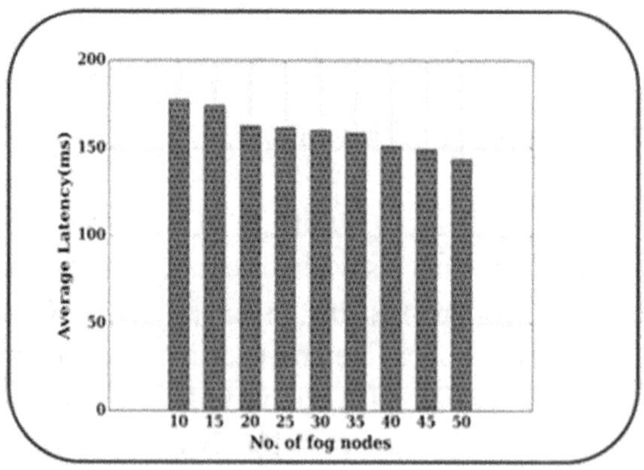

5. CONCLUSIONS AND FUTURE RESEARCH DIRECTION

In our paper, we have proffered a hybrid approach using coded caching based federated learning to create a learning to all popular files in the Fog node with time type content popularity. As such, by framing the placement problem and utilizing the learning of federation, deployment strategies are derived through collaborative learning. The proposed approach addresses a stable low level transmission, and a general prediction model on fog which is conducted locally through user devices to demonstrate that the federated learning framework is capable of handling time fluctuation in popularity. The simulation findings also showed that the performance was harmed by simply focusing on global multicast sharing, which is poor and overlooks variations in content popularity. The privacy of the data will be loosely packed in this situation when federated learning has been applied because federated learning model is meant to be run locally on user device. So when it will be performed at fog, third party sources can also see the learning model data. So, the future direction for this paper will be to ensure greater privacy preservation. The numerical results attain from the experimentation in terms of cache hit rate, CPU Usage, throughput and latency assert the proposed approach as a promising paradigm for further research to be carried out in this context.

REFERENCES

Ahvar, E. (2021). Next Generation of SDN in Cloud-Fog for 5G and Beyond-Enabled Applications: Opportunities and Challenges. *Network (Bristol, England), 1*, 28–49.

Alam, T. (2021). Cloud-Based IoT Applications and Their Roles in Smart Cities. *Smart Cities*, *4*(3), 1196–1219. DOI: 10.3390/smartcities4030064

Alojail, M. (2020). Fog Computing Mitigate Limitations of Cloud Computing. *International Journal of Recent Technology and Engineering*, *8*(5), 1732–1736. DOI: 10.35940/ijrte.E6199.018520

Atlam, H. F., Walters, R. J., & Wills, G. B. (2018). Fog Computing and the Internet of Things: A Review. *Big Data and Cognitive Computing*, *2*(2), 1–18. DOI: 10.3390/bdcc2020010

Bai, B., Li, W., Wang, L., & Zhang, G. (2019). Coded Caching in Fog-RAN: B Matching Approach. *IEEE Transactions on Communications*, *67*(5), 3753–3767. DOI: 10.1109/TCOMM.2019.2896026

Dang, T. D., & Hoang, D. (2017). A Data Protection Model for Fog Computing. *Proceedings of the Second International Conference on Fog and Mobile Edge Computing (FMEC)*, 32-38. DOI: 10.1109/FMEC.2017.7946404

Gnaneswar, N., Hadresh, G., & Pdinesh, V. (2020). A Comparison Analysis of Fog And Cloud Computing, DOI: DOI: 10.31221/osf.io/y7db2

Habibi, P., Farhoudi, M., Kazemian, S., Khorsandi, S., & Leon-Garcia, A. (2020). Fog Computing: A Comprehensive Architectural Survey. *IEEE Access : Practical Innovations, Open Solutions*, *8*, 69105–69133. DOI: 10.1109/ACCESS.2020.2983253

Hong, H. (2017). From Cloud Computing to Fog Computing: Unleash the Power of Edge and End Devices. *Proceedings of the IEEE International Conference on Cloud Computing Technology and Science (CloudCom)*, 331–334. DOI: 10.1109/CloudCom.2017.53

Jiang, Y., Huang, W., Bennis, M., Zheng, F. (2020), Decentralized Asynchronous Coded Caching Design and Performance Analysis in Fog Radio Access Networks, IEEE Transactions on Mobile Computing, 19(3), 540–551.

Khan, S., Parkinson, S., & Qin, Y. (2017). Fog computing security: A review of current applications and security solutions. *Journal of Cloud Computing (Heidelberg, Germany)*, *6*(19), 1–22. DOI: 10.1186/s13677-017-0090-3

Khumalo, N., Oyerinde, O., & Mfupe, L. (2020). Reinforcement Learning Based Computation Resource Allocation Scheme for 5G Fog-Radio Access Network. *2020 Fifth International Conference on Fog and Mobile Edge Computing (FMEC)*, 353–355. DOI: 10.1109/FMEC49853.2020.9144787

Luan, T. (2015). Fog Computing: Focusing on Mobile Users at the Edge. *Computer Science*.

Mijuskovic, A., Chiumento, A., Bemthuis, R., Aldea, A., & Havinga, P. (2021). Resource Management Techniques for Cloud/Fog and Edge Computing: An Evaluation Framework and Classification. *Sensors (Basel)*, *21*(5), 1–22. DOI: 10.3390/s21051832 PMID: 33808037

Pengfei, H., Sahraoui, D., Huansheng, N., & Tie, Q. (2017). Survey on fog computing: Architecture, key technologies, applications and open issues. *Journal of Network and Computer Applications*, *98*, 27–42. DOI: 10.1016/j.jnca.2017.09.002

Sheikh, S., Haghi, M., Kashani, M., & Mahdipour, E. (2022)... *Multimedia Tools and Applications*, *81*, 1997–2042. DOI: 10.1007/s11042-021-11423-9 PMID: 34690529

Shukla, S., Hassan, M. F., Tran, D. C., Akbar, R., Paputungan, I. V., & Khan, M. K. (2021). Improving latency in Internet-of-Things and cloud computing for real-time data transmission: A systematic literature review (SLR). *Cluster Computing*, *26*(5), 2657–2680. DOI: 10.1007/s10586-021-03279-3

Siddiqi, M. A., Yu, H., & Joung, J. (2019). 5G Ultra-Reliable Low-Latency Communication Implementation Challenges and Operational Issues with IoT Devices. *Electronics (Basel)*, *2019*(8), 1–18. DOI: 10.3390/electronics8090981

Silva, C. (2019). On the Location of Fog Nodes in Fog Cloud Infrastructures. *Sensors (Basel)*, *19*(11), 24–45. DOI: 10.3390/s19112445 PMID: 31146339

Winnie, Y. (2018). Enhancing Data Security in IoT Healthcare Services Using Fog Computing. *proceedings of the International Conference on Recent Trends in Advance Computing (ICRTAC)*, 200–205. DOI: 10.1109/ICRTAC.2018.8679404

Yousefpour, A., Fung, C., Nguyen, T., Kadiyala, K., Fatemeh, J., Jalali, A., Niakanlahiji, J. K., & Jue, J. P. (2019). All one needs to know about fog computing and related edge computing paradigms: A complete survey. *Journal of Systems Architecture*, *98*, 289–330. DOI: 10.1016/j.sysarc.2019.02.009

Yu, W., Liang, F., He, X., Hatcher, W. G., Lu, C., Lin, J., & Yang, X. (2018). A Survey on the Edge Computing for the Internet of Things. *IEEE Access : Practical Innovations, Open Solutions*, *6*, 6900–6919. DOI: 10.1109/ACCESS.2017.2778504

Chapter 17
AI-Powered Tools to Enhance the Stages of Software Development

S. Roobini
https://orcid.org/0000-0002-4104-1875
SNS College of Technology, India

M. Kavitha
https://orcid.org/0009-0003-1203-1904
Sri Krishna College of Engineering and Technology, India

Hema Deenadayalan
https://orcid.org/0000-0002-8586-2907
Sri Ramakrishna College of Arts and Science for Women, India

A. Muthusamy
https://orcid.org/0000-0003-1889-0630
Kongu Engineering College, India

ABSTRACT

The rapid evolution of Artificial Intelligence (AI) has significantly impacted the software development lifecycle (SDLC), introducing tools that enhance efficiency, accuracy, and innovation. This chapter examines the integration of AI-powered tools across SDLC stages, including planning, design, coding, testing, deployment, and maintenance. AI automates tasks like code generation, bug detection, and test case creation, reducing errors and accelerating development. It also enhances decision-making, fosters team collaboration, and optimizes resources through predictive analytics and intelligent project management tools. The chapter highlights AI's role in software quality improvement, using machine learning to detect anomalies

DOI: 10.4018/979-8-3693-9356-7.ch017

and predict failures early. Ethical and security challenges are addressed, stressing responsible AI use and human oversight. By chapter's end, readers will understand how AI-powered tools reshape software development, enabling the creation of robust, scalable, and user-friendly applications while navigating ethical and quality challenges effectively.

I. INTRODUCTION

The field of software development is evolving rapidly, propelled by advancements in artificial intelligence (AI). Once viewed as a distant future possibility, AI technologies are now a central part of the software development process, automating tasks, improving accuracy, and driving efficiency in ways that were previously unimaginable. From early planning stages through to deployment and ongoing maintenance, AI-powered tools are reshaping traditional workflows and enabling developers to achieve higher levels of productivity and innovation.

The software development lifecycle traditionally consists of several distinct phases: planning, coding, testing, deployment, and maintenance. Each phase presents unique challenges, such as managing complex project requirements, identifying and fixing bugs, and ensuring that software systems can scale effectively. In order to overcome these obstacles, AI has become a potent ally. By harnessing machine learning, natural language processing, and data analytics, AI-driven tools are capable of performing complex tasks that were once the sole domain of human developers. This not only speeds up the development process but also helps to reduce human error, enhance code quality, and improve overall software performance.

This chapter aims to explore the integration of AI tools at each stage of the software development lifecycle, illustrating how these tools are transforming the industry and pushing the boundaries of what is possible. In the planning phase, for example, AI-driven project management tools can help teams organize resources more effectively, predict potential roadblocks, and optimize project timelines. During coding, intelligent code assistants can suggest code snippets, detect errors in real-time, and even generate code autonomously, allowing developers to focus on more strategic and creative tasks. Similarly, AI has revolutionized software testing by automating repetitive test cases, identifying vulnerabilities, and providing insights that can prevent issues before they arise.

The adoption of AI-powered tools within the deployment and maintenance phases is equally impactful. AI enhances deployment processes by optimizing CI/CD pipelines, facilitating faster and more reliable releases, and enabling automated monitoring of system performance. In the maintenance stage, AI helps predict system failures, proactively manage security threats, and optimize performance, ensuring a more stable and efficient software product.

As we explore each phase in detail, this chapter will provide a comprehensive look at the tools, techniques, and best practices for implementing AI in software development. Through real-world examples and case studies, we will illustrate the transformative power of AI and discuss the implications of this technology for the future of the software industry. By understanding the potential of AI-powered tools, software developers, project managers, and IT leaders can better prepare for an era where AI is not just an enhancement, but a fundamental component of the software development process.

1.1 Challenges

This chapter's main objective is to examine the ways that artificial intelligence (AI) is transforming the software development lifecycle by offering effective tools and methods for increasing productivity, streamlining processes, and improving the overall quality of software. AI-powered solutions are becoming essential in assisting developers, testers, and project managers in addressing difficulties more efficiently throughout the development cycle as software development continues to grow more complicated and demanding.

II. THE SOFTWARE DEVELOPMENT LIFE CYCLE (SDLC)

The Software Development Life Cycle (SDLC) is a detailed strategy that outlines how to create, maintain, upgrade, and replace certain software. The life cycle lays out a plan for enhancing the overall quality and process of software development.

2.1 Stages of SDLC

The Software Development Life Cycle (SDLC) outlines the tasks that software engineer or developer must do at different phases. Barenkamp (2020), guarantees that the finished product can satisfy the needs of the client and stay within the allocated budget. Thus, prior knowledge of this software development process is essential for a software developer. These seven phases make up the SDLC, which consists of the following stages:

1. Planning and Requirements Gathering

The planning step of the SDLC is when you gather business requirements from stakeholders or customer. The feasibility of developing the product, income possibilities, production costs, end-user needs, etc. are all assessed during this phase. We can utilise a feature prioritisation framework that considers the software/update's value, cost, development time, and other criteria to appropriately determine what should be made, what should not be made, and what should be made first. We can proceed to the next stage once it has been determined that the software project is possible to develop, meets user needs, and aligns with stakeholder and corporate objectives.

2. Define Requirements

In order for the development team to convert the information gathered during the planning and analysis phase into exact requirements, this step is crucial. A software requirement specification (SRS) or product specification, a use case document, and a requirement traceability matrix document are among the significant papers that are developed using this approach as a guide.

3. Design

The system design, programming language, templates, platform to be used, and application security measures are all included in the software design document (SDD), which is an improved version of the initial plan and vision. One can also use this to create a flowchart showing how the program reacts to user input. Creating a prototype model is commonly an essential phase in the design process. A pre-production version allows the team to make adjustments and preview how the final product will look, saving the trouble of rewriting the code.

4. Implementation (Coding)

A pre-production version allows the team to make adjustments and preview how the final product will look, saving the trouble of rewriting the code. The product's basic development begins at this point. As outlined in the DDS design, developers utilize a dedicated programming language for this task. Therefore, it is crucial that the coders adhere to the guidelines established by the association. Compilers, interpreters, debuggers, and other traditional programming tools are also used at this point. According to software rules, some well-known languages are used, such as Python, Java, C/C++, etc. A substantial amount of work and specific development tools may be needed at this stage of the SDLC. Setting up a defined timeline and milestones is essential for the software developers to understand the expectations and for tracking progress during this phase.

5. Testing and Debugging

After the product has been produced, testing is necessary to ensure that the software operates flawlessly. Only a small amount of testing is done, despite all stages of the SDLC. At this point, any likely defects are monitored, addressed, and retested. To make sure the software product works as intended, your quality assurance team must do validation testing prior to putting it into the production environment. Additionally, the testing procedure might assist in resolving any significant security and user experience problems. It is possible to test software in a virtual setting.

6. Deployment

The final product is distributed in stages in accordance with the organization's plan following extensive testing. After that, it is put to the test in an actual industrial setting. Making sure it runs smoothly is crucial. The company distributes the entire product if it works successfully. Deployment can be planned and automated based on the kind. One can use a limited number of canary releases if it's just implementing a feature upgrade. The main aim of the deployment phase is to facilitate a smooth and successful transition from the development environment to the production environment. Additionally, at this point, any lingering flaws in the software are quickly fixed. By collecting and taking into account client feedback, the SDLC process is further improved.

7. Maintenance and Monitoring

According to its structure, the software development life cycle (SDLC) ends with the maintenance phase. However, as the industry transitions to a more agile software development technique, maintenance is only a stage of future development. Users could discover faults and bugs during the maintenance step that were overlooked during the previous testing stage. To improve user experience and retention, these problems must be resolved. For any new features one might wish to include in upcoming release or upgrade, the SDLC phases can easily be restarted.

2.2 AI's Role in Each Stage

Artificial intelligence (AI) is bringing about a profound change in software development. Advanced AI technologies have brought about a substantial evolution in software development processes, resulting in solutions that are more intelligent, scalable, and efficient. Bruhin (2024) examines the significant influence of artificial intelligence on contemporary software development. AI is expected to be extremely beneficial to every facet of contemporary software organizations, and by integrating it into various parts of the software development process, can enhance it. AI is therefore changing the way developers approach their projects, from automating tedious jobs to streamlining intricate procedures.

1. AI in Requirements Gathering Phase

Large volumes of data may be automatically collected and analysed by AI-powered systems from a variety of sources, including user activity, market trends, and customer feedback. This makes it easier for developers to obtain thorough and up-to-date information about customer requirements. Additionally, AI can be used to speed up the process of gathering prerequisites and reduce the amount of human interaction in the planning portion. Natural Language Processing (NLP) has become a potent technology that can better analyse and comprehend stakeholder inputs, making it easier to capture and document requirements in a more organised and precise way.

Key Contributions

- NLP for Requirement Extraction
- Sentiment Analysis for Stakeholder Priorities
- Requirement classification and Prioritization
- Intelligent Requirement Validation and Consistency Checks
- Automated Requirement Documentation
- Continuous Feedback Loop with Stakeholders

2. AI in Planning Phase

In the planning phase, AI plays a significant role in project management, resource allocation, and risk prediction. AI-driven tools analyze historical data, previous project trends, and current resource availability to help project managers forecast timelines, allocate resources, and identify potential risks. Kumar (2024) improves project planning accuracy and creates a strong foundation for development.

Key Contributions

- Predictive analytics for project timelines and budgets
- Automated requirement analysis and refinement
- Risk Assessment and Mitigation
- Dynamic Task Prioritization and Scheduling
- Enhanced Communication and Collaboration
- Real-Time Monitoring and Adjustment of Project Plans

3. AI in Software Design Phase

AI improves the software design phase process by increasing the precision, effectiveness, and creativity of design activities. This helps to build a solid architectural basis for future development. The prototype's output can be assessed by machines by comparing it to preset benchmarks. In essence, this technique uses predictive analytics, which compares the results of the software prototype with historical data (the goals) to generate forecasts. Furthermore, Lindeman (2024) details that, AI can run simulations and validate designs to find possible defects or performance problems early on. This makes that the finished design is dependable and thoroughly tested.

Key Contributions

- Automated Design Suggestions and Prototyping
- Architecture Optimization and Validation
- Intelligent Component Reuse and Design Patterns
- User Experience Enhancement through Behavior Analysis
- Predictive Modeling for Design Decisions
- Automatic Code Generation for Design Specifications
- Real-Time Collaboration and Documentation

4. AI in Development Phase

AI speeds up software development and lowers errors during the development phase by improving productivity, code quality, and teamwork. With features like error detection, auto-completion, and intelligent code recommendations, AI is revolutionising the coding stage and enabling developers to create code more quickly and accurately. Code assistants and other AI models provide real-time suggestions based on the context of the code being written.

AI-driven coding greatly reduces the time and resource requirements of activities, allowing developers to write and comprehend code more quickly, produce code samples and documentation, and use natural language to communicate requirements. Boilerplate code can be produced more quickly and easily with the help of more sophisticated AI techniques that can even generate code from natural language descriptions.

Key Contributions

- Intelligent Code Assistance and Auto-Completion
- Automated Code Generation
- Code Review and Error Detection
- Automated Testing Integration

- Enhanced Collaboration and Knowledge Sharing
- Predictive Analytics for Performance Optimization
- Real-Time Feedback and Continuous Improvement
- Automated Documentation Generation

5. AI in Testing Phase

AI plays a crucial role in the testing phase by automating the creation, execution, and analysis of tests. AI-driven testing systems create test cases, anticipate possible flaws, and pinpoint high-risk code segments. Testing resources can be allocated more effectively by using machine learning models to examine test results and find trends in the occurrence of bugs. By giving priority to the most important test cases, AI also helps to maximize test coverage by cutting down on testing time and increasing accuracy. Faster and continuous testing, total automation without human intervention, more robust testing capabilities, lower maintenance costs and time, and higher return on investment are just a few advantages that developers may enjoy with AI-driven testing, sometimes referred to as autonomous testing.

Key Contributions

- Automated Test Case Generation
- Intelligent Test Prioritization
- Regression Testing Optimization
- Defect Prediction and Bug Detection
- Automated UI and Functional Testing
- Performance Testing and Bottleneck Identification
- Test Data Generation and Management
- Root Cause Analysis and Failure Prediction
- Continuous Testing in CI/CD Pipelines

6. AI in Deployment Phase

By automating deployment, decreasing human intervention, and minimizing errors, artificial intelligence (AI) helps pipelines for continuous integration and continuous deployment (CI/CD). Monitoring technologies driven by AI continuously evaluate the performance of applications, identify irregularities, and offer insights to stop problems before they affect users. AI algorithms can optimize rollout management and A/B testing for minimal disruption, which improves deployment tactics. It goes without saying that when we connect AI through the machine learning process, machines may also be employed to process the deployment status. New software upgrades may be deployed automatically and effectively with AI-driven continuous deployment solutions, guaranteeing a seamless and ongoing release process.

AI improves productivity, dependability, and flexibility through proactive problem-solving, resource allocation optimisation, and deployment process automation.

Key Contributions

- Automated Continuous Integration/Continuous Deployment Pipelines
- Predictive Resource Allocation and Scaling
- Intelligent Rollouts and Deployment Strategies
- Automated Performance Monitoring and Issue Detection
- Root Cause Analysis for Deployment Failures
- Real-Time Security Monitoring and Threat Detection
- Rollback Automation and Self-Healing Systems
- User Behavior Analysis and Feedback Loops

7. AI in Maintenance Phase

AI tools actively monitor systems to spot problems and anticipate possible breakdowns before they happen during the maintenance period. Anomaly detection models and predictive analytics aid in identifying anomalous activity, and AI-powered security solutions look for weaknesses and keep an eye out for online dangers. AI guarantees that software stays reliable, safe, and up to date while reducing down-time by automating routine maintenance operations. AI is capable of identifying performance bottlenecks and suggesting optimisations for increased software efficiency by analysing performance indicators and user input. Furthermore, based on user activity and comments, the system can identify the best patches and upgrades, guaranteeing that they are useful and pertinent.

Key Contributions

- Predictive Maintenance and Failure Prevention
- Automated Issue Detection and Root Cause Analysis
- Self –Healing Capabilities
- Continuous Security Monitoring and Threat Detection
- Performance Optimization and Resource Management
- Automated Patch Management and Updates
- User Behavior Analysis for Continuous Improvement
- Knowledge Management and Intelligent Documentation

AI turns the maintenance phase into a proactive, responsive procedure by combining automation, intelligent monitoring, and predictive analytics. This improves software performance, security, and dependability, which raises user happiness and lowers maintenance expenses over time. Through these contributions, AI not only streamlines each stage of the SDLC but also enables a more agile and efficient development process.

III. AI-POWERED TOOLS FOR EACH STAGE OF THE SDLC

In order to improve productivity, accuracy, and efficiency, AI-powered tools are being included into all phases of the Software Development Life Cycle (SDLC). Efimova (2024) explains the kinds of AI tools that complement each stage of the SDLC are broken down as follows:

3.1 Planning and Requirements Gathering

Prototyping, often known as the conceptual phase, is the first step in the software development life cycle. This stage necessitates the highest level of human involvement in order to comprehend user needs and translate them into functional models. AI technologies and methods greatly minimize the need for human participation, spot flaws early in the conceptualization phase, and expedite the process as a whole. The following are some AI tools that can be used to create prototypes that are more secure and effective:

3.1.1 Natural Language Processing Tools

Tools for natural language processing (NLP) are useful during the Software Development Life Cycle's (SDLC) requirements gathering and analysis stage. By using AI to process vast amounts of text, they are able to effectively extract needs from a variety of sources, including documents, meeting minutes, and even voice inputs. Martelli (2024), the key NLP tools are:

i. IBM Watson

Purpose: IBM Watson NLP can extract particular needs based on context, evaluate text, and identify important concepts, entities, and sentiment.

Use: It is particularly helpful for translating unstructured requirements into organized formats, detecting stakeholder priorities, and processing long documents.

ii. Google Cloud Natural Language

Purpose: The goal is to process and evaluate textual data in order to identify entities, sentiment, and syntax.

Use: Assists requirements teams with classifying needs, prioritizing them according to sentiment or recognized critical areas, and extracting crucial information from lengthy documentation.

iii. Microsoft Azure Text Analytics

Purpose: The goal is to use natural language processing (NLP) to extract insights from texts, such as sentiment analysis, entity recognition, and key word extraction.

Use: By examining text-based requirements papers or consumer feedback, it makes it easier to comprehend the needs of stakeholders.

iv. Requirements Assistant by IBM DOORS Next

Purpose: Examines requirements documents for discrepancies, unclear passages, and other problems.

Use: Assists teams in improving accuracy and clarity by detecting ambiguous terminology, identifying missing information, and refining requirements.

v. ReQtest

Purpose: An AI-powered requirements management solution for tracking, tracing, and prioritizing requirements.

Use: Effectively manages requirements through classification, dependency analysis, and requirement prioritization according to project goals.

vi. Acrolinx

Purpose: The goal is to use AI to evaluate requirements documentation's tone, consistency, and clarity of information.

Use: Assures that requirements are unambiguous, consistent, and simple for all parties involved to grasp, which is essential for preventing miscommunications while the project is being developed.

vii. Jama

Purpose: AI-Powered Insights for Jama Software Requirements Management

The goal is to assist teams in gathering, organizing, and analyzing requirements with an AI-enhanced requirements management platform.

Use: By identifying possible hazards and providing predictive insights regarding requirements stability, Jama's AI capabilities facilitate change management.

viii. Spacetime NLP

Purpose: uses natural language processing to analyze vast volumes of text data in order to find relationships, sentiment, and entities.

Use: Assists in extracting requirements from large text sources, such as emails, customer feedback, and legacy documentation, guaranteeing thorough requirement coverage.

ix. QRA's QVScribe

Purpose: Analysis of ambiguity, complexity, and inconsistency needs is the goal.

Use: Reduces the possibility of misunderstandings in later stages by highlighting ambiguous or imprecise criteria and suggesting modifications.

x. Specmate

Purpose: Ensures alignment between requirements and test cases by employing natural language processing (NLP) to generate test cases from requirements.

Use: Facilitates seamless transitions to the testing phase by assisting teams in confirming that requirements are precise and testable.

3.2 Design

Popular tools used in the **Design Phase** of the Software Development Life Cycle (SDLC). These tools support UI/UX design, prototyping, wireframing, architecture planning, and documentation, enabling teams to create comprehensive and well-structured designs.

3.2.1 AI-Assisted Design Tools

According to Anguilar (2021), AI tools in design and prototyping help automate the transformation of ideas and sketches into functional interfaces, offer design improvements, and recommend optimized architectural solutions. These tools can significantly streamline and enhance the software design process.

i. Sketch2Code by Microsoft

Purpose: The goal is to expedite the process of turning hand-drawn design graphics into HTML code so that working prototypes may be created more quickly.

Application: Sketch2Code allows designers to input sketches of website or app layouts, and it will examine the pictures, identify design elements, and produce HTML code that mirrors the original layout. As a result, the prototype process is accelerated and less human coding is required.

Benefit: It enables designers and developers to rapidly iterate on ideas by cutting down on the time and technical expertise required to translate design concepts into code.

3.2.2 Generative Design and Prototyping Tools

i. Figma with AI Plugins

Purpose: Supports collaborative design and AI plugins offer suggestions for color palettes, layout adjustments, and font pairings.

Application: Uses machine learning to suggest color palettes, font pairings, and layout adjustments, ensuring that designs are visually appealing and meet UI/UX best practices.

Benefit: Enhances UI/UX design by automating visual and layout suggestions based on best practices.

ii. Adobe XD with Adobe Sensei

Purpose: Integrates Adobe Sensei, an AI tool that provides smart suggestions for animations, color schemes, and layout adjustments.

Application: Provides AI-powered features like auto-animate and voice prototyping, as well as layout suggestions to streamline the design process.

Benefit: Speeds up design workflows with auto-animate, voice prototyping, and AI-generated design recommendations.

iii. Sketch

Purpose: Assists designers in producing interactive prototypes and high-fidelity user interface designs, emphasizing responsive layouts.

Application: A vector-based design tool used mostly for wireframing, prototyping, and UI/UX design.

Benefit: Excellent for creating desktop, online, and mobile application interfaces.

enables consistent design across screens and projects by offering a library of reusable parts and symbols. Facilitates seamless developer collaboration by integrating with plug-in for design handoff.

iv. InVision

Purpose: Its primary goal is to facilitate design collaboration, feedback gathering, and version control, which makes it perfect for team-based design projects.

Application: A design and prototyping collaborative platform that enables designers to produce interactive prototypes and mockups.

Benefit:

- Enables designers to model the user experience with interactive, clickable prototypes.
- Offers real-time versioning, comments, and feedback, allowing stakeholders to evaluate collaboratively.
- Enables integration with other design programs, such as Sketch and Figma, and is frequently used to show designs to developers or clients.

v. Axure RP

Purpose: Suitable for more intricate or sophisticated applications, it enables sophisticated, high-fidelity prototyping that emphasizes functionality and interactions.

Application: A program for producing intricate user flow diagrams, interactive prototypes, and wireframes.

Benefit:

- Frequently employed for creating apps with intricate forms, logic, or multi-step procedures.
- Supports sophisticated prototype features like state-based interactions, dynamic panels, and conditional flows.
- Assists product managers and designers in creating wireframes and precise processes, which can act as thorough development blueprints.

3.2.3 Wireframing and Mockup Tools

i. Balsamiq

Purpose: This low-fidelity wireframing tool's goal is to swiftly produce simple interface mockups.

Application: Wireframes in the sketch style that communicate structure and layout without delving into specifics are made with Balsamiq. It's very helpful for early design ideation and brainstorming.

Benefits

- **Speed:** Because of Balsamiq's simplicity, designers can produce wireframes fast without becoming bogged down by aesthetics.
- **Emphasis on Layout:** By maintaining low-fidelity designs, Balsamiq assists teams in concentrating on structure and utility as opposed to aesthetics.
- **Easy Collaboration:** It is a good way to get input early in the design process since it is easy for stakeholders who are not involved in the design process to understand.

ii. Lucidchart

Purpose: An all-purpose diagramming tool for making wireframes, system diagrams, and flowcharts.

Application: For both high-level and thorough design documentation, Lucidchart is frequently used to create wireframes, user flows, and system architecture diagrams. Teams can collaborate on diagrams in real time because it's collaborative.

Benefits

- **Encourages Complex Diagrams:** Lucidchart is perfect for extensive workflow mapping and system architecture visualization because of its variety of templates and diagram possibilities.
- **Collaboration in Real Time:** Remote and cross-functional cooperation is made easier by the ability for multiple team members to modify and comment on designs at once.
- **Integration with Other Tools:** Adding diagrams to documentation is made simple with Lucidchart's integrations with Google Workspace, Atlassian, Slack, and other programs.

iii. Moqups

Purpose: An online tool that helps teams create and refine layouts through wireframing, mockups, and diagramming.

Application: To illustrate user journeys and design concepts, Moqups is used to generate interactive wireframes, prototypes, and flow diagrams. It is perfect for rapid design iterations since it facilitates the switch from wireframe to prototype.

Benefits

- **All-in-One Design Tool:** Teams may design, test, and iterate with Moqups's unified environment for wireframing, prototyping, and flowcharting.
- **Usability:** Both designers and non-designers can easily utilize it thanks to its user-friendly drag-and-drop interface.
- **Interactive Prototypes:** Before full production starts, teams can provide stakeholders a preview of the product by including interactive connections and transitions.

3.2.4 Architecture and System Design Tools

i. Microsoft Visio

Purpose: Visio is primarily used for visualizing intricate systems, workflows, and organizational structures. It is also helpful for planning data flow, workflows, and system architecture during the design stage.

Application: A vector graphics and diagramming tool frequently used to create organizational charts, network diagrams, and flowcharts.

Benefits

- **Workflow and System Diagrams**: Create and record organizational structures, data processes, and system flows.
- **Cooperation:** Teams can examine and update designs in a collaborative setting by sharing and editing diagrams.
- **Integration:** Makes data imports and updates easy by integrating seamlessly with other Microsoft products, including Excel, PowerPoint, and SharePoint.

ii. Enterprise Architect (Sparx Systems)

Purpose: It is perfect for organized, in-depth design work because it is utilized for model-based systems engineering (MBSE), requirements management, and extensive UML modeling.

Application: A full-featured modeling tool for managing and visualizing intricate business and software processes.

Benefits

- **Use BPMN and UML Modeling:** Supports industry standards for high-level design and architectural planning, including Business Process Model and Notation (BPMN), Unified Modeling Language (UML), and others.
- **Traceability** from requirements to development is made possible by managing requirements in conjunction with system models.
- **Simulation and Analysis:** It is appropriate for developing reliable system models because it enables early validation through integrated model simulation.

iii. Draw.io (diagrams.net)

Purpose: Offers a user-friendly, accessible platform for rapid diagramming, which is frequently utilized for informal, group-based design projects.

Application: A free online diagramming tool that's frequently used to create network diagrams, flowcharts, and other visual designs.

Benefits

- **Fast Diagramming:** Without requiring sophisticated tools, teams can quickly produce organizational charts, ER diagrams, and flowcharts.
- **Collaboration:** Teams may work together in real time on diagrams using Draw.io's cloud-based sharing features, which interface with Google Drive, GitHub, and other platforms.
- **Flexibility:** It is perfect for early-stage design ideation, workflow visualization, and rapid documentation preparation because to its adaptability and simplicity of usage.

iv. Visual Paradigm

Purpose: Supports a variety of diagrams for requirements management, database design, and system design, and is utilized in software development and business modeling.

Application: A complete modeling and design tool that adheres to several modeling standards, including BPMN, ERD, and UML.

Benefits

- **From beginning to end Modeling:** Using UML, SysML, and ERD diagrams, Visual Paradigm covers every step of the SDLC, from requirement analysis and design to implementation and documentation.
- **Support for Scrum and Agile:** offers integrated agile tools that work with design workflows, like sprint planning and user stories.

- **Reverse engineering** is perfect for legacy system documentation and refactoring efforts since it can produce UML diagrams from code and vice versa.

3.3 Coding

In the **Coding Phase** of the SDLC, AI tools help developers write, debug, optimize, and review code more efficiently. Nag (2024) scouts some popular AI-powered tools used in this phase:

3.3.1 Code Generation and Assistance

i. GitHub Copilot

Purpose: Code snippets, functions, and complete code blocks are generated by the system using comments and the surrounding code context in order to help developers.

Application: An AI-powered code completion tool built on OpenAI's Codex concept that integrates with well-known IDEs like Visual Studio Code.

Benefits

- **Boosts Output:** helps developers finish code more quickly by offering code ideas in real-time.
- **Multiple Language Support:** Compatible with a number of programming languages, including Ruby, Go, TypeScript, JavaScript, and Python.
- **Promotes Standardized Coding Practices:** Frequently makes recommendations for commonly used patterns and libraries.
- To **improve learning,** new coders can watch AI-generated suggestions to understand grammar and coding patterns.

ii. Tabnine

Purpose: With sophisticated, real-time code completions can anticipate entire lines or blocks based on context, the goal is to assist developers in writing code more quickly.

Application: A code auto completion tool driven by AI that makes context-aware recommendations to increase developer productivity.

Benefits

- **Language Compatibility:** More than 20 programming languages are supported, and it interfaces with well-known IDEs like Visual Studio Code, IntelliJ, and Sublime Text.
- **Customization:** Makes the tool flexible for team standards by enabling developers to set it up for particular coding patterns and styles.
- **Privacy & Security:** Suitable for sensitive applications, it provides a local-only mode where code suggestions are generated without sending data outside.
- **Efficiency Gains:** Speeds up coding and lessens developer fatigue by requiring fewer keystrokes.

iii. CodeT5

Purpose: The goal is to improve and automate operations related to code creation, interpretation, and translation. This will be especially helpful when working in multilingual development environments or while revising code.

Applications: code completion, code summarization, and language translation. Salesforce's transformer-based AI model was created especially for NLP and programming activities.

Benefits

- **Code Generation and Translation:** This tool is helpful for learning new languages or for cross-language development because it can translate code between languages.
- **Code Summarization:** Produces brief code summaries to aid developers in comprehending complex functions or legacy code more quickly.
- **Improved Code Understanding:** Helps with refactoring by seeing related patterns, which makes the code easier to maintain.
- Multiple programming language learning, code simplification, and documentation are all examples of versatile use cases.

iv. OpenAI Codex

Purpose: Assisting developers by producing, translating, and reworking code and building complete apps from plain language instructions is the goal.

Application: GitHub Copilot's AI model, Codex, is taught especially to comprehend and produce code, which makes it useful in a variety of automation and development scenarios.

Benefits

- **Natural Language to Code Conversion:** This tool helps both developers and non-developers automate chores or create prototypes by translating simple English instructions into code.
- **Broad Language Support:** It can be used with projects that require many languages because it supports more than a dozen programming languages.
- The development cycle is accelerated by enhanced prototyping, which aids in the rapid creation of functioning snippets and prototypes.
- **Learning and Exploration:** Provides an intuitive means for users to test out new programming languages, functions, or concepts.

3.3.2 Code Review and Quality Analysis

i. DeepCode

Purpose: The goal of this AI-powered code review tool is to provide recommendations for structural code enhancements that aid in the improvement of system architecture.

Application: Makes sure the project follows best practices and effective structures by analyzing code for possible enhancements and making recommendations for modifications to optimize software architecture.

Benefit: Supports the design's architectural integrity by assisting in making sure the code complies with best standards.

ii. Amazon CodeGuru

Purpose: Provide best practices and architectural recommendations derived on an analysis of related projects and codebases.

Application: Offers AI-powered suggestions for improving code quality and speed. It may examine code, identify errors, and suggest architectural adjustments that improve the resilience of the program.

Benefit: Helps developers and architects make data-driven decisions for long-term stability by enhancing the software's architecture's scalability, security, and efficiency.

3.3.3 Automated Code Documentation

i. Kite

Purpose: With its intelligent code completions and recommendations for developers, particularly in Python, Kite is an AI-powered code completion and suggestion tool that aims to increase productivity.

Application: It provides instant documentation lookups and is mostly used in code editors to help developers by anticipating and automatically completing code depending on context.

Benefits

- **Enhanced Coding Speed:** Reduces keystrokes and speeds up the coding process by suggesting complete code snippets.
- **Contextual Recommendations:** increases accuracy by using machine learning to evaluate the code's context and offer pertinent completions.
- **Documentation Assistance:** Makes it simple for developers to comprehend unknown code or libraries by automatically retrieving and displaying documentation for a variety of functions and libraries within the editor.
- **Supports Several Languages:** Kite is multilingual and supports JavaScript, Java, and a number of other languages, despite being optimized for Python.

ii. Code2Doc

Purpose: An AI solution called Code2Doc helps developers maintain current and comprehensible documentation with little manual labor by automatically creating documentation from code.

Application: Used to automatically generate structured documentation, summaries, and thorough code comments for functions, classes, and complete projects. It is beneficial for teams and big codebases where maintaining uniformity in documentation is essential.

Benefits

- **Less Work in Documentation:** creates explanations and summaries automatically, saving developers time on documentation duties.
- **Boosts the Readability of Code:** makes complicated code structures easier for others to understand by turning them into readable and understandable documentation.
- **Enhances Collaboration:** Team members can swiftly comprehend each other's code without requiring lengthy handovers when documentation is up to date.

3.3.4 Container Management and Deployment Intelligence

i. KubeFlow

Purpose: The goal of the open-source KubeFlow platform is to assist developers in creating, implementing, and overseeing Kubernetes machine learning workflows. Model training, testing, and deployment in containerized systems are all streamlined as part of the machine learning process.

Application: KubeFlow helps teams to execute machine learning workloads on Kubernetes clusters, which facilitates the scaling, automation, and management of ML models in production. It is mostly utilized in machine learning and data science projects.

Benefits

- **ML Lifecycle Management from Start to Finish:** It is a complete system that supports the entire machine learning workflow, from data processing and model training to deployment and monitoring.
- **Flexibility and Scalability:** Makes use of Kubernetes to expand resources as needed, enabling the effective training of complicated models and big datasets across dispersed clusters.

ii. Aqua Security

Purpose: Aqua Security is a cloud-native security platform focused on securing containerized applications, microservices, and Kubernetes environments. It uses AI-driven techniques to detect vulnerabilities, ensure compliance, and protect against runtime threats.

Application: Widely used for security in containerized and Kubernetes-based applications, Aqua Security provides tools for vulnerability scanning, runtime security, and compliance enforcement.

Benefits:

- **Comprehensive Container Security**: Protects containerized applications from the build phase through deployment to runtime, reducing risks throughout the SDLC.
- **Automated Vulnerability Management**: Scans containers, images, and configurations for vulnerabilities, and applies security policies automatically, helping prevent security issues from reaching production.

- **Runtime Protection**: Monitors and protects containers and Kubernetes workloads in real-time, offering runtime defenses against attacks like privilege escalation and anomalous behavior.
- **Compliance and Policy Enforcement**: Supports compliance with industry standards (e.g., NIST, CIS) by enforcing policies for security best practices, ensuring applications meet regulatory requirements.

3.4 Testing

In the **Testing and Debugging** phases of the SDLC, Amalfitano (2023) AI tools can greatly improve efficiency and accuracy by identifying bugs, optimizing performance, and enhancing overall software quality. Here are some AI-powered tools and how they're applied in these phases:

3.4.1 AI-Powered Automated Testing

i. Applitools

Purpose: A visual testing tool driven by AI.

Application: Applitools is a UI/UX testing application that takes screenshots of various devices and browsers and compares them to find discrepancies.

Benefits

- Automatically identifies UI inconsistencies.
- Reduces the need for manual visual testing by offering insights on cross-platform compatibility.

ii. Testim

Purpose: AI-powered automated functional testing.

Application: Develops, executes, and oversees automated tests, utilizing AI to modify tests in response to user interface modifications.

Benefits

- Reduces false positives, improving test stability.
- uses self-healing characteristics to expedite the production and maintenance of tests.

iii. Mabl

Purpose: A platform for intelligent end-to-end testing.

Applications: Mabl use AI to test web apps for functionality, regression, and performance.

Benefits

- Makes using natural language processing to create tests easier.
- Maintenance is reduced via self-healing tests that adjust to changes in the code.

iv. Sauce Labs

Purpose: The goal is cross-device and cross-browser testing.

Application: Sauce Labs manages and optimizes test execution in a variety of scenarios by utilizing AI.

Benefits

- Compatible with a large variety of devices and browsers.
- Enhances test performance, optimizes test suites, and offers AI insights for debugging.

3.4.2 Intelligent Bug Detection and Fixing

i. DeepCode by Synk

Purpose: AI-driven debugging and code analysis.

Application: Real-time code analysis to find errors, weaknesses, and code smells.

Benefits

- During debugging, it offers proactive security and bug identification.
- Increases developer productivity by providing repair recommendations.

ii. Microsoft Azure

Purpose: A tool for monitoring and debugging.

Application: Monitors apps, identifies problems, and spots irregularities using AI.

Benefits

- Offers real-time monitoring of application performance.
- Identifies possible problems and bottlenecks, enabling focused debugging.

iii. CodeGuru by AWS

Purpose: AI-driven performance profiler and code review tool.

Application: Examines code to discover any problems and offer comments on performance and quality.

Benefits

- Identifies performance snags and suggests fixes.
- Finds errors and inefficiencies in the code, improving its quality.

iv. Sentry

Purpose: Debugging and error tracking in real time.

Application: AI-powered tool that keeps an eye out for runtime faults in programs and provides error stack traces to aid in debugging.

Benefits

- Offers useful information about manufacturing errors.
- Minimizes debugging time by assisting in the identification of error patterns.

v. Rollbar

Purpose: The tool's purpose is to monitor and debug errors.

Application: Classifies and ranks mistakes using machine learning.

Benefits

- Real-time alerts increase debugging efficiency.
- Gives high-impact errors priority so that developers can concentrate on important problems first.

vi. Diffblue Cover

Purpose: Unit tests for Java programs are automatically generated by the AI-powered tool Diffblue Cover. It is intended to assist developers find possible flaws early in the development cycle and increase test coverage.

Application: Unit tests for Java applications are mostly created by development teams during the coding and testing stages. It reduces manual testing labor by automating the generation of tests directly within the source.

Benefits

- **Increased Test Coverage:** Diffblue Cover automatically generates thorough unit tests, boosting code reliability and test coverage.
- **Time savings:** Allows developers to concentrate on other things by accelerating the test creation process through autonomous test generation.
- **Early Bug Detection:** Unit test coverage can be increased to help find and fix problems early, which minimizes rework and downstream debugging.
- **Simple Integration:** It is possible to include it into CI/CD pipelines, guaranteeing continuous test creation and upkeep for every code update.

vii. SmartBear TestComplete

Purpose: Teams may design automated tests for desktop, web, and mobile apps with SmartBear's functional test automation platform, TestComplete. Both scripted and scriptless test creation are supported.

Application: TestComplete is widely used during the testing phase and is appropriate for performance, regression, and functional user interface testing. Python, VBScript, JavaScript, and other programming languages are among those it supports.

Benefits

- **Cross-Platform Testing:** Provides thorough test coverage for a range of application types by enabling automated testing across desktop, web, and mobile platforms.
- Both non-technical users and seasoned developers can utilize it thanks to its support for both codeless test development and scripted automation.
- **Object Recognition:** Makes use of AI-powered objects recognition to enable tests to adjust to UI changes, cutting down on test failures and maintenance time.
- **Integration with CI/CD Pipelines:** It is possible to incorporate it into CI/CD workflows, which facilitates rapid feedback for iterative development and continuous testing.

3.4.3 Defect Prediction and Analysis

i. Sealights

Purpose: A quality intelligence tool called Sealights assists in monitoring code coverage, evaluating the impact of tests, and locating untested or dangerous code throughout the SDLC.

Application: Sealights is utilized for quality evaluation, test impact analysis, and test optimization. It is especially useful in settings where code changes often since it guarantees that testing efforts are concentrated on the most impactful regions.

Benefits

- In order to save time and money, **Test Impact Analysis** determines which parts of the code are affected by recent modifications and ranks the tests appropriately.
- **Better Test Coverage:** Offers information about code coverage, highlighting untested sections and concentrating on high-risk code to increase test reliability and coverage.
- **Collaboration** is streamlined when QA, development, and management teams all agree on risk areas and set priorities for testing.
- **Decreased Testing Costs:** Cuts down on pointless testing by concentrating primarily on the areas of the codebase impacted by recent changes, maximizing the usage of test resources.

ii. SonarQube

Purpose: SonarQube's goal is to continually scan code for errors, vulnerabilities, security flaws, and code smells. SonarQube is a tool for code quality and security analysis.

Application: To assess code quality in real-time during the coding and testing stages, SonarQube is frequently utilized. Numerous CI/CD technologies are integrated with it, and it offers ongoing security and code health feedback.

Benefits

- **Improved Code Quality:** Produces cleaner, easier-to-maintain code by validating it against predetermined quality standards.
- By locating flaws in the code, **security vulnerability detection** assists teams in resolving security concerns at an early stage of development.
- **CI/CD integration:** Easily integrates with CI/CD tools, allowing for continuous quality feedback and automatic code analysis with every code change.
- **Multiple Languages Supported:** SonarQube is adaptable to a variety of development contexts thanks to its support for over 25 programming languages.

3.4.4 Intelligent Test Automation

i. Selenium with ML

Purpose: Intelligent test automation is achieved by enhancing Selenium with Machine Learning (ML). Selenium-based tests incorporate machine learning to increase test efficiency, stability, and adaptability.

Application: Selenium combined with machine learning is used to test web applications automatically, especially for user interface testing. By enabling tests to self-heal and adjust to dynamic web elements, machine learning (ML) improves Selenium's functionality.

Benefits

- **Self-Healing Tests:** Selenium tests can adjust to small UI changes without malfunctioning thanks to machine learning, which lessens the requirement for ongoing test maintenance.
- **Improved Stability:** By dynamically identifying and choosing the optimal locators, machine learning models can increase test stability and decrease faulty tests.
- **Efficient Use of Resources:** Optimizes the time and resources used for debugging and rerunning tests by lowering the frequency of false test failures.
- **Increased Test Coverage:** By identifying high-priority test cases through user interactions and behavior analysis, machine learning can increase test coverage for crucial features.

ii. Tricentis Tosca

Purpose: A model-based tool for automating tests.

Applications

- Facilitates scriptless automation for both regression and functional testing.
- Enables continuous testing through integration with CI/CD processes.

Benefits

- Reduces reliance on scripting knowledge, which is a benefit.
- Enables model-driven testing to increase test coverage.

iii. Katalon Studio

Purpose: For API, web, and mobile testing, the goal is to offer a comprehensive test automation solution.

Applications

- AI-assisted test design and implementation.
- Analytics for test insights are built in.

Benefits

- Using a single platform, automation is made simpler.
- Improves test efficiency by offering practical insights.

iv. AI-based TestNG with ML Integration

Purpose: Intelligent test case prioritization for Java unit testing driven by AI.

Applications

- Key features include the analysis of test case execution history using machine learning models.
- Test order is optimized according to areas that are prone to defects.

Benefits

- Prioritizes important tests, which cut down on execution time.
- Strengthens the ability to spot defects.

v. Functionize

Purpose: To use AI to automate web application testing

Applications

- Natural Language Processing (NLP) for test case creation is one of the main features.
- Adaptable and self-healing testing.

Benefits

- One advantage is that it enables non-technical users to create tests.
- Uses adaptive automation to reduce the amount of test maintenance.

vi. IBM Rational Functional Tester (RFT)

Purpose: AI-driven tool for functional and regression testing.
Applications

- Automatic script adaptation and UI change detection using AI.
- Many languages and platforms are supported.

Benefits

- Lowers the need to maintain test scripts.
- Improves compatibility between programs.

3.5 Deployment

Software release to production environments, configuration management, scalability assurance, and problem-solving are all part of the SDLC's deployment phase. During this stage, AI tools optimize performance, expedite deployment procedures, and guarantee seamless rollouts. Pothukuchi (2023), a list of AI tools utilized during the deployment phase is provided below, along with information on their uses, advantages, and applications:

3.5.1 CI/CD Pipeline Automation

Sauvola (2024) inspects tools that focus on automating the continuous integration and continuous delivery pipelines:

i. Spinnaker

Purpose: The goal of Spinnaker is to provide a continuous delivery platform with AI capabilities for rollbacks and deployment automation.

Application: Supports canary and blue/green releases, two multi-cloud deployment techniques.

Benefits

- AI-powered monitoring for in-the-moment reversal decision-making.
- Uses sophisticated deployment techniques to lower risk.
- Improves multi-cloud installations' dependability.

ii. Harness

Purpose: The goal is to provide a continuous delivery platform powered by AI that simplifies deployment.

Application: Provides sophisticated rollback and verification tools for deployment management.

Benefits

- AI-powered monitoring to find irregularities after deployment.
- Minimizes downtime through error detection and automated rollbacks.
- Streamlines intricate deployment processes.

iii. Azure DevOps with AI Integration

Purpose: Offers a collection of DevOps tools to facilitate intelligent deployment management and CI/CD pipelines.

Application: Automates Azure application deployment, testing, and monitoring.

Benefits

- Makes use of AI to forecast deployment hazards and enhance efficiency.
- Automates the rollout of apps and environment provisioning.
- Simplifies version control and release administration.

iv. AWS CodeDeploy

Purpose: The goal is to automate the deployment of programs to on-premises servers or Amazon Web Services (AWS).

Application: Simplifies updates for apps in a variety of settings.

Benefits

- AI-powered resource usage optimization.
- Reduces human mistake by using automated deployment scripts.
- Adapts easily to changing production settings.

v. Jenkins with AIPlugins

Purpose: In order to facilitate continuous integration and continuous delivery (CI/CD), Jenkins is a well-known open-source automation server. Soft (2024), Jenkins expands its automation capabilities to incorporate predictive analytics, performance optimization, and intelligent decision-making by including AI plugins.

Application

- Smart Build Control
- Uses AI-driven analysis to find unstable or faulty tests.
- Pipeline Enhancement
- Tracking and Finding Anomalies:
- Analyzing Feedback

Benefits

- Increased Efficiency of the Pipeline
- Improved Dependability
- Quicker Reaction Times
- Resource and Cost Optimization
- Well-Informed Choice Making

3.5.2 Predictive Analysis for Rollbacks

Tools that use AI for predicting deployment risks and automating rollback processes:

i. New Relic Applied Intelligence

Purpose: The application's performance is tracked both during and after deployment.

Application: For post-deployment fault, performance bottleneck, and anomaly detection.

Benefits

- AI-powered performance degradation notifications.
- Gives useful information for problem-solving.
- Improves the end-user experience by lowering incidents linked to deployment.

ii. Dynatrace

Purpose: The goal of Dynatrace is to monitor applications, infrastructure, and deployments using artificial intelligence.

Applications: Performance optimization and deployment monitoring are provided by the application.

Benefits

- Provides examination of the underlying causes of deployment problems.

- Automatically identifies and fixes issues.
- Increases scalability by dynamically adjusting resource allocation.

3.6 Maintenance and Monitoring

The Software Development Life Cycle's (SDLC) maintenance and monitoring phase is concerned with making sure the program continues to function properly after it has been deployed. This stage uses AI techniques to assist identify irregularities, anticipate possible problems, improve performance, and minimize downtime. A thorough rundown of AI-powered tools for this stage may be found below:

3.6.1 Anomaly Detection in Logs and Metrics

i. Datadog

Purpose: Datadog is a platform for cloud-based analytics and monitoring.
Applications

- Keeps an eye on metrics, traces, and system logs for irregularities.
- Gives apps, databases, and infrastructure complete visibility.

Benefits

- Abnormal pattern detection in real time.
- Alerts prior to escalation for mistakes or performance problems.
- Makes the system more reliable by using automated insights.

ii. Splunk

Purpose: Log management and machine data analysis platform is the goal.
Applications

- Looks for odd patterns in logs and metrics.
- Monitors how the system behaves in various dispersed situations.

Benefits

- AI-driven insights for identifying anomalies.
- Central log analysis to facilitate speedier troubleshooting.

- Predictive analytics in order to foresee such problems.

3.6.2 Predictive Maintenance

i. IBM Watson AIops

Purpose: AI-powered IT operations management system is the goal.
Applications

- Predicts failures by analyzing past system performance data.
- Automatically generates warnings and suggestions for preventative measures.

Benefits

- Reduces unscheduled downtime.
- Uses trend analysis to maximize resource use.
- Enables quicker problem solving through root-cause analysis driven by AI.

ii. Moogsoft

Purpose: Moogsoft's goal is to use AI for anomaly identification and incident management.
Applications

- Links incidents and alarms to determine the underlying reasons.
- Gives forecasted information about probable system faults.

Benefits

- By grouping related events together, alert fatigue is decreased.
- Workflows for incident resolution that are automated.
- Enables real-time AI analysis to improve operational efficiency.

3.6.3 User Feedback and Sentiment Analysis

i. MonkeyLearn

Purpose: The goal is to provide a machine learning platform for text analysis.
Applications

- Examines comments left by users on social media, reviews, and polls.
- Detects patterns in user sentiment and reoccurring problems.

Benefits

- Encourages customer-focused enhancements.
- Makes setting priorities for problems and improvements easier.
- Provides practical insights that increase user pleasure.

ii. Lexalytics

Purpose: An NLP platform for text analytics and sentiment analysis.
Applications

- Extracts significant patterns from massive amounts of textual data.
- Examines consumer reviews to find sentiment and issues.

Benefits

- Assists teams in comprehending consumer problems.
- Offers insights based on data to enhance products and services.
- Improves decision-making for efficiently handling user feedback.

3.7 Documentation and Knowledge Management

The SDLC's documentation and knowledge management process entails producing, preserving, and arranging vital project data to facilitate productive teamwork and information exchange. It guarantees that all interested parties have access to current, accurate resources. These solutions ensure that the project's knowledge base is a valued asset throughout its lifecycle by streamlining the documentation process, enhancing accessibility, and promoting effective team decision-making.

3.7.1 Automatic Documentation Generation

i. Sphinx

Purpose: The goal of Sphinx is to transform docstrings and code comments into organized documentation.

Applications

- Produces technical documentation for projects utilizing Python.
- Multiple output formats (such as HTML and PDF) are supported.

Benefits

- Makes authoring documentation less labor-intensive.
- The documentation up to date with changes to the code.

ii. Doxygen

Purpose: By reading code annotations, Doxygen generates documentation for a range of programming languages.

Applications

- Records extensive undertakings with several participants.
- Uses AI integration to identify lacking documentation and preserve version history.

Benefits

- Improves documentation clarity and consistency.
- Saves time by updating the codebase automatically when it changes.

3.7.2 Intelligent Search and Knowledge Retrieval

i. Guru

Purpose: Knowledge management platform driven by AI.

Applications

- Easily searchable and centralizes team knowledge.
- Ranks and prioritizes information that is often accessed using machine learning.

Benefits

- Fast access to important data speeds up the onboarding process.
- Cuts down on the amount of time spent looking for project-related information.

ii. Confluencc

Purpose: A platform for knowledge sharing and collaborative documentation.
Applications

- Uses AI to improve search capabilities so that pertinent documents may be quickly retrieved.
- Maintains centralized access to all project-related documentation.

Benefits

- Encourages better teamwork.
- Makes ensuring that current project knowledge is easily accessible.

3.7.3 Documentation Enhancement

i. Microsoft Azure QnA Maker

Purpose: The goal of Microsoft Azure QnA Maker is to transform current documentation into an interactive format with questions and answers.
Applications

- Develops chatbot-like user interfaces for user manuals or frequently asked questions.
- Improves non-technical users' access to documentation.

Benefits

- Improves the usability and engagement of documentation.
- Enhances assistance for external consumers as well as internal teams.

IV. THE BENEFITS OF AI-POWERED TOOLS IN SOFTWARE DEVELOPMENT

Software development has changed as a result of artificial intelligence (AI), which increases productivity, lowers mistakes, and fosters creative thinking. These days, AI-powered instruments are essential to contemporary development procedures since they provide a number of advantages that optimize processes and enhance results suggested by Chafik (2020).

i. Quicker Development Cycles

Code creation, debugging, and testing are among the repetitive chores that AI-powered solutions automate. By managing these time-consuming tasks, developers may concentrate on their primary creativity and logic. With context-based intelligent suggestions, tools like IntelliCode and GitHub Copilot let developers write code more quickly.

ii. Improved Quality of Code

Code is examined by AI algorithms for any mistakes, inefficiencies, and weaknesses. By spotting problems before they become more serious, static analysis tools like SonarQube or DeepCode aid in upholding high levels of quality. Strong, clear, and maintainable code is guaranteed by these technologies.

iii. Cost-Effectiveness

AI technologies drastically lower development costs by increasing productivity and automating operations. Real-time analytics and predictive maintenance also reduce downtime, guaranteeing efficient resource utilization.

V. CHALLENGES AND CONSIDERATIONS IN ADOPTING AI TOOLS

i. Data Privacy and Security

Integrating AI tools often requires granting access to sensitive codebases or data, raising concerns about information security. Ciniselli (2024) professes that organizations need robust protocols to protect intellectual property and customer data when using AI systems. Careful vetting of AI vendors and their data handling practices is crucial. Consider implementing data anonymization techniques or using on-premises AI solutions for highly sensitive projects.

ii. Reliability of AI Models

The output quality of AI tools depends heavily on their training data. Biased or incomplete datasets can lead to unreliable results or perpetuate existing biases. It's important to critically evaluate AI-generated suggestions and not blindly trust them. Regular auditing and retraining of AI models with diverse, high-quality data can help improve reliability over time.

iii. Skill Gap

Effectively leveraging AI tools requires new skills and knowledge. Developers and teams need training to understand AI capabilities, limitations, and best practices for integration. Organizations should invest in upskilling programs and consider hiring AI specialists to bridge the knowledge gap. Creating internal AI champions can help drive adoption and share expertise across teams.

iv. Ethical Considerations

The increasing use of AI in software development raises ethical concerns about potential job displacement and the creation of opaque decision-making systems. It's crucial to approach AI adoption with a human-centric mindset, focusing on augmenting human capabilities rather than replacing them.

VI. FUTURE TRENDS IN AI-POWERED SOFTWARE DEVELOPMENT

i. Autonomous Development

Increased use of natural language processing for code generation, allowing developers to describe desired functionality in plain language and have AI generate corresponding code snippets or even entire programs. Eames (2024) explores that AI-assisted debugging and error detection, with intelligent systems analyzing code in real-time to identify potential issues, suggest fixes, and optimize performance. Automated testing and quality assurance powered by AI, capable of generating comprehensive test cases, simulating user interactions, and identifying edge cases human testers might miss.

ii. AI-Driven DevOps

AI-driven project management and resource allocation, optimizing team productivity by assigning tasks based on individual strengths and predicting potential bottlenecks or delays. Intelligent code refactoring and optimization, with AI systems suggesting improvements to code structure, efficiency, and readability based on best practices and project-specific requirements. Personalized IDE experiences that adapt to individual developer preferences and coding styles, offering tailored suggestions and auto-completions.

iii. AI for Code Security

AI-powered security analysis to identify vulnerabilities and potential exploits in real-time during the development process. Automated documentation generation, creating comprehensive and up-to-date documentation based on code analysis and developer comments. Intelligent code review systems that provide detailed feedback on code quality, adherence to coding standards, and potential improvements. AI-assisted API integration, simplifying the process of incorporating third-party services and libraries into applications.

iv. Human AI Collaboration

Human-AI collaboration is an exciting frontier that offers immense potential for innovation and progress. Humans excel at creative thinking, emotional intelligence, and complex decision-making, while AI systems are adept at processing vast amounts of data, identifying patterns, and performing repetitive tasks. Recognizing and leveraging these complementary abilities can lead to powerful synergies. Define specific areas where AI can augment human capabilities and vice versa. This clarity helps avoid confusion and ensures that both human and AI contributions are maximized. Ensure that AI systems provide clear explanations for their outputs and decision-making processes. This transparency builds trust and allows humans to better understand and validate AI-generated results.

VII. CONCLUSION

The software development lifecycle has been completely transformed by AI-powered technologies, which provide unmatched efficiency, accuracy, and creativity. These technologies enable teams to concentrate on creativity and problem-solving by automating monotonous processes, enhancing code quality, and facilitating more intelligent project management. The advantages of adoption greatly exceed the disadvantages, even in the face of obstacles including integrating difficulties, moral dilemmas, and training needs. Businesses that strategically use AI technologies can achieve revolutionary results by developing high-caliber, flexible software solutions that satisfy the needs of a constantly changing digital environment. Software development is being revolutionized by AI-powered technologies that improve scalability, speed up operations, and decrease errors. Developers may concentrate on creativity and problem-solving with the help of these technologies, which automate monotonous activities and offer predictive insights. Their increasing significance in the industry is shown by their involvement in revolutionizing the software development lifecycle.

To enhance their processes and results, developers and teams are urged to investigate and implement AI-powered solutions. Despite the significant advantages, issues including integration difficulties, moral dilemmas, and training requirements must be addressed. Teams may create software solutions that flourish in a changing digital environment and open up new possibilities by carefully and strategically integrating AI.

REFERENCES

Amalfitano, D., Faralli, S., Rossa, J. C., & Matalonga, S. (2023). Artificial Intelligence Applied to Software Testing: A Tertiary Study. *ACM Computing Surveys*, *56*(3), 1–38. DOI: 10.1145/3616372

Anguilar, A. R., Hernandez, J. O., Garcia, A. J., & Limon, X. (2021).Software Design and Artificial Intelligence: A Systematic Mapping Study. *International Conference in Software Engineering Research and Innovation,* 54-60.

Barenkamp, M., Rebstadt, J., & Thomas, O. (2020). Applications of AI in classical software engineering. *AI Persepectives*, *2*(1), 1–15. DOI: 10.1186/s42467-020-00005-4

Bruhin, O., Ebel, P., Mueller, L., Li, M. M., & Manhai, M., Genai, & Muller, L. (2024). GenAI and Software Engineering: Strategies for Shaping the Core of Tomorrow's Software Engineering Practice. *International Conference on Information Systems,* 1-17.

Chafik, N., & Benchekroun, A. (2020). Integrating Artificial Intelligence in Software Engineering: Enhancements and Challenges in the Development Lifecycle. *Iconic Research and Engineering Journals*, *3*(12), 253–265.

Ciniselli, M., Puccinelli,N., Qiu, K., & Grazia, L.D. (2024).From Today's Code to Tomorrow's Symphony: The AI Transformation of Developer's Routine by 2030. *Computer Papers*, 25-39.

Eames, T., Markus, F., Patricia, L., & Justus, B. (2024). International Workshop on Green and Sustainable Software. *VU Research Portal,* 1-9.

Efimova, D. (2024, August 15). Generative AI Application Across the Software Development Lifecycle. *epam.*

Kumar, S. (2024, May 6). Understanding the Application and Impact of AI in Software Development Life Cycle. *DZone*.

Lindeman, M.J. (2024, August 9). The AI-SDLC Phases for Systems that Include an AI Model. *Pieces for Developers*.

Lu, H., Li, Y., Chen, M., Kim, H., & Serikawa, S. (2018). Brain intelligence: Go beyond artificial intelligence. *Mobile Networks and Applications*, *23*(2), 368–375. DOI: 10.1007/s11036-017-0932-8

Martelli, K., Cao, N., & Cheng, B. (2023). *How generative AI can revolutionize the software development lifecycle*. KPMG.

Nag, S. (2024, September 11). Generative AI and the changing face of Software Development Lifecycle. *Calsoft.*

Pothukuchi, A. S., Kota, L. V., & Mallikarjunaradhya, V. (2023). Impact of Generative AI on the Software Development Life Cycle (SDLC). *International Journal of Creative Research Thoughts*, *11*(8), 287–291.

Sauvola, J., Tarkoma, S., Klemettinen, M., Riekki, J., & Doermann, D. (2024). Future of Software with Generative AI. *Automated Software Engineering*, *31*(26), 25–32.

Soft, V. (2024, January 24). Generative AI in Software Development Life Cycle (SDLC). *V2Soft Innovation through. Intelligence.*

Sorte, W. B., Joshi, P., & Jagtap, V. (2015). Use of Artificial Intelligence in Software Development Life Cycle: A state of the Art Review. *International Journal of Technology Management*, *3*(3), 398–403.

Ulfsnes, R., Moe, N.B., Stray, V., & Skarpen, M. (2024). Transforming Software Development with Generative AI: Empirical Insights on Collaboration and Workflow. *Generative AI for Effective Software Development*, 219-234.

Wagner, J. (2023, August 15). AI Tools for the Software Development Process. *Stoplight.*

Zelianko, Y. (2024, May 15). The Transformative Impact of AI in Software Development: A Survey – Based Analysis. *Techreviewer.*

Compilation of References

Abirami, T., Ananthi, K., Venice, J. A., Chandru, R., & Rathish, C. R. (2024). The Impact of 5G Technology on the Digital Supply Chain and Operations Management Landscape. In *Applications of New Technology in Operations and Supply Chain Management* (pp. 289-311). IGI Global.

Acemoglu, D., & Restrepo, P. (2018). Artificial intelligence, automation, and work. In *The economics of artificial intelligence: An agenda* (pp. 197–236). University of Chicago Press.

Adadi, A., & Berrada, M. (2018). Peeking inside the black-box: A survey on explainable artificial intelligence (XAI). *IEEE Access : Practical Innovations, Open Solutions*, *6*, 52138–52160. DOI: 10.1109/ACCESS.2018.2870052

Ahvar, E. (2021). Next Generation of SDN in Cloud-Fog for 5G and Beyond-Enabled Applications: Opportunities and Challenges. *Network (Bristol, England)*, *1*, 28–49.

Ajiga, D., Okeleke, P. A., Folorunsho, S. O., & Ezeigweneme, C. (2024). Enhancing software development practices with AI insights in high-tech companies. IEEE Software Engineering Institute, Technical Report TR-2024-003.

Ajiga, D., Okeleke, P. A., Folorunsho, S. O., & Ezeigweneme, C. (2024). The role of software automation in improving industrial operations and efficiency. *International Journal of Engineering Research Updates*, *7*(1), 22–35. DOI: 10.53430/ijeru.2024.7.1.0031

Al Dallal, J. (2015). Identifying refactoring opportunities in object-oriented code: A systematic literature review. *Information and Software Technology*, *58*, 231–249. DOI: 10.1016/j.infsof.2014.08.002

Alam, T. (2021). Cloud-Based IoT Applications and Their Roles in Smart Cities. *Smart Cities*, *4*(3), 1196–1219. DOI: 10.3390/smartcities4030064

Al-Asili, A. (2024). The Impact of AI on Unit Testing within CICD Processes for Software Development.

Ali, O. (2024). Popular API Technologies: REST, GraphQL, and gRPC.

Ali, H., & Hussain, A. (2023). Exploring generative AI for automated code generation: Opportunities and challenges. *International Journal of Software Engineering and Knowledge Engineering, 33*(1), 115–135. DOI: 10.1142/S0218194023500024

Ali, J. M. (2023). AI-driven software engineering. *Advances in Engineering Innovation, 3*(1), 17–21. DOI: 10.54254/2977-3903/3/2023030

Alimjon, D. (2022). Problems of data replication in distribution systems. *ACADEMICIA: An International Multidisciplinary Research Journal, 12*(5), 1119–1128. DOI: 10.5958/2249-7137.2022.00585.7

Alizadehsani, Z., Gomez, E. G., Ghaemi, H., González, S. R., Jordan, J., Fernández, A., & Pérez-Lancho, B. (2021). Modern Integrated Development Environment (IDEs). In Lecture notes in networks and systems (pp. 274–288). DOI: 10.1007/978-3-030-78901-5_24

Allamanis, M., Barr, E. T., Bird, C., & Sutton, C. (2018). A survey of machine learning for big code and naturalness. *ACM Computing Surveys, 51*(4), 1–37. DOI: 10.1145/3212695

Alojail, M. (2020). Fog Computing Mitigate Limitations of Cloud Computing. *International Journal of Recent Technology and Engineering, 8*(5), 1732–1736. DOI: 10.35940/ijrte.E6199.018520

Alsamhi, S. H., Ma, O., & Ansari, M. S. (2019). Survey on artificial intelligence based techniquesfor emerging robotic communication. *Telecommunication Systems, 72*(3), 483–503. DOI: 10.1007/s11235-019-00561-z

Alshahrani, S., & Althobaiti, A. (2023). A review of generative AI techniques for software engineering. *MDPI Information, 17*(2), 62. DOI: 10.3390/info17020062

Alshammari, F. (2022). Trends in Intelligent and AI-Based Software Engineering Processes: A Deep Learning-Based Software Process Model Recommendation Method. *Computational Intelligence and Neuroscience, 2022*, 1–11. Advance online publication. DOI: 10.1155/2022/1960684 PMID: 36248934

Alzubi, J., Nayyar, A., & Kumar, A. (2018). Machine learning from theory to algorithms: An overview. *Journal of Physics: Conference Series, 1142*(1), 012012. DOI: 10.1088/1742-6596/1142/1/012012

Alzyadat, W., Al-Madi, M., Muhairat, M., Al-Madi, N., & Altarawneh, F. (2023). A Roadmap for Artificial Intelligence Augmented Software Development Life Cycle: Aspects of Knowledge Vaporization. *2023 International Conference on Information Technology: Cybersecurity Challenges for Sustainable Cities, ICIT 2023*. DOI: 10.1109/ICIT58056.2023.10226133

Amalfitano, D., Faralli, S., Hauck, J., Matalonga, S., & Distante, D. (2023). Artificial Intelligence Applied to Software Testing: A Tertiary Study. *ACM Computing Surveys*, *56*(3), 1–38. DOI: 10.1145/3616372

Anderson, M. R., Cafarella, M., Jiang, Y., Wang, G., & Zhang, B. (2014). An integrated development environment for faster feature engineering. *Proceedings of the VLDB Endowment International Conference on Very Large Data Bases*, *7*(13), 1657–1660. DOI: 10.14778/2733004.2733054

Andrade, E. C., Andrade, S., & Vital, S. (2021). A survey of AI-driven testing methods for software systems. *ACM Computing Surveys*, *54*(2), 1–35. DOI: 10.1145/3447028

Anguilar, A. R., Hernandez, J. O., Garcia, A. J., & Limon, X. (2021).Software Design and Artificial Intelligence: A Systematic Mapping Study. *International Conference in Software Engineering Research and Innovation,* 54-60.

Anwar, R., & Bashir, M. B. (2023). A Systematic Literature Review of AI-based Software Requirements Prioritization Technique. *IEEE Access : Practical Innovations, Open Solutions*, *11*, 143815–143860. DOI: 10.1109/ACCESS.2023.3343252

Araújo, A., Mamede, H. S., Filipe, V., & Santos, V. (2022). An integrated approach using robotic process automation and artificial intelligence as disruptive technology for digital transformation. In European, Mediterranean, and Middle Eastern Conference on Information Systems (pp. 438-450). Springer Nature Switzerland.

Araújo, A., Mamede, H. S., Filipe, V., & Santos, V. (2022, December). An Integrated Approach Using Robotic Process Automation and Artificial Intelligence as Disruptive Technology for Digital Transformation. In European, Mediterranean, and Middle Eastern Conference on Information Systems (pp. 438-450). Cham: Springer Nature Switzerland.

Arundel, J., & Domingus, J. (2019). *Cloud Native DevOps with Kubernetes: building, deploying, and scaling modern applications in the Cloud.* O'Reilly Media.

Asaad, J., & Avksentieva, E. (2023). Review of ways to apply machine learning methods in software engineering. E3S Web of Conferences. .DOI: 10.1051/e3sconf/202344907018

Asatiani, A., & Penttinen, E. (2016). Turning robotic process automation into commercial success - case opus capita. *Journal of Information Technology Teaching Cases*, *6*(2), 67–74. DOI: 10.1057/jittc.2016.5

Asquith, A., & Horsman, G. (2019). Let the robots do it! – taking a look at robotic process automation and its potential application in digital forensics. *Forensic Science International. Reports*, *1*, 100007. DOI: 10.1016/j.fsir.2019.100007

Atlam, H. F., Walters, R. J., & Wills, G. B. (2018). Fog Computing and the Internet of Things: A Review. *Big Data and Cognitive Computing*, *2*(2), 1–18. DOI: 10.3390/bdcc2020010

AWS. (2024). *Cloud native architecture best practices*. Amazon Web Services Technical Documentation.

Azure, M. (2024). *Enterprise cloud-native transformation guide*. Microsoft Documentation.

Baglini, R., & Hjorth, H. (2021). Natural Language Processing 4 All (NLP4All): A New Online Platform for Teaching and Learning NLP Concepts. *Proceedings of the 5th Workshop on Teaching Natural Language Processing*, 2021, 28–33. DOI: 10.18653/v1/2021.teachingnlp-1.3

Bai, B., Li, W., Wang, L., & Zhang, G. (2019). Coded Caching in Fog-RAN: B Matching Approach. *IEEE Transactions on Communications*, *67*(5), 3753–3767. DOI: 10.1109/TCOMM.2019.2896026

Bajaj, Y., & Samal, M. (2023). Accelerating Software Quality: Unleashing the Power of Generative AI for Automated Test-Case Generation and Bug Identification. *International Journal for Research in Applied Science and Engineering Technology*, *11*(7), 345–350. Advance online publication. DOI: 10.22214/ijraset.2023.54628

Balalaie, A., Heydarnoori, A., & Jamshidi, P. (2016). Microservices architecture enables devops: Migration to a cloud-native architecture. *IEEE Software*, *33*(3), 42–52. DOI: 10.1109/MS.2016.64

Banaee, H., Ahmed, M. U., & Loutfi, A. (2013). Data mining for wearable sensors in health monitoring systems: A review of recent trends and challenges. *Sensors (Basel)*, *13*(12), 17472–17500. DOI: 10.3390/s131217472 PMID: 24351646

Bank of America. (2021). Erica: The AI-driven virtual assistant. Retrieved from https://www.bankofamerica.com/

Baqar, M., & Khanda, R. (2024). The Future of Software Testing: AI-Powered Test Case Generation and Validation. arXiv preprint arXiv:2409.05808.

Barenkamp, M., Rebstadt, J., & Thomas, O. (2020). Applications of AI in classical software engineering. *AI Perspectives*, *2*(1), 1–15. DOI: 10.1186/s42467-020-00005-4

Barocas, S., Hardt, M., & Narayanan, A. (2019). Fairness and machine learning. Retrieved from https://fairmlbook.org/

Basel Committee on Banking Supervision. (2020). Guidelines: The use of technology in banking supervision. Bank for International Settlements. Retrieved from https://www.bis.org/

Basher, M. A., & Roy, P. C. (2011). Introducing an e-Health card for developing countries: A case study of Bangladesh. Stockholms Universiteit. http://www.diva-portal.org/smash/get/diva2:428633/FULLTEXT01.pdf

Bavota, G., Panichella, S., Tsantalis, N., & Canfora, G. (2014). Recommending refactorings based on team Co-maintenance patterns. In *Proceedings of the 29th ACM/IEEE International Conference on Automated Software Engineering (ASE 2014)*. DOI: 10.1145/2642937.2642948

Behjati, R., Arisholm, E., Bedregal, M., & Tan, C. (2019). Syn- thetic Test Data Generation Using Recurrent Neural Networks: A Position Paper. 2019 IEEE/ACM 7th International Workshop on Realizing Artificial Intelligence Synergies in Software Engi- neering (RAISE). DOI: 10.1109/RAISE.2019.00012

Belle, V. (2023). Knowledge representation and acquisition for ethical AI: Challenges and opportunities. *Ethics and Information Technology*, *25*(1), 22. Advance online publication. DOI: 10.1007/s10676-023-09692-z

Bharathi, V., Natraj, N. A., Gopinath, S., & Kiruthikaa, R. (2024). Advanced Computer Vision Techniques for Accurate Measurement in Unmanned Mobile Robots. *Measurement Science Review*, *24*(5), 188–192. DOI: 10.2478/msr-2024-0025

Binns, R., Veale, M., Van Kleek, M., Shadbolt, N., & O'Hara, K. (2018). 'It's reducing a human being to a percentage': Perceptions of justice in algorithmic decisions. *Proceedings of the 2018 CHI Conference on Human Factors in Computing Systems*, 1-14. DOI: 10.1145/3173574.3173951

Bird, C., Ford, D., Zimmermann, T., Forsgren, N., Kalliamvakou, E., Lowdermilk, T., & Gazit, I. (2022). Taking Flight with Copilot. *ACM Queue; Tomorrow's Computing Today*, *20*(6), 35–57. DOI: 10.1145/3582083

Blanchfield, B. B., Heffernan, J. L., Osgood, B., Sheehan, R. R., & Meyer, G. S. (2010). Saving billions of dollars - and physicians' time - by streamlining billing practices. *Health Affairs*, *29*(6), 1248–1254. DOI: 10.1377/hlthaff.2009.0075 PMID: 20430822

Borges, A. F., Laurindo, F. J., Spínola, M. M., Gonçalves, R. F., & Mattos, C. A. (2021). The strategic use of artificial intelligence in the digital era: Systematic literature review and future research directions. *International Journal of Information Management*, *57*, 102225. DOI: 10.1016/j.ijinfomgt.2020.102225

Boru, D., Kliazovich, D., Granelli, F., Bouvry, P., & Zomaya, A. Y. (2015). Energy-efficient data replication in cloud computing datacenters. *Cluster Computing*, *18*(1), 385–402. DOI: 10.1007/s10586-014-0404-x

Boudi, A., Bagaa, M., Pöyhönen, P., Taleb, T., & Flinck, H. (2021). AI-based resource management in beyond 5G cloud native environment. *IEEE Network*, *35*(2), 128–135. DOI: 10.1109/MNET.011.2000392

Boukerche, A., Tao, Y., & Sun, P. (2020). Artificial intelligence-based vehicular traffic flo prediction methods for supporting intelligent transportation systems. *Computer Networks*, *182*, 107484. DOI: 10.1016/j.comnet.2020.107484

Brown, T., Mann, B., Ryder, N., Subbiah, M., Kaplan, J., & Dhariwal, P. (2020). Language models are few-shot learners. *Advances in Neural Information Processing Systems*, *33*, 1877–1901.

Bruhin, O., Ebel, P., Mueller, L., Li, M. M., & Manhai, M., Genai, & Muller, L. (2024). GenAI and Software Engineering: Strategies for Shaping the Core of Tomorrow's Software Engineering Practice. *International Conference on Information Systems,* 1-17.

Brynjolfsson, E., & Mcelheran, K. (2016). The Rapid Adoption of Data-Driven Decision-Making. *The American Economic Review*, *106*(5), 133–139. DOI: 10.1257/aer.p20161016

Bullock, S., Morecroft, C. W., Mullen, R., & Ewing, A. B. (2017). Hospital patient discharge process: An evaluation. *European Journal of Hospital Pharmacy. Science and Practice*, *24*(5), 278–282. DOI: 10.1136/ejhpharm-2016-000928 PMID: 31156958

Burnaev, E., Mironov, E., Shpilman, A., Mironenko, M., & Katalevsky, D. (2023). Practical AI Cases for Solving ESG. *Sustainability (Basel)*, *15*(17), 12731. Advance online publication. DOI: 10.3390/su151712731

Cai, F., Zhu, N., Hc, J., Mu, P., Li, W., & Yu, Y. (2019). Survey of access control models and technologies for cloud computing. *Cluster Computing*, *22*(3), 6111–6122. DOI: 10.1007/s10586-018-1850-7

California Legislative Information. (2020). California Consumer Privacy Act (CCPA). Retrieved from https://leginfo.legislature.ca.gov

Camacho, D., Gálvez, G., Molina, J. M., & De La Torre, R. (2015). Automated testing of cloud services with genetic algorithms. *Software, Practice & Experience, 45*(9), 1277–1305. DOI: 10.1002/spe.2278

Carino, S., & Andrews, J. H. (2015). Dynamically Testing GUIs Using Ant Colony Optimization. *ASE, 2015*, 138–148. DOI: 10.1109/ASE.2015.70

Cavoukian, A. (2018). Privacy impact assessments: An essential tool for the development of AI applications. Information and Privacy Commissioner of Ontario. Retrieved from https://www.ipc.on.ca

Chafik, N., & Benchekroun, A. (2020). Integrating Artificial Intelligence in Software Engineering: Enhancements and Challenges in the Development Lifecycle. *Iconic Research and Engineering Journals, 3*(12), 253–265.

Chan, A. T. S., Cao, J., Chan, H., & Young, G. (2001). A web-enabled framework for smart card application in health services. *Communications of the ACM, 44*(9), 76–82. DOI: 10.1145/383694.383710

Charanya, R., & Aramudhan, M. (2016, February). Survey on access control issues in cloud computing. In *2016 International Conference on Emerging Trends in Engineering, Technology and Science (ICETETS)* (pp. 1-4). IEEE.

Chen, L., "Quantum AI Algorithms: Advancements for Complex Problem Solving."

Cheng, Q., Sahoo, D., Saha, A., Yang, W., Liu, C., Woo, G., . . . Hoi, S. C. (2023). Ai for it operations (aiops) on cloud platforms: Reviews, opportunities and challenges. arXiv preprint arXiv:2304.04661.

Cheng, Y., Chen, J., Huang, Q., Xing, Z., Xu, X., & Lu, Q. (2023). Prompt Sapper: A LLM-Empowered Production Tool for Building AI Chains. *ACM Transactions on Software Engineering and Methodology*. Advance online publication. DOI: 10.1145/3638247

Chen, J. H., & Asch, S. M. (2017). Machine Learning and Prediction in Medicine - Beyond the Peak of Inflated Expectations. *The New England Journal of Medicine, 376*(26), 2507–2509. DOI: 10.1056/NEJMp1702071 PMID: 28657867

Chen, Y., & Rodriguez, M. (2024). AI integration challenges in cloud-native environments: A systematic review. *Journal of Cloud Computing (Heidelberg, Germany), 12*(2), 145–162.

Chen, Z., Fang, Z., & Tan, Q. (2019). Machine learning-based test prioritization for Android applications. *IEEE Access : Practical Innovations, Open Solutions, 7*, 160194–160205. DOI: 10.1109/ACCESS.2019.2951166

Chen, Z., & Monperrus, M. (2019). A literature study of embeddings on source code. *ACM Computing Surveys*, *51*(3), 1–27. DOI: 10.1145/3190507

Chirra, D. R. (2020). AI-Based Real-Time Security Monitoring for Cloud-Native Applications in Hybrid Cloud Environments. *Revista de Inteligencia Artificial en Medicina*, *11*(1), 382–402.

Chittala, S. (2024). ORCHESTRATING THE CLOUD: AI-ENHANCED RELEASE AUTOMATION IN KUBERNETES ENVIRONMENTS. [IJRCAIT]. *INTERNATIONAL JOURNAL OF RESEARCH IN COMPUTER APPLICATIONS AND INFORMATION TECHNOLOGY*, *7*(2), 864–878.

Choi, J., An, G., & Yoo, S. (2024). Iterative Refactoring of Real-World Open-Source Programs with Large Language Models. In Lecture Notes in Computer Science (including subseries Lecture Notes in Artificial Intelligence and Lecture Notes in Bioinformatics). DOI: 10.1007/978-3-031-64573-0_4

Chowdary, V. H. D., Shanmukh, A., Nikhil, T. P., Kumar, B. S., & Khan, F. (2024, May). DevOps 2.0: Embracing AI/ML, Cloud-Native Development, and a Culture of Continuous Transformation. In *2024 4th International Conference on Pervasive Computing and Social Networking (ICPCSN)* (pp. 673-679). IEEE.

Christopoulou, A., Giakoumakis, E. A., Zafeiris, V. E., & Soukara, V. (2012). Automated refactoring to the Strategy design pattern. *Information and Software Technology*, *54*(11), 1202–1214. DOI: 10.1016/j.infsof.2012.05.004

Ciniselli, M., Puccinelli,N., Qiu, K., & Grazia, L.D. (2024).From Today's Code to Tomorrow's Symphony: The AI Transformation of Developer's Routine by 2030. *Computer Papers*, 25-39.

Cloud, H. (2011). The nist definition of cloud computing. National institute of science and technology, special publication, 800(2011), 145.

Cloud, G. (2024). *Implementing AI in cloud-native applications*. Google Cloud Documentation.

Confidently, L. A. O., Chakraborty, M., & Kundan, A. P. (2021). Monitoring Cloud-Native Applications.

Convolbo, M. W., Chou, J., Lu, S., & Chung, Y. C. (2016, December). DRASH: A data replication-aware scheduler in geo-distributed data centers. In *2016 IEEE International Conference on Cloud Computing Technology and Science (CloudCom)* (pp. 302-309). IEEE.

D'Onofrio, D. S., Fusco, M. L., & Zhong, H. (2023). *CI/CD Pipeline and DevSecOps Integration for Security and Load Testing (No. SAND-2023-08255). Sandia National Lab.* SNL-NM.

da Silva, G. H. G., Holanda, M., & Araujo, A. (2016, June). Data replication policy in a cloud computing environment. In 2016 11th Iberian conference on information systems and technologies (CISTI) (pp. 1-6). IEEE.

Dai, P., Yang, L., Wang, Y., Jin, D., & Gong, Y. (2023). Constructing Traceability Links between Software Requirements and Source Code Based on Neural Networks. *Mathematics, 11*(2), 315. Advance online publication. DOI: 10.3390/math11020315

Dang, T. D., & Hoang, D. (2017). A Data Protection Model for Fog Computing. *Proceedings of the Second International Conference on Fog and Mobile Edge Computing (FMEC)*, 32-38. DOI: 10.1109/FMEC.2017.7946404

Dastin, J. (2020). Amazon scraps AI recruitment tool that showed bias against women. Reuters. Retrieved from https://www.business-standard.com/article/international/amazon-scraps-secret-ai-recruiting-tool-that-showed-bias-against-women-118101000204_1.html

Davidson, K., Smith, R., & Lee, J. (2024). AI-driven DevOps: Impact on deployment efficiency and resource utilization. *Cloud Computing Research, 15*(3), 78–92.

Davis, C. (2019). *Cloud Native Patterns: Designing Change-Tolerant Software*. Simon and Schuster.

De Donato, L., Flammini, F., Marrone, S., Mazzariello, C., Nardone, R., Sansone, C., & Vittorini, V. (2022). A survey on audio-video based defect detection through deep learning in railway maintenance. *IEEE Access : Practical Innovations, Open Solutions, 10*, 65376–65400. DOI: 10.1109/ACCESS.2022.3183102

Dehaerne, E., Dey, B., Halder, S., De Gendt, S., & Meert, W. (2022). Code generation using machine learning: A systematic review. *IEEE Access : Practical Innovations, Open Solutions, 10*, 82434–82455. DOI: 10.1109/ACCESS.2022.3196347

Deng, S., Zhao, H., Huang, B., Zhang, C., Chen, F., Deng, Y., & Zomaya, A. Y. (2024). Cloud-native computing: A survey from the perspective of services. *Proceedings of the IEEE.* DOI: 10.1109/JPROC.2024.3353855

Derezińska, A. (2018). A Structure-Driven Process of Automated Refactoring to Design Patterns. In Advances in Intelligent Systems and Computing. DOI: 10.1007/978-3-319-67229-8_4

Derezinska, A., & Sygocki, D. (2023). Review of Automated Code Refactoring of C# Programs. In *Proceedings of the 18th Conference on Computer Science and Intelligence Systems (FedCSIS 2023)*. DOI: 10.15439/2023F7277

Devalla, S., & Yogix, M. (2023). Building Trust in AI -A Simplified Guide to Ensure Software Quality. Journal of Soft Computing Paradigm. .DOI: 10.36548/jscp.2023.3.001

Devarajan, Y. (2018). A Study of Robotic Process Automation Use Cases Today for Tomorrow's Business. *International Journal of Computers and Technology*, *5*(6), 12–18.

DevOps Research Group. (2024), DevOps Research & Assessment. (2024). Accelerate state of DevOps report. Google Cloud. https://cloud.google.com/devops/state-of-devops

Dong, H., Zhang, C., Li, G., & Zhang, H. (2024). Cloud-Native Databases: A Survey. *IEEE Transactions on Knowledge and Data Engineering*, *36*(12), 7772–7791. DOI: 10.1109/TKDE.2024.3397508

Dorsey, E. R., & Topol, E. J. (2016). State of Telehealth. *The New England Journal of Medicine*, *375*(2), 154–161. DOI: 10.1056/NEJMra1601705 PMID: 27410924

Doshi-Velez, F., & Kim, B. (2017). Towards a rigorous science of interpretable machine learning. arXiv preprint arXiv:1702.08608. https://doi.org//arXiv.1702.08608DOI: 10.48550

Duan, Y., Edwards, J. S., & Dwivedi, Y. K. (2019). Artificial intelligence for decision making in the era of Big Data–evolution, challenges and research agenda. *International Journal of Information Management*, *48*, 63–71. DOI: 10.1016/j.ijinfomgt.2019.01.021

Durelli, V. H. S., Sampaio, S. A., & Garcia, V. C. (2020). Toward AI-based software testing: The roles of machine learning techniques. *IEEE Software*, *37*(4), 37–43. DOI: 10.1109/MS.2020.2987712

Dwivedi, Y. K., Hughes, L., Ismagilova, E., Aarts, G., Coombs, C., Crick, T., Duan, Y., Dwivedi, R., Edwards, J., Eirug, A., Galanos, V., Ilavarasan, P. V., Janssen, M., Jones, P., Kar, A. K., Kizgin, H., Kronemann, B., Lal, B., Lucini, B., & Williams, M. D. (2021). Artificial Intelligence (AI): Multidisciplinary perspectives on emerging challenges, opportunities, and agenda for research, practice and policy. *International Journal of Information Management*, *57*, 101994. DOI: 10.1016/j.ijinfomgt.2019.08.002

Dzedzickis, A., Subačiūtė-Žemaitienė, J., Šutinys, E., Samukaitė-Bubnienė, U., & Bučinskas, V. (2021). Advanced applications of industrial robotics: New trends and possibilities. *Applied Sciences (Basel, Switzerland)*, *12*(1), 135. DOI: 10.3390/app12010135

Eames, T., Markus, F., Patricia, L., & Justus, B. (2024). International Workshop on Green and Sustainable Software. *VU Research Portal,* 1-9.

Efimova, D. (2024, August 15). Generative AI Application Across the Software Development Lifecycle. *epam.*

Engeström, Y. (2000). Activity theory as a framework for analysing and redesigning work. *Ergonomics*, *43*(7), 960–974. DOI: 10.1080/001401300409143 PMID: 10929830

Enterprise Technology Review. (2024). Cost analysis of AI implementation in DevOps. Technology Economics Quarterly, 8(1).

Erler, M. (2024, August). Sustainable Computing for AI & Cloud Native Workloads. In *2024 IEEE Hot Chips 36 Symposium (HCS)* (pp. 1-24). IEEE Computer Society. DOI: 10.1109/HCS61935.2024.10664662

Esteva, A., Kuprel, B., Novoa, R. A., Ko, J., Swetter, S. M., Blau, H. M., & Thrun, S. (2017). Dermatologist-level classification of skin cancer with deep neural networks. *Nature*, *542*(7639), 115–118. DOI: 10.1038/nature21056 PMID: 28117445

European Commission. (2018). General Data Protection Regulation (GDPR). Retrieved from https://ec.europa.eu

European Commission. (2021). Proposal for a regulation on artificial intelligence. Retrieved from https://ec.europa.eu

European Union. (2018). General Data Protection Regulation (GDPR). Retrieved from https://eur-lex.europa.eu

Faishal, M., Mathew, S., Neikha, K., Pusa, K., & Zhimomi, T. (2023). The future of work: AI, automation, and the changing dynamics of developed economies. *World Journal of Advanced Research and Reviews*, *18*(3), 620–629. DOI: 10.30574/wjarr.2023.18.3.1086

Feng, S., Chen, Z., Li, L., & Su, Z. (2020). CodeBERT: A pre-trained model for programming and natural languages. *Proceedings of the 2020 Conference on Empirical Methods in Natural Language Processing (EMNLP),* 1536–1547. DOI: 10.18653/v1/2020.findings-emnlp.139

Feng, X., Guo, C., Jiao, T., & Song, J. (2022). A maturity model for AI-empowered cloud-native databases: From the perspective of resource management. *Journal of Cloud Computing (Heidelberg, Germany), 11*(1), 39. DOI: 10.1186/s13677-022-00318-1

Fitzgerald, J. (2018). Patient engagement through digital health platforms. *Health Affairs, 37*(6), 930–935. DOI: 10.1377/hlthaff.2018.0037

Freeda, R. (2024). Test suite optimization under multi-objective constraints for software fault detection and localization: Hybrid optimization-based model. *International Journal of Software Testing, 10*(1), 151–166. DOI: 10.3233/WEB-220131

Freeda, R. A., & Rajendran, P. S. (2023). An Overview of Efficient Regression Testing Prioritization Techniques Based on Genetic Algorithm. In Dutta, P., Chakrabarti, S., Bhattacharya, A., Dutta, S., & Shahnaz, C. (Eds.), *Emerging Technologies in Data Mining and Information Security. Lecture Notes in Networks and Systems* (Vol. 490). Springer., DOI: 10.1007/978-981-19-4052-1_39

Freeda, R. A., & Rajendran, P. S. (2023). Test Suite Minimization for Regression Testing Using Keyword Match Technique. In Joshi, A., Mahmud, M., & Ragel, R. G. (Eds.), *Information and Communication Technology for Competitive Strategies (ICTCS 2022). ICTCS 2022. Lecture Notes in Networks and Systems* (Vol. 623). Springer., DOI: 10.1007/978-981-19-9638-2_24

Gadde, H. (2022). AI-Enhanced Adaptive Resource Allocation in Cloud-Native Databases. *Revista de Inteligencia Artificial en Medicina, 13*(1), 443–470.

Ganesan, P., & Sanodia, G. (2023). Smart Infrastructure Management: Integrating AI with DevOps for Cloud-Native Applications. *Journal of Artificial Intelligence & Cloud Computing. SRC/JAICC-E163. DOI: doi. org/(2) E163 J Arti Inte & Cloud Comp, 2*(1), 2-4.DOI: 10.47363/JAICC/2023

Garcia, S., "Autonomous Systems' Moral Dilemmas: Navigating Ethical Territories."

Garousi, V., Joy, N., & Keleş, A. B. (2024). AI-powered test automation tools: A systematic review and empirical evaluation. arXiv preprint arXiv:2409.00411.

Ghazal, T. M., Hasan, M. K., Alshurideh, M. T., Alzoubi, H. M., Ahmad, M., Akbar, S. S., Al Kurdi, B., & Akour, I. A. (2021). IoT for smart cities: Machine learning approaches in smart healthcare—Areview. *Future Internet, 13*(8), 218. DOI: 10.3390/fi13080218

Ghorbani, M. A. (2023). AI tools to support design activities and innovation processes.

Ghosh, S., Bandyopadhyay, A., Sahay, S., Ghosh, R., Kundu, I., & Santosh, K. C. (2021). Colorectalhistology tumor detection using ensemble deep neural network. Engineering Applications ofArtificial Intelligence, 100, 104202.

Gil, G., Corujo, D., & Pedreiras, P. (2021, September). Cloud native computing for industry 4.0: Challenges and opportunities. In *2021 26th IEEE international conference on emerging technologies and factory automation (ETFA)* (pp. 01-04). IEEE.

Ginsburg, G. S., & Phillips, K. A. (2018). Precision medicine: From science to value. *Health Affairs, 37*(5), 685–692. DOI: 10.1377/hlthaff.2017.1624 PMID: 29733705

Gnaneswar, N., Hadresh, G., & Pdinesh, V. (2020). A Comparison Analysis of Fog And Cloud Computing, DOI: DOI: 10.31221/osf.io/y7db2

Goul, M., Henderson, J. C., & Tonge, F. M. (1992). The emergence of artificial intelligence as a reference discipline for decision support systems research. *Decision Sciences, 23*(6), 1263–1276. DOI: 10.1111/j.1540-5915.1992.tb00448.x

Grechanik, M., Fu, C., & Xie, Q. (2019). Automatically testing large-scale distributed systems using machine learning techniques. *ACM Transactions on Software Engineering and Methodology, 28*(2), 1–35. DOI: 10.1145/3313623

Guizzo, G., Petke, J., Sarro, F., & Harman, M. (2021, May). Enhancing genetic improvement ofsoftware with regression test selection. In 2021 IEEE/ACM 43rd International Conference onSoftware Engineering (ICSE) (pp. 1323-1333). IEEE.

Gupta, R., "Interpretable AI: Understanding Complex Models."

Habibi, P., Farhoudi, M., Kazemian, S., Khorsandi, S., & Leon-Garcia, A. (2020). Fog Computing: A Comprehensive Architectural Survey. *IEEE Access : Practical Innovations, Open Solutions, 8*, 69105–69133. DOI: 10.1109/ACCESS.2020.2983253

Hacker, P. (2018). The right to be forgotten: A comprehensive analysis. *Harvard Law Review, 131*(5), 1208–1240. DOI: 10.2307/26561013

Haghighat, M., Zonouz, S., & Abdel-Mottaleb, M. (2015, November). CloudID: Trustworthy cloud-based and cross-enterprise biometric identification. *Expert Systems with Applications, 42*(21), 7905–7916. DOI: 10.1016/j.eswa.2015.06.025

Hall, M., Khojaye, M. A., Walkinshaw, N., & McMinn, P. (2014). Establishing the source code disruption caused by automated remodularisation tools. In *Proceedings of the 30th International Conference on Software Maintenance and Evolution (ICSME 2014)*. DOI: 10.1109/ICSME.2014.75

Hallur, G., ... (2023). Seamless mobility: Innovating the digital service landscape in telecom industry. In Proceedings of Fifth International Conference on Computing, Communications, and Cyber-Security (IC4S 2023). Springer. DOI: 10.1007/978-981-97-2550-2_14

Hallur, G.. (2024). Navigating the infotainment landscape: Status and regulations in the digital age. *2024 International Conference on Advances in Data Engineering and Intelligent Computing Systems (ADICS)*, 1-6. DOI: 10.1109/ADICS58448.2024.10533560

Hamioud, S., & Atil, F. (2015). Model-driven java code refactoring. *Computer Science and Information Systems*, *12*(2), 375–403. DOI: 10.2298/CSIS141025015H

Hao, D., Zhang, C., & Xie, X. (2018). Test selection in continuous integration using machine learning. *Proceedings of the 40th International Conference on Software Engineering (ICSE 2018),* 1000-1011. DOI: 10.1145/3180155.3180189

Hasterok, C., & Stompe, J. (2022). PAISE® – process model for AI systems engineering. at - Automatisierungstechnik, 70, 777 - 786. .DOI: 10.1515/auto-2022-0020

Hat, R. (2024). Red Hat named a leader in 2024 Gartner® Magic Quadrant™ for cloud application platforms. Red Hat Blog. https://www.redhat.com/en/blog/red-hat-named-leader-2024-gartnerr-magic-quadranttm-cloud-application-platforms

Hemmati, H., & Arcuri, A. (2015). Empirical analysis of the effectiveness of search-based test automation. *Automated Software Engineering*, *22*(2), 211–243. DOI: 10.1007/s10515-014-0154-5

Henning, S. (2023). Scalability Benchmarking of Cloud-Native Applications Applied to Event-Driven Microservices. DOI: 10.21941/kcss/2023/2

Herrera, B. (2024). *Cloud-Native Applications and Their Role in Supporting Agile Hardware Development* (Doctoral dissertation, Massachusetts Institute of Technology).

Himmelstein, D. U., Jun, M., Busse, R., Chevreul, K., Geissler, A., Jeurisssen, P., & Woolhandler, S. (2014). A comparison of hospital administrative costs in eight nations: Us costs exceed all others by far. *Health Affairs*, *33*(9), 1586–1594. DOI: 10.1377/hlthaff.2013.1327 PMID: 25201663

Hong, H. (2017). From Cloud Computing to Fog Computing: Unleash the Power of Edge and End Devices. *Proceedings of the IEEE International Conference on Cloud Computing Technology and Science (CloudCom)*, 331–334. DOI: 10.1109/CloudCom.2017.53

Hourani, H., Hammad, A., & Lafi, M. (2019, April). The impact of artificial intelligence on software testing. In *2019 IEEE Jordan International Joint Conference on Electrical Engineering and Information Technology (JEEIT)* (pp. 565-570). IEEE. DOI: 10.1109/JEEIT.2019.8717439

HSBC. (2019). AI in risk management: A transformative approach. Retrieved from https://www.hsbc.com

IEEE. (2020). Ethically aligned design: A vision for prioritizing human well-being with artificial intelligence and autonomous systems. Retrieved from https://ethicsinaction.ieee.org

Imazato, A., Higo, Y., Hotta, K., & Kusumoto, S. (2017). Finding Extract Method Refactoring Opportunities by Analyzing Development History. In *Proceedings of the International Computer Software and Applications Conference*. DOI: 10.1109/COMPSAC.2017.129

Incident Management Forum. (2024). *Benchmark report on incident resolution in AI-enabled systems*. IMF Publications.

Issac, R., Muni, R., & Desai, K. (2018). Delineated analysis of robotic process automation tools. Proceedings of 2018 2nd International Conference on Advances in Electronics, Computers, and Communications, ICAECC 2018, 0-4. DOI: 10.1109/ICAECC.2018.8479511

Issac, R., Dantas, A., & Perez, I. J. (2011). Towards a model driven robotic process automation approach. In *2011 IEEE Symposium on Computational Intelligence in Migratory Applications (CIMA)* (pp. 1-7). IEEE.

Ivaki, N. R., & da Silva, P. M. G. (2024). AI-BASED INTRUSION DETECTION MECHANISMS FOR CLOUD-NATIVE SERVICES. Cherukuri, B. R. (2024, February). Development of Design Patterns with Adaptive User Interface for Cloud Native Microservice Architecture Using Deep Learning With IoT. In *2024 IEEE International Conference on Computing, Power and Communication Technologies (IC2PCT)* (Vol. 5, pp. 1866-1871). IEEE.

Iyenghar, P., Otte, F., & Pulvermueller, E. (2022). AI-guided Model-Driven Embedded. *Software Engineering*, •••, 395–404. DOI: 10.5220/0011006200003119

Jabbari, R., bin Ali, N., Petersen, K., & Tanveer, B. (2016). What is DevOps? A systematic mapping study on definitions and practices. In Proceedings of the scientific workshop proceedings of XP2016 (pp. 1-11).

Jenkins. (2024). Jenkins AI and plugin development documentation. The Jenkins Project. https://www.jenkins.io/

Jha, S., Tiwari, P., Gupta, S. N., & Gupta, V. (2022). Natural Language Processing for Small Businesses and Future Trends in Healthcare. In Studies in computational intelligence (pp. 311–324). DOI: 10.1007/978-981-16-8012-0_24

Jha, A. K. (2018). Health information technology and the quality of health care. *Journal of the American Medical Association, 319*(9), 831–833. DOI: 10.1001/jama.2018.1079

Jiang, Y., Huang, W., Bennis, M., Zheng, F. (2020), Decentralized Asynchronous Coded Caching Design and Performance Analysis in Fog Radio Access Networks, IEEE Transactions on Mobile Computing, 19(3), 540–551.

Jiang, L., & Khoo, S.-C. (2014). Vector abstraction and concretization for scalable detection of refactorings. In *Proceedings of the ACM SIGSOFT Symposium on the Foundations of Software Engineering*.

Jiwani, A., Himmelstein, D., Woolhandler, S., & Kahn, J. G. (2014). Billing and insurance-related administrative costs in United States' health care: Synthesis of micro-costing evidence. *BMC Health Services Research, 14*(1), 1–9. DOI: 10.1186/s12913-014-0556-7 PMID: 25540104

Jones, R. (2024). The Impact of AI on Secure Cloud Computing: Opportunities and Challenges. *The Indonesian Journal of Computer Science, 13*(4). Advance online publication. DOI: 10.33022/ijcs.v13i4.4383

Jordanov, J., & Petrov, P. (2023). Domain Driven Design Approaches in Cloud Native Service Architecture. TEM Journal. https://doi.org/DOI: 10.18421/tem124-09

JPMorgan Chase. (2020). COiN: Revolutionizing fraud detection. Retrieved from https://www.jpmorganchase.com

Juan, J., & Mason, B. (2019). Implementing Quality Assurance in Cloud-Native Applications: Challenges, Strategies, and Best Practices. *International Journal of Advanced Engineering Technologies and Innovations, 1*(4), 283–293.

Jyothi, A. P., Shankar, A., Narayan, J. R. A., Maniyar, H., & Ambarkhane, S. (2024). Robotic process automation: In-depth analysis of advanced automation techniques and technologies. In 2024 IEEE International Conference on Contemporary Computing and Communications (InC4) (Vol. 1, pp. 1-6). IEEE.

Jyothi, A. P., Shankar, A., Narayan, J. R. A., Maniyar, H., & Ambarkhane, S. (2024, March). Robotic Process Automation: In-Depth Analysis of Advanced Automation Techniques and Technologies. In 2024 IEEE International Conference on Contemporary Computing and Communications (InC4) (Vol. 1, pp. 1-6). IEEE.

Kalech, M., & Stern, R. (2018). Using model-based diagnosis to improve software testing. U.S.Patent No. 9,934,131. Washington, DC: U.S. Patent and Trademark Office.

Kanchepu, N. (2023). Cloud-Native Architectures: Design Principles and Best Practices for Scalable Applications. *International Journal of Sustainable Development Through AI. ML and IoT*, *2*(2), 1–21.

Kang, H., Nembhard, H. B., Rafferty, C., & Deflitch, C. J. (2014). Patient flow in the emergency department: A classification and analysis of admission process policies. *Annals of Emergency Medicine*, *64*(4), 335–342.e8. DOI: 10.1016/j.annemergmed.2014.04.011 PMID: 24875896

Kanipriya, M., Sugumaran, D., Pandiyarajan, V., Yogananda, B. S., Selvakumar, P., & Mohan, S. (2024, January). Analysis of Electromyography Signals for Control of Mechanical Prosthesis using Machine Learning Techniques. In 2024 2nd International Conference on Intelligent Data Communication Technologies and Internet of Things (IDCIoT) (pp. 1059-1067). IEEE.

Karanam, R. (2024). SECURING CLOUD-NATIVE APPLICATIONS: A HOLISTIC APPROACH. [IJCET]. *INTERNATIONAL JOURNAL OF COMPUTER ENGINEERING AND TECHNOLOGY*, *15*(4), 692–702.

Kashani, Z. M., & Briand, L. C. (2017). Machine learning applications in software testing: A systematic literature review. *Empirical Software Engineering*, *22*(6), 2933–2977. DOI: 10.1007/s10664-017-9511-4

Katalon. (2024). The state of software quality report 2024. Katalon Research. https://katalon.com/reports/state-quality-2024

Kaur, J., & Gill, N. S. (2019). *Artificial Intelligence and deep learning for decision makers: a growthhacker's guide to cutting edge technologies*. BPB Publications.

Kellermann, A. L., & Jones, S. S. (2013). What it will take to achieve the as-yet-unfulfilled promises of health information technology. *Health Affairs*, *32*(1), 63–68. DOI: 10.1377/hlthaff.2012.0693 PMID: 23297272

Kernbach, J. M., Hakvoort, K., Ort, J., Clusmann, H., Neuloh, G., & Delev, D. (2021). The Artificial Intelligence Doctor: Considerations for the Clinical Implementation of Ethical AI. *Acta Neurochirurgica. Supplementum*, *257–261*. Advance online publication. DOI: 10.1007/978-3-030-85292-4_29 PMID: 34862549

Kerrigan, N. (2024). *Enabling a Digital Birmingham: an evaluation of the Birmingham Digital Inclusion Strategy*. Birmingham City University.

Kessler, M., & Pugh, M. (2023). Artificial intelligence in software development: A survey of the field. *ACM Computing Surveys*, *55*(4), 75. Advance online publication. DOI: 10.1145/3542036

Keszocze, O., Soaked, M., Kuksa, E., & Drechsler, R. (2013). Lips: An IDE for model driven engineering based on natural language processing. 2013 1st International Workshop on Natural Language Analysis in Software Engineering, NaturaLiSE, 2, 31–38. DOI: 10.1109/NAturaLiSE.2013.6611718

Khaled, H., & Ahmed, M. (2020). Applying machine learning to optimize automated test case generation for web applications. *Journal of Systems and Software*, *159*, 110438. DOI: 10.1016/j.jss.2019.110438

Khan, S., "Human-Robot Collaboration: AI's Role in Robotics."

Khan, B., Fatima, H., Qureshi, A., Kumar, S., Hanan, A., Hussain, J., & Abdullah, S. (2023). Drawbacks of Artificial Intelligence and Their Potential Solutions in the Healthcare Sector. *Biomedical Materials & Devices*, *1*(2), 1–8. DOI: 10.1007/s44174-023-00063-2 PMID: 36785697

Khan, M. F. I., Mahmud, F. U., Hoseen, A., & Masum, A. K. M. (2024). A New Approach Of Software Test Automation Using Ai. *Yingyong Jichu Yu Gongcheng Kexue Xuebao*, *21*(1), 559–570.

Khan, S., Parkinson, S., & Qin, Y. (2017). Fog computing security: A review of current applications and security solutions. *Journal of Cloud Computing (Heidelberg, Germany)*, *6*(19), 1–22. DOI: 10.1186/s13677-017-0090-3

Khashabi, D., Sammons, M., Zhou, B., Redman, T., Christodoulopoulos, C. E., Srikumar, V., Rizzolo, N., Luo, L. R. G., Do, Q., Tsai, C., Roy, S., Mayhew, S., Feng, Z., Wieting, J., Yu, X., Song, Y., Gupta, S., Upadhyay, S., Arivazhagan, N., . . . Roth, D. (2018). CogcompnLP: Your Swiss army knife for NLP. LREC 2018 - 11th International Conference on Language Resources and Evaluation, 541–549.

Khumalo, N., Oyerinde, O., & Mfupe, L. (2020). Reinforcement Learning Based Computation Resource Allocation Scheme for 5G Fog-Radio Access Network. *2020 Fifth International Conference on Fog and Mobile Edge Computing (FMEC)*, 353–355. DOI: 10.1109/FMEC49853.2020.9144787

Kılıç, H. (2017). *Kamuda Bulut Bilişim Kullanımına Yönelik Risk Analizi ve Yönetimi, Uzmanlık Tezi, (yayımlanmamış)*. Çevre ve Şehircilik Bakanlığı.

Kim, M., Ryu, S., & Kwon, K. (2021). AI-based static analysis for automated software testing. *Information and Software Technology*, *128*, 106518. DOI: 10.1016/j.infsof.2020.106518

Kosińska, J., Baliś, B., Konieczny, M., Malawski, M., & Zieliński, S. (2023). Toward the observability of cloud-native applications: The overview of the state-of-the-art. *IEEE Access : Practical Innovations, Open Solutions*, *11*, 73036–73052. DOI: 10.1109/ACCESS.2023.3281860

KPMG. (2015). AHP I Healthcare-India (No. 1). https://assets.kpmg/content/dam/kpmg/in/pdf/2016/09/AHPIHealthcare-India.pdf

Krasniqi, R., & Do, H. (2023). Generalizability of NLP-based Models for Modern Software Development Cross-Domain Environments. 2023 IEEE/ACM 2nd International Workshop on Natural Language-Based Software Engineering. https://doi.org/DOI: 10.1109/NLBSE59153.2023.00009

Kratzke, N. (2022). Cloud-Native Applications and Services. *Future Internet*, *14*(12), 346. DOI: 10.3390/fi14120346

Kripalani, S., LeFevre, F., Phillips, C. O., Williams, M. V., Basaviah, P., & Baker, D. W. (2007). Deficits in communication and information transfer between hospital-based and primary care physicians: Implications for patient safety and continuity of care. *Journal of the American Medical Association*, *297*(8), 831–841. DOI: 10.1001/jama.297.8.831 PMID: 17327525

Kruk, M. E., Gage, A. D., Joseph, N. T., Danaei, G., García-Saisó, S., & Salomon, J. A. (2018). Mortality due to low-quality health systems in the universal health coverage era: A systematic analysis of amenable deaths in 137 countries. *Lancet*, *392*(10160), 2203–2212. DOI: 10.1016/S0140-6736(18)31668-4 PMID: 30195398

Kumar, A. (2024). AI-driven innovations in modern cloud computing. arXiv preprint arXiv:2410.15960.

Kumar, S. (2024, May 6). Understanding the Application and Impact of AI in Software Development Life Cycle. *DZone*.

Kumar, S., & Smith, P. (2024). Cloud-native architecture adoption trends. *Journal of Cloud Engineering*, *9*(1), 23–45.

Kuner, C. (2017). *The General Data Protection Regulation: A commentary*. Oxford University Press.

Lacity, M., Willcocks, L., & Craig, A. (2016). Robotic process automation at Telefónica O2. *MIS Quarterly Executive*, *15*(1), 21–35.

Lang, H., Tian, H., Li, D., Niu, Z., & Wen, L. (2022, August). Design of A Cloud Native-Based Integrated Management Platform for Smart Operation of Multi-Business Buildings. In *2022 14th International Conference on Intelligent Human-Machine Systems and Cybernetics (IHMSC)* (pp. 169-173). IEEE. DOI: 10.1109/IHMSC55436.2022.00047

Larson, E., Sharma, J., Bohren, M. A., & Tunçalp, Ö. (2019). When the patient is the expert: Measuring patient experience and satisfaction with care. *Bulletin of the World Health Organization*, *97*(8), 563–569. DOI: 10.2471/BLT.18.225201 PMID: 31384074

Laszewski, T.. (2018). *Cloud Native Architectures: Design high-availability and cost-effective applications for the cloud.* Packt Publishing Ltd.

Lee, J., "AI and Creativity: The Impact of GANs in Art Generation."

Lee, C. L., Chao, C. T., Chu, W. H., Hung, M. Y., & Lee, J. K. (2022). Accelerating AI Applicationswith Sparse Matrix Compression in Halide. *Journal of Signal Processing Systems for Signal, Image, and Video Technology*, •••, 1–14.

Lee, K., & Kim, J. (2023). Examining generative AI's influence on source code quality and development processes. *Journal of Software Engineering Research and Development*, *11*(1), 5. Advance online publication. DOI: 10.1186/s40411-023-00204-4

Li, B. H., Hou, B. C., Yu, W. T., Lu, X. B., & Yang, C. W. (2017). Applications of artificial intelligence in intelligent manufacturing: A review. *Frontiers of Information Technology & Electronic Engineering*, *18*(1), 86–96. DOI: 10.1631/FITEE.1601885

Li, D., & Du, Y. (2017). *Artificial intelligence with uncertainty*. CRC press. DOI: 10.1201/9781315366951

Li, L., Wang, D., Shen, X., & Yang, M. (2009). A method for combinatorial explosion avoidance of AI planner and the appli- cation on test case generation. *CiSE, 2009*, 1–4.

Lima, R., da Cruz, A. M. R., & Ribeiro, J. (2020, June). Artificial intelligence applied to software testing: A literature review. In *2020 15th Iberian Conference on Information Systems and Technologies (CISTI)* (pp. 1-6). IEEE. DOI: 10.23919/CISTI49556.2020.9141124

Lindeman, M.J. (2024, August 9). The AI-SDLC Phases for Systems that Include an AI Model. *Pieces for Developers*.

Lin, J. W., Chen, C. H., & Chang, J. M. (2013). QoS-aware data replication for data-intensive applications in cloud computing systems. *IEEE Transactions on Cloud Computing*, *1*(1), 101–115. DOI: 10.1109/TCC.2013.1

Liu, H., Zong, J., Wang, Q., Liu, Y., & Yang, F. (2022, April). Cloud native based intelligent RAN architecture towards 6G programmable networking. In *2022 7th International Conference on Computer and Communication Systems (ICCCS)* (pp. 623-627). IEEE.

Liu, J., & Zhang, L. (2023). The impact of generative AI on software development efficiency: A case study approach. *Journal of Software (Malden, MA)*, *35*(2), e2367. DOI: 10.1002/smr.2367

Liu, P., Zhang, X., Pistoia, M., Zheng, Y., Marques, M., & Zeng, L. (2017). Automatic Text Input Generation for Mobile Testing. *ICSE*, *2017*, 643–653. DOI: 10.1109/ICSE.2017.65

Liu, Z., Roberts, R. A., Lal-Nag, M., Chen, X., Huang, R., & Tong, W. (2021). AI-based language models powering drug discovery and development. *Drug Discovery Today*, *26*(11), 2593–2607. DOI: 10.1016/j.drudis.2021.06.009 PMID: 34216835

Li, Z., Huang, X., & Zhang, M. (2022). AI-powered testing of autonomous driving systems: Challenges and approaches. [TOSEM]. *ACM Transactions on Software Engineering and Methodology*, *31*(2), 1–44. DOI: 10.1145/3474126

Lu, Q., Zhu, L., Xu, X., Whittle, J., & Xing, Z. (2022). Towards a Roadmap on Software Engineering for Responsible AI. 2022 IEEE/ACM 1st International Conference on AI Engineering – Software Engineering for AI (CAIN), 101-112. DOI: 10.1145/3522664.3528607

Lu, Y., Bian, S., Chen, L., He, Y., Hui, Y., Lentz, M., . . . Zhuo, D. (2024). Computing in the Era of Large Generative Models: From Cloud-Native to AI-Native. *arXiv preprint arXiv:2401.12230.*

Luan, T. (2015). Fog Computing: Focusing on Mobile Users at the Edge. *Computer Science.*

Lu, H., Li, Y., Chen, M., Kim, H., & Serikawa, S. (2018). Brain intelligence: Go beyond artificial intelligence. *Mobile Networks and Applications*, *23*(2), 368–375. DOI: 10.1007/s11036-017-0932-8

Machireddy, J. R., Rachakatla, S. K., & Ravichandran, P. (2022). Cloud-Native Data Warehousing: Implementing AI and Machine Learning for Scalable Business Analytics. *Journal of AI in Healthcare and Medicine*, 2(1), 144–169.

Madakam, S., Holmukhe, R. M., & Jaiswal, D. K. (2019). The future digital workforce: Robotic process automation (RPA). *Journal of Information Systems and Technology Management, 16*, 1–17. DOI: 10.4301/S1807-1775201916001

Mahendru, L., ... (2024). Smart driving: Leveraging IoT for automotive innovation. 2024 5th International Conference on Electronics and Sustainable Communication Systems (ICESC), 377-380. DOI: 10.1109/ICESC60852.2024.10689748

Maiti, P., ... (2024). Decentralized defenses: A framework for 5G IoT security in Industry 4.0 using blockchain crowdsourcing. 2024 3rd International Conference on Sentiment Analysis and Deep Learning (ICSADL), 534-538. DOI: 10.1109/ICSADL61749.2024.00093

Mansouri, N. (2016). Adaptive data replication strategy in cloud computing for performance improvement. *Frontiers of Computer Science, 10*(5), 925–935. DOI: 10.1007/s11704-016-5182-6

Mansouri, N., Javidi, M. M., & Zade, B. M. H. (2021). Hierarchical data replication strategy to improve performance in cloud computing. *Frontiers of Computer Science, 15*(2), 1–17. DOI: 10.1007/s11704-019-9099-8

Marakkoottathil, M., Venkatesh, R., & Natraj, N. A. (2024). A Quantitative Study on Cloud Computing in the UAE: Identifying and Addressing Adoption Barriers. In *Analyzing and Mitigating Security Risks in Cloud Computing* (pp. 66–90). IGI Global. DOI: 10.4018/979-8-3693-3249-8.ch004

Marr, B. (2020). How JPMorgan Chase is using AI to improve fraud detection. Forbes. Retrieved from https://www.forbes.com

Martelli, K., Cao, N., & Cheng, B. (2023). *How generative AI can revolutionize the software development lifecycle*. KPMG.

Master, S., ... (2024). Unleashing creativity: The business potential of generative AI. 2024 2nd World Conference on Communication & Computing (WCONF), 1-6. DOI: 10.1109/WCONF61366.2024.10692266

Mathew, D., Shukla, V. K., Chaubey, A., & Dutta, S. (2021). Artificial Intelligence: Hope for Future or Hype by Intellectuals? 2021 9th International Conference on Reliability, Infocom Technologies and Optimization (Trends and Future Directions), ICRITO 2021. DOI: 10.1109/ICRITO51393.2021.9596410

Mealha, D., Preguiça, N., Gomes, M. C., & Leitão, J. (2019, March). Data replication on the cloud/edge. In *Proceedings of the 6th Workshop on Principles and Practice of Consistency for Distributed Data* (pp. 1-7).

Meghanathan, N. (2013). Review of access control models for cloud computing. *Computer Science & Information Science*, *3*(1), 77–85. DOI: 10.5121/csit.2013.3508

Memon, A. M. (2004). Using tasks to automate regression testing of GUIs. In *IASTEDInternational Conference on Artificial Intelligence and Applications-AIA* (pp. 477-82).

Mihaljević, B., Radovan, A., & Žagar, M. (2024). An analysis of generative artificial intelligence tools usage to adapt and enrich software development courses. In International Conference on Education and New Developments 2024 (pp. 553-557).

Mijuskovic, A., Chiumento, A., Bemthuis, R., Aldea, A., & Havinga, P. (2021). Resource Management Techniques for Cloud/Fog and Edge Computing: An Evaluation Framework and Classification. *Sensors (Basel)*, *21*(5), 1–22. DOI: 10.3390/s21051832 PMID: 33808037

Milea, N. A., Jiang, L., & Khoo, S.-C. (2014). Scalable detection of missed cross-function refactorings. In *Proceedings of the 2014 International Symposium on Software Testing and Analysis (ISSTA 2014)*. DOI: 10.1145/2610384.2610394

Miller, K., & Mun, J. (2023, July). Cyber technologies, machine learning, additive manufacturing, and cloud in the box to enable optimized maintenance processes in extreme conditions. In International Conference on Human-Computer Interaction (pp. 672-684). Cham: Springer Nature Switzerland.

Miller, R. (2020). California Consumer Privacy Act (CCPA) compliance strategies. *Privacy Law Journal*, *8*(2), 45–59.

Miller, R., & Davis, T. (2024). Machine learning applications in DevOps monitoring. *Cloud Technology Review*, *11*(2), 112–128.

Miloudi, I. E., Yagoubi, B., & Bellounar, F. Z. (2021, October). A Survey of Dynamic Replication Strategies in Cloud Computing Systems. In *2021 International Conference on Networking and Advanced Systems (ICNAS)* (pp. 1-6). IEEE. DOI: 10.1109/ICNAS53565.2021.9628963

Ministry of Health and Family Welfare. (2018). Ministry of Health and Family Welfare Hospitals in the Country. https://pib.gov.in/PressReleasePage.aspx?PRID=1539877

Mitchell, B. S. (2023). Cloud Native Software Engineering. arXiv preprint arXiv:2307.01045.

Moghadam, M. H. (2019). Machine Learning-assisted Perfor- mance Testing. ESEC/SIGSOFT FSE 2019, 1187–1189.

Morgan, L. (2024). AI governance in DevOps environments. *Risk Management Quarterly, 16*(4), 67–82.

Mukhamediev, R., Popova, Y., Kuchin, Y., Zaitseva, E., Kalimoldayev, A., Symagulov, A., Levashenko, V., Abdoldina, F., Gopejenko, V., Yakunin, K., Muhamedijeva, E., & Yelis, M. (2022). Review of Artificial Intelligence and Machine Learning Technologies: Classification, Restrictions, Opportunities and Challenges. *Mathematics, 10*(15), 2552. Advance online publication. DOI: 10.3390/math10152552

Müller, H., & Schneider, A. (2023). Trends in generative AI for software engineering: Challenges and opportunities. *Software, Practice & Experience, 53*(1), 7–24. DOI: 10.1002/spe.3176

Nag, S. (2024, September 11). Generative AI and the changing face of Software Development Lifecycle. *Calsoft*.

Nandanwar, R., ... (2024). Stitching data threads: Impact of artificial intelligence on fashion evolution. 2024 4th International Conference on Innovative Practices in Technology and Management (ICIPTM), 1-6. DOI: 10.1109/ICIPTM59628.2024.10563840

Narayanan, A., Bonneau, J., & Felten, E.. (2016). *Bitcoin and cryptocurrency technologies: A comprehensive introduction*. Princeton University Press.

Nassar, A., & Kamal, M. (2021). Ethical dilemmas in AI-powered decision-making: A deep dive into big data-driven ethical considerations. *International Journal of Responsible Artificial Intelligence, 11*(8), 1–11.

Ng, H., & Tan, W. (2019). Personal data protection act (PDPA) compliance in Singapore. Singapore. *Law Review, 35*(1), 20–30.

Nguyen, H. (2021). *Machine Learning Model Management using Cloud-Native Technologies for IoT* (Master's thesis).

Nguyen, T. N. (2023). Statistical Models and Machine Learning to Advance Code Completion: Are We There Yet? In Natural computing series (pp. 121–153). DOI: 10.1007/978-981-19-9948-2_5

Nguyen-Duc, A., Cabrero-Daniel, B., Przybylek, A., Arora, C., Khanna, D., Herda, T., . . . Abrahamsson, P. (2023). Generative Artificial Intelligence for Software Engineering—A Research Agenda. arXiv preprint arXiv:2310.18648.

NIST. (2013). *Cloud Computing Standards Roadmap*. National Institue of Standards and Tecnology Special Publication.

Nithiyanantham, K. K., ... (2024). Crop health monitoring for precision agriculture using IoT-based sensors in drones. In Lecture Notes in Electrical Engineering (pp. 875-890). DOI: 10.1007/978-981-97-3442-9_62

OECD. (2019). OECD principles on artificial intelligence. Retrieved from https://www.oecd.org

Olabanji, D., Fitch, T., & Matthew, O. (2023). Cloud-native architecture portability framework validation and implementation using expert system. [IJASCSE]. *International Journal of Advanced Studies in Computer Science and Engineering, 12*(4).

Oyeniran, O. C., Adewusi, A. O., Adeleke, A. G., Akwawa, L. A., & Azubuko, C. F. (2023). AI-driven devops: Leveraging machine learning for automated software deployment and maintenance. *DevOps Journal, 5*(2), 89–104.

Oyeniran, O. C., Modupe, O. T., Otitoola, A. A., Abiona, O. O., Adewusi, A. O., & Oladapo, O. J. (2024). A comprehensive review of leveraging cloud-native technologies for scalability and resilience in software development. *International Journal of Science and Research Archive, 11*(2), 330–337. DOI: 10.30574/ijsra.2024.11.2.0432

Pandi, S. B. (2023). Artificial intelligence in software and service lifecycle.

Panichella, S., Palomba, F., & Zaidman, A. (2018). The impact of deep learning techniques on software quality assurance. *IEEE Software, 35*(6), 56–62. DOI: 10.1109/MS.2018.290110430

Pan, Y. (2016). Heading toward Artificial Intelligence 2.0. *Engineering (Beijing), 2*(4), 409–413. DOI: 10.1016/J.ENG.2016.04.018

Paradkar, A. M., Sinha, A., Williams, C., Johnson, R. D., Outter- son, S., Shriver, C., & Liang, C. (2007). Automated functional conformance test generation for semantic web services. ICWS 2007, 110–117

Pashchenko, D. (2023). *Early Formalization of AI-tools Usage in Software Engineering in Europe: Study of 2023*. International Journal of Information Technology and Computer Science., DOI: 10.5815/ijitcs.2023.06.03

Patel, A. et al., "Evolving AI Ethics: Adversarial Robustness in Neural Networks."

Patil, B., ... (2024). Artificial intelligence powered paradigm shift: Revolutionizing digital marketing. 2024 4th International Conference on Innovative Practices in Technology and Management (ICIPTM), 1-6. DOI: 10.1109/ICIPTM59628.2024.10563450

Patrício, L., de Sousa Costa, C. R., Varela, L., & Cruz-Cunha, M. M. (2024). Literature review on the sustainable implementation of Robotic Process Automation (RPA) in medical and healthcare administrative services. *Procedia Computer Science*, *239*, 166–176. DOI: 10.1016/j.procs.2024.06.159

Paul, D., Namperumal, G., & Selvaraj, A. (2022). Cloud-Native AI/ML Pipelines: Best Practices for Continuous Integration, Deployment, and Monitoring in Enterprise Applications. *Journal of Artificial Intelligence Research*, *2*(1), 176–231.

Pengfei, H., Sahraoui, D., Huansheng, N., & Tie, Q. (2017). Survey on fog computing: Architecture, key technologies, applications and open issues. *Journal of Network and Computer Applications*, *98*, 27–42. DOI: 10.1016/j.jnca.2017.09.002

Pentyala, D., Manduva, V. C., & Devarasetty, N. (2021). Cloud-Native Data Engineering: Improving Reliability Through AIOrchestrated Operations. *International Journal of Advanced Engineering Technologies and Innovations*, *1*(3), 94–128.

Performance Analytics Review. (2024). Metrics processing in enterprise environments. Technical Performance Quarterly, 7(2).

Perry, N., Srivastava, M., Kumar, D., & Boneh, D. (2022). Do Users Write More Insecure Code with AI Assistants? *Proceedings of the 2023 ACM SIGSAC Conference on Computer and Communications Security*. DOI: 10.1145/3576915.3623157

Pinciroli, R., Ali, A., Yan, F., & Smirni, E. (2020). Cedule+: Resource management for burstable cloud instances using predictive analytics. *IEEE Transactions on Network and Service Management*, *18*(1), 945–957. DOI: 10.1109/TNSM.2020.3039942

Polamarasetti, A. (2021). Data Science Innovations for Cloud-Native AI Applications. *International Journal of Machine Learning Research in Cybersecurity and Artificial Intelligence*, *12*(1), 292–324.

Polese, M.. (2023). Empowering the 6G cellular architecture with Open RAN. *IEEE Journal on Selected Areas in Communications*.

Pölöskei, I. (2022). MLOps approach in the cloud-native data pipeline design. *Acta Technica Jaurinensis*, *15*(1), 1–6. DOI: 10.14513/actatechjaur.00581

Pothukuchi, A. S., Kota, L. V., & Mallikarjunaradhya, V. (2023). Impact of Generative AI on the Software Development Life Cycle (SDLC). *International Journal of Creative Research Thoughts*, *11*(8), 287–291.

Prabhu, S.. (2024). Elevating business experiences: AI-powered chatbots reforming marketing and e-commerce. In Singh, D. (Eds.), *Transforming the Financial Landscape with ICTs* (pp. 1–27). IGI Global., DOI: 10.4018/979-8-3693-1503-3.ch001

Pradhan, P. R., Limaye, G., & Jhaveri, R. H. (2022). Artificial intelligence in software testing: A systematic review. *Journal of King Saud University. Computer and Information Sciences*. Advance online publication. DOI: 10.1016/j.jksuci.2022.04.012

Pramod, D. (2022). Robotic process automation for industry: Adoption status, benefits, challenges and research agenda. *Benchmarking*, *29*(5), 1562–1586. DOI: 10.1108/BIJ-01-2021-0033

Prangon, N. F., & Wu, J. (2024). AI and Computing Horizons: Cloud and Edge in the Modern Era. *Journal of Sensor and Actuator Networks*, *13*(4), 44. DOI: 10.3390/jsan13040044

Prasad, S., & Murthy, G. S. (2017). Adaptive test automation using AI-based techniques: A new approach. *Proceedings of the International Conference on Automation, Computing and Communication Systems (ICACCS 2017)*, 346-352. https://doi.org/DOI: 10.1109/ICACCS.2017.7829987

Rajkomar, A., Dean, J., & Kohane, I. (2018). Machine learning in medicine. *The New England Journal of Medicine*, *380*(14), 1347–1358. DOI: 10.1056/NEJMra1814259 PMID: 30943338

Raj, P., Vanga, S., & Chaudhary, A. (2022). *Cloud-Native Computing: How to Design, Develop, and Secure Microservices and Event-Driven Applications*. John Wiley & Sons. DOI: 10.1002/9781119814795

Ramakrishnan, T., Mohan Gift, M. D., Chitradevi, S., Jegan, R., & Subha Hency Jose, P. Nagaraja, Rajneesh Sharma H.N., Selvakumar P., Sintayehu Mekuria Hailegiorgis, (2022). "Study of Numerous Resins Used in Polymer Matrix Composite Materials", Advances in Materials Science and Engineering, vol. 2022, Article ID 1088926, 8 pages, 2022. DOI: 10.1155/2022/1088926

Raman, R., & Kumar, P. (2018). India achieves WHO recommended doctor population ratio: A call for a paradigm shift in public health discourse! NCBI. https://www.ncbi.nlm.nih.gov/pmc/articles/PMC6259525/

Rane, J.. (2024). *Influence of digitalization on business and management: A review on artificial intelligence, blockchain, big data analytics, cloud computing, and internet of things*. Generative Artificial Intelligence in Agriculture, Education, and Business.

Raychev, V., Bielik, P., & Vechev, M. (2016). Probabilistic model for code with decision trees. *Proceedings of the 43rd Annual ACM SIGPLAN-SIGACT Symposium on Principles of Programming Languages,* 731–744. DOI: 10.1145/2983990.2984041

Reddy, A. K., Alluri, V. R. R., Thota, S., Ravi, C. S., & Bonam, V. S. M. (2021). DevSecOps: Integrating Security into the DevOps Pipeline for Cloud-Native Applications. *Journal of Artificial Intelligence Research and Applications*, *1*(2), 89–114.

Reddy, A., Indragandhi, V., Ravi, L., & Subramaniyaswamy, V. (2019). Detection of Cracks anddamage in wind turbine blades using artificial intelligence-based image analytics. *Measurement*, *147*, 106823. DOI: 10.1016/j.measurement.2019.07.051

Report, T. A. (2024), Katalon, The state of software quality report 2024. https://katalon.com/reports/statc-quality-2024

Research, I. B. M. (2024). *Predictive analytics in cloud environments: A technical review*. IBM Technical Library.

Rodgers, M., Mukherjee, S., Melamed, B., Baveja, A., & Kapoor, A. (2024). Solving business problems: The business-driven data-supported process. *Annals of Operations Research*, *332*(1), 705–741. DOI: 10.1007/s10479-023-05770-z

Rodriguez, N., "Advancements in NLP: Contextual Understanding in Language Models."

Sabin, J., Khan, W., Subbe, C. P., Franklin, M., Abulela, I., Khan, A., & Mohammed, H. (2016). ' The time it takes how doctors spend their time admitting a patient during the acute medical take. *Clinical Medicine (London, England)*, *16*(4), 320–324. DOI: 10.7861/clinmedicine.16-4-320 PMID: 27481373

Salunkhe, S. D., & Patil, D. (2016, August). Division and replication for data with public auditing scheme for cloud storage. In *2016 International Conference on Computing Communication Control and automation (ICCUBEA)* (pp. 1-5). IEEE.

Sauvola, J., Tarkoma, S., Klemettinen, M., Riekki, J., & Doermann, D. (2024). Future of Software with Generative AI. *Automated Software Engineering*, *31*(26), 25–32.

Scriven, A., Kedziora, D. J., Musial, K., & Gabrys, B. (2023). The technological emergence of automl: A survey of performant software and applications in the context of industry. Foundations and Trends® in Information Systems, 7(1-2), 1-252.

Sebrechts, M., Volckaert, B., Turck, F., Yang, K., & Al-Naday, M. (2022). Fog Native Architecture: Intent-Based Workflows to Take Cloud Native toward the Edge. *IEEE Communications Magazine*, *60*(8), 44–50. DOI: 10.1109/MCOM.003.2101075

Selvakumar, P. (2023). Biomedical applications of polymers in biosensors, cancer vaccines and drug delivery systems. *Biopolimery i Kletka*, *39*(4), 245–256. DOI: 10.7124/bc.000AA0

Selvakumar, P., Mariappan, P., Shunmugam, S., Paul, R., & Jabez, S. (2024). Removal of chemicals from effluent using photobioreactor technology to improve environmental and health impacts. *Zeitschrift für Physikalische Chemie*, *2024*(7), 1295–1302. Advance online publication. DOI: 10.1515/zpch-2023-0450

Seo, C., Yoo, D., & Lee, Y. (2024). Empowering Sustainable Industrial and Service Systems through AI-Enhanced Cloud Resource Optimization. *Sustainability (Basel)*, *16*(12), 5095. DOI: 10.3390/su16125095

Sergeyuk, A., Titov, S., & Izadi, M. (2023). Dataset for "In-IDE Human-AI Experience in the Era of Large Language Models; A Literature Review" paper [Dataset]. In Zenodo (CERN European Organization for Nuclear Research). DOI: 10.5281/zenodo.10290921

Seth, D., Nerella, H., Najana, M., & Tabbassum, A. (2024). Navigating the Multicloud Maze: benefits, challenges, and Future trends. International Journal of Global Innovations and Solutions (IJGIS).

Shahamiri, S. R., Kadir, W. M. N. W., Ibrahim, S., & Hashim, S. Z. M. (2011). An automated framework for software test oracle. *Information and Software Technology*, *53*(7), 774–788. DOI: 10.1016/j.infsof.2011.02.006

Sheikh, S., Haghi, M., Kashani, M., & Mahdipour, E. (2022)... *Multimedia Tools and Applications*, *81*, 1997–2042. DOI: 10.1007/s11042-021-11423-9 PMID: 34690529

Shekhar, S. S. (2019). Artificial intelligence in automation. *Artificial Intelligence*, *3085*(06), 14–17.

Shirgaonkar, M., Shinde, A., Sankpal, P., & Gutte, V. (2022, March). Cloud computing security using cryptographic algorithms. In 2022 6th International Conference on Computing Methodologies and Communication (ICCMC) (pp. 31-37). IEEE.

Shortliffe, E. H., & Cimino, J. J. (2013). *Biomedical informatics: Computer applications in health care and biomedicine* (4th ed.). Springer.

Shukla, S., Hassan, M. F., Tran, D. C., Akbar, R., Paputungan, I. V., & Khan, M. K. (2021). Improving latency in Internet-of-Things and cloud computing for real-time data transmission: A systematic literature review (SLR). *Cluster Computing*, *26*(5), 2657–2680. DOI: 10.1007/s10586-021-03279-3

Siddiqi, M. A., Yu, H., & Joung, J. (2019). 5G Ultra-Reliable Low-Latency Communication Implementation Challenges and Operational Issues with IoT Devices. *Electronics (Basel)*, *2019*(8), 1–18. DOI: 10.3390/electronics8090981

Silva, C. (2019). On the Location of Fog Nodes in Fog-Cloud Infrastructures. *Sensors (Basel), 19*(11), 24–45. DOI: 10.3390/s19112445 PMID: 31146339

Singh, A. (2023). Optimization of the Cloud-Native Infrastructure using. *Artificial Intelligence.*

Singh, A., Suri, B., & Kaur, S. (2020). Artificial intelligence and machine learning-based testing: The next frontier for software testing. [IJACSA]. *International Journal of Advanced Computer Science and Applications, 11*(3), 101–107. DOI: 10.14569/IJACSA.2020.0110312

Singh, J., Goyal, S. B., Kaushal, R. K., Kumar, N., & Sehra, S. S. (2024). *Applied Data Science and Smart Systems.* Taylor & Francis Group.

Sivathapandi, P., Paul, D., & Sudharsanam, S. R. (2021). Enhancing cloud-native CI/CD pipelines with AI-driven automation and predictive analytics. *Australian Journal of Machine Learning Research & Applications, 1*(1), 226–265.

Sivathapandi, P., Paul, D., & Sudharsanam, S. R. (2021). Enhancing Cloud-Native CI/CD Pipelines with AI-Driven Automation and Predictive Analytics. *Australian Journal of Machine Learning Research & Applications, 1*(1), 226–265.

Smith, J., & Patel, R. (2024). AI-driven infrastructure management efficiency. *Cloud Computing Engineering, 8*(3), 234–251.

Snyder, M. P.. (2019). Precision medicine: Personalized, problem-solving approach. *Science, 362*(6417), 208–210. DOI: 10.1126/science.aav4060

Snyder, M., Kircher, M., & Wylie, T. (2019). Precision medicine: The role of genomics in patient care. *Annual Review of Medicine, 70*, 113–130. DOI: 10.1146/annurev-med-041917-044452

Soft, V. (2024, January 24). Generative AI in Software Development Life Cycle (SDLC). *V2Soft Innovation through. Intelligence.*

Sorte, W. B., Joshi, P., & Jagtap, V. (2015). Use of Artificial Intelligence in Software Development Life Cycle: A state of the Art Review. *International Journal of Technology Management, 3*(3), 398–403.

Soyjaudah, K. M. S., Catherine, P. C., & Coonjah, I. (2016, April). Evaluation of UDP tunnel for data replication in data centers and cloud environment. In 2016 international conference on computing, communication and automation (ICCCA) (pp. 1217-1221). IEEE.

Srihith, I., Varaprasad, R., Mohan, Y., Srinivas, T., & Sravanthi, Y. (2022). A Review on New Challenges in AI and Software Engineering. International Journal of Advanced Research in Science. *Tongxin Jishu*. Advance online publication. DOI: 10.48175/IJARSCT-7137

Srivastava, P. R., & Baby, K. (2010). Automated software testing using metahurestictechnique based on an Ant Colony Optimiza- tion. *ISED*, *2010*, 235–240.

Srivastava, P., & Khan, R. (2018). A review paper on cloud computing. *International Journal of Advanced Research in Computer Science and Software Engineering*, *8*(6), 17–20. DOI: 10.23956/ijarcsse.v8i6.711

Stahmann, P. (2024). AI-based Real-time Anomaly Detection in Digitized Production: Characterization and Socio-technical Facilitation of Decision-making (Doctoral dissertation, Universität Osnabrück).

Steyvers, M., & Kumar, A. (2023). Three Challenges for AI-Assisted Decision-Making.. Perspectives on psychological science: a journal of the Association for Psychological Science, 17456916231181102..DOI: 10.1177/17456916231181102

Sun, D. W., Chang, G. R., Gao, S., Jin, L. Z., & Wang, X. W. (2012). Modeling a dynamic data replication strategy to increase system availability in cloud computing environments. *Journal of Computer Science and Technology*, *27*(2), 256–272. DOI: 10.1007/s11390-012-1221-4

Sunyaev, A., Kaletsch, A., Mauro, C., & Krcmar, H. (2009, May). Security analysis of the German electronic health card's peripheral parts. In ICEIS (3) (pp. 19-26). DOI: 10.5220/0001854000190026

Surabhi, M. C. (2013). Natural languagc pinnovativc framework integrates advanced machine learning algorithms with IoT sensor networks to optimize energy consumption in green buildings. DOI: 10.1007/978-3-031-35915-6_25

Suresh Babu, C. V., & Akshara, P. M. (2024). Revolutionizing Conversational AI: Unleashing the Power of ChatGPT-Based Applications in Generative AI and Natural Language Processing. In A. Obaid, B. Bhushan, M. S., & S. Rajest (Eds.), Advanced Applications of Generative AI and Natural Language Processing Models (pp. 228-248). IGI Global. DOI: 10.4018/979-8-3693-0502-7.ch011

Suresh Babu. (2023). *C.V.* Artificial Intelligence and Expert Systems, Anniyappa Publicaitons.

Suresh Babu, C. V., & Barath Kumar, S. (2024). Navigating the Terrain: Current Challenges and Solutions in Integrating Generative AI Into Education. In Hai-Jew, S. (Ed.), *Generative AI in Teaching and Learning* (pp. 274–290). IGI Global., DOI: 10.4018/979-8-3693-0074-9.ch011

Suresh Babu, C. V., & Moses, C. (2024). Reinventing Customer Support: Unleashing ChatGPT's Potential for Personalized Engagement and Responsible AI Implementation. In Bansal, R., Ngah, A., Chakir, A., & Pruthi, N. (Eds.), *Leveraging ChatGPT and Artificial Intelligence for Effective Customer Engagement* (pp. 93–110). IGI Global., DOI: 10.4018/979-8-3693-0815-8.ch006

Suresh Babu, C. V., & Suruthi, G. (2024). Unravelling the Evolution of Generative AI in Communication Education: A Historical Journey Into Human-Machine Communication. In Elmoudden, S., & Wrench, J. (Eds.), *The Role of Generative AI in the Communication Classroom* (pp. 55–71). IGI Global., DOI: 10.4018/979-8-3693-0831-8.ch003

Surianarayanan, C., & Chelliah, P. R. (2023). Demystifying the Cloud-Native Computing Paradigm. In *Essentials of Cloud Computing: A Holistic, Cloud-Native Perspective* (pp. 321–345). Springer International Publishing. DOI: 10.1007/978-3-031-32044-6_12

Svyatkovskiy, A., Deng, S. K., Fu, S., & Sundaresan, N. (2020, November). Intellicode compose: Code generation using transformer. In *Proceedings of the 28th ACM joint meeting on European software engineering conference and symposium on the foundations of software engineering* (pp. 1433-1443).

Svyatkovskiy, A., Zhao, Y., Fu, S., & Sundaresan, N. (2020). Pythia: AI-assisted code completion system. *Proceedings of the 25th ACM SIGKDD International Conference on Knowledge Discovery & Data Mining,* 2727–2735.

Swain, V. K., Panigrahi, R., Sahu, K. K., & Padhy, N. (2024). Revealing MOVE METHOD: Machine Learning-driven Real-time Refactoring Identification for Enhanced Software Quality. In *Proceedings of the 4th International Conference on Emerging Systems and Intelligent Computing (ESIC 2024).* DOI: 10.1109/ESIC60604.2024.10481609

Tahirkheli, A. I., Shiraz, M., Hayat, B., Idrees, M., Sajid, A., Ullah, R., Ayub, N., & Kim, K. I. (2021). A survey on modern cloud computing security over smart city networks: Threats, vulnerabilities, consequences, countermeasures, and challenges. *Electronics (Basel), 10*(15), 1811. DOI: 10.3390/electronics10151811

Tamanampudi, V. M. (2021). AI and DevOps: Enhancing pipeline automation with deep learning models for predictive resource scaling and fault tolerance. *Distributed Learning and Broad Applications in Scientific Research*, *7*, 38–77.

Tamimi, A. A., Dawood, R., & Sadaqa, L. (2019, April). Disaster recovery techniques in cloud computing. In *2019 IEEE Jordan International Joint Conference on Electrical Engineering and Information Technology (JEEIT)* (pp. 845-850). IEEE. DOI: 10.1109/JEEIT.2019.8717450

Tao, C., Gao, J., & Wang, T. (2019). Testing and quality validation for ai software–perspectives,issues, and practices. *IEEE Access : Practical Innovations, Open Solutions*, *7*, 120164–120175. DOI: 10.1109/ACCESS.2019.2937107

Tatineni, S., & Chakilam, N. V. (2024). Integrating Artificial Intelligence with DevOps for Intelligent Infrastructure Management: Optimizing Resource Allocation and Performance in Cloud-Native Applications. *Journal of Bioinformatics and Artificial Intelligence*, *4*(1), 109–142.

Theodoropoulos, T., Rosa, L., Benzaid, C., Gray, P., Marin, E., Makris, A., Cordeiro, L., Diego, F., Sorokin, P., Girolamo, M. D., Barone, P., Taleb, T., & Tserpes, K. (2023). Security in Cloud-Native Services: A Survey. *Journal of Cybersecurity and Privacy*, *3*(4), 758–793. DOI: 10.3390/jcp3040034

Thiruvasagam, G., & Vettriselvan, R. (2021). What is after COVID-19?: Changing economies of the shipping industries and maritime education institutions. In 21st Annual General Assembly, IAMU AGA 2021 - Proceedings of the International Association of Maritime Universities (pp. 96–110).

Thompson, M., "AI for Climate Change: Enhanced Prediction Models."

Thompson, R., & Lee, K. (2024). Performance optimization in cloud-native environments. *Journal of Cloud Architecture*, *10*(1), 45–62.

Tirupati, K. K.. (2024). Improving Database Performance with SQL Server Optimization Techniques. *Modern Dynamics: Mathematical Progressions*, *1*(2), 450–494.

Tiwari, P., Goyal, R., & Sharma, S. (2021). A comprehensive review on code generation using deep learning techniques. *International Journal of Artificial Intelligence & Applications*, *12*(3), 45–61.

Topol, E. J. (2019). *Deep medicine: How artificial intelligence can make healthcare human again*. Basic Books.

Tufano, M., Agarwal, A., Jang, J., Moghaddam, R. Z., & Sundaresan, N. (2024). AutoDev: Automated AI-driven development. arXiv preprint arXiv:2403.08299.

UK Government. (2018). Data Protection Act 2018. Retrieved from https://www.legislation.gov.uk

Ulfsnes, R., Moe, N.B., Stray, V., & Skarpen, M. (2024). Transforming Software Development with Generative AI: Empirical Insights on Collaboration and Workflow. *Generative AI for Effective Software Development*, 219-234.

Usman, A., Schadek, R., & Theel, O. (2017, January). A Novel Highly Available Data Replication Strategy exploiting Data Semantics, Coding Techniques and Prior At-Hand Knowledge. In 2017 IEEE 22nd Pacific Rim International Symposium on Dependable Computing (PRDC) (pp. 301-310). IEEE.

Uzule, K., & Verina, N. (2023). Digital barriers in digital transition and digital transformation: Literature review. *Economics and Culture*, *20*(1), 125–143. DOI: 10.2478/jec-2023-0011

Vall, R., & Araya, F. (2023). *Exploring the Benefits and Challenges of AI-Language Learning Tools*. International Journal of Social Sciences and Humanities Invention., DOI: 10.18535/ijsshi/v10i01.02

Van Der Aa, H., & Leopold, H. (2021). 10 Supporting RPA through natural language processing. In De Gruyter eBooks (pp. 187–200). DOI: 10.1515/9783110676693-010

Vaswani, A., Shazeer, N., Parmar, N., Uszkoreit, J., Jones, L., Gomez, A. N., Kaiser, L., & Polosukhin, I. (2017). Attention is all you need. *Advances in Neural Information Processing Systems*, *30*, 5998–6008.

Vedurada, J., & Krishna Nandivada, V. (2018). Identifying refactoring opportunities for replacing type code with subclass and state. *Proceedings of the ACM on Programming Languages*. DOI: 10.1145/3276508

Velayutham, S., & Shanmugam, G. (2021). Artificial Intelligence assisted Canary Testing of Cloud Native RAN in a mobile telecom system.

Vemulapalli, G. (2024). *Cloud Data Stack Scalability: A Case Study on Migrating from Legacy Systems*. International Journal of Sustainable Development Through AI. *ML and IoT*, *3*(1), 1–15.

Vest, J. R. (2010). Health information exchange: The key to achieving meaningful use. *Journal of the American Medical Informatics Association : JAMIA*, *17*(5), 489–494. DOI: 10.1136/jamia.2010.001024

Vettriselvan, R., & Vinodhan, V. (2022). Promotional strategies for gender equity in maritime sector: Maritime education institutions. In *Proceedings of the International Association of Maritime Universities Conference*.

Vijayakumar, G., Rajkumar, M., Rajiv Chandar, N., Selvakumar, P., & Duraisamy, R. (2024). Muniyandi Rajkumar, Rajiv Chandar N, Selvakumar P and Ramesh Duraisamy, (2024). Environmentally friendly TDS removal from waste water by electrochemical ion exchange batch-type recirculation (EIR) technique. *Environmental Science. Water Research & Technology, 10*(4), 826–835. DOI: 10.1039/D3EW00793F

Vijay, S. A. (2014). Reducing and optimising the cycle time of patients discharge process in a hospital using six sigma DMAIC approach. *International Journal of Qualitative Research, 8*, 169–182.

Vira, T., Colquhoun, M., & Etchells, E. (2006). Reconcilable differences: Correcting medication errors at hospital admission and discharge. *Quality & Safety in Health Care, 15*(2), 122–126. DOI: 10.1136/qshc.2005.015347 PMID: 16585113

Wager, K. A., Lee, F. W., & Glaser, J. P. (2021). *Health care information systems: a practical approach for health care management.* John Wiley & Sons.

Waghambare, M. A., Prabhu, S., & Ashok, P. (2024). Artificial Intelligence (AI)-Powered Chatbots for Marketing and Online Shopping. In *Digital Technologies in Modeling and Management: Insights in Education and Industry* (pp. 21-39). IGI Global.

Waghambare, M., Prabhu, S., Ashok, P., & Natraj, N. A. (2024). Elevating Business Experiences: AI-Powered Chatbots Reforming Marketing and E-Commerce. In *Transforming the Financial Landscape With ICTs* (pp. 1-27). IGI Global.

Waghambare, M. A.. (2024). Artificial intelligence (AI)-powered chatbots for marketing and online shopping. In Prakasha, G. S. (Eds.), *Digital Technologies in Modeling and Management: Insights in Education and Industry* (pp. 21–39). IGI Global., DOI: 10.4018/978-1-6684-9576-6.ch002

Wagner, J. (2023, August 15). AI Tools for the Software Development Process. *Stoplight.*

Wang, Y., Qiu, X., Zhang, C., Mi, W., Li, L., & Ji, Y. (2009, September). Effective data replication in heterogeneous structured P2P networks. In 2009 5th International Conference on Wireless Communications, Networking and Mobile Computing (pp. 1-4). IEEE.

Wang, F.. (2017). A review of blockchain technology applied to smart grids: Challenges and opportunities. *IEEE Access : Practical Innovations, Open Solutions, 5*, 2077–2086. DOI: 10.1109/ACCESS.2017.2651582

Wang, F., Casalino, L. P., & Khullar, D. (2017). The role of predictive analytics in health care: A review of current literature and future directions. *Health Affairs*, *36*(3), 421–428. DOI: 10.1377/hlthaff.2016.1103

Wang, F., Yang, S. C., & Yang, Y. L. (2011). Regression Testing Based on Neural Networks and Program Slicing Techniques. In Wang, Y., & Li, T. (Eds.), *Practical Applications of Intelligent Systems. Advances in Intelligent and Soft Computing* (Vol. 124). Springer., DOI: 10.1007/978-3-642-25658-5_50

Wang, H., Casalino, L. P., & Khullar, D. (2017). Managing third-party vendors in healthcare. *Health Management Review*, *42*(3), 250–260. DOI: 10.1097/HMR.0000000000000156

Wang, S., Huang, L., Gao, A., Ge, J., Zhang, T., Feng, H., Satyarth, I., Li, M., Zhang, H., & Ng, V. (2022). Machine/deep learning for software engineering: A systematic literature review. *IEEE Transactions on Software Engineering*, *49*(3), 1188–1231. DOI: 10.1109/TSE.2022.3173346

Wang, Y., Chen, L., & Liu, H. (2023). Generative AI for source code generation: Current trends and future directions. *IEEE Software*, *40*(2), 62–70. DOI: 10.1109/MS.2023.10176168

Wei, Z., Xie, X., Zhan, J., & Zhang, J. (2022). Towards better code generation models: A survey of current trends and future directions. *ACM Transactions on Software Engineering and Methodology*, *31*(2), 1–28.

Wen, L., Qian, H., & Liu, W. (2022). Research on Intelligent Cloud Native Architecture and Key Technologies Based on DevOps Concept. *Procedia Computer Science*, *208*, 590–597. DOI: 10.1016/j.procs.2022.10.082

Williams, E. et al., "Privacy-Preserving AI: Decentralized Learning Architectures."

Williams, R.. (2024). Predictive maintenance in cloud systems. *Infrastructure Management Review*, *13*(4), 178–195.

Wilson, M., & Chang, L. (2024). Transparency in AI-driven DevOps decisions. *Ethics in Technology*, *9*(2), 89–104.

Winnie, Y. (2018). Enhancing Data Security in IoT Healthcare Services Using Fog Computing. *proceedings of the International Conference on Recent Trends in Advance Computing (ICRTAC)*, 200–205. DOI: 10.1109/ICRTAC.2018.8679404

Witte, R., Sateli, B., Khamis, N., & Rilling, J. (2011). Intelligent Software Development Environments: Integrating Natural Language Processing with the Eclipse Platform. In Lecture notes in computer science (pp. 408–419). DOI: 10.1007/978-3-642-21043-3_49

Xu, J., Yang, P., Xue, S., Sharma, B., Sanchez-Martin, M., Wang, F., Beaty, K. A., Dehan, E., & Parikh, B. (2019). Translating cancer genomics into precision medicine with artificial intelligence: Applications,challenges and future perspectives. *Human Genetics*, *138*(2), 109–124. DOI: 10.1007/s00439-019-01970-5 PMID: 30671672

Xu, Y., Liu, X., Cao, X., Huang, C., Liu, E., Qian, S., Liu, X., Wu, Y., Dong, F., Qiu, C.-W., Qiu, J., Hua, K., Su, W., Wu, J., Xu, H., Han, Y., Fu, C., Yin, Z., Liu, M., & Zhang, J. (2021). Artificial intelligence: A powerful paradigm for scientific research. *Innovation (Cambridge (Mass.))*, *2*(4), 100179. DOI: 10.1016/j.xinn.2021.100179 PMID: 34877560

Yahav, E. (2023). Towards AI-Driven Software Development: Challenges and Lessons from the Field (Keynote). *Proceedings of the 31st ACM Joint European Software Engineering Conference and Symposium on the Foundations of Software Engineering*. DOI: 10.1145/3611643.3633451

Yamamoto, K., "AI-Enabled Precision Medicine: Revolutionizing Disease Diagnosis."

Yang, C., Liu, Y., & Yin, C. (2021). Recent advances in intelligent source code generation: A survey on natural language-based studies. *Entropy (Basel, Switzerland)*, *23*(9), 1174. DOI: 10.3390/e23091174 PMID: 34573800

Yarlagadda, R. T. (2018). The RPA and AI automation. International Journal of Creative Research Thoughts (IJCRT), 2320-2882.

Yogish, D., Manjunath, T. N., & Hegadi, R. S. (2019). Review on Natural Language Processing Trends and Techniques Using NLTK. In Communications in computer and information science (pp. 589–606). DOI: 10.1007/978-981-13-9187-3_53

Younis, Y. A., Kifayat, K., & Merabti, M. (2014). An access control model for cloud computing. *Journal of Information Security and Applications*, *19*(1), 45–60. DOI: 10.1016/j.jisa.2014.04.003

Yousefpour, A., Fung, C., Nguyen, T., Kadiyala, K., Fatemeh, J., Jalali, A., Niakanlahiji, J. K., & Jue, J. P. (2019). All one needs to know about fog computing and related edge computing paradigms: A complete survey. *Journal of Systems Architecture*, *98*, 289–330. DOI: 10.1016/j.sysarc.2019.02.009

Yu, S., Wang, C., Ren, K., & Lou, W. (2010, March). *Achieving secure, scalable, and fine-grained data access control in cloud computing. In 2010 Proceedings IEEE INFOCOM*. Ieee.

Yu, W., Liang, F., He, X., Hatcher, W. G., Lu, C., Lin, J., & Yang, X. (2018). A Survey on the Edge Computing for the Internet of Things. *IEEE Access : Practical Innovations, Open Solutions*, *6*, 6900–6919. DOI: 10.1109/ACCESS.2017.2778504

Zelianko, Y. (2024, May 15). The Transformative Impact of AI in Software Development: A Survey – Based Analysis. *Techreviewer.*

Zhang, Y., Bajpai, Y., Gupta, P., Ketkar, A., Allamanis, M., Barik, T., Gulwani, S., Radhakrishna, A., Raza, M., Soares, G., & Tiwari, A. (2022). Overwatch: learning patterns in code edit sequences. Proceedings of the ACM on Programming Languages, 6(OOPSLA2), 395–423. https://doi.org/DOI: 10.1145/3563302

Zhang, C., & Lu, Y. (2021). Study on artificial intelligence: The state of the art and future prospects. *Journal of Industrial Information Integration*, *23*, 100224. DOI: 10.1016/j.jii.2021.100224

Zhang, J., & Tao, D. (2020). Empowering things with intelligence: A survey of the progress, challenges, and opportunities in artificial intelligence of things. *IEEE Internet of Things Journal*, *8*(10), 7789–7817. DOI: 10.1109/JIOT.2020.3039359

Zhang, L., & Liu, W. (2024). AI monitoring systems in cloud environments. *Cloud Security Journal*, *12*(3), 156–171.

Zhao, L., Alhoshan, W., Ferrari, A., Letsholo, K. J., Ajagbe, M. A., Chioasca, E.-V., & Batista-Navarro, R. T. (2021). Natural language processing for requirements engineering: A systematic mapping study. *ACM Computing Surveys*, *54*(3), 1–41. DOI: 10.1145/3444689

Zheng, X., & Zhao, Y. (2023). The role of generative AI in modern software engineering: Trends and predictions. *ACM Transactions on Software Engineering and Methodology*, *32*(4), 1–32. DOI: 10.1145/3571847

Zhu, S., Yu, T., Xu, T., Chen, H., Dustdar, S., Gigan, S., ... & Pan, Y. (2023). Intelligent computing: the latest advances, challenges, and future. Intelligent Computing, 2, 0006.

Zhu, X., Zhou, B., Hou, L., Chen, J., & Chen, L. (2008). An Experience-Based Approach for Test Execution Effort Estima- tion. 2008 The 9th International Conference for Young Computer Scientists. DOI: 10.1109/ICYCS.2008.53

Zong, Y., & Chen, C. (2023). AI-assisted code generation: A systematic review of the state of the art. *Journal of Systems and Software*, *207*, 110–123. DOI: 10.1016/j.jss.2023.111234

Zulkifli, N. I. (2024). Optimizing Data Flow and Integration for High-Performance Analytics: A Security-Centric Architecture Framework to Improve Efficiency and Decision-Making Across Domains. *Advances in Intelligent Information Systems*, *9*(10), 17–32.

About the Contributors

Pethuru Raj PhD is working at the Edge AI division of Reliance Jio Platforms Ltd. (JPL) Bangalore. Previously. worked in IBM Global Cloud Centre of Excellence (CoE), Wipro consulting services (WCS), and Robert Bosch Corporate Research (CR). I have gained over 23 years of IT industry experience and 9 years of research experience. Finished the CSIR-sponsored PhD degree at Anna University, Chennai and continued with the UGC-sponsored postdoctoral research in the Department of Computer Science and Automation, Indian Institute of Science (IISc), Bangalore. After that, I was granted two international research fellowships (JSPS and JST) to work as a research scientist for 3.5 years in two leading Japanese universities. I am focusing on some of the emerging technologies such as the Internet of Things (IoT), Artificial Intelligence (AI) Model Optimization Techniques, Prompt Engineering for Large Language Models (LLMs), Efficient, Explainable and Edge AI, Blockchain, Digital Twins, Cloud-native and Edge computing, Green and Generative AI, Reliability and Platform Engineering, 5G/6G, etc.

Ramamurthy Venkatesh has industry experience of about 33 years. He is currently heading NETS International Communications, a regional System Integrator for IT/Telecom services as CEO with more than 230+ employees, serving leading telcos and enterprises. NETS is one of the reputed UAE-based system integrators providing new-generation Infrastructure Solutions and Digital Solutions covering Enterprise IT, Cloud, Cybersecurity, Automation and Managed Services and Solutions. After graduating as a telecommunication engineer, he started his six-year short services career as an Indian Air Force officer in 1988. His later engagements in India include roles such as Technical Head Product Manager, and Manager - Projects for another ten years with some of the leading telecom service providers. After moving to UAE in 1999, he was employed with the region's leading telecom services provider – Etisalat for 15 years. During this tenure, his responsibilities and roles included Project Management of Fixed & Mobile Network rollout projects and vendor and partner management till year 2014. Then he joined NETS International Group with offices in multiple countries and currently as CEO of NETS UAE, he is leading an enthusiastic team of Senior managers and Business Unit heads for driving high-performance business deliverables through the delivery of a portfolio of digital solutions and services. With a keen passion for teaching and mentoring, he is also visiting/adjunct faculty in select B-Schools in India and UAE including SP Jain Global, MAHE Manipal, Skyline University, Westford School of Management and corporate training programs. His research interests include cloud IoT, Blockchain, AI/ML, Quantum computing, Cybersecurity and so on.

N.A. Natraj is an Assistant Professor at SIDTM in Symbiosis International University, India. My academic chronicles include Ph, D. in Electronics and Communication Engineering from Karpagam Academy of Higher Education, Coimbatore. I have 12 years of Teaching and Research experience in the Institutes of India and Zambia. My research interests include Wireless Sensor Networks, the Internet of Things, 5G, Communication Networks, Machine Learning and Blockchain. I hold publications in reputed Journals and have published patents in the mentioned research fields. I have completed certifications in domains like 5G, IoT, Digital Forensics and Blockchain from various organizations like Stanford, Europe Open University, Qualcomm, University of London, etc.

Rathinaraja Jeyaraj is a post-doctoral fellow at the University of Houston-Victoria, Texas, USA. Previously, I was a post-doctoral associate at the Kyungpook National University, Daegu, South Korea. I received my PhD in Distributed Systems from the Department of IT, National Institute of Technology Karnataka, India. I have Collaborated and assisted in developing research proposals with professors in the University of Pittsburgh, Florida International University, and the University of Houston. I have completed multiple research projects at the School of Computer Science and Engineering, Kyungpook National University and have published them in various reputed journals. Unboxing, manipulating and applying machine and deep learning algorithms to solve problems in cloud-IoT, CV, NLP, and interdisciplinary research domains, although broad, capture my current research interests most accurately. These rapidly growing avenues are promising prospects to expand my current expertise while applying my knowledge, skills, and experience gained post-Ph.D.

***

Adeyinka Kehinde Iyioluwa is a dedicated student pursuing a degree in Information and Communication Engineering. With a strong passion for artificial intelligence and technology, Adeyinka has authored several academic papers, focusing on topics such as AI applications and data security. Currently, Adeyinka is actively involved in research related to privacy and security management practices in computer science

Adeyinka Taye Iyinoluwa is a passionate researcher and academic with a strong background in Information and Communication Engineering. Known for a deep interest in technology and its transformative impact, Adeyinka is driven by a commitment to advancing innovative solutions in the field of education and beyond.

Harishchander Anandaram completed a PhD in bioengineering, an M.Tech., and a B.Tech. in bioinformatics from the Sathyabama Institute of Science and Technology, Chennai, in 2020, 2011, and 2009. In his bachelor's and master's theses, he worked on analysing resistance in HIV protease inhibitors based on molecular mechanics and machine learning studies, a collaborative project with IIT Madras. In his PhD thesis, he worked on pharmacogenomics and miRNA-regulated networks in psoriasis, a collaborative project with Georgetown University, USA; JIPMER, India; CIBA, India; and ILS, India. His thesis illustrated a multi-disciplinary approach by combining computational biophysics and molecular biology machine learning. While doing a PhD, he had the opportunity to collaborate with international researchers and have publications in reputed international journals in bioinformatics and systems biology. He has received the prestigious "Young Scientist Award" from "The Melinda Gates Foundation" for his research abstract on "The Implications of miRNA Dynamics in Infectious Diseases.". To date, he has reviewed more than 200 manuscripts in systems biology.

A. Muthusamy is currently working as an Assistant Professor, Department of Computer Technology, Kongu Engineering College, Erode, He received his Ph.D. degree in Computer Science from Bharathiar, University, Coimbarore. He received his master degree in M.C.A from K.S.R. College of Engineering affiliated to Anna University, Chennai. He received his bachelor degree in B.Sc. Computer Science from Sri Kandhan College of Arts and Science affiliated to Periyar University, Salem. Having 13+ years of experience in Teaching & Research and 3 years of experience in IT sectors. Life time member ISTE, IIT (D) campus, New Delhi, Microsoft, USA. His area of research includes Data Mining and Text Mining. He is a Reviewer of 30 National / International Journals, IEEE& Springer conferences. An inspired writer, he has authored 20 Research papers, 1 Patent, 4 Book Chapters and 15 Technical presentations.He received honors and awards from various Institutions.

Subash Banala is a dedicated Senior Manager, Cloud Architect, and Security; AI/ML Engineer who combines technical expertise with strategic leadership to drive impactful results. With over 19 years of experience in the tech industry, Subash is known for his hands-on approach to solving complex problems and guiding teams through the ever-evolving landscape of cloud technology, security, and artificial intelligence. Since joining Capgemini America in 2022, Subash has been at the forefront of developing innovative cloud, security, AI/ML, and FinOps solutions. As a Senior Manager, he is responsible for overseeing day- to-day operations, managing project activities, and ensuring that the organization's technology infrastructure is not just robust but also future-ready. His efforts have led to significant advancements in technology and operational efficiency, contributing to over $1.8 million in cost savings and revenue growth. Subash is passionate about integrating AI/ML into everyday business processes, using data analytics to predict outcomes and make smarter, more proactive decisions. Before Capgemini, Subash honed his skills at IBM Pvt Ltd., where he specialized in Security Vulnerability Management, Middleware, and Cloud Technologies. As a Subject Matter Expert (SME), he led key initiatives to strengthen security protocols and implement advanced cloud solutions. Subash's work helped protect critical assets, enhance security measures, and support clients across industries like Retail Banking, automobile, credit cards, and Payment Systems. His expertise in designing secure and scalable cloud environments is not just about technology—it's about understanding the business impact and making sure that the solutions he delivers are aligned with the client's goals. Beyond his day-to-day work, Subash is also a recognized thought leader. He has authored research articles published in leading journals, sharing insights on the latest trends in cloud computing, security, and AI/ML. His passion for knowledge extends to the stage as well, where he has participated as a speaker at various conferences. Subash enjoys engaging with the tech community, sharing his experiences, and discussing practical solutions to the challenges businesses face today. He believes that technology should empower people, simplify processes, and create opportunities for innovation. Subash's commitment to the tech field is further underscored by his recognition as a Senior Member of the IEEE, an honor that reflects his significant contributions to technology and engineering. He is continually looking for ways to stay ahead of the curve, leveraging his knowledge and experience to push the boundaries of what's possible in cloud architecture and security. Academically, Subash holds a bachelor's degree in Electronics and Communication Engineering from Gulbarga University, which laid the foundation for his technical career. He values lifelong learning and often encourages his teams to stay curious, continuously explore new technologies, and never stop asking questions.

Vaishnavi Bhardwaj is a student in the Department of CSIT at Siksha O Anusandhan University, India

C.G. Balaji is an educator and researcher focused on advancing computer engineering and technology. He is currently working as an Assistant Professor in Symbiosis Institute of Digital and Telecom Management, Symbiosis International (Deemed University), Lavale, Pune. He holds a Ph.D. in Information and Communication Engineering from College of Engineering Guindy, Anna University, Chennai-25 and has over nine years of teaching experience. His expertise includes Next Generation Networks, Wireless/Mobile Networks, Network Convergence, Internet of Things and Software Defined Networks. He motivates students and creates innovative educational materials, emphasizing collaboration to explore new areas in computer science and engineering. He believes in a reciprocal learning process where both he and his students gain knowledge from each other. His research covers Device-to-device Communication, and Efficient Data Offloading Strategies in Next Generation Networks. He has published several papers in reputed journals and holds patents in intelligent healthcare systems and IoT solutions. As a member of IAENG, IEI, ISTE, and CSTA – INDIA, he actively contributes to academic committees and initiatives. Committed to continuous learning, he holds certifications in Industry 4.0, Outcome-Based Learning, Patent Creation, and Data Science, and participates in faculty development programs to stay current with field advancements.

Madhavi Damle is a professional with a diverse academic background, holding industry experience of 17 years and academic postgraduate teaching experience of 15 years. She holds degrees in B.Sc. in Physics and a B.Sc.Tech in Computer Science and Communication, an MBA and a PhD in Knowledge Management, Innovation Management, Digital Transformation and strategy as the areas of expertise. She has expertise in teaching technology management and Digital Transformation. Dr. M. Damle has been associated with prestigious institutions like Symbiosis Institute of Digital & Telecom Management (SIDTM), Pune, and SVKM's Narsee Monjee Institute of Management.

Hema Deenadayalanis currently working as an Assistant Professor, Department of Computer Science, Sri Ramakrishna College of Arts & Science for Women, Coimbatore, Tamilnadu. She received her Ph.D. degree in Computer Science from AvinashilingamUniversity, Coimbarore. She received her master degree in M.C.A from Bharathidasan University, Trichy. She received her bachelor degree in B.Sc. Computer Science from SeethalakshmiRamaswami Collegeaffiliated to BharathidasanUniversity, Trichy. Having 6+ years of experience in Teaching & Research. Her research interests are Machine Learning, Artificial Intelligent, Internet of Things, Semantic Web and Data Mining. She has published 8 research papers in Journals and presented 6 research papers in various National and International Conferences.

G. Rajeswari is an Assistant Professor in the School of Computing at Sathyabama Institute of Science and Technology. With a distinguished academic background, she holds a Doctorate from the College of Engineering Guindy, Anna University, Chennai. Dr. Rajeswari has made significant contributions to the academic community through her research, publishing papers in reputed journals. Driven by a passion for teaching and research, she continues to inspire and mentor students while advancing knowledge in the field of computer science.

Vallapureddy Harika vharika606@gmail.com Dept. of Computer Science and Engineering Stanley College of Engineering & Technology for Women, India

Harsh Jain is an undergraduate student in the Department of Computer Science and Engineering at SRM Institute of Science and Technology, Ramapuram, Chennai.

Kavitha M. was born in Coimbatore, TamilNadu, India, in 1984. She completed her Phd in 2022. She received M.Tech IT degree from College of Guindy, Chennai, in the year 2009. She received B.E CSE degree from Coimbatore Institute of Engineering and Information Technology, Coimbatore. Currently she is working as Associate Professor at Sri Krishna College of Engineering and Technology, Coimbatore. Her research areas are Cloud computing, Data mining and IoT. She has published more than 20 research papers in International and National Journals and more than three papers in National and International Conferences.

N. Janaki is currently working in the Dept of EEE at VISTAS. She has published research articles in various journals and conferences.

P. Selvakumar is currently an Associate Professor in the Department of Science and Humanities at Nehru Institute of Technology, Coimbatore, Tamil Nadu, India. Since 2023, he has served as the Department IQAC Coordinator at the institute. Prior to joining Nehru Institute of Technology, he held positions as an Assistant Professor in the Department of Science and Humanities various engineering colleges in Coimbatore, Tamil Nadu, India, spanning from 2011 to 2023. Dr.P. Selvakumar's academic and research interests lie primarily in the field of phytochemistry. He has made significant contributions to his field, with an impressive record that includes 30 journal publications, 12 patents, and 20 conference papers. Additionally, he has organized 5 seminars and conferences, further demonstrating his commitment to academic and scientific exchange. Throughout his career, Dr. P.Selvakumar has been recognized for his dedication and excellence in teaching, having been honored with several awards, including the Best Teacher Awards. He holds a prominent position in the academic community, contributing actively to research.

Srimanta Pandit is a Senior Consultant at Protiviti, specializing in business process management and digital transformation solutions. With an MBA from Symbiosis Institute of Digital & Telecom Management (SIDTM), Pune, he brings expertise in Appian and Microsoft Power Platform. Based in Abu Dhabi, United Arab Emirates, Srimanta plays a key role in helping organizations optimize their processes and implement cutting-edge technology solutions. His skills focus on driving business efficiency through digital platforms and process automation

Sudheer Panyaram is a seasoned expert with 18 years of experience in implementing Enterprise applications across different industries like Automotive, Manufacturing, Aviation, Healthcare, Utilities and Finance and has recently ventured into the emerging field of quantum computing. Sudheer played a pivotal role in integrating SAP solutions with evolving digital transformation initiatives, such as cloud migrations and data analytics, making businesses more efficient and agile. Sudheer led many large-scale digital transformation initiatives such as ERP implementations, Building Customer centric Commerce Applications, Optimizing supply chain operations, Scaling up Inventory, Supply chain planning and Execution platforms, Integrating MES platforms with Enterprise and Consumer applications, Establishing SOX controls, Finance applications and driving business transformations, including cloud migrations that have resulted in world-class customer experiences, significant cost savings, and outstanding improvements in operational efficiency, and revenue gains. Sudheer enjoys working at Technology driven startup companies. Sudheer has worked in EV start-up companies where he has leveraged his domain acumen combined with Technology Experience to Build scalable Enterprise IT applications, Digital & Finance software by leveraging cutting edge technologies SAP S4 Hana cloud, AI/ML & IOT. He is a visionary in the automotive industry, specializing in artificial intelligence (AI), machine learning (ML), and quantum computing. With a background in computer science and engineering, Sudheer joined automotive companies like Rivian and Fisker. Early in his career, he realized the transformative potential of AI and ML in optimizing vehicle manufacturing, autonomous driving, and predictive maintenance. He realized the transformative potential of AI and ML in optimizing vehicle manufacturing, autonomous driving, and predictive maintenance. Sudheer's experience includes designing and deploying machine learning models to solve intricate problems, improving predictive analytics, and integrating AIML solutions with existing SAP ERP frameworks. These models not only enhance data- driven decision-making but also contribute to the strategic advancement of manufacturing processes. They play a critical role in transforming manufacturing operations through cutting-edge technology and expert SAP ERP guidance. In addition to that, Sudheer also developed expertise in researching Quantum computing applications and its usage in solving enterprise business problems in the area like Logistics optimization, Manufacturing, Battery Cells & Finance modelling. Sudheer's unique combination of ERP experience and forward-thinking approach positions him as a leader in leveraging quantum computing to push the boundaries of what's possible in enterprise technology. His work focuses on integrating quantum solutions to tackle real- world business challenges, making him a pioneer in the field.

Narayan Patra is working as an Associate Professor in the Department of CSIT at Siksha O Anusandhan University, India

Sivaram Ponnusamy is a distinguished academic and researcher with expertise in computer science, electrical engineering, and business management. With qualifications such as a B.E. in Electrical and Electronics Engineering, an M.E. in Computer Science, a Ph.D., and an MBA in Project Management, he serves as a professor and research supervisor in engineering colleges and universities, specializing in artificial intelligence and computer science. Dr Ponnusamy has filed multiple patents in cutting-edge technologies, ranging from remote voting systems to AI-based attendance management and environmental analysis tools. His work includes editing several Scopus-indexed books on AI applications, digital twin technology, and women's safety, with ongoing international projects in AI research. As an active member of various professional bodies, including IAENG and ISOC, he also contributes as a reviewer for reputed journals. Recognized for his academic contributions, he was awarded by the Thanjavur District Collector for developing an innovative Android-based meeting management tool. Additionally, Dr. Ponnusamy frequently chairs international conferences and conducts seminars on the latest technological trends, making significant contributions to AI, machine learning, and software development. He is the research supervisor for several research scholars, and his IGI-Global Profile URL is https://www.igi-global.com/affiliate/sivaram -ponnusamy/449070.

Sushree Bibhuprada B. Priyadarshini ((Ph.D in Computer Science and Engineering) is currently working as an Asst. Prof. in Dept. of Computer Science and Information Technology at Institute of Technical Education and Research. She is the recipient of Orissa State Talent Scholarship and NRTS scholarship. She has got the certificate of Merit in Brigade Talent Search Exam. She has received the "All Round the best Student of the year". She has secured the highest marks in Computer Science and Data Processing from ITER in 2011-13 and was awarded for "Best

Poster Presentation" in the Workshop on "Monitoring of Research of Ph. D. Scholars. She has received the "Best Student Paper Award" in 15th International Conference on Information Technology, IEEE at IIIT. She has been invited and selected as the Keynote Speaker of International Conference of Innovative Applied Energy, St. Cross College, Oxford University. Besides, she is the Member of IAENG, SDIWC, CSTA. She is also working as reviewer in International Journal of Engineering Research & Technology and IEEE Consumer Electronics journal. She has around 24 publications including IET, IEEE, Elsevier, Springer, IGI Global etc.

Joyce S is currently working as an Associate Professor in Sathyabama Institute of Science and Technology Chennai.She has specialized in Human Resource Management and Marketing and has been into academics for the past 15 years. Published 10 Research papers and Indexed in Scopus.

R. Vettriselvan, an Associate Professor, AMET University, specialized in HRM and Marketing. He is acting as Mentor, Saraswathi Institute of Medical Sciences, Hapur. He served as Review Board member, National Council for Higher Education, Malawi, Head of the Department, School of Commerce and Management Studies, St. Eugene University, Zambia, and Director, Research and Publication, St. John the Baptist University, Malawi. He has published 25 books and 93 articles in peer reviewed journals and edited book chapters. Under his guidance two have completed and five are pursuing their PhD.

Achlendra Raj is a Project Management Consultant at Capgemini, specializing in delivering high-quality solutions in project management and digital transformation. With an MBA from Symbiosis Institute of Digital & Telecom Management (SIDTM), Pune, he brings expertise in agile methodologies, being a certified SAFe Agilist. Based in Pune, Maharashtra, India, Achlendra is dedicated to driving efficiency and innovation in the tech industry through effective project management practices.

Palanivel Rathinasabapathi Velmurugan is associated with BSBI, Berlin, as a professor in the Human Resource Management and Finance Stream. Prior to joining BSBI, he held the designation "Head" Faculty of Management at Sharda University, Uzbekistan, Central Asia, and "Dean of Arts" assignments at DMI St. John the Baptist University, Malawi, Central Africa. Also, he has been associated earlier with DMI St. Eugene University in Zambia, MAM Business School and various Engineering Colleges in India. He has a Ph.D. in Management from Mannonmanium Sundaranar University in India. Besides this, he holds an MBA Degree from SRM University in India and a BE Chemical Engineering degree from Annamalai University in India. Also, he completed six NPTEL Certificate

Programs conducted by various IITs in India. He brings with him 15 years of rich working experience in teaching and research. Furthermore, he has a keen interest in the Case Method of teaching and research. He is an academic out of passion. Not only that, but he also takes a keen interest in guiding Ph.D. students. He has supervised three Ph.D. research scholars under his supervision at DMI St. Eugene University in Zambia.

Kishor Kumar Reddy, currently working as Associate Professor, Dept. of Computer Science and Engineering, Stanley College of Engineering and Technology for Women, Hyderabad, India. He has research and teaching experience of more than 10 years. He has published more than 50 research papers in National and International Conferences, Book Chapters, and Journals indexed by Scopus and others. He is an author for 2 text books and 7 co-edited books. He acted as the special session chair for Springer FICTA 2020, 2022, SCI 2021, INDIA 2022 and IEEE ICCSEA 2020 conferences. He is the corresponding editor of AMSE 2021 conferences, published by IoP Science JPCS. He is the member of ISTE, CSI, IAENG, UACEE, IACSIT

Jimmy Carter R is a dedicated Assistant Professor of Business Administration at Bishop Heber College, Trichy, Tamil Nadu, India, who brings a wealth of knowledge and practical expertise to the classroom, shaped by his prior experience in the corporate sector. With a strong academic foundation and hands-on exposure to real-world business dynamics, he specializes in areas such as strategic management, organizational behavior, and entrepreneurial development. His teaching philosophy emphasizes bridging the gap between theory and practice, ensuring students are well-prepared to tackle modern business challenges. Known for his innovative teaching techniques and commitment to student growth, Mr.Jimmy fosters critical thinking and leadership skills among his students. In addition to his teaching responsibilities, he actively engages in research, academic collaborations and professional development initiatives, contributing significantly to the field of business education and inspiring the next generation of business leaders.

Roobini S. is a dedicated research scholar currently doing her PhD in data analytics in Healthcare sector in Anna University, Chennai, under the guidance of Dr. M. S. Kavitha in the year 2024. She received M.E degree from PSG College of Technology in the year 2017, Coimbatore. Roobini has secured TANCET scholarship during her P.G. course and pursued Best Project Award in P.G Course. She received B.E degree from SNS College of Technology. She served as Assistant Professor at Sri Krishna College of Engineering and Technology, Coimbatore. Her research areas are predictive analytics, deep learning and AI. She has published book chapters, design patents, book and research articles in International Conferences and Journals. Roobini has extensive experience in developing and deploying AI solutions underscores her dedication to solving real-world challenges through technology. With a diverse range of skills and a strong passion for technological advancement, she aims to make significant contributions to the field of predictive analytics in healthcare.

S. Menaka is an Assistant Professor in the Department of Computer Science and Engineering at SRM Institute of Science and Technology, Ramapuram, Chennai. She earned her Ph.D. in October 2024 from Saveetha University, Chennai, India. Previously, she completed her M.E. in Computer Science and Engineering at T.J.S. Engineering College in 2015, securing the 7th rank in Anna University for her postgraduate studies. Her undergraduate degree in Information Technology was obtained from RMD Engineering College, Chennai, in 2008, where she ranked 27th in Anna University. Dr. Menaka's research interests span Machine Learning, Deep Learning, and Computer Vision. She has presented numerous research papers at national and international conferences and published articles in reputed journals. Additionally, she has contributed to academia as a reviewer, editorial board member for journals and conferences, and as a resource person for seminars conducted by various universities.

S. Umamaheswari is an accomplished academician and researcher with over 18years of experience in teaching and research. She joined Sathyabama Institute of Science and Technology as a Lecturer in 2008 and earned her Ph.D. in Business Administration from the same institution in 2017. Her research expertise spans,Marketing, Human Resource Management, Operations Management, and Finance. She has authored more than 25 research papers, published a book, and contributed three book chapters. Her research has received 192 Google Scholar citations and 36 Scopus citations.

M. Swathi Sree, Assistant Professor, Department of Computer Science and Engineering currently working in Stanley College of Engineering and Technology for Women since 2019. She is currently Pursuing Ph.D in Computer Science and Engineering in KL University and she completed her Post Graduation in 2015 from JNTUH. She possesses excellent experience in both teaching and research. She got Elite Certificate in NPTEL (Machine Learning). Her research interest area is Machine Learning. She has publications in Scopus, IJR, IJSDR, IGI global in addition she has a patent granted.

C.V. Suresh Babu is a pioneer in content development. A true entrepreneur, he founded Anniyappa Publications, a company that is highly active in publishing books related to Computer Science and Management. Dr. C.V. Suresh Babu has also ventured into SB Institute, a center for knowledge transfer. He holds a Ph.D. in Engineering Education from the National Institute of Technical Teachers Training & Research in Chennai, along with seven master's degrees in various disciplines such as Engineering, Computer Applications, Management, Commerce, Economics, Psychology, Law, and Education. Additionally, he has UGC-NET/SET qualifications in the fields of Computer Science, Management, Commerce, and Education. Currently, Dr. C.V. Suresh Babu is a Professor in the Department of Information Technology at the School of Computing Science, Hindustan Institute of Technology and Science (Hindustan University) in Padur, Chennai, Tamil Nadu, India. For more information, you can visit his personal blog at https://sites.google .com/view/cvsureshbabu/.

Arun Kumar Udayakumar received his Ph.D in the field of Electrical Engineering and his area of research includes Power Quality Improvement, Brushless DC Motor Drives, Artificial Intelligence, Internet of Things and Optical Sensors & Electronics and solar absorbers. He currently works as a professor and researcher at Karpagam Academy of Higher Education (Deemed to be University), Coimbatore, India. He has published around 50 papers in well reputed journals and conferences including, IEEE, Springer, Elsevier and American Scientific Publishers. He has also received funds from Texas Instruments, Bengaluru, India, towards his research project entitled "Implementation of Sliding Mode based Position Sensorless Drive for PMSM" qualifying for quarter final in "Texas Instruments Innovation Challenge, India Design Contest 2015". He has also received $300 worth components from DST - Texas Instruments, towards his research work in PMSM. As a reviewer, he has reviewed more than 100 articles from various journals including IEEE, Springer and Elsevier. He has also served as an editorial board member and advisory committee member for various IEEE international and national conferences.

B. Sundaravadivazhagan is a distinguished researcher and educator in Information and Communication Engineering, with over 23 years of academic and research experience. He earned his Ph.D. from Anna University, Chennai, in 2016. A Senior Member of IEEE, he is also affiliated with ISACA, ISTE, and ACM. He has published more than 85 research papers in SCI and Scopus-indexed journals and contributed to multiple international conferences. His expertise spans AI, Deep Learning, IoT, Cybersecurity, and Wireless Networks. He has received research grants from Oman's TRC and serves on academic committees, including at Amrita University and Saveetha School of Engineering.

Kurella Vaishnavi vaishnavikurella25@gmail.com Stanley College of Engineering & Technology for Women, India Dept. of Computer Science and Engineering

Nithin Shiva Vanka is an AI enthusiast with a strong passion for exploring and developing innovative solutions through technology. I am deeply interested in the potential of AI to transform industries and improve everyday life. With hands-on experience in various technical fields, I focus on continuous learning and enjoy working on projects that harness the power of AI to address real-world challenges and drive meaningful change.

Mecit Yuzkat worked as a research assistant at Yıldız Technical University, Department of Computer Engineering between 2013-2022. He wrote his master's thesis titled "A process mining system for process analysis and discovery" in the field of process mining, which is a sub-branch of data mining. He has conference and article publications in this field. He completed his PhD in the field of classification of biomedical images using deep learning methods. He has studies in Q1 journals within the scope of SCI regarding his PhD study. He has received many trainings such as project development and management. Now he continues to work as a manager and researcher in projects in the field of artificial intelligence at Health Institutes of Turkey. He has been responsible for the laboratory of logic, electronics, circuit and microprocessor courses at Yıldız Technical University for many years.

Index

A

AI Automation 91, 101, 217, 219, 235, 299, 304
AI-Driven DevOps 58, 69, 205, 207, 215, 223, 233, 234, 235, 474
AI Ethics 214, 230, 392, 393, 400
AI in software development 88, 95, 104, 107, 111, 119, 120, 165, 175, 193, 194, 196, 437, 473, 476, 477
AI-Powered 17, 28, 29, 36, 55, 57, 68, 69, 71, 72, 73, 74, 75, 77, 80, 81, 91, 118, 121, 123, 126, 133, 134, 135, 136, 137, 138, 139, 140, 141, 142, 144, 146, 147, 148, 149, 150, 151, 152, 153, 154, 155, 156, 157, 158, 159, 160, 161, 162, 163, 164, 165, 166, 167, 168, 171, 172, 173, 184, 188, 210, 220, 229, 237, 238, 242, 243, 244, 248, 250, 251, 263, 264, 266, 267, 268, 269, 270, 273, 277, 279, 280, 282, 284, 287, 291, 308, 309, 379, 382, 383, 401, 402, 435, 436, 437, 440, 443, 444, 445, 447, 452, 454, 455, 457, 459, 460, 464, 465, 466, 467, 468, 472, 473, 474, 475
AI-Powered Software Development 473
AI-Powered Tools 72, 123, 133, 134, 138, 139, 144, 146, 155, 156, 157, 158, 160, 161, 162, 163, 164, 165, 171, 172, 184, 210, 237, 238, 263, 268, 280, 435, 436, 437, 444, 452, 457, 467, 472
Algorithmic Bias 156, 378, 380, 381, 384, 385, 386, 392, 395, 396, 397, 403, 404
Anomaly Detection 13, 63, 67, 72, 73, 133, 135, 137, 139, 145, 151, 152, 153, 156, 160, 164, 169, 203, 214, 215, 216, 218, 219, 224, 225, 227, 228, 238, 239, 240, 245, 250, 285, 382, 443, 466, 467
API Usage Recommendations 38, 39
Artificial Intelligence (AI) 1, 2, 6, 7, 8, 18, 24, 26, 27, 28, 29, 30, 35, 46, 47, 52, 53, 54, 55, 56, 57, 58, 63, 68, 69, 71, 74, 75, 80, 81, 82, 83, 84, 85, 92, 95, 100, 108, 114, 115, 118, 132, 136, 138, 139, 140, 143, 146, 149, 153, 158, 160, 162, 167, 168, 172, 174, 175, 177, 178, 186, 187, 196, 198, 199, 203, 204, 211, 212, 213, 218, 219, 221, 222, 229, 233, 234, 237, 240, 242, 243, 245, 247, 252, 258, 259, 260, 261, 263, 264, 269, 282, 283, 284, 285, 286, 287, 288, 290, 291, 292, 293, 296, 297, 300, 308, 327, 328, 340, 351, 353, 377, 378, 379, 381, 384, 387, 395, 398, 401, 405, 407, 408, 411, 435, 436, 437, 439, 442, 466, 472, 476, 477
Automated Debugging 48, 49, 121, 122
Automated Testing Frameworks 217, 352
Automation 5, 7, 23, 27, 31, 33, 43, 49, 50, 57, 60, 61, 62, 63, 66, 69, 71, 74, 79, 82, 83, 85, 88, 89, 90, 91, 92, 94, 95, 97, 98, 101, 102, 103, 107, 118, 121, 122, 130, 133, 134, 136, 143, 152, 163, 165, 166, 167, 176, 201, 203, 204, 206, 207, 208, 209, 210, 211, 212, 214, 217, 219, 225, 228, 229, 230, 231, 232, 233, 234, 235, 240, 241, 246, 248, 251, 253, 254, 255, 256, 257, 263, 264, 265, 266, 267, 268, 269, 270, 271, 276, 277, 280, 282, 285, 286, 287, 291, 295, 296, 297, 298, 299, 300, 302, 303, 304, 305, 306, 307, 309, 310, 311, 312, 316, 317, 318, 319, 321, 322, 324, 325, 326, 327, 328, 329, 331, 332, 333, 336, 337, 338, 339, 340, 341, 342, 344, 345, 349, 350, 351, 352, 353, 354, 355, 375, 379, 382, 383, 390, 401, 442, 443, 444, 453, 456, 460, 462, 463, 464, 465

C

Cloud Computing 27, 59, 75, 83, 85, 90, 91, 134, 135, 154, 157, 167, 168, 174, 183, 204, 205, 208, 233, 234, 327, 357, 358, 359, 361, 362, 363, 364,

365, 366, 367, 368, 369, 372, 373, 374, 375, 376, 379, 412, 413, 415, 417, 432, 433
Cloud Native 26, 83, 84, 85, 86, 166, 167, 168, 199, 205, 221, 222, 233, 296, 308
Cloud-Native Architecture 82, 84, 88, 134, 137, 142, 166, 229, 234, 318
Cloud-Native DevOps 203, 204, 205, 206, 207, 208, 209, 211, 214, 215, 217, 219, 222, 223, 224, 225, 226, 227, 229, 232
Cloud-native Software 57, 58, 59, 63, 67, 82, 87, 89, 90, 93, 95, 96, 133, 134, 135, 136, 137, 138, 139, 140, 146, 155, 156, 157, 158, 160, 161, 163, 164, 165, 171, 172, 173, 174, 175, 179, 181, 182, 183, 184, 186, 191, 197, 295, 296, 297, 298, 299, 302, 303, 304, 305, 307, 317, 325, 333, 351, 352, 378, 379, 381, 401, 402
cloud-native software engineering 57, 58, 59, 63, 67, 82, 87, 89, 90, 95, 96, 133, 134, 135, 136, 137, 138, 139, 140, 146, 155, 165, 172, 173, 175, 179, 182, 183, 197, 296, 297, 299, 302, 304, 305, 307, 317, 325, 333, 352
Cloud-Native Technologies 84, 180, 192, 208, 296, 352, 378, 379, 380, 381, 383, 384, 401, 402, 404, 405
Code Analysis and Generation 36
Code Aware Suggestions 37, 38
Code Completion 34, 37, 38, 39, 40, 41, 50, 55, 118, 119, 120, 121, 123, 132, 177, 187, 193, 293, 452, 453, 455
Coded Caching 411, 412, 414, 416, 417, 419, 420, 421, 423, 430, 431, 432
Code Generation 31, 36, 50, 89, 90, 92, 93, 95, 97, 100, 101, 102, 104, 107, 109, 110, 114, 115, 117, 120, 121, 123, 124, 125, 126, 128, 129, 130, 131, 132, 133, 136, 139, 146, 149, 157, 158, 160, 163, 164, 166, 169, 194, 284, 293, 435, 441, 452, 453, 473
Codex Model 120, 121, 146
Continuous Integration/Continuous Delivery 103
Continuous Integration/Continuous Deployment (CI/CD) 137, 149, 150, 158, 443

D

Data-driven 7, 69, 76, 77, 81, 134, 136, 137, 146, 168, 238, 241, 244, 248, 286, 288, 295, 306, 317, 325, 327, 339, 346, 350, 378, 379, 381, 406, 454
Data-driven Decision-making 69, 325, 327, 379, 406
Data Privacy 19, 130, 160, 162, 163, 165, 183, 208, 222, 223, 226, 232, 263, 283, 290, 348, 352, 369, 378, 380, 381, 384, 386, 387, 388, 393, 394, 395, 396, 397, 399, 400, 404, 472
data replication 357, 358, 359, 360, 361, 362, 364, 367, 374, 375, 376
Debugging 45, 46, 47, 48, 49, 50, 101, 102, 108, 121, 122, 126, 127, 150, 228, 241, 275, 276, 277, 278, 279, 284, 439, 457, 458, 459, 460, 462, 472, 473
Deep Learning 1, 2, 4, 9, 14, 16, 17, 22, 30, 33, 34, 36, 40, 54, 63, 67, 83, 95, 120, 121, 123, 124, 125, 126, 130, 132, 135, 169, 172, 198, 200, 206, 208, 215, 216, 217, 219, 223, 225, 235, 258, 259, 282, 293, 340, 401
DevOps 26, 58, 60, 61, 62, 65, 66, 69, 70, 72, 74, 83, 85, 86, 96, 101, 103, 165, 166, 174, 180, 190, 200, 203, 204, 205, 206, 207, 208, 209, 210, 211, 214, 215, 217, 219, 220, 221, 222, 223, 224, 225, 226, 227, 228, 229, 230, 231, 232, 233, 234, 235, 247, 248, 255, 256, 264, 267, 276, 279, 280, 290, 465, 474
Digital Transformation 58, 135, 296, 298, 309, 315, 328, 330, 340, 353, 379

E

Ethical AI Integration 378, 398, 400, 404
Ethical Challenges 93, 352, 377, 378, 381, 384, 386, 389, 396, 397, 402

F

Federated Learning 2, 19, 22, 24, 140, 152, 160, 164, 208, 411, 412, 414, 418, 419, 420, 421, 423, 431
Fog Computing 411, 412, 413, 414, 415, 416, 417, 421, 432, 433

G

Generative AI 32, 54, 87, 88, 89, 90, 91, 92, 93, 94, 95, 96, 97, 98, 99, 101, 102, 104, 105, 106, 107, 108, 110, 111, 112, 114, 115, 165, 176, 198, 476, 477

H

Hospital Admission and Discharge Processes 297, 305, 315, 325, 326, 337, 338

I

implementation challenges 140, 207, 351, 433
Intelligent Code Generation 136, 146, 149, 157
Intelligent Project Management 435, 475

L

Learning from Coding Patterns 39

M

Machine Learning 1, 2, 4, 5, 7, 9, 12, 13, 14, 17, 27, 29, 30, 33, 34, 36, 37, 42, 44, 48, 49, 50, 55, 57, 58, 63, 67, 69, 71, 72, 73, 75, 76, 77, 80, 81, 84, 85, 102, 103, 109, 112, 117, 118, 119, 120, 121, 122, 123, 124, 125, 126, 130, 132, 136, 137, 138, 139, 141, 143, 144, 145, 146, 149, 150, 151, 152, 153, 154, 155, 158, 159, 162, 166, 168, 172, 186, 198, 199, 200, 201, 207, 209, 210, 211, 212, 213, 215, 217, 218, 219, 220, 227, 229, 230, 231, 234, 239, 240, 243, 244, 246, 247, 250, 253, 254, 258, 259, 264, 266, 268, 281, 282, 284, 288, 289, 293, 297, 304, 327, 339, 340, 379, 381, 382, 391, 392, 395, 401, 406, 407, 408, 418, 419, 435, 436, 442, 447, 455, 456, 459, 462, 463, 469, 470
Microservices 57, 58, 60, 61, 63, 65, 66, 67, 73, 74, 77, 78, 79, 85, 88, 89, 90, 94, 98, 101, 133, 134, 135, 136, 138, 141, 143, 144, 145, 146, 147, 153, 156, 157, 158, 163, 166, 177, 180, 186, 190, 199, 204, 205, 206, 208, 219, 220, 229, 296, 299, 304, 309, 311, 333, 341, 352, 379, 456

N

Natural Language Processing 1, 3, 4, 7, 9, 14, 16, 20, 22, 31, 34, 35, 36, 50, 52, 53, 54, 55, 56, 67, 69, 93, 102, 109, 112, 114, 117, 124, 128, 132, 136, 140, 141, 142, 146, 149, 158, 169, 172, 201, 206, 248, 250, 264, 289, 293, 340, 379, 381, 395, 436, 440, 444, 445, 446, 458, 463, 473
Neural Networks 2, 4, 9, 10, 12, 17, 21, 40, 120, 124, 130, 175, 176, 198, 200, 201, 216, 258, 261, 340, 407

O

Operational Efficiency 135, 155, 204, 205, 212, 232, 298, 327, 339, 341, 344, 378, 379, 381, 383, 384, 395, 401, 404, 468

P

Patient Experience 298, 316, 327, 329, 338, 346
Predictive Analytics 1, 7, 17, 57, 63, 67, 85, 136, 137, 138, 141, 142, 143, 144, 149, 152, 158, 159, 168, 204, 207, 209, 210, 215, 220, 227, 230, 234, 239, 241, 242, 244, 246, 248, 255, 256, 257, 264, 266, 268, 270, 280, 285, 310, 311, 378, 379, 381, 382,

396, 401, 402, 404, 409, 435, 440, 441, 442, 443, 444, 465, 468
Project Management 110, 129, 283, 286, 287, 288, 435, 436, 440, 474, 475

Q

Quality Assurance 5, 23, 30, 136, 139, 167, 176, 180, 188, 190, 201, 237, 238, 239, 240, 241, 242, 243, 245, 246, 247, 248, 251, 252, 253, 254, 255, 257, 277, 280, 282, 285, 439, 473

R

Regulatory Compliance 13, 78, 320, 388, 391, 395, 396, 397, 398, 401, 402, 404
Risk Management 234, 286, 319, 323, 378, 379, 381, 382, 388, 389, 396, 397, 401, 402, 404, 407
Robotic Process Automation 296, 297, 299, 302, 303, 304, 305, 306, 317, 325, 328, 329, 332, 336, 338, 339, 342, 344, 350, 352, 353, 354, 355, 401

S

Scalability 5, 15, 16, 24, 41, 43, 45, 46, 47, 58, 59, 60, 61, 62, 65, 69, 75, 82, 84, 89, 92, 93, 94, 95, 98, 103, 111, 117, 128, 129, 135, 136, 138, 140, 141, 142, 143, 144, 145, 149, 150, 155, 156, 158, 162, 163, 164, 169, 172, 173, 177, 180, 181, 183, 186, 187, 193, 199, 204, 205, 208, 223, 227, 230, 231, 232, 251, 266, 269, 270, 273, 278, 296, 299, 303, 304, 309, 335, 336, 344, 352, 365, 366, 379, 380, 454, 456, 464, 467, 475
Serverless Computing 57, 66, 161, 304
Software development 29, 30, 31, 32, 33, 37, 41, 43, 45, 50, 51, 52, 54, 56, 58, 60, 61, 70, 79, 84, 87, 88, 89, 93, 94, 95, 98, 99, 100, 101, 102, 104, 105, 106, 107, 108, 109, 110, 111, 112, 114, 117, 118, 119, 120, 123, 126, 129, 130, 131, 133, 134, 135, 136, 137, 138, 140, 142, 143, 146, 147, 149, 155, 156, 157, 158, 160, 161, 163, 164, 165, 166, 167, 171, 172, 173, 174, 175, 176, 177, 178, 179, 181, 182, 183, 184, 186, 187, 191, 193, 194, 195, 196, 197, 200, 204, 206, 231, 232, 240, 242, 246, 247, 248, 250, 251, 252, 264, 266, 270, 280, 283, 284, 285, 288, 290, 291, 297, 298, 299, 303, 333, 343, 351, 435, 436, 437, 439, 440, 441, 444, 446, 451, 467, 472, 473, 475, 476, 477
Software engineering 31, 52, 53, 54, 57, 58, 59, 63, 64, 67, 82, 87, 88, 89, 90, 91, 94, 95, 96, 97, 101, 109, 110, 111, 112, 114, 115, 117, 118, 120, 128, 129, 130, 131, 132, 133, 134, 135, 136, 137, 138, 139, 140, 146, 152, 155, 156, 160, 163, 164, 165, 166, 168, 169, 172, 173, 174, 175, 176, 177, 178, 179, 181, 182, 183, 184, 193, 195, 196, 197, 198, 199, 200, 281, 282, 283, 284, 286, 287, 289, 290, 291, 292, 293, 296, 297, 299, 302, 304, 305, 307, 317, 325, 333, 352, 375, 476, 477
Software Quality Assurance 245, 246, 247, 248, 251, 252, 253, 282
Software testing 27, 54, 166, 175, 198, 201, 237, 238, 239, 241, 243, 244, 248, 252, 254, 255, 256, 257, 259, 260, 263, 264, 270, 281, 282, 285, 436, 476
Source code creation 87, 89, 92, 93, 107, 112

T

TabNine 36, 117, 119, 121, 123, 135, 139, 147, 148, 149, 156, 157, 158, 159, 452
Test Automation 27, 71, 167, 240, 241, 254, 255, 257, 263, 264, 265, 266, 267, 268, 269, 270, 277, 280, 282, 460, 462, 463

www.ingramcontent.com/pod-product-compliance
Lightning Source LLC
LaVergne TN
LVHW080352011026
849161LV00009B/2281